HANDBOOK OF INTERNATIONAL MANAGEMENT

Edited by

INGO WALTER

New York University and INSEAD

Associate Editor

TRACY MURRAY

University of Arkansas

WILEY

JOHN WILEY & SONS

New York • Chichester • Brisbane • Toronto • Singapore

Library of Congress Cataloging in Publication Data:

ISBN 0-471-60674-X

Printed in the United States of America

10 9 8 7 6 5 4 3 2 1

PREFACE

The international dimensions of business have become an everyday fact of life for corporations, consumers, and governments in virtually every country. The notion that firms can operate in a purely domestic environment is today an anachronism and a prescription for trouble. One industry after the other is becoming truly global in nature, as manufacturing is spread around the world according to the principles of competitive advantage. New players are emerging, even as existing players are forced from the market. The services industries are becoming global as well, particularly banking and finance, insurance, professional services, transportation, and tourism. Neither business strategy nor public policy can any longer be formulated in the absence of careful consideration of the international dimensions.

The *Handbook of International Business* was first published in 1982 to aid in interpreting international developments and to link them into the formulation of sound approaches to the global market. This volume, and the companion *Handbook of International Business,* which focuses on developments in the global environment of the business firm, represents an extensively revised and expanded edition of the original work.

This volume deals with managerial issues confronting firms doing business internationally. This incudes managing parent-subsidiary relations, international marketing and market research, political risk assessment, conflict management and legal dimensions, managing the international finance and accounting functions, international sourcing, technology transfer, organization design, as well as planning and strategy development.

Credit for the contents of the *Handbook,* of course, belongs to the various authors who have taken great care to present their subjects in a careful and understandable manner. As editors, we set out to design a volume that would meet practitioner needs, select authors, and edit the results. Criticism for errors of omission therefore rests with us.

INGO WALTER
TRACY MURRAY

New York, New York
Washington, D.C.
April 1988

CONTENTS

CONTRIBUTORS

JEAN BODDEWYN is Professor of International Business and Coordinator of International Business Programs at Baruch College, City University of New York. He holds a Commercial Engineer degree from the University of Louvain (Belgium), an M.B.A. from the University of Oregon, and a Ph.D. in Business Administration from the University of Washington (Seattle). His teaching centers on international business, management, and marketing; while his present research interests and consulting activities deal with international business-government relations, corporate external affairs, disinvestments, and advertising. Major publications include *Comparative Management and Marketing* (1969), *World Business Systems and Environments* (co-author, 1972), *Public Policy Toward Retailing: An International Symposium* (co-editor and co-author, 1972), *Western European Policies Toward U.S. Investors* (1974), *International Business-Government Communications* (co-author, 1975), *European Industrial Managers: West and East* (editor, 1976), *International Divestment: A Survey of Corporate Experience* (1976), *Multinational Government Relations: An Action Guide for Corporate Management* (1977), and *Comparison Advertising: A Worldwide Study* (1978) and *Advertising Self-Regulation and Outside Participation: A Multinational Comparison* (1988). He is a member of the Academy of International Business, International Studies Association, and the Academy of Management. He is also the author of a series of international surveys of advertising regulations, conducted for the International Advertising Association.

MICHAEL Z. BROOKE is a freelance author and managing director of Brooke Associates (Manchester) Ltd., a company which undertakes contract writing, training programs and consultancy for business. He began research into international corporate strategies in 1963 at the University of Manchester Institute of Science and Technology where he was Director of the International Business Unit which he founded in 1970. In that year he published his first book on the subject—*The Strategy of Multinational Business*—in collaboration with H. Lee Remmers (Professor at the European Institute of Business Administration, INSEAD, Fontainebleau). Since then he has published 16 books, mainly on international trade and investment, as well as over 100 articles. He has held visiting professorships in the University of South Carolina and Queen's University in Kingston, Canada. He has also lectured or conducted seminars in 14 countries.

JAMES BURTLE has been Professor of Economics at Iona College, New Rochelle, N.Y. since 1982. Before joining Iona College, he was managing editor of the International Country Risk Guide, a publication of International Reports, New York. The risk guide, an advisory service for leading companies and financial institutions world-wide, establishes risk ratings for 90 countries based on political evaluations and analysis of economic and financial data. Mr. Burtle was vice-president in the economics department of W.R. Grace and Company 1958–1980. At W.R. Grace one of his main concerns was as adviser to the Grace treasury department on foreign exchange operations. While at Grace he also maintained a foreign exchange advisory service for 12 major U.S. companies. Prior to joining W.R. Grace he was a member of the economics division of the International Labor Office in Geneva, Switzerland. He is a graduate of the University of Chicago with B.A. and M.A. degrees in economics. Mr. Burtle is co-author with the late Sidney Rolfe of *The Great Wheel, The International Monetary System* (1975). He has written numerous articles on international economics and finance for scholarly and financial publications. Mr. Burtle has had adjunct teaching positions at Columbia University, New York University, and other universities. He has been a director of Predex Corporation (exchange rate forecasting) and a member of the Advisory Committee to the U.S. Office of Management and the Budget on the presentation of U.S. Balance of Payments Statistics. He has testified before the Senate Banking Committee on international monetary reform and the operation of foreign exchange markets.

FREDERICK D. S. CHOI is Professor of Accounting and International Business at New York University and received his Ph.D. degree from the University of Washington. He has previously taught at the Cranfield School of Management, the University of Hawaii, the University of Washington, The Japan-American Institute of Management Science, the European Institute of Business Administration (INSEAD), and served as a member of the First American Visiting Team to establish the National Center for Industrial Science and Technology Management Development in the Peoples Republic of China. Dr. Choi's research interests center on the accounting issues associated with multinational entities including the performance evaluation of foreign operations, exchange risk management, financial innovations, and international financial analysis. On several editorial boards, Dr. Choi is a consultant to industry, the accounting profession and academic institutions. He is the author or co-author of 10 books and over 50 articles. His recent books include *International Accounting* (under revision with G. Mueller), *Frontiers of International Accounting* with G. Mueller (1985), and *Accounting and Financial Reporting in Japan* with K. Hiramatsu (1987).

C. SAMUEL CRAIG is Professor of Marketing and Associate Dean for Academic Affairs at New York University's Graduate School of Business Administration. He has taught at the Ohio State University, College of Administrative Sciences, and Cornell University, Graduate School of Business Administration. He received a B.A. from Westminster College in 1965, an M.S. from the University of Rhode Island in 1967, and a Ph.D. from the Ohio State University in 1971. Dr. Craig has done considerable work in the areas of advertising, assessing communication effectiveness, the diffusion of innovation, and international marketing. He worked for IBM's Data Processing Division and currently is a consultant to a number of major corporations. Dr. Craig is author or co-author of over 50 articles and technical papers. He is co-author of *Consumer Behavior: An Information Processing Perspective* (1982) and *International Marketing Research* (1983), with Susan Douglas.

STANLEY M. DAVIS has a Ph.D. in Sociology from Washington University. He is a business advisor and writer about the management and organization of large corporations. He has worked with senior management of many global companies on matters of strategy implementation, organization design, corporate vision and values, and management development. His clients have included Apple, Arco, Chase Manhattan Bank, Chemical Bank, Citibank, Herman Miller, Mercedes Benz of North America, Metropolitan Life, Primerica, Olivetti, Sun Microsystems, Wang, and Xerox.

Dr. Davis is the author of six books, including *Matrix, Managing and Organizing Multinational Corporations,* and *Managing Corporate Culture.* His new book, *Future Perfect,* is an exploration of management in the future, and is to be published in 10 languages beginning in October, 1987.

Dr. Davis is the President of Stanley M. Davis Associates of Boston, from which he conducts his research, writing, consulting, seminar, speech, training, and video activities. He was on the faculty of the Harvard Business School for 11 years, Columbia University for two years, and has been Research Professor at Boston University for eight years. He is a Principal of the MAC Group Inc., a Cambridge-based consulting firm, and a member of the Board of Trustees of the Boston Ballet. He resides and works in Chestnut Hill, Massachusetts.

SUSAN DOUGLAS is currently Professor of Marketing and International Business at the Graduate School of Business Administration of New York University. Previously, she was a member of the faculty at the Centre d'Enseignement Superieur des Affaires at Jouy-en-Josas, France, and was Professor of Management (Associated) at the European Institute of Advanced Studies in Management in Brussels. She received a B.A. and an M.A. from the University of Manchester in the United Kingdom, graduated from the Institute des Sciences Politiques, Paris, in 1963, and obtained a Ph.D. from the Wharton School of the University of Pennsylvania in 1969. Other teaching experience includes the University of Louvain, Belgium, the University of the Witwatersrand, Johannesburg, and the Tatung Institute of Technology, Taipei, Taiwan. Her principal areas of research are cross-national consumer behavior, international market research, and strategic planning for the multinational markets. She has published extensively in these areas in leading journals in the United States and Europe, including the Journal of Marketing, the Journal of Marketing Research, the Journal of Consumer Behavior, and European Research. Recent publications include "A Cross-National Analysis of Country of Origin Effects on Product Evaluations" (with Johny Johansson and Ikiyiro Nonaka, 1985) and "The Myth of Globalization" (with Yoram Wind, 1987) and is co-author of a book on International Marketing Research with C. Samuel Craig. Dr. Douglas has served as consultant to a number of companies in the United States, Europe, and the Far East, including Robinson Associates in Philadelphia, S.A.E.D.E.D.C. in Paris, Canadean in London, and Tatung Industries in Taiwan. She has held research grants from the Marketing Science Institute in Cambridge, the U.S. Department of Agriculture, and the Delegation Generale des Recherches en Sciences Sociales, Paris.

LOWELL DWORIN has a Ph.D. in physics from Columbia University and a Ph.D. in business administration from the University of Michigan. He is an Assistant Professor in the College of Business Administration of the University of Texas at Austin, where he teaches courses in taxation in the Master of Professional Accountancy program. Among the courses he has taught are Multinational Taxation, Taxation of Partnerships and Corporations Filing Consolidated Returns, and Oil and Gas Taxation. He is engaged in a study of the taxation of international oil and gas exploration and production for the U.S. Department of the Treasury. His earlier work for the Treasury

Department and the Bureau of Business Research at the University of Texas at Austin dealt with the taxation of deep-sea mining and the relationship between manufacturing investment and employment in Texas and national economic conditions. He is a member of the editorial board of *The Accounting Review.*

EDWARD B. FLOWERS is an Associate Professor of Economics and Finance in the College of Business Administration of St. John's University, New York. He has conducted research on oligopoly theories of direct foreign investment and on the causes for changes in world business cycle synchronicity. Dr. Flowers is the author of a text on corporate finance which is illustrated with over 30 computer-generated comprehensive, interrelated models of the firm. He has recently studied the economy of Taiwan on a grant from the Pacific Cultural Foundation, focusing on the potential for Taiwan's direct investment in the United States and on the modernization of Pacific Basin financial institutions. Dr. Flowers has also served as a Foreign Policy Office for the Office of the Assistant Secretary for International Affairs of the U.S. Treasury Department, Washington, D.C.

THOMAS N. GLADWIN is Associate Professor of Management and International Business at the Graduate School of Business Administration of New York University, where he is also the director of the "International Business Negotiation Exercise." He received a Ph.D. in Business Administration from the University of Michigan in 1975.

Dr. Gladwin teaches courses on international business negotiation, conflict management, global strategic management, and environmental analysis. He is the author of three dozen articles in the field of international business and three books: *Environment, Planning and the Multinational Corporation, Multinationals Under Fire: Lessons in the Management of Conflict,* with Ingo Walter, and *Environmental Aspects of the Activities of Transnational Corporations: A Survey.*

Dr. Gladwin has been active in executive programs at General Electric, IBM, Peat Marwick, American Express, AMAX, Combustion Engineering, Chase Manhattan Bank, Arden House, Gulf International Bank (Bahrain), Danish Management Center, Swedish Institute of Management, Grupo Catho (Brazil), and the Federation of Korean Industries. He has served as a consultant to the U.N. Centre of Transnational Corporations, Center for Public Resources, World Commission on Environment and Development, and to numerous multinational enterprises.

MICHAEL GRUSON is a member of the New York Bar and since 1973 a partner of the law firm Shearman & Sterling, New York where he is primarily engaged in the representation of foreign banks.

Dr. Gruson received his legal education in Germany (University of Mainz, LL.B. 1962; Freie Universität, Berlin, Dr. Jur. 1966) and in the United States (Columbia University, M.C.L. 1963; LL.B. 1965). He is a director and a member of the faculty of the Center of Transnational Legal Studies at the University of Illinois, Champaign-Urbana, which conducts annual seminars for public sector attorneys in Latin America and China. He is presently Vice Chairman of the Committee on Banking Law and Chairman of the Subcommittee on Legal Opinions of the International Bar Association.

He has published a book, *Die Bedürfniskompetenz* (legislative jurisdiction) (1967), is co-editor of the book *Sovereign Lending: Managing Legal Risk* (1984), and co-author of the book *Legal Opinions in International Transactions* (1987). In addition, he has lectured, and published articles in professional journals, on issues of choice-of-law, jurisdiction, banking law, and international financing law.

STEPHEN J. KOBRIN is Professor of Management at the Wharton School of the University of Pennsylvania. He holds a B. Mgt. E. degree from Rensselaer Polytechnic Institute, an M.B.A. from Wharton, and a Ph.D. from the University of Michigan. His research interests focus on: international business-government interaction; international strategic management, international political-economy; and environmental assessment. Major publications include: *Foreign Direct Investment, Industrialization, and Social Change* (1977); *Political Risk: A Review and Reconsideration* (1979); *Foreign Enterprise and Forced Divestment in the LDCs* (1980); *Managing Political Risk Assessment* (1982); *International Expertise in American Business* (1984); *Diffusion as an Explanation of Oil Nationalization* (1985); and *Testing the Obsolescing Bargaining Hypothesis in the Manufacturing in Less Developed Countries* (1987).

KONRAD W. KUBIN is Associate Professor of Accounting at Virginia Polytechnic Institute and State University. He studied in three countries and received his Certificate of Candidacy (B.S. equivalent) from Erlangen-Nürnberg University, his M.B.A. from the University of Colorado, and in 1972 his Ph.D. from the University of Washington. At Virginia Tech Dr. Kubin was instrumental in developing a graduate course in international accounting. He has delivered and published numerous papers on international accounting in the United States as well as abroad, has been a member of the American Accounting Association's International Accounting Committee, and currently serves as an officer of its International Section. Dr. Kubin is a CPA in the Commonwealth of Virginia. His business experience includes working for three years for a German public accounting firm and serving as a consultant to a "Big 8" CPA firm in France, Belgium, and Germany. He also was a Visiting Exchange Professor at the Politechnika Warszawska and the Oskar Lange Academy of Economics in Wroclaw, Poland. He is a former recipient of a Fulbright Grant and received the 1979 Outstanding Faculty Vice President Award from Beta Alpha Psi, national honorary and professional accounting fraternity.

DUANE KUJAWA (Ph.D., Business Administration, University of Michigan, 1970) is Professor of Management and International Business and Associate Dean, School of Business Administration, University of Miami, Coral Gables. He has researched and published considerably on industrial relations and employment issues related to multinational enterprise. Publications include *International Labor Relations Management in the Automotive Industry: A Comparative Study of Chrysler, Ford and General Motors* (1971), *Management and Employment Practices of Foreign Direct Investors in the United States* (1976), *Employment Effects of Multinational Enterprises: A United States Case Study* (1980), *Production Strategies and Practices of Foreign Multinationals in the United States* (1981), *Japanese Multinationals in the United States* (1986), and "Foreign Sourcing Decisions and the Duty to Bargain Under the NLRA" (1972). Dr. Kujawa has lectured extensively in the United States at universities, before professional associations, and in executive development programs. Additionally, he has traveled and taught in West Germany, Japan, Venezuela, Colombia, and throughout Central America. Consultancies have included government agencies, international organizations, academic institutions, and corporations.

FRANCIS A. LEES is Professor of Economics and Finance and former Chairman of Department at St. Johns University. He taught at Fordham University and at the University of Maryland. He received his A.B. from Brooklyn College, his M.A. from St. Louis University, and his Ph.D. degree in 1961 from New York University. Dr. Lees' principal areas of research include international finance, international banking, and international economic relationships. He has published papers in professional journals in these fields and is the author of 11 books and monographs including five published by The Conference Board. His most recent book is *Foreign Multinational Investment in the United States* (1986). At the present time his research interests focus on international banking and financial risk faced by corporate borrowers, and Brazilian Economic Development. Dr. Lees has been awarded a Fulbright Grant (1987–88) to carry out research in Brazil. He has served as a consultant to The Conference Board, New York Clearing House Association, New York State Education Department, Central Bank for Cooperatives, Royal Commission on Electric Power (Toronto), and Point of Purchase Advertising Institute. Dr. Lees served in the U.S. Army.

KATHERIN MARTON is Associate Professor of Business Economics and International Business in the School of Business, Fordham University, New York. Professor Marton is the author of numerous articles on multinational corporations and technology transfer. She received an M.Sc. degree from the University of Minnesota, and doctorate degrees from the University of Vienna and from the Graduate School of Business Administration, New York University.

RICHARD W. MOXON is Associate Professor of International Business at the University of Washington. He holds B.S. and M.S. degrees in engineering from Stanford University, and a DBA from Harvard University. He has also taught at Stanford, INSEAD and management schools in Latin America. He is the Educational Director of the Pacific Rim Bankers Program. Professor Moxon's research and teaching are focused on international competition and the management of international operations. His recent research has been on international competition in the commercial aircraft industry, international strategic business alliances, negotiations between multinational corporations and developing countries, and the management of export operations by small high technology companies.

TRACY MURRAY received a Ph.D. from Michigan State University in 1969 and is now Phillips Petroleum Company Distinguished Professor of International Economics and Business, University of Arkansas. His past positions include Economic Affairs Officer, U.N. Conference on Trade and Development (UNCTAD), 1971–73; Associate Professor, Graduate School of Business Administration, New York University, 1974–78; Visiting Scholar, U.S. International Trade Commission 1987–88; and economic consultant to U.N. Conference on Trade and Development (UNCTAD) (1975, 1979, 1981, 1982, 1984–86), Organization of American States (1977 to present), Executive Office of the White House (USTR) (1979), Government of Colombia (1980, 1981), Government of Argentina (1980), U.N. Industrial Development Organization (UNIDO) (1981–86), U.N. Development Program (UNDP) (1984–84), and World Bank (1985–86). He received an IBM Post-Doctoral Fellowship for International Business Studies (1976) and lecture grants from the U.S. Information Agency (USIA) to Argentina, Brazil, Colombia, Egypt, Fed. Rep. of

Germany, Hong Kong, India, Indonesia, Malta, Papua-New Guinea, Philippines, Singapore, and Yugoslavia. Dr. Murray has published numerous scholarly papers on international trade theory and policy, statistical methodology and applications, and in particular, trade problems of developing countries; his research has also been published in documents issued by governments and international organizations and in book form.

MICHÉAL Ó'SÚILLEABHÁIN is a Statutory Lecturer in the Department of Economics, University College, Cork, Ireland. Having graduated from the National University of Ireland in 1959, he pursued postgraduate studies at the Institute for World Economics, Kiel, Germany, and was awarded his Dr. So. Pol. degree in the Economics Faculty of Kiel University for a dissertation on international agricultural trade. Following his return to Ireland in 1967 he was at first concerned with policy issues in European economic integration. In more recent years, his teaching and research reflect a strong interest in interdisciplinary collaboration. He is currently assisting a colleague at the Technical University of Munich in editing a book on a case method approach to solving weakly structured problems. Having published conference papers on foreign direct investment in the food, pharmaceutical, and electronic products industries, he has recently completed a book on empirical aspects on intraindustry trade.

SAMUEL RABINO is Associate Professor, Marketing Group; Faculty Coordinator, High Technology MBA Program. Professor Rabino, who came to the College of Business Administration in 1982 from Boston University School of Management, holds an A.B. from Hebrew University in Jerusalem and M.B.A. and Ph.D. degrees from New York University. He taught previously at Bernard Baruch College and at Manhattan College. The author of numerous articles on international marketing, export incentive programs, product planning, and brand strategies and development, Professor Rabino has been a consultant to the Department of Commerce in Washington, D.C.; the Nestlé Corporation; the Gillette Corporation; the First National Bank of Boston; Elscint, Inc.; and Times Mirror Cable T.V., among others. He currently conducts research in the areas of diffusion of innovation and optimizing pricing strategies for media sellers. Professor Rabino has served as the regional vice president of the Academy of International Business.

FRANKLIN R. ROOT is Professor of International Business and Management at the Wharton School. A graduate of Trinity College, he has an M.B.A. from the Wharton School and a Ph.D. from the University of Pennsylvania. Professor Root has lectured in several countries in the fields of international business and economics. He has served on the faculties of the University of Maryland (1950–1955), the Copenhagen School of Economics and Business Administration (1963–1964), and the Naval War College (1967–1968). During the summer of 1970, he was Regional Advisor on Export Promotion for the Economic Commission for Latin America in Santiago, Chile. Professor Root has engaged in extensive consulting with business and government agencies. He has published over 50 articles and has written three books: *Strategic Planning for Export Marketing, International Grade and Investment* (Fifth Edition), and *Entry Strategies for International Markets.* Professor Root has conducted executive seminars throughout the United States and abroad on foreign market entry strategies and political risk management. He is a past

President of the Academy of International Business and current Dean of the Fellows of the Academy of International Business.

ALAN M. RUGMAN is Professor of International Business at the University of Toronto. Previously he was Professor and Director of the Centre for International Business Studies at Dalhousie University. He has been a visiting professor at Columbia Business School, London Business School, Harvard University and the University of Hawaii. Born in England in 1945, Dr. Rugman came to Canada in 1968 and became a Canadian citizen in 1973. He earned his B.A. from Leeds University in 1966, the M.Sc. from London University in 1967 and the Ph.D. from Simon Fraser University in 1974. He has published numerous articles and books dealing with the financial, economic and managerial aspects of multinational enterprises. His books include: *Multinationals in Canada* (1980), *Inside the Multinationals* (1981), *New Theories of the Multinational Enterprise* (ed.) (1982), *Multinationals and Technology Transfer* (ed.) (1983), *Multinationals and Transfer Pricing* (ed.) (1985), *International Business* (co-author, 1985), *Megafirms* (co-author, 1985), and *Administered Protection in America* (co-author, 1987). Dr. Rugman is a member of Canada's International Trade Advisory Committee and has been a consultant to both private sector companies and government agencies. He has been selected for inclusion in *Who's Who in the World, Who's Who in the East,* and the *Canadian Who's Who*.

RANA K.D.N. SINGH is President, International Industrial and Licensing Consultants, Inc., New York, and formerly served as Director, Centre for Science and Technology for Development at the United Nations.

INGO WALTER is the Dean Abraham L. Gitlow Professor of Economics and Finance at the Graduate School of Business Administration, New York University, and holds a joint appointment as the Societé de Banques Suisses Professor of International Management INSEAD, Fontainebleau, France. He has been on the faculty at New York University since 1970. From 1971 to 1979, he was Associate Dean for Academic Affairs, serving as Chairman of International Business from 1980 to 1983, and as Chairman of Finance from 1983 to 1985. Professor Walter received his A.B. and M.S. degrees from Lehigh University and his Ph.D. degree in 1966 from New York University. He previously taught at the University of Missouri St. Louis, where he was Chairman of the Department of Economics. Dr. Walter's principal areas of research include international trade policy, international banking, environmental economics, and economics of multinational corporate operations. He has published papers in various professional journals in these fields and is the author or editor of 16 books, the most recent of which is *Global Competition in Financial Services,* published in 1988. He has served as a consultant to various U.S. and foreign government agencies, international institutions, banks and corporations, among them the National Academy of Sciences, Organization for Economic Cooperation and Development, United Nations, World Bank, British Petroleum, the General Electric Company, Philip Morris International, Swiss Bank Corporation and Morgan Guaranty Trust Company. He is a Director of the Hartwell Funds and the Trade Policy Research Centre, London.

KENNETH D. WEISS is a marketing and international trade consultant, now on leave from the State University of New York, college at Old Westbury to work on an investment development project in La Paz, Bolivia. He has previously held positions as President of TREICO (foreign trade consultants), senior trainer for the World Trade Institute in New York, trade-promotion training officer for the United Nations in Africa, foreign-trade information adviser to the government of Honduras, marketing-development adviser in Colombia for the Council of the Americas, and project coordinator in South Korea for the International Marketing Institute. He has also taught international business and marketing at Laredo State University in Texas and operated an export-management company. Mr. Weiss received an M.B.A. degree from Stanford University in 1965. He is a member of Beta Gamma Sigma, scholastic honorary society, and was awarded a life membership in Alpha Kappa Psi, professional business fraternity. He received special training in export promotion from the U.S. Department of Commerce and the International Trade Center (UNCTAD/GATT) in Geneva. Mr. Weiss has written books and magazine articles on international trade and has lectured on export promotion in more than 20 countries. He is conversant in English, French, and Spanish.

CLAS WIHLBORG is Associate Professor of Finance and Business Economics at the University of Southern California. He received his Ph.D. degree from Princeton University in 1977 and previously taught at New York University Graduate School of Business Administration and the Claremont Graduate School. Dr. Wihlborg's principal areas of research include international corporate finance and international monetary economics. He has published papers in professional journals in these areas and is the editor of *Exchange Risk and Exposure* (with Richard M. Levich, 1980). Recently he published a book, *Macroeconomic Uncertainty: International Risks and Opportunities for the Corporation* (with Lars Oxelheim, 1987) which extends the conventional methods for measuring and managing exchange rate and interest rate risk to developing a comprehensive strategy for managing uncertainty about the macroeconomic environment of the firm.

THE MULTINATIONAL ENTERPRISE

CONTENTS

THE MULTINATIONAL ENTERPRISE

Alan M. Rugman

The emergence of large multinational enterprises (MNEs) has changed the face of international business in the last 30 years. Today some 500 multinational enterprises control over half of the world's exchange of manufactured goods and services (Stopford and Dunning, 1983). There are now over 10,000 MNEs, but the largest 500 account for at least 80 percent of all foreign direct investment. In 1981, the total value of the sales of these 500 MNEs amounted to over US $2,700 billion—over 20 percent of the world's gross domestic product and over half of its traded output. These large MNEs come mainly from Europe, the United States, and Japan. (See Exhibit 1.)

The managers of these giant MNEs wield enormous economic and political power, and entire nations have experienced the effects of global competition between them. Even the United States has felt the repercussions of international competition. It is no longer just a home base for overseas investment, but is also a host nation. U.S. MNEs must now fight foreign rivals at home and abroad for market share and profitability. This section will discuss the determinants of such multinational activity, that is, the reasons for international production and distribution.

DEFINITION OF THE MULTINATIONAL ENTERPRISE

A multinational enterprise (MNE) is defined as an organization that engages in the production and distribution of goods and/or services in two or more nations. The MNE thereby controls the operations of at least one subsidiary in a foreign nation. It is an economic organization which operates an internal market across international borders. (For alternative definitions of the MNE, see Hood and Young, 1979; Rugman, 1981, and Stopford, 1982.)

Today, control over international distribution is equally important to production, since firms compete globally in both the domestic and foreign markets of rivals. The strength of MNEs can be in distribution or production; marketing advantages are as valuable as technological ones. For example, of the 20 largest Canadian-owned, mature, resource-based MNEs identified and discussed in Rugman and McIlveen (1985), all but one have marketing-based advantages. The exception, Northern Telecom, is a traditional MNE, owing its success to high technology. Most of the world's largest MNEs, from the United States, Europe, and Japan, engage in such high-tech industries. It is here that the fight for survival against global competition is at its strongest.

EXHIBIT 1   THE WORLD'S LARGEST 500 MULTINATIONAL ENTERPRISES

Home Country		Number of MNEs
United States		242
Europe		172
UK	67	
Germany	33	
France	20	
Sweden	16	
Switzerland	10	
Netherlands	7	
Italy	6	
Belgium	4	
Austria	3	
UK/Netherlands	2	
Others	4	
Japan		62
Canada		18
Australia		3
South Africa		3
	Total	500

Source.   Calculated from John M. Stopford, *The World Directory of Multinational Enterprises 1982–83,* London: Macmillan, 1983.

Note.   Stopford defines an MNE as an industrial corporation with over U.S. $1 billion of sales in 1981 if it meets one of three criteria: (1) at least 25 percent equity in at least 3 foreign subsidiaries; (2) at least 5 percent of sales from foreign investments and (3) at least U.S. $75 million in sales from foreign operations.

UNDERSTANDING THE MNE

The appropriate theory of the MNE is a firm level theory. It is necessary to understand the determinants of foreign direct investment (FDI) at the firm level rather than at the industry level. Data on FDI are often recorded at industry level, but industries are statistical abstractions, whereas firms are real, live MNEs, where managers, workers, and stockholders all have a stake in their operation. Also discussed here will be the nature of the MNE as an economic organization, the sources of its competitive advantages, and its relations with government. More detailed treatment of the organizational structures of MNEs appears elsewhere in this volume.

The approach in this section will be to use the "new theories" of the MNE as a basis for understanding the motives for FDI in a world of global competition and economic interdependence. The new theories of the MNE used here are developments of the transaction costs theory of Coase (1937) and Williamson (1975), as applied to MNEs by Teece (1981 and 1982) and Hennart (1982). Of particular interest is *internalization theory,* as explained in Rugman (1981) and Rugman et al. (1985). For antecedents of internalization theory, see Buckley and Casson (1976), and Dunning (1977). Internalization theory is similar to the eclectic approach of Dunning (1979, 1981), see Rugman (1982, especially Chapter 1), Rugman (1985), and Dunning and Rugman (1985). For recent surveys of internalization theory, see Buckley and Casson (1985) and Rugman (1986).

REASONS FOR MNEs

Why does FDI take place? It does so only when it is less costly to service foreign markets by FDI than by exporting or licensing. Normally, a firm has a choice between at least these three methods of international transactions.

In a frictionless world of perfect competition, the firm can contract at "arm's length" prices, whenever such competitive prices exist or are feasible for the firm. Foreign markets can be serviced by exports or licensing. Unfortunately for many products, especially intermediate products such as knowledge, there are no arm's length prices. The firm then has to overcome the market imperfection implicit in the lack of arm's length prices. In this case, it makes an internal market, using a hierarchical structure to control the allocation and distribution of resources and goods within the firm. Foreign markets can now be serviced by foreign direct investment, in addition to exporting or licensing.

Contractual arrangements with independent foreign partners are favored when there are high costs associated with internalization, and relatively lower costs with licensing. This occurs, for example, when the risk of dissipation of the firm-specific advantage of the MNE is small, and when the costs of incurring contractual agreements are relatively low. Transaction costs exist for the MNE in making a contract with another firm. They include the conceptual costs of creating a contractual agreement plus the operational costs of administering and enforcing it. For the MNE, these transaction costs are often high since it lacks information about the foreign nation, while the other party to the contract has some environmental familiarity. For the partner, the costs are also high due to lack of knowledge about all the details and elements of the product, process, or service being purchased.

It is apparent that FDI originates at the firm level when a typical MNE has to determine the relative costs of internalization versus contracting (assuming that the arm's length choice of exporting is even more costly to the firm due to various other market imperfections such as tariffs and other barriers to trade). Furthermore, it is a convenient starting point to assume that international exchanges by MNEs in the same industry group will be motivated by a similar set of factors, that is, all MNEs will seek the most efficient mode of exchange, subject to the information constraints imposed upon them. These environmental, or country-specific factors, can be taken as parameters to start with.

HOW TO MODEL THE MNE

To explain the motivation of FDI, it is necessary to simplify by assuming the exogeneity of the country-specific advantage (CSA) and other environmental parameters. This approach is different from that of Kojima (1978) and others who emphasize the locational, trade-specific characteristics of FDI. For a criticism of Kojima's macroeconomic-based theory of FDI, see Gray (1982). Instead of this trade theory view of the world, it is necessary to build a microeconomic industrial organization theory of the MNE.

It has been demonstrated in Rugman (1981, 1985) that free trade and MNEs are alternative mechanisms for allocating goods and services to worldwide markets. When barriers to trade exist (such as tariffs or other government-induced market imperfections), the internal market of the MNE replaces the external market of trade. When this occurs, much of interindustry trade is replaced by intraindustry trade and FDI (undertaken by MNEs).

The reasons for trade in homogeneous products are determined by differences in relative goods prices between nations. These rely on traditional Ricardian explanations of comparative advantage, or upon a neoclassical-based Heckscher-Ohlin-Samuelson (H-O-S) trade model of differences in relative factor endowments. In these trade models, the country-specific advantage (CSA) is the determining factor. These models of trade work only when market imperfections are assumed away, or at least when the general characteristics of internationally competitive markets are not distorted by gross deviations from a neoclassical-type equilibrium.

The reasons for MNEs, on the other hand, are determined by the need to internalize a firm-specific advantage (FSA), as explained in detail later. The FSAs arise for the MNEs when there are either natural or government-imposed transaction costs. Internalization takes the form of foreign direct investment (FDI) when there are barriers to trade (which deny exporting) or a risk of dissipation of the FSA (which denies licensing). As a special case, some MNEs engage in offshore assembly to take advantage of cheap foreign labor, a situation where the foreign CSA is a dominant consideration to the MNE.

MNEs perform intraindustry trade, which in the literature of international economics, builds upon the analysis of market imperfections, specifically trade in differentiated products (for example, see Krugman, 1983). Intraindustry trade arises because a good (or "industry" in terms of the H-O-S model) has many characteristics. The simple H-O-S model looks at goods as a homogeneous product, but in reality, there are heterogeneous characteristics in goods and services. Intraindustry trade by MNEs has grown rapidly in the post World War II period, but the economics literature has been slow to advance theoretical arguments which serve to reconcile trade theory with the reality of the MNE.

Two arguments have been advanced by trade economists; they revolve around factors on the production side and the consumption side. First, the product differentiation of the good, and the related need for the product to be produced by large firms which enjoy scale economies, is an explanation of MNEs and intraindustry trade. This is because scale is a type of market imperfection in terms of the H-O-S model. Second, on the consumption side, it has been observed that there is increasing congruence of consumers tastes, especially in the high income advanced nations of the Northern Hemisphere, between which most trade and MNE activity takes place.

Within this framework of an exogenous CSA, the strategic choices open to MNEs in the same industry grouping can be considered only in terms of the limited choice of entry mode between exporting, foreign direct investment, and licensing. While it is important for MNEs to reevaluate their firm-specific advantages (FSAs), market niches, and other attributes, it is not feasible to model these ongoing FDI choices as other than changes in the original FDI decision, such that a new set of entry modes needs to be considered. However, this still permits some analysis of how industry rivals operate on a worldwide basis and of how FDI occurs. Here the recent work of Michael Porter (1980) on competitive strategy provides useful clues to FDI when adapted to a global context.

In particular, Porter's identification of entry and exit barriers is a useful method of classifying changes in FDI due to dynamic adjustments in the FSAs of MNEs. Due to their internal markets, MNEs are better equipped to bypass both entry and exit barriers (such as R&D, advertising, and scale economies) than are domestic or host country rivals. This ability of MNEs to move into new world markets, switch modes, and enter and exit at lower costs than domestic firms, is an important reason for the increase in FDI on a global basis. One result is an increase in cross investments, or two-way FDI which is following the growth of MNEs in general. Cross-FDI is a response to the changing FSAs of MNEs and to the increase in global competition. Today, MNEs (each with an FSA) in the same industry will operate in different nations, when there is no apparent difference in the CSAs, such that traditional trade explanations of international activity are insufficient in explaining trade and investment patterns.

THE THREE TYPES OF MNEs

The MNE is a multiplant firm and the key decision is where the boundary falls between the allocation of resources in either an internal market or a regular (external) market. MNEs will occur when their internal markets experience lower transaction costs than those that arise in operating an arm's length market (Rugman, 1981 and Caves, 1982). MNEs are of three types:

1. Horizontally integrated multiplant firms.
2. Vertically integrated multiplant firms.
3. Diversified multiplant firms and conglomerates (which reduce risks).

HORIZONTALLY INTEGRATED MNEs.   Horizontally integrated MNEs have a transactional advantage in using a hierarchical administrative structure to control their international production. Firms use their internal markets when these either have lower costs or generate higher revenues, that is, they have lower net costs, than any alternative market or contractual system. This principle applies internationally and explains the need for MNEs.

Usually each horizontally integrated MNE has a special FSA in the form of an intangible advantage or asset. The FSA can be in the form of technological knowledge, management skills, or marketing know-how. Often the FSA is patented. Each MNE attempts to differentiate its product or service, therefore, the first question to ask when examining an MNE is about the nature of its unique FSA.

The natural market imperfections identified by Caves (1971, 1982) as facing horizontally-integrated MNEs are of two general types. First, the public goods nature of knowledge, which leads to the appropriability problem first identified for the MNE by Johnson (1970) and Magee (1975). Second, information impactedness, opportunism, and buyer uncertainty aspects of market failure raised by Williamson (1976) in a domestic context and applied in an international context by others. These transaction costs are classic reasons for the internalization of markets by MNEs.

The Pharmaceutical MNEs.   As an example of the application of the concept of internalization to FDI it is interesting to study the pricing of pharmaceuticals by horizontally integrated MNEs. There is an externality in the production and pricing of pharmaceuticals. Multinational drug firms engage in expensive R&D to find, produce, and market a new product. It costs up to $70 million to put a new drug on the market, with most of this expense due to the animal and human testing required to guarantee the safety of the product in order to pass strict government health regulations.

These huge expenses need to be recovered by the MNE so it places a patent on the product. This gives the firm exclusive property rights over the manufacture and distribution of the product in the domain of the patent. In nations where patents are not respected, or when the MNE fears that licensing or a joint venture can lead to dissipation of its FSA, then the MNE has an incentive to keep the proprietary knowledge within the firm. It does this by making an internal market, that is, the firm keeps control of the knowledge by using wholly-owned subsidiaries to supply host nation markets with a brand name product. Multinational drug firms thereby appropriate a fair return on their investments and bring their new health-related products to consumers around the world.

We would expect to observe a high degree of FDI in the drug industry due to the need for internalization as a protection against dissipation of the FSA of the MNE. Each nation's drug MNEs have the same incentives for internalization, so intra-industry investments take place, as a response to both natural and unnatural market imperfections.

There is some potential for rent-seeking behavior of the MNEs. They have a monopoly over the use of the knowledge, and the more effective their method of internalization of the FSA on a worldwide basis, then the greater the opportunity for rents to be earned. However, data on the profitability of drug MNEs reveal that they do not earn excess profits over time, nor is there any evidence of systematic exploitation of host nations. This is partly explained by the problem facing drug MNEs; that of ongoing R&D expenses in the search for the few successful new product lines.

There is a probability distribution of successful drug innovations (just as there is for oil wells or mines). Many drugs are impossible to market as they are not sufficiently different from competitive products. Others provide little revenue to the firm due to their inability to pass standards, regulatory codes, or other restrictions. Only a few drugs are successful and these have to finance future investments. The dynamic FSA of a drug MNE relies on costly ongoing R&D in new product lines.

Host Government Policy on Drug MNEs. Recent policy actions in Canada have severely affected the drug industry in that nation. This is discussed in detail in Gordon and Fowler (1983). In the early 1970s, both the Canadian federal and provincial governments enacted legislation for compulsory licensing by MNEs to generic producers. The MNEs were given only three years to sell their product in the Canadian market before they were required to license host country generic producers, who in return paid the MNEs a small royalty of 4 percent on sales.

The effect of this compulsory licensing requirement was to virtually destroy R&D in the drug industry in Canada. It became prohibitively expensive for MNEs to maintain any R&D capacity in Canada, since patents on new drugs would not be respected for a long enough period to recover development costs. Therefore, R&D in Canadian subsidiaries decreased drastically with parent MNEs taking over R&D where there was no risk of appropriation by the host nation of the FSA in knowledge of the MNE at such a low price. Such environmental changes in the Canadian CSAs disrupted the normal pattern of FDI. This regulation of the MNEs by changing the CSAs is being repeated elsewhere.

Paradoxically it is impossible for a viable Canadian-owned drug industry to develop since the Canadian market (of 24 million people) is too small to support the huge development costs of new drugs. Canada lacks scale economies in R&D, production, and marketing. As other nations, especially developing nations (such as India), Italy, and the eastern European countries, do not respect international patents, it is not feasible for a Canadian-based MNE to rely on foreign sales or production to recover its costs of drug development. Recognition of some of these problems led Canada in 1986 to moderate its regulations. In order to encourage more R&D by MNEs, they were allowed a longer patent period.

In the future, FDI in pharmaceuticals may well be reduced by the breakdown of internationally accepted patent laws. As other forms of international servicing, such as licensing or exporting are not feasible due to the risk of dissipation of the knowledge advantage of the MNE, world welfare and health losses will be experienced. Only by respecting the property rights of MNEs, whatever the nationality of the parent company, will it be feasible for brand name drug producers to recover their position in host nations such as Canada. Without internalization it is not possible for MNEs to provide social benefits in the form of R&D, employment, taxes, and health services.

VERTICALLY INTEGRATED MNEs. The second area in which the modern theory of the MNE is relevant for an understanding of the determinants of FDI is for vertically integrated MNEs, such as oil or mineral resource firms. In the case of vertically integrated multiplant firms, the internal market can be used to establish control and minimize transaction costs. This gives another sort of FSA to the MNE. Let us look at oil firms as a case study of vertically integrated MNEs.

Petroleum MNEs. In the case of petroleum companies, the type of FSA that may be controlled within the MNE is always one determined by external market imperfections. Petroleum firms engage in vertical integration in response to both natural and government-induced market imperfections. Their control over sources of supply and over markets is justified when an FSA needs to be generated in order to bypass a host of transaction costs involving supply uncertainties, logistics and search costs. The optimal rate of development of an oil field requires coordination of the production (refining) and marketing function in a dynamic sense. This is best achieved within a firm, where accurate information about all these functions can be assembled. Such knowledge is not freely available, and the internalization of extraction, refining, and marketing by the MNE gives it a special type of FSA. This assignment of property rights permits it to protect its company information and gives the firm a knowledge advantage.

There are four stages of vertical integration: Extraction, transportation, refining, and distribution. Control of the supplies and markets is needed to allow the crucial capital intensive refining stage to operate at full capacity. An oil MNE can put together this package at lower costs than the market. The MNEs have managed to continue this process even after OPEC disrupted the extraction stage in 1973 and 1979. The oil MNEs retained control over distribution, so they were able to pass on to consumers the higher costs of crude oil. In return, the oil MNEs only required stable supplies of oil; price did not matter. Of course, over the last ten years the bargaining over crude oil prices has moved away from firms and toward governments. Yet the oil MNEs still retain the general ability to overcome the set of transaction costs, so their role as internalizers will continue in the future.

One of the key benefits of an MNE is that a subsidiary has access to the large set of crude oil supplies owned by its multinational parent. If there is a disruption to part of the supply, action can be taken by the parent to minimize the effect on any one affiliate. Also, an affiliate can always renew its contracts for supplies of crude oil. During times of crisis, a firm with no ongoing relationship with a supplier of crude oil may have difficulty in obtaining adequate supplies of crude oil at any price.

Another benefit for the subsidiary is access to new research and technology produced within the MNE; activities which are controlled and centralized in the parent firm but used optimally by all affiliates. While there are no theoretical problems with the concept of making internal markets, practical issues may arise when it is applied internationally. The key problem is that of sovereignty. The host nation often has a viewpoint different from that of the parent firm. The host nation may look at the same picture as the multinational firm and its subsidiary but interpret it differently. It is for this reason that FDI puzzles governments, but is accepted as a natural phenomenon by MNEs.

DIVERSIFIED MNEs.   The third type of multiplant MNEs are *diversified* MNEs. These are explained by the principles of international diversification and have been discussed in Rugman (1979). The focus upon financial diversification means that conglomerate activity can also be included in this category of MNEs. Conglomerates from different countries often engage in cross-FDI, for example, FDI by MNEs in the same industries but across different countries.

MNEs, by the very nature of their international operations, are engaged in risk pooling. They are exposed to less variation in sales than are uninational firms confined to a single (domestic) market. Although international diversification is an explanation based on financial factors instead of real asset factors it is still relevant to explain MNE activities since risk pooling is an excellent reason for cross-industry investments.

Reasons for International Diversification.   The international diversification relevant here is that in which market imperfections (in the form of information costs and government regulations) in the international capital market enter to constrain simple portfolio diversification (which individuals could do themselves by buying into the stock indexes of various nations). The individual has information and research costs. There is also political risk, exchange risk, and other environmental uncertainties to be considered.

The MNE is a potential surrogate vehicle for individual financial asset diversification since it is already operating internationally and the business cycles of nations do not move in perfect tandem. The advantages of real asset diversification of MNEs arise since MNEs avoid market imperfections by internalization. This has an implication for FDI, since there is a type of FSA involved in the financial diversification achieved by the specific MNE. Each MNE is a portfolio of assets, with an FSA something like a brand name, since the FSA is unique to each individual MNE. There is a close linkage between the role of the MNE as an international diversifier and the growth of two-way FDI in recent years.

MNEs IN SERVICE SECTORS

FDI occurs in service sectors as well as in manufacturing sectors. For example, the theory of the MNE has been shown to explain activities in the international hotel industry (see Casson (1982) and Dunning and McQueen (1982)). The latter demonstrate that MNEs in the hotel industry have ownership specific advantages (or FSAs) in the form of high quality, reliable and efficient "experience goods" (services) which reduce the transaction costs (buyer uncertainty) of customers. These internalized knowledge advantages are slightly different but are common to all major hotel MNEs, for example Holiday Inn, Inter-Continental, Hilton, Sheraton, and Trusthouse Forte.

Cross-investment in the hotel sector is taking place, despite the prevalence of U.S. owned MNEs. Dunning and McQueen report that the United States has 50 percent of foreign associated hotels, France 15 percent, Britain 15 percent but West Germany only 2 percent. Country-specific factors help to determine this degree of foreign ownership; a multiplant domestic base being required for overseas hotel chains. An example of FDI in the United States is Canadian ownership of the Four Seasons hotel chain, and the purchase of the Howard Johnson hotels by Imperial Tobacco of Britain (subsequently sold in 1985).

To promote horizontal integration, FDI will exist, indeed prevail, in international banking. Each multinational bank has an intangible knowledge advantage which lowers such transactions costs as opportunism and buyer uncertainty. FDI in banking will increase as the FSAs become more apparent. We notice that European, Canadian, and Japanese multinational banks are increasing their presence on world markets, although U.S. banks still dominate. Grubel (1977) and Rugman (1979) have discussed this in detail.

IMPLICATIONS OF THEORY FOR POLICY

The theory of internalization has been shown to offer powerful insights into the linkages between MNEs, intraindustry trade, and FDI. Internalization builds upon earlier theories such as Vernon's (1966) product cycle and Dunning's (1981) eclectic theory of the MNE. These two models of the MNE, however, are too broad; a convenient simplification is required to explain and predict FDI, such as the assumption of exogeneity in the CSAs. This is not a radical departure from the literature, since both the product cycle and eclectic approaches use the key element of internalization theory, namely the importance of market imperfections (which leads to identification of the FSAs). Thus it can be inferred that all of these theories of the MNE are useful variations in explaining FDI. Also relevant will be other theories of the MNE which have focused upon one or another type of market imperfection, a point made in the context of the general nature of internalization theory in Chapter 2 of Rugman (1981). As market imperfections persist, indeed increase, we can expect more FSAs to develop, leading to even more FDI in the future.

From this comes a simple but penetrating insight into the policy issues raised by MNEs. As a limiting case FDI will disappear with the removal of the market imperfections which generate it. In a world of perfect markets and no externalities, that is where knowledge can be priced on a regular market and no government-imposed imperfections exist, then there is not a logical reason for the MNE. Indeed free trade is all that occurs in such a first best world. Since transaction costs and government regulations do exist in practice, then it is evident that all policy discussion is about second best measures. What policy means in this context is unclear. All we can do is look to the first-best solution as a guideline. For example, if GATT can liberalize trade by removing tariff (and today nontariff barriers) then the motives for FDI are simultaneously reduced. If the market imperfections can be removed *at source*, the MNEs and FDIs will fade away.

To the extent that MNEs are replacements for the best world of free trade, they increase allocative efficiency. Internal markets are a method of getting towards the elusive benefits of perfect markets. In a world of transaction costs and government imperfections arm's-length market prices simply do not exist for many goods and services. Internalization is an efficient response (from the perspective of the firm and its management) to such market imperfections. To the extent that FDI is done in the internal market of MNEs it can be concluded that FDI is efficient, when compared to the second-best world from which it springs.

PERFORMANCE OF MNEs. The world's largest MNEs are identified in the Appendix. Exhibit A1 reports the profits of the 18 largest U.S. MNEs; Exhibit A2, the profits of the largest European MNEs; and Exhibit A3 those of the largest 18 Japanese. Also reported in Exhibit A4 are profits of the largest 18 Canadian MNEs, although these are smaller than the other three sets.

Data on the performance of the world's largest MNEs reveal that they are efficient in the sense that they earn a normal rate of return. Summary data on the performance of the 18 largest U.S., 18 largest European, 18 largest Japanese, and 18 largest Canadian MNEs are reported in Exhibit 2 for the period 1970–1983. Profits are shown by the ROE (defined as net income after taxes divided by the value of stockholders' equity). For more detail see Rugman and McIlveen (1985). The standard deviation (SD) of these earnings over the period is also recorded. This is a proxy for the total risk of earnings of each set of MNEs over the period.

These groups of MNEs earn mean profits which are insignificantly different from uninational (domestic) firms of similar size. The reason that the European MNEs average ROE is lower than that of other nations is due partly to the inclusion of 14 state-owned enterprises (SOEs) in the group (Rugman, 1983). It has also been demonstrated that U.S. MNEs had more stable profits than non-MNEs of similar size over the 1960–69 period, and that this benefit of international diversification applies as a general principle (Rugman, 1979).

EXHIBIT 2   PERFORMANCE OF THE WORLD'S LARGEST MULTINATIONALS, 1970–1983

	1970–1983	
	ROE	S.D.
United States	12.9	5.5
Canada	12.0	5.8
Japan	10.5	4.6
Europe	8.5	4.8

Source.   Adapted from Exhibit 3 in Rugman and McIlveen (1985).

Intraindustry trade and FDI is also important for small open economies, such as Canada, Belgium, Switzerland, and so on. These nations lack a domestic market of sufficient size to provide indigenous firms with scale economies and the full benefits of specialization. Instead, many small scale plants with short production runs exist. These inefficient plants only survive due to the protection of a tariff or nontariff barrier. Yet, as the world moves toward trade liberalization, with the GATT rounds reducing nominal tariffs, some of this protection is disappearing and firms are having to engage in contracting out and other types or rationalization in order to achieve greater economies of specialization. This increases the amount of FDI.

SUMMARY AND CONCLUSIONS

FDI is a replacement for trade. The explanation for increasing FDI activity is to be found by considering the plethora of natural and government induced "unnatural" market imperfections which lead to the development of internal markets by MNEs.

The trade and industrial "policies" of nations are often the very causes of MNE activity. MNEs and changes in FDI react to governmental policies, rather than initiate them. When governments create distortions in the marketplace (for distributional, regulatory or other nonefficiency reasons) they are effectively signalling for replacement internal markets, which the MNEs provide and FDI signifies.

FDI is the result of world-wide innovation as MNEs use internal markets to retain their FSAs. MNEs provide goods and services to consumers which embody this intangible asset, thereby transferring technology and increasing global economic welfare. Diffusion of technological know-how is confined to MNEs and the consumers of their products until the products become relatively standardized, at which time the risk of dissipation of the FSAs becomes negligible and indigenous producers in host nations take over the provision of the product or service.

The United States, like other nations, benefits from FDI, since this is a replacement for international trade with the MNE being a vehicle for efficient worldwide allocation and distribution. Clearly, in the long-run, efficient industrial development is dependent upon the acceptance of FDI. Even in the protectionist atmosphere of the United States, it does not pay to restrict inward FDI, for the same reasons of economic efficiency that outward U.S. FDI has always been supported. FDI is superior to short-term interventionist policies which preserve the interest of owners and workers at the expense of national economic welfare.

The symmetry of MNEs to free trade is a guiding light in the jungle of government intervention, regulation, and restriction of international economic activity. If formal protection, nontariff barriers to trade or other restrictions on trade increase, then MNEs or contractual arrangements will increase. The lesson of the MNE in the last 30 years is that as restrictions are imposed on trade then alternative methods of international exchange will develop in order to prevent the contraction of world welfare.

SOURCES AND SUGGESTED REFERENCES

Buckley, Peter J., and Mark Casson. *The Future of the Multinational Enterprise.* Basingstoke and London: Macmillan, 1976.

———. *The Economic Theory of the Multinational Enterprise.* London: Macmillan, 1985.

Casson, Mark. *Alternatives to the Multinational Enterprise*. London: Macmillan, 1979.

———. "Transaction Costs and the Theory of the Multinational Enterprise," *New Theories of the Multinational Enterprise*. Edited by Alan M. Rugman. London: Croom Helm, and New York: St. Martin's Press, 1982.

——— (ed.). *The Growth of International Business*. London: George Allen and Unwin, 1983.

Caves, Richard E. "International Corporations: The Industrial Economics of Foreign Investment," *Economica* 38 (1971): 1–27.

———. *Multinational Enterprise and Economic Analysis*. Cambridge and New York: Cambridge University Press, 1982.

Coase, Ronald H. "The Nature of the Firm," *Economica* 4 (1937): 336–405.

Dunning, John H. "Trade, Location and Economic Activity and the MNE: A Search for an Eclectic Approach," *The International Allocation of Economic Activity. Proceedings of a Nobel Symposium held in Stockholm*. Edited by Bertil Ohlin et al. London: Macmillan, 1977.

———. "Explaining Changing Patterns of International Production: In Defence of the Eclectic Theory," *Oxford Bulletin of Economics and Statistics* 41 (November 1979): 269–296.

———. *International Production and the Multinational Enterprise*. London: George Allen and Unwin, 1981.

Dunning, John H., and Matthew McQueen. "The Theory of the MNE and the International Hotel Industry," *New Theories of the Multinational Enterprise*. Alan M. Rugman (ed.). London: Croom Helm, and New York: St. Martin's Press, 1982.

Dunning, John H. and Alan M. Rugman. "The Influence of Hymer's Dissertation on the Theory of Foreign Direct Investment," *American Economic Review* (May 1985): 228–32.

Gladwin, Thomas N. and Ingo Walter. *Multinationals Under Fire* (New York: John Wiley, 1980).

Gordon, Myron, and David Fowler. "The Performance of the Multinational Drug Industry in Home and Host Countries: A Case Study," Charles P. Kindleberger and David B. Audretsch (eds.), *The Multinational Corporation in the 1980s*. Cambridge, MA: MIT Press, 1983.

Gray, H. Peter. "Macroeconomic Theories of Foreign Direct Investment," *New Theories of the Multinational Enterprise*. Alan M. Rugman (ed.). London: Croom Helm, and New York: St. Martin's Press, 1982.

Grubel, Herbert G. "A Theory of Multinational Banking," *Banca Nazionale del Lovoro Quarterly Review* (December 1977).

Hennart, Jean-Francois. *A Theory of Multinational Enterprise*. Ann Arbor, MI: University of Michigan Press, 1982.

Hood, Neil and Stephen Young. *The Economics of Multinational Enterprises*. London: Longman, 1979.

Johnson, Harry G. "The Efficiency and Welfare Implications of the International Corporation," *The International Corporation*. Edited by Charles P. Kindleberger. Cambridge, MA: MIT Press, 1970.

Kojima, Kiyoshi. *Direct Foreign Investment: A Japanese Model of Multinational Business Operations*. London: Croom Helm, 1978.

Krugman, Paul. "The 'New Theories' of International Trade and the Multinational Enterprise," *The Multinational Corporation in the 1980s*. Charles P. Kindleberger and David B. Audretsch (eds.). Cambridge, MA: MIT Press, 1983.

Magee, Stephen P. "Information and the Multinational Corporation: An Appropriability Theory of Direct Foreign Investment," *The New International Economic Order*. Edited by Jagdish N. Bhagwati. Cambridge, MA: MIT Press, 1977.

Porter, Michael G. *Competitive Strategy.* New York: Free Press, 1980.

Rugman, Alan M. *International Diversification and the Multinational Enterprise.* Lexington: D.C. Heath, 1979.

———. *Multinationals in Canada: Theory, Performance and Economic Impact.* Boston: Martinus Nijhoff, 1980.

———. *Inside the Multinationals: The Economics of Internal Markets.* London: Croom Helm, and New York: Columbia University Press, 1981.

——— (ed.). *New Theories of the Multinational Enterprise.* London: Croom Helm, and New York: St. Martin's Press, 1982.

——— (ed.). "The Comparative Performance of U.S. and European Multinational Enterprises, 1970–79," *Management International Review* 23:2 (1983): 4–14.

———. "The Determinants of Intra-Industry Direct Foreign Investment," Asim Erdilek (ed.), *Multinationals as Mutual Invaders: Intraindustry Direct Foreign Investment.* London: Croom Helm, 1985: 38–59.

———. "New Theories of the Multinational Enterprise: An Assessment of Internalization Theory," *Bulletin of Economic Research* 38:2 (May 1986): 101–118.

Rugman, Alan M. and John McIlveen. *Megafirms: Strategies for Canadian Multinationals,* Toronto: Methuen, 1985.

Rugman, Alan M., Donald J. Lecraw, and Laurence Booth. *International Business.* New York: McGraw-Hill, 1985.

Stopford, John M. *The World Directory of Multinational Enterprises 1982–83,* London: Macmillan, 1982.

Stopford, John M. and John H. Dunning. *Multinationals: Company Performance and Global Trends.* London: Macmillan, 1983.

Teece, David J. "The MNE, Market Failure and Market Pioneer Considerations," *Sloan Management Review* (Spring 1981).

———. "A Transactions Cost Theory of the Multinational Enterprise." University of Reading Discussion Paper in International Investment and Business Studies. No. 66 (September 1982). Published in Casson (1983).

Vernon, Raymond. "International Investment and International Trade in the Product Cycle," *Quarterly Journal of Economics* 80 (May 1966).

Williamson, Oliver E. *Markets and Hierarchies: Analysis and Antitrust Implications:* A Study in the Economics of Internal Organizations. New York: Free Press, 1975.

EXHIBIT A1   PERFORMANCE OF THE 18 LARGEST U.S. MULTINATIONALS

Firm	1983 Sales (Cdn. millions)	1973–1983	
		ROE	S.D.
Exxon	$110,205	14.5	4.8
General Motors	92,809	12.9	7.5
Mobil	67,953	13.1	5.2
Ford	55,320	10.5	7.6
IBM	50,000	19.5	2.5
Texaco	49,861	11.7	5.3
E.I. du Pont de Nemours	44,024	11.6	4.3
Standard Oil of California	34,022	13.1	4.4
General Electric	33,346	16.2	3.7
Gulf	33,077	10.0	4.4
Occidental Petroleum	23,788	14.8	12.3
Philips Petroleum	18,976	14.3	4.7
Sun	18,330	12.8	4.2
United Technologies	18,254	11.6	3.9
Tenneco	17,861	12.2	4.5
ITT	17,614	10.9	3.2
Chrysler	16,476	6.7	13.6
Proctor and Gamble	15,495	16.5	2.8
Average		12.9	5.5

Sources.   *Fortune* 500 U.S. Industrials Annual Reports

EXHIBIT A2 PERFORMANCE OF THE 18 LARGEST EUROPEAN MULTINATIONALS

Firm	(Country)	1983 Sales (Cdn. millions)	1970–1983 ROE	S.D.
Royal Dutch/Shell	Neth./U.K.	$100,238	15.9	5.4
British Petroleum[1]	U.K.	61,218	12.0	7.5
ENI[1]	Italy	31,137	2.1	4.6
Unilever	U.K./Neth.	25,251	11.6[2]	6.0
Francais de Petroles	France	22,835	10.5	11.4
Elf-Aquitaine[1]	France	22,633	12.6	8.3
Philips	Netherlands	20,131	5.2	2.7
Siemens	Germany	19,567	8.4	1.6
Volkswagenwerk[1]	Germany	19,528	5.1	6.7
Daimler-Benz	Germany	19,487	18.1	10.9
Bayer	Germany	18,188	8.2	3.5
Hoechst	Germany	18,116	6.5	3.6
Renault[1]	France	18,003	1.9	3.4
Fiat	Italy	18,002	3.9[3]	3.4
Nestle	Switzerland	16,554	7.5	4.7
BASF	Germany	16,448	6.7	4.3
BAT Industries	Britain	15,036	12.1	2.2
Thyssen	Germany	14,063	5.3	4.5
Average			8.5	4.8

Sources. *Fortune* International 500 Non-U.S. Industrial Corporations and Stopford, John M. *The World Directory of Multinational Enterprises 1982–83,* London: Macmillan, 1982.

[1] state-owned or controlled
[2] 1970–1982
[3] 1970–1979

EXHIBIT A3   PERFORMANCE OF THE 18 LARGEST JAPANESE MULTINATIONALS

Firm	1983 Sales (Cdn. millions)	1970–1983 ROE	S.D.
Toyota Motor	$22,556	15.1	3.8
Matsushita Electric Industrial	20,805	12.0	3.7
Hitachi	19,666	11.7	3.1
Nissan Motor	19,535	12.6	3.3
Mitsubishi Heavy Industries	14,828	7.6	3.6
Nippon Steel	14,443	9.1	5.5
Toshiba	11,801	7.4	6.7
Honda Motor	10,916	15.4	4.9
Nippon Kokan	7,799	9.0	4.7
Mitsubishi Electric	7,625	10.3	3.7
Toyo Kogyo	7,529	8.3	5.3
Nippon Electric (NEC)	7,196	9.4	4.5
Sumitomo Metal	6,834	9.9	6.3
Kobe Steel	6,079	8.3	4.7
Sanyo Electric	5,942	11.0	3.2
Kawasaki Steel	5,701	10.1	7.5
Sony	5,656	13.8	5.2
Ishikawajima-Harima	4,652	8.5	3.2
Average		10.5	4.6

Sources. Fortune International 500 Non-U.S. Industrial Corporations and Stopford, John M. *The World Directory of Multinational Enterprises 1982–83,* London: Macmillan, 1982.

EXHIBIT A4   PERFORMANCE OF THE 18 LARGEST CANADIAN MULTINATIONALS

Firm	1979–1983 Average Sales (Cdn. millions)	1970–1983 ROE Percent	S.D. Percent
Alcan	$5,879	10.3	7.5
Seagram	3,169	10.2	1.6
Noranda	2,867	13.2	9.4
Hiram Walker	2,867	11.6	4.0
NOVA	2,665	12.5	1.9
Northern Telecom	2,573	13.8	6.7
Massey Ferguson	2,542	4.9	6.6
Macmillan Bloedel	2,143	8.5	7.3
Moore	2,141	17.3	2.0
Inco	1,929	9.5	7.4
Genstar	1,861	14.1+	6.3+
Domtar	1,684	11.4	7.7
Abitibi Price	1,577	10.5	7.0
AMCA	1,515	12.0	6.7
Molson	1,434	15.8	2.4
John Labatt	1,432	15.0	2.5
Consolidated-Bathurst	1,386	13.4	8.8
Mean	2,279	12.0	5.8

Source.   Corporate Annual Reports

ENTERING INTERNATIONAL MARKETS

CONTENTS

ENTERING INTERNATIONAL MARKETS

Franklin R. Root

Today companies need to plan for growth and survival in a world of global competition. Many companies will choose to remain at home to confront international competitors in once-familiar domestic markets. But other companies will choose to meet their competitors in foreign markets (as well as in domestic markets) by going international in one or more ways. To do so, they will need to design and carry out entry strategies that can sustain a continuing presence in foreign markets.

THE ELEMENTS OF FOREIGN-MARKET-ENTRY STRATEGY

THE NEED TO PLAN. A foreign-market-entry strategy is a comprehensive plan that lays down the objectives, resources, and policies that will guide a company's international business over a period of time long enough to achieve a sustainable growth in world markets. The time horizon for an entry strategy should be distant enough to compel company managers to raise and answer fundamental questions about the direction and scope of their international business. For most companies the entry-strategy time horizon will be 3 to 5 years.

Managers in small and medium-sized companies tend to view strategic planning for foreign-market entry as something only large companies can afford to do because they think it calls for elaborate techniques applied by expert planners to mountains of data acquired by costly research. But this is a misconception. Planning foreign-market entry is actually a process of deciding on the direction of a company's international business by combining reason with empirical knowledge. It forces managers to examine critically all assumptions about foreign markets and competition. Once a company accepts the *idea* of strategic planning, it can surely find a way to plan foreign-market entry—however limited its resources may be. Indeed, no company can afford *not* to think systematically about where its international business should be three to five years from now, because it will be competing against strategy-minded Japanese, European, and other firms. Without an entry strategy, a company is confined to short-run, ad hoc responses to changing markets and competition. Such a "sales" approach to foreign markets is no longer a viable form of international business.

CONSTITUENT PRODUCT/MARKET PLANS. A company's overall foreign-market-entry strategy is an aggregation of several individual product/market strategies. Managers need to design an entry strategy for *each* product and *each* foreign market. Differences among foreign markets make highly risky the assumption that a particular entry strategy would draw the same response across different products or different country markets. This statement does not gainsay the desirability of identifying clusters of *similar* country markets that can be entered with the same strategy. Indeed, market clustering is a natural outcome of the reconciliation by managers of the constituent product/market plans to form a company's overall foreign-market-entry strategy.

The constituent plans call for decisions on the following issues:

1. The target product and target foreign market.
2. The company's objectives and goals in the target market.
3. The entry mode to penetrate the target foreign country.
4. The marketing plan to penetrate the target market in the target country.
5. The control system to monitor performance in the target country/market.

These entry decisions are interdependent, making the planning process iterative, with several feedback loops. For instance, the evaluation of alternative entry modes may bring about a revision of market objectives or even start a search for a new target country. Or the design of the marketing plan may call into question an earlier preference for a particular entry mode. Once operations begin in a foreign target market, variances in performance may lead managers to revise any or all of the other entry decisions. Thus managers should regard planning for foreign-market entry as a continuing, open-ended process.

This section addresses primarily the third and fifth entry issues: the choice of an entry mode and the revision of foreign-market-entry strategies to sustain market performance. Section 3 examines the other entry issues, particularly the formulation of a marketing plan to gain penetration of a foreign target market.

FOREIGN-MARKET-ENTRY MODES. A foreign-market-entry mode is an institutional arrangement that enables a company to transfer its products, technology, management, and other resources to a foreign *country*. The need to penetrate a country as well as a market is unique to international business because in domestic business a company is already located inside the country that contains its market. Since an entry mode that is successful for one country may not be successful for another, managers need to decide on the most appropriate entry mode for each target country.

Foreign-market-entry modes may be classified as follows:

1. Export entry modes:
   a. Indirect.
   b. Direct agent/distributor.
   c. Direct branch/subsidiary.
   d. Other.
2. Contractual entry modes:
   a. Licensing.
   b. Franchising.

      c. Technical agreements.
      d. Service contracts.
      e. Management contracts.
      f. Construction/turnkey contracts.
      g. Contract manufacture.
      h. Coproduction agreements.
      i. Other.
3. Investment entry modes:
      a. Sole venture: new establishment.
      b. Sole venture: acquisition.
      c. Joint venture: majority.
      d. Joint venture: 50–50.
      e. Joint venture: minority.

In deciding on the most appropriate entry mode for a particular product and target foreign country, managers need to consider several, often conflicting, external forces in the target country as well as several factors internal to the company.

Target-country factors include *market factors* (such as sales potential, competition, and distribution channels), *production factors* (such as the quality, quantity, availability, and cost of inputs for local production) and *political, economic,* and *sociocultural factors* (such as government policies toward international trade and investment, geographic distance, attributes of the economy, and the cultural "distance" between the home and target-country societies).

How managers respond to external country factors in choosing an entry mode depends on factors internal to the company. They include *product factors* (such as degree of differentiation, pre- and post-purchase services, technological intensity, and the need for adaptation), and *resource/commitment factors* (such as resources in management, capital, technology, and functional skills, and the willingness to commit them to foreign markets).

The diversity of forces and the need to assess their strengths and future directions combine to make the entry-mode decision a complex process with many trade-offs among alternative entry modes. To deal with this complexity, managers can benefit from an analytical model that facilitates systematic comparisons of entry modes with respect to a particular product and target country. This model is offered later, after the reader has become acquainted with the general advantages and disadvantages of the different entry modes.

ENTERING FOREIGN MARKETS THROUGH EXPORTS

EXPORTING AS A LEARNING EXPERIENCE. Most manufacturers enter international business for the first time as exporters. By using an indirect channel, a manufacturer can begin exporting with low start-up costs, modest risks, and the prospect of early profits on sales. He can then step up his effort over time by penetrating new country markets, adding new export products, and eventually moving on to direct export channels. Exporting allows a manufacturer, therefore, to test the acceptance of his products in foreign markets in an exploratory, experimental fashion. And so, exporting becomes an international learning experience that carries a company into a growing commitment to international business.

Licensing and investment entry modes can seldom offer manufacturers the advantages of exporting as a first learning experience. Although they may have low start-up costs, licensing arrangements are not good learning experiences because the foreign-licensee firms have full control over the marketing of licensed products. Thus the licensee stands as a buffer between the licensor (manufacturer) and the foreign market. Furthermore, licensing may create a future competitor in world markets, a contingency that is likely to be overlooked by the neophyte international company. In contrast, equity investment in local production can provide an intense learning experience, but only at a high risk. Investment entry calls for a much-higher commitment of resources than exporting and is much-more exposed to political risks. Moreover, the information and experience needed by managers to make good investment decisions are simply unavailable to the neophyte international company.

As managers gain knowledge and experience from export operations, they also learn to assess the true risks of international business as distinguished from its imagined risks. They are inclined to move, therefore, toward entry modes that offer greater control over the marketing effort in target countries. They may also discover that some excellent foreign-market opportunities can be exploited only through licensing, investment, or other nonexport entry modes. The story of a small building-products manufacturer (call him Alpha) reveals this process of growing international involvement.

Alpha entered foreign markets for the first time in 1965 by exporting to Europe and Australia, and now has distributors in all the major industrial countries. In the late 1960s, Alpha negotiated licensing agreements in Europe, Japan, and South Africa. The Japanese licensee later became a joint-venture partner. As sales reached substantial volumes in certain countries, Alpha began to establish local production facilities. It opened its first plant in Europe in 1970 and its second plant in Australia the following year. By the early 1970s, Alpha was getting about 80 percent of its income from foreign operations, which included exporting, licensing, joint ventures, and wholly owned subsidiaries in countries on all continents.

Although few manufacturers become as dependent on international business, Alpha's story is representative of how many companies have developed their international business. It may help managers in neophyte international firms to know that even the giant multinational manufacturers got their start in international business as exporters.

GETTING STARTED: INDIRECT EXPORTING

Indirect and Direct Export Channels. In exporting to a target country, a company may use any of several export channels. Exhibit 1 illustrates the principal channels.

The primary distinction among the alternative export channels is the presence or absence of export middlemen in the home country. Channels that utilize domestic intermediaries are called *indirect* because the manufacturer does not export on his own but instead relies on an export middleman. Channels that utilize foreign agents or distributors, the manufacturer's own foreign sales facilities, or any other channels that circumvent domestic export middlemen are called *direct*. With direct channels, the manufacturer carries on his own export operations.

There are several kinds of domestic export middlemen: export merchants who deal mainly in staple goods, resident foreign buyers and commission houses who source products for export, exporting manufacturers who take on complementary lines, international trading companies, and export management companies. In the United States, the most important middleman is the export management company.

EXHIBIT 1

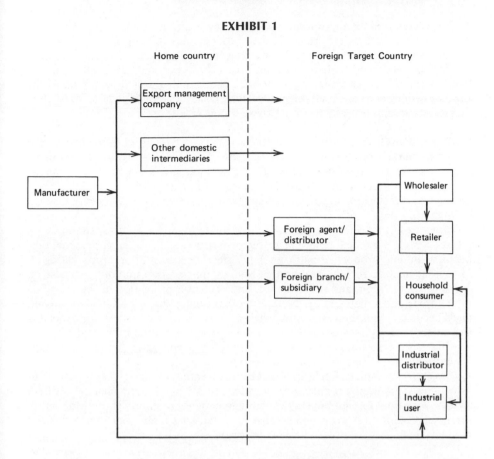

A U.S. Department of Commerce study of 5,000 manufacturing companies in 1978 disclosed five major obstacles to exporting: (1) lack of knowledge of how to find foreign agents and distributors, (2) lack of knowledge about foreign markets, (3) lack of interest in foreign markets, (4) fears of not getting paid, and (5) lack of adequate personnel (U.S. Dept. of Commerce, 1978). Manufacturers who want to export but experience one or more of the other obstacles should consider using an export management company to handle their export business.

Export Management Companies.   An export management company (EMC) is a specialist in international marketing that acts as the export department for several manufacturers in noncompetitive lines. In the United States there are some 800–1,000 EMCs who represent some 10,000 manufacturers and account for about 10 percent of U.S. manufactured exports.

EMCs vary greatly in size, product/market specialization, services, and experience. The representative EMC is small (one or two individuals in management and sales), relies on foreign agents or distributors rather than on its own foreign sales offices, takes title to its clients' products, specializes in certain geographic areas (such as Europe or Latin America), handles lines in three or more industries, and is willing to accept exclusive rights for a single country (Brasch, 1978).

The selection of an appropriate EMC is a key decision. Manufacturers need to identify EMCs that have experience in their product lines and target foreign markets, and then screen the candidate EMCs for the most suitable one. Information on EMCs may be obtained from trade publications, the U.S. Department of Commerce, and EMC associations.[1] After signing a contract, the manufacturer should support the EMC by helping to draw up a foreign-marketing plan, by supplying sales aids (such as literature and samples), and by promptly servicing export orders.

DIRECT EXPORTING.   Indirect exporting gives the manufacturer immediate access to foreign markets through the marketing networks of EMCs and other export intermediaries. But the other side of the coin is the manufacturer's lack of control over his foreign sales. A manufacturer who wants to exploit foreign markets aggressively will move on to direct exporting after gaining his initial international exposure through indirect exporting.

Direct exporting offers the manufacturer the following specific advantages: (1) greater control over the foreign-marketing plan (pricing, advertising, personal selling, distribution, product services, etc.), (2) greater concentration of marketing effort on the manufacturer's own product line, (3) quicker information feedbacks on markets, competition, and performance, and (4) better protection of the manufacturer's trademarks, patents, goodwill, and other intangible property. These advantages become actual, however, only when a manufacturer organizes for exporting and commits the resources necessary for an active penetration of foreign markets. The higher start-up costs and risks of direct exporting compared to indirect exporting can only be justified by greater marketing effectiveness.

The most-common channels in direct exporting are those using foreign agents or distributors and foreign branches or subsidiaries. A less common channel is direct contact with final foreign buyers through company representatives working out of the home country, an arrangement that is generally suitable only for industrial products (including services) with high unit values.

Deciding on the Direct Export Channel.   In deciding on a direct export channel, managers need to make decisions on three levels: (1) *Performance specifications*— what should the channel do? (2) *Channel type*—which alternative channel most closely matches the performance specifications? (3) *Channel member*—which intermediary (particular agent, distributor, or branch/subsidiary manager) in the most appropriate channel type is best qualified to carry out the foreign-marketing plan?

Channel-performance specifications indicate what the export manager wants in geographic market coverage in the target country, the intensity of that coverage, sales and promotional efforts, inventory and delivery systems, customer credit, product services (such as installation, maintenance, and repairs), and other channel performance. These specifications will depend on the company's product line, its objectives, its resources, and its foreign-marketing plan.

Performance specifications provide guidelines for the choice of the right channel type. For most manufacturers, the first step in this selection process is a comparison of the branch/subsidiary channel against the agency/distributor channel. The former requires the manufacturer to establish his own sales operations in the target country.[2] The major advantage of this channel type is greater control over the foreign-marketing plan; its major disadvantage is higher fixed costs. The choice between these two channel types, therefore, rests on a comparative assessment of their respective sales and costs over the entry-planning period. Manufacturers tend to use an agent/distributor channel for early export entry because of its lower start-up costs. If so, the second screening step compares foreign agents against foreign distributors in the target country.

A foreign agent is an independent middleman who represents the manufacturer in the target market. As an agent, this middleman does not take title to the manufacturer's product but rather sells that product on a commission basis. Furthermore, an agent seldom holds inventory (beyond samples) or extends credit to customers. Usually the manufacturer receives orders from his agent and then ships directly to the foreign buyer. A foreign agent, therefore, is essentially a salesman.

In contrast, a foreign distributor is a merchant who buys the manufacturer's product for resale to other middlemen or to final buyers. The distributor performs more functions than the agent (such as maintaining inventories, extending credit, servicing orders, and providing after-sales services), and he also assumes the ownership risks. His compensation is his profit margin on resale of the manufacturer's product.

In choosing between an agent and a distributor, export managers need to determine their profit contributions over the entry-planning period by estimating their respective sales and costs. In addition to the expected profit contribution of the channel, managers should also consider control, risk, and other nonprofit channel specifications.

The most attractive export channel today may become obsolete tomorrow as changes occur in markets, competition, channel systems, and public policy, as well as in a manufacturer's own products, resources, and entry strategy. For this reason manufacturers should avoid getting locked into a particular channel, and they need to monitor channel performance continually to know when new channel arrangements become desirable.

Choosing a Foreign Agent or Distributor.   Finding good agents or distributors is a recurring problem for export managers. It is recommended that they begin the recruitment process by drawing up an agent (distributor) profile that lists all the desirable features of an agent (distributor) in a particular foreign target market. Exhibit 2 suggests the nature of such a profile.

Manufacturers are well advised to make the final selection of a foreign agent or distributor only after personal interviews with the best prospects. Interviews are the most reliable way for manufacturers to gain a feel for a particular agent (distributor) and his organization. But interviews should come only after desk research has identified the best candidates. The time and expense needed for a careful selection of an agent or distributor is justified by the critical importance of this decision. An old saying in exporting goes: "Your line is only as good as your foreign representative."

A final point on export entry. The manufacturer's agreement with his foreign representative should be a written contract that clearly sets forth the rights and obligations of both parties. Provisions relating to sole and exclusive rights, competitive lines, the resolution of disputes, and contract termination are of particular importance. A written agreement is most needed when things go wrong. It cannot, of course, insure that things will go right. Much of an export manager's job is the "care and feeding" of his foreign representatives—a never-ending task of building and sustaining an export-channel team that works together in a common endeavor.

EXHIBIT 2   ELEMENTS OF A MANUFACTURER'S PROFILE FOR EVALUATING PROSPECTIVE FOREIGN DISTRIBUTORS

Lines handled
Experience with manufacturer's or similar product line
Trading areas covered
Size of firm
Sales organization
Physical facilities
Willingness to carry inventories
After-sales service
Knowledge and use of promotion
Reputation with suppliers, customers, and banks
Record of sales performance
Cost of operations
Financial strength and credit rating
Relations with local government
Knowledge of English and other relevant languages
Knowledge of business methods in manufacturer's country
Overall experience
Willingness to cooperate with manufacturer

EXPORT OPERATIONS.   It is beyond the scope of this section to describe export operations, but certain features deserve some comment: documentary requirements, price quotations, payment arrangements, and organization.*

Export Documents.   The variety of export documents appears as a formidable obstacle to the newcomer in international business. Fortunately, manufacturers can call on international-freight forwarders to prepare most documents (as well as arranging shipment) and on banks for assistance in handling documents relating to international payments. Export documents must be prepared meticulously in the correct number of copies and at the right time. With the assistance of forwarders and banks, new export managers can learn quickly all they need to know about documentation.

Probably the single most important document is the ocean (or airway) *bill of lading* issued by an international carrier. Apart from serving as a receipt for goods delivered to the carrier and a contract for its services, the bill of lading controls possession of the shipment. When made out to the exporter's own order, it becomes a document of title necessary to obtain the goods at the foreign point of destination.

Export Price Quotations.   Standard price quotations are widely used in exporting. The two most important codifications are *International Commercial Terms* (Incoterms) adopted by the International Chamber of Commerce, and *Revised American Foreign Trade Definitions* adopted by the Chamber of Commerce of the United States. Manufacturers should specify one of these codes in making export price quotations and negotiating export sales contracts.

---

* Useful publications on export operations include *Exporters' Encyclopaedia:* Small Business Administration, 1979; Dowd, 1977; and the *Foreign Trade Handbook.*

The most-common price quotations are *ex named point of origin* (ex factory, ex mill, ex warehouse, etc.), *f.a.s.* (free along side), and *c.i.f.* (cost, insurance, freight). Under an ex quotation, the exporter quotes a price that applies only at the named point of origin with the importer assuming all the responsibility and cost to transfer the merchandise to the ultimate foreign destination. A close variant of this quotation is f.o.b. (free on board) named inland carrier at named inland point, under which the exporter prices his goods as loaded on a specified carrier. An f.a.s. quotation includes delivery of the manufacturer's goods alongside a designated vessel (that is, within reach of its loading tackle) with the importer responsible for all subsequent movement of the goods. Under a c.i.f. quotation, the manufacturer's price covers the cost of the goods, the marine insurance, and all transportation charges to the foreign port of entry.

The quotation easiest for the manufacturer to prepare is ex point of origin, but importers generally prefer a c.i.f. quotation. F.a.s. is a good compromise because it is not difficult for the manufacturer to prepare and for the importer to use in calculating his landed cost. Manufacturers should be flexible in price quotations; it is inexcusable to lose a sale because of unwillingness to quote f.a.s. or c.i.f.

Payments Arrangements. The exporter assumes two nonpayment risks: (1) default by the importer, and (2) inconvertibility resulting from exchange restrictions imposed by the host government. Hence exporters need to check out not only the importer but also the convertibility of the importer's currency. A third risk is the foreign-exchange risk from variations in the rate of exchange. The exporter can avoid this risk by quoting the price in his own currency, a practice that is usually open to U.S. manufacturers given the international role of the dollar. When the exporter does quote his price in a foreign currency, he can hedge against the foreign-exchange risk by using the forward exchange market. In most circumstances, the exporter should hedge rather than speculate on foreign-exchange rates.

Ranked by a rising risk of nonpayment, the alternative forms of international payment are (1) cash in advance, (2) irrevocable, confirmed letter of credit, (3) documentary draft, (4) open account, and (5) consignment. An *irrevocable, confirmed letter of credit* enables the exporter to draw his draft (bill of exchange) against a domestic bank without recourse, an arrangement amounting to payment at the time of shipment.[3] With the *documentary draft* form of payment, the exporter draws his draft against the importer and sends it along with the negotiable bill of lading and other documents through his bank for collection. The importer can obtain the bill of lading (and therefore the goods) only after paying the draft or accepting it for later payment when the exporter extends credit. Because of the high risk, open-account and consignment-payment terms should be restricted to the exporter's own foreign affiliates or to old customers in convertible-currency countries.

In today's competitive markets, manufacturers need to be flexible in their payments arrangements, balancing risk against opportunity. Dogmatic insistence on letter-of-credit terms will lose sales to competitors who are offering credit under documentary drafts. U.S. manufacturers can obtain export credit insurance against both commercial and political risks from the Foreign Credit Insurance Association (FCIA).

Export Organization. A company just starting out in direct exporting is most likely to establish an export department staffed by an export manager and a few assistants. This "built-in" department depends on other departments for order filling, accounting, credit approval, and other support activities. Although a good way to gain export experience with low start-up costs, the built-in export department should be viewed as a transitional device to be replaced later with a full-function export department or division.

Another aspect of export organization is the authority granted to the export manager. Too commonly that authority is limited by constraints (particularly in pricing and promotion) that weaken the export manager's ability to exploit foreign-market opportunities. Manufacturers who want an aggressive export strategy need aggressive export managers with the authority and resources to plan and execute that strategy.

ENTERING FOREIGN MARKETS THROUGH LICENSING AND OTHER CONTRACTUAL ARRANGEMENTS

Companies may enter foreign markets under a wide variety of contractual arrangements: licensing, franchising, technical agreements, service contracts, construction/turnkey contracts, contract manufacture, coproduction agreements, and others. Licensing is by far the most common contractual arrangement.

INTERNATIONAL LICENSING.   The essence of an international licensing agreement is the transfer of industrial property rights (patents, trademarks, and/or proprietary know-how) from a licensor in one country to a licensee in a second country. Industrial property rights are seldom assigned or sold outright to a foreign company. The usual practice is for the licensor to allow the licensee to use the rights for a specified period of time in return for a royalty compensation.

Manufacturers may license foreign companies for reasons that have little or nothing to do with foreign-market entry. Licensing may be viewed as simply a way of obtaining incremental income on "shelf" technology that has already been written off against domestic sales. Or a manufacturer may agree to exchange technology with a foreign counterpart, a practice known as cross-licensing. Again, manufacturers may license abroad to get legal protection for their patents and trademarks in countries where they must be "worked" to remain valid or to guard against infringement. Multinational companies commonly license their own foreign subsidiaries to establish legal ownership of industrial property, to facilitate repatriation of income, or to satisfy home and host governments. These uses of licensing do not concern us here; we are interested in licensing as a way of entering foreign markets.

Advantages and Disadvantages of Licensing as a Primary Entry Mode.   Licensing offers the manufacturer both advantages and disadvantages as a primary entry mode. Compared to export entry, the most evident advantage of licensing is the circumvention of import restrictions and transportation costs in penetrating foreign markets. Instead of transferring physical products to a target country, the manufacturer transfers intangible property rights and technology. In contrast to investment entry, the outstanding advantages of licensing are low entry costs and low direct risks. Although licensing incurs transfer costs, it requires no fixed investment by the manufacturer. For the same reason, licensing arrangements are exposed to far fewer political risks than foreign investments.

The most critical disadvantage of licensing as an entry mode is the licensor's lack of control over the licensee's marketing program. Although the licensor ordinarily maintains quality control over the licensed product, he does not control the licensee's volume of production or marketing strategy. The market performance of the licensed product, therefore, depends on the motivation and ability of the licensee. A second disadvantage is the lower absolute size of returns from licensing compared to returns from export or investment. In the representative agreement, licensing revenues take the form of running royalties over the life of the agreement. Today royalty rates seldom exceed five percent of the licensee's net sales, and agreements seldom run beyond 5–10 years.

Another disadvantage of licensing is its exclusivity. Ordinarily, a licensing agreement grants to the licensee exclusive rights to use the technology or trademark in the manufacture and sale of specified products in the licensee's country. For the duration of the agreement, therefore, the licensor is prevented from marketing those products in the licensee's country by using another entry mode, such as export or investment. This *opportunity cost* is particularly irksome when the licensee fails to exploit market opportunity. For example, in 1956 a U.S. manufacturer of construction materials granted to a Japanese firm an exclusive license for 20 years to manufacture and sell one of its specialty products that was highly successful in the United States. It so happened, however, that the Japanese firm failed to promote the product, paying it only marginal attention. Since the licensing agreement did not provide for a minimum royalty, the licensor received very little income. Nonetheless, the U.S. manufacturer was precluded from entering the Japanese market until the expiration of the agreement in 1976 (Ricks et al., 1974, p. 40).

The opportunity cost of foresaken income may be substantial even when the licensee does a very good job. For instance, a U.S. manufacturer of technical products granted a British firm not only an exclusive license to manufacture and sell its products in the United Kingdom but also an exclusive right to sublicense its know-how in all other foreign countries. At the time, the manufacturer had no plans to go abroad, and the licensing arrangement promised a continuing royalty income without the need for any foreign investment. Within a few years, the British licensee had sublicensed firms in several countries who, in turn, exploited very attractive market opportunities. Restricted to modest licensing royalties, the U.S. manufacturer could only watch his products creating much more income for the British licensee and the sublicensees (Mace, 1966, p. 76).

Licensing can also generate another kind of opportunity cost—the creation of a competitor in third markets or even in the manufacturer's home market at a later time.

Manufacturers can somewhat alleviate opportunity costs in licensing through contractual provisions that require minimum royalties or make possible the termination of the agreement because of poor performance. They can also participate more in their licensees' success by receiving some compensation in the form of equity or by an option to buy equity in licensee firms. In this way licensing entry may be transformed into investment entry. But the best safeguard is for managers to make licensing decisions only in the context of a comprehensive foreign-market-entry strategy.

For manufacturers who want an aggressive exploitation of foreign markets, licensing is generally a third-best entry strategy. Only when export or investment entry are not feasible or appropriate because of external or internal factors does licensing become attractive to such firms. This is most likely to be the case for developing and communist countries where exports may be kept out by import restrictions and, at the same time, investment entry may be barred by government policy, or the market may be too small or political risks too high to justify it. Small manufacturers are more attracted to licensing than large manufacturers because it is a low-commitment entry mode.

International licensing is most commonly combined with other entry modes. Indeed, the majority of licensing agreements by U.S. manufacturers are with their own foreign subsidiaries. Licensing is also frequently associated with joint ventures in which the licensor has an equity position. Licensing/equity mixes are popular because they allow the manufacturer to benefit from the growth of the licensee firm to a much higher degree than with a pure licensing agreement. Licensing may also be used by the manufacturer to source products for sale on world markets. Despite its limitations as a *primary* entry mode, therefore, licensing has become a flexible *secondary* entry mode that can be combined with other entry modes to form a mixed entry mode superior to its individual constituents.

Profitability Analysis of a Proposed Licensing Venture. Many manufacturers view international licensing as a marginal activity that does not warrant a careful evaluation of its benefits and costs. This attitude fosters bad licensing decisions. Managers should decide on licensing as a primary entry mode for a target foreign country only after comparing licensing with alternative entry modes with respect to profitability, risk, and strategy objectives. Not to do so is to treat licensing as an ad hoc, tactical decision when it is truly a strategic decision that will determine a company's long-run participation in a target market and possibly in third markets as well. We offer an approach to profitability analysis of alternative entry modes later on in this section.

Negotiating and Managing Licensing Agreements. Apart from helping managers to decide on the desirability of licensing entry for a particular target country, profitability analysis can also help managers negotiate better licensing agreements. It can provide an understanding of the licensor's objectives, the value of the technology package to the licensee, and the many trade-offs among the elements of a licensing agreement.

The signing of the licensing contract ends formal negotiations, but it is only the start of the licensing venture. In most ventures, the licensee will require continuing technical support from the licensor who, in turn, will have a continuing interest in helping the licensee achieve market success. Manufacturers, therefore, should view their international licensing arrangements as *nonequity* joint ventures that join together the strengths of the two partners in pursuit of a common goal—the creation of a sustainable role in the target market.

OTHER CONTRACTUAL ENTRY MODES. In addition to licensing, several other contractual entry modes have become prominent in recent years, particularly in doing business with developing and communist countries. We can offer here only some brief comments on these arrangements.

International Franchising. Unlike conventional licensing, the franchisor licenses a *business system* to an independent franchisee in a target foreign country. The franchisee carries on a business under the franchisor's trade name and in accordance with policies and practices laid down by the franchise agreement. In the decade 1965–75, over 200 U.S. companies established 11,000 franchise outlets in foreign markets (Business International, 1977, p. 52). Through franchising, Holiday Inn, McDonald's, Kentucky Fried Chicken, Avis, and many other U.S. firms have become household names in scores of countries. The classic international franchisor, of course, is Coca-Cola. International franchising has become, therefore, a powerful entry mode for companies that have products and services that can be reproduced by independent franchisees.

Contract Manufacturing.   In contract manufacturing, an international firm negotiates a long-term arrangement with a company in the foreign target country to manufacture a product for subsequent sale by the international firm. To get the product manufactured to its own specifications, the international firm usually transfers technology to the contract manufacturer.

Contract manufacturing can offer several advantages to the U.S. manufacturer as a mode of foreign-market entry. It requires only a modest commitment of capital and management resources compared to investment entry, avoids the political problems of local ownership, and allows the manufacturer to exercise full control over the foreign-marketing program. On the other hand, the manufacturer may find it difficult or impossible to locate a good contract manufacturer (especially in developing countries), he must often provide substantial technical assistance to bring the contract manufacturer up to desired quality levels, and—as in licensing—he may be creating a future competitor.

Management Contracts.   Under an international management contract, a company undertakes the day-to-day management of an independent enterprise in a foreign target country. In return for its management services, the company ordinarily receives fees over the fixed life of the contract.

Manufacturers usually enter management contracts only in conjunction with other arrangements, such as joint ventures or turnkey projects, because they seldom see themselves as primary suppliers of management services. Apart from fees, management contracts can provide manufacturers with a way of controlling foreign ventures in which their ownership is zero or minimal.

Turnkey Construction Contracts.   Under a turnkey project, a company provides not only engineering and construction services but also the additional services needed to bring the project up to the point of operation before it is turned over to the owner. At times a company may also operate the project for a transition period, an arrangement called *turnkey plus*. In short, a turnkey contract calls for the international transfer of a package of services—engineering, construction (often including financing), training, and (possibly) management.

Coproduction Agreements.   Coproduction is a kind of nonequity joint venture that is prominent in East-West business. Under a long-term contract, the Western company provides technology, components, and other inputs to a communist state enterprise in return for a share of the resulting production, which it then markets in the West. A U.S. manufacturer may gain several advantages from a coproduction agreement, including the sale of equipment and other products to the communist enterprise, a low-cost source of products for sale in the West, licensing royalties, and presence in a communist country that can generate future business. But these advantages must be weighed against certain possible disadvantages—the failure of the communist partner to maintain quality standards or meet delivery schedules, difficulties in protecting technology from disclosure, and the creation of a future competitor in third markets. Coproduction arrangements are very attractive to communist countries because payments to the Western companies come out of production rather than out of scarce foreign exchange.

ENTERING FOREIGN MARKETS THROUGH INVESTMENT IN LOCAL PRODUCTION

ADVANTAGES AND DISADVANTAGES OF INVESTMENT ENTRY.   Companies invest abroad in production for three fundamental reasons—to acquire minerals and other raw materials through exploitation of natural resources, to source manufactured products at a low cost for use or sale at home and in third countries, and to build a logistical base for the penetration of a local market in the target country. Our interest here is with the third group of investors who use investment as a mode of foreign-market entry.

· Through investment entry, a company can establish a full-function enterprise in the target country and thereby exploit its competitive advantages to a higher degree than is ordinarily possible through export or contractual entry modes. Investment entry allows a company to control the foreign-marketing program and to gain logistical advantages that may arise from the circumvention of import barriers, savings in transportation costs, or lower production costs. Because of its manifold advantages, investment entry has become the hallmark of the multinational corporation.

Investment entry also poses certain disadvantages. Compared to other entry modes, it requires a far greater commitment of capital, management, and other company resources. This higher commitment, in turn, means a higher exposure to business and political risks. Substantial start-up costs, long payback periods, and the cost of disinvestment in the event of failure must also be considered disadvantages of investment entry. Again, managers need more information to make good investment decisions than is true of export and licensing decisions. In particular, investment becomes a high-risk entry mode when the investor has no prior experience in the target country. Understandably, therefore, manufacturers are inclined to invest in a country only after gaining knowledge and experience through export or contractual entry modes.

THE DECISION TO INVEST IN A TARGET COUNTRY.   The investment-entry decision is the outcome of a lengthy process that ordinarily involves several managers from different functions and at different levels of the company organization. We can structure this process as a sequence of checkpoints that must be passed before the final approval of a foreign-investment proposal: (1) Should we investigate the foreign-investment proposal? (2) Is the present investment climate in the target country acceptable? (3) Will the investment climate remain acceptable over our strategic planning period? (4) Will the investment project meet return on investment and other objectives after taking account of business and political risks? If not, can we redesign the project to make it acceptable? (5) Have our entry negotiations with the host government reached a satisfactory outcome?

Probably the most critical checkpoint is the first one—the decision to investigate. The usual form of a positive decision to investigate is the creation of a management team drawn from marketing, finance, engineering, and other relevant functions. Not only is investigation costly in management time and money, it also tends to generate a commitment to invest. That is to say, the management team is quite likely to become a champion of the investment project. Before making a decision to investigate a proposal in depth, therefore, managers should review the alternative entry modes available to the company, including alternative investment modes (*de novo* versus acquisition and sole venture versus joint venture). Such a review helps prevent a premature decision to investigate by safeguarding against tunnel vision that considers only the investment proposal in question.

Following the decision to investigate, the next two checkpoints call for a thorough evaluation of both the present and future investment climates of the target country. The investment climate includes all the political, social, economic, and other environmental factors that can have a significant effect on the profitability and safety of the project over its planning horizon. Managers need to identify the critical or "killing" variables in the investment climate, and then assess their present and likely future behavior. Because so many critical variables relate to the political system and government of the host country, an assessment of the future investment climate is mainly an assessment of *political risk:* Will the current rules of the game (e.g., ownership rights, the right to import raw materials and parts used in production, and the right to repatriate profits) remain acceptable over the project's time horizon? To answer this question, managers should make explicit judgments on the stability of government policies and the political system in general.

If the investment climate checkpoints are passed, managers can turn to a full investigation of the project's economic feasibility—the market, production and supply, labor, capital sourcing, tax, and other factors. The recommended approach to measure the expected return on investment is a discounted cash-flow analysis with adjustments for political and other risks.

The last checkpoint is negotiations with the host government. Increasingly, governments are establishing screening systems to insure that foreign investment projects contribute net economic and social benefits to the host country. It has become vital, therefore, for managers to know the investment-screening criteria used by the government of a target country. Then it is often possible to design an investment project so as to enhance its acceptability by the host government and, at the same time, maintain its profitability.

The checkpoints identify the key elements of the investment-entry decision. But, in practice, that decision is seldom the outcome of a successive consideration of checkpoints. It is more likely to be a process with many twists, turns, and iterations. In most instances, managers will run through checkpoints several times before deciding on negotiations with the host government. And those negotiations can sometimes lead back to a general reassessment of the investment climate and project before the decision process comes to an end.

INVESTMENT ENTRY THROUGH ACQUISITION.   A foreign-investment proposal may be a proposal to acquire a firm in the target country rather than start a venture from scratch. The checkpoints apply to all forms of investment entry, but acquisition entry has its own special features. Our interest here is with horizontal acquisition (the product line is similar to the investor's) the dominant purpose of which is entry into a foreign target market.

Advantages and Disadvantages of Acquisition Entry.   Acquisition entry offers a company several *potential* advantages compared to new-venture entry. They are only potential advantages because they depend critically on the choice of the acquired firm. A poor choice can transform a potential advantage into an actual disadvantage.

The most evident advantage of acquisition entry is a faster start in the target country. The investor gains control over a going concern with a product line, manufacturing facilities, managers, workers, and customers. To achieve the same market penetration through a new venture could take several years. For the same reason, acquisition entry promises a quicker return on investment. But this advantage presumes that the acquired firm is viable or can be made viable through a "quick fix" by the investor. Moreover, even when the acquisition is a good one, the time needed to fit it to the policies and operations of the investor company can easily take a year or more. In the event of a poor acquisition, the start-up period may exceed that of a new venture. One mistake is the acquisition of a firm with a product line radically different from the investor's. As an entry mode, the basic purpose of a foreign acquisition should be market diversification—not product diversification.

Through acquisition entry, an international company may also obtain a scarce resource that would be more costly to mobilize in a venture started from scratch. This resource can be any one or several of the acquired firm's assets—a product line, a manufacturing facility, goodwill, a dealer network, a work force, managers, technology, and so on. But once again, a poor acquisition can turn this advantage into a disadvantage. For example, a U.S. housewares company, frustrated by its inability to get distribution for its exports to West Germany, acquired a local housewares manufacturer. Unfortunately, this strategy backfired because the manufacturer also suffered from a weak distribution system. As a consequence, the U.S. company not only failed to solve its export distribution problem but also created a new problem—what to do with the products of its new German subsidiary.[4] To conclude on this point, if an international company is seeking a specific resource through an acquisition, it needs to make certain that an acquisition candidate actually possesses that resource and that it will become available to the investor after the acquisition is made. Other potential advantages of acquisition entry include a lower overall cost than building from scratch, synergistic effects on the investor's other operations, and the elimination of a competitor.

Acquisition entry may run into obstacles that are absent or weaker for new ventures. Acquisitions by foreign investors are opposed by many host governments because they eliminate locally owned enterprises. This negative policy is most prominent in developing countries, but it is also encountered in certain industrial countries, notably Australia, Canada, France, and Japan. For example, the French government is inclined to reject acquisitions involving "sensitive" industries (such as computers) or industry leaders.[5] Foreign acquisitions can also be blocked by U.S. antitrust policy, as shown by the attempt of Rockwell International to take over Serck Ltd., a British manufacturer of industrial valves.[6]

Finding a good acquisition candidate can take a great deal of time and money. In some countries, good candidates are simply not available. Further, the assessment of candidates is often arduous because of peculiar accounting systems, false or deceptive financial records, and the concealment of problems by local owners and managers.

Acquisition Strategy.   A study of 407 acquisitions in Europe by U.S. and European firms over the period 1965–1970 concluded that the payoff from acquisitions was lower than the payoff from investments in new manufacturing plants and the risk of failure was high. Only half of the acquisitions were rated successful by managers (Kitching, 1974). It is prudent, therefore, for an international company to evaluate acquisition entry from the perspective of an overall foreign-market-entry strategy.

If acquisition is judged the best way to enter a target country, then managers should articulate an acquisition strategy that specifies and ranks objectives; identifies the desired features in a candidate firm; and provides guidelines for pricing, financing, and assimilating the acquired firm. The proper execution of a good acquisition strategy can bring an international company an ongoing enterprise that has immediate access to a target market and can form a base for future market development.

INVESTMENT ENTRY THROUGH JOINT VENTURES. Joint-venture entry occurs when an international company invests in a business enterprise in a target country together with a local partner firm. The foreign investor may hold a majority, a minority, or half of the joint venture's equity. Joint ventures are usually started from scratch, but they may also result from the purchase of equity in an existing local firm.

Advantages of Joint Ventures. In developing and communist countries, joint ventures may be the only investment-entry mode available to international companies because host governments prohibit sole ventures. Many governments also prohibit majority joint ventures. Since the most common reason for joint-venture entry is host-government policy, it follows that in many instances joint ventures are viewed by international managers as second-best to sole ventures. Nonetheless, joint ventures can offer foreign investors certain advantages apart from host-government acceptance.

By contributing capital to the joint venture, the local partner reduces the foreign partner's investment outlay and risk exposure. But the local partner's most valuable contribution is his knowledge of the local business environment and his ongoing contacts with local customers, suppliers, banks, and government officials. That is why joint ventures can be attractive to companies with little experience in foreign operations. It is also why many U.S. manufacturers have entered joint ventures in Japan even when sole-venture entry was open to them. In some cases, a joint venture may be the only way for an international company to gain an acceptance of its products by local middlemen and customers. The story of a U.S. manufacturer of poultry feed who invested in a sole venture in Spain illustrates this point. After production got underway, the manufacturer discovered he could not sell his feed because local poultry growers and feed producers were linked by generations-old business ties, resembling a closely knit family. In effect, the chicken-feed market was barred to newcomers. To circumvent this problem, the manufacturer bought several chicken farms in Spain only to learn that no one would buy his chickens. At last report, the manufacturer was thinking about buying restaurants in Spain! Clearly, the manufacturer could have avoided this sad experience by entering a joint venture with a Spanish feed company (Ricks et al., 1974, pp. 24–25). Summing up, the local partner's resources combined with those of the foreign partner can sometimes exploit a target market more effectively than a sole venture.

Disadvantages of Joint Ventures. International managers commonly complain that joint ventures dilute their control over foreign operations. Even with majority joint ventures, international managers must accommodate the interests of local partners. The importance of control ultimately depends on a company's international strategy. One study of joint ventures concluded that companies attempting to penetrate multiple-country markets with a narrow product line found joint ventures an obstacle to the creation of global marketing and production systems. In contrast, companies that were continually introducing new products into foreign markets over several product lines showed a high tolerance for joint ventures (Franko, 1971).

Management control need not be synonymous with the degree of ownership. International companies may achieve a dominant control even over minority joint ventures in several ways. If, for example, a joint venture is continually dependent on the foreign partner for a critical input (say, technology), then that partner can exert a decisive control regardless of the ownership split. A minority foreign partner can also gain significant control through formal arrangements, such as the issuance of voting and nonvoting equity shares, bylaws that give him the right to select key executives or veto key decisions, or a management contract.

Choosing the Right Partner.   After managers have decided on a joint venture as the most appropriate entry mode for a target country, the most critical decision is the choice of a local partner. Joint ventures are often compared to marriages, and like marriages they frequently founder on the rocks of divorce.

Managers should first determine what they want the joint venture to accomplish in the target country over a strategic planning period, and how the joint venture fits into their overall international business strategy. Next they need to find out the objectives and policies of the prospective local partner, as well as the resources he would bring to the joint venture. Only after agreement on the purpose of the joint venture should managers go on to negotiate specific issues—ownership shares, the allocation of management responsibilities, profit reporting, dividend policy, the settlement of disputes, and others. If all the issues are not resolved during negotiations, they are certain to return at a later time. But even a comprehensive joint-venture agreement marks only the end of the venture's beginning. The venture will prosper only if the partners trust each other and continually support their common endeavor.

DECIDING ON THE RIGHT ENTRY MODE

THREE DECISION RULES.   We have now reviewed several foreign-market-entry modes. As we have seen, each mode has its general advantages and disadvantages. But managers must move from the general to the specific: They must decide on an entry mode for a particular product and for a particular foreign country/market. To do so, they may follow one of three different decision rules.

The *naive rule* is for managers to use the *same* entry mode, such as agent/distributor exporting, for all target countries. Because country markets and entry conditions are heterogeneous, this rule leads managers to forsake promising markets that cannot be penetrated with their single entry mode or to end up in markets with an inappropriate mode.

The *pragmatic rule* is for managers to find an entry mode that "works." In most instances, managers start by assessing export entry, and only if such entry is infeasible do they go on to assess another mode. This rule avoids the two pitfalls of the naive rule, and it also saves management time and effort. But it fails to lead managers to the most appropriate mode. A workable mode is not necessarily the right mode.

The *strategy rule* is for managers to decide on the right entry mode as a key element in a company's foreign-market-entry strategy. It is the most difficult rule to follow because managers must make systematic comparisons of alternative entry modes. But the payoff is better entry decisions.

AN APPLICATION OF THE STRATEGY RULE.   It should be evident from our discussion of the different entry modes that the choice of a particular mode for a target country is influenced by many, often conflicting, forces. It is, therefore, a complex strategic decision that demands management judgment.

Our approach to the entry decision is an interpretation of the strategy rule: Choose the entry mode that maximizes profit contribution over the strategic planning period within the constraints of company resources, risk, and nonprofit objectives. Managers initiate this approach by screening all entry modes for *feasibility:* Is it possible for my company to enter the target country with this mode? Next managers make three comparisons of the workable modes that survive this screening—profit contribution, risk, and nonprofit objectives. Then these comparisons are brought together to form an overall comparative assessment. This final ranking of alternative entry modes requires managers to decide on trade-offs among profits, risks, and objectives. The principal advantage of this approach is that it compels managers to compare alternative modes and thereby directs them toward the right mode.

MONITORING FOREIGN-MARKET-ENTRY STRATEGIES

In this section we have focused our attention on one element of a foreign-market-entry strategy—the choice of an entry mode. We now close with a brief reference to another element—a control system that monitors the performance of the overall strategy.

International managers should establish performance standards for the current budgetary period that reflect their strategic objectives in target country/markets. Deviations between planned and actual performance become warning signals that trigger an investigation of causes. Only after that is done can managers take proper remedial action. More generally, strategic planning for foreign-market entry is a continuous process involving the assessment of past performance as well as changes in the international business environment. The right strategy for today may not be the right strategy for tomorrow. The evolution of a company's international business should describe a sequence of entry strategies designed by managers to create and sustain a presence in markets throughout the world.

NOTES

1. The National Federation of Export Management Companies, located in New York City, is the association of the regional trade associations. The U.S. Department of Commerce has published a *Directory of U.S. Export Management Companies.*
2. The distinction between a sales branch and a sales subsidiary is purely legal: A branch has the same legal identity as the parent company, whereas a subsidiary has its own legal identity. Whether a company chooses to use a branch or a subsidiary is a legal and tax question—not a marketing question.
3. The details of letter of credit and other international payments arrangements may be obtained from banks. The major banks have publications in this field, such as *Financing of U.S. Exports* by the First National Bank of Chicago.
4. *Princess Housewares GmbH (A)* (Boston: Intercollegiate Case Clearing House, 1968).
5. "French Acquisition Climate Remains Highly Charged," *Business International,* April 13, 1979, pp. 113–114.

6. "Rockwell International: Reaching for the Automotive Market Abroad," *Business Week,* May 5, 1980, p. 87.

SOURCES AND SUGGESTED REFERENCES

Brasch, J.J. "Export Management Companies," *Journal of International Business Studies,* Spring–Summer 1978.

Business International. *International Licensing.* New York: BI, 1977.

Contractor, Farok. *International Technology Licensing: Compensation, Costs and Negotiation.* Lexington, MA: Lexington Books, 1981.

Czinkota, Michael R., ed. *Export Management.* New York: Praeger Publishers, 1982.

Exporters' Encyclopedia. New York: Dun & Bradstreet International, annual.

Foreign Trade Handbook. Chicago: Dartnell Corporation, latest edition.

Franko, L.G. "Joint Venture Divorce in the Multinational Company," *Columbia Journal of World Business,* May–June 1971.

Kitching, John. "Winning and Losing with European Acquisitions," *Harvard Business Review,* March-April 1974.

Mace, M.L. "The President and International Operations," *Harvard Business Review,* November–December 1966.

Newbould, G.D., P.J. Buckley, and J.C. Thurwell. *Going International: The Experience of Smaller Companies Overseas.* New York: Wiley, 1978.

Poynter, Thomas A. *Multinational Enterprises and Government Intervention.* London: Croom Helm, Ltd., 1985.

Ricks, D., M. Fu, and J. Arpan. *International Business Blunders.* Columbus, OH: Grid, Inc., 1974.

Root, Franklin R. *Entry Strategies for International Markets.* Lexington, MA: Lexington Books, 1987.

Rosson, Philip J. and Stanley D. Reid, eds. *Managing Export Entry and Expansion.* New York: Praeger Publishers, 1987.

Small Business Administration. *Export Marketing for Smaller Firms,* 4th ed. Washington, D.C.: U.S. Government Printing Office, 1979.

U.S. Dept. of Commerce. *Export Promotion Strategy and Programs,* study prepared by the Industry and Trade Organization. Washington, D.C.: Dept. of Commerce, 1978.

INTERNATIONAL MARKETING MIX

CONTENTS

INTERNATIONAL MARKETING MIX

Samuel Rabino

MARKETING MIX AND MARKETING STRATEGY

Effective management of international marketing-mix strategy is a key ingredient of a successful enterprise. The caliber of a firm's product-market strategy and its execution separates the high performers from the low performers. Differences in market share, in technological accomplishments, in customer loyalty, in product innovation, in quality of the product manufactured, in sales growth, in after-tax profit, in return on investment, and in reputation and image all tend to derive to a large extent from a well-developed strategy and execution of marketing-variables decisions.

Luck and Ferrell (1979) suggest that strategic planning, the determination of strategies, should take place in three phases:

1. Marketing objectives—the creation of a viable, sustainable customer base and market for the firm's products/services.
2. Policies—the rules that guide the selection of strategies as well as the subsequent actions that implement them.
3. Strategies—the fundamental means of reaching the objectives.

The discussion will concentrate on the third stage—identifying and selecting marketing strategies—but a prerequisite to that stage is the sound and explicit determination of objectives and policies.

THE MARKETING MIX. Marketing consists of an integrated strategy that is aimed at providing customer satisfaction. To do this, a company has certain demand-influencing variables that together constitute the marketing mix. The mix includes the product or service offered by the firm, the distribution channels used (e.g., wholesalers, distributors, retailers) to make the product available to customers, the price charged for the product, advertising and sales promotion, and personal selling effort. The four marketing-mix variables—product, distribution, promotion, and price—are traditionally viewed as controllable, that is, variables that are under the control of the firm and can influence the level of consumer response.

In the following sections, each of the marketing-mix variables will be discussed separately. Subsequently, implications for marketing planning will be derived.

PRODUCT DECISIONS. Two issues are particularly relevant for the development of international product plans. The first involves a decision between a product-differentiation or a market-segmentation approach; the second deals with product life-cycle analysis.

Product differentiation provides one basis upon which a supplier can appeal to selective buying motives. Products may be perceived to be different by buyers; these differences can be real or imaginary. Simply stated, products are different if the consumer believes they are different. When a company designs a single marketing mix and directs it at an entire market for a particular product, it is using a market, or undifferentiated, approach. For example, Levi, Wrangler, and Lee use essentially the same appeal and the same products in all of Western Europe ("Blue Jeans," 1975). Frequently a company will attempt to use promotional efforts to differentiate its products from competitors' products. It hopes to establish in customers' minds the superiority and preferability of its product compared to competing brands. Thus Levi, in an effort to differentiate its products, markets them in Europe with the theme "The Original Jeans."

The product life cycle refers to a sales pattern that most successful products undergo. The sales pattern is frequently described in terms of four stages: introduction, growth, maturity, and decline. In the introduction stage, the product is new in the marketplace. Sales begin to build as initial buyers become aware of the product, try it, and ultimately decide to adopt it. As interest in the product expands, the product moves into its growth stage, characterized by a rapid increase in sales. Other firms, attracted by a potential market opportunity, introduce similar products, which expand both the availability of the product and marketing efforts aimed at increasing sales. As sales continue to expand, the product moves into the maturity stage. Competition is typically keen as the market reaches a saturation, or leveling-off, point. Severe price competition often prevails, thus reducing profits. After reaching a maturity stage, the sales of some products actually decline from their peak-sales level and the product may enter a period of decline.

The product life-cycle concept is important for two reasons. First, it applies in an international as well as a domestic marketing situation. Products are introduced in export markets, create a market or capture market share, attract competitors, and finally may be squeezed out of a market. Second, and perhaps more important, many firms attempt to expand sales and prolong the growth and maturity phases of the life cycle by seeking new markets in other countries. The general approach is to find a product strategy that meets the needs of foreign customers at a reasonable cost to the firm. According to Keegan (1980), five policy alternatives can be used to expand international markets.

Strategy One: Product-Promotional Extension. This is the easiest marketing strategy to implement and probably the most profitable one. The strategy entails selling in every country in which the company operates exactly the same product with the same advertising and promotional themes and appeals that it uses in the United States. Pepsi Cola, for example, has been successful in selling the same product with standard promotional themes in a variety of markets. Pepsi has estimated that the cost of preparing ads would be raised substantially by tailoring promotions to each foreign market. Although this strategy has worked for soft drinks, other American firms have run into problems trying to export prepared foods that do not fit local preferences. A case in point is the unsuccessful effort by a

U.S. company to capture the British cake-mix market. It offered U.S.-style cake mix with fancy frosting only to discover that English consumers prefer their cake at tea time, and that the cake they prefer is dry, spongy, and suitable for being picked up with the left hand while the right hand manages a cup of tea.

The advantages of this strategy lie not only in the substantial economies associated with standardization of marketing communication, but also in cost saving resulting from manufacturing economies of scale and the elimination of product R&D costs.

Strategy Two: Product Extension—Promotional Adaptation. This strategy involves selling the same product in foreign markets but adapting it to local conditions. American firms marketing analgesics in Japan sell essentially the same product under a somewhat different theme. The copy theme for Bufferin, for example, is "gentle for your stomach," whereas in the United States it is positioned primarily as a headache reliever ("Marketing in Japan," 1978).

As with the product-promotion strategy, the principal appeal of this strategy is its relatively low cost, because R&D and manufacturing costs remain the same. The only costs incurred are those associated with the development of different promotional strategies.

Another example is Colgate's introduction of a soap bar to Mexico. Colgate has put its Irish Spring formula on sale in Mexico in a new "double protection" bar soap called Nordiko. The choice of the Nordiko (as opposed to Irish Spring) was based on the assumption that it projected a fresh and cool image to the Mexican consumers ("Colgate's Nordiko," 1976).

Strategy Three: Product Adaptation—Promotional Extension. This approach to international product planning extends without change the basic communications strategy developed for the United States, and adapts the American product to local use conditions. Exxon (then Esso), for example, adapted its gasoline to meet different climate conditions in foreign markets, but used its famous "Put a tiger in your tank" promotion in all areas.

Strategy Four: Dual Adaptation. When the sociocultural and economic conditions are such that using the same product and/or promotion is rendered impossible, a strategy of adaptation of both the product and the communications efforts is suggested. Brazil, for example, had been one of the world's leading importers of Scotch whiskey until about five years ago, when the military government began to tax heavily all imports it considered "superfluous." Brazilian and other manufacturers came up with a score of new brands, all bottled, and some even distilled in Brazil. The products are sweeter than the traditional Scotch whiskey and are promoted as thirst-quenching, cooling drinks ("Scotch: On the Rocks," 1978).

Strategy Five: Product Invention. Perhaps the most risky market expansion strategy is to try to invent something to meet the special needs of overseas customers. Colgate, for example, saw potential in the estimated 600 million people in the world who wash clothes by hand. To tap this market, they developed an inexpensive (less than $10), plastic, hand-powered washer that has the tumbling action of a modern automatic machine. This product has sold well in Mexico and could help expand the demand for Colgate's laundry detergent.

Although there is no specific criterion for selecting one strategy over another so that a company's profits will be maximized over the long run, marketing research of multinational markets should result in a set of decision rules aiding a company in the selection of the optimal strategy. The first step in formulating an international product policy is the identification and definition of the potential market for the product. Prospective buyers have to be identified. Their ability to buy through income, credit, or other means has to be ensured, as well as their willingness to buy. Often marketing-opportunity analysis must delve into many attitudinal, experiential, and life-style aspects of individuals in order to determine how best to sort out those who do not want to buy from those who do. In Italy, for example, purple is considered a negative color and labels bearing female religious figures are considered poor taste ("Adapting Export Packaging," 1979). Obviously, the final strategy decision should be consistent with corporate objectives (e.g., geographic expansion), research and development capacities, and financial constraints.

PRICING DECISIONS.   Efficient pricing of goods and services is often a critical factor in the successful operation of a firm. Although the basic pricing ingredients—costs, competition, demand, and profit—are the same for all firms, the optimum mix of these factors varies according to the nature of products, markets, legal and ethical constraints, and corporate objectives.

Price is of unique strategic importance to marketing planners for a number of reasons. It is an important consideration in matching firm resources and supplies to buyer demand. "Unlike product, promotion, and distribution, price can be adjusted quickly and frequently to match supply or demand fluctuation" (Luck and Ferrell, 1979).

Pricing strategies are influenced by a variety of factors that affect ultimate price decisions. These factors may be more involved than traditional microeconomic determinants such as supply, demand, and competitive considerations, and can include such considerations as internal corporate policies and the stage in the product life cycle.

Pricing strategies of U.S. manufacturers affect the competitive posture of the United States in export markets as well as the level of export involvement. It has been observed that more than 90 percent of U.S. manufacturers have never developed export markets (Lang, 1968). Part of the reason for the limited export performance by U.S. firms lies in pricing policies. The export-pricing policy most frequently used by U.S. companies is a cost-plus method (Keegan, 1980). To use this method, a fixed dollar amount is added to the cost of an item to yield a selling price. This amount is the markup designed to cover overhead expenses and produce a profit for a firm. This approach clearly does not take into account competitive conditions in export markets.

Two important disadvantages are associated with the cost-plus approach, according to Keegan. First, it ignores demand elasticity, which changes seasonally along a business cycle. Theoretically, we can be in a situation of rising costs and an upswing of the economy while the economies of other exporting countries are depressed or lagging behind the United States and the costs of factors of production are cheaper. Second, and perhaps an even more serious problem with markup pricing, is the tendency to apply the same average markup percentage to broad classes of goods with little or no regard for possible differences in price sensitivity. In both situations the exporter might miss an opportunity in an export market where a relatively low price would have resulted in large orders.

Cateora and Hess (1979) observe that pricing, from the standpoint of the international marketer, is probably the most complicated decision variable among the four marketing-mix variables. Its sensitivity to variations in the competitive conditions, taxation procedures, legislation, intracompany competition, and monopolistic purchasers make the issue of who sets a price for a product more and more important. It appears that there are three alternative positions a company can take toward worldwide pricing (Keegan, 1980), as follows:

1. *The ethnocentric pricing policy.* This policy states that the price of a product will be the same alternative whether it is sold domestically or in export markets. Obviously this approach does not take into account demand sensitivity in the various product markets.

2. *The polycentric pricing policy.*   This policy is used in a situation in which a subsidiary or affiliate is entitled to pursuing policies that are independent of the parent company. The flexibility of this approach allows for more maneuverability in responding to local market conditions. One disadvantage that is associated with this approach is that local managers do not benefit from corporate experience and more sophisticated types of analyses that the parent company could have provided.

3. *The geocentric pricing policy.*   This is an approach that is less flexible than the polycentric approach and yet not as rigid as the ethnocentric pricing policy. The assumption here is that there are some local market factors that should be recognized, but the local decision making is accompanied by headquarters' guidance. A case in point is TRW's pricing strategy. TRW's Automotive Worldwide Group puts pricing to final consumers in the hands of its operating subsidiaries. Local prices are determined by the local marketplace. Similarly, at American Can International, pricing to customers is left to the local affiliates. Headquarters is available for assistance on pricing matters, and affiliates may call if they so wish (*Managing Global Marketing,* 1976).

In the final analysis, companies have tried to keep a fairly tight rein on local decision making. A relatively unified pricing structure, one that operates if not worldwide, at least regionally, aids in discouraging source switching by customers (if free access to various sources is permitted by the company) and minimizes counterproductive competition among various subsidiaries for third-market business.

ADVERTISING.   Marketing communications are attempts by a firm to influence the behavior of the markets for its products and services. According to Kotler (1980), advertising consists of nonpersonal forms of communications to target buyers and publics conducted through paid media under clear sponsorship.

Kleppner (1980) states that advertising may be geared toward the following:

1. Increasing the frequency of use of a product.
2. Increasing the variety of uses of a product.
3. Adding a new product to a well-known line.
4. Reinforcing credibility of important claims.
5. Launching a special promotional campaign.
6. Turning a disadvantage into an advantage.

7. Dispelling a misconception.
8. Enhancing the image of a company (corporate advertising).

One of the most basic marketing objectives is the creation of repeat-purchase behavior or brand loyalty. Brand loyalty implies a repeat purchase on the basis of preference rather than habit. Once a brand loyalty has been established with an identifiable consumer group, the next objective is to increase the rate of consumption. The advertising of most consumer packaged goods (e.g., detergents) includes just such a theme. Experience has shown that it is easier to interest old customers in buying more of a product than to find new ones. Clorox, for example, long known as a bleach, is now promoted as an efficient disinfectant to encourage sales to its existing customers.

Promotion can be used when adding a line in order to benefit from the reputation the firm has generated for its brands. Similarly, advertising efforts are used to enhance or fine tune implementation of other marketing objectives and programs.

The last application area, corporate advertising, is deemed by this writer to be especially important in the context of international marketing. Given the suspicions and controversy surrounding the operations of multinationals, especially in developing countries, it appears that corporate advertising, that is, advertising aimed at creating a favorable corporate image rather than selling a particular product, could be particularly useful. Exxon's corporate advertising, for example, emphasizes its educational and training programs around the world.

Advertising Strategy.   Ultimately, advertising strategy entails two broad groups of decisions. The first is the writing of a copy platform. It sets forth the actual themes and claims to be used, and usually includes the mood of an ad and expressions of product features. The second decision set, media planning, involves media-mix decisions, that is, the selection of a combination of television and radio programs, magazines, newspapers, and other media vehicles that will maximize profits, given a budget constraint.

Quantitative models have been developed to help structure and evaluate media and audience data. Obviously the development of media models is predicted on an understanding of the appropriateness of media vehicles and a knowledge of how media are matched with markets. In general, advertisers prefer media whose audience characteristics are closest to the profile of market characteristics of their consumers (Sissors, 1971). Characteristics by which the target population may be identified include demographic, psychographic, and purchase-behavior variables. The goal for international advertisers is to direct market-research efforts toward data about the available media in a desired export market and the demographics or psychographic profiles of local target markets. Media availability and target-market characteristics will dictate the selection of a media mix with an optimal combination of cost and exposure value.

A central component in the development of an advertising plan is the creation of the appeal or the message to be communicated to the target audience. Since the appeal is usually expressed in a combination of words and a picture, language and cultural barriers complicate the task of the international advertiser. The problem involves not only different languages but also different connotations of expressions that are meaningful in one setting but not in another. Thus "Body by Fisher" became "Corpse by Fisher" in some translated versions, and Pepsi's "Come alive" came out instead "Come out of the Grave" (Dunn, 1976).

Stages of Development.   Another important variable to be considered in international-advertising planning is the target export market's stage of economic development. There is a clear association between advertising volume as a percentage of GNP and the general level or stage of economic development of a country—the higher the general level in a country, the higher is the proportion of income spent on advertising (Keegan, 1980). One general implication for the exporting firm or a multinational is that the per capita spending on advertising can be used as a rough indicator of the relative importance of advertising vis-á-vis other elements of the marketing mix.

Regional differences exist also in terms of media availability. Literacy, for example, influences the relative effectiveness of print medium vis-á-vis other media (e.g., radio). Radio and television services either may not be offered or may be offered so minimally that they cannot really be considered viable media options. Promotion in India is a case in point. Half of the total advertising spending is aimed at the literate middle-class urban citizen. However, when aiming ads at the illiterate rural segment of the population, advertisers screen commercials at movie houses. Radio is only a secondary medium, since most government-controlled radio stations are not permitted to carry commercials. Although television stations are allowed to carry commercials, advertisers consider television to be too expensive a medium ("India Offers," 1978).

In general, the proportion of advertising spent on print is relatively low in Latin America and high in the Middle East and Africa. Television expenditures, as a percentage of all advertising, are notably above average in Asia and very low in the Middle East and Africa. Radio receives a higher-than-average proportion of expenditures in the Middle East, Africa, Latin America, and Australia/New Zealand in comparison with the United States, Canada, and Europe (Keegan, 1980). These spending patterns can be used as one guideline when planning and developing a media-mix in any given region.

COORDINATING INTERNATIONAL ADVERTISING.   Peebles et al. (1978) suggest six steps to govern the conduct of the international-advertising effort. These steps or decision rules are aimed at circumventing the "standardized versus localized" debate (a worldwide standardized advertising campaign versus a custom-tailored, country-specific campaign).

As shown in Exhibit 1 the steps are as follows:

1. *Marketing and advertising strategy and objectives.*   At this stage, the home office and its subsidiaries jointly clarify their understanding of the firm's marketing objectives. In many cases, subsidiary management will be able to offer valid and useful insights when establishing objectives. Recurrent themes may alert the home office to market problems and opportunities of which they were previously unaware.

2. *Individual market input.*   Based upon the home office's reaction to their strategies and objectives, each separate market builds a tentative advertising campaign. A sufficient amount of visual material and copy must be prepared to indicate the primary creative thrust of the campaign. The home office will review all the campaigns and offer suggestions.

3. *Testing.*   Each campaign is market tested in its particular country. The home office will review the test results and offer comments and suggestions.

4. *Campaign review.*   Based upon market test results and the home office critique of those results, subsidiaries develop their campaigns to presentation

EXHIBIT 1   FRAME WORK FOR PROGRAMMED MANAGEMENT APPROACH

1. Strategy and Objectives

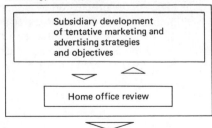

2. Individual Market Input

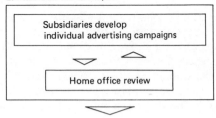

3. Testing

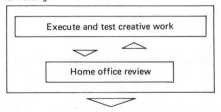

4. Campaign Review

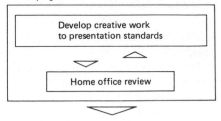

5. Budget Approval

6. Campaign Implementation

Source.   Peebles, 1978.

standards. Each subsidiary's campaign is then submitted to the home office for review and approval or modification.

5. *Budget approval.*   Final budget approval for each subsidiary is delayed until the home office evaluates the campaign.

6. *Implementation.*   Upon reviewing budget approval, the subsidiaries may start a full-scale campaign implementation. Media commitments may be made and final production work begins.

An overall campaign resulting from this approach may be highly standardized, or it may be a campaign consisting of several elements aimed at unique market conditions.

CHANNEL-OF-DISTRIBUTION DECISIONS.   Distribution is concerned with organizing systems of transportation, storage, and communication so that goods and services will be readily available to customers (Dalrymple and Parsons, 1980). The objective is to minimize the costs of storing and shipping merchandise while maintaining or improving sales to the ultimate user. Perhaps more than any other marketing-mix variable, distribution decisions are the least controllable by an exporting firm or a parent company's headquarters. Furthermore, the search for a reliable distributor is considered to be one of the most important barriers to exporting for small companies. Ultimately, channel decisions determine how the firm will reach its target markets, and thus the choice and performance of the channel are major determinants of the firm's financial performance. It is important, therefore, to review some of the complex issues surrounding the selection and evaluation of middlemen.

Middlemen.   The selection of middlemen for use in distribution channels should be based on sales and profit considerations. There are four key determinants of channel strategy: market targets, the marketing program, product or service characteristics, and corporate skills and resources.

According to Cravens et al. (1980), direct distribution whereby a manufacturer performs all channel functions by making contact with consumers and/or industrial and institutional end users through a salesforce or by mail, is favored when consistent with the following type of setting: Target markets include a few large customers or customers concentrated geographically, a major component of the marketing program is personal selling, the product is complex (e.g., computers) and requires the manufacturer's personnel in selling and maintenance, and the manufacturer possesses sufficient skills and financial resources to accommodate direct distribution.

When attempting to reach a more diffuse customer base with products that are frequently purchased in small amounts by a variety of users (e.g., food items), where promotion through advertising is more effective than personal selling, or when corporate capabilities are limited, the use of intermediaries becomes a more realistic option.

One of the most effective and economical ways of locating foreign representation, especially for the smaller firm, is by utilizing the services of the Department of Commerce ("Locating Foreign," 1979). Computer files containing information on more than 150,000 importing firms, trade lists, trade missions, and other services are all available to the prospective buyer and should aim him or her in getting exposure in export markets through intermediaries. Consider the lucrative Middle Eastern market. Black & Decker, Beecham, Union Carbide, Unilever, Nestlé, Kraft, General Electric, and Gillette all have one thing in common: they rely on independent distributors to sell their products ("Developing Middle East," 1977). Union Carbide, for example, works with seven trading companies in the Arabian Gulf area to market the full range of consumer products. Its industrial products currently are sold direct by product specialists, working out of regional headquarters in Athens, because of their high level of specialization.

In general, a strategy of using a single distributor is recommended to the new exporter who is still ambivalent about involvement in foreign markets and when product acceptability is uncertain. After a product "takes off" in the export market, there might be a justification for opening a local selling branch or agency, or employing more distributors. This pattern of evolution in distribution approaches typifies, for example, the market behavior of U.S. firms operating in the United Kingdom ("Surveying," 1979). Firms new to the market find it more convenient to appoint one distributor to cover the whole country. Later, in order to achieve greater market penetration, other distributors may be appointed. A number of larger U.S. firms maintain their own sales organizations in the United Kingdom as familiarity with the British market increases. Others appoint sales agents who are manufacturers of similar or contemporary products and take on additional items on a commission basis.

It is clear that channel decisions are particularly difficult to implement and supervise from the home country just because, as a general rule, the longer the channel, the more middlemen there are, and the less the control in the export market is. Different cultural and economic systems further aggravate this problem. Legal constraints, such as the laws governing termination of foreign distributors' services, sometimes limit the use of such distributors and might lead to a costly establishment of a selling branch by the exporting firm.

In conclusion, it should be recognized that a proper distribution strategy offers a firm the best means of reaching its export market. Although some companies may find that going directly to consumers is more appropriate than using intermediaries, many are compelled either to form new channels or to become members of existing channels. When selecting a foreign distributor it becomes critically important to refer to data sources provided by organizations such as the United Nations or the U.S. Department of Commerce. They can help provide information on issues such as reputation and quality or service provided by a foreign distributor as well as the legal/economic environments.

STANDARDIZED VERSUS DIFFERENTIATED (CUSTOMIZED) MARKETING MIX STRATEGY

The dilemma of whether or not a firm operating in the international marketplace can sell its product without changing product, promotion, price, and place, and still earn a good return is not a new one. However, it appears that more product categories successfully cross borders with minimal adaptation efforts that renew the interest and the evaluation of the conditions facilitating standardization of international marketing strategy.

Essentially the problem could be articulated as follows: How does one negotiate between the need to develop a marketing strategy which addresses the unique considerations of a particular country/market and pressures to reduce costs and expenses in order to achieve competitive edge in that market. Employing international

media and advertising has been successful in diminishing the role cultural difference plays in consumer buying decisions for several product categories. The upshot
is that for these categories manufacturers can develop a standardized "selling point"
message which would be equally effective in several international markets. Included
among these product categories are: personal computers, video equipment, health
food, fitness clothing and equipment, beer and low alcohol beverages, convenience
foods, toys, and financial services (Hulse, 1984). A recent conference attempted to
deal with this issue, and opinions of some of the participants are presented next.

Kotler proposes the development of a customization index which measures the
product, buyer behavior, and environmental dissimilarities between the source and
target countries to show the magnitude of the discrepancy and to allow the manager
to decide whether it is significant enough to require a differentiated strategy. Typically, adaptation is required in four of the following elements: (1) labeling, (2)
packaging, (3) materials, (4) color, (5) name, (6) product features, (7) advertising
theme, (8) advertising media, (9) advertising execution, (10) price, and (11) sales
promotion. Thus, for example, sales of Barbie dolls in Japan zoomed from near zero
to 2 million units after Mattel allowed the Japanese importer to change the extremely western look of the doll. Simon-Millers offers Kentucky Fried Chicken,
sushi, Exocet missiles, Mirage fighter planes, and Kalashnikov rifles as examples of
global products. She suggests that a reason for the success of global product strategy
is that customers will tend to prefer a good price/quality ratio to a highly customized
but less cost-effective item. Porter suggests a combination of standardization and
customization. He divides international marketing coordination into three basic
forms:

- Similar methods across countries such as common brand, product positioning,
  and service standards.
- Transfer of know-how among countries, such as market-entry approach, or
  customer/market information.
- Integration of effort across countries—international account management, for
  instance.

Porter concludes that upstream value activities, such as marketing, sales, and
service, are more difficult to standardize globally than downstream activities such as
R&D and production. The same product can serve different segments in different
countries. If one country is basically high-end, and another is mostly low-end, there
is still some overlap; a product in the middle could serve the lower segments of the
first country and the higher segments of the second one. Wind proposes a mix of
global, regional, local, and segmented brands. As an alternative, the entire portfolio
can be segmented, producing local, regional, and global segments (Marketing News,
1985).

INDUSTRIAL VERSUS CONSUMER MARKETING

Defining and analyzing markets is an early activity in developing a marketing strategy. "To the marketer, a market is the set of all individuals and organizations who are
actual or potential buyers of a product or service" (Kotler, 1980). This section
focuses on the opportunities originating from the fact that consumers differ.

Segmentation is the strategy of developing different marketing programs directed to different market subgroups or segments. These market subgroups are the market targets. A market target is any group of potential customers toward whom a company decides to direct its marketing efforts. A company may choose to view all potential customers within a product market as sufficiently similar to treat it as a single market, for example, developing one marketing strategy for all the Arab countries in the Middle East.

Other market-target options involve separating potential customers within product markets into different groups based on some demand-related characteristic. For example, somewhat different marketing campaigns could be developed for France than for England. In such a situation, different marketing mixes would be designed for different target markets. Thus the essence of marketing strategy becomes the fine tuning of the market mix according to the target market to which it is applied.

The objective of the marketer is to know and understand the market or submarket. In this context two general types of markets will be discussed: the consumer market and the industrial market. These markets are essentially distinguished on the basis of the buyers' role and motives rather than the characteristics of the purchased product. Consumers are individuals and households buying for personal use. Industrial buyers purchase for the purpose of producing.

In the following section, the motives and reasons for buying decisions in consumer- and industrial-market settings will be discussed. Gaining insight into the dynamics of the decision process will result in a better fit between the desired target market (e.g., individual consumers, organizations) and the marketing mix of the exporting firm. Applications of buying-behavior information generally have the following two objectives. The first is to make demand predictions. The other objective is demand diagnosis, which is concerned with describing what markets are like and explaining why management should expect certain kinds of market behavior to take place.

BUYING MOTIVES AND BEHAVIOR IN THE CONSUMER MARKET.   The consumer market buys products and services to satisfy a variety of needs—physiological, psychological, social, and spiritual. Literature of consumer behavior is very extensive and relies on clinical and social psychology, economics, and sociology. Only factors that can clearly be related to marketing-mix variables will be discussed here. According to Kotler (1980), the major factors influencing consumer buying behavior are in turn as follows:

1.   Buyer characteristics.
2.   Product characteristics.
3.   Seller characteristics.
4.   Situational characteristics.

The objective of the international marketer is to collect information about each of these factors.

Buyer Characteristics.   Cultural, social, personal, and psychological factors are relevant to buyer characteristics. Thus, for example, mood is very extensively used as a theme in Japanese advertising and reflects the cultural characteristic of avoiding confrontation. "Interestingly, one spot might look very much like another mood spot, yet Japanese viewers seem to clearly note the difference" (*Advertising Age,* "Marketing in

Japan," 1978). Social factors include the influence of other people in the consumer's life, particularly the reference groups, family roles, and status. Reference groups, for example, are all those groups that influence an individual's attitudes, opinions, and value system. A reference group's opinions of a product or service could be important in influencing a buyer's decision. Continuing the Japanese example, one observes that a larger part of the advertising efforts is directed toward a group rather than toward the individual, since the Japanese, particularly the men, feel themselves to be part of a group. Hence, "we" and "us" are popular pronouns in ad copy.

Another way of analyzing group influence on individual buying behavior is to examine the social stratification or social classes in a given country. Separation of classes can lead to important differences in behavior within the same culture. Many American companies that aim their marketing programs at the middle class can appeal to the same target market in other cultures. In Latin America, for example, the emerging middle class is expected to be more receptive to work-saving appliances, convenience foods, and disposable items—product concepts that until recently were not particularly meaningful in societies consisting primarily of two classes: the very poor, who had no purchasing power, and the very rich, who preferred luxury items ("Is the Well," 1977).

Personal factors include the consumer's age, sex, occupation, economic circumstances, life style, and personality. The worsening economic conditions in the United Kingdom, for example, resulted in the introduction of Economy Fish Fingers by the market leader, Birds Eye. An economy pack, the product was modified by a gradual reduction of the amount of cod in it ("Today's European Consumer," 1977). An earlier attempt to use cheaper cuts of fish failed because the consumers were not ready for such a radical downgrading.

Finally, psychological characteristics include consumers' motivations, perceptions, attitudes, and beliefs.

Product Characteristics.   Various characteristics of the product influence buying decisions—color, styling, quality, price, and taste. For food items, backup services might also influence consumer decisions. The marketer has control over these product attributes and can design or rearrange them so that the appeal of the product to the target market of interest will be maximized.

Seller Characteristics.   Characteristics of the seller will also influence the buying-decision outcome. The seller in this context could be the manufacturer. The reputation associated with his name, with the retail outlet, or with the combination of the two is critical. The image of the manufacturer's reliability and the retailer's knowledgeability, friendliness, and service are considerations important to buying decisions.

Situational Characteristics.   Various situational factors influence the buying decision. Climate, seasonability, weather, economic outlook, current fads, and other variables that the manufacturer does not control but has to contend with, all have an impact.

BUYING MOTIVES AND BEHAVIOR IN THE INDUSTRIAL MARKET.   The differences between industrial and consumer buying stem largely from the fact that the industrial buyer is responsible to an organization. The characteristics of the organization become important influences on buying decisions. Size will dictate quantity needs, for instance. Furthermore, there are typically fewer buyers in industrial markets than in consumer markets, which makes it possible to offer more personalized services (Cravens et al., 1980).

Several individuals may be involved in the industrial buying process, including product users, top management, purchasing agents, financial specialists, and research-and-development specialists. This complicates the decision process. Industrial buyers are likely to have greater training and technical knowledge about the product in question. Thus the American firm exporting industrial products must offer a marketing mix that is more technical than that of consumer marketing.

As in consumer marketing, many theories have been advanced to explain how industrial buyers make their purchase decisions. A widely accepted model of industrial buying behavior is that of Webster and Wind (1972). According to this model, the variables influencing industrial buying decisions can be classified as belonging to one of the two following categories: task and nontask. Each set contains four classes of variables as illustrated in Exhibit 2.

The task category includes variables that are directly related to the buying problem. The emphasis here is on maximizing the economic objectives of the buyer, such as favoring a supplier with the lowest total cost or more reliable after-sale maintenance. The nontask category includes variables that extend beyond the buying problem. Personal motives such as ego enhancement or risk aversion are more important here.

One implication of this model for the American seller is the need to evaluate the foreign buyer from the perspectives of both economic incentive and the human and social aspects.

Equally important is the evaluation of the four classes of variables that appear in both categories: environmental, organizational, interpersonal, and individual.

Environmental Factors.   These factors are external to the organization, where buying decisions are influenced by the level of primary demand, economic outlook, the cost of borrowing, the rate of technological change, political and regulatory developments, and competitive developments. These environmental influences are normally beyond the control of both buyer and seller and have to be considered as given.

Organizational Factors.   Each company spells out objectives, policies, procedures, structures, and systems to guide the buying process. Buying decisions are affected by the company's systems of reward, authority, status, and communication.

EXHIBIT 2   CLASSIFICATION AND EXAMPLES OF VARIABLES INFLUENCING ORGANIZATIONAL BUYING DECISIONS

Type of Influence	Task	Nontask
Individual	Desire to obtain lowest price	Personal values and needs
Social	Meetings to set specifications	Informal, off-the-job interactions
Organizational	Policy regarding local suppliers preference	Methods of personal evaluation
Environmental	Anticipated changes in prices	Political climate in an election year

Source.   Webster and Wind, 1972.

Interpersonal Factors.   These factors involve the interaction of several persons of different status, authority, empathy, and persuasiveness in the company. It would be very difficult for the American seller to know in advance how interpersonal factors work in a particular company.

Individual Factors.   Individual factors are all those factors that influence individuals' preferences and choice rules, such as demographic characteristics and general attitudes toward risk taking (Kotler, 1980).

The model described could be used as a framework for developing marketing and selling strategies aimed at industrial buyers. The marketing practitioner should be aware of these four buying determinants and conduct an in-depth analysis of how these factors affect the specific target market for his product.

In the international market setting, environmental influences on buying behavior, including economic, technological, physical, political, legal, and cultural factors, could be the most important determinants of values and norms of the client organization. An understanding of them is essential. American suppliers should also be aware of the personal risks involved in industrial buying. The decision maker runs the risk that the product that is purchased will not perform satisfactorily. He also incurs the psychosocial risk of how other members of the organization will view the decision (Moriarty and Galper, 1978). Since perceived risk plays a dominant role in the individual's decision-making process, the industrial marketer must evaluate all aspects of the marketing mix in terms of their impacts on perceived risk.

UNCONTROLLABLE VARIABLES AND MARKETING-MIX DECISIONS

Marketing strategy consists of target-market selection and the offering of a marketing mix. Marketing-mix variables are viewed as uncontrollable variables, or variables that are influenced and manipulated by internal managerial decisions. Thus, for example, management has, to a large degree, control over the characteristics of the product it manufactures, the price it sets, the media it selects, and the distributor it uses. The degree to which an optimal mix of marketing variables could be developed by a firm is limited, however, by uncontrollable variables—factors that the firm has to contend with without really being able to influence them, at least in the short run.

These variables are as follows:

1. Cultural and social factors.
2. Political and legal factors.
3. Economic factors (conditions).

CULTURAL AND SOCIAL FACTORS.   Cultural and social considerations are probably the most constraining uncontrollable variables when marketing in a foreign setting. There are various definitions of culture, but there are three aspects of culture on which there is widespread agreement: "It is not innate, but learned; the various facets of culture are interrelated—you touch a culture in one place and everything else is affected; it is shared and, in effect, defines the boundaries of different groups" (Hall, 1977). Culture has a profound effect on the political-economic system in any given country.

In general, the firm's long-run survival depends upon how it relates to conditions in its environment. Each of these conditions is capable of presenting a firm with constraints and opportunities that are relevant to its operations. Maintaining effectiveness depends upon the adjustment of strategy and structure to constraints imposed by the environment. Although this holds true both domestically and internationally, the task of matching firm to environment is more difficult in an international setting.

The cultural setting of any given foreign market includes diverse areas such as language, religion, local values and attitudes, education, social order or classes, politics, law, and technology and material culture, that is, the role of technology in the cultural and economic development process. Each of these factors, by itself or by interacting with other factors, can significantly influence the effective application of a marketing mix in any foreign setting. International-business literature has been evaluating the interaction of business, especially the multinational firm, and the cultural environment for many years. In our context it is germane to suggest to the firm contemplating introduction of products in a foreign setting some guidelines by which it can evaluate the receptivity of a foreign culture to its marketing offerings.

One approach describing the process by which a product that is new to a given foreign market is accepted locally was developed by Sheth and Sethi (1977). They link acceptability to the degree of resistance to change of any given culture. The less resistant to change a culture is, the easier is the application of the relevant marketing mix.

Although societies and cultures differ externally, unique identifying features exist that position various cultures on a continuum of social change—from traditional to developed societies. The criterion for placing a society at a point on the continuum is the amount of resistance to change—the lower the degree of resistance to change, the higher a society will place on the continuum (Sheth and Sethi, 1977). Sheth and Sethi suggest that an understanding of the process by which different cultures move on the continuum can help in understanding and predicting the circumstances under which a given product or idea tends to be accepted in a society. A propensity to change is contingent upon the nature of the product and how it fits with traditional and social values of a given society.

Innovation and Change.   International marketing efforts can be viewed as engaging a process of innovation and change. Products are introduced to a foreign target market in combination with a marketing-mix strategy. This marketing effort involves a communication about the innovation with identifiable source, channel, and message components. Communication about the product influences the country's propensity to change, as well as generating an evaluation of the product. The product is evaluated according to its ability to satisfy a set of relevant criteria for the product class. However, the influence of communication on either the propensity to change or the evaluation of the product is limited by two major constraints. The first constraint relates to the selectivity with which potential customers process information. Unless the culture is ready for a change, customers will be insensitive to communication on the new product and will pay little attention to it. Similarly, unless the product is favorably perceived by a culture, the acceptability of a communication will be minimal.

The second constraint relates to the compensatory manner in which a country's change agents and opinion leadership exert influence on propensity to change and product evaluation. If the adoption tendency is strong, the innovation will be tried. Satisfaction resulting from a trial may lead to the creation of product loyalty.

In general, the long-run adoption of an innovation will influence both the propensity to change and product evaluation. If there is satisfaction with the product over the long run, the propensity to change will be affected. Satisfaction will lead to greater receptivity to change and more-favorable predisposition toward the exporting firm or the manufacturer that introduced the innovation.

LEGAL ENVIRONMENT.   The laws of a society are one dimension of its culture. They present a more concrete manifestation of its attitudes and cultural norms and usually reflect its religious tradition. Because laws reflect the culture that gave birth to them, one finds great diversity among the laws of different nations (Terpstra, 1978).

One framework to evaluate the legal environment of international marketing has been developed by Terpstra. Pertinent dimensions are: (1) U.S. laws, and (2) domestic laws of each of the firm's foreign markets.

U.S. Laws and International Marketing.   The international marketing considerations most affected by U.S. laws are exporting, antitrust, and organization and ownership arrangements.

Exporting.   The U.S. has a variety of controls on export trade. Since many of these controls reflect the ever-changing international and domestic climate, we shall allude here only to the kinds of control imposed.

One type of control relates to the country involved. Generally there are restrictions on trading with communist countries. Another control relates not to the prospective export market but to the nature of the product. For certain types of products considered strategic or sensitive, there are tighter controls and even prohibition. Products such as nuclear weapons, armaments, and components used for surveillance of communications fall into this category. Another set of restrictions applies to pricing. Specifically, the Internal Revenue Service can examine and have a voice in the price set for exports to foreign subsidiaries.

Antitrust.   The U.S. antitrust laws affect the foreign business activities of American companies. The opinion and practice of the United States Justice Department is that even if an act is committed abroad, it falls within the jurisdiction of U.S. courts if the act produces consequences within the United States. One exception is the Export Trade Act. The act specifically excludes from antitrust prosecution the cooperation of competitive firms in the development of foreign markets. This antitrust exemption is subject to two qualifications. The first is that collaboration in export markets will not affect competition with the United States. The second is that in their business practices abroad, American firms must follow the same standard of behavior that is required in the United States.

In addition to some exemptions from the antitrust legislation, the government offers exporters some tax incentives. One such incentive is the Domestic International Sales Corporation (DISC). A DISC is a domestically based subsidiary for export sales. When a DISC is set up, it enjoys tax benefits on a portion of the income derived from export sales.

Foreign Laws and International Marketing.   The legal system of a foreign market country affects all marketing-mix variables. The object here is not to list all possible constraints, but to highlight some important considerations that should be included in any analysis prior to a target market selection.

Product.   Many regulations affect product and product-related issues such as packaging, in order to ensure local consumers of the products' purity, safety, or performance. The issue of product liability is becoming more and more important. Despite significant variations in rules from one country to another, the evolution everywhere is in the direction of more constraints, and the rate of change toward higher standards of liability is accelerating. In fact, the Common Market countries are now considering international agreement on rules for product liability that are significantly tougher than most existing national laws (Siegmund, 1978).

Price.   In some countries the concept of monopolistic competition is not as threatening as it is in the United States. As a result, one may find price agreements between businesses. Price controls also constrain pricing strategies of international marketers. For example, in the mid 1960s, France had an economy wide price freeze.

Distribution.   According to Commerce Department experts, the most problematic distribution issue concerns the local laws governing the relationship between the exporting firm and its foreign distributors. When disagreement between an exporter and a distributor occurs, these laws typically override the provisions in the contract and can make the severing of an undesirable relationship with a foreign agent or distributor very painful for the exporting firm because of the indemnification it is obliged to make. Occasionally a termination, even if carried out according to the requirements of the local law, may result in protracted litigation or unwarranted settlement when the foreign agent utilizes the nuisance possibilities in the often ambiguous legislation ("Lessening Terminal Rules," 1978). It is, therefore, crucial to gain information on the agency-termination laws of various countries as well as to include specific features protecting the export firm in any representational agreement. The foreign-business-practices division of the Office of International Finance and Investment of the Department of Commerce provides such information and sample guides for the preparation of agreements.

Promotion.   Most nations have some kind of laws regulating advertising, and advertising regulation takes several forms. Moreover, Boddewyn (1980) suggests that there is a global spread of advertising regulation, so that not only do U.S. regulatory developments quickly spread abroad (e.g., the issues of imposing corrective ads and of restricting children in ads), but other countries' discomforts with advertising are having an effect here. Boddewyn identifies seven key factors that influence the global multiplication of advertising regulation. These factors and major regulatory developments are listed in Exhibit 3. The implications of this phenomenon for corporate decision makers are a need for more self-regulation, collaborating with consumer organizations, lobbying and public advocacy, and revision of some marketing and promotion policies.

POLITICAL ENVIRONMENT.   Corporate involvement in international business ranges from minor exporting operations to investment in factories and total control of the marketing infrastructure in an overseas market. The more a firm commits

EXHIBIT 3   REGULATORY TRENDS IN INTERNATIONAL ADVERTISING

Key Regulatory Factors	Major Regulatory Developments
Consumer protection (e.g., against untruthful, unfair, misleading ads)	Prior substantiation of advertising claims is becoming the norm
Protecting competitors (e.g., against the misuse of comparison and cooperative advertising)	Growing product restrictions affect their advertising
	More informative ads are in order
Environmentalism (e.g., against outdoor advertising)	Advertising language is being restricted
Civil rights (e.g., against sexist ads)	"Vulnerable" groups, such as children, are becoming the particular target of advertising regulations
Religion (e.g., against the advertising of contraceptives)	
Standards of taste and decency (e.g., against sexy ads)	More groups and people can now sue advertisers
	Penalties are getting stiffer
Nationalism (e.g., against the use of foreign languages, themes, and illustrations)	

Source.   Boddewyn, 1980.

resources in the form of direct investment in manufacturing abroad, the more it should be attuned to the political environment. In this context, the firm should be aware of the potential confrontation it might face with a host government. Kobrin (1978) takes the position that the root of this conflict lies in the fact that the scope and objectives of the firm and state differ. The firm's interest lies in allocating and utilizing resources so as to maximize profits on a global basis. The state's interest lies in achieving objectives such as growth, employment, stability, and so forth for itself.' Four potential conflict areas can be identified as follows:

1. *Control.*   By accepting a subsidiary of a foreign parent, the host country gives up some degree of control over its industrial and economic affairs.
2. *Protection from Outside Threats.*   If multinationals are viewed as exploiting elements of the local population, hostility against the outside threat can be aroused.
3. *Cultural-Change Agents.*   Foreign firms can be viewed by both individuals and society at large as a threat to the established culture.
4. *Affronting National Pride.*   Corporate skills and technical know-how and resources may be painfully obvious and resented by local nationals.

Kobrin suggests that the political risk that the firm must be concerned with involves home, host, and third-country relationships and their mutual and often complex interactions.

Operations may be disrupted by internal conflict; restrictions on repatriations may limit profits or even result in expropriations. It is suggested, therefore, that some risk estimates be introduced into the analysis of any investment decision overseas. The result of such analysis would affect not only the type of international involvement (e.g., exporting vs. direct investment), but marketing-mix strategies (e.g., owning a distribution channel vs. using an agent, developing a somewhat-modified product in the home country vs. developing a product manufactured specifically for host-country target markets).

ECONOMIC ENVIRONMENT.   There are a number of criteria by which one can assess the impact of the economic environment on marketing mix decisions. The stage of economic development appears to be particularly appropriate, since it suggests the kind of options that the international marketers has when assembling marketing-mix variables. Economic conditions are related to the existence of mass media as well as the level of education, literacy, and consumption patterns. Rostow (1971) identifies five stages or five sequential categories of economic development as follows:

Stage 1.   The traditional society. Countries in this stage lack the capability of significantly increasing the level of productivity. Another characteristic is a low degree of literacy.

Stage 2.   The preconditions for takeoff. During this stage the advances of modern science are beginning to be applied in agriculture and production. The development of transportation, communications, power, education, health, and other public undertakings are begun in a small but important way.

Stage 3.   The takeoff. Human resources and social overhead have been developed to sustain steady development. Agricultural and industrial modernization lead to rapid expansion in these areas.

Stage 4.   The drive to maturity. Modern technology is extended to all fronts of economic activity.

Stage 5.   The age of mass consumption. This stage leads to a shift in the leading economic sectors toward durable consumer goods and services. Real income per capita rises to the point where a large number of people have significant amounts of discretionary income.

Economies of most developing countries fall into one of the first three categories. The industrialized countries fall into the last two categories. In general, the less developed the country, the smaller the size of potential markets, defined geographically or based on per capita income. The distribution networks in less developed countries are minimal. The more advanced the economy, the more flexibility the international marketer has in terms of segmenting target markets by offering different price points, a number of product lines, various media mixes, and shopping outlets at alternative distribution networks.

PLANNING THE INTERNATIONAL MARKETING MIX

DEVELOPING A MARKETING MIX.   Initial market-scanning probing should indicate to an exporting firm or a multinational whether or not some potential exists for penetration in a new foreign market. External documentary sources such as the information offered by U.S. Department of Commerce field offices, company executives based abroad in company subsidiaries, affiliates, branches, distributors, suppliers, and government official scan all aid in one form or another in providing initial information about a market.

Keegan (1980) suggests a general framework for the collection of data in international markets. This framework includes 25 information categories, which are listed in Exhibit 4. The framework is comprehensive and particularly suits the needs of a multinational interested in the creation of an ongoing global data base. For our purpose, the most relevant research needs are listed in section I of the exhibit and include information on market potential, consumer and customer attitudes and behavior, channels of distribution, communication and market services, new products, and every other aspect of competitive sales and operations.

We will take this analysis one step further under the assumption that a *geographic* target market has been identified as a potential area of interest for the firm. Such a designation should result from the interaction of two factors: corporate objectives (e.g., penetration into the lucrative Middle East market) and preliminary research (e.g., exploratory contacts with local distributors, information about activity and competing firms). Once a target market has been identified, more comprehensive research, such as that proposed by Keegan (1980), should be undertaken to develop a segmentation strategy and to examine whether or not the needs of segment(s) could be satisfied by

EXHIBIT 4   TWENTY-FIVE CATEGORIES FOR A GLOBAL BUSINESS INTELLIGENCE SYSTEM

Category	Coverage
I. MARKET INFORMATION	
1. Market potential	Information indicating potential demand for products, including the status and prospects of existing company products in existing markets
2. Consumer/customer attitudes and behavior	Information about attitudes, behavior, and needs of consumers and customers of existing and potential company products. Also included in this category are attitudes of investors toward a company's investment merit
3. Channels of distribution	Availability, effectiveness, attitudes, and preferences of channel agents in company's system or a competitor's system, or of independent distributors; wholesalers, retailers, and so on
4. Communications media	Media availability, effectiveness, and cost
5. Market sources	Availability, quality, and cost
6. New products	Nontechnical information concerning new products for a company (this includes products that are already marketed by other countries), ideas, and market potential
7. Competitive sales	Sales performance of competitve products
8. Competitive marketing programs and plans	Marketing programs and plans (sales promotions, advertising, area coverage, etc.) for existing and new products
9. Competitive products	Prices and features for existing and proposed products
10. Competitive operations	Information relating to a competitor's operating capability. Employee morale, transfers, production efficiency, and so on.
11. Competitive investments	Information concerning competitive investments, expansion plans, or moves. New capacity, investment proposals, indications of manufacturing resource commitments

EXHIBIT 4   *(Continued)*

Category	Coverage
II. PRESCRIPTIVE INFORMATION	
12. Foreign exchanges	Information concerning changes or expected changes in foreign-exchange rates by exchange-control authorities and immediate influences upon these authorities
13. Foreign taxes	Information concerning decisions, intentions, and attitudes of foreign authorities regarding taxes upon earnings, dividends, and interest
14. Other foreign prescriptions	All information concerning local, regional, or international-authority guidelines, rulings, laws, decrees other than foreign-exchange and tax matters affecting the operations, assets, or investments of a company
15. U.S. government prescriptions	U.S. government incentives, controls, regulations, restraints, etc., affecting a company
III. RESOURCE INFORMATION	
16. Manpower	Availability of individuals and groups. Employment candidates, sources, strikes, etc
17. Money	Availability and cost of money for company uses
18. Raw material	Availability and cost
19. Acquisitions and mergers	Leads or other informationn concerning potential acquisitions, mergers, or joint ventures
IV. GENERAL CONDITIONS	
20. Economic factors	Macroeconomic information dealing with broad factors, such as capital movements, rate of growth, economic structure, and economic geography
21. Social factors	Social structure of society, customs, attitudes, and preferences
22. Political factors	"Investment climate," meaning of elections, political change
23. Scientific technological factors	Major developments with broad but relatively untested implications
24. Management and administrative practices	Management and administrative practices and procedures concerning such matters as employee compensation, report procedure
25. Other information	Information not assignable to another category

Source.   Keegan, 1980.

developing appropriate marketing mix(es) while simultaneously meeting corporate objectives. To this end, a framework for international marketing planning has been developed as shown in Exhibit 5.

This framework meets two needs of the firm contemplating foreign-market penetration: market description and market diagnosis. Given rules by which the firm will decide whether or not it is worth its while to exert marketing efforts in the

EXHIBIT 5   INTERNATIONAL MARKETING-MIX PLANNING

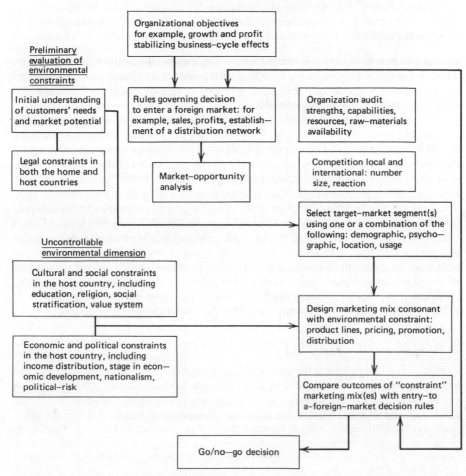

target market of interest, it can now focus on identifying and developing a segmentation scheme. Typically, the variables used to segment and describe a market are demography, location, site, and usage. Each of the variables will be discussed briefly.

Demographic Variables.   Markets can be segmented or described according to age, sex, income, family size, religion, social class, and other variables. Existence of many young people, for example, could influence a decision of sporting-goods manufacturers to enter a market.

Psychographic Variables.   These variables can be used as supplements to demographic variables. The focus here is on general buyer habits, lifestyles, and attitudes as they might be related to a specific product class or consumption in general. People's attitudes toward leisure time might influence a decision to introduce "time saving" products or establish a fast-food chain.

Geographic Variables. A decision to enter a market can be based on geography and population density. For example, entering a market in a developing country may depend on proximity to a transportation center, or a marketer may concentrate only on urban areas where the more educated and affluent middle class is likely to be found.

Product-Usage Variables. A market can be divided on the basis of product usage. Thus a market may be divided into users and nonusers. Users may be classified further as heavy, moderate, or light. A separate campaign could be developed for each of these segments or subsegments.

Once a market description or a segmentation scheme is developed, a marketing mix should be developed taking into account company resources, external uncontrollable constraints, and the segment's descriptors (demographic, psychographic, etc.) and requirements. Obviously, the net result would be a mix that is not optimal. The more restricted the international market planner is by the uncontrollable variables, the fewer options he has in terms of assembling the most effective mix. The firm should therefore compare what it can do, given the various environmental constraints and the cost of market penetration, to the decision rules it established beforehand with regard to satisfactory marketing and profit outcomes. After evaluating what can and cannot be done, the firm might very well conclude that the options it has in terms of marketing mix are very limited, and it cannot develop an effective marketing mix. Such a diagnosis should lead to a no-go decision.

Often, though, appropriate market research will lead to the identification of untapped markets that will increase the likelihood of a market penetration.

SOURCES AND SUGGESTED REFERENCES

"Adopting Export Packaging to Cultural Differences." *Business America* (1979), pp. 1–7.

Boddewyn, "The Global Spread of Advertising Regulations," paper presented at the regional meeting of the Academy of International Business in New York, January 1980.

Cateora, R. and M. Hess. *International Marketing.* Homewood, IL: Richard D. Irwin, 1979.

"Colgate's Nordiko Aims at P&G in Mexico." *Advertising Age,* Vol. XLVII, No. 45 (1976), p. 27.

Cravens, W., E. Hills, and B. Woodruff. *Marketing Decision Making.* Homewood, IL: Richard D. Irwin, 1980.

Criswell, B. "Is the Well Going Dry? Try Getting off the Main Drag." *Advertising Age,* Vol. XLVIII, No. 23 (1977), p. 56.

Dalrymple, J. and J. Parsons. *Marketing Management.* New York: Wiley, 1980.

Dunn, S. W. "Effect of National Identity on Multinational Promotional Strategy in Europe." *Journal of Marketing,* Vol. XL (1976), pp. 50–57.

Giberga, M. "Lessening Terminal Risks with Overseas Agents." *Commerce America* (September 1978), pp. 30–33.

Hall, T. *Beyond Culture.* Garden City: Anchor, 1977.

Hulse, Carolyn. "Popular Categories Cross Cultural Boundaries." *Advertising Age* (12/24/1984), p. 17.

"India Offers a Diverse, Complex Advertising Market." *Advertising Age,* Vol. XLIX, No. 28 (1978), p. 96.

Keegan, J. *Multinational Marketing Management.* 2nd ed., Englewood Cliffs, NJ: Prentice Hall, 1980.

Kleppner, O. *Advertising Procedure.* 7th ed., Englewood Cliffs, NJ: Prentice Hall, 1980.

Kobrin, J. "The Political Environment," in V. Terpstra, ed. *The Cultural Environment of International Business,* Cincinnati: South-Western, 1978.

Kotler, P. *Marketing Management*. 4th ed., Englewood Cliffs, NJ: Prentice-Hall, 1980.

"Locating Terminal Rules with Overseas Agents," *Commerce America* (April 1979), pp. 6–8.

Luck, J. and O. C. Ferrel. *Marketing Strategy and Plans*. Englewood Cliffs, NJ: Prentice Hall, 1979.

Managing Global Marketing. New York: Business International Publications, 1976.

"Marketing in Japan," *Advertising Age*, Vol. XLIX, No. 3 (1978), pp. 43–90.

Moriarty, T. and M. Galper. *Organizational Buying Behavior: A State-of-the-Art Review and Conceptualization*. Cambridge: Marketing Science Institute, 1978.

Peebles, M., K. Ryans, Jr., and I. R. Vernon. "Coordinating International Advertising." *Journal of Marketing*, Vol. XLII, No. 1 (1978), pp. 28–34.

Rostow, W. *The Stages of Economic Growth*. 2nd ed., Cambridge: Cambridge University Press, 1971.

"Scotch: On the Rocks." *Advertising Age*, Vol. XLIX, No. 28 (1978), p. 96.

Sheth, N. and S. Sethi. "A Theory of Cross Cultural Behavior" in G. Woodside, N. Sheth, and P. Bennet, eds., *Consumer and Industrial Buying Behavior*, New York: North-Holland, 1977.

Shilling, A. "Developing Middle East is all it Claims to Be, A New Frontier." *Advertising Age*, Vol. XLVIII, No. 28 (1977), pp. 64–110.

Siegmund, J. *Current Developing in Product Liability Affecting International Commerce*. Staff Study, Washington, D.C.: Department of Commerce, 1978.

Sissors, J. "Matching Media with Markets." *Journal of Advertising Research*, Vol. XI (1971), pp. 39–43.

"Standardization—No Standard for Global Marketing." *Marketing News*, September 27, 1985, pp. 3–4.

"Surveying the United Kingdom's Distribution and Sales Channels." *Business America* (1979), pp. 12–14.

Terpstra, V. *The Cultural Environment of International Business*, Cincinnati: South-Western, 1978.

"Today's European Consumer: Skeptical and Uncertain Target." *Advertising Age*, Vol. XLVIII, No. 12 (1977), p. 24.

Webster, E. and Y. Wind. "A General Model for Understanding Organizational Buying Behavior." *Journal of Marketing*, Vol. XXXVI (1972), pp. 12–19.

Zahn, P. "Blue Jeans Marketers Battle for Share in Europe." *Advertising Age*, Vol. XLVI, No. 34 (1975), p. 63.

INFORMATION FOR INTERNATIONAL MARKETING DECISIONS

CONTENTS

INFORMATION FOR INTERNATIONAL MARKETING DECISIONS

Susan P. Douglas
C. Samuel Craig

As competition for world market share intensifies in many industries, such as automobiles, steel, watches, apparel, and electronics, attention to international marketing strategy becomes even more crucial. Lack of familiarity with foreign environments, coupled with the greater degree of uncertainty in operation across national boundaries implies, however, a high level of risk. Collection of relevant information can aid in reducing the level of risk and thus lead to more effective international business decisions.

Information is required for two types of decision-making situations: (1) when a company is considering initial entry into international markets, and (2) when a company has existing operations in foreign markets. In the first case, information is required to determine (1) which countries, product markets, and target segments to enter, and (2) what mode of entry (i.e., export, direct sales, joint venture) to use in each country and product market. In the second case, information is needed (1) to monitor changes in the business environment of the different national markets where the company has operations, and (2) to determine the appropriate allocation or reallocation of resources across different countries, products, and target segments.

The type of information needed in these two decision-making situations is somewhat different. For the first set of decisions, heavy reliance is placed on the use of secondary data, in particular, macrocountry indicators such as GNP, population, measures of country political stability, and financial risk. These enable assessment of the investment climate in a country, as well as marketing threats and opportunities. In addition, data concerning specific product markets and competition should be obtained where available.

The plethora of information relating to international markets suggests, however, the importance of selectivity in collecting such information. Not only are high costs associated with collecting and processing information in relation to a multiplicity of international markets, but in addition, the human mind has a limited capacity to handle, organize, and interpret information on this scale. The collection of information for international business decisions should thus be guided by the specific requirements of each type of decision. Such an explicit focus avoids both decision making based on inadequate or inaccurate data and the collection of an overabundance of unnecessary or little-used information.

The second set of decisions not only requires, or rather assumes, the availability of such secondary market data, but also requires internal company data relating to sales and performance within each national market. In addition, projections of sales and performance data are needed in order to assess future market potential in each country and product market. The specific types of information which can aid in making both sets of decisions are next discussed in more detail.

First, the different types of information required for making international marketing decisions are identified. Alternative sources of these data and their relative merits and limitations are then discussed. Finally, the various uses of this information both in relation to initial market entry and in reallocating resources across countries and product markets are examined.

COLLECTING INFORMATION FOR STRATEGIC INTERNATIONAL MARKETING DECISIONS

In making strategic international marketing decisions, three types of information are required:

1. Secondary data relating to the national investment and market environment.
2. Internal company data relating to past sales and performance.
3. Estimates of projected sales and market potential.

The specific data and relevant sources for each of these categories are examined next in more detail.

DATA RELATING TO THE NATIONAL INVESTMENT CLIMATE AND MARKET ENVIRONMENT

Information Sources.   An important type of data needed in making international business decisions unique to international, as opposed to domestic, business relates to the national business-investment climate and environment. These data can be obtained from a variety of secondary sources, including Frost and Sullivan, the Economist Intelligence Unit, Euromonitor, the United Nations, and Predicasts.

The Economist Intelligence Unit, for example, publishes 92 quarterly reports covering 165 countries. These provide a business-oriented analysis of the latest economic indicators and trends in each country. Annual country profiles for these countries covering the economic and political structure together with key economic and trade statistics are also published, as well as a world outlook which provides forecasts of key political and economic trends.

Frost and Sullivan also publishes information on key economic and social variables for 120 countries contained in their country data base, and country facts publications which are updated quarterly. This includes economic variables such as GDP, per capita GDP, inflation, exports, as well as social data such as energy consumption and imports, population growth, literacy, and unionization.

EXHIBIT 1 EUROMONITOR INTERNATIONAL MARKETING DATA (1984)

POPULATION
Population distribution
Total population
Population trends
Vital statistics
Demographic breakdowns by sex
Demographic breakdowns by age
Population estimates
Demographic breakdowns by nation

EMPLOYMENT
Employment indicators
Economically active population
Employment by activity
Employment by age
Employment by status

PRODUCTION
Food indices
Land use
Livestock
Meat
Animal and fishery products
Fruit and vegetables
Cereals
Forestry products and other crops
Processed foods
Beverages
Tobacco products
Energy
Electrical energy
Minerals
Metals and building materials
Soaps and detergents
Motor vehicles
Domestic appliances
Textiles
Footwear
Clothing

TRADE
Balance of trade
Imports by origin
Exports by destination
Imports of basic commodities
Exports of basic commodities

TRADE (con't)
Imports of foodstuffs
Imports of beverages
Imports of manufactured goods

ECONOMY
Main economic indicators
GDP—trade
GDP—origin
GDP—distribution
Defence
Exchange rates

STANDARD OF LIVING
Wages
Prices
Costs
Ownership levels

CONSUMPTION AND MARKET SIZES
Food
Beverages and tobacco
Durables
Industrial materials and energy

RETAILING
Retail sales
Number of retail outlets

CONSUMER EXPENDITURE
Total consumer expenditure
Consumer expenditure by nation

HOUSING, HEALTH, AND EDUCATION
Housing and households
Health
Education

COMMUNICATIONS
Culture
Road transport
Shipping and railways
Mass media
Postal services and telephones

TOURISM AND TRAVEL
Receipts and expenditure
Arrivals and accommodation

Euromonitor publishes a broad range of indicators. These are contained in two volumes, one relating to European markets, the other to all other countries. The indicators available in relation to international markets are shown in Exhibit 1. The information and data available for European markets is considerably more detailed than that for other markets. The major limitations of the data are that they are not computerized nor updated very frequently.

The U.N. and UNESCO yearbooks provide extremely detailed statistics for an extensive number of countries, focusing predominantly on economic and demographic data such as income, population, literacy, educational levels, and birth, death, and marriage rates. The major limitation of these data, although extremely detailed and carefully collected, is that they do not always focus on information of the greatest relevance to marketing decisions. Emphasis is placed on analysis of past trends, rather than the projection of future trends, which is required for international business decisions.

The World Bank also publishes a number of statistics for 128 countries throughout the world (World Bank, 1987). These include basic indicators such as population, G.N.P. per capita, inflation, literacy, food production, as well as statistics relating to the economy, that is, growth of production by sector, growth of consumption, trade movements, capital movements, and various demographic and social statistics. These are carefully compiled, in some cases using U.S. or UNESCO data, and are highly reliable. On the other hand, they suffer from the same limitations as the U.N. data, namely, their general economic focus and lack of up-to-dateness.

The Worldcasts division of Predicasts also contains information on national income, population, the labor force, industrial production, trade and service, and government. Their main focus, however, has been on commodity and product-market data for industries such as chemicals, metals, instruments, transportation equipment, and fabricated products—the export-oriented industries. These are also projected by country for selected product markets, notably that for industrial goods. In general, one-, two-, three-, and four-year projections are developed.

Data Accuracy, Equivalence, and Interpretation.   There is, nonetheless, considerable variation in data from one source to another, as is evident from the range of values reported for a given statistic such as GNP per capita, number of television sets in use, vehicle registration, or number of retail institutions. In addition, accuracy of data varies from country to country. Data from the United States and the highly industrialized nations are likely to have a higher level of accuracy than that from developing countries. This is largely due to the mechanisms for collecting data. In the United States and other industrialized nations, relatively reliable and sophisticated procedures for collecting population or industry census data, national accounting, or other macrodata are utilized. In developing countries, however, such data may be based on estimates or rudimentary procedures with a high component of measurement error.

Measurement units are also not necessarily equivalent from country to country. In the case of income, for example, annual income figures in France and Belgium are likely to include the thirteenth month—a bonus automatically received by all salaried workers—hence providing a measurement construct different from that in other countries. Similarly in some countries, such as the United Kingdom, use of a company car is provided to many employees as a fringe benefit. Consequently, registration of personal-vehicle ownership does not necessarily provide an accurate reflection of "actual" levels of personal-vehicle ownership.

Interpretation of apparently equivalent measures also poses a number of problems. Comparisons of GNP per capita, may, for example, be misleading. Differences in personal taxation structures and in relative prices imply, however, that purchasing-power parity is not necessarily equivalent. Studies (Kravis et al., 1986) adjusting national income statistics for purchasing-power parity have tended to result in significant readjustment of apparent relative wealth, especially for developing economies.

An important limitation to all of these data in assessing market potential is that they relate to the general business environment. In addition, individual companies will require, wherever feasible, data relating to specific product markets, and a linking of the macroindicators to these markets.

A valuable source of product-market data is the U.S. Department of Commerce. Of key interest among these publications are: (1) global market surveys, in-depth reports covering behavior characteristics, trade barriers, market share figures, end-use analysis, and trade contracts, in 20 to 30 of the best country markets for a specific industry such as computers and peripheral equipment, machine tools, laboratory instruments, food processing and packaging equipment, etc.; these are updated regularly for all markets covered in an export overview for the industry; (2) export statistics profiles—tables of U.S. exports for a specific industry, analyzing export products and by-products, country-by-country, over each of the last five years; and (3) market share reports, which compare export performance of U.S. goods in a specific country with those from 13 other major supplier markets, covering both short- and long-term trends. The focus in these publications is on certain industries, particularly those with export potential.

In collecting information to assess market entry, a company should, therefore, collect information relating to both the macrocountry environment, and the specific product market.

In essence, four major categories of information relevant to market-entry decisions may be identified as follows:

1. Indicators of *risk* associated with operation in an overseas market.

2. Indicators of market *potential* and control.

3. Indicators of *costs* of exploiting market potential, which also vary with different modes of operation.

4. *Product*-specific market data.

Risk Factors.   Three major types of risk may affect the success or profitability of operations in a foreign environment.

1. *Political risk.*   These include the imposition of restrictions or regulations of the operations of foreign corporations by host governments as well as internal political instability and insurrections. While expropriation has attracted considerable attention, its extent has been limited and appears to have declined substantially in recent years in favor of other measures of control and regulation (Kobrin, 1984). Use of a variety of different approaches such as expert

opinion, Delphi techniques and impressions, as well as quantified approaches using multiple indicators has, however, been recommended (Rummel and Heenan, 1978). Syndicated services for evaluating risk are also available, such as Business Environment Risk Index, the Business International Index or Frost and Sullivan's World Political Risk Forecasts.

2. *Financial and foreign-exchange risks.* These include factors such as the rate of inflation, currency depreciation, or restrictions on capital flows and repatriation of earnings. Again, a variety of commercial services are available. These include services for predicting foreign-exchange rates in the long run, such as those provided by the major international banks (i.e., Chemical Bank, Citibank) or specialized econometric forecasters such as Chase Econometrics, Data Resources, Inc., or the Wharton Econometric Forecasting Associates. The accuracy and reliability of these services has been extensively investigated, and shows variation depending on the currency and time horizon (Levich, 1983). Also provided by other sources are summary indicators such as the biannual rating of 109 countries' creditworthiness by 75–100 international bankers, published in the *Institutional Investor.*

3. *Legal and regulatory factors.* These include factors such as import-export restrictions on various forms of ownership, modes of operation, tariff barriers, product regulation, and legislation. Information on these generally has to be analyzed on a country-by-country basis for a specific product category, and is found in sources such as the *Price Waterhouse Information Guides,* or Dun & Bradstreet's *Exporters' Encyclopedia,* which contain information on foreign commerce, language, weights and measures, price controls, distributor agreements, marking and labeling, and commercial practices.

Some illustrative examples of variables that might be included under each of these categories are shown in Exhibit 2. It should be noted, however, that these are illustrative only, and in each case the variables specifically relevant for a particular company or product will need to be determined.

Indicators of Market Potential. The second set of variables are surrogate indicators for market growth and development. These include the following:

EXHIBIT 2   RISK FACTORS

Political Factors
   Internal political stability
   Communist influence
   Expropriation risks
   Host-government attitudes to foreign investment

Legal Factors
   Import-export restrictions
   Legal systems
   Restrictions on ownership

Financial factors
   Rate of inflation
   Capital-flow restrictions
   Foreign-exchange risk

1. *Demographic characteristics.*   Here factors such as population size, rate of population growth, degree of urbanization, and age structure and composition can be obtained from U.N. data, demographic and other statistical yearbooks, or from the other information sources previously cited.

2. *Economic characteristics.*   These are essentially factors such as GDP or GNP per capita, rates of growth, income distribution, and so forth. Again, information on such factors can be obtained in most international data banks.

3. *Geographic characteristics.*   Here factors such as the physical size of the country, climatic, and topographical conditions need to be considered. These are most likely to be found in geographic atlases. Information on climate can also be obtained from tourist guidebooks.

4. *Technological characteristics.*   In this category are included factors such as the level of technological education, of consumer education and literacy and existing production or consumption technology. This can be obtained from a variety of sources such as the U.N. Yearbooks of Industrial Statistics, Labor Statistics, and National Accounts, or the regional market atlases published by Business International and Europa Publications. These contain information on production in the extractive and manufacturing industries, agricultural production, labor productivity, hours worked by operatives, as well as other social and economic data. The level of consumption technology can be evaluated from the level of household-appliance ownership, the number of libraries and museums, consumption of newsprint, or expenditure on higher education. Technological development can be evaluated from the existence of more sophisticated industries such as electronics or microprocessing, and from the level of energy consumption, and productivity indexes, which are found in most data sources.

5. *Sociocultural characteristics.*   These include factors such as dominant cultural values and life-style patterns, linguistic fragmentation, and cultural or ethnic homogeneity. Here considerably greater difficulty is likely to be encountered in obtaining relevant data and developing quantitative indicators. Information on aspects such as linguistic fragmentation or the number of ethnic or subcultural groups can be obtained from U.N. demographic and statistical handbooks. However, the extent to which this provides evidence of market potential is not always clear. More detailed studies of cultural values and life-style patterns have been conducted in relation to a number of countries, typically the more industrialized countries (de Vulpian, 1986; Shainwald, 1984). Interpretation of the implications for product potential and marketing strategy is, however, not always clear (Douglas and Macquin, 1977).

Some illustrative examples of relevant factors to be included from these categories are shown in Exhibit 3. Again, however, it should be emphasized that these are only illustrative, and the specific indicators will depend on the product market and the individual company.

Costs of Market Operation.   The third set of variables includes factors relating to the infrastructures that affect the costs of operating in a specific country environment. These are of two kinds: (1) *integrative networks,* which affect the feasibility or

**EXHIBIT 3   BUSINESS AND MARKET
ENVIRONMENT INDICATORS**

Demographic characteristics
  Size of population
  Rate of population growth
  Degree of urbanization
  Population density
  Age structure and composition of population

Geographic characteristics
  Physical size of country
  Topographical characteristics
  Climate conditions

Economic factors
  GNP per capita
  Income distribution
  Rate of growth of GNP
  Ratio of investment to GNP

Technological factors
  Level of technological skill
  Existing production technology
  Existing consumption technology
  Education levels

Sociocultural factors
  Dominant values
  Life-style patterns
  Ethnic groups
  Linguistic fragmentation

---

desirability of utilizing specific types of marketing programs and strategies, and (2) *basic resource requirements,* which affect the feasibility or costs associated with different modes of operation within a given national market.

Integrative Networks.   A variety of factors might be included here, as for example, the availability of television advertising, commercial radio networks, and supermarkets or other self-service outlets, the development of the transportation network and the communication system, and the existence of banking, financial, and credit services, advertising agencies, or market-research organizations. Information on these factors can be obtained from a variety of sources. Information relating to the number of television sets or radios owned, mail flow per capita, newspaper circulation, transportation statistics (such as kilometers of railroads, roads, ton kilometer of freight per kilometer of road or railroad), number of commercial and consumer motor vehicles, and number of wholesalers and retailers are available in most international data sources. Information relating to service industries is, however, likely to have to be obtained from the relevant international or national association, for example the International Advertising Association (IAA), the International Association of Department Stores, or the local chamber of commerce.

Resource Requirements.   Essentially cover three basic categories as follows:

1. *Physical resources,* such as electricity, energy, or water. Again information on the availability of these, for example, electricity production or energy consumption, can be obtained from most international data sources. More detailed information relating to specific regional and site availability is, however, likely to require more detailed investigation.

2. *Human resources,* such as the availability of labor, work skills, management training, and attitudes. Once again, aggregate information on the size of the labor force, levels of productivity, or hourly wages, is contained in sources such as the U.N. Statistical Yearbooks, but specific regional or industry availability will require more explicit investigation.

3. *Capital resources,* such as financial and capital resources and technology availability and sophistication. As in the preceding two cases, aggregate information on, for example, capital formation and financial markets is available in sources such as *International Financial Statistics.* Technology can be assessed in terms of the existence of high-technology industries. Again, however, the relevancy of these to specific industries and companies will require further examination.

Examples of both types of variables are noted in Exhibit 4. But again, as in the case of the two preceding variable sets, the examples are illustrative only, and the specific indicators selected are contingent on the specific product and company and the mode of operation or market entry that is envisaged.

EXHIBIT 4   INFRASTRUCTURE REQUIREMENTS

Integrative networks
   Transportation infrastructure
   Distribution network
   Availability of mass media, TV, radio, magazines
   Availability of communication networks, mail services
   Existence of other marketing or functional organizations

Basic resources
   Physical
      Electricity
      Energy
      Water
   Human
      Availability of labor
      Work skills of labor
      Management training and attitudes
   Capital
      Financial resources
      Technological capabilities
      Housing for expatriate labor

DATA RELATING TO THE PRODUCT MARKET
AND COMPANY PERFORMANCE

Market Size and Structure. In addition, wherever feasible, data relating to the specific product market should be collected. These should include information with regard to product usage, usage of complementary and substitute products, and competitive market structure. The relevant types of variables are essentially the same as those that would be used to assess potential-market size and structure in relation to the domestic market.

Product-Usage Data. Here information relating to levels of product ownership for durable products, or sales-purchase and repeat-purchase rates for nondurables, is desirable. Availability of such data is likely to depend on the development of the product market and the specific country. Nielsen data can, for example, be obtained for most major industrialized countries. The Economist Intelligence Unit also publishes studies relating to different products such as shoes, confectionery, and radios in various European countries. In developing countries such as the African countries or the Asian markets, greater difficulty is likely to be encountered in obtaining such data.

Usage of Complementary or Substitute Products. Data relating to usage of complementary products, for example, automobiles for tires, cameras for film, or substitute products such as margarine for butter may be useful. Similarly, data on bourbon consumption might be collected by companies marketing Scotch whiskey. Difficulties are likely to be encountered in collecting such data as in relation to product usage. Data for some industries, for example, the construction industry or major industrial markets, are readily available. In relation to consumer goods, such as soft drinks or electronic toys, much may depend on the state of market development.

Competitive Market Structure. Data relating to the competitive market structure should also be collected. This might include, for example, the number and size of competitors in the marketplace, their sales volume and rates of growth, relative market share, and so forth. Again, the feasibility of obtaining such data is likely to vary significantly with the specific product. In industrial markets, some data may be obtained from company reports or trade sources. In developing countries these may, however, be scanty. In consumer-goods industries in general, greater difficulty is likely to be encountered, as firms often have diverse product lines and do not break down aggregate figures on this basis.

Some illustrative indicators are shown in Exhibit 5. Specific operational definitions will, however, need to be established for each product market.

Company Sales and Product-Market Performance. Internal company data are also an important component of the information system. The same types of information needed to evaluate domestic marketing decisions are required. The exact information required, however, is likely to vary considerably from company to company depending on the nature of existing operations. Regardless of interfirm variation in information requirements, they should include aggregate measures of market performance, for example, return on investment, market share as a percentage of total industry sales, market share relative to the top, or leading three, competitors, trends in market share, marketing expenditure relative to sales ratios, or growth in sales by product line.

EXHIBIT 5 PRODUCT-SPECIFIC INDICATORS

Product usage
  Sales volume of product
  Ownership of product

Usage of complementary or substitute products
  Sales volume of complementary products
  Existence of user industries
  Sales of substitute products

Competition
  Number of firms
  Sales analysis
  Growth rate of competing firms

Depending on the size of the market, these may be broken down to reflect territorial or regional measures of performance, for example, market-share estimates and trends by specific geographic regions, sales and sales trends by region, expenditure relative to sales ratios by region, and so forth. Measures of performance relative to specific marketing variables or tasks such as sales force advertising, sales promotion, pricing, and distribution efficiency should also be included.

These data will only be available in relation to the specific national or product markets in which the company is already involved and are essentially needed for decisions relating to the reallocation of resources and effort across different country and product markets.

Collection of data for international operations and incorporation of these data into the information system initially appears relatively straightforward. Data comparability from one country to another presents a major obstacle. It is important to realize that a value or number supplied by a subsidiary in one country is not necessarily identical to the supposedly comparable figure supplied by a subsidiary in another country. Consequently, values or figures need to be adjusted into equivalent units so they can serve as a meaningful input for marketing decisions.

Sales-volume measures, for example, may be expressed in real or monetary units. Real units, although accurately reflecting the number sold, may be misleading in that the nature of the product can vary from country to country corresponding to different market requirements. Automobiles and pharmaceutical products, for example, frequently require modification to conform to specific national product regulations, thus entailing different costs.

Monetary units may thus be doubly misleading. The price of the product may not only reflect design differences, but in addition, differences in pricing policy, transfer-pricing practices, and local taxation rules, for example, a value-added tax. In addition, monetary units require conversion by an appropriate exchange rate. This gives rise to further difficulties to the extent that exchange rates are floating and may sometimes artificially reflect shifts in capital funds or temporary balance of payments. Procedures or mechanisms that adjust for such factors are thus required.

These difficulties are further compounded by variations in accounting procedures and standards in different countries. Costs may not be estimated in the same way or may include different expense items. Countries have different rates of social security payment and methods for allocating and billing these. Some adjustment has to be made to make calculation of sales force costs as a percentage of total sales comparable.

Even seemingly unambiguous measures of performance such as market share may be misleading. The definition of the relevant product market may vary from country to country as in the case of soft drinks or pharmaceuticals, thus understating or overstating a firm's share of the market. In examining sales response to various marketing-mix elements, differences in distribution channels and their efficiency, media availability and effectiveness, and market structure and pricing have to be taken into consideration. Distribution channels, such as supermarkets, used in one country may not exist in another, and hence distribution costs will be higher. Advertising sales ratios may be affected by the availability of various media and their reach. In some countries, television advertising may not be available. Consequently, print or radio media may be more widely used. Media mixes thus vary considerably, rendering strict comparison of advertising and sales ratios of limited value.

Sales and Demand Projections. In addition to estimating current market potential, estimates of future market potential and growth are also required to evaluate future rates of return. This is important when considering initial market entry because of the high costs and uncertainty associated with entering new markets. Such estimates are also necessary in countries where a company has existing market operations to assess whether resources and effort should be shifted from one product market and country to another.

If the company has been involved in the product market a sufficient time for historical data to be available, procedures similar to those followed in the domestic market can be used. For example, time-series trend analysis, or double-exponential smoothing analyses can be conducted. Since the application is identical to that in the domestic-market situation, these are not discussed here.

If, however, management is considering entry into new markets or is in the initial stages of market development, other procedures will be required. Often many of these markets, particularly in developing countries are likely to be small and fragmented, and limited data are available (Moyer, 1968). The small size of the markets, as well as the difficulty and high costs of undertaking research under such conditions, suggests that techniques commonly used in domestic markets, such as surveys of buying intentions or market tests are likely to be prohibitively expensive. In some cases, they may in fact be infeasible. Consequently, low-cost rudimentary procedures are likely to be required.

Data-extrapolation techniques offer considerable potential in this regard, since they make use of experience and data collected in one or more countries to develop estimates or forecasts of potential in other countries. Such extrapolations may either be made using time-series or cross-sectional data.

It is important to note that use of extrapolation techniques requires a number of assumptions concerning the relevance in one country of data collected in another country. First, it requires that countries be equivalent units or comparable in certain relevant respects. Thus, for example, extrapolation between countries that have similar market structures or demand characteristics is likely to be the most successful. Secondly, it assumes that the measurement units are comparable or equivalent in all countries. Thus, for example, if monetary units are used, their currency equivalents have to be established. Even if real units are utilized, equivalence has to be established, since these may not be defined similarly in different countries. Thirdly, it assumes that the relationship between demand determinants and sales is the same in all countries, that is, if GNP is related to cement consumption in one country, it will be related to cement consumption in another country. Finally, it requires that product classes are comparable and equivalent in all countries. For example, comparability of different shampoo variants or soft drinks in all countries has to be established. Furthermore, if projections over time are to be made, it requires that the rate of change in all markets be approximately equivalent.

Lead-Lag Analysis.   The first and most simplistic method of data extrapolation is lead-lag analysis. This is based on the use of time-series data from one country to project sales in other countries. It assumes that determinants of demand in the two countries are identical and the only factor that separates them is time. Sales trends in France, for example, can be predicted on the basis of sales trends in the United States, with a lag of x years. Exhibits 6 and 7 show this for television sets in the United States, the United Kingdom, and West Germany. This method is, however, generally not widely used, because of the difficulty of identifying the relevant time lag. Furthermore, the accuracy of the estimate is open to some question. It is likely to be most effective in the case of innovations, which have the same penetration rate in different countries.

Shift-Share Analysis.   Another technique which can be used to screen for products with high export potential and identify high opportunity markets for these products is shift-share analysis (Green and Allaway, 1985). This is based on import data statistics for a given set of products and countries over a certain time period. The actual growth in imports for a product within this set is then compared with the average growth for the overall product set. Products with a higher than average growth rate (i.e. a positive net shift), are considered to have the highest export potential, and similarly, countries with above average import growth for these products, to offer the most attractive export opportunities.

Barometric Analysis.   A third technique, which relies on the use of cross-sectional data, is analogous to the use of barometric procedures in domestic sales forecasting. This assumes that if there is a relationship between the product category and a gross indicator in one country, the same relationship will hold in other countries. Exhibit 8 shows the relationship between glass consumption and GNP in different countries.

**EXHIBIT 6   PERCENTAGE OF HOUSEHOLDS
OWNING TELEVISION SETS**

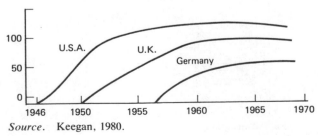

Source.   Keegan, 1980.

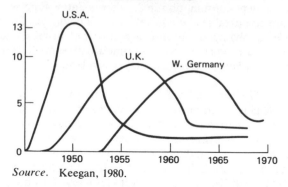

EXHIBIT 7 YEARLY PERCENTAGE INCREASE IN HOUSEHOLD OWNERSHIP OF TELEVISION SETS

Source. Keegan, 1980.

Various models can be applied to these data, including linear regression, logarithmic, exponential, or more complex models, to develop relevant model parameters, as in Exhibit 9. These can then be used to predict sales based on level of GNP in other countries.

An analogous procedure, which has been effectively used in relation to consumer markets, is the development of multiple-factor indexes. Thus rather than using one factor such as GNP to predict sales, a number of different variables are included in

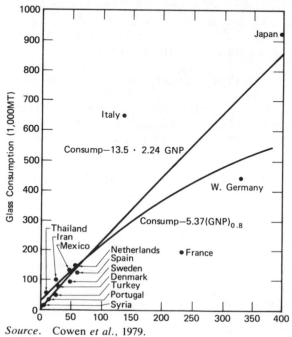

EXHIBIT 8 GLASS CONSUMPTION AND GNP

Source. Cowen *et al.*, 1979.

EXHIBIT 9   REGRESSION MODELS FOR PREDICTING GLASS CONSUMPTION BASED ON GNP

Country	Glass Consumption (metric tons)	GNP ($ Billion)
Syria	15	3
Portugal	36	13
Thailand	46	11
Turkey	50	23
Denmark	74	26
Iran	95	28
Sweden	99	48
Mexico	128	50
Netherlands	138	58
Spain	132	59
France	197	230
West Germany	454	330
Italy	686	135
Japan	1,230	393

$$\text{Model I} \quad C = A + B(\text{GNP}) = 13.5 + 2.24\text{GNP}$$
$$\text{Model II} \quad C = A(\text{GNP})^B = 5.37(\text{GNP})^{.8}$$

the model. Dickensheets (1963) has, for example, developed a multiple-factor index for refrigerators with larger storage capacity, consisting of 11 indicators including food-shopping habits, number of supermarkets and self-service food stores, auto ownership, consumption of frozen foods, per capita private-consumption expenditure, employment of women, availability of domestic help, availability of consumer credit, cost of electricity for residential use, dwelling construction and size of new dwellings, and refrigerator saturation in high-income families. Where weights for each factor are developed, these indexes can be used to rank countries in terms of their attractiveness or market potential.

Segment Extrapolation.   A modified version of the barometric procedure is segment extrapolation. The barometric procedure assumes that certain gross indicators are related to aggregate market potential. In some cases, there may be different market segments, in which different factors underlie demand. Alternatively, different market segments may have different levels or rates of market penetration.

In the first case, different indicators will have to be developed for each market segment. In the case of diesel engines for small boats, for example, there may be two potential markets—that for pleasure boats and that for fishing boats. In the first case, the relevant indicators might include per capita disposable income; in the second case, the length of the coastline or estimates of fish haul would be more appropriate. Similarly, in the case of hotels, there may be two potential market segments—one for tourist, and one for business travel. The first may be estimated on the basis of the number of tourists traveling to different countries; the second on the basis of growth in GNP.

In the second case, where different market segments have different rates of consumption or market penetration, extrapolation by segment, rather than for the total market, is desirable. This is particularly likely to occur in relation to up-scale luxury goods such as expensive wristwatches or pens. If market penetration of expensive wristwatches is related to income, the number of units sold to different income groups can be identified in one country, for example, the United States. The number of household units in each of these income groups is then identified in the second country and multiplied by the relevant group penetration rate to obtain potential-market size by subgroup. This is shown in Exhibit 10.

Similarly, in relation to industrial markets, different user industries can be identified, and rates of penetration in each of these industries determined for one country. The number of companies in each of these industries in another country can then be assessed and multiplied by the relevant penetration rate in order to determine potential-market size. In the case of minicomputers the key user industries might be financial institutions or commercial data-processing and market-research companies.

This technique can be further refined by breaking down companies within each of these industries by size, sales volume, or other factors indicative of sales potential. Penetration rates in each of these within-industry segments can then be estimated in the base country. The number of companies in each of these segments in the second country is determined and multiplied by the relevant segment-penetration rates. For example, in estimating market potential for microwave ovens in the industrial sector, three major groups of potential users might be identified—hotels, fast-food chains, and restaurant chains. For hotels, the number of units likely to be purchased might vary with the number of rooms. Sales potential can be estimated by size class in the base country. The number of hotels in each size class can then be estimated in the second country from tourist-board data or tourist guides. This can be multiplied by the relevant-size-class sales-potential figure to obtain market-potential estimates. This is shown in Exhibit 11. Similarly in the case of fast-food chains, if the number of units purchased varies with sales volume, penetration rates can be estimated by these segments in the base country. Again, these rates can be multiplied by the number of chains in each segment in the second country to obtain market-potential estimates.

Econometric Forecasting Models.   More complex forecasting models can also be developed using econometric procedures. These typically require both cross-sectional

EXHIBIT 10   PREDICTING SALES OF WRISTWATCHES

| | Country 1 | | Country 2 | |
Household Income	Number Sold Annually	×	Number Household Units (thousands)	=	Potential Sales Volume (units)
$35,000 and over	0.51		240	=	122
$30,000–34,999	0.47		300	=	141
$25,000–29,999	0.39		310	=	121
$20,000–24,999	0.38		600	=	228
$15,000–19,999	0.35		580	=	203
$10,000–14,999	0.21		610	=	128
$ 5,000– 9,999	0.20		1920	=	384
$ Under 4,999	0.19		2040	=	388
					1715

EXHIBIT 11   ESTIMATING MARKET POTENTIAL OF MICROWAVE OVENS BY USER SEGMENT (MARKET SEGMENT—HOTELS)

Number of Rooms	Number of Units Purchased	×	Hotels	Potential Market
50–100	5		200	1000
30– 49	2		100	200
<30	0		50	0
				1200

and time-series data. The cross-sectional data might relate variation in sales to macroindicators such as population, income, literacy, and proportion of the population in agriculture (Armstrong, 1970). Data on these indicators and sales can then be collected over time for selected countries. Regression analysis can be used to identify causal relationships and develop model parameters. The model can then be used to predict sales in other countries or to project sales over time in the same country where predictions for the macroindicators can be obtained. Another model (Lindberg, 1982), primarily intended to predict demand for consumer durables, uses time series data on personal consumer expenditure on the good and the level of saturation (i.e., number of households owning at least one unit) in selected countries to predict growth in demand for the good in other countries.

Such models do require the availability of historical sales data. Furthermore, they assume that extrapolation of these data is relevant in predicting future trends. This is likely to be the case only in relation to a relatively limited number of products that are in the mature phase of the product life cycle. In addition, trends, and hence underlying relationships between sales and indicators, often change very rapidly in foreign markets. Consequently, such techniques are likely to be often subject to substantial error. The models are complex to develop, and frequent updating of relevant model parameters is required.

The Macrosurvey.   A technique likely to be particularly effective in developing countries, where there is low market potential, predominantly in scattered rural areas, is the macrosurvey (Carr, 1978). A differentiation scale first has to be developed, consisting of different indicators, or relevant combinations, each of which corresponds to a level of market potential. For example, in Exhibit 12, the presence of a church in a village might indicate that a sales call would be worthwhile, but the community might need to have several telephones before it was considered worthwhile to establish a distribution facility.

Data has then to be collected on the presence or absence of these various items. This may be accomplished by aerial photography, or in some cases, the equivalent of the *Yellow Pages* can be useful. The most comprehensive approach would include a community visit in order to complete and update the index. An example of a scale developed to assess the potential for U.S. products in rural Thailand is shown in Exhibit 13.

USING INTERNATIONAL MARKETING INFORMATION

The four types of information about the international business environment can be used in two distinct decision-making situations—where management is contemplating

EXHIBIT 12   GUTTMAN SCALE OF DIFFERENTIATION FOR 24 MEXICAN VILLAGES

Step Number	Item Content	Proportion Discriminated
1	Named and autonomous locality group	1.00
2	One or more governmentally designated officials; more than one street	.92
3	One or more organizations in village	.88
4	A church	.84
5	A school building; a government organization; Mass said in the village more than annually	.80
6	A functional school	.76
7	Has access to a railroad or informant voluntarily includes railroad in list of village needs	.63
8	Access to electric power; informant estimates that a majority have electricity; six or more streets	.46
9	Railroad station; four or more bus or train trips daily	.41
10	School has four or more grades	.37
11	Village has a public square; village market patronized by people in other villages	.29
12	Doctor; priest resides in village; 10 or more streets; school has six or more grades; six or more stores; two or more television sets in village; public monument	.20
13	Has one or more telephones	.16
14	Forty percent or more have radios; settlement area one square mile or more	.12
15	Secondary school; 20 or more stores	.08
	(Coefficient of scalability is .92)[a]	

Source. Carr, 1978.
[a]The coefficient of scalability is a measure that "varies from 0 to 1, and should be above .6 if the scale is truly unidimensional and cumulative."

market entry, and where the company already has operations in overseas markets. For a company considering international market expansion, information is needed to determine *which* countries or markets to enter, and *how* to enter—what mode of operation to use in entering these markets. For the company already in international markets, information is required to monitor business environment change and to assess how to reallocate resources and effort across different national boundaries and product markets. In the latter case, data relating to the product market and to company performance is also required. These information requirements are next discussed in more detail.

MARKET ENTRY AND MODE OF ENTRY DECISIONS.   For companies entering international markets for the first time, a dual decision has to be made concerning the appropriate combination of countries and modes of entry to be used. This requires

EXHIBIT 13   DIFFERENTIATION SCALE OF RURAL THAILAND AND ASSOCIATED MARKETS

Step Number	Item Content	Estimated Population	Markets
1	Market square	1,000–3,000	Piece-good cloth and light agricultural implements (e.g., shovels)
2	Fairground; agricultural support shops (e.g., hand forges, wheel wrights); food shops	3,000–8,000	Manufactured clothes (e.g., work clothes, sandals); canned/dried foods (e.g., evaporated milk, dried shrimp and squid); radios, bicycles, and mopeds
3	Raimie *fiber* mill and pond; Buddhist temple; elementary school; urban support shops (e.g., auto-repair shop)	5,000–10,000	Service for mopeds; hardware, (e.g., hammers, saws, roofing material); school supplies; one-man motorized agricultural equipment (e.g., front-end tiller)
4	Government administration building; ambulatory health care; secondary school; police services	7,000–10,000	Window/door-screen material, glass; social dresses; primitive plumbing equipment (e.g., lavatories, shower heads, etc., with support piping)
5	Raimie *sack* mill and water reservoir; high school and/or technical college; sewer-and water-purification systems	22,000–30,000	Light-industrial machinery (welding, pipe-threading equipment); air conditioning; cement; construction services; office supplies and equipment

Source.   Carr, 1978.

the collection of information to assess the investment climate and market potential in all countries to be considered.

Evaluating Market Entry.   A major problem in the initial stages of international market entry is the bewildering array of countries and markets which could be entered. Since it is clearly prohibitive to examine all possible countries and markets, an initial screening procedure to determine which countries to investigate in depth is required. Secondary data can provide the basis for this evaluation, in conjunction with a screening or scanning routine developed to evaluate countries on relevant variables (Douglas et al., 1972). This screening procedure is modeled after the management decision-making process, selecting relevant variables and weighting them according to their perceived importance to management to rank countries in terms of priority for further investigation.

A modified version of the conceptual framework used to develop this procedure integrating international information needs is outlined in Exhibit 14. Three stages in the procedure may be identified. First, a number of preliminary screening criteria for eliminating countries are identified. Next, criteria for evaluating countries and

EXHIBIT 14 A CONCEPTUAL FRAMEWORK FOR COUNTRY/MODE-OF-ENTRY SELECTION

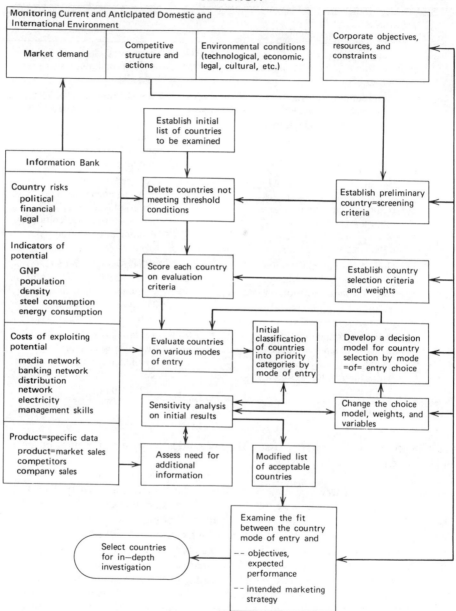

Source. Adapted from Douglas *et al.*, 1972.

the weights to be assigned to them under different modes of operation or entry are determined. Finally, countries are evaluated, based on these criteria, utilizing information relating to the general business and investment climate and, where available, to the specific-product market. A sensitivity analysis is then conducted to assess the robustness of the classifications.

Step 1: Preliminary-Screening Criteria. The first step in the macroevaluation phase is to establish the preliminary-screening requirements. These consist of go–no-go criteria applied by management to establish the feasible list of countries for the evaluation process. This assumes that countries may be excluded from further consideration on the basis of certain attributes.

Two types of attributes may be relevant as follows:

1. *Prohibitions* or restrictions on the sale of specific products or services by foreign companies, for example, firearms or narcotics, or restrictions by home governments on marketing to certain countries, as for example, to the Soviet Union.

2. *A priori* rules of thumb established by management for eliminating countries. The latter may reflect ideological or political influences, for example, a U.S. company might eliminate South Africa, or a company selling pork products might eliminate Moslem countries. They might also reflect the need for a minimum level of demand or market size. For example, a manufacturer of fur coats might eliminate countries with tropical climates, or a cigarette manufacturer, countries below a certain level of GNP per capita or population size. The specific criteria will depend on the nature of the product market and corporate objectives. Companies marketing similar products will not necessarily use similar sets of criteria. Interest and willingness to trade with communist countries or to assume risk may vary with the individual company. In any given situation, therefore, the onus is on management to identify the set of relevant criteria.

Step 2: Selecting Variables and Determining Weights for Evaluating Countries.

Identifying Relevant Variables. The second step is to determine which country characteristics are to be used in evaluating marketing opportunities and how these should be weighted. Following the four information components identified earlier, four types of variables need to be taken into consideration in evaluating international markets:

1. The *risks* associated with operating in a given national or product market.
2. The market *potential* and growth of the country and the specific product market.
3. The *costs* of operating in that environment.
4. The strength of potential *competition.*

The variables listed earlier (in Exhibits 2, 3, 4, and 5) provide some illustrative characteristics that might be used in evaluating international marketing opportunities. Information relating to each of these can be obtained from the sources indicated previously. In each specific case, however, the specific variables to be included need to be carefully selected by management based on the nature of the product market and corporate objectives.

Establishing the Relative Importance of Each Variable. Once the relevant variables to be included have been selected, the weights to be assigned to each of these have to be determined. These are likely to vary from company to company. For example, one company may be willing to accept a higher degree of political risk and less economic stability than another company. Similarly, a company emphasizing a mass-media approach may attach importance to a well-developed communication structure or the existence of television advertising. This implies that the weights should be provided by the judgments of relevant decision makers within the firm. Such judges should be selected on the basis of their involvement and importance in decisions to enter international markets. Various procedures may be utilized to generate and analyze these weights, such as a Delphi technique, conjoint or trade-off analysis, or rank-order or interval scaling.

Determining the Mode of Entry. Country-selection decisions are also affected by, and interact with, the mode-of-entry, or operation, decision. The importance of tariff barriers is, for example, critical when exporting, and may encourage local production. Similarly, factors such as the level of local technological, mechanical, or managerial skills are substantially more important if local production is being envisaged as opposed to licensing or exporting.

The variables included in the evaluation procedure and the importance attached to them therefore need to be adjusted according to the mode of entry. Judges or decision makers can be asked to select and weight variables under different modes of operation and entry as, for example, exporting, licensing, contract manufacturing, joint venture, or local production. Where significantly different variables or weights are assigned for different modes of entry, these can then be incorporated into the evaluation model.

Step 3: Country Evaluation and Sensitivity Analysis. Countries can then be evaluated based on these variables using information from the international information bank and ranked according to their score. If more than one set of weights is used, evaluations can be made sequentially based on the different sets. The highest ranking obtained for the country on any one of these sets is then retained as its score. The rank orderings of countries and the implied financial investment is then reviewed and the initial list of countries for in-depth evaluation selected.

The robustness of this procedure and overall congruence with initial management objectives is then examined. A sensitivity analysis is conducted using simulation procedures to evaluate the explicit and implicit decision rules used by management and their implications. At the same time, the need for more accurate information on countries where minor changes either in the value of variables or their weights would affect acceptance or rejection may be assessed. Particular attention is focused on cases that would shift the country dramatically from a high-priority to a medium- or low-priority zone.

The possibility of collecting additional information or redefining information needs may then be considered. A reevaluation of countries may be introduced, leading to the development of a modified list of acceptable countries.

Finally, the congruence of the procedure with initial management objectives is assessed. The rank ordering of countries with top priority for in-depth investigation is then examined. Each country ranking implies a specific mode of entry or operation, for example, exporting to Venezuela, local production in the Philippines. The compatibility of this country/mode-of-entry alternative with initial management expansion and financial objectives can be assessed. If the country rankings do not appear to be consistent with these objectives, reassessment of the procedure is required. More explicit incorporation of financial or other investment criteria may, for example, be desirable.

Other procedures can be developed for evaluating target countries based on secondary data. They may vary in the degree of complexity and sophistication, depending on company size and resources available for international market evaluation. Simple country-rating schemata may, for example, be used or more intricate models developed incorporating political and financial-risk analysis (Stobaugh, 1969). In either case, however, careful selection of country indicators relevant to the specific company or product market and the availability of an appropriate information bank is crucial to effective country-market assessment.

REALLOCATION DECISIONS.   For companies already involved in international markets, decisions with regard to the reallocation of resources and effort across different countries and product markets also need to be made. These require (1) the monitoring of environmental change in different countries, and (2) assessing relative profitability in different countries and product markets.

Monitoring Environmental Change.   Monitoring environmental change requires surveillance of a number of key indicators. These should be carefully selected and tailored to the specific product or range of products with which management is concerned. Two types of indicators are required. The first monitors the general health and growth of a country and its economy and society; the second, those aspects of the specific product market. Again, information with regard to these indicators can be obtained from the sources previously cited.

The first type of indicator might include factors such as the growth of GNP, population growth, percentage of GDP in agriculture, level of steel or cement consumption, imports of gasoline, or employment in service industries. In this context, it is helpful to include not only indicators that relate to the general economic and business trends and market growth, but also financial data, such as the rate of inflation or balance-of-payments figures and foreign-exchange rates, which provide indicators of the health of the financial climate. These are likely to be particularly critical when a company is involved in exporting or in sourcing across international boundaries.

The second type of indicator might include data relating to product sales in units and in dollar volume, market-share data, prices of leading competitors, number and growth of user industries, and so forth. If such data is not available or the product market is not well developed, surrogate indicators of potential demand may be developed, such as those discussed earlier. In the case of marine engines for small boats, for example, the length of the coastline in miles might provide an appropriate indicator, whereas for corn pickers, the acreage or annual volume of corn production might be suitable. Similarly, minicomputer industries might be concerned with the growth of the service sector of the economy. In each case, however, the particular indicators to be included should be tailored to the specific objectives and strategy of the company and the nature of the product market. Companies reluctant to assume financial risk might, for example, place greater emphasis on financial indicators and rates of inflation.

Reallocating Resources and Management Time and Effort across Different Regions, Countries, and Product Markets. Companies already involved in international markets also need to reassess periodically the allocation of resources and management time and effort across different regions, countries, and product markets. This may be desirable either because of changes in market conditions in a given country, for example, in inflation rates, or in economic growth, which affect profitability. Alternatively, management decisions to diversify or to enter new product markets or new countries may stimulate such a reevaluation.

Profitability in existing markets and countries thus has to be assessed relative to that anticipated from entering new product markets or expanding the current company product line in new countries. In addition to short-term profitability, a critical input to the resource-allocation decision is sales trends in each country or product market. These provide an indication of how resources and marketing effort should be shifted over time to anticipate changing conditions and to help ensure the long-term viability of the firm's international operations. As indicated earlier, in areas where the firm has a history of operations, sales-forecasting techniques similar to those employed domestically can be used. When new countries are being considered, methods of sales forecasting outlined earlier can be utilized.

Current profitability levels coupled with the sales forecast may suggest the desirability of reallocating resources from the product markets and countries in which the company is currently operating to other product markets and countries.

The international-product-portfolio model provides an appropriate conceptual framework for examining this decision and for determining the appropriate mix of countries, product markets, and operational modes for the firm. Various alternative formulations of this model have been developed, ranging from the simpler Boston Consulting Group portfolio model (Larreche, 1978) or the McKinsey/GE business screen to the more-complex, risk-return models (Wind, 1982).

Following the Boston Consulting Group portfolio model, product markets can be characterized on the basis of market share and market growth (Day, 1977), both of which are assumed to be linked to profitability. Applying this model to international markets, the growth rate for a given product market in each country and the company's market share can be examined. Assuming that world market share is a major objective, resources and effort should be shifted from countries with low rates of market growth to countries with high rates of market growth to enable the company to maintain or increase long-run global market share (Larreche, 1978). This does, however, necessitate availability or development of information relating to product-market growth and could be developed from historical data.

Similarly, the McKinsey/GE business screen can be applied to countries rather than products (Harrell and Kiefer, 1981). In this approach, products are assessed on two dimensions—business strength and industry attractiveness—analogous to the market share and growth dimensions used in the Boston Consulting Group model. In the case of screening countries, these dimensions are replaced by the company's competitive strength in a given country and the country's attractiveness. Multiple factor scales to assess a company's position on each of these dimensions are then developed based on management experience. Countries are then rated on these scales and their position plotted in a two dimensional matrix. This analysis can provide insights for resource allocation or investment decisions. Countries with low ratings both on attractiveness and competitive strength may be candidates for disinvestment. Similarly, resources may be diverted from countries rating high on competitive strength but low on attractiveness, to those rating high on attractiveness but weak in competitive strength.

Neither of these approaches take into consideration the possibility of cost economies for multiproduct companies nor of counterbalancing growth rates in different product markets. Companies may also prefer to concentrate efforts in countries with similar market characteristics, so that standardized strategies can be used in different countries throughout the world, thus reducing costs associated with strategy adaptation and development. This may also be true if there are significant costs of country-market entry or when products have shared marketing costs—for example, when they share a common sales force or distribution network, or have a common brand identification (Doyle and Gigengil, 1976). Assessment of such economies does, however, require information, providing a breakdown of current and projected production and marketing costs for each product at different levels of output in each country considered.

A more complex approach is to follow a risk-return portfolio model (Wind and Douglas, 1981). This assumes that the allocation of effort to different product markets is based on the expected rate of return from each product market and the risks associated with operating in a given market. Risk can be limited by the mode of operation within a country. Licensing, for example, reduces the level of risk, though with a commensurate limitation on rate of return. The optimal combination of countries, target segments, and product markets, and modes of operation to maximize profitability relative to a given level of risk has thus to be evaluated in relation to all product markets and countries under consideration.

This approach requires information related to the rates of return and risks associated with each of the components of the portfolio. A number of measures can be used to evaluate returns, such as net present value, ROI, net cash flow, or any other measure of performance for each product line in all countries to be considered. Attention needs to be paid to obtaining data that are comparable from one country to the next, particularly where the product line or segment differs and hence the basis for allocating overhead costs differs. Equally, accounting procedures or fiscal authority requirements may vary, generating data that are not strictly comparable from one country to another.

Risk can be evaluated based on a number of indicators as discussed in relation to financial, political, and legal risks. Then the best set of alternative portfolios, can be selected, given some assumptions concerning the nature of risk management is willing to accept. In countries or product markets in which the company is not currently operating, management judgements with regard to the potential attractiveness and risks associated with these markets can be obtained, applying an hierarchical approach (Saaty, 1980). This enables extension of the range of portfolios to be considered beyond the product markets and countries where the company has current operations. Expansion into new product markets, segments and countries can thus be evaluated as well as divestment in other products or countries.

The impact of alternative international scenarios, for example, expected rates of inflation or sharp or moderate rises in oil prices, on expected rates of return has also to be taken into consideration. Since a variety of different scenarios may be feasible, estimation of the most likely scenarios and the probability of their occurrence may be desirable. Once these scenarios have been identified, their impact on specific product markets and also on individual countries has to be determined. Use of expert opinion or Delphi techniques may be effective.

The complexity of this approach, and in particular its information requirements, suggests that at this point in its development it is most likely to be appropriate only for multinational corporations with a highly diversified product line. In this case, the range of alternatives is sufficiently large, and hence potential impact on profitability of reallocating resources substantial enough to warrant the cost and complexity of the data collection and assessment required. Other companies may prefer to use the less complex procedures, which have less stringent information and estimation requirements.

CONCLUSIONS

Collection of information is a key element in developing and implementing effective international marketing strategies. In particular, it is important to gather information relating to macroeconomic indicators in order to monitor the business-investment climate and marketing environment in different countries throughout the world.

Companies committed to international markets and global market expansion should develop an international information bank. This should link relevant macroeconomic, social, political, and technological indicators and information to internal company sales and market-performance data. Analyses of these data provide important input into decisions relating to market entry and the reallocation of resources on a global scale.

In domestic markets, an effective information system is essential to success. Because of the rapidly changing nature of international markets, the development of an efficient information system is even more important if the company is to remain a viable force in world markets. Yet even companies whose main focus is on domestic markets cannot afford to ignore international developments. The plight of the U.S. textile, television, automobile, and watch industries serves to underscore the importance of monitoring international development. Adoption of a global perspective in business is thus increasingly essential as the pace accelerates toward the emergence of a world economy and globally integrated markets.

SOURCES AND SUGGESTED REFERENCES

Armstrong, J.S. "An Application of Econometric Models to International Marketing," *Journal of Marketing Research,* Vol. VII, No. 2 (1970), pp. 190–198.

Carr, R.P. "Identifying Trade Areas for Consumer Goods in Foreign Markets," *Journal of Marketing,* Vol. XII (1978), pp. 76–80.

"Country Credit Bounces Back," *Institutional Investor,* March 1983.

Cowen, J., R.R. Galan, F. Gallione, B. Gardner, C. Sullivan, and J.C. Tshishimbi. *International Expansion of PPG, Float Glass Technology.* Unpublished working paper, 1979.

Day, G.S. "Diagnosing the Product Portfolio," *Journal of Marketing,* Vol. XLII (1977), pp. 29–38.

Dickensheets, R.J. "Basic and Economical Approaches to International Marketing Research," *Proceedings, American Marketing Association.* Chicago: American Marketing Association, 1963.

Douglas, S.P., P. LeMaire, and Y. Wind. "Selection of Global Target Markets: A Decision-Theoretic Approach," *Proceedings of the XXIII ESOMAR Congress,* September 1972.

——— and A. Macquin. *L'Utilisation du Style de Vie dans le Media Planning.* Paris: Jours de France, 1977.

Dun & Bradstreet. *International Exporters' Encyclopedia.* New York: Dun & Bradstreet, annual edition.

The Economist Intelligence Unit. *Marketing in Europe,* Special Reports. London: The Economist Intelligence unit.

———. *Country Reports Service,* quarterly. London: The Economic Intelligence unit.

———. *Country Profiles,* annual. London: The Economic Intelligence unit.

———. *World Outlook,* annual. London: The Economic Intelligence unit.

Euromonitor Publications Ltd. *European Marketing Data and Statistics.* London: Euromonitor Publications Ltd., annual edition.

———. *International Marketing Data and Statistics,* annual edition.

Frost and Sullivan, *Country Facts,* quarterly.

———. Political Risk Yearbook, annual.

Green, R.C. and A.A. Alloway. "Identification of Export Opportunities: A Shift-Share Approach," *Journal of Marketing,* Vol. 49, Winter 1985.

Harrell, G. and R. Keifer. "Multinational Strategic Market Portfolios," *MSU Business Topics,* Winter 1981.

International Financial Statistics. Washington, D.C.: International Monetary Fund.

Keegan, W.J. *Multinational Marketing Management,* 4th ed. Englewood Cliffs, NJ: Prentice-Hall, 1988.

Kobrin, S. "Expropriation as an Attempt to Control Foreign Firms in LDCs: Trends from 1960 to 1979," *International Studies Quarterly,* 28, 1984.

Kravis, I.B., A. Heston, and R. Summers. *World Comparisons on Purchasing Power and Real Production.* New York: UN, 1986.

Larreche, J.C. "The International Product Market Portfolio," S. Jain, ed., *Research Frontiers in Marketing: Dialogues and Directions,* Proceedings of the American Marketing Educators' Conference. Chicago: American Marketing Association, 1978.

Levich, R.M. "Currency Forecasters Lose Their Way," *Euromoney,* 1983.

Lindberg, B.C. "International Comparison of Growth in Demand for a New Durable Consumer Product," *Journal of Marketing Research,* Vol. XIX, August 1982.

Moyer, R. "International Market Analysis," *Journal of Marketing Research,* Vol. V (1968), pp. 353–360.

Predicasts. *Worldcasts.* Cleveland: Predicasts Annual.

"Rating Country Risk," *The Institutional Investor,* biannual.

Rummel, R. and D. Heenan. "How Multinationals Analyze Political Risk," *Harvard Business Review,* Vol. LVI (1978), pp. 67–76.

Saaty, T. *The Analytic Hierarchy Process.* New York: McGraw-Hill, 1980.

Shainwald, R. "A Marketing Profile of the Japanese Consumer," paper presented at the annual meeting of the Academy of International Business, Cleveland, Ohio, October 17–20, 1984.

Stobaugh, R. "How to Analyze Foreign Investment Climates," *Harvard Business Review,* Vol. XLVI (1969), pp. 100–108.

The Price Waterhouse Information Guides, *Doing Business in . . . Value Added Tax,* etc.

United Nations. *The Demographic Yearbook.* New York: United Nations, annual edition.

——. *Yearbook of Industrial Statistics.* New York: United Nations, annual edition.

——. *Yearbook of Labor Statistics.* New York: United Nations, annual edition.

de Vulpian, *The RISC Observer.* Paris, 1986.

Wind, Y. *Product Policy:* Reading, MA: Addison-Wesley, 1982.

——. and S. Douglas. "International Portfolio Analysis and Strategy: The Challenge of the '80s," *Journal of International Business Studies,* Fall 1981.

World Bank. *The World Bank Report.* Baltimore: Johns Hopkins University Press, annual edition.

MARKETING RESEARCH IN THE INTERNATIONAL ENVIRONMENT

CONTENTS

MARKETING RESEARCH IN THE INTERNATIONAL ENVIRONMENT

Susan P. Douglas
C. Samuel Craig

Prowess in domestic markets does not necessarily transfer to international markets. There are countless examples of blunders made by otherwise knowledgeable and successful companies entering international markets for the first time. Philip Morris, for example, tried unsuccessfully to convert Canadian smokers to one of its popular U.S. cigarette brands. Traditionally, Canadians have favored so-called Virginia-type tobacco blends, and despite a substantial advertising and promotional campaign, they retained their preference. General Mills encountered a similar misfortune with its Betty Crocker cake mixes in the U.K. market. The English housewife simply could not believe that a mix would be able to produce the exotic devil's food cake pictured on the package (Ricks et al., 1983). In both cases, adequate prior market research would have revealed such potential problems.

Why do companies not engage in adequate market research? The answer lies in part in a lack of sensitivity to the differences in consumer tastes, preferences, and response patterns in foreign markets. The high costs associated with research in overseas markets and sometimes the lack of adequate research competence constitute further barriers to international market research. In addition, the conceptual, methodological, and organizational problems associated with such research in many cases lead companies to doubt its value.

Such attitudes are, however, largely unwarranted. Although it is true that research in international markets is often more expensive, of lower quality, and less reliable than comparable data in the U.S. market, it is nonetheless, essential to collect such data. Only with the aid of such information can effective international marketing strategies be developed and the costly mistakes of Philip Morris, General Mills, and numerous other shortsighted companies be avoided.

Secondary information sources useful in relation to market entry and resource allocation decisions are discussed elsewhere in this volume. This chapter provides some guidelines for the collection of primary data in international markets, focusing in particular on multicountry research. Issues arising in relation to single-country research in foreign markets are not examined here, since they are similar to those in domestic market research, and are covered adequately elsewhere (Cochran, 1977; Green, 1978; Green and Tull, 1988; Lehmann, 1985; Sudman, 1976).

In this section, the major issues in designing multicountry research are examined first. Next the types of data and the associated sampling issues are discussed. Instrument design and alternative data-collection procedures are then covered. Finally, the main conclusions are highlighted.

ISSUES IN CONDUCTING INTERNATIONAL MARKETING RESEARCH

Two views are commonly held with regard to the design of international market research. The first holds that international market research is essentially the same as domestic market research. The second, on the contrary, conceives of international market research as a very different type of operation from single-country research, requiring a fund of experience and a combination of skills very different from that required for research in one country. The truth lies between these two extremes, as the same basic principles and procedures apply. However, the problems that arise, although present to some degree in domestic market research, are magnified in conducting international research. To indicate more specifically what difficulties may be encountered, the various types of international market research are first examined, and the issues arising both from a managerial and a research standpoint are outlined.

TYPES OF INTERNATIONAL MARKETING RESEARCH.   The significance of problems arising in international marketing research depends on the specific type of international market research being conducted. In general, four types of international market research may be identified: (1) single-country research, (2) independent multicountry research, (3) sequential multicountry research, and (4) simultaneous multicountry research (Barnard, 1976). Single-country research is that undertaken in one country by a foreign company. Independent multicountry research is that undertaken by subsidiaries of multinational organizations in different countries and not coordinated across countries. In both of these cases, as noted previously, the issues encountered are similar to those in domestic market research, and hence are not discussed further in this context.

In sequential multicountry research, research is conducted first in one country and then in other countries. This is attractive insofar as lessons learned in one country can be applied in another. This procedure may increase the efficiency of research, as the key findings of earlier studies influence the focus of later ones. In addition, costs are spread over a longer period.

Simultaneous multicountry research is research conducted at the same time in different countries, coordinated across countries. This is the most difficult to undertake and is particularly difficult to organize and coordinate. It tends to entail high costs and be relatively time-consuming. Consequently, although a growing number of such studies are beginning to be undertaken, they are still relatively rare.

A number of conceptual and methodological issues also hamper the execution of such research. In the first place, the relevant unit of analysis, that is, country, group of countries, and target segments has to be selected. Then appropriate sampling and data-collection procedures have to be determined, in particular, whether the same procedures will be used in each country or location. Designing a research instrument that provides comparable results and is of equivalent reliability is a further consideration, particularly in view of the need for linguistic and stimulus translation from one context to another. Despite such difficulties, multicountry research is essential to the development of effective international marketing strategy and in making many tactical decisions with regard to foreign markets. These are discussed next in more detail.

MANAGERIAL ISSUES IN INTERNATIONAL MARKETING RESEARCH.   Research is an important input into a number of international marketing decisions. In the first place, research may be undertaken to estimate demand in foreign markets. Second, it may be designed to determine appropriate bases of international market segmentation. Research may also be required to determine whether various marketing-mix elements such as advertising and pricing should be standardized across countries or adapted to the idiosyncrasies of specific national or product markets. Finally, it is an important element in developing long-run strategy with regard to international markets.

Demand Estimation.   Here, two types of research may be required. First, research may be required to estimate the income elasticity of demand. This measures the relationship between the amount demanded of various goods and economic progress, or, more specifically, how demand for goods changes with changes in levels of income (Moyer, 1968). This may aid in indicating how demand for a product will increase or decrease as income levels rise in different countries. Second, research may be required to estimate current demand, examining current market penetration, that is, the number of customers currently owning or purchasing the product, and repurchase rates. Similarly, surveys of purchase intentions and expected purchase rates may be undertaken to estimate future potential.

International Segmentation Decisions.   An important decision in developing international marketing strategy is how to segment international markets. Here, a key decision is whether to segment markets on a country-by-country basis and then identify relevant segments within countries as in domestic markets (Wind and Douglas, 1972). Alternatively, transnational segments cutting across national boundaries may be appropriate. This requires investigation of whether the response patterns of similar segments or customer groupings, such as businessmen, teenagers, or upper-socioeconomic-status consumers in different countries are more similar to each other than to other segments within the same countries.

Research to determine the appropriate base for market segmentation may also be required. Here it is important to assess whether similar bases of segmentation can be used in different countries. Although in some countries certain benefit or life-style segments may be viable, these may not exist or be reached easily in other countries.

Marketing-Strategy Development.   In developing international marketing strategy, a fundamental decision is whether a global, as opposed to a country-specific, positioning strategy is selected. Products and concepts developed in relation to a specific national market need to be evaluated in other national markets to see whether they can be launched in these markets. In particular, evaluation of whether modification, either in the physical characteristics of the product or of its positioning relative to competing products and selected target segments, is required. Equally, research to determine whether and how concepts and products, for example, automobiles, can be developed specifically for multicountry markets may be desirable.

Appropriate operationalization of such positioning strategies in terms of marketing-mix tactics must also be examined. This requires testing the effectiveness of using the same advertising theme and copy or similar sales-promotion tools in each country. Research to assess whether price elasticities are similar in different countries, and hence similar pricing strategies can be used, may also be desirable. In relation to media and distribution decisions, the infrastructures are likely to differ from country to country and hence limit the feasibility of utilizing similar strategies.

Strategic Marketing Planning. Research can also provide much valuable information in developing long-run marketing strategy. Here, two major strategic issues need to be considered. The first concerns the selection of appropriate countries, product markets, target segments, and modes of operation in each of these markets for long-run market growth. This requires identification of opportunities in different countries and product markets (as well as assessment of the ease of effective market penetration and exploitation). The second concerns the extent to which similar product positioning strategies can be used and hence marketing strategies standardized across different countries, and economies of scale achieved relative to world markets. This requires assessment of the efficacy of standardized relative to country-specific product lines and communication appeals in different country markets.

Research can thus aid in making more effective strategic and tactical decisions relative to international markets. Observational and qualitative data can be useful in the exploratory stages of research and market entry. Survey research is, however, likely to constitute the primary mode of investigation in overseas markets, providing relevant quantitative information on which to base decisions. Consequently, the primary focus of this chapter is on the issues and problems arising in the design of survey research.

ISSUES IN DESIGNING INTERNATIONAL MARKETING RESEARCH. Conducting research in multicountry markets is considerably more complex than conducting research in a domestic market. Traditional marketing-research concepts, designs, and measures are often ill suited and inadequate to cope with the problems encountered in a multicountry environment. In particular, the need to establish the conceptual and linguistic equivalence of measurement instruments and their interpretation gives rise to problems.

Many of the concepts, measurement instruments, and procedures to administer these have been developed and tested in the United States. Their relevance and applicability in other countries is, however, far from clear. Explicit administrative and analytic procedures for modifying and testing the relevance of concepts and measures developed in one country should thus be incorporated into the research design. In addition, procedures should enable the identification of concepts and measures unique to a specific country or culture. More specifically, it is suggested that a hybrid approach should be adopted (Wind and Douglas, 1980). Concepts and measures developed and tested in one national or cultural context, for example, life-style statements, are then translated and adapted for use in other countries and contexts. Constructs and measures unique to a specific country or culture should also be identified. This suggests a need to conduct exploratory research to identify country-specific constructs and to test the applicability of those used in other national contexts. The relevance of both sets of measures, using either internal- or external-validation criteria, are then examined to determine what should be incorporated in the design. Potential biases associated with the use of various instrument administration and analysis procedures need also to be taken into consideration. Data-collection techniques such as personal interviewing, telephone, or mail surveys differ from country to country in terms of their reliability and sources of bias (Webster, 1966).

Elimination of cultural bias from data interpretation is also an important issue. Individual researchers are likely to interpret data in terms of their own cultural self-referent (Lee, 1966). Consequently it is desirable to develop research procedures allowing for participation of researchers from all cultures or countries investigated in both the development of research instruments and the stage of the data analysis and interpretation.

Although such procedures add considerably to research costs and time required to conduct the research, they are nonetheless important in developing more reliable and better-quality data for international marketing decisions. This is a necessary consideration insofar as much of the data available for making international marketing decisions tends to be scantier, of poorer quality, and less reliable than that available for domestic marketing decisions.

ORGANIZATIONAL ISSUES IN INTERNATIONAL MARKETING RESEARCH.   In organizing and coordinating international marketing research, two main issues can be identified. The first concerns the extent to which research is centralized or decentralized within a corporation and is managed and organized by local subsidiaries or, alternatively, central headquarters. The second is whether in-house resources of a research department located either at central headquarters or locally are utilized, or external research services purchased from a large international research organization or from local suppliers.

The Degree of Centralization in Research.   The appropriate degree of centralization depends, to a large extent, on the organizational structure of the company, the nature of the decision, and the level and location in the organization where the decision is to be made.

Three major approaches to organizing international marketing research may be identified: (1) centralized, (2) coordinated, and (3) decentralized (Ewen, 1981). Centralized research, directed and controlled at corporate headquarters, may be most appropriate where the purpose of the research is to provide input into corporate policy and strategic decision making. There is, however, a danger of misinterpreting local nuances and downplaying environmental factors. In coordinated research, an outside research agency is used to design and coordinate research conducted in different countries with some participation from management in local subsidiary operations. In the case of decentralized research, responsibility for the establishment of research specifications and organization is delegated to local country management, once broad guidelines have been established by corporate headquarters. This may, however, result in the collection of data that are not comparable across countries as well as substantial emphasis on local country-specific issues.

Where a centralized mode of organization is adopted, the research unit at corporate headquarters establishes the specifications for the research that is to be conducted in each country. Secondary data or fieldwork may be purchased from an outside organization, that is, a local research agency or organization, but data analysis and interpretation is conducted at headquarters. This approach provides maximum control and also ensures comparability in data across countries. In addition, it may help to hold down costs.

On the other hand, there is the danger of ethnocentric cultural bias. Central headquarters will prefer a uniform research design with minimal adaptation to differences in local conditions, since this facilitates control of research (Adler, 1975). Problems of communication and coordination can, however, arise between corporate headquarters and local operating units who may complain of a lack of attention to specific local factors and environmental conditions.

In the case of coordinated organization, corporate headquarters will participate in the definition of the research to be conducted, but an external research agency or organization will spell out the details of the research design, take charge of the administration and coordination of the fieldwork in different countries and data analysis. This may result in some of the same problems of communication and coordination between corporate headquarters and local operating units if responsibility for research design and field operations is delegated to an external agency. This can, to some extent, be alleviated by requesting management or research staff in local operating units to participate in the research design, data collection, and analysis. It may also result in problems with regard to lack of comparability in the data, if modifications are made locally in research design or data collection procedures.

The third major alternative is decentralization. Here, corporate headquarters establishes research objectives in broad terms, and leaves the detailed specifications of the research design and management of the research process to local country operating units. Local management is thus responsible for data collection and analysis. Based on this, they would then present a report on relevant findings to corporate headquarters.

The primary advantage of this type of approach is that it provides optimal adaptation to differences in local market conditions, and in research capabilities and services in different countries. However, problems with regard to comparability in research design or data collection procedures may arise. In addition, an inclination to adopt a country-specific perspective and to focus on aspects specific to a given national environment may occur. This can, to some extent, be alleviated by establishing international or regional coordinating committees and meetings (Adler, 1975). Such procedures can, however, add to administrative costs, as well as prolonging the research process. Scheduling of fieldwork and reports also need to be coordinated, to ensure comparability in the timing of the research. Sometimes, this can give rise to difficulties, due to operation across geographic distances and international boundaries. Delays can, for example, occur in mailing or receipt of data and reports. Standardized procedures for coding and categorization of data, as well as for data analysis and report preparation, may also be desirable in order to ensure comparability (Franzen and Light, 1976). Development of standardized procedures is in fact often critical to ensure effective communication and coordination of local research.

The organization of international research should thus strike a delicate balance between centralization and direction of research from central headquarters, and decentralization or local autonomy in research design and implementation. The former may result in lack of attention to specific loyal idiosyncrasies and problems of implementation. The latter is likely to lead to research and data that are not comparable across countries. In particular, mechanisms to ensure effective communication and control between local operating units and central administrative units are essential.

In-House versus External Research Services.   A second issue concerns the use of internal research capabilities versus the purchase of external research services. Here it is unlikely that many companies will have the in-house expertise to design and implement research for all international markets. The need for familiarity with the local research environment and multiple linguistic competence is typically critical for effective field research. Consequently, unless a study entails predominantly desk research, purchase of outside services is likely to be required.

International research organizations vary considerably in terms of size and the range of services offered. Some are highly specialized, such as Nielsen, and SAMI, which provide information on market share. Others are large full-service organizations offering worldwide research services including consumer, industrial, agricultural, and feasibility studies, and various data-collection and data-processing services. Sometimes these are carried out by local branch offices (Research International has, for example, offices in 29 countries) and sometimes by traveling multilingual executives using quality local suppliers.

Some organizations specialize in particular product markets. IMS International, the second-largest research organization in volume of sales, is the dominant researcher in the pharmaceutical area, and offers audits and doctor panels worldwide. Other organizations specialize in qualitative market research, including discussion groups and projective techniques.

Most research tends to be ad hoc, that is, focusing predominately on product development and testing, attitude and image studies, and qualitative studies, as shown by the profile of the "typical" research market in Exhibit 1. In more industrialized countries, however, a higher proportion is spent on continuous, that is, audit or monitoring research, since understanding of the market, the primary purposes of ad hoc research, has already been gained. There is, of course variation from country to country in the type of research. In Australia, Malaysia, Denmark, and Finland there is substantial use of omnibuses. Equally, there are changes over time. In India, for example, there is less product testing than previously, as market monitoring and understanding of consumer tastes has grown.

Choice of organizations or type of service depends to a large extent on the type of research required, and in particular, the degree of methodological sophistication required. In the case of exploratory market research, use of traveling research executives and qualitative research may be appropriate. If more extensive ad hoc market surveys are required, use of one of the large international full-service organizations with offices in the countries to be investigated may be desirable. Similarly, if highly specialized research is required as, for example, in pharmaceuticals, use of organizations specialized in the product market is likely to be preferable.

In purchasing outside services, an important consideration is whether to purchase all services from the same supplier, or whether to "patch together" services from different suppliers. Use of a single supplier helps in building a working relationship and minimizes the administrative effort required, but can lead to a monopoly situation. As Exhibit 1 indicates, only a limited number of companies provide a range of services and are likely to cover all countries desired. Consequently, either such organizations are used or services are purchased from multiple suppliers, that is, medium and small ad hoc agencies. This will, however, entail substantial costs, inconvenience, and difficulties for management. Use of different suppliers for different projects and types of research (i.e., qualitative vs. survey research) may, however, be desirable.

**EXHIBIT 1 PROFILE OF "TYPICAL" RESEARCH MARKET
(BY VALUE IN %)**

Continuous research	35
Ad hoc research	
Habit/attitude/image studies	15
Product development and testing (quantitative)	15
Qualitative	10
Industrial/agricultural/pharmaceutical/other nonconsumer	10
Others	5
Media research	5
Omnibuses	5

**EUROPEAN MARKET RESEARCH MARKET STRUCTURE
(BY VALUE IN %)**

Country	*Ad Hoc*	Continuous
Austria	62	38
Belgium	52	48
Denmark	75	25
Finland	60	40
France	69	31
West Germany	65	35
Greece	75	25
Ireland	67	33
Italy	50	50
Netherlands	65	35
Norway	55	45
Portugal	59	41
Spain	47	53
Sweden	48	52
Switzerland	59	41
United Kingdom	65	35

Source. Barnard, 1978.

TYPES OF DATA FOR INTERNATIONAL MARKETING RESEARCH

In collecting data for international marketing decisions, two types of data may be considered—secondary and primary. Secondary data are data already available and collected for other purposes, such as GNP or income data, or the Pan European Survey of Executives. Primary data are those expressly collected as input to a specific decision. In an international context these data are highly complementary in nature. Secondary data are frequently used in the early stages of research to identify countries and target segments and product markets to be examined. Primary data are collected in subsequent phases of research to determine appropriate marketing strategies and tactics to reach these segments and product markets.

SECONDARY DATA. The various sources of secondary data are covered in an earlier section of this handbook, and hence will not be reexamined here. The principal advantages of these data are their ready availability and low cost. They may eliminate the need to undertake primary data collection and provide some initial indication of the attractiveness of various markets.

The disadvantage of such data is that they are typically collected on a region, country, or region-within-country basis, and hence may not be comparable. This is the case even in relation to such vital data as population and GNP. In addition, these data are frequently somewhat out of date, which is often a critical limitation given the rapid pace of change in many international markets. They also tend to be macroindicators relating to factors such as income, population, the economy, or social trends, rather than the more specific market data required for marketing decisions.

The major problem is, however, that the data are aggregated across regions, countries, or regions within countries and thus tend to give the illusion of homogeneity. This masks the existence of wide diversity within many regions and countries. In Europe, for example, the wealthiest regions in the Common Market, Hamburg, had a per capita income in 1980 of 193 compared with 45 for the poorest region, Eastern Greece. Similarly, data relating to aggregate values, living patterns, and socio-cultural change, as for example, that provided by the RISC organization (de Vulpian, 1986) or the *Reader's Digest European Survey* hide significant differences with regard to values or living standards among different sectors of the population.

In general, therefore, it is important to realize that although the country has traditionally been used as the relevant unit for defining the target population, this may not necessarily be appropriate. Countries are often highly heterogeneous with regard to a variety of factors such as language diversity, socioeconomic and technological development, social cohesion, and wealth. Consequently, the relevant target population might be subgroupings within countries such as cities, regions, communities, or cultural and minority subgroups such as teenagers, businessmen, blue-collar workers, or career women.

Since these groups face similar problems and decision situations from country to country, they may be expected to have similar behavior and response patterns (Douglas, 1976). In some cases these may be closer to those of a comparable segment in another country than to other groups within the same country (Thorelli et al., 1975). Consequently, the relevant target population may consist of such segments considered transnationally or on a global basis.

For some purposes, clusterings of countries may exhibit similar patterns of behavior, and hence the country cluster is the relevant target population. In the automobile industry, for example, regional groupings of countries often define the relevant target market, because of the existence of economies of scale and the need for integration of small markets. The same also applies to the pharmaceutical industry.

PRIMARY DATA.   Once secondary-data sources have been examined and have provided some initial indication about the nature of different markets, the next step is to collect primary data, tailored to meet information needs relating to specific management decisions. In particular, primary data are likely to be required in order to make tactical decisions for example, market segmentation or marketing-mix decisions relative to the extent to which strategies can be standardized across countries, or need to be adapted to specific national market conditions. Such data are also desirable in making long-term strategic target market selection decisions.

A first step in the collection of such data is the development of an appropriate sampling plan. Here two main issues are important: (1) the *representativeness* and

(2) the *comparability* of the samples relative to the target population. In the multinational context, choice of appropriate sampling procedures is particularly complex, since it often involves sampling at multiple levels as well as determining the sequencing of sampling at each of these levels. Furthermore, cost considerations are often an important issue, and may dominate decisions relating to the choice of sampling procedures.

In designing a sampling plan, the first step is to find an appropriate sample frame for the target population. Then the appropriate respondents have to be selected. Next, techniques for sampling have to be selected, the sample size determined and procedures for dealing with sampling nonresponse established. Each of these steps is next discussed in more detail.

Selecting the Sampling Frame.   Once the target population to be sampled has been established, the sampling frame, or list of population elements from which the sample is to be drawn, has to be determined. In an international context, this frequently presents difficulties because of limited availability and inherent limitations of sampling frames such as electoral or municipal lists, directories, telephone books, or mailing lists available in domestic market research. When available, they frequently do not provide adequate coverage, particularly in less developed countries, and hence give rise to frame error.

The most aggregate level at which a sampling frame can be constructed is the world; the next level consists of geographic regions such as Europe or Latin America. Following this is the country, and the geographic units or other subgroups within countries, for example, regions, cities, precincts, neighborhoods, or local associations and community groups.

The level at which the sampling frame is developed will depend in part on the specific product market and research objectives and the availability of lists at each level. The sequencing of research and whether, for example, one region or country is investigated first and then another will also determine the appropriate level for constructing a sampling frame. The advantages and limitations of each of these levels as sampling frames are next discussed in more detail.

World.   The first level at which a sampling frame may be developed is the world. This is likely to be appropriate in industrial markets, such as injection molders, surgical equipment, machine tools, and mainframe computers. In industrial markets, worldwide or regional lists of manufacturers can be obtained from sources such as Bottin International, which registers names and addresses of over 300,000 firms in 110 countries under 1,000 product classifications, by trade and by country, or Dun and Bradstreet's *World Marketing Directory,* which lists firms in 133 countries, and *Kelly's Manufacturers and Merchants Directory,* which lists firms in the United States and other major trading countries in the world. In some cases, trade associations are able to provide such information. These are listed in the *World Guide to Trade Associations.*

Use of a world sampling frame is likely to be relatively rare in the case of consumer research. It might, however, occur if the target population is a relatively small transnational market segment. For example, subscribers to the *National Geographic* or American Express card holders might be appropriate sampling frames for testing a new foreign-travel publication or readers of the *Economist* for business services. Similarly, subscribers to *European Research* might be an appropriate sampling frame for testing new market-research services. The major restriction on the use of sampling frames that transcend national boundaries is thus likely to be the availability of appropriate sampling lists of the target population.

Country Groupings. The next level for developing a sampling frame is that of country groupings. These are most likely to be regional. As in the case of global sampling frames, regional sampling frames are most likely to exist in industrial markets. Regional listings of manufacturing companies, banks, and other organizations, such as the *Directory of European Associations* may, for example, be found, particularly in the more-developed countries.

In some cases, however, regional sampling frames suitable for consumer markets may also be available. *Paris Match,* for example, has an extensive number of subscribers throughout Europe, while news and business magazines as *Fortune, Newsweek,* and *BusinessWeek* have started to develop regional editions. But it is important to note that these will generate a relatively particular sample, and hence relevance to the desired target population needs to be assessed.

Country. The country is the most commonly used level for developing a sampling frame in multicountry research. Here frames such as electoral lists, population censuses, and telephone books can be utilized. It should, however, be recognized that such sampling frames are not always available, particularly in developing countries, and in addition coverage will vary.

Sampling frames commonly used in U.S. market research, such as electoral or municipal lists, census tract and block data, or telephone listings, are often not available or are not current in other countries. For many years, for example, neither Cairo nor Tehran, with populations of 8 and 5 million respectively, have had a telephone book. Some countries, notably in Southeast Asia and Africa, lack any type of population lists, and hence sampling frames have to be constructed from scratch. In many cities in South America and Asia, even street maps are not available, and in extreme cases (for example, Saudi Arabia) streets have no names and houses are not numbered.

Different biases may also be inherent in different sampling frames. In many countries outside the United States, for example, use of telephone lists (except in the case of industrial research) will provide a relatively skewed sample. Similarly, use of block data will not necessarily ensure a random sample, and may result in underrepresentation of lower socioeconomic respondents living in caves, hovels, or riverboats.

Subcountry Groupings. The next level of sampling frames is subgroups within countries. These might be geographic units such as cities or neighborhoods, or ethnic, racial, cultural, age, or demographic subgroupings such as Catholics, Protestants, Blacks, Indians, foreigners of different origins, children, cat owners, members of the PTA, or senior citizens. Similarly, in an organizational context, specific industries or organizations within certain regions might constitute the relevant population.

The availability of an appropriate sampling frame is likely to vary with the specific subgrouping. For geographic units, this is likely to pose the least problem, if maps or local electoral lists can be obtained. In some countries, however, even such frames may not be available. Information on demographic groupings will generally be available from census data, and religious groups from church membership or organizations. Greater difficulties may be encountered getting information on other ethnic groups unless there are local ethnic organizations.

The Choice of Respondent.   Once the sampling frame has been determined, the specific respondents to be sampled have to be determined. Here, as in domestic market research, an important consideration is whether a single respondent is used or whether multiple respondents will be required, for example, husbands, wives, and children in the family, or buyers, users, prescriptors, and gatekeepers in organizations.

This decision depends to a large extent on the degree of involvement of different participants in purchase decisions. In organizations, for example, the purchasing agent may merely act as the agent in making purchases, whereas actual decisions about what to purchase are made by a buying committee or are influenced by the user. Similarly, in the household the housewife may act as the agent in purchasing food and groceries, but choice decisions may be heavily influenced by other family members and explicit purchase requests or feedback on choices may be important. Consequently, multiple respondents may be desirable.

Identification of the relevant respondent(s) in each country is also an important consideration, since these may vary from country to country. In some countries, for example, there may be a tendency among organizations toward highly centralized decision making. Hence the industrial buyer may be merely an agent. In Anglo-Saxon cultures, on the other hand, there is a greater tendency to delegate authority. Consequently, the buyer may play an important role.

Similarly, among upper socioeconomic families in Latin American or Asian countries and among white non-Afrikaaner South African families, the maid is frequently responsible for purchasing food and groceries. Therefore, relevant participation in purchase decisions is difficult to ascertain. This is in marked contrast to the family decision making common in relation to grocery purchasing in the United States, or the housewife-dominated decision making more prevalent in Europe. Prior examination of such factors is therefore necessary to determine appropriate choice of respondent(s).

Sampling Procedures.   The next step is to determine appropriate sampling procedures. Here a first consideration is whether research is to be undertaken in all countries and contexts, or whether results and findings are generalizable from one country or context to another.

Ideally, research should be conducted in all countries and contexts in relation to planned marketing operations. In some cases, given the high costs of multicountry research, management may consider it desirable to use findings in one country as a proxy for another. For example, market response patterns in Scandinavian countries may be sufficiently similar to sample only one of these countries. Similarly, response patterns in the Netherlands may be sufficiently close to those in Germany to generalize from a survey of the Dutch to the German market. It is, however, important to realize that such a procedure is fraught with danger. Even though previous experience suggests that response patterns are the same in both countries, this may change, or not be relevant in relation to the specific case examined.

Furthermore, there is a trade-off between the number of countries in which research is undertaken and the depth or quality of the research. Either a limited number of countries can be investigated in depth or a larger number can be studied, but less extensively. This often becomes an important issue when the sampling lists have to be developed or extensive interviewer training is required. Consequently, substantial costs may be entailed in generating reliable, good-quality data, and it may be more desirable to investigate a single or limited number of countries rather than several countries with less reliable methods.

Differences in the cost-effectiveness of research organizations from one country to another is often an important consideration in this regard. Costs do not always parallel wage rates in each country. As Exhibit 2 indicates, research costs vary considerably from one country to another in Europe. Based on an ESOMAR survey, costs of conducting quantitative research (based on an index of estimated cost of four types of surveys—a usage and attitude study, an advertising test, a package test, and a product test) were highest in Switzerland and Sweden, and lowest in Belgium and Greece. Qualitative research, based on an index of group discussion and depth interview costs, was highest in France and Norway and lowest in Austria and Greece. Consequently, it may be desirable to select a country where research organizations are more cost-effective or to use these as the preferred location from which to conduct international market research.

The importance attached to representativeness as opposed to comparability is a consideration. Data can be collected that are representative of the countries or contexts studied, drawing, for example, probability or quota samples. Such samples are, however, unlikely to be equivalent with regard to variables such as income, education, age, or size, or organization, structure, and industry, because the underlying distribution of these variables varies from country to country. If, on the other hand, the samples are comparable and matched on key background characteristics, national representativeness will be lost.

The selection of sampling procedures is related to decisions with regard to how the data will be collected. Use of mail questionnaires requires, for example, the existence of a mailing list, whereas personal interviews facilitate the use of cluster

EXHIBIT 2   RESEARCH COSTS IN EUROPE: 1982

Quantitative (Average of Four Indices)		Qualitative (Average of Two Indices)		Overall Rating (Average of Six Indices)	
Country	Index	Country	Index	Country	Index
1 Switzerland	147	1 France	134	1 Switzerland	135
2 Sweden	125	2 Norway	132	2 France	127
3 France	123	3 Netherlands	126	3 Sweden	118
4 West Germany	116	4 Switzerland	112	4 Netherlands	115
5 Netherlands	109	5 Denmark	107	5 Norway	111
6 Italy	106	6 Sweden	105	6 West Germany	107
7 Norway	101	7 Spain	101	7 Italy	100
8 Great Britain	96	8 Great Britain	99	8 Denmark	98
9 Denmark	94	9 West Germany	89	9 Great Britain	97
10 Spain	93	10 Italy	89	10 Spain	96
11 Finland	76	11 Belgium	87	11 Belgium	78
12 Austria	75	12 Finland	84	12 Finland	78
13 Belgium	73	13 Austria	73	13 Austria	74
14 Greece	68	14 Greece	63	14 Greece	66

Source.   Smalofsky, 1983

sampling. In establishing sampling procedures, a decision has to be made about whether random or purposive sampling should be used. The sample size has to be determined, as well as procedures for dealing with nonresponse.

Sampling Techniques. The distinction between probabilistic sampling and purposive sampling is an important one. In probabilistic sampling, each respondent in the target population has an equal chance of being in the sample. In purposive, or judgmental, sampling some criteria are established on the basis of which respondents are selected. Although in domestic market research, random, or probabilistic, sampling is generally considered to be the most desirable, this is not always the case in international market research. Difficulties of obtaining reliable sampling frames and costs associated with their development suggest that other methods such as judgment or convenience sampling may be more cost effective. Alternatively, samples matched across countries with regard to key background characteristics may be desired, suggesting the use of quota sampling.

Random Sampling. A major problem with the use of random sampling in international market research is that it requires the existence of a frame or list. Respondents are then picked at random from this list, selecting, for example, every nth name or person successively, until the desired sample size is obtained. These respondents constitute the sample population and are then questioned by personal interview, mail, or telephone. This technique is, however, difficult to apply in many developing countries because of the limited availability of appropriate sampling frames.

In cases where no adequate sampling frame is available, an alternative procedure is to use the *random walk* method. The interviewer then also becomes the sampler. The interviewer is provided with a walk route and instructed to select every nth house to interview (Frey, 1970). This actually sounds easier than it is, since the interviewer may have difficulty following the route or determining exactly what constitutes a "dwelling unit" in urban slums or villages, or where buildings include multiple dwelling units. Such difficulties suggest why random sampling, although from a statistical standpoint the only valid procedure, has frequently been replaced by the use of purposive or judgmental sampling.

Judgmental Sampling. Another procedure is to select respondents based on judgment. This may be particularly appropriate in certain industrial markets, where "experts" can provide valuable information, as for example in the aerospace industry or where specific individuals are known to have key influence. The sales force is often a valuable source of information, since they know customer needs and interests, though care should be taken in using them, for example, to obtain quantitative estimates of sales potential. Importers or export agents may also be used as "key informants," though some bias may be introduced reflecting their own self-interests.

This procedure may also be used in consumer markets, notably in developing countries. Here, questioning of village elders, priests, or other local authority figures may provide a reliable method of obtaining information about the number of inhabitants, current purchase behavior, and problems. This may be particularly desirable in countries with high levels of illiteracy, where the purpose of the research is to estimate sales potential rather than response to alternative marketing strategies.

Quota Sampling. A procedure commonly used in both industrialized and developing countries is quota sampling. The number of respondents required within a given category (e.g., in consumer research, in different age or income groups, working vs. nonworking wives, or in industrial markets, industry or firm size) is specified. Again, this procedure is particularly likely to be appropriate for industrial markets, where, depending on the product, customers are likely to be found in specific industries. Although this procedure ensures that the sample will be representative on the selected quota characteristics, there is clearly a danger that these characteristics are systematically associated with other factors, which will introduce confounding effects (Campbell and Stanley, 1963).

In a comparison of consumer innovators in France and the United States, for example (Green and Langeard, 1975), the French population was stratified along the variables of age, income, education, and employment status to ensure equivalence to the U.S. population on these characteristics. This stratification, rather than any fundamental differences in innovative behavior, may account for their lower levels of communication about grocery products and less television viewing compared with the U.S. sample, since they come from the more-sophisticated, better-educated elite of the French population.

Convenience Sampling.   Another alternative is to use convenience sampling. This implies selecting any respondent who is readily available. In developing countries, for example, convenience sampling in the marketplace provides a low-cost procedure for generating a sample (Mayer, 1978). Given the difficulties and costs of developing reliable sampling frames in such countries, this is often appropriate for developing a sample that although not strictly representative, may nonetheless be free of any systematic bias.

Sometimes in cross-national research, sample designs involve a mix of different approaches. In industrial market research, for example, specific industries may be selected for investigation and then quota sampled within each industry. Similarly, different regional units or areas, for example, certain major cities in industrialized countries, or villages in developing countries, may be selected. Then random-walk or block sampling within the city, or judgmental sampling of village elders can be applied.

Sample Size.   Another important decision concerns the appropriate sample size. Here, assuming a fixed budget, there is a trade-off between the number of countries or contexts sampled, the sample size within each country, and the extensiveness of the data collected from each respondent. As in many domestic market-research projects, a choice has to be made between small samples and high-quality in-depth research or larger samples and less extensive data.

Use of statistical procedures to determine appropriate sample size poses some difficulties, since to apply these procedures, some estimation of population variance is required (Cochran, 1977). In many cases these may not be available or where available may differ from one country to another. Hence appropriate sample sizes can only be determined on a country-by-country, rather than transnational, basis. Sample sizes may thus in many cases be determined arbitrarily, on an ad hoc basis. Management may, for example, decide that samples of 200–300, or 20 focus groups in each country, are required.

Diversity with regard to other factors within country units also needs to be taken into consideration. Differences with regard to the distribution of key determinants and related variables or sampling characteristics such as income, age, and education are likely to arise. This suggests that larger-than-normal sample sizes are likely to be required to test for the impact of differences in these variables on cross-national findings. This does, however, entail high sampling costs and hence may pose difficulties from a budgetary standpoint. Use of large sample sizes such as those in the *Reader's Digest European Survey* or the Leo Burnett/International lifestyle survey, are, therefore, rare.

Small sample sizes may, however, be defensible, particularly in the exploratory stages of research, where there is likely to be less concern with representativity. Use of large samples, although increasing statistical reliability and reducing random error, may increase error from nonsampling sources (Lipstein, 1975; Frey, 1970). Additional interviewers will be required, as well as additional coders, thus increasing the possibility of errors from interviewing and data processing. Consequently, additional quality controls will be required, necessitating expenditures to train competent interviewers and to supervise editing and coding. This is likely to pose problems in international market research, particularly in developing countries, where the quality of fieldwork may be frequently poor, and availability of trained interviewers or qualified research organizations limited.

Comparability of Sample Composition. A key issue in developing a sampling design is the importance attached to the representativity as opposed to the comparability of the samples. If samples are drawn that are representative of the target population, they are unlikely to be comparable with regard to certain key characteristics such as income, age, and education. This can create a problem if, as is frequently the case, such variables affect the behavior or response pattern studied. For example, in comparing interest in tropical fruit in different countries, income or education might be important factors affecting response. Mistaken inferences about national differences or similarities in interest in tropical fruits might, therefore, be made, when these reflect differences between samples in income distribution, rather than "true" national differences. One might, for example, conclude there was lack of adequate market potential, when in fact a small high-income segment constituted a potential spearhead for market entry. Equally, a myriad of other factors, such as life-style patterns or subcultural influences, may vary across countries. These introduce a confounding effect that may make it extremely difficult to isolate the impact on the behavior studied.

Statistical procedures can be used to evaluate the impact of different sample compositions on results. Either univariate or multivariate analysis of covariance can be conducted, with the different countries or target populations being entered as experimental units and the sampling characteristics as covariates. Tests of the significance of the covariates indicate whether findings are attributable to differences in the composition of national samples. Covariance analysis can also be used to adjust national means for differences in sampling characteristics, so that the impact of such variables is removed from the analysis, as well as identifying the strength of the association for specific variables. Initial applications of this procedure (Douglas, 1980) suggest, however, that substantial differences in composition will be required before there is a significant effect on results.

Comparability in Sampling Procedures. A further issue is whether the same sampling procedures are used. Sampling procedures vary in reliability from one country to another. Thus rather than using identical sampling procedures and methods in each country, it may be preferable to use different methods or procedures that have equivalent levels of accuracy or reliability (Webster, 1966). If, for example, in one country random sampling is of known validity and in another country quota sampling is known to be of equivalent validity, the results will be more comparable in terms of response rate and quality of response if two different procedures are used than if the same sampling procedure were used. Similarly, it is not safe to assume that if the same sampling procedures are used in each country with known biases, the results will automatically be comparable (Holt and Turner, 1970). A sampling procedure underestimating commercial travelers might have a different effect in various countries because of a different incidence of commercial travelers. Thus the results would not be comparable.

Similarly, costs of sampling procedures may differ from country to country. Cost savings achieved by using the same method in many countries and centralizing analysis, coding and so forth, may be outweighed by use of the most efficient sampling method in each country. For example, in one country random sampling may necessitate the purchase of a special list at a high price, whereas in another country quota sampling produces acceptable results at half the cost. Consequently it may be more appropriate to use the quota method in the latter country while using random sampling in the first.

Differences in sampling methods can also be utilized to provide a check on the reliability of results and potential bias in different methods. In one industrial survey, different sampling procedures with different sources of potential bias were used in five different countries (Webster, 1966). A constant pattern was found on one of the main variables studied, namely, the percentage of firms in each size category owning the test product. If the same sampling procedure had been utilized in each country, this might not have been detected.

In brief, therefore, use of similar sampling procedures will not necessarily ensure comparability of results, since each procedure is subject to different types of bias, and these vary from country to country. Deliberate variation of procedures, on the other hand, if intelligently used, can provide a means for checking the validity of results and detecting biases inherent in different types of procedures.

INSTRUMENT DESIGN

Once sampling procedures have been set up to obtain the desired data, the next step is the design of the research instrument. Here, as in other aspects of international market research, a key issue is to establish the comparability of the research instrument in different countries and cultural contexts. In so doing, it is important to ensure that the research instrument is adapted to the specific national and cultural environment and is not biased in terms of any one country or culture. Such bias may enter in both the design and development of the instrument, as well as in its application and scoring.

Bearing such factors in mind, the issues arising in instrument design for multi-country research are first examined. The main focus is on survey research and questionnaire design, since these are the methods predominantly used in multicountry research. The various sources of response bias associated with survey instruments are discussed. Issues with regard to instrument translation and use of verbal and nonverbal stimuli are then covered. Finally, different methods of instrument calibration and scoring procedures are discussed.

ISSUES IN INSTRUMENT DESIGN. In designing a research instrument for survey research, the key aspects concern: (1) the method of approach to the respondent, that is, how the sponsorship and/or purpose of research is presented and the degree of confidentiality promised, (2) how questions are formulated and in what sequence or order they are asked, and (3) what response format is used, and (4) whether these are precoded or unstructured (Oppenheim, 1966). In multicountry research, instrument design becomes even more complex because of the multilinguistic and sociocultural contexts.

Equivalence of comparability of the content, that is, behavior and topics studied, has to be established. Different response biases may also tend to be more or less prevalent, or be a source for concern in different countries and cultures. Operation in multilingual and cultural contexts also implies that instruments, whether verbal or nonverbal, will need to be translated so that they have equivalent meaning in each context. High levels of illiteracy imply that use of nonverbal stimuli instead of, or in conjunction with, verbal stimuli may be desirable. Finally, differences in perception and ability to grasp both verbal and nonverbal stimuli imply that response scales and formats will need to be designed to eliminate or reduce bias arising from such sources. It may also be desirable to include a test that alerts the researcher to the presence of such biases.

Functional Equivalence.   In examining the equivalence of the research context, a first issue to be considered in conducting international marketing research is that the behaviors studied may not necessarily be *functionally* equivalent and have the same role or function in all countries and contexts studied (Berry, 1969). Thus, for example, although bicycles are predominantly used for recreation in the United States, in the Netherlands, as in various developing countries, they provide a basic mode of transportation. This implies that in designing the research instrument, the relevant competing product set will need to be defined differently in the two contexts. In the United States it will include other recreational products, whereas in the Netherlands it will include alternative modes of transportation.

Similarly, in examining different components of life style in different countries or cultures, apparently similar activities may have different functions. In some countries such as the United States, for example, adult education may be regarded a leisure activity, whereas in other contexts, for example, Japan, it is designed to improve work performance. In the same way, whereas shopping is predominantly a work activity in the United States, in other cultures and countries, it is an important aspect of social life.

Conceptual Equivalence.   Another and related issue is that of the *conceptual* equivalence of different attitudes and behavior in different countries and contexts. A personality trait such as aggressiveness may not be relevant in all countries and cultures, or may be expressed in different types of behavior, hence requiring different measures. Some attitudes or behavior may be unique to a specific country or culture. The concept of *philotimo,* or conformity to norms and values of the in-group, and the importance attached to making sacrifices to family, friends, and others is, for example, unique to the Greek culture (Triandis and Vassilou, 1972).

Examination of this issue is particularly necessary in relation to attitudinal, psychographic, and life-style variables, which cannot be objectively measured. Even where the same construct is identified, it may best be tapped by different types of statements in different cultural settings. Innovativeness, for example, may be a relevant construct in both the United States and France. In the United States it is commonly measured by self-designated measures and statements such as "I frequently talk about new products with friends and neighbors," or "I am generally the first among my friends to buy a new product." In France, however, to be innovative is not socially valued, and in addition, new food products or brands are not a common topic of discussion (Green and Langeard, 1975). Consequently, use of behavioral rather than attitudinal measures will be preferable.

Similarly, social interaction is measured in the United States by statements such as "We frequently dine with friends." This is not appropriate to measure social interaction in other cultural contexts, such as developing countries, where dining with friends is not a common practice, and meals are taken almost exclusively with the family. Social interaction may take other forms such as participation in communal dancing or other festivities.

Such problems can also arise in relation to behavioral variables. For example, the question "Are you engaged?" has a different meaning in different cultures (Berent, 1965). In the United Kingdom it implies a formal commitment to be married, whereas in Italy and Spain it merely means having a boyfriend or girlfriend.

Category Equivalence.   Equivalence with regard to different categories also has to be established. Product class definitions may, for example, differ from one country to another. In the soft-drink and alcoholic-beverage market, for example, forms of soft drinks such as carbonated sodas, fruit juices, and powdered and liquid concentrates vary significantly from one culture to another. In Mediterranean cultures, for example, beer is considered to be a soft drink (Berent, 1975). Similarly, in the dessert market, items that are included will vary substantially, ranging from apple pie, jellies, and ice cream to baklava, rice pudding, and zabaglione. In some societies, cakes or cookies are included as desserts, whereas in China sweet items do not form part of the meal. This implies that what is included in the relevant competing product set will vary. Careful attention to such factors is thus an important consideration when designing concept or product tests, or alternatively, developing product-related measures.

Equivalence has also to be considered in relation to demographic characteristics. In the case of marital status, for example, in various African countries it is not uncommon for a man to have several wives, and in some cases women may have several husbands. Occupational categories also do not always have strict equivalence in all countries. Occupations may also have different status categories in different countries and societies. Priests and ministers, for example, often occupy higher prestige categories in the less-developed than in the more literate industrialized nations. Similarly, the social prestige attached to government administrative positions or to being a lawyer varies from society to society.

POTENTIAL SOURCES OF RESPONSE BIAS.   Once the equivalence or comparability of the content of the research has been established, the next step is to design the research instrument. First, it is important to establish a method of approach and questionnaire administration that avoids generating a response bias. Here four major types of bias can be identified: that (1) arising from a respondent's desire to be socially acquiescent, (2) arising from the topic being considered, (3) arising from specific response styles such as yea-saying, and (4) associated with specific categories or types of respondents.

Social Acquiescence or Courtesy Bias.   The desire to provide the socially desirable response, and in cases where an interviewer is present to give the response wanted by the interviewer, is particularly prevalent in certain countries and contexts. This type of bias appears to be particularly common in Asia, everywhere from Japan to Turkey (Mitchell, 1965). Some of the effects of this bias can be reduced by concealing sponsorship of the study, more effective training of interviewers, and more careful wording of questions to avoid use of "moral" or judgmental wording. In particular, it is important to maximize the ease of providing a socially unacceptable response by prefacing questions with phrases such as, "Some people feel this way, some people feel that way—how do you feel?"

Topic Bias.   Differences also arise with regard to topics that are socially sensitive in different national and cultural contexts. Willingness to respond to questions about income or discuss topics such as sex or alcoholism vary from one country or culture to another. In the Scandinavian countries, for example, respondents are considerably more willing to admit to overdrinking than in Latin countries (Lovell, 1973). In India, sex tends to be a taboo topic.

This suggests the need to identify what topics are socially sensitive in each country and cultural context. Measures to reduce bias from this source, as, for example, by collecting observational data or using an influential sponsor or improved interviewer probing techniques, can thus be introduced.

Response Style.   Differences in response-style bias from country to country also occur. Studies have, for example, found variation in the existence of yea-saying and nay-saying (Chun et al., 1974) and also in tendencies to use extreme points in verbal ratings (Douglas and LeMaire, 1974). Another study, applying multiple-scaling devices, suggested, however, that such tendencies were "true" responses, rather than an artifact of the scaling device (Crosby, 1969).

This suggests the need to use multiple-scaling instruments such as unipolar and bipolar scales as well as Likert or other types of scales to check for the existence of such biases. In addition, where scales equivalent to the Crowne-Marlowe measure (Crowne and Marlowe, 1964) or other similar scales measuring social acquiescence, and adapted to specific cultural environments are available, these should also be included.

Respondent Characteristics.   Differences in response bias have also been found to be related to certain respondent characteristics. These appear in general to be the same in different countries and cultures. Yea-saying and nay-saying biases, have, for example, been found, in other countries as in the United States, to be stronger among women, the less-educated, and respondents of lower socioeconomic status (Landsberger and Saavedra, 1967). Item nonresponse has also been found to be related to similar factors, namely, sex, age, and education (Douglas and Shoemaker, 1979) in nine European countries.

This suggests that the distribution of different national samples on variables such as income and education will need to be examined, to identify the extent to which such factors are likely to affect the comparability of results. In general, however, preliminary research indicates that substantial differences in such distributions will be required, before there is any significant effect (Douglas and Shoemaker, 1979).

INSTRUMENT DEVELOPMENT AND QUESTION FORMULATION.   Once the mode of approach to avoid response bias has been determined, the next step is to develop an instrument and decide how questions should be posed. In this context, high levels of illiteracy in many developing countries suggest that use of nonverbal stimuli may be desirable. In addition, administration of the instrument in multilinguistic and cultural contexts will require translation to ensure instrument comparability.

Use of Nonverbal Stimuli.   Where research is conducted in countries or cultures with high levels of illiteracy, as for example, Africa and the Middle East, (Exhibit 3) it is often desirable to use nonverbal stimuli such as show cards. Questionnaires can be administered orally by an interviewer, but respondent comprehension will be facilitated if pictures of products or concepts or test packs are provided.

Show cards such as those shown in Exhibit 4 and 5 can, for example, be used in concept testing or to assist in answering product-usage questions. Product samples can also be shown to respondents. A drawback of this approach is that respondents tend to become irritated if the samples are removed for the next interview. Consequently, it is wise to be able to leave a free sample or alternative reward (Corder, 1978).

Even where literacy levels are high, it may be desirable to use nonverbal stimuli as a complement to verbal stimuli to provide a check on instrument equivalence and potential biases from instrument translation and adaptation to different linguistic and cultural contexts.

EXHIBIT 3   LEVELS OF LITERACY IN SELECTED LOW AND MIDDLE INCOME COUNTRIES

Country	Year	Percentage of Illiteracy
Low-Income Countries[1]		
Ethiopia	1970	95.8
Somalia	1980	93.9
Mali	1976	90.6
Niger	1980	90.2
Togo	1970	84.1
Nepal	1975	80.8
Middle-Income Countries[2]		
Yemen Arab Republic	1980	91.4
Mauritania	1976	82.6
Liberia	1974	79.0
Morocco	1971	78.6
Saudi Arabia	1980	75.4
Yemen (PDR)	1973	72.9
Papua New Guinea	1971	67.9
Nigeria	1980	66.0
Egypt	1976	61.8

Source.   UNESCO, Statistical Yearbook 1984

[1] (GNP per capita, $120–$400)

[2] (GNP per capita, $400–$1,430)

EXHIBIT 4   SHOW CARDS

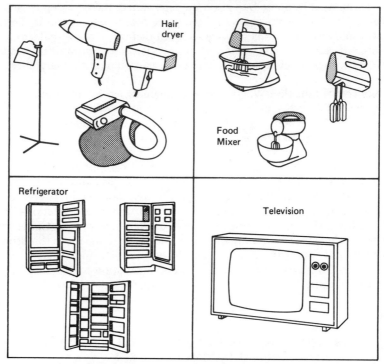

Source.   Market Research Africa, in Corder, 1978.

Instrument Translation.   Both verbal and nonverbal stimuli require translation for use in different linguistic and cultural contexts. Where a verbal instrument is used, a procedure widely advocated in the social sciences is that of *back-translation* (Brislin, 1970; Werner and Campbell, 1970). A questionnaire is translated from the initial or base language by a native speaker of the language of translation and then retranslated back into the original language by a native speaker of that language.

Although useful in identifying translation errors, back-translation is not always totally effective (Brislin, 1970). Bilinguals often develop a particular language structure and usage and hence may not translate into the idiom commonly used by the mass of the population. Furthermore, back-translation assumes the existence of equivalent terms and concepts in all languages and that a "totally loyal" translation is required. This may not always be the case. The terms *fair play* and *lonesomeness* are, for example, difficult to render in German (Brislin et al., 1973). Also, in some cases it may be more desirable to translate into equivalent colloquial phrases, rather than attempting to make a "totally" faithful and accurate translation.

Such considerations suggest that use of *parallel* translation may be desirable (Frey, 1970). A committee of translators conversant with at least two of the languages employed can then go through successive iterations of translation and retranslation. In international market research, members of different local research organizations could be used. This could result in *decentering* of the original questionnaire (Werner

EXHIBIT 5   INTERVIEW SHOW CARD USED IN CONSUMER SURVEY IN SOUTH AFRICA[a]. (ASSIST TO ANSWER QUESTION "WHAT IS YOUR SEWING MACHINE USED FOR?")

Source.   Singer Sewing Machine Company, New York.
[a]This freehand style of drawing proved to have good appeal in interviews conducted in developing countries.

and Campbell, 1970), so that the terminology is equally comprehensible in all language contexts, and the dominance of one language structure and cognitive context is eliminated.

In addition, in countries such as Belgium, India, Canada, and South Africa that have multilanguage subgroups, separate versions of the questionnaire or research instrument will need to be developed. Even if the linguistic subgroup can understand another language, as is, for example, often the case in more-developed countries such as Belgium or Canada, translation into the local idiom will enhance willingness to respond and to provide complete and accurate answers.

Even if nonverbal stimuli such as pictures, show cards, or graphics, are used, the equivalence of their meaning in each context has to be evaluated. Although it might appear that pictorial stimuli are universal, this is not always the case. The Bantu of South Africa, for example, do not distinguish between blue and green. Consequently, use of these colors to distinguish between two objects or symbols would be of no avail. Similarly, African blacks do not always interpret Western three-dimensional perceptual cues correctly, which may give rise to some difficulties in the use of pictures and scenes. Interpretation of meaning attached to colors, shapes, or objects varies from country to country and culture to culture, and hence may affect perception of pictures, scenes, and other visual stimuli. The symbolism evoked by color, for example, varies widely from country to country. In Japan, white is a color of mourning, whereas in Malaysia green symbolizes danger and in other Asian countries, infidelity. Consequently, product, package, or picture stimuli may be inappropriately interpreted, or different associations may be evoked.

Studies of word associations with basic objects such as table, dark, man, mountain, house, deep, and soft among West European subjects (Rosenzweig, 1961) have generally found these to be highly similar. It is, however, questionable whether the same similarities would be found if a more diverse set of countries were studied. Similarly, at lower levels in the hierarchy of associations, for example, specific products such as dining tables or low-sudsing detergents, or in relation to brands, it is likely that much greater diversity will be found.

RESPONSE FORMAT. Although it is generally recognized that instruments need to be designed to eliminate bias due to content and mode of presentation to the respondent, there is generally less appreciation of biases that may arise from response format and recording procedures. These are examined further in the following sections.

Scoring Device. In designing response format, an important consideration is whether different or similar response formats should be used. It has, for example been argued that different response scales, adapted to specific cultural and educational traditions will be required. Thus, for example, in France a 20-point scale is commonly used in rating performance in primary and secondary schools. Such scales are, however, somewhat cumbersome, and existing studies suggest that little bias will be introduced by use of 5- or 7-point rating scales common in U.S. research (Douglas and LeMaire, 1974).

In countries with low literacy levels, where responses are to be scaled, some ingenuity will be required in the development of appropriate response-recording devices. Although interviewers can pose questions and record categorical responses concerning behavior and background characteristics, some difficulties can arise in obtaining response to attitudinal questions, where indication of position on a scale by the respondent is required.

One such scale is the *Funny Faces* scale, which has been used to good effect among blacks in South Africa (Corder, 1978). This is shown in Exhibit 6. Respondents are shown a concept, or given an attitudinal statement, and asked to indicate their degree of agreement or interest by indicating their position on this scale. Another device is the use of a wooden notched scale. The ends of the scales are explained to the respondent. These may, for example, represent positive or negative positions with regard to certain attitudinal statements. Respondents are then asked to indicate their positions by placing a stick in one of the notches on the scale.

Steps of a ladder can also be used to indicate the various response alternatives open to respondents (Cantril, 1965). Respondents are shown a sketch of a ladder and asked to indicate their position with respect to steps on the ladder. In countries or cultures where ladders are not known, other items can be substituted. For example, for Zulus a picture of a mountain with successive terraces was substituted. This

**EXHIBIT 6   THE FUNNY
FACES SCALE**

Very happy

Happy

Not happy but
also not unhappy

Unhappy

Very unhappy

Source.   Corder, 1978.

represented the different stages or steps in climbing the mountain and was a much more familiar set of alternatives.

Techniques in which respondents define their positions relative to the cultural self-norm or to a self-defined response continuum may also be appropriate. In developing life-style measures, for example, adaptation of methods developed in other social sciences such as Cantril's self-anchoring scale (Cantril and Free, 1962) may be desirable. Here the individual indicates his own anchor point and its position or distance from a culture-specific stimulus set. In the research conducted by Cantril (1965), concerns of different kinds were studied. Yet although this eliminates cultural differences, it also eliminates differences in adaptation relative to the cultural norm.

Use of scaling instruments that have been tested in different countries and cultures and are believed to be culture free, such as Osgood's semantic differential (Osgood et al., 1975), may also be desirable. These are, however, somewhat rare, particularly in relation to scales commonly used in marketing research. One exception is the adaptation of the Myers and Warner Colloquial and Formal Rating Scales for use in France (Angelmar and Pras, 1978). Similar adaptation and testing of verbal rating scales should be undertaken before they are used in other countries or linguistic contexts.

Scoring Procedures.   Procedures to avoid bias in the recording and scoring of the response are also required (Meade and Brislin, 1973; Straus, 1969). These can arise as a result of random errors, such as incorrect recording by the interviewer or respondent, or because of some systematic source of error. Although the former can only be reduced by improved design of the research instrument, clearer, more graphic scales or greater attention to interviewer training and procedures to eliminate systematic bias can be incorporated into the research design.

An important source of systematic error that is a potential danger in international marketing research arises from the cultural self-referent bias (Lee, 1966). Thus a researcher of a specific nationality or culture may tend to interpret data in terms of his own cultural self-referent or cultural values. This is best resolved by the use of multiple judges, each with different self-referents, to interpret the data, and in the case of open-ended or qualitative data, to develop appropriate coding or categorization schema. For example, in a two-country/culture study, one monolingual judge from each country or culture should be used, and two bilingual judges, each a native speaker from a different country. An iterative, back-checking process, similar to that used in linguistic translation, can then be applied to ensure decentering of interpretation and elimination of the cultural self-referent bias (Werner and Campbell, 1970).

Furthermore, given the existence of differences in response set and respondent bias in different countries and cultures, use of different standards of scoring and interpretation may be desirable (Straus, 1969; Cunningham et al., 1977). Measures can thus be culturally *ipsatized,* that is, the identical measure is used, but standards for scoring and interpretation differ across countries and cultures. For example, if results are being compared between an Irish and a British sample, where the Irish may be expected to respond to items in a more emotional manner, the data can be ipsatized by national group.

An alternative procedure is normalization. Thus rather than using raw scores for individuals in the analysis, differences from the country mean are utilized. For each variable, country averages are computed. An individual's score on each variable is then deducted from the country average and used as input in the comparative analysis. This procedure will, however, clearly only be necessary if responses are not elicited relative to a cultural self-norm.

Once the instrument has been designed to ensure comparability or equivalence across all countries and contexts studied and to minimize response bias from administration in different national and cultural contexts, the next step is to determine appropriate procedures for its administration in these different contexts.

DATA-COLLECTION PROCEDURES

In determining how to implement the research design, decisions have to be made with regard to appropriate data-collection techniques, for example, survey, experimentation, depth interviewing, observation, and so forth, and also their execution. This depends to a large extent on the purpose of the research. This may be either exploratory, that is, designed to identify relevant constructs to be examined in subsequent phases of research, or concerned with more-precise estimation as, for example, predicting new-product response, or testing advertising effectiveness. As noted previously, research in developed countries tends to be predominantly ad hoc or audit research and there is less need to conduct exploratory research. In developing countries, however, where little is known about market trends, it is often important to conduct exploratory or qualitative research.

Where exploratory research is to be undertaken to identify relevant concepts or product classes, or attitudes and behavior relative to these, unstructured data-collection techniques such as protocols, depth interviews, and focus groups can be particularly useful. Such techniques avoid the imposition of a cultural bias, since no prespecified conceptual model is imposed *a priori* by the researcher. Rather the respondent(s) is left to respond freely in selecting criteria or attitudinal statements most relevant to him. The specific terminology used by respondents when thinking about products, sources, or purchase situations, may be identified (Douglas et al., 1981). On the other hand, the burden of interpretation is placed on the researcher to identify concepts, attitudes, or behaviors that are considered relevant. Consequently, in order to eliminate any potential cultural bias, it is generally desirable, as in the case of instrument design, to make use of multiple judges from different cultural and linguistic backgrounds when interpreting the data. Although collection of these data is relatively simple, care in supervision of data-collection procedures in order to minimize potential reactivity is required. Experience in data interpretation is also important and will require skilled and well-trained researchers.

If more precise quantitative estimation is required, survey research is likely to be more appropriate. As noted previously, the survey has traditionally been the instrument most frequently used in international marketing research. It does, however, require the availability of trained interviewers and a field-research organization. Such services are generally available in most countries in the world, either from local research organizations or the major international market research organizations, though the way in which they are organized may vary.

In determining appropriate data-collection procedures, decisions have to be made about how the survey should be administered. As in domestic research, three major alternatives can be identified: mail, personal interview, and telephone. In making this choice, care needs to be taken to ensure that reliable good-quality data are generated. Here a number of factors have to be taken into consideration. These are examined next in more detail.

SURVEY-ADMINISTRATION TECHNIQUES.   In domestic market research, relative cost, length of survey, and time constraints largely determine the choice of questionnaire-administration procedures. In international markets, however, other aspects such as availability of mailing lists and trained interviewers, the quality of the postal service, levels of literacy, or private telephone ownership also affect the decision. Of particular importance, especially in consumer research in developing countries are low levels of literacy (see Exhibit 3). These, coupled with lower wage levels, often dictate frequent use of personal interviewing. The advantages and disadvantages of each method in international markets are next discussed in more detail.

Mail Surveys.   Mail surveys can typically be used effectively in industrial market research. Mailing lists such as those of Bottin International or directories for specific industries are generally available. The key problems are to identify the relevant respondent within a company and to personalize the address to increase the likelihood of response. Appropriate sponsorship or prior telephone verification can also aid in increasing response rates.

In consumer research, and particularly in developing countries, use of mail surveys may give rise to some problems. As in the case of sampling frames, mailing lists may not exist or sources such as telephone directories may not provide adequate coverage.

Available lists such as magazine subscription lists or membership-association lists may be skewed to better educated segments of the population. In addition, in some countries, the effectiveness of mail surveys is limited by low levels of literacy, reluctance of respondents to respond to mail surveys, and extremely inefficient mail services. In countries with high levels of illiteracy, the proportion of the population likely to be reached by mail survey is limited. Even in countries where levels of literacy make use of mail surveys feasible, reluctance to respond and a tendency to regard surveys as an invasion of privacy may limit their effectiveness. Inefficiency of mail services constitutes a further hazard in using mail surveys in other countries. In several Latin American countries, for example, it is estimated that a substantial proportion of domestic mail is never delivered, while Italy is notorious for the inefficiency of its mail service.

Thus although mail surveys may be effectively used in industrial market research, in consumer research they may be appropriate only in industrialized countries. Here levels of literacy are high, and mailing lists are readily available. In other countries they may only be appropriate if it is desired to reach a relatively up-scale and well-educated segment of the population. Thus although costs of administering mail surveys appear low on a per-questionnaire mailed-out basis, low response rates or poor quality data in developing countries may render such surveys less cost effective than other methods of data collection.

Telephone Interviewing.   Telephone interviewing is a method of questionnaire administration that has developed substantially in the United States in recent years. The availability of WATS lines and special volume rates have changed the economics of telephone interviewing as opposed to other methods of administration. Furthermore, use of telephone interviewing from a centralized location facilitates control over the interviewers. This has been found increasingly to be a problem in personal-interview surveys.

In industrial market research, use of telephone surveys may be quite effective. The majority of businesses, other than some small or itinerant retailers or craftsmen, are likely to have telephones. It is important, as in the case of mail surveys, to be able to identify the relevant respondent(s). This is, however, facilitated in telephone surveys by the ability to conduct initial probing or ask preliminary screening questions. Willingness to respond may, however, depend on relative time pressures at work and the desired target population. Where the target population is upper management, some resistance is likely to be encountered unless substantial interest in the survey can be aroused. Use of personal contacts, or obtaining sponsorship from some appropriate organization or association may also be desirable.

In consumer research, the feasibility of using telephone surveys varies from country to country. In countries such as Egypt and Morocco there are less than two telephones per 100 inhabitants, and in Chile and Brazil, 6 and 8 per 100 respectively. Even in relatively affluent societies such as Italy and Spain there are only 43 and 36 public and private telephones per 100 inhabitants, and in Portugal only 18. Volume rates and grouped lines such as those in the United States are rarely available, though in Europe, several research organizations now offer computer-steered telephone interviewing throughout Europe from a central location such as the Netherlands (de Houd, 1982). Telephone interviewing has also been used successfully in Europe in tracking consumer acceptance and satisfaction with automobiles (Smith and Watson, 1983).

Telephone linkages vary substantially in quality and are often inadequate for efficient interviewing. As in the case of mail surveys, respondents may be reluctant to respond to strangers or to questions posed by an anonymous interviewer, and may be unaccustomed to lengthy conversations. Consequently, telephone surveys may only be appropriate where the research is designed to reach relatively up-scale consumer segments, people who are accustomed to business transactions by telephone, as for example, doctors and lawyers. In addition, the questionnaire needs to be short, simple, and easily administered by telephone.

Personal Interviewing.   The third method of administering questionnaires is by personal interview. In industrial marketing research, personal interviewing is likely to be the dominant mode. Response to mail surveys may tend to be low and adaptation cannot be made to specific company situations. In telephone interviews only limited information can be obtained from certain respondents and in relation to specific nonconfidential topics. Furthermore, probing is carried out less effectively. In consumer research, for the reasons noted previously, that is, lack of mailing lists, inadequate mail services, and high levels of illiteracy, personal interviewing will often be required.

In personal interviewing, a key problem is the interaction between the interviewer and the respondent. In international market research this is affected by a number of factors. These vary from country to country and can affect the quality of data obtained. As noted previously, attitudes toward questioning by strangers, feelings that interviewing constitutes an invasion of privacy, and suspiciousness about the interviewer's motivations vary from country to country or culture to culture. This affects the willingness of respondents in both industrial and consumer surveys to participate or cooperate in surveys, as does the extent to which respondents will deliberately conceal information or give false answers.

In industrial marketing research, willingness to participate and provide information may depend to a large extent on the competitiveness of the market environment. In certain countries or with certain product markets such as pharmaceuticals or electronics, management may be considerably more reluctant to provide information than in product markets such as crafts, etc. In the former case, suspicion may be aroused that information may leak to competition, or be used to the company's detriment. In consumer surveys in Latin countries, and in the Middle East, interviewers are regarded with considerable suspicion. In Latin countries, where tax evasion is a national pastime, interviewers are often suspected of being tax inspectors. In the Middle East, at-home interviews with housewives may have to be conducted in the evening when husbands are at home, though growing success with discussion groups is reported.

An important factor in deciding whether or not to use personal interviewing is the availability of trained interviewers. In certain developing countries, the availability of field staff is open to some question. There may be a lack of competent trained professional interviewers. This is often the case in cultures such as the Middle East where it is not acceptable for women to hold such posts. This implies that interviewers will have to be recruited and trained expressly for a specific piece of research. Political and social surveys conducted in developing countries have typically found recruitment of socioeconomically up-scale individuals in leadership positions to be desirable. Thus, for example, village headmen, teachers, and country prefects have been found to be good interviewers (Frey, 1970). In such situations extensive training programs have to be developed prior to the survey, and standard procedures for interviewing developed.

Yet even in more-developed countries, attention to interviewer training and briefing and debriefing is desirable to ensure the maximum response rate and to avoid bias arising from interviewer-respondent interaction. This is particularly desirable when the interview involves open-ended or complex questions and tasks such as, for example, projective techniques or multidimensional scaling.

The personal interview is typically the most expensive method of questionnaire administration. It is, however, the method most commonly used outside the United States. Lack of sampling frames, higher rates of response, and low wage rates in developing countries often offset the higher costs. Furthermore, in countries with low levels of literacy, personal interviewing is mandatory. The improved quality of the data is also a major consideration.

DATA QUALITY.   An important consideration in collecting data in multicountry research is the quality of the data obtained. The sampling plan can be set up to ensure comparability of the samples from country to country. The instrument may be well designed to avoid cultural bias. Effective survey administration procedures may be established. Yet there may still be a number of underlying problems that need to be carefully evaluated.

Little is known concerning factors that affect rates of nonresponse or the quality of data provided by respondents in other countries. With a few rare exceptions, the reliability of data obtained in cross-national research has been little investigated, using either test-retest, or interjudge-reliability procedures. It is, nonetheless, critical that checks of this type be included as standard procedure in multicountry research. As in domestic research, two major sources of error in survey research can be identified—sampling and nonsampling error. Problems arising from sampling error can generally be readily identified and hence pose somewhat less of a threat to the quality of data than the problems arising from the somewhat invidious nature of nonsampling error.

Nonsampling Error.   Nonsampling error can arise as a result of the individual respondent's unwillingness to respond accurately and completely, his personality and response set, purposeful misreporting of data, faulty recall, respondent fatigue, interviewer error, the interaction between the interviewer and the respondent, or other extraneous factors. Since these sources of bias have been discussed in relation to questionnaire administration, they are not discussed further here.

Sampling Error

Survey Nonresponse.   Differential rates of nonresponse to surveys can affect the quality of the data. Again, some evidence exists to indicate differences in the rates of nonresponse to surveys in different nations (Almond and Verba, 1963) and also among different categories of respondents. In the classic Almond and Verba study, the percentages of the samples actually interviewed were United Kingdom, 59 percent; Mexico, 60 percent; Italy, 74 percent; Germany, 74 percent; and the United States, 83 percent. This, however, is a more significant problem in mail and telephone interviewing, and can be more effectively controlled in personal interviewing except in countries where there are high rates of refusal. This problem is compounded by the inadequacies of many sampling frames discussed earlier.

Available evidence tends to suggest that background characteristics of nonrespondents are likely to be the same. Samples will thus be underrepresented with regard to the same segments, for example, low-income or less-educated consumers. It is, therefore, important to make adjustments for such factors to ensure comparability of samples and that national representativeness is not lost. This can be corrected by double-sampling on high nonresponse segments. If, however, other factors such as suspiciousness of interviewers or hostility towards surveys underlie nonresponse, the relevant determinants and their impact will need to be investigated in each specific case.

Little research also appears to have been conducted into ways to increase rates of nonresponse in other countries or in multicountry surveys. One study of elites found that use of large incentives increased response and improved the probability of providing complete responses (Godwin, 1979). Other standard procedures, such as personalization, sponsorship, and follow-ups are also used in other countries, although little has been published with regard to their relative effectiveness.

The efficacy of several return-increasing techniques in South America and Africa has also been examined (Eisinger et al., 1974). In Kenya and the Ivory Coast, the effects of registration and personalization in a mail survey were examined. In neither case did personalization significantly increase returns, though registration increased returns by eight percent in Kenya. Registration was also found to increase returns in Venezuela and Argentina. In all cases, follow-up mailings increased return rates. This is comparable to similar findings in the United States.

Reliability of the Data. Another issue is the reliability of data obtained in cross-national surveys. Here the prime concern is whether the same result is obtained when a measure is repeated in a different context, fashion, or time. Despite all efforts to design an instrument that is adapted to all countries and cultures, it may not be equally reliable in all these contexts. Similarly, different forms, for example, of attitudinal or life-style measures, may vary in their level of reliability. The stability of data over time is yet another consideration.

Despite its significance, the reliability of the data in cross-national research has received little attention. Available evidence suggests, however, that the reliability of data varies from country to country. Studies of public opinion data, have, for example, investigated the reliability of data on age and education in the United Kingdom and the United States over time (Schreiber, 1975/76). For age, 91 percent of the U.S. sample, and 98 percent of the British sample gave consistent reports in both waves of measurement. However, for education the figure was only 74 percent in the U.S. sample. Another study based on self-administered questionnaires to couples in five countries from two linguistic groupings, the United States, the United Kingdom, France, Belgium, and Canada, found generally somewhat higher levels of reliability for ten background characteristics ranging from a low of 84 to 100 percent. Reliability did, however, vary from country to country, though no systematic or consistent patterns emerged (Davis et al., 1981).

Reliability has also been found to vary with the type of data. The same five-country study found reliability to be greater for background data than behavioral data, and this in turn more reliable than attitudinal data. In the first two instances, comparisons of husband-wife reports were used as measures of reliability, whereas in the third instance, attitudinal variables, a measure of internal consistency was applied to multiple-item attitudinal constructs. As in the case of background characteristics, the level of reliability was found to vary from country to country, though again there was no systematic tendency for any particular national sample or language group to exhibit high or low reliability across different variables of the same type.

Such findings suggest that in addition to efforts to design instruments so as to control and minimize nonequivalence from one country or context to another, attention should also be directed toward monitoring the reliability of these instruments. This requires that reliability be investigated routinely in cross-national surveys, just as interview verification and examination of sampling errors are an accepted part of research practice. Adjustments for unreliability can also be made, but entail complex statistical procedures (Bagozzi, 1980; Griliches, 1974).

CONCLUSION

International marketing research provides an essential input into the design of effective strategies for international operations. Further, it aids in decisions concerning appropriate tactics to be used in different country markets. In particular, research is required to evaluate long-run market potential relative to different countries, product markets, and target segments. Research can also aid in determining appropriate modes of market segmentation, that is, by country or across countries, as well as relevant bases for market segmentation. Decisions with regard to the adaptation of marketing-mix tactics to specific national environments should also be research based. Finally, research provides a valuable input for long-run strategic planning and selection of countries, product markets, target segments, and modes of operation for long-run market growth.

The heart of the research design is the sampling plan and the research instrument. The sampling plan has to be developed to ensure that accurate and reliable data are collected in the most cost-effective manner. An appropriate balance between comparability of samples and representativeness of the target population has to be maintained. Instruments should be designed to ensure as far as possible comparability across countries and cultural contexts. In particular, elimination of cultural bias in the instrument itself and in its analysis is an important consideration.

In analyzing data from multicountry research, a number of problems arise because of multiple levels of measurement units, that is, countries, industries, companies, respondents within companies, and households, particularly when these vary in their underlying composition (i.e., different buying centers, household composition, etc.). The hierarchical character of the research design (i.e., across countries and target segments, and different levels of product markets and product lines) adds further to the difficulties of analysis. This implies that use of a multistage hierarchical approach will frequently be required. Data are first analyzed *separately* for each unit examined, and then *across* all the units studied (Frey, 1970). Although tedious and time consuming, this has the advantage of tailoring the analysis to, and gaining understanding of, the specific problems or situations in each country or context before integrating findings across countries. However, more efficient analysis awaits development of adequate multivariate statistical techniques that can effectively deal with the complex hierarchical nature of multinational data.

International marketing operations clearly emerge as one of the major trends of the 1980s. Yet existing research procedures and organization appear ill-suited to aid management in meeting new developments in the internationalization of business operations. Although the high costs and conceptual and methodological difficulties associated with international marketing research appear to constitute a barrier, the expected payoff is high. Collection of better and more reliable information is an important step in improving international marketing decisions. Thus increased attention to the design and execution of international market research constitutes an important priority in the agenda of the international marketer.

SOURCES AND SUGGESTED REFERENCES

Adamopoulos, J. "The Dimensions of the Greek Concept of Philotimo," *Journal of Social Psychology,* Vol. X (1977), pp. 313–314.

Adler, L. "Managing Marketing Research in the Diversified Multinational Corporation." E.M. Mazze, ed. *Marketing in Turbulent Times and Marketing: The Challenges and the Opportunities—Combined Proceedings.* Chicago: American Marketing Association, 1975.

———— and C.S. Mayer. "Meeting the Challenge of Multinational Marketing Research," W. Keegan and C. Mayer, eds. *Multinational Product Management.* Cambridge, MA: Marketing Science Institute, 1976.

Almond, G. and S. Verba. *The Civic Culture: Political Attitudes and Democracy in the Nations.* Princeton: Princeton University Press, 1963.

Anderson, B.R. "On the Comparability of Meaningful Stimuli in Cross-Cultural Research," *Sociometry,* Vol. XXX, No. 2 (1967), pp. 127–136.

Angelmar, R. and B. Pras. "Verbal Rating Scales for Multinational Research." *European Research,* Vol. VI (1978), pp. 62–67.

Bagozzi, R.P. *Causal Models in Marketing.* New York: Wiley, 1980.

Barnard, P. "The Role and Implementation of International Marketing Research," *International Marketing Research Seminar.* Brussels: ESOMAR, 1976.

————. "Market Research in the World Economy," *Marketing Research Society Newsletter,* No. 150 (1978), pp. 9–14.

————. "The World of Research," *Marketing Research Society Newsletter,* No. 171 (1980), pp. 31ff.

Berent, P.H. "International Research Is Different," E.M. Mazze, ed. *Marketing in Turbulent Times and Marketing: The Challenges and the Opportunities—Combined Proceedings.* Chicago: American Marketing Association, 1975.

Berry, J.W. "On Cross-Cultural Comparability," *International Journal of Psychology,* Vol. IV (1969), pp. 119–128.

Bottin International, U.S.A. 5714 West Pico Boulevard, Los Angeles, CA 90019.

Boyd, H.W., R.E. Frank, W.F. Massy, and M. Zoheir. "On the Use of Marketing Research in the Emerging Economies," *Journal of Marketing Research,* Vol. I (1964), pp. 20–25.

Brislin, R. "Back-Translation for Cross-Cultural Research," *Journal of Cross-Cultural Psychology,* Vol. I (1970), pp. 185–216.

————, W.J. Lonner, and R.M. Thorndike. *Cross-Cultural Research Methods.* New York: Wiley, 1973.

Campbell, D.T. and J. Stanley, *Experimental and Quasi-Experimental Design and Research.* Chicago: Rand McNally, 1973.

Cantril, H. *The Pattern of Human Concerns.* New Brunswick, NJ: Rutgers University Press, 1965.

———— and L.A. Tree. "Hopes and Fears for Self and Country," *American Behavioral Scientist,* Vol. VI supplement (1962), p. 8.

Chun, K.T., J.B. Campbell, and J. Hao. "Extreme Response Style in Cross-cultural Research: a Reminder," *Journal of Cross-Cultural Psychology,* Vol. V (1974), pp. 464–480.

Cochran, W.G. *Sampling Techniques.* New York: Wiley, 1977.

Corder, C.K. "Problems and Pitfalls in Conducting Marketing Research in Africa," B. Gelb, ed. *Marketing Expansion in a Shrinking World.* Proceedings of American Marketing Association Business Conference. Chicago: American Marketing Association, 1978.

Crosby, R.W. "Attitude Measurement in a Bilingual Culture," *Journal of Marketing Research,* Vol. VI (1969), pp. 421–426.

Crowne, D.P. and D. Marlowe. *The Approval Motive: Studies in Evaluative Dependence.* New York: Wiley, 1964.

Cunningham, W.H., I. Cunningham, and R.T. Green. "The Ipsative Process to Reduce Response Set Bias," *Public Opinion Quarterly,* Vol. XLI, No. 3 (1977), pp. 379–394.

Davis, H.L., S.P. Douglas, and A.J. Silk. "Measure Unreliability: A Hidden Threat to Cross-National Marketing Research," *Journal of Marketing,* Spring 1981, pp. 98–108.

de Houd, Maurice. "Internationalized Computerized Telephone Research: Is It Fiction?" *Market Research Society Newsletter,* 19 January 1982, pp. 14–15.

Douglas, S.P. and P. LeMaire. "Improving the Quality and Efficiency of Life-style Research," XXV ESOMAR Congress, Budapest.

———. "Cross-National Comparisons and Consumer Stereotypes: A Case Study of Working and Non-Working Wives in the U.S. and France," *Journal of Consumer Research,* Vol. III (1976), pp. 12–20.

——— and R. Shoemaker. "Item Non-Response in Cross-National Surveys," *European Research,* October 1981.

———. "Adjusting for Sample Characteristics in Multi-Country Survey Research," *Proceedings, 9th Annual Meeting of the European Academy for Advanced Research in Marketing.* Edinburgh, 1980.

———, C.S. Craig, and J.P. Faivre. "Protocols in Consumer Research: Problems, Methods and Uses," J. Sheth, ed. *Research in Marketing,* Vol. V. Greenwich, CT: JAI Press, 1981.

Dun and Bradstreet, *Principal International Businesses, The World Marketing Directory.* New York: Dun and Bradstreet, 1987.

Eisinger, R.A., W.P. Janicki, R.L. Stevenson, and W.L. Thompson. "Increasing Returns in Mail Surveys," *Public Opinion Quarterly,* Vol. XXXVII (1974), pp. 124–130.

Encyclopedia of Associations. Detroit: Gale Research Company, Book Tower, 1980.

Ewen, J.W. "Industrial Research in International Markets," American Marketing Association/Market Research Society Conference, New York, October 1981.

Franzen, M.P. and L. Light. "Standardize Process Not Programs," *International Marketing Research* seminar. Brussels: ESOMAR, 1976.

Frey, F. "Cross-Cultural Survey Research in Political Science," *The Methodology of Comparative Research,* R.E. Holt and J.E. Turner, eds. New York: The Free Press, 1970.

Godwin, R.K. "The Consequences of Large Monetary Incentives in Mail Surveys of Elites," *Public Opinion Quarterly,* Vol. XLII (1979), pp. 378–387.

Goodyear, J. "The World of Research," *Marketing Research Society Newsletter,* No. 171 (1980), pp. 81ff.

Green, P.E. *Mathematical Tools for Applied Multivariate Analysis.* New York: Academic Press, 1978.

——— and D.S. Tull. *Research for Marketing Decisions,* 5th edition. Englewood Cliffs, NJ: Prentice-Hall, 1988.

Green, R. and E. Langeard. "A Cross-National Comparison of Consumer Habits and Innovator Characteristics," *Journal of Marketing,* Vol. XLIX (1975), pp. 34–41.

Griliches, Z. "Errors in Variables and Other Inobservables," *Econometrika,* Vol. XLII (1974), pp. 971–998.

Holt, R.T. and J.E. Turner, eds. *The Methodology of Corporative Research.* New York: Free Press, 1970.

Kelly's Manufacturers and Merchants Directory. New York: Kelly's Directories, annual edition.

Landsberger, H.A. and A. Saavedra. "Response Set in Developing Countries," *Public Opinion Quarterly,* Vol. XXXI, No. 2 (1967), pp. 214–229.

Lee, J.A. "Cultural Analysis in Overseas Operations," *Harvard Business Review,* Vol. XLIV (1966), pp. 106–114.

Lehmann, D.R. *Market Research and Analysis,* 2nd edition. Homewood, IL: Richard D. Irwin, 1985.

Linton, A. and S. Broadbent. "International Life-Style Comparisons," *European Research,* Vol. III, No. 2 (1975), pp. 51–56, 84.

Lipstein, B. "In Defense of Small Samples," *Journal of Advertising Research,* Vol. XV (1975), pp. 33–42.

Lovell, M.R. "Examining the Multinational Consumer," *Developments in Consumer Psychology.* Maidenhead: ESOMAR, 1973.

Mayer, C.S. "Multinational Marketing Research: The Magnifying Glass of Methodological Problems," *European Research,* Vol. 6 (1978), pp. 77–84.

Meade, R.D. and R.W. Brislin. "Controls in Cross-Cultural Experimentation," *International Journal of Psychology,* Vol. VIII, No. 4 (1973), pp. 231–238.

Mitchell, R.E. "Survey Materials Collected in Developing Countries: Sampling Measurement and Interviewing: Obstacles to Intra- and Inter-National Comparisons," *International Social Science Journal,* Vol. XVII, No. 4 (1965), pp. 186ff.

Moyer, R. "International Market Analysis," *Journal of Marketing Research,* Vol. IV (1968), pp. 353–60.

Oppenheim, A.N. *Questionnaire Design and Attitude Measurement.* London: Heineman, 1966.

Osgood, C.E., W.H. May, and M.S. Miron. *Cross-Cultural Universals of Affective Meaning.* Urbana, IL: University of Illinois Press, 1975.

Pike, K. *Language in Relation to a Unified Theory of the Structure of Human Behavior.* The Hague: Mouton, 1966.

Poortinga, Y.M. "Some Implications of Three Different Approaches to Intercultural Comparison," *Applied Cross-Cultural Psychology,* J.W. Berry and W.J. Lonner, eds. Amsterdam: Swetts and Zeitlinger, 1975.

Reader's Digest. *A Survey of Europe Today—the peoples and markets of sixteen European countries.* London: Reader's Digest, 1970.

Ricks, D.M., Y.C. Fu, and J.S. Arpan. *International Business Blunders.* Columbus, OH: Grid, 1983.

Rosenzweig, M.R. "Comparisons of Word Association Responses in English, French, German and Italian," *American Journal of Psychology,* Vol. LXXIV (1961), pp. 347–360.

Rusby, P. "Europe, One Market for Market Research," *European Research,* Vol. II (1974), pp. 22–28.

Schreiber, E.M. "Dirty Data in Britain and the U.S.A., the Reliability of 'Invariant' Characteristics Reported in Surveys," *Public Opinion Quarterly,* Vol. XXXIX, No. 2 (1975/76), pp. 493–506.

Smith, R.P. and A.J.K. Watson. "Product Excellence on a Complex Product through Telephone Interviewing," *European Research,* January 1983, pp. 11–18.

Straus, M.A. "Phenomenal Identity and Conceptual Equivalence of Measurement—A Cross-Cultural Comparative Research," *Journal of Marriage and the Family,* Vol. XXXI, No. 2 (1969), pp. 233–239.

Sudman, S. *Applied Sampling.* New York: Academic Press, 1976.

Thorelli, H., H. Becker, and J. Engledow. *The Information Seekers: An International Study of Consumer Information and Advertising Image.* Cambridge, MA: Ballinger, 1976.

Triandis, H.C. *The Analysis of Subjective Culture.* New York: Wiley, 1972.

——— and V. Vassilou. "A Comparative Analysis of Subjective Culture," H.C. Triandis, *The Analysis of Subjective Culture.* New York: Wiley, 1972.

UNESCO. *Statistical Yearbook,* annual edition.

U.S. Department of Commerce, Bureau of the Census. *Statistical Abstract of the United States.* Washington, D.C.: U.S. Government Printing Office, annual edition.

de Vulpian, A. *The RISC Observer.* Paris, 1986.

Webster, L. "Comparability in Multi-Country Surveys," *Journal of Advertising Research,* Vol. VI (1966), pp. 14–18.

Werner, O. and D.T. Campbell. "Translating Working Through Interpreters and the Problems of Decentering," *A Handbook of Method in Cultural Anthropology,* R. Naroll and R. Cohen, eds. New York: Columbia University Press, 1970.

Wind, Y. and S.P. Douglas. "International Market Segmentation," *European Journal of Marketing,* Vol. IX (1972), pp. 17–25.

———. "Comparative Consumer Research: The Next Frontier," *European Journal of Marketing,* 1981 (special issue on comparative marketing).

"World of Research," *Marketing Research Society Newsletter,* June 1980.

World Guide to Trade Associations, Vols. 1 and 2. Detroit: Gale Research, annual.

MANAGEMENT OF THE INTERNATIONAL MARKETING FUNCTION

CONTENTS

MANAGEMENT OF THE INTERNATIONAL MARKETING FUNCTION

Kenneth D. Weiss

TARGET MARKET SELECTION

SELECTING TARGET COUNTRIES. The international marketer who shoots at the world in general, like pointing a shotgun at a flock of birds, is unlikely to score a hit. He will do much better if he aims at specific targets.

Which Countries Import. A simple approach to market selection is to suppose that the highest-potential markets for a product are countries that normally import substantial quantities of it. Import statistics are found in several publications, including the following:

1. Organization for Economic Co-operation and Development (OECD) "Micro-tables," on microfilm, which give current, detailed import and export statistics of the 24 OECD member countries.
2. United Nations publications, including *Commodity Trade Statistics,* the *International Trade Yearbook,* the *World Trade Annual,* and the U.N. Food and Agriculture Organization's *FAO Trade Yearbook.*
3. U.S. Department of Commerce *Market Share Reports,* commodity series, which give for a single commodity the level of imports, main suppliers, and U.S. market share in each major importing country; and other USDC publications that show U.S. exports by product and by country.

It is usually possible through desk research to identify the nations that import a product, with quantities, values, supplying countries, and major trends. Some drawbacks are that very specific products may be buried in larger product groups, international trade statistics are never entirely accurate, and target-market decisions should not be based on statistics alone.

Market Indicators. A second approach to target-market selection is the use of market indicators; for example, an indicator of the size of a national market for nurses' caps is the number of nurses in a country. A source of many market indicators is the annual International Bank for Reconstruction and Development's *World Development Report*. This report reveals, for example, that the mid-1982 population of Nigeria was 91 million, increasing by 2.6 percent per year, and there was one nurse for every 4040 persons. If each nurse will purchase, on the average, 3 caps a year, the 1986 market potential is about 60,000 caps.

This approach can be very useful as a starting point, although it doesn't consider local production, import competition, or economic, social, political, or legal factors that may affect sales of a product.

Marketing Considerations.   After selecting *possible* target markets from statistics or indicators, a number of marketing considerations should be examined. These can be summarized as follows:

1. *Suitability of product,* including brand name, label, package, instructions, and warranty. Some pertinent questions are, "Will my product have to be adapted to a different type of electrical current?" "Will my brand name sound appealing in another language?" "Will my label and instructions have to be translated?" and "Will the terms of my warranty have to be changed?"

2. *Ability to meet the price,* considering the costs of production, delivery, and market access.

   a. Most manufacturers know how their *cost structures* compare with those in other producing countries, and many can make comparisons of the approximate *per unit* costs of raw materials, labor, capital, administration, and taxes.

   b. *Delivery costs* depend on several factors, including quantities shipped, traffic on the route, competition among shipping companies, and distance. The increasing variety of air and ocean freight services makes it important to look for and negotiate the lowest rates for acceptable levels of service.

   c. *Market access* includes import duties and quotas, import and foreign exchange licenses, and other restrictions. An exporter can ascertain his access to a specific market by contacting the consulate of that country or the U.S. Department of Commerce country specialist in Washington, D.C.

3. *Ability to promote and distribute* the product in the foreign market. Several publications, such as the U.S. Department of Commerce *Overseas Business Report* series, contain information on distribution and promotion in each country. Some distribution systems, for example those in Japan, are hard for a foreign firm to get a product into. Also, some countries, as in Eastern Europe, lack advertising agencies and media or have laws that make it difficult to mass market a consumer-convenience good.

4. *Potential for achieving a substantial market share.* This potential depends on many factors including local and import competition and the image of a firm's products in the target market. The U.S. image is a strong competitive advantage for some products, such as blue jeans, but is less beneficial for other products, like consumer electronics.

5. *The economic situation,* specifically, whether a country can pay for its imports and the extent to which it allows foreign investors to take out earnings in hard currency. Most international banks have systems of rating countries on their ability to meet foreign-exchange obligations. More specifically, the

Chase World Information Service gives statistics on the payment terms used for each country by most American exporters and on the delays experienced in receiving payment under letters of credit and bills of exchange.

6. *The political situation,* as an indication of a country's future stability. The country-rating systems of international banks consider the possibility of internal upheavals or external aggression, which can lay waste to the most carefully planned marketing campaign. Less dramatically, political conditions can result in product-safety laws, price controls, or restrictions on advertising that may seriously hamper marketing activities. A case in point is the Kenyan manufacturer who was left with a warehouse full of miniskirts when his market country, Uganda, suddenly outlawed this form of dress.

INTERNATIONAL MARKET SEGMENTATION.   The term *market segmentation* is used in two ways in international marketing—to segment the world and to segment a particular country. In addition, there is the concept of the *international market segment.*

Segmenting the World.   For marketing purposes, countries can be grouped according to many different criteria. For example, grouping by *language* would put French-speaking countries in one segment, Spanish-speaking countries in another segment, and so on. This is useful to firms selling language-dependent products such as books and greeting cards.

Some other segmentation criteria that can be used are the following:

1. Religion.
2. Political/economic system.
3. Level of development.
4. Climate.
5. Geographical location (the most common).

Segmenting the world may lead to grouping countries that are in different geographic areas, and even to splitting countries. For example, segmentation based on level of development would place the whites of South Africa with advanced countries and the nonwhites with the emerging nations. This in turn can affect the way a firm is organized for international marketing.

Segmenting Foreign Markets.   Any national market can be segmented according to a number of variables, which are summarized by Kotler (1980):

1. *Geographic,* including region, city size, and climate.
2. *Demographic,* including age, sex, income, and so forth.
3. *Psychographic,* including social class, life-style, and personality.
4. *Behavioristic,* including product benefits sought, rate of usage, and sensitivity to changes in price, advertising, or other elements of the marketing mix.

Of course these categories often overlap. For example, a segmentation of Cyprus based on ethnic background would produce a geographic division of the Turkish population and the Greek population.

Geographic segmentation is useful wherever people in different parts of a country have very different purchasing behavior, for example, the sophisticated customers of Bogotá compared with the Colombian *campesinos.*

Demographic segmentation has many uses overseas, such as suggesting small package sizes for small German families and visual advertisements for poorly educated Haitians. In fact, the "illiterate" segment would include 90 percent of the adult population in about 15 countries.

Psychographic segmentation can consider attitudes toward foreign goods and the "westernization" or modernization that such goods often bring or accelerate. In traditional societies such as Japan or Saudi Arabia, most customers for many products are in the "westernized" market segment.

Behavioristic segmentation is vital internationally. A bicycle used for delivering groceries will be very different from one used for racing, although the two might operate on the same street. A refrigerator in many countries must be decorative, because it will be placed where visitors to the house can see it. The consumers who are least loyal to national, or traditionally imported, brands may be the logical targets of market-introduction publicity campaigns.

The information needed to segment foreign markets is becoming increasingly available from international, national, state, and local government organizations, local and international market-research firms, and foreign companies and trade associations.

One danger in market segmentation is the temptation to overdo it by formulating unique marketing plans for segments too small to warrant them. Adaptations in product, pricing, promotion, and distribution should be thought of as investments, each with a payback potential or net present value.

International Market Segments.   The concept of international market segments is transnational. It recognizes that consumers located in various countries but having similar purchasing characteristics, can be reached by similar marketing procedures.

This concept is especially relevant to marketers of *industrial products.* For example, a supplier of small gasoline engines might single out the following worldwide market segments:

Builders of small boats.

Producers of motorcycles, snowmobiles, and related products.

Manufacturers of lawn mowers, grass trimmers, and other outdoor tools.

This firm would then organize internationally by *market segment.*

The concept is relevant also to some consumer markets. There are people in all countries who like to have the best Scotch whiskey, the most prestigious perfume, the finest wristwatches, and weekly news in English. These international market segments respond worldwide to similar products, prices, promotion, and distribution.

Targeting Specific Customers.   International customers can be categorized as either industrial users that import for their own account, including military and other government organizations, or industrial users and private consumers, who are reached through intermediaries (including state trading corporations in socialist countries).

Prospective customers can be identified from directories, and their purchasing behavior ascertained by market research. Two very useful directories are *Bottin Europe* and *Bottin International,* which list for each country federal government ministries, industry federations having foreign-trade departments, domestic and foreign chambers of commerce, principal manufacturing and importing companies, state trading corporations, and a great deal of other useful information. Also, Dun & Bradstreet's *Principal International Businesses* covers the entire free world. There are several other useful general directories.

More specific information is available for individual countries and industries. A country example is the *Standard Trade Index of Japan,* published by the Japan Chamber of Commerce and Industry. An industry example is the *World Aviation Directory,* by the Ziff Davis Publishing Company in New York; it describes civil air carriers, aviation/aerospace and components manufacturers, overhaul facilities, and relevant publications and government organizations (including air forces) in all countries.

Industrial users of a product can often be identified from publications of national trade associations, membership lists of chambers of commerce and/or industry (in some countries chamber membership is obligatory), or lists maintained by government ministries. These sources usually give only the companies' names, addresses, telephone numbers, and perhaps main products and activities. Additional information, such as years in business or approximate size, must usually be obtained by field research. Importers, import agents, brokers, wholesalers, and retailers that channel merchandise to individual consumers can be identified from publications such as the *Director of British Importers,* or the U.S. Department of Commerce *Foreign Traders Index* and *Trade Lists.* These publications, however, do not tell a marketer which organizations can handle his product effectively or which *will be willing* to handle it. This kind of information is obtained through field data collection.

INTERNATIONAL PRICING

Global Pricing Strategy. An important question in international pricing strategy is whether to maintain one price worldwide, a unique price in each market, or some intermediate system. The answer depends largely on the number of producing facilities a company operates and the number of markets it sells in.

One World Price. Many firms that produce in only one country and sell to many establish a uniform export price, f.o.b. factory or port of lading. Warren Keegan (1980) calls this "ethnocentric pricing."

The uniform export price is often, but not always, below the normal domestic selling price. This can be justified by the following arguments:

Competition is more severe in foreign markets.

The country-of-origin price must be low to compensate for the high cost of moving goods overseas.

Foreign customers should not be charged for purely domestic expenses, such as advertising and delivery in the home country.

Export sales are really extra, or incremental, sales, so only incremental costs plus profit must be covered (export pricing based on incremental costs may violate antidumping laws, which exist in most countries).

There are several advantages to a uniform export price:

It is the simplest. Price quotations can be given quickly and easily.

An export price list can be published and distributed to foreign representatives and customers.

The firm can pay more attention to nonprice elements of the marketing mix.

There is of course a major disadvantage to setting one world price—inflexibility. It will surely be too low for some markets and too high for others, thus depriving the firm of larger margins in the first case and larger sales volumes in the second.

Some firms that have sources from several countries also try to establish uniform prices, f.o.b. country of origin, although this implies a different profit margin at each plant because of differences in production costs. With this system producing firms try to allocate production to the lowest-cost plant, whereas customers prefer to buy from the location from which transportation cost and import duties are the lowest.

It is rare for a firm to try to maintain a uniform worldwide price, c.i.f. port of unlading or closer to the consumer. This is difficult even within common-market areas because of different freight rates, disparate local price levels, and fluctuations in currency exchange rates. One product for which the price to the consumer can be adapted immediately to exchange-rate fluctuations is the weekly news magazine, the publishers of which can change its price every week in any country by simply printing the new price on the cover.

Different Price in Each Market. To set and maintain a different price for each market requires a degree of market knowledge and control that few firms possess. The companies best equipped to do this are multinationals, such as the Coca-Cola Company, that produce in nearly every country in which they sell. This system of *market differentiated pricing* is described by Richard Robinson (1978). Its main advantage is that price can be adjusted according to consumer characteristics and competitive conditions in each country.

Separate pricing for each market is almost always done at the local level, as it is hard for a world, or even a regional, headquarters staff to know enough about conditions in each country to set the most profitable price. Also it is very hard for a headquarters organization to control price once the products leave the company-owned portion of the distribution channel.

Some potential difficulties with market-differentiated prices are jealousies and unauthorized reselling. A foreign representative may be jealous of his counterparts in other countries who pay lower prices than he does, and a representative who pays low prices may make unauthorized sales through alternate distribution channels in countries where prices are higher. There are laws in some regions that make it difficult for a company to prohibit such reselling.

Intermediate Pricing Policies. At least three alternatives are available:

A Different F.O.B. Factory (or F.O.B. Port of Lading) Price from Each Producing Unit. This is a cost-based pricing policy that favors lower-cost producing units, although higher-cost factories can still sell because of cheaper transportation, quicker delivery, or other advantages.

Delivery from Free Zones.   Goods can be shipped from different producing units to free-trade zones, as in Panama, and all buyers can be quoted the same price, F.O.B. free zone. It is even possible to use a free zone as a *basing point* for c.&f. or c.i.f. prices. For example, a customer in Buenos Aires could be given a c.&f. price for delivery from Panama, even though the goods were actually shipped from a factory elsewhere.

Same Final Sale Price throughout a Region.   This system can be used, for example, with heavy industrial equipment throughout the Andrean Common Market. Buyers within the market area are likely to compare price quotations with each other, and the goods, once installed, cannot easily be reshipped to another region in which prices may be higher.

THE PRICE POSITION OR LEVEL.   A firm that is using market-differentiated prices should determine its products' *price position* in each market country. This is where a product's price fits in the spectrum of prices of all competing products.

High Price Position.   High price levels can be used if a firm's image and the quality of its products are equal or superior to those of the best of the competition. A firm must be able to sell enough at the high price to meet its profit objectives. This is facilitated if the product has new or unique characteristics that allow it to be *differentiated* from the competition. As in domestic markets, a new product may be sold initially at a high price in order to *skim* the cream.

Medium Price Position.   Medium prices for consumer goods can be used in countries where the middle class is substantial (it is still small in many less developed countries). Marketing competition in the middle of the price range is often active and varied, with special price offers, new product developments, and promotional campaigns, all based on market research. Firms selling industrial goods abroad often select middle price levels and compete by means of product information, personal selling, and service.

Low Price Position.   An international marketer can choose a low price position if he is able to sell profitably at the bottom of the price range, and if he can capture a large enough share of the market to meet his profit objectives. Often firms choose *penetration* prices because they are the simplest competitive weapon to use, but they are also the easiest for competitors to duplicate. This can result in competitive pressure to lower prices still further.

Barter.   When merchandise is not sold for cash, but is bartered for other goods, the question of price is still important. A barter deal usually involves fixing a monetary value per unit for each kind of merchandise to be included in the transaction. Then the exchange is, for example, $500,000 worth of tractors for $500,000 worth of grain.

Transfer Pricing.   Special difficulties with pricing arise in intracompany sales from one country to another. The exporting country would like a high transfer price to maximize taxable profits within its borders. The importing country, however, would prefer a low transfer price to maximize taxable profits there (although the customs department in the importing country would frown on unjustifiably low prices). The company, for its part, would like to show the most profit in the country with the lowest tax rates.

There is a trend toward the general acceptance of *arm's length* transfer prices, which means that goods moving intracompany from one country to another are priced as if the transaction were between unrelated business entities.

WORKING BACK TO FIRST COST.   A firm that selects a *price position* in the target market must work back to determine its f.o.b. factory price and then decide whether it can profitably sell at that level. The process for an exporter using a normal consumer goods distribution channel is explained in the following section.

Foreign retail price:

Less retail markup and freight equals *foreign wholesale price;*

Less wholesale markup and freight equals *importer's price;*

Less importer's markup equals *landed cost;*

Less customs clearance and duty equals *c.i.f. port of unlading;*

Less international shipping and insurance equals *f.o.b. vessel, port of lading;*

Less freight forwarding and documents charges equals *f.a.s. vessel, port of lading;*

Less delivery to pier equals *f.o.b. shipping point,* packed for export.

There may also be charges for port warehousing, special handling, etc.

In deciding whether it can meet a calculated price f.o.b. shipping point, a firm should consider the cost of financing as well as any export incentives such as Domestic International Sales Corporation (DISC) or Foreign Sales Corporation (FSC) tax deferments.

Standard Multipliers.   Firms that do business often with the same countries may develop standard multipliers for estimating prices. For example, an exporter of frozen beef from Kansas City to Japan might determine that the Tokyo retail price multiplied by 0.2 will give a close approximation of the f.o.b. packing house price.

The multiplier system can be used also to estimate prices forward. For example, a Dallas manufacturer of machine tools might determine that its normal export prices times three give the approximate final sales price to a customer in Bogotá.

OTHER CONSIDERATIONS.   Some other factors to consider in international pricing are price changes, currency of quotation, terms of payment, confirming houses, and bidding on international tenders.

Price Changes.   Price *increases* in foreign markets are often made necessary by increases in manufacturing, transportation, or other costs, or by inflation in market countries. Occasionally price *decreases* are made possible by reductions in import duties, or are made necessary by increased competition.

Care must be taken to advise all foreign representatives before a price change is to take place and to honor former prices for all sales made before the effective date of an increase.

In countries with high rates of inflation, prices can be averaged over time to make increases less frequent. That is, in a country where the rate of inflation is 10 percent per month, prices can be increased by 20 percent every two months. They will be too high right after an increase, and then too low, but there will be fewer disruptive changes.

Price control in several countries restricts price increases, and violations of price-control regulations can have serious consequences for a foreign-owned firm.

Currency of Quotation.   A very high proportion of world exports is paid for in U.S. dollars. For exporters, however, the safest currency of quotation is the one that is least likely to be devalued before payment is received. This implies quoting in the currencies of countries with low inflation rates, such as Switzerland.

It is possible to quote in a currency at a fixed exchange rate. For example, an American exporter to Brazil can agree to quote in cruzeiros at the rate of exchange on the day the contract was signed. Then the importer will be able to pay in cruzeiros, but if a devaluation takes place before payment is made he will have to pay enough cruzeiros to give the exporter a fixed number of dollars.

Finally, when receiving foreign currencies in payment for merchandise, an exporter can *hedge* to protect himself against devaluation. For example, an exporter who is to receive 1 million yen in 90 days, can sell the yen for dollars, at a discount, for delivery in 90 days. Of course the discount will be large if the banking community thinks the yen is likely to go down against the dollar.

Terms of Payment.   International terms of payment are extremely important, to the point that credit is often more critical than price itself. The following general comments can be made with respect to exporting:

Open account sales save time and money, and can be used when both the customer *and his country* are known to be able and willing to pay.

Time drafts give the exporter, as assurance of payment, the customer's signature on a bank document. To dishonor a draft is quite shameful in some countries, but unfortunately not in all.

Sight drafts are safe in theory, but there are hazards. An importer may choose to claim his merchandise late, or not at all, and a country's banking system may be slow in making payment.

Letters of credit can be secure payment instruments; however, they are costly, and they bind the exporter to rigid terms. A letter of credit issued by a reliable foreign bank can be factored, or the exporter can borrow against it.

Cash in advance is sometimes obtained for small or special orders, or from unknown customers, or in periods when merchandise is in short supply. Many foreign importers maintain bank accounts in the United States or Western Europe to facilitate making cash payments.

The Confirming House.   For sales to customers or countries that have poor credit ratings an exporter can try to arrange for payment through a confirming house. European confirming houses are well acquainted with African markets, for example, and can evaluate credit risks much more effectively than less experienced American exporters.

International Tenders.   Major international tenders from foreign government organizations usually specify the currency of quotation and the payment terms. The main task in preparing a quotation is to evaluate the competing firms and their probable price offerings. The practice of bidding high to cover extraordinary payments to foreign agents is now restricted by the Business Practices and Records Act, and by laws in several countries.

PRODUCT CONSIDERATIONS

PRODUCT DESIGN AND QUALITY.   A major question in international marketing is whether to standardize a product for the world or adapt it to each market area. The usual answer is that a firm should standardize as much as possible to reduce expenses, while adapting where it must to increase sales. The ideal procedure would be to compare the projected costs with the expected benefits of each adaptation in product design, quality, packaging, and service.

Design Considerations.   The design of a product for international markets is influenced by many factors including the way in which it will be used, conditions of use, consumer preferences, and legal and economic conditions.

The use of a product varies from place to place. For example, candles can be purchased for entertaining, lighting, or other purposes. The design varies according to the *type of use.*

Conditions of use also affect product design. Very rough roads require strong suspension systems on motor vehicles; high altitudes necessitate low-pressure tennis balls, and so forth.

Consumer preferences vary enormously from country to country; for example:

The *size* of chairs is larger in Sweden than in Indonesia.

The *scent* of detergent is milder in the Middle East than in most parts of Europe.

Color preferences are many and surprising, including *green* crosses on medical supplies in South Korea and *black* false teeth in Thailand.

The *taste* of soft drinks is sweeter in many countries than in the United States.

Laws such as product-safety regulations can influence the design of toys and other products, and *economic conditions* can require designs that lend themselves to low-cost production techniques.

Quality Considerations.   The important point about quality is that it should be *appropriate* for the market and the price position at which a firm is aiming. A firm can price itself out of a market by making its product quality unnecessarily high, or it can damage its reputation by selling goods of very low quality.

Often *industrial goods* must be of high quality even in countries in which private consumers buy mainly on price. This is because buyers of industrial goods everywhere are more sophisticated than the average household consumer. They are better able to judge quality and to appreciate the drawbacks of installing shoddy machines and equipment.

Standards and Specifications.   Most countries now have industrial standards institutes that publish nationally accepted standards for each product. These are often patterned after those of a leading industrial nation.

An important service for international marketers of manufactured products is *Technical Help to Exporters,* from the National Technical Information Service in Springfield, Virginia. This service provides manufacturers and exporters with information about the standards, certification requirements, and regulatory agencies that will affect sales of their products in foreign countries.

Some of the more common product adaptations for foreign markets pertain to electrical characteristics (voltage and cycles) and sizes (metric).

Patent Protection.   Patent laws around the world are varied and often complicated. In general, an international marketer should seek to have his product patented in every country in which he plans to sell as soon as a decision is made to go ahead. According to *Foreign Business Practices* (1985), the United States benefits from the Patent Cooperation Treaty, the European Patent Convention, the Inter-American Convention of 1910 on Inventions, Patents, Designs and Models, and a number of bilateral agreements. These conventions serve basically to place a foreign firm in the same position as a domestic firm with regard to patents in a signatory country.

There are also agreements in Western Europe that make it possible to obtain patent coverage in several countries by filing only one application. Even so, a firm must be alert to keep its patent protection in force in each market country for as long as the law allows. This is true in both civil-law and code-law countries.

The complexity of international patent laws makes it advisable to use a competent international attorney to obtain and maintain protection.

BRAND AND TRADEMARK.   A great deal of attention is given to the *selection* and *protection* of brand names and trademarks in international marketing, especially in the past few years.

Selection of Names and Trademarks.   An alternative chosen by many companies is the uniform *worldwide* company and/or product identification. Such identification helps build the image of firms such as *Kodak,* whose products are often purchased by international travelers, and *Exxon,* which has just five letters including two high-visibility *X*'s. The main criteria for a worldwide name are that it be memorable and that it not have an offensive or derogatory meaning in any major language.

Many other firms *translate or adapt* their brand names to make them more acceptable in various target markets. Terpstra (1978) gives seven variations of the name of an ethical drug product of the Eli Lilly Company. This is an intermediate policy between the worldwide brand and complete adaptation.

Complete adaptation means using in each country or region a brand name and a trademark that seem ideal for that market area. This policy deprives a product of the image of strength associated with multinational firms, but gives it the appearance of local ownership. It may be the best policy in countries in which nationalistic feelings are high and the image of multinational firms is unfavorable.

The use of *private or store brand* merchandise is growing in most developed countries, and may be a means of market entry for a manufacturing firm that does not have the expertise or the money to promote its own brand.

Although some unbranded products are for sale the world over, the use of *generic* products is mainly a U.S. phenomenon. Both brand consciousness and brand loyalty are higher in most foreign countries than in the United States.

Protection of Names and Trademarks.   The United States is a party to the Paris Union International Convention for the Protection of Industrial Property, the Madrid Agreement Concerning the International Registration of Trademarks, and other multinational conventions. Their basic purpose is to allow an individual or firm to register a trademark under the same conditions as a citizen of the country in which registration is being made. The agreements also contain a *right of priority* clause, which gives the first owner of a trademark in any participating country six months in which to file for registration in other participating countries.

Even though brands and trademarks can be protected indefinitely if they continue to be used, *imitation* and *counterfeiting* are both common. There are many examples of imitation brands, with just one or two letters different from the well-known originals, and outright counterfeiting of products such as *Levi's* and *Apple*. A firm's representatives around the world must remain alert for imitation and counterfeit merchandise and should be ready to initiate or recommend the most effective correction action.

PACKAGE AND LABEL.   Usually at least some adaptations are made in the packages and labels of products to be sold in foreign markets. Several factors affect this process, as described in the following sections.

Handling Conditions.   The way in which a product will be handled affects the amount of *protection* a package must provide. Products to be sold in rural stores in developing countries are often subject to rough and frequent handling, and thus need stronger packaging.

Shopping Habits.   In countries where people are in the habit of shopping every day, *package sizes* are smaller than in the United States. Also customers in this type of country usually like to *see* the merchandise they are buying. This leads to greater use of transparent packaging.

Laws.   Most countries have at least some laws that affect labeling and packaging. Examples are requirements that a product's contents be shown on the label, or that an opaque container be filled to at least a specified percent of its capacity. When an exported product reaches a foreign country and does not meet all legal requirements, it is usually stopped by customs and the exporter and the importer usually blame each other for their mutual oversight.

Extent of Self-Service.   In countries where self-service has not yet become the accepted way of retailing, packages and labels do not need to have the promotional impact that is required in other countries.

Consumer Preferences.   People's tastes with regard to design and color vary widely from place to place. A company marketing laundry detergent in Somalia tested the package with many different illustrations, showing Somali women at different socioeconomic levels, wearing different clothes, and engaged in different activities. The outcome was an illustration of a decidedly middle class woman wearing a brightly colored striped dress and hanging very white clothes on a clothesline.

Economic Conditions.   Poor economic conditions dictate the use of small package sizes, relatively inexpensive packaging, and, if possible, reusable containers.

Creating the Label and Package.   In a majority of countries there are no qualified package-design consultants. International marketers often have packages and labels designed in world or regional headquarters and then tested locally by market-research firms.

For some types of products such as French perfume, Japanese cameras, and Italian wines, the country image as a producer of that product is so strong that very little adaptation must be made in the package or label. For products for which a country is not noted, such as Russian wine and American *sake,* the *appearance* of the product in the retail store is exceptionally important.

INSTRUCTIONS, WARRANTIES, AND SERVICE.   These three aspects of the product may have little effect on *initial* sales, but they are paramount for repeat sales of both industrial and consumer goods.

Instructions.   Several countries, such as Venezuela, require that product instructions be provided in the local language. A product like a transistor radio, which can be sold worldwide with little or no adaptation, may be packaged with an instruction sheet printed in six or eight different languages. Instructions to be read in foreign countries should be exceptionally simple, clear, and complete.

Warranties.   A product warranty can be uniform throughout the world or it can vary from country to country. Some factors that favor nonuniform warranties are the following:

> **Location of Manufacture.**   One factory may not be able to achieve the same product quality as others.
>
> **Condition of Use.**   Marine engines may break down more in salt water than in fresh water, more in industrial applications than if used by individual consumers.
>
> **Competition and Promotion.**   A firm may *have* to offer an attractive warranty because the competition is doing so, or it may *choose* to offer an attractive warranty as a promotional tool.

A company using nonuniform warranties must limit service under warranty to a specified market area, that is, the country of purchase. Thus an African customer who buys a television set in Europe might not be able to have it serviced under warranty in his home country.

Service.   It is shortsighted, and in some countries illegal, to sell a product without maintaining adequate service facilities and inventories of parts. Service facilities usually have to be maintained in each country because it is time-consuming, risky, and expensive to ship products across national boundaries for servicing. There are some exceptions, as when photocopiers used in Mexico are sent to the United States for repair.

Whether servicing is done in company-owned service centers or by independent distributors, two very difficult problems are *training* and *control.* Training of servicemen is done through manuals, visits to the service centers by home office personnel, and training courses at national, regional, or world headquarters. Control is carried out through inspections, reporting systems, and sometimes follow-up with customers who have had products repaired.

Some multinational suppliers of industrial goods such as elevators emphasize *preventive maintenance* more abroad than in their home countries. This is done to minimize the frequency of breakdowns, repairs, and costly rush shipments of replacement parts.

INTERNATIONAL PRODUCT STRATEGY.   Some important aspects of international product strategy are product cycles, the product line, and product development.

Product Cycles.   There are two theories relating to international product cycles. One is the familiar theory that every product goes through several phases from introduction to extinction, and a product's natural life can be extended by marketing techniques. The international application is that a product's life can also be extended by taking it to countries in which it will still be appreciated. Chamber pots, washboards, and kerosene stoves are still in demand in some parts of the world.

The other product-cycle theory holds that a new product is first manufactured and sold in its country of origin. Then it is exported. Then it is manufactured and sold both domestically and abroad. Finally it is manufactured abroad and imported to its country of origin, which by that time should be starting the cycle all over again with another new product.

The Product Line.   Multinational firms usually do not try to market all their products and models in every country. This holds true for exporters, but to a lesser degree.

Firms usually try to sell in each country the products that best fit the market and meet competition. Local subsidiaries are often given autonomy, subject to approval by or consultation with a central office, to choose the products and models that they will actively market.

Product Development.   International operations promote product development by providing many new sources of product ideas. Often a distributor in Asia will come up with a product variation that will meet a need in Latin America, Europe, or worldwide.

The work of new-product research and development is usually done at the regional or world level, especially if technically sophisticated processes are involved. There is however a trend toward decentralization of R&D, partly in response to pressure from countries that would like to increase their technological capabilities. *Product testing* is usually done at the regional or local levels. This helps prevent the introduction of new products or product developments into countries for which they are not well suited.

INTERNATIONAL DISTRIBUTION

DISTRIBUTION FUNCTIONS.   A channel of distribution must serve both information functions and physical functions. Furthermore, movement through the channel must be efficient in both directions—outward to the customer and inward to the international marketer.

Information Functions.   The kinds of information that move *out* through a channel of distribution include product data, prices, promotion and special offers, and changes in products, prices, and warranties. Information that moves *in* from the customer includes market data, inquiries, credit verifications, orders, and suggestions of product changes.

A channel that does not facilitate the passage of information becomes an opaque door that separates the international marketer from his customers.

Physical Functions.   Physical flows out through a channel of distribution include products, parts, service, documents, and financing. The physical flow inward is payment.

The channel selected must be able to perform the specific functions that are required to market a particular product. That is, if sales of a product require large local inventories, the channel must be able to maintain them. If service is important, the channel must provide adequate service facilities.

TYPES OF DISTRIBUTION CHANNELS.   Firms engaged in exporting can use either direct or indirect channels of distribution. The tendency is for firms to begin with indirect channels and progress to more direct ones. Firms that are truly committed to international marketing want the market knowledge and control that usually result from direct distribution.

Channels In the Home Country.   If a firm sells directly from its home country to a foreign market, it is said to be involved in *direct* exporting. There are, however, many kinds of *indirect* channels. Sales can be made to the *buying office of a multinational firm* in the home country. They can be made to the *buying office* of a foreign government or to the *buying agent* of a foreign retail organization. They can be made to an *export merchant* or *trading company,* which buys for its own account and resells abroad. They can be made through *export agents* or *brokers.* A firm's products can be exported by another firm that carries complementary goods. The U.S. Department of Commerce gave this a name—the "piggyback" system. A company can join with producers of similar products in a Webb-Pomerene Association, which permits joint exporting that would otherwise be in violation of antitrust laws. There are now about 30 active Webb-Pomerene Associations handling such products as woodchips, dried fruit, and motion pictures. Finally, a company can form its own *Foreign Sales Corporation* (FSC). This is an offshore subsidiary that can export American products worldwide. There is no corporate income tax on a portion of the FSC's profits.

Channels in the Market Country.   Distribution channels vary greatly, even in neighboring countries, as shown by Terpstra in Exhibit 1. The activities of multinational firms are slowly reducing these differences. Some noticeable trends are toward a smaller role for middlemen who do not take title; toward larger wholesale and retail organizations; and toward shorter (more direct) marketing channels. These trends do not appear in all countries or with regard to all products.

Large volumes of business and large individual sales in foreign markets are often made directly to government organizations, major industrial users, and large retailing organizations. Such transactions may be arranged by seller's *agents* or by company-owned sales offices in the market country. Smaller volumes of business are usually handled through agents or brokers to wholesalers and industrial distributors, or through importer-distributors to industrial users and retailers. There are numerous variations of these basic channels.

Finally, there are some instances of *direct* export sales *by mail order.* This method seems to be used mostly for selling articles of clothing to countries having

EXHIBIT 1   VARIATIONS IN EUROPEAN DISTRIBUTION CHANNELS BY PRODUCT AND COUNTRY[a]

	Furniture		Domestic Appliances		Books and Stationery		Textiles		Footwear		Clothing	
	France	U.K.	Germany	Netherlands	Belgium	Netherlands	Belgium	U.K.	Germany	U.K.	France	U.K.
Department and variety stores	8.3	13.2	15.6	11.1	25.1	5.3	6.2	10.2	23.8	14.5	17.4	20.6
Multiple chain stores	4.8	26.9	16.8	22.6	9.1	33.4	7.2	16.0	16.0	48.5	4.1	50.7
Mail order	3.1	12.8	24.9	1.5	6.3	3.9	2.5	12.0	0.7	14.0	3.2	10.3
Cooperatives	2.2	7.8	2.3	0.3	0.1	0.3	0.8	3.6	0.2	3.6	1.2	2.8
Independents and street trade	81.6	39.2	40.3	64.5	59.4	57.1	83.3	58.2	59.1	19.4	74.1	15.6

[a]Percentage of sales in each channel.
Source. Terpstra (1978), p. 363. Adopted from *Vision* magazine, June 1975, p. 38.

well-developed postal systems, especially where textile products imported in quantity face quotas or high import duties.

Selecting a Distribution Channel.   The selection of a distribution channel is very important because of the difficulty of changing a channel once it is established. A more complete discussion of channels selection can be found in Majaro (1977).

   Some of the factors to consider in selecting an international distribution channel are the following:

   The Functions It Has to Perform.   If product sales must be financed, the channel should be strong financially, and so forth.

   The Firm's Objectives and Financial Ability.   A firm that plans to compete actively in a foreign market for several years and is financially strong should consider setting up a company-owned distribution system.

   Channels Used in the Market.   At times it is nearly impossible to enter a market except through the traditional distribution system. At other times the traditional system is effectively closed to a new foreign competitor, and an alternate distribution scheme must be used.

In general, distribution channels are more direct for industrial products, large sales orders, large selling and/or buying organizations, and goods that are expensive, sophisticated, perishable, custom-made, or in frequent need of service.

SELECTING FOREIGN REPRESENTATIVES.   If the distribution channel is to include independent distributors or agents in market countries, they must be selected with great care because (1) the firm will be known in the market country by the quality of its representatives, (2) the firm's success in the market will depend largely on the work of its representatives, and (3) once named, an agent or distributor may be very hard to replace, because of personal, business, and legal considerations. In theory, the various components of a distribution channel should form an integrated system that functions smoothly for the benefit of all concerned.

Identifying Potential Representatives.   Potential foreign representatives can be identified from U.S. Department of Commerce *Trade Lists,* national, international, and industry directories, and personal contacts and market research. Their credentials can be checked through bank and trade references, U.S. Department of Commerce *World Trade Directory Reports,* credit-reporting agencies such as Dun & Bradstreet International, and/or personal visits.

Criteria for Selection.   The following are some important factors to consider in the selection of foreign representatives:

   Availability and interest in the firm's products. This can be a difficult criterion, because qualified agents and distributors in major market countries have their desks piled high with letters from would-be suppliers throughout the world.

   Market knowledge that can help the supplier to properly adapt its products and marketing techniques.

The ability to represent a firm adequately, by virtue of management capabilities, areas covered, customers served, product lines carried, sales organization, auxiliary services, and financial strength.

The right "chemistry" with executives of the supplying firm to facilitate understanding and cooperation toward the achievement of mutually beneficial objectives.

Contracting with Foreign Representatives.   An international representation agreement is normally set forth in a written contract—usually enforceable under the laws of the country in which it is to be executed. Some of the usual provisions of such contracts are the following:

Legal nature of the contract—commercial representation.

Parties to the contract—names, addresses, and whether contracting parties are signing as individuals or for their business firms.

Authentic text—if in more than one language, which one is official.

Dates of entering into force and of termination.

Products covered.

Territory included.

Whether the foreign representative will have exclusive sales rights to the covered products.

Kinds of customers included and kinds exempted (if any).

Rights and obligations of the supplying firm to accept or reject orders, provide information, establish factories in the contractual territory, protect the rights of the representative, prevent competition from unauthorized imports and counterfeit brands, assist with sales promotion and advertising, and pay travel or other expenses of the representative.

Rights and obligations of the representative to protect his supplier's interests, to take or not take legal actions in the supplier's name, to observe the supplier's standard conditions of sale, to refrain from handling competing products (unless expressly permitted), to maintain merchandise inventories, to provide after-sale service and spare parts, to provide market and credit information, to advertise and sell, to protect the supplier's industrial property rights, and to assist with collections (if working as an agent).

Commission arrangement (for an agency agreement) or mark-up/discount (for a distributorship agreement).

Provision for termination of the agreement.

Legal jurisdiction.

Absence of conflicting agreements.

Arbitration of disputes.

WORKING WITH FOREIGN REPRESENTATIVES.   The following are some of the considerations involved in working with foreign representatives, once a contract has been signed:

Training.   Both agents and distributors need in-depth understanding of the company's products and how to sell them. Adequate training not only helps the representatives do a better job, but assures them that the supplying firm is concerned about their performance.

Objectives.   Yearly sales objectives, by product and area or type of customer, should be worked out during face-to-face meetings with each representative. This can be difficult because in many countries the concepts of detailed planning, objective reporting, and early corrective action are not widely accepted.

Consultation.   There should be planned, regular two-way communications between the supplying firm and its foreign representatives. Although improvements in international telephone and telex, and electronic communications have led to dramatic increases in their use, periodic written reports and personal visits are still vital.

Assistance.   Serious international marketers strive to assist their foreign representatives by accepting special product orders, sending technicians to help at trade fairs and with special problems, sending missionary salesmen to participate in calls on important customers, giving top priority to urgent shipments, providing catalogs, ad mats, and cooperative advertising, extending credit whenever possible, and trying to eliminate mistakes in production, shipping, and documentation.

INTERNATIONAL PHYSICAL DISTRIBUTION.   International physical distribution is a complex, multimodal world of logistics, shipping, insurance, warehousing, and documentation. The following sections describe some of the important considerations.

Order Processing.   Processing and filling an order involves various departments of a company—sales, shipping, credit, and perhaps manufacturing. The work of these departments must be coordinated to reduce intracompany conflict and costly mistakes. It is common in small firms for the international-sales department to have to rely on credit and shipping departments that are oriented toward the domestic market and lack both interest and expertise in the international area.

Packing and Marking.   International shipments by sea require special packing in order to reduce damage from pilferage, breakage, and water. The marking of crates and containers follows generally accepted practices, but many countries have peculiar marking requirements. Export-packing, freight-forwarding, shipping, and insurance companies have valuable expertise in this field.

Documentation.   In spite of frequent efforts to simplify the paperwork involved in international shipments, correct documentation is an exacting and time-consuming process. All documents produced by the supplying firm should be double-checked for accuracy, and all documents produced by the freight forwarder should be examined as soon as they are received. This is especially important when shipping under letters of credit.

Also, the supplying firm should carefully check the import documentation requirements of each country to which it is shipping. Useful information can be obtained from customers abroad, consulates of the market country, freight forwarders, Croner's *Reference Book for World Traders,* the Bureau of National Affairs *Export Shipping Manual,* the Dun & Bradstreet *Exporter's Encyclopedia,* and *Shipping Digest.* There are several new computer programs that can facilitate export processing and paperwork.

Shipping.   The use of *air* freight, both to and within international markets, has been increasing dramatically. The high cost of air freight is offset by its speed, relative safety from breakage and pilferage, simpler packing and documentation require- . ments, and lower insurance costs. In many countries, air freight reaches customers who are practically inaccessible by surface transportation.

In *marine* shipping it appears that the conference system is gradually breaking apart, thus increasing the opportunities for negotiation of rates, routes, and schedules. Also, nonvessel-owning common carriers and shippers' associations are adding to the shipping options for exporters.

International *surface* transportation is now dependable throughout Western Europe, but still faces serious difficulties in many parts of the developing world.

Insurance.   A number of countries now require that import shipments be insured by local firms. Thus, c.i.f. shipping terms are giving way to c.&f. The exporter should normally insist on *proof* that the importer has purchased adequate insurance coverage. If the exporter feels that he might bear liability for loss or damage even though insurance coverage was not his responsibility, he can purchase *contingent insurance* to be sure there is adequate, effective coverage. Most insurance coverage is all-risk, warehouse to warehouse, for 110 percent of the c.i.f. value of a shipment.

Warehousing.   International firms often make use of bonded warehouses, or warehouses in free zones. Product inventories have to be especially well controlled, and special packing may be needed for storage in very cold, hot, or humid climates. Many ports and terminals lack adequate cold-storage facilities. Also many warehouses in developing countries are short of materials-handling equipment. This calls for smaller and lighter shipping units and stronger packing.

Multimodal Distribution.   There is a clear worldwide trend toward the use of large containers, land bridges, roll-on roll-off, barge-aboard-ship, trailer-on-flat-car, and related equipment that can reduce the costs of export packing, insurance, shipping, and warehousing.

INTERNATIONAL PROMOTION

ADVERTISING.   International advertising is done at all levels—world, region, country, and locality. Variations in media and message from one place to another make this a very challenging function of international marketing management. Total expenditures on advertising vary from well over $100 per person per year in the United States to almost zero in some of the least-developed countries. The *media mix* also varies enormously according to the availability of media, legal restrictions, rates of literacy, and consumers' habits.

Print Media.   International advertising is done at the *world* level through publications such as *Trade Channel* and *Worldwide Projects*. These publications reach selected audiences in wide geographic areas and are used for advertising products that are to be distributed worldwide.

Some examples of *regional* publications are *Visión* for Latin America, *Arab Business* for the Middle East, and *Jeune Afrique* for French-speaking African countries.

Most advertising in these publications is directed at industrial users or sophisticated household consumers.

Most developed countries have a variety of *national* newspapers or magazines, and most developing countries have one or more of them. The advertising content of these varies with the country and publication.

Throughout the world, most print media advertising is done in local newspapers and, where available, specialized magazines. One aspect that varies a great deal from country to country is the use of color in local newspapers and magazines. Some publications emphasize color; others do not offer it, while still others do, but lack the color separation and printing techniques and equipment for accurate reproduction. In general, foreign countries are not yet making extensive use of in-ad couponing or newspaper inserts.

Broadcast Media.   *Radio,* including AM, FM, and shortwave, is perhaps the most universal advertising medium. There are in Western Europe several *regional* stations that reach most of the European Common Market and carry advertising by multinational firms. There is also a great deal of transborder radio coverage, for example, Laredo stations reach the English-speaking audience in northern Mexico and French stations broadcast to the French-speaking portion of Switzerland.

Advertisers and advertising agencies around the world seem to reach their highest levels of creativity when working with radio. An unlimited mixture of music, voices, tempos, volumes, and approaches appeals to target audiences.

Some difficulties with this advertising medium in many countries are fragmentation of the market by a large number of competing stations and the lack of adequate information on listenership. This often results in "overkill," by advertising on more stations than should be necessary to reach a given sales objective.

Television has now reached nearly all countries, and color broadcasting is available in most developed and many developing nations. There is a large amount of transborder television reception, such as programs from Jordan reaching over to Arabic-speaking residents of Israel. The growth of cable systems and satellite dish reception is adding to the internalization of TV advertising.

A difficulty with television in many countries is the poor quality of local production. Multinational firms that do local advertising often have the story-board made up locally, then have the ad produced in a country that has high-quality facilities, and then have it reviewed and/or tested at the local level before being broadcast. Another important difficulty is legal restriction of television advertising. In several countries TV stations are noncommercial; advertising is not allowed at all, except perhaps "public service" announcements by official organizations. In other countries advertising is allowed, but severely restricted. Examples of such restrictions are no ads for liquor or tobacco products, none directed to children, and none during peak viewing hours.

Other Advertising Media.   Newspaper, magazine, radio and television ads are supplemented in most countries by billboards, fliers, loudspeaker announcements, transportation placements, movie theater advertising, direct mail, point-of-purchase advertising, and ads positioned in football stadiums and other public places. The motoring public is attracted by billboard ads wherever they are legal, and most market-economy countries now have firms that own and rent billboard space.

Movie theater advertising is useful in many countries in which a routine form of entertainment is to see a movie each week. The same messages can be used both in movie theaters and on television if the viewers' characteristics are not markedly different. The development of point-of-purchase advertising follows closely the introduction of self-service. Window signs, "shelf-talkers," and other forms of point-of-purchase advertising are used to reinforce messages placed in the mass media.

Advertising Agencies.   There are now qualified local advertising agencies in nearly all countries, and many international agencies offer virtually worldwide coverage. There is a trend by multinational firms to give more of their advertising to the large agencies, most of which are headquartered in the United States, Japan, and Great Britain.

Advertising that is standardized at the world or regional level (except perhaps for language translation) is usually developed by international agencies. Many local agencies have prospered, however, because of in-depth knowledge of local thought patterns, nuances of language, media coverages, and rate structures. It is common to have ads *produced* by international agencies but *placed* by local firms.

SALES PROMOTION.   International sales promotion takes three principal forms—trade fairs and exhibitions, trade missions, and contests and premiums.

Trade Fairs and Exhibitions.   A great deal of international sales promotion is done through trade fairs and exhibitions held throughout the world. They are especially important in countries with centrally planned economies, in which other methods of generating sales may be severely restricted.

National fairs open to the general public (often similar to state and county fairs in the United States) are useful for showing new consumer products or increasing brand awareness. Much more important, however, are specialized industry fairs, usually held annually in industrialized countries and closed to the general public. There are several reasons for attending and exhibiting in these fairs—to introduce new products, to see what the competition is doing, to carry out informal market research, to generate inquiries and sales, and to acquire or support local agents/distributors. Information on important fairs can be found in the Bill Communication, Inc. *Exhibits Schedule,* published annually. Also important are foreign-trade exhibitions sponsored by the U.S. Department of Commerce, state government agencies, associations of exporters, chambers of commerce, and individual firms. These are held in U.S. trade centers, hotel rooms, and other facilities in major market cities.

The key words for success in all trade exhibitions are *preparation, execution,* and *follow-up.* Successful exhibitors take care to identify their target customers and invite them specifically to their stands or booths, and to select products that will be of interest to those customers. With technical products it is important to have the exhibit manned at all times by both *technical* and *sales* personnel who can speak the languages of their target customers. Interpreters can be hired to work at exhibitions, but direct communication is highly preferable. Finally, successful exhibitors keep records of their conversations with all promising visitors and follow up as soon as possible.

Contests and Premiums.   The promise of something for nothing has universal appeal, especially in countries in which economic conditions are difficult and public lotteries are common. The variety is endless, from small bills (currency) packed randomly in cereal boxes to a free battery with a new transistor radio. In several countries the governments have determined that contests and premiums are *too* effective, economically wasteful, and unfair, and have responded with laws that restrict the maximum value of prizes and other conditions of this kind of sales promotion. It is important to check the legality of a special promotion in each country before putting it into effect.

PUBLIC RELATIONS AND PUBLICITY.   National pride, and prejudice, make public relations an important function in foreign-owned firms worldwide. Publicity is often combined with public relations or with advertising. A highly oversimplified definition of these two terms is that *public relations* means doing nice things for people, and *publicity* means telling them about it.

Public Relations.   A firm has many "publics" in each country in which it operates—suppliers, customers, each level of government, the military, religious organizations, students, and the population in general. A very bad image with any of these groups can diminish sales and jeopardize the firm's future in a particular country. In addition, global communications have helped social concerns to become contagious. A campaign against a product in one country can quickly spread to others. In particular, a small campaign against the marketing of infant formula led to a United Nations resolution on marketing practices.

World, regional, and national public relations personnel should continually monitor the attitudes of a firm's various publics about (1) foreign business in general, and (2) the firm in particular. This can be done by watching news media and talking with leaders of the various publics and with alert foreign diplomats and company employees.

Public relations, then, is both *preventive* and *corrective. Preventive* activities include minimizing environmental pollution from company operations, educating consumers to minimize hazardous misuse of the firm's products, giving expatriate employees training in the local language, and buying uniforms for a local baseball team. *Corrective* activities include quickly changing commercials that have been found to be offensive to any segment of the population, taking steps to reduce sales of products that are driving local competitors out of business, and counteracting calls of exploitation by showing how much the firm is contributing to the local economy through its purchases, wages, and taxes.

Publicity.   A very effective way for a firm to improve its image or its sales at the retail level is through stories and articles in the news media. Personal and written contact with media executives can result in published or broadcast information that has high impact. Many companies issue regular press releases about product improvements, key local employees, new distributors, and other favorable aspects of their operations.

In many countries there is a direct and open link between advertising and publicity, as when a magazine editor promises an article on a new product in return for so many inches of paid advertising. The manager of promotion in each country should understand the local system and how it works.

PERSONAL SELLING.   Personal selling has two dimensions in international marketing—export and missionary salespersons sent by the home office, and local salespersons in the market country.

Export Sales Personnel.   A person in charge of selling a nontechnical product in a region of the world may have to be on the road as much as 90 percent of the time. His tasks are to sell directly to major buyers and/or to support and train local agents and distributors.

This person should have complete knowledge of the company and its products, because on foreign travels he will not have backup support readily at hand. He should know also the language and culture of the countries to which he is traveling. One simple blunder, like pointing the sole of his shoe at a buyer in South Korea or complimenting a consumer's wife in Spain, could cost him a sale. Finally, the international salesperson should know the buying history of each of his customers and each country's production, consumption, imports, exports, customs duties, and regulations concerning his product.

The export salesperson should continually gather market information, both in his office and on the road. In the field he will also have to motivate foreign representatives, settle disputes involving the company, its representatives, and its customers, and resolve any technical problems that may have arisen.

The carrying of *commercial samples* from country to country has been simplified by the *carnet,* which is available from the New York office of the International Chamber of Commerce.

Foreign Sales Personnel.   Products that rely on *supply push* (as opposed to *demand pull*) marketing strategies need personal selling. Unfortunately the sales profession suffers in many countries from a lack of prestige. Adequate training, compensation, and foreign travel have improved the image somewhat, but in many countries young people from "good" families are still reluctant to go into sales.

Except in very unusual circumstances, foreign salespersons are company employees and are thus subject to minimum-wage, severance-pay, and other laws in each country. The best ways of motivating them vary greatly from one culture to another. In Japan, for example, company-wide recognition of good performance can have more effect than a substantial commission.

The supervision of field sales personnel presents special difficulties in countries where loose supervision is taken as a sign of disinterest, and tight supervision as a signal of distrust. Sales managers must be selected with great care, especially where personal selling is to be emphasized and the salespersons are from different ethnic groups which might be feuding with each other or have very different cultural characteristics.

OTHER ASPECTS OF PROMOTION.   Some other aspects of promotion that should be considered are standardization or adaptation, planning and budgeting, and the promotional mix.

Standardization or Adaptation.   Advertising *media plans* cannot be standardized at the world level; however, *messages* can be if they appeal to *universal buying motives.* The standard message can be adapted in each country as required. Worldwide standardization saves a great deal of expense, but does not lead to maximum sales.

The details of successful sales-promotion, public-relations, and publicity activities can be communicated to each country office for information and possible adoption. Personal-selling knowledge and techniques are similar around the world. Whether sales training is done at the country level or at higher levels depends largely on the product's complexity.

Planning and Budgeting. The main aspect of promotional planning that can be standardized is the *method* of setting the total amount to be spent. The firm can decide to use *competitive parity, percentage of sales, task-objective,* or some other method, and can apply that method to each national operation. Of course there should be flexibility to adapt to special circumstances, as when the percentage of sales method is being used and competitors in a given country are substantially increasing their promotional expenditures.

The Promotional Mix. This term refers to the relative emphasis to be placed on advertising, sales promotion, public relations, publicity, and personal selling. A simple answer is to follow the trade custom and do whatever is normal for a given product in a given country. A more useful (but more complex) answer is to try to assess the costs and benefits of money spent on each type of promotion. This is especially difficult in the case of public relations, which may not directly produce any sales, but which may ultimately make the difference between staying in a country and having to leave it.

ORGANIZATION, PLANNING, AND CONTROL

ORGANIZATION FOR INTERNATIONAL MARKETING. The concept of organizing for international marketing can be thought of in two ways—the place of international operations in the organization, and the way in which the international operation is structured internally.

The Place of International Operations. If a firm is not committed to international operations, but is only exporting as opportunities arise, it can simply expand the roles of its domestic sales, shipping, credit, and other divisions to include foreign markets. This is inexpensive, but is also risky because domestic operating personnel may not understand or care about foreign markets, and there may be conflicts because of a lack of leadership and coordination.

At a higher level of commitment, the firm can organize a separate international department. It may have only administrative and sales personnel at first, but these can be followed by experts in international shipping and credit. Later, personnel can be added to take care of international market research, licensing, finance, personnel, and other functions.

A firm that becomes fully committed to serving international markets can create a specialized subsidiary such as the **IBM** World Trade Corporation. This kind of subsidiary is a nearly self-contained business entity in charge of international operations, and relates with the parent company almost at arm's length except at the highest levels.

There is one more stage in the placement of international operations—to become a world company. A world headquarters is established to supervise the various divisions, including the former home office. This world headquarters may be with or near the former home office, or it may be in a different country that offers simple organizational procedures and low corporate income taxes.

Internal Structure of International Operations. There are four basic ways of structuring a firm's international operations—by function, geographically, by type of product, and by type of customer. Most firms use a combination of two or more of these systems. In a functional form of organization, the head of international marketing might supervise international sales, international credit, and so forth. He might also be in charge of any sales offices in other countries. His responsibility would include all products sold abroad and all foreign markets.

In a *geographic* form of organization international operations are simply divided by market areas, for example, Eastern Europe, Western Europe, the Middle East, and the Andean Group countries. Each area can contain from 1 to about 50 countries, which do not necessarily have to be contiguous. For example, an area of responsibility might be "developed countries in Africa and Asia" or "all Spanish-speaking countries in Latin America and the Caribbean."

In organization by *type of product,* an office products firm might set up international paper products, desk accessory, and photocopier divisions. Each of these would perform the functions required to market its assigned products throughout the world.

Organization by *type of customer* is important when similar customers have similar needs and are scattered in several countries. A producer of pneumatic tires, for example, might have its international marketing organization divided to cater to (1) automobile and truck manufacturers, (2) producers of construction equipment, (3) manufacturers of bicycles and small trailers, and (4) the aftermarket.

In practice, firms that do large volumes of international business compound these various structures. That is, a large firm might have its international operations structured first by function; then the major functions, such as international sales, could be broken down geographically. Finally, each of these geographic groups could be subdivided by type of product or customer.

INTERNATIONAL MARKETING PLANNING.   Successful international marketing normally requires detailed, long-range, worldwide profit planning. Haphazard international selling with the objective of maximizing profits each year in every market does not produce optimum benefits.

Detailed Profit Planning.   A firm's sales, profit, market share, or other objectives usually follow its organizational structure. That is, if a firm's international operations include an export sales department that is divided geographically and then by product, its specific export sales objectives will be set by geographic area and then by product.

Types of Objectives.   *Sales and profit* targets can be set globally, then broken down by region and country (if the firm is organized on a geographic basis). Planners at the world level set the overall goal and then meet with regional managers to allocate it to the regions. Then each regional goal is divided among the countries or areas that make up that region. On the contrary, the managers of the smallest marketing units can be asked to make their projections first. Then these can be combined into regional and finally world totals. In practice, planning discussions usually move simultaneously both up and down the corporate structure until world, regional, and national goals are set.

Market share objectives are more likely to be set at the local level, where planners can take full account of forecasts and opinions as to future market conditions. There are some firms, like Bic, that talk in terms of shares of the *world* market, but this approach is useful only for firms that are major competitors in a large number of countries.

A firm can set as its goal a minimum *return on investment* from each market area or type of product. In doing so, however, it should keep in mind the concept of long-term, worldwide planning, which will be discussed later in this section.

It is common to combine two or more objectives. For example, an automobile manufacturer in Argentina might plan on a 20 percent market share in year X with a return on investment of at least 18 percent. The use of multiple objectives can help prevent a local manager from taking actions that make him look good in the short run, but will hurt the company's future profitability.

Strategies and Tactics. If a firm is to meet its international marketing objectives, its managers must develop product, price, distribution, and promotion *strategies* for specific products and markets. Detailed tactics are thus planned to implement the strategies.

For example, a firm that intends to capture 15 percent of a foreign market for greeting cards might develop the following strategies:

Product. Use single fold only, make some cards with no text and others with very brief messages (written, not just translated, locally); sell only single cards, and wrap each one in cellophane; use standard local sizes.

Price. Maintain price to consumer about two thirds of the way up the range of prices in the market. Give retailers a discount that is slightly larger than average; give wholesalers a normal discount.

Distribution. Distribute through normal channels, but try for more market penetration by placing cards in medium-price general-merchandise stores.

Promotion. Give dealers display racks. Concentrate on radio, year-round, peaking before major holidays.

Detailed tactics to carry out these strategies would include, for example, the *media plan* giving radio stations to be used, the advertising schedule and budget, and major themes.

Long-Range Profit Planning. Many new ventures lose money in their first year or two. This is even more true with international operations because it takes considerable investment in time and money to acquire a full understanding of laws that affect marketing and *the extent to which* they are enforced in each country, to hire the required sales, service, and other personnel, train them adequately, and move in any necessary expatriate staff members, to establish distribution, whether company-owned or through independent representatives, including warehousing and service facilities, to build up a supply of products and parts, to gain familiarity with a new and distant market that may have very different characteristics from the home market, and to persuade industrial customers that the firm is there for the long haul; that it won't pull out suddenly and leave them with unserviceable products. It may also take time to ride out a period of political uncertainty, as during recent years in Chile and El Salvador.

A classic book on this subject is *Strategic Planning for Export Marketing,* by Franklin W. Root (1964). It stresses the need for *5-year* profit plans, which may include planned losses during the initial years in new foreign markets.

Worldwide Profit Planning.   Domestic firms sometimes continue to market an unprofitable product because it is a vital part of a lucrative line, or continue to sell in an unprofitable area if it is important to the company's overall strategy. The case with international marketing is similar. A firm may want to stay with an unprofitable product or market country to make it harder for competition to gain a foothold, to be in the market and ready when economic or political conditions improve, to not leave any gaps in a market area such as the European Community, or to pick up or test ideas that may be useful in other areas. This international gathering and application of ideas has been called *synergism*—the whole greater than the sum of its parts.

CONTROL OF INTERNATIONAL MARKETING.   Control in international marketing is the complement of planning. It requires systematic collection and feedback of information so the firm will know whether it is meeting its objectives, and if not, where and by how much it is failing. If any objectives are not being met, the situation should be analyzed, and corrective action taken at the earliest possible moment.

SOURCES AND SUGGESTED REFERENCES

Arab Business. London: International Communications, 1975- (monthly).

Bill Communications, Inc. "Exhibits Schedule," *Successful Meetings* magazine annual.

Bottin Europe. Paris: Didot-Bottin, 1978.

Bottin International. Paris: Didot-Bottin, 1979. 2v.

Brandon's Shipper & Forwarder. N.Y.: New York Foreign Freight Forwarders and Brokers Association, 1929- (weekly).

Bureau of National Affairs, Inc. *International Trade Reporter; Export Shipping Manual.* Wash., D.C., 1947- 3v.

Croner's Reference Book for World Traders. Queens Village, N.Y., 1949-.

Day, A.J. *Exporting for Profit.* London: Graham & Trotman (International Publications Service), 1976.

Dun & Bradstreet *Exporters' Encyclopedia: World Marketing Guide.* N.Y.: Dun & Bradstreet International. Annual.

Dun & Bradstreet, Inc. *Principal International Businesses.* N.Y., 1974- Annual.

Food and Agriculture Organization of the United Nations. *Trade Yearbook.* Rome, 1958-.

International Bank for Reconstruction and Development. *World Development Report 1984.* New York: Oxford University Press, 1985.

International Marketing Institute, *Export Marketing for Smaller Firms,* 4th ed. Washington, D.C.: Small Business Administration, 1979.

Jeune Afrique. Paris, Groupe J.A., 1960- (weekly).

Kahler, R. *International Marketing,* 4th ed. Pelham Manor, NY: South-Western, 1977.

Keegan, *Multinational Marketing Management.* Englewood Cliffs, NJ: Prentice-Hall, 1974.

Kotler, P. *Principles of Marketing.* Englewood Cliffs, NJ: Prentice-Hall, 1980.

Majaro, S. *International Marketing: A Strategic Approach to World Markets.* New York: Wiley, 1977.

Organization for Economic Cooperation and Development. *Import/Export Microtables*. Paris, 1975-.

Robinson, R.G. *International Business Management*. Hinsdale, IL: Dryden Press, 1978.

Root, F.R. *Strategic Planning for Export Marketing*. Scranton, PA: International Textbook, 1966.

Standard Trade Index of Japan. Tokyo, Japan Chamber of Commerce and Industry, 1979.

Successful Export Strategy. Proceedings of a conference sponsored by the London Chamber of Commerce and Industry and The Institute of Export. London: Graham & Trotman, 1977.

Terpstra, V. *International Marketing*, 2nd ed. Hinsdale, IL: Dryden Press, 1978.

Trade Channel. Amsterdam, Trade Channel Organization, 1946- (monthly).

United Nations. Statistical Office. *Statistical Papers:* Series M. (Commodity Trade Statistics). NY, 1949-. Irregular.

United Nations. Statistical Office. *Yearbook of International Trade Statistics*. NY, 1951-. Annual.

U.S. Dept. of Commerce. Domestic and International Business Administration. *Overseas Business Reports*. Wash., D.C., GPO.

U.S. Department of Commerce. *Foreign Business Practices*. Washington, DC: U.S. Government Printing Office, 1985.

Vision. Grand-Saconnex, Switzerland, m.d.- (11/yr.).

World Aviation Directory. Wash., American Aviation Pubs., 1940-. v.1-. Biennial.

World Trade Annual. Prepared by the Statistical Office of the United Nations. N.Y., Walker & Co. 5v.

Worldwide Projects. Westport, Conn., Intercontinental Pubs., 1967- (6/yr.).

COUNTRY-RISK ASSESSMENT

CONTENTS

COUNTRY-RISK ASSESSMENT

Ingo Walter

International business involves a wide variety of inherent risks. Export markets, carefully developed and nurtured, may suddenly collapse because of internal changes in target markets, imposition of exchange controls, or protectionist trade-policy measures. Imports of raw materials, components and parts, or capital equipment may face restricted supplies or major increases in cost due to shifting conditions—economic or political—in principal supplier countries. International lending may face restrictions on repayment of interest and principal, rescheduling, or outright default. Contracts to build turnkey plants abroad may face abrupt cancellations; licensing arrangements may face restrictions on fee remittances; and foreign direct investment may be subject to nationalization, expropriation, confiscation, indigenization, or a variety of domestic measures in host countries that seriously impair profitability.

Such risks are essentially related to economic and political conditions that exist in countries—or in politically sovereign national states. They can also spill over from one country to another, or affect several countries at once, thereby limiting the ability of firms to diversify away from the risks inherent in country conditions. It is generally agreed that exposure to such risks in international business has risen over the years, requiring banks, manufacturing firms, insurance companies, and others to devote increasing resources to analyzing country-related conditions and ensuring that returns are adequate to compensate them for the risks involved. This is the task of *country-risk assessment,* which has received a great deal of attention by banks, corporations, and others engaged in international business and exposed to shifting country conditions.

ELEMENTS OF COUNTRY-RISK ASSESSMENT

A simple view of the problem focuses on risk that arises out of structural (supply-side) elements, demand-side and monetary elements, and external economic and political developments, as well as the quality of the national economic management team and the domestic political constraints bearing upon decision makers. One might begin with a relationship such as the following:

$$Y + M = A + X$$

representing real flows of goods and services in an economy, where Y is output, M is imports, A is domestic absorption (consumption, investment, and public-sector spending) and X is exports, all in real terms. Clearly, supply-side changes in Y with unchanged demand will require shifts in imports or exports—reduced production capabilities, for example, mean either increased imports or a more limited capacity to export. In a similar way, demand-side shifts affecting A with unchanged supply can be examined—increased government spending will, for example, have to be met from expanded imports or will deflect export production to meet domestic needs. Monetary variables can affect the picture as well—growth in the domestic money supply will, unless reflected in exchange rates, tend to raise A relative to Y and, therefore, increase M, decrease X, or both.

In order to bring the money side into the picture explicitly, we can develop an equally simple equation describing international financial flows:

$$VX - VM - DS + FDI + U - K_0 = DR - NBR.$$

Here VX and VM represent the money value of exports and imports, respectively. DS represents debt-service payments to foreigners (usually part of VM in conventional balance-of-payments accounting); FDI is net flows of nonresident foreign direct investments; U represents net flows of private and public-sector grants such as foreign aid. K_0 is net capital flows undertaken by residents, DR is the change in international reserves of the country in question, and NBR is its net borrowing requirement. An overall negative balance on the left side of the equation clearly means that the country will have to increase its foreign borrowing or use up some of its international reserves. At the same time, increases in foreign borrowing will mean increases in DS in future time periods.

Tying the two equations together are typical "country scenarios." For example, a government comes under political pressure to increase spending for domestic social purposes. It does so by running a fiscal deficit, which it finances by issuing government bonds, most of which may end up in the asset portfolio of the central bank, which in turn has paid for them by increasing the money supply (central-bank liabilities). This puts upward pressure on the general price level in the economy, which the government is reluctant to see reflected in a depreciation of its currency— the disequilibrium exchange rate being secured through exchange controls or central-bank intervention on foreign-exchange markets. The whole process is likely to show up as an increase in A offset by an increase in M and/or a decrease in X in the first equation, the financial flows appearing in the second equation as a net reduction in $(VX - VM)$ financed by a reduction in reserve holdings DR (the central bank's external assets) and/or an increase in net borrowing abroad NBR (e.g., the central bank's external liabilities). Many other such scenarios could be sketched out. The problem is to ascertain what each of them may mean for the different variables we have identified as they evolve over time, particularly DS and NBR. This, together with the underlying political scenarios, is the essence of getting a fix on the expected value and variance of an organization's exposure in a particular country. How can this be accomplished?

Effective country-risk assessment ideally requires the employment of a true "renaissance person"—exceedingly intelligent, a holder of doctorates from respectable institutions in economics, political science, sociology, psychology, and perhaps a few other fields as well, totally objective, with a great deal of common sense. In addition to being well traveled, he or she should be up to date on developments in all countries of interest to the bank (and in other countries that might affect them) and personally acquainted with key policy makers. Obviously, there are few such individuals. The question is whether international banks or corporations *as institutions* can in some way put together all of these qualities, using "ordinary" individuals and traditional organizational linkages to assemble a superior ability to forecast the future of countries.

STRUCTURAL ASPECTS.   The question here is whether developments in the internal workings of a national economy, both on the supply and demand sides, will seriously threaten markets, profitability, or the ability to service a country's external obligations. We are interested first in the linkages between the supply-side's ability to produce export, import-competing, and nontraded goods, and in the qualitative and quantitative dimensions of the labor force, the capital stock, the natural resource base, technology, and entrepreneurship that combine to determine this capability. At the same time we are interested in the contributions of real-capital inflows to these supply capabilities made possible by foreign borrowing, foreign direct investment, and other types of financial transfers.

Historical measures of supply-side economic performance abound: labor-force growth and participation rates, unemployment rates, migration and labor-force distributional trends, savings and investment trends, productivity trends, natural resource availability, and the like. The quality, timeliness, and comparability of the relevant data vary widely, but the real problem obviously lies in ascertaining whether the past is likely to be a good guide for the future. Here a great deal of judgment is required in order to identify and project, for example, various types of quantitative or qualitative labor-supply ceilings and possible market disruptions, social and economic infrastructure bottlenecks, capital-adequacy problems, natural resource constraints. Of prime importance is the evaluation of government policies that will influence domestic savings and investment, capital flight and foreign direct investment, risk-taking and entrepreneurial activity, supply conditions in labor markets, the adequacy of economic and social infrastructure, exploitation, and forward processing of natural resources—the entire underlying complex of incentives and disincentives built into the nation's fiscal and regulatory system. In many cases such policies are anchored in government planning documents; an assessment of the degree of realism embodied in these plans may be quite important—government attempts to force the supply side of an economy into a mold that does not fit, but to which a political commitment has been made, can lead to severe domestic and international distortions in the real sector, ballooning of external borrowing, and ultimately, debt-service problems.

On the demand side, we are as interested in factors affecting taxes, government expenditures, transfer payments, and the overall fiscal soundness of the public sector, as we are in prospective patterns of demand for goods and services from the private and export sectors. Once again, historical data series covering consumption spending, government taxation and expenditures, gross national product or gross domestic product, and other conventional economic indicators are usually available on a reasonably timely basis to permit an evaluation of the demand picture over a number of years. But forecasts depend, in large part, on the ability to predict government demand management and income-distribution policies, as well as exogenous demand-side shocks that may emanate from the foreign sector, or other sources, changing expectations.

In attempting to develop a defensible prognosis of the structural aspects of country futures, the analyst must start from a complete information base about the historical track record of the domestic economy and its current situation, and then try to project both the demand-side and supply-side dimensions. This may not be a serious problem in the short term, where the exogenous and policy elements are relatively fixed, but the sources of error multiply as the forecasting period is extended, and few or none of the important determinants of economic performance can be considered constant. What will happen to taxes, transfers, government regulation, the pattern of subsidies and other market distortions, consumption and saving patterns, investment incentives, treatment of foreign-owned firms, and similar factors 5 to 10 years into the future? Everything is up for grabs, and forecasting has to rely in large measure on the basic competence of the policymakers, their receptivity to outside advice, and the pattern of social and political constraints under which they operate. Assuming the cast of characters remains the same, past experience in macroeconomic management and reactions to outside shocks may not be a bad guide to the future, but this assumption itself is often open to question.

MONETARY ASPECTS.   A part of the task of projecting future country scenarios— and some would contend the most important part—lies in the monetary sector. Whereas most country analyses contain extensive descriptions of the national financial system, the critical factors obviously relate to prices and exchange rates. Useful indicators are the domestic monetary base, the money supply, net domestic credit, and available price indexes, together with net foreign official assets and net foreign debt. Monetary disturbances may originate domestically or from the foreign sector (e.g., major increases in external reserves that become monetized). Apart from their inflationary and exchange-rate aspects, of course, such disturbances may also have real-sector influences on consumption and savings, capital formation, income distribution, expectations, and the like.

Once again, whereas the mechanisms relating monetary developments to country-risk problems are well understood, and the requisite data usually more readily available than most others, near-term assessments are far easier than formulating a defensible long-range outlook. It is possible to evaluate the relationship of the existing exchange rate to some hypothetical market-determined rate based on a calculated purchasing-power-parity index, and to project this deviation for the near term based on relative inflation trends. The larger the degree of currency overvaluation, for example, the greater the need for increased external borrowing, as well as the likelihood of reserve losses and/or the prospects for a tightening of controls on international trade and payments. Much more difficult is the task of forecasting government responses to problem situations in the monetary sphere—devaluation, liberalization of controls, domestic monetary stringency, and the like—and particularly the timing of such measures. In the longer term, the problem once again boils down to the competence of the monetary policy makers and the political pressures bearing upon them.

EXTERNAL ECONOMIC ASPECTS.   Because of the importance of foreign-exchange availability in projecting debt service, country assessments usually must pay a great deal of attention to outside factors affecting a country's balance of payments and external finance. On the export side, this requires evaluation of both long-term trends and short-term instabilities. Increasing product and market diversification might be a sign of greater export stability and reduced vulnerability to shifting economic and political conditions, or protectionist trends in a country's major markets. Shifts in the ratio of exports to gross national product may signal changing future balance-of-payments conditions, and an analysis of demand and supply characteristics for major export products may indicate possible sources of future instability in export receipts. Domestic export-supply constraints and export-competing demand elements link back into the analysis of structural problems, outlined above. Export policies set by the national government and by governments of competing exporters may also be important, along with exchange-rate policies. In general, we are interested here in alignment of a country's exports with its international competitive advantage, diversification of export risk, and home and third-country policies that might pose a threat to future export earnings.

On the import side as well, concern must focus on both long-term trends and short-term instabilities. The ratio of imports to gross national product, for example, says little about country risk, but abrupt and sizable shifts in this ratio may be important. The ability to compress imports in times of balance-of-payments trouble may be considered in terms of measures such as the ratio of food and fuel to total imports, or the ratio of food, fuel, intermediate goods, and capital equipment to total imports. Import-price volatility, supplier concentration among trading partners, and trends in import-replacement production are among the other measures that can help identify risk elements originating on the import side. Here, as in the case of exports, we are also interested in the policy context—the structure of effective tariff and nontariff protection and its impact on domestic resource allocation and efficiency in production.

We have already noted the importance of foreign direct investment for the supply side of a national economy in terms of its contribution to aggregate and sectoral capital formation, technology transfer, development of human resources, management and entrepreneurial activity, access to markets, and access to supplies—the traditional multinational corporate "bundle" of services. Besides the balance-of-payments gains associated with capital inflows, induced exports, and import-replacement production, outflows may occur through induced imports of goods and services and profit remittances. Each foreign-investment project evidences a more or less unique balance-of-payments profile, in magnitude as well as in timing.

Policies affecting foreign direct investment (e.g., taxation, restrictions on earnings remittances, indigenization pressures, nationalization, and expropriation) may seriously alter this profile and thereby influence country prospects as viewed by international lenders as well. Multinational companies are often extraordinarily sensitive to changes in national-policy environments, and because they can portend change in the overall creditworthiness of countries as a whole, shifts in foreign-direct-investment patterns deserve careful attention, as do capital outflows on the part of domestic residents; these are frequently highly sensitive to the domestic outlook, especially in times of possible discontinuous policy changes.

Finally, it may be important to analyze the magnitude and types of grants and concessional loans that a country receives from abroad, and prospective future developments in these flows. Here domestic developments in the donor countries, donor-recipient relations, and the economic and political attractiveness of the recipient for such transfers may be important. Moreover, is there a "lender of last resort"? Countries of strategic or economic importance are obviously prime candidates for future intergovernmental "rescues" that may, to some extent, backstop private bank-lending exposure in severe problem situations and increase the interest of major financial powers in successfully concluding resolution of country problems.

LIQUIDITY ASPECTS. The aforementioned issues usually involve medium- and long-range forecasts of such aggregates as the balance of trade, the current account, and various other "flow" measures. These will naturally be reflected in a country's future international reserve position and in its access to international financial markets for future financing needs. Near-term "liquidity" assessments generally focus on such measures as changes in a country's owned reserves and International Monetary Fund (IMF) position and on ratios, such as reserves to monthly imports, intended to indicate in some sense the degree of "cushioning" provided by reserve holdings. Ability to borrow additional sums abroad, or to refinance existing debt, naturally depends on the projected state of financial markets and assessment of country creditworthiness by international banks and official institutions at the time of need. Favorable financial-market and country conditions sometimes lead to "preemptive" borrowing to restructure outstanding debt at market terms and to build up reserves for future use or to improve future creditworthiness.

Analysis of the size and structure of country indebtedness and debt-service payments is equally important in this regard. Ratios such as total debt to exports or to gross national product, and long-term public debt to exports or to gross national product are used in virtually all country analyses, as are the amount and trends in overall external indebtedness, current versus term debt, and total and short-term bank claims. The *debt-service ratio*—debt-service payments to exports or "normal" exports—is perhaps the most common and can be criticized on various grounds. For example, by using only exports in the denominator, it ignores the potentially equivalent contributions of import substitution to debt-service capabilities. A particular debt-service ratio (e.g., .3) may mean entirely different things for different countries as far as creditworthiness is concerned. Additionally, the ratios of foreign-capital inflows to debt-service payments, exports plus capital inflows and aid receipts to current debt, vital imports plus debt-service payments to exports plus capital inflows and aid receipt (*compressibility ratio*), and the reciprocal of the average maturity of external debt (*rollover ratio*) are commonly used.

All such ratios must be interpreted cautiously and have different meanings for different countries and for the same country at different times and stages of development. There are no valid rules of thumb. The skill lies in the interpretation of any ratios used, particularly changes therein, and in the specific context of particular country situations. Yet even if a good analyst recognizes the limitations of some of the more pedestrian indicators, they may nevertheless figure heavily and perhaps mechanically into how the market views the situation in a debt-rollover context and, therefore, may have to be monitored carefully.

POLITICAL ASPECTS. Besides domestic structural and monetary factors and external stock and flow variables, country analysis related to term exposure always requires astute political forecasting. Most closely related to the economic variables just reviewed, of course, is the "competence" or "wisdom" of the economic managers, which, insofar as it relates to the cast of characters on the stage, is basically a political matter. Small changes in the actors can cause enormous changes in the quality of the play. There is also the question whether the technocrats have a full political mandate to "do what is necessary" from a debt-service point of view, and ultimately whether the government itself is firmly enough in the saddle and has the political "guts" to carry it out. Recent "horror stories" ranging from Turkey and Zaire to Jamaica, Peru, and Poland illustrate the critical importance of evaluating and forecasting the political "overlay" of national economic policy making—the degree of resolve, the power base, and the tools available for implementing sound policy decisions. Banks and corporations that are leaders in country analysis generally place a great deal of stress on this particular dimension, which requires an entirely different sort of prognostication and information base than some of the more mechanical aspects of the problem. Beyond this, there are more fundamental political developments that need to be sorted out, monitored, and forecast as well.

Internal political change may range from gradual to abrupt, systemic to nonsystemic, and cataclysmic to trivial in terms of its importance to international firms. For example, political drift to the right or left may mean a great deal in terms of the internal and external workings of the national economy and the quality of economic management, as the recent history of countries like Brazil, Mexico, Chile, and Sri Lanka nicely demonstrates. The symptoms make themselves felt in domestic fiscal and monetary policies, relations with foreign countries, pressures for nationalization or indigenization of foreign direct investments, imposition of exchange controls, and the like. Adverse shifts in this respect may result in soaring imports, reduced capacity to export, drying-up of foreign direct investment, capital flight, aid cutoffs, and problems in accessing international capital markets. The point is that it is necessary to fix on the direction, magnitude, and timing of political drift, if any, before very much that is sensible can be said about future macroeconomic scenarios.

A more dramatic version of the same thing relates to violent internal political conflict, which may ultimately produce the type of political "drift" discussed previously, but in the meantime may have serious direct economic consequences as well. Strikes, terrorism, sabotage, and popular insurrection may seriously disrupt the workings of the national economy, with potentially dramatic consequences for the balance of payments. Export industries like tourism are particularly sensitive to such problems. The direct and indirect import requirements of government anti-insurgency efforts can be significant as well. It is obviously necessary to assess the strength of both the insurgency movement and the government in order to forecast the duration and outcome of the conflict, which, if it results in systemic change, may even lead to repudiation of external debt. As the Iranian case shows, such forecasts are as treacherous as they are critical to the whole process of country analysis. The assassination of South Korean President Park Chung Hee illustrates the extreme range of possible outcomes of a discrete event of political violence, from total insignificance to a fundamental political and economic overthrow of the existing order.

External political conflict can likewise take a variety of forms, ranging from invasion (Afghanistan) and foreign-inspired or foreign-supported insurgency (Zaire, Morocco, Tunisia) to border tension and perceived external threats (Peru, Israel, Thailand). Threats from abroad often require far-reaching domestic-resource reallocation in the form of an inflated defense establishment—causing probable adverse trade shifts—and for most countries involve large direct foreign-exchange costs as well. Military hardware, human resources, and infrastructure in an economic sense generally have low or negative productivity in terms of the domestic economy or the balance of payments. Such distortions alone may have a serious bearing on the risk profile of a country as viewed from abroad.

These problems reside in both *potential* and *actual* external conflict. The latter simply makes the various distortions worse—to the extent that the costs are not absorbed by foreign political allies—to which must be added the supply-side possibilities of physical and human resource destruction and dislocation, obsolescence, and reconstruction costs that are not partly offset by reparations or aid receipts. Even if external political conflict is won, there may be derivative internal political upheavals and possibly sizable costs of occupation. If the conflict is lost, continued internal resistance and reparations obligations may have a debilitating effect on the home economy, quite apart from the possibility of debt repudiation by the successor regime. All such assessments have to be undertaken in probabilistic terms, but they are of far more than casual interest in exporting to, investing in, or lending to countries like South Korea, Taiwan, Thailand, Yugoslavia, Pakistan, and even Malaysia and Singapore.

Shifting political alliances, regional political developments, and bilateral relations over such peripheral issues as human rights and nuclear proliferation can provide additional sources of political conflict. All are heavily influenced by global, regional, and national political events. Heavy lending exposure in Eastern Europe and China (insofar as the banks are not backstopped by their home governments) carry with them risks related to both future political developments and the ability of the borrowers to sever links to Western trade and financial markets at acceptable economic cost to themselves.

Political forecasting is an art that, despite its central role in plotting the creditworthiness future of countries, remains in its infancy. Indexes of political stability developed by political scientists say little that is very reliable about the future or the ultimate implications for traders, investors, or lenders. The more-sophisticated projections and even on-line information systems detailing possible sources of internal and external political conflict, although useful and necessary, usually leave the critical judgments largely up to the user of the information. There are also problems in the completeness and currency of political information, and the inevitable biases embedded in external and in-house information that consensual approaches such as the "Delphi" technique have only begun to attack. It is not surprising, therefore, that political forecasts by banks and others "missed" on dramatic cases like Iran, Egypt, and South Korea, or less-dramatic ones like Zaire and Turkey. It hardly means, however, that significant advances cannot still be made.

DESIGNING A COUNTRY-RISK INSTRUMENT

From a managerial perspective, a key question is how the results of country assessment can be boiled down to *ratings* that can be effectively used in decision making. Clearly, to adequately describe a country's prospects fully would require an extensive and detailed narrative backed up by large quantities of economic data and forecasts. Such extensive and relatively unstructured "country studies" would clearly lack usability in business decision making. Moreover, they would be relatively noncomparable among countries and highly sensitive to differences in competence among country analysts. Some technique, therefore, may have to be found to organize as much country information as possible and boil it down into usable form. This is the task of *country-risk rating* systems.

Exhibit 1 presents an instrument that might be used to construct a country-risk rating. It involves assigning judgmental values to a series of factors, compiling them

EXHIBIT 1   COUNTRY-ANALYSIS INSTRUMENT

ECONOMIC ELEMENTS

Supply Capability and Resiliency

Describe numerically the prospects during the next 7–10 years the following elements of the supply side of the national economy.

	Favorable			Unfavorable	
	1	2	3	4	5

Labor-force quantity
Labor-force quality
Labor-supply bottlenecks
Labor-supply disruptions
Savings rate
Financial intermediation[1]
Investment levels (domestic)
Economic infrastructure[2]
Social infrastructure[3]
Agricultural development
Natural resources
Energy
Foreign direct investment
Productivity
Entrepreneurship
Character of the people
Supply-side summary:
  Real-growth potential
  Emergence of bottlenecks
  Ability to withstand adverse shocks

Demand and Monetary Factors

Describe numerically the prospects during the next 7–10 years for the following elements of the aggregate demand and monetary characteristics of the national economy.

Aggregate-demand factors:	Favorable			Unfavorable	
	1	2	3	4	5

Consumer spending
Investment spending
Government spending
Net foreign demand[4]
Income-redistribution pressure
Government deficit

Monetary factors:	1	2	3	4	5

Money-supply growth

Demand-side summary:	1	2	3	4	5

Unemployment
Inflation rate
Realized GNP growth[5]

EXHIBIT 1 *(Continued)*

Economic policy makers:	1	2	3	4	5

Assessment of competence

External Balance

Describe numerically the prospects during the next 7–10 years for the country's balance of payments.

Trade:	Favorable			Unfavorable	
	1	2	3	4	5
Export growth					
Export diversification[6]					
Import growth					
Import diversification[7]					
Import compressibility[8]					

Financial flows:	1	2	3	4	5
Investment flows (net)					
Foreign-aid receipts					
Capital flight					
Foreign-borrowing ability					

Reserves and debt:	1	2	3	4	5
Size of foreign debt					
Debt service "burden"[9]					
External reserves					
IMF position[10]					

Exchange rate:	1	2	3	4	5
Deviation from market rate[11]					

External-balance summary:	1	2	3	4	5
Balance of trade					
Terms of trade[12]					
Balance of payments					
External reserves					
Foreign debt					

POLITICAL ELEMENTS

Leadership Change

Mark the combination that seems to describe best the country's leadership:

	Democratically elected majority party	Democratically elected majority coalition	Non-democratically elected ruling party/ coalition/faction	No real ruling party/ coalition/faction
Leadership in power for past 4–5 years				
Leadership in power for less than 4–5 yrs.				
Leadership facing fragmented opposition				

EXHIBIT 1 *(Continued)*

Leadership facing
strong, organized
opposition

	Low				High
	1	2	3	4	5

Describe numerically the level
of violence displayed during
demonstrations, riots, or
strikes by both demonstrators
and police (army?) during the
past 2–3 years

Describe numerically the level
of terrorism (both internally
and abroad, by organizations
belonging to the country)

Goal Change

	YES	NO	DON'T KNOW
Fundamental issues are being debated and the leadership is deeply divided over them			

(If the answer is YES, answer the following:)

	YES	NO
Does the content of these debates touch on matters of economic policy?	☐	☐
Although it does not touch on matters of economic policy, the debates themselves strongly influence the leadership's economic policies	☐	☐

(If the answer is NO, answer the following:)

	YES	NO
Although fundamental issues are not being debated, they do exist and are potentially divisive	☐	☐
Strong pressure groups within the country are likely to bring up requests or demands whose implementation requires a drastic change in officially stated systemic goals	☐	☐

Policy Change

	Yes				No
	1	2	3	4	5

The way laws, regulations, rules, and
orders are implemented has changed over
the last 4–5 years

Administrative procedures are currently
being revised and changed

EXHIBIT 1 *(Continued)*

The need for a thorough administrative reform having deep implications on how rules are implemented is felt

Capability

How to you rate the country's . . .

	Favorably			Unfavorably	
	1	2	3	4	5

Efforts to set up and manage an efficient educational system (elementary and high schools, vocational schools, institutes of higher learning)?

Efforts to use its natural resources (land reclamation, extraction of minerals, etc.)?

Efforts to utilize its human capital (providing employment and incentives to specialists, financing research, etc.)?

Efforts to enforce its own laws (prevention and punishment of crime)?

Efforts to avoid and prevent deviance or morally condemnable behavior?

Efforts to cope with environmental problems (pollution, health, etc.)?

Welfare programs?

Other programs for the underprivileged?

Wage and price policy?

Ability to project a good image of the government among its own citizens?

Ability to project a good image abroad?

Ability to convince the public opinion of the worthiness of its own government?

Ability to cope with internal natural emergencies (earthquakes, drought, etc.)?

Ability to cope with social and political emergencies (strikes, terrorism, etc.)?

Ability to respond effectively to explicit military threat from abroad?

Structural Differentiation

Does the political system have specialized structures able to perform the following activities:

	Low specialization			High specialization	
	1	2	3	4	5

    rule making
    rule implementation
    rule adjudication (tribunals)

Does the political system have specialized structures able to convert popular demands and widely felt needs into suitable outputs

EXHIBIT 1 *(Continued)*

(a new law, an administrative reform, etc.) through the following activities:

	1	2	3	4	5

rule making
rule implementation
rule adjudication

Ideological Polarization

Check the existence of the following:

	Low 1	2	3	4	High 5

Opposing groups characterized by widely differing systems of thought
Historically rooted cleavages among groups
Intolerance among groups and unwillingness to compromise
Use of violence justified and encouraged by the opposing groups

Subsystem Autonomy

	Low 1	2	3	4	High 5

Amount of political participation allowed through elections and party/trade-union activism (or whatever group has an official status)

Amount of political participation allowed or tolerated through demonstrations, propaganda, lobbies, professional associations, etc. (informal interest groups)

Level of the activity actually occurring

Internal Political Summary

	Favorable 1	2	3	Unfavorable 4	5

Prospects for domestic political violence

Prospects for "systemic" political change

Prospects for adverse economic effects of emerging political change

Mandate given to economic policy makers

External Political Factors

	Favorable 1	2	3	Unfavorable 4	5

Prospects of border warfare

Geopolitical tension spillovers

Regional political alliances

Economic warfare

EXHIBIT 1 *(Continued)*

COUNTRY-REVIEW SUMMARY

	1	2	3	4	5	Weights*a*	Products
Economy: supply side							
Economy: demand side							
Balance of payments, reserves, debt							
Competence of economic policy makers							
Internal political							
External political							
TOTALS						100	

WEIGHTED COUNTRY RATING

PROJECT-SPECIFIC FACTORS

Aside from the overall country profile you have developed by running through the foregoing analysis, is there anything about the proposed project that might cause you to alter your assessment of risk?

Yes   No

If so, is your assessment of project-specific risk higher or lower than that applying to the country as a whole?

Higher   Lower

By how much (%)?

Why?

Explanatory Notes

[1] Adequacy of existing or prospective financial institutions to channel savings into investment.
[2] For example, rail lines, highways, port facilities, telecommunications, etc.
[3] For example, schools, hospitals.
[4] Exports minus imports.
[5] Outlook for *actual* (as opposed to *potential*) GNP growth.

EXHIBIT 1   *(Continued)*

6   Diversification across export markets and products.
7   Diversification across import sources of supply (trading partners).
8   Imports of "necessities" like food and fuel (which cannot be reduced under adversity) as
    a percentage of total imports.
9   For example, debt-service payments as a percent of exports.
10   Net borrowings from the International Monetary Fund.
11   Is the currency "overvalued" or "undervalued," as projected?
12   Movement of export prices relative to import prices.
*a*Assign weights to factors A through F in this column according to your assessment of the
relative importance of each summary factor. Weights must add up to 100. Then multiply the
value you have assigned to each factor by its weight, and add all of the products for items A
through F. Your total ("weighted country rating") will lie somewhere between 100 (most
favorable) and 500 (least favorable).

into aggregates, and then compiling the aggregates into an overall summary "score."
This involves the assignment of weights, either explicit or implicit, to the various
factors. This process may involve a great deal of subjectivity, and it is not at all
certain that the same weights should be assigned to each country—since the relative
importance of individual factors differs as potential sources of risk from one country
to the next.

What the country-risk-rating approach contributes in usability, it often loses in
capturing highly country specific sources of risk. For example, few country-risk-rating
systems succeeded in forecasting the 1977 Iranian revolution or its consequences for
international business transactions. For this reason, dependence on such "weighted
checklist" or "scoring" systems can be quite hazardous. It is recommended that this
kind of approach be used only as a preliminary "screen" to identify countries that
should be further reviewed in depth with specific reference to the kind of exposure
contemplated.

RISK ASSESSMENT AND INTERNATIONAL
BUSINESS DECISIONS

Given the nature of the country-evaluation problem within the context of decisions
in international lending and investing, and the available techniques, it is useful to
discuss briefly the institutional setting within which this process occurs. Exhibit 2 is
a simplified schematic of a decision system that will vary, to some extent, among
international firms or banks. The solid lines represent reporting relationships, and
the dashed lines represent information flows. Information on cross-border exposure
can be maintained by a monitoring system at the head office. Care must be taken
that exposure is correctly measured in the light of third-country guarantees, insurance, and certain other factors that might be considered to shift the locus of risk.
Exposure data should be updated frequently and made available to responsible
officers along with any country limits decided upon by management.

The degree of decentralization of decision making differs substantially among
international corporations and banks. However, the need to secure competitive advantages through close client contact, quick response times, and adequate decision

EXHIBIT 2   SETTING, MONITORING, AND EVALUATING INTERNATIONAL RISK EXPOSURE

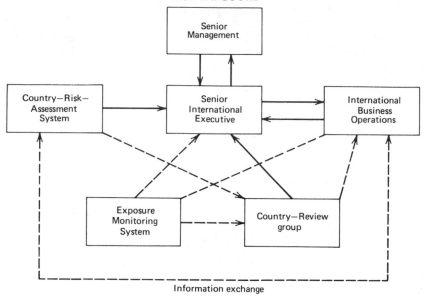

Information exchange

authority often leads to greater decentralization. This puts a premium on the existence of some type of centralized system that assures that objective risk evaluation is in fact undertaken, yet at the same time does not itself unduly restrict the activities of the enterprise in a highly competitive marketplace. In any case, there will normally be a substantial two-way exchange of information between those responsible for the system and line managers insofar as they are not one and the same. In the event that a major project is contemplated, if a shift in existing exposure limits seems justified by profitability trends, or if an alteration in the perceived riskiness of exposure develops, an ad hoc country-review group may be formed, consisting of responsible officers, senior executives with regional responsibility, country economists and other country specialists, and possibly other interested individuals under the chairmanship of the firm's senior international corporate officer or his designee. Such a review group may make a recommendation of appropriate action in the case involved. The purpose is to bring together as many different viewpoints as possible, often with conflicting opinions—for example, between the country economist emphasizing the risks and executives emphasizing business opportunities, competitive positioning and the associated returns. Ultimate responsibility lies with the senior international corporate officer who reports directly to top management and is charged with monitoring and planning the bank's international loan or investment portfolio within broad policy guidelines.

In the design of a country-analysis function, the emphasis clearly must be on the fact that it is the beginning, not the end, of the task. Approaches that try to be overly precise risk triggering arguments among users over irrelevant points. Those that are too general may fail to concentrate on the true sources of risk in country exposure and on the specific concerns facing a particular bank or corporation. Risk to medium- and long-term loan or investment exposure requires a far more complex analysis than risk to short-term lending or to exporting. The twin temptations of "quick and dirty" and "overloaded" country assessments often seem to confront international enterprises. The first approach promises mechanical shortcuts and the use of low-priced talent to grind out results at reasonable cost, but often appears to succeed only in producing nonsense—there really is no substitute for high-quality analysis, flexibility, judgment, and familiarity. The second approach may rely on well-qualified internal personnel at high cost, yet encounter a dangerous narrowing of country expertise, possibly cause dissension, and create bottlenecks in the decision-making process.

The conflicting demands of country assessment—ranging from high levels of usability, auditability, and comparability and the need to capture exceedingly complex and country-specific qualitative judgments over extended periods of time, to the need to avoid abuse of the results in decision making—probably mean that there is no such thing as an "ideal" system. "Appropriate" systems will certainly differ for different banks or corporations. The key may reside as much on the *human resources* side as on the *technology* side. To train line bankers or corporate executives in using reasonably unsophisticated yet sensible country assessments properly and in being sensitive to changing country-risk profiles as they go about their business may in the end contribute more to sound decisions than comparable resources devoted to the design and implementation of more-elegant systems. This would appear to follow from the view of multinational corporations' and banks' general competitive advantage as "information factories" to which their global operations and headquarters-affiliate links are ideally suited. The exercise of country assessment should be an integrated managerial process that focuses the network of information and actively involves individuals with different functions and perspectives. The exercise will thus have intangible benefits all its own, quite apart from its more visible output in the form of defensible country-by-country evaluations. Mechanization and decentralization of the country review process will tend to cut down and perhaps eliminate this benefit and may thereby help to stifle an environment conducive to sound international business decisions.

SOURCES AND SUGGESTED REFERENCES

Duff, D. and I. Peacock. "A Cash Flow Approach to Sovereign Risk Analysis," *The Banker,* Vol. XXI (1979), pp. 34–39.

Gladwin, T.N. and I. Walter. *Multinationals Under Fire: Lessons in the Management of Conflict,* New York: John Wiley & Sons, 1980.

Goodman, S.H. (ed.). *Financing and Risk in Developing Countries.* New York: Praeger, 1978.

Goodman, S.H. "How the Big Banks Really Evaluate Sovereign Risks," *Euromoney,* Vol. VIII (1977), pp. 41–46.

Haner, F.T. "Rating Investment Risks Abroad," *Business Horizons,* Vol. III (1979), pp. 34–42.

Heffernan, Shelagh A. *Sovereign Risk Analysis.* Winchester, MA: George Allen & Unwin, 1986.

Hofer, C.W. and T.P. Haller. "Globescan: A Way to Better International Risk Assessment," *Journal of Business Strategy,* Vol. II (1980), pp. 68–75.

Kobrin, S.J. "Political Risk: A Review and Reconsideration," *Journal of International Business Studies,* Vol. XI (1979), pp. 44–61.

Nagy, P. *Country Risk: How to Assess, Quantify and Monitor It.* London: Euromoney Publications, 1978.

Nagy, P. "Quantifying Country Risk: A System Developed by Economists at the Bank of Montreal," *Columbia Journal of World Business,* Vol. XIII (1979), pp. 44–60.

Puz, R. "How to Tell When a Country Shifts from A-1 to E-5," *Euromoney,* Vol. IX (1978), pp. 123–37.

van Agtmael, A. "Evaluating the Risks of Lending to Developing Countries," *Euromoney,* Vol. VII (1976), pp. 88–96.

POLITICAL RISK EVALUATION

CONTENTS

POLITICAL RISK EVALUATION

Stephen J. Kobrin

In any business, setting objectives, strategic planning, and managing day-to-day operations requires assessment of the external environment: economic conditions, demographic trends, technological progress, competitive strategies, cultural mores, changes in government, and regulatory action. Assessment entails *both* analysis of the present and prediction of the future.

The need to deal with external factors poses a series of "risks" for the firm. Improper understanding of current conditions can result in the failure to exploit potentially profitable markets. The failure to predict, or simply to understand, change can lead to the erosion of competitive position, legal problems, or regulatory pressure. Both inaccurate analyses and unanticipated changes can result in the unexpected—in variation or risk.

Risks emanating from the external environment are political if they relate to the exercise of power or authority in society. That includes: (1) the determination of the degree of state control of the economic system; (2) the formulation of laws and regulations; (3) the competition of various societal groups for influence over resources; (4) the struggle for authority—democratic or otherwise; (5) the expression of opposition—peaceful or violent; and (6) the various forms of international interaction including diplomacy, multilateral agreements, and war.

To the extent a firm's asset base, strategy, or operations are potentially effected by these sorts of events, it faces political risks. While they often take the form of actions of government—as the ultimate authority—they may reflect pressures from other groups in society or conflict between them. They may also result from the struggle among societal groups for power and authority, or even its absence. A tariff, for example, may be imposed by government against its will because of pressures from threatened industries. International firms have been caught, in a variety of ways, in the struggle by blacks for power in South Africa; the virtual absence of authority in Lebanon has destroyed the market and business environment in that country.

Political risks can result in the loss of assets, force undesirable changes in strategy or organization, compromise the firm's ability to market or service its products, and limit access to revenues and profits. Political risks can affect a wide range of business transactions including manufacture, export, construction contracts, services such as accounting and consulting, and finance such as bank lending to private or public debtors. This chapter will not deal with the political or country risks associated with financial transactions (see Chapter 7 by Ingo Walter), but with those associated with tangible operations such as manufacture, export, or construction by international companies. The focus will be on risks to the assets, strategy, and operations of industrial firms.

STRATEGY AND POLITICAL RISK

As firms become international, they enter new countries and find that foreign operations account for a greater proportion of assets, employees, and sales. Internationalization also has strategic implications. As foreign operations grow in importance, most firms find that they must change the way they look at the world; they come to see themselves as global actors in a world-market.

Some industries are characterized by a competitive environment that requires global integration whether it be standardization of products, coordination of manufacturing, centralization of purchasing, or unification of research and development. Operations in individual countries are not independent of each other, but fit into a coherent system-wide whole.

In other industries, firms compete on a market-by-market basis. They see themselves as global firms, but the pressures to respond to national differences—social, cultural, or political—are so great that integration is limited and they see their world as a series of relatively independent national markets.

While the pressure to integrate varies substantially across industries, most international firms have to exploit at least some of the benefits of multinationality to survive. The barriers to strategic integration and coordination of operations, however, are legion. The world of the international firm is comprised of a very large number of independent and sovereign states with their own ideas about how an economy should be organized, their own objectives and interests, and their own strategies, including the appropriate role of international firms. While integration may make sense to the firm, it may run counter to any given state's objectives. The argument that rationalization of manufacturing will reduce costs may ring hollow in a country that will bear the burden of reduced employment.

Thus international firms face pressures to integrate strategy and operations, and countervailing pressures to fragment—to respond differently in each country. Setting objectives, developing strategy, and managing operations requires *simultaneous* evaluation of technical, economic, and business factors and the external environment. The assessment of external environments is an essential part of strategic planning, not simply a step in the evaluation of "political risk."

The other side of that coin is that political risks can not be determined independently of strategy. A country's requirement for local production may be catastrophic to an integrated automobile producer or computer manufacturer, but may not even affect a manufacturer of processed foods that uses only local materials in a simple production process. The same political event or act may affect only in-country operations of some foreign firms, but may reverberate throughout the world-wide structures of those that are more tightly integrated. Disorder that interrupts operations may affect not just one plant, but others dependent on it for components or finished products. Thus the impact of events will vary considerably depending on the degree of integration and on the firm's strategy.

In summary, it is impossible to consider political risk without taking strategy into account. In some cases, what we call political risks may be a government reacting to the firm's (worldwide) strategy. In others, the impact of events on a firm may vary from trivial to critical, depending on strategy. While there are certainly exceptions where events affect every foreign firm in a country—such as the socialist revolution in Cuba or the civil war and anarchy in Lebanon—political risks result from the interaction of a particular firm and its environment. Firms with different asset bases, organizations, and strategies may face very different risks at the same time and place.

IMPACT ON THE FIRM.   As noted, some political events may affect all firms in a country. Classic examples are nationalizations that are designed to transform a market into a socialist economy, such as those in Cuba (1960), Algeria (1967–72), Angola (1975), or Chile (1971–73). A civil war or even widespread strife may threaten assets, personnel, or disrupt or destroy distribution channels or markets.

Yet even in these circumstances, there are significant differences in *impacts* on firms. While there is obviously a loss of potential business, the effect of the expropriation of a bank depends on its balance of assets and liabilities. The significance of a given market varies by industry; in some firms, losses are confined to the country at issue, while in others they affect worldwide operations.

Social revolution, however, is not the typical political event of interest to business firms. Most do not affect all foreign investors, but only specific industries, firms, or even projects. Furthermore, the asset base, strategy, and nature of operations of a firm all determine the likelihood that external events will affect a project, the form those impacts will take, and their potential cost. Vulnerability to political risk depends on a project's strategy and structure.

A construction firm, for example, operating in a country for a fixed and relatively short period of time to complete a specific project faces a limited number of risks. It is concerned primarily with repudiation, nonpayment, unfair calling of guarantees, events that increase costs or prevent timely completion, and threats to the safety of personnel.

Similarly, an "export platform"—that is, a company producing a very labor intensive product for export in low labor cost countries—faces few potential risks. These operations require minimal capital investment, are typically quite mobile, and may not be the sole source of supply for the firm. Political risks are limited to the immediate effects of disruption of operations, the value of the inventory on hand, and perhaps most important, barriers to import into target markets.

An oil firm operating under a production contract faces a broader range of risks, but can still define political risk succinctly: ". . . the likelihood that the company will not be able to develop and dispose of reserves on the terms stipulated in the initial project proposal." Events of concern include, stringent tax terms, additional operating controls, restrictions on production or export, and changes in accounting rules.[1]

Manufacturing firms may face the greatest variety of potential risks. They generally enter a country because of long-term business opportunities and many develop sizeable asset bases over time. A very wide range of events, regulations, policy changes, and other requirements can result in undesired changes in strategy, organization, or operations, and constrain achievement of objectives at either the local or worldwide level.

It should be clear from this discussion that political risks occur *within* the firm as a result of external events. The events themselves are of interest *only* if they produce an impact on one or more projects. Political risks result from the interaction of politics in the outside world with the particular configuration of assets, objectives, strategies, and operations that characterize a given company. The probability of events affecting a firm, the way in which they do, and their potential cost, all depend on the firm's strategy and the nature of its operations. It makes little sense to talk about political risk in a country unless you have a specific project in mind.

SOURCES OF POLITICAL RISK.   When we talk about sources of political risk we are describing a range of events that could potentially affect business firms. Under some conditions, they may not have a significant business impact; under others, they may affect only some industries and firms. The effects may be positive as well as negative, and their costs (or benefits) will vary substantially. The discussion that follows is *not* intended to be comprehensive, nor is it an attempt to develop a scheme to classify political risks. Rather, it is intended to illustrate the range and types of events that can produce costly effects: that is, compromise assets, strategy, or operations. Sources of political risks can be found at the global or regional level, they result from interstate relations, and they are produced by home and host country policies.

The Global or Regional Level.   Some sources of political risk are pervasive resulting from widespread trends or events. The energy "crunch" of the 1970s was worldwide affecting firms in virtually every country. (The shortage, however, did not affect all firms equally, nor did it affect all negatively. Those in the oil industry, and others producing goods or services that helped conserve energy, did quite well.)

Regional trends and conflicts are sources of political risks. An excellent example is the Arab-Israeli dispute which has had a variety of repercussions for business firms. Some have been caught directly in the web of violence—facilities destroyed during military attacks, offices outside of the mid-East bombed by terrorist groups, travel compromised because of concerns over air piracy, and the like. Other companies, probably a much larger number, have been caught in the political disputes that emanate from the conflict. The attempt by the Arab states to boycott Israel commercially and then extend it to a secondary and tertiary boycott of firms in third countries dealing with Israel, caused many companies to make hard choices and, in the U.S. case, to risk running afoul of American anti-boycott legislation.

Interstate Relations.   Political risks can also result from interstate relations. War is the most obvious, if not the most important, example. Firms operating in Argentina during the Falklands conflict were affected in a number of ways. Virtually every business firm in Hong Kong is affected by the agreement between Great Britain and China to return that colony to the latter's sovereignty.

Perhaps the most important interstate source of political risks results from home countries attempting to apply or extend their policies extraterritorially to international firms. The U.S. provides some excellent examples.

A number of American firms found that sales by subsidiaries abroad to countries proscribed under the *Trading with the Enemy Act* were considered illegal by their government, even though the subsidiary's host country found the transactions legal or even desirable. The cases have resulted in difficult situations in countries such as Canada and France,[2] where application of the Trading with the Enemy Act was considered as U.S. interference in domestic affairs, and the companies involved were caught between two conflicting sets of orders from home and host country governments. Similarly, the American government's attempt to enforce a boycott of the Soviet gas pipeline to Western Europe in 1982, by prohibiting the sale of products produced by American firms or technology under license from American firms, caused widespread difficulties.

The United States certainly is not the only government to attempt to extend its reach extraterritorially through the web of its multinational firms. Home country governments have attempted to restrict flows of investment abroad, prevent transfers of technology deemed to threaten military or economic security, enforce economic boycotts of political opponents (i.e., South Africa, Rhodesia, and Cuba), and in general apply political and economic policies to international business transactions.

Host Countries. Firms tend to be most concerned about political risks in host countries and most political risk analyses are motivated by new investment opportunities or significant changes in current operating environments. Some political risks affect virtually every firm (or every foreign firm) operating in a country. Classic examples of these *macrorisks* are the revolutionary transformation of a social and economic system, such as in Cuba in 1960; devastating civil war, as in Lebanon; and long term instability resulting in sharp shifts in policy, as in Argentina.

While macrorisks are often dramatic and newsworthy, their actual incidence is limited. A study of expropriation in 79 less developed countries found that in most countries, expropriation affected only a small percentage of foreign investors; less than fifteen countries were classified as "mass expropriators" who nationalized all or even most of their foreign firms. In the vast majority of countries, expropriations involved only a minority of foreign investors and were targeted at specific industries.[3] For example, when many of the oil producing countries nationalized that industry in the 1970s, other sectors were not affected.

Furthermore, nationalization is no longer the best example of political risk, as its incidence has declined dramatically since 1976.[4] While there are entirely too many examples of civil war and civil strife in countries where international firms operate, they too are the exception rather than the rule. Most political risks are less dramatic and much more specific. They are *microrisks*, resulting from policies affecting only certain industries or firms whose impact and cost varies significantly given different strategies.

Most of the "risks" faced by firms result from the normal—if not always ordinary—processes of government. They result from adverse policies or regulations (an increase in the minimum wage or taxes), performance controls designed to promote internal development or macroeconomic objectives (local production or ownership requirements), attempts to resolve balance of payments difficulties (export requirements), competition among domestic interest groups (requirements for increased labor participation in management or barriers to import), and the like.

Most political risks result from conflicts between the strategy and objectives of the firm and of the host country. A multinational, for example, may review its manufacturing operations in Europe and realize that competitive pressures require nationalization; the closing of older inefficient plants, expansion of others, and the integration of production regionally. Governments in countries where plants are to be closed may well object, especially if unemployment is high and the manufacturing base is deteriorating. The result is likely to be conflict and political risks, taking the form of forced deviations from strategy or even retaliation against the company and its products.

Similarly, in developing countries, development policies may call for local production when it is inefficient from the firm's point of view, or export requirements may conflict with a company's global strategy. It is reasonable to think of political risks as a government's response to a firm's strategy—of its attempt to achieve its objectives by exerting control over a company's structure, strategy, or operations.

POLITICAL RISK AS A BARGAINING PROCESS. A good deal of experience has shown that vulnerability to *micro* political risks is often determined by the relative bargaining power of the firm and the host government. If a company has technology the country needs or can generate exports, it may be less vulnerable to constraints. A computer firm, for example, that can bring otherwise unavailable technology and generate exports may be able to sustain 100 percent ownership of a subsidiary when other foreign investors are forced to accept joint ventures.[5]

Whether constraints result from lengthy negotiations or are imposed as a result of action by the administration or legislature, they typically reflect at least an implicit bargaining process. They reflect the relative bargaining power of the firm and the host country.

A firm's sources of leverage flow from its technology, managerial skills, exports or access to world markets, and ability to mobilize capital. A country's bargaining power is based on its natural resources, the availability of cheap and productive labor, the attractiveness of its market, its geographic location, and its political environment. Relative bargaining power is also affected by the competitiveness of the industry, the competition among other countries for foreign investment, and the degree of global integration in the industry.

One would expect that a firm that (1) can supply needed technology that is difficult to find elsewhere, (2) that faces little competition in its industry, and (3) that can promise access to world markets would be much less vulnerable to political risks than one in a mature industry characterized by intense competition that produces only for the local market. An industry that is truly global—where it is difficult to compete based on operations in a single national market—limits the range of constraints available to a host country. If an industry is globally integrated, a local subsidiary is not an independent entity; its value is dependent on its role as a unit in the company's worldwide operations. That fact alone may significantly constrain the host country's bargaining power.

With the exception of infrequent, if dramatic, events such as the Iranian revolution, it is critically important to differentiate between sources of political risk and impacts on the firm. Whether environmental events affect a firm and the costs of any impacts that do occur are dependent on a particular company's configuration and strategy. Vulnerability to political risk must be determined at the project level.

USES OF POLITICAL RISK ANALYSIS

Political risk analyses typically are undertaken in response to a specific corporate need: (1) The firm may face a decision about an investment in a country and require an analysis of political risks; (2) The planning cycle may require country assumptions or a brief analysis of the business environment; or (3) Significant changes in important countries may well prompt an urgent request from management asking "what does that mean for us?"

Too frequently, political analyses are reactive and not well integrated into the managerial process. They do not consider their ultimate use or usefulness.

INVESTMENT DECISIONS.   Any significant investment decision requires analysis of the business environment. While in extreme cases there may be concern over the safety of assets or personnel, in most instances firms are interested in the impact of the political process on opportunities, costs, and the variability of cash flows or risks.

If the analysis is to be of use in investment decision making, it must deal with questions—in terms of both form and substance—that are asked in the capital budgeting process. While it is not reasonable to expect a rigorously quantified analysis at this point, it is reasonable to expect that political risk analyses deal with relatively specific impacts on cash flows, allow at least some rough estimate of probabilities, and provide information on a year-by-year basis.

STRATEGIC PLANNING.   Political risk analysis too often plays a role in the strategic planning process and not in the determination of strategies. While any plan must be based on a reasonable assessment of the business environment in the country of concern, environmental assumptions are just the beginning. Strategy and political risks must be determined simultaneously. First, the political environment may place limits on strategic options. Second, and just as important, it is impossible to analyze or forecast political risk in the abstract. With the exception of the *macrorisks* discussed above, political risks generally arise in *response* to a specific strategy.

Furthermore, as many industries become increasingly integrated globally, it is dysfunctional to consider political risks on an independent country-by-country basis. Constraints imposed on a project in a single country may well affect operations in a number of others. In fact, the actual risks may be much greater up or down stream— due to the effects of an interruption of supply—than in the country in question.

OPERATIONS.   Existing operations are a neglected area in political risk analysis. Few firms maintain ongoing analyses of countries to help managers with the multitude of choices that operations entail. Yet many of these are affected by the political environment, and one can certainly envision choices of alternatives that could be influenced by political factors. While continuous political analyses may not be either practical or desirable, efforts can be made to sensitize operating managers to the political environment and its impact on the firm.

TRAVEL.   Political analyses are often requested as background for trips abroad by top corporate management. These provide general country background, an assessment of the current situation, and perhaps background on the people that the manager is likely to meet.

EVALUATING POLITICAL RISK

Evaluating political risks entails: scanning the environment (i.e., gathering information); analyzing that information to develop estimates of potential impacts on the firm; and communicating those estimates to the final user effectively.

SCANNING.   Politics is a complex process of human interaction and how you view it often depends on where you sit. It is rare, if not impossible, for any single individual or group to have an unbiased overview of the environment. In general, there are no objective observers—only multiple views of the process from the perspective of individual participants. Elected officials, members of the opposition, labor unions, student groups, local business people, the military, foreign investors, and diplomats are all likely to have slightly—or not so slightly—different views of what is going on.

That has a number of important implications for environmental scanning. First, analysts need to talk with individuals representing as many different points of view as possible. Even highly placed government officials are likely to have biased and partial views of the situation, often overestimating their own power and assuming that their view of reality *is* reality.

Second, there is absolutely no point in "averaging the answers." If individual responses and opinions represent different views, forcing a single estimate or scenario out of the data will result in a significant loss of valuable information. What is important is to retain and explain the diversity, determine how various groups see the situation, and understand the reasons for their differences.

Managers are interested in the potential *impact* of the external environment on the firm: on assets, strategy, and operations. Information about the environment itself is no more than raw data in most instances. Scanning entails a great deal more than gathering information, which quickly can become overwhelming and confusing. Effective scanning requires information that will be useful in estimating political risks; impacts that result from the interaction of the firm and the external environment. Thus, effective scanning entails posing relevant questions to information sources— questions whose answers allow the analyst (or the manager) to make judgments about political risk to the *project* in question. This is discussed in detail later.

INFORMATION SOURCES.   Generally, information is obtained from either human sources or various forms of secondary data. Evidence indicates that managers prefer the former—information coming from someone who has direct experience or other expertise pertaining to the problem at hand.

Human Sources.   Most managers consider their primary source of information about political environments, particularly in host countries, to be colleagues within their firm: country managers, regional executives, and others with international responsibilities or experience. First and foremost is the *subsidiary manager*—the person responsible for a given country. The advantages of country managers are considerable. They are immersed in the local environment—often they are host country nationals—who are, or should be familiar with what is going on. They have access to people and information that is not available elsewhere, and are familiar with the firm, its organization, and strategy.

It is this dual role that makes subsidiary managers so valuable as sources of information about potential political risks. They are the *only* individuals who are part of both the host country environment and the firm, thus uniquely qualified to gauge potential impacts of the former on the latter.

Yet, subsidiary managers also bring limitations to political risk analysis: (1) Their primary role is not political analyst, but manager. Their evaluations of the environment cannot help but be influenced by their objectives; it is unreasonable to expect that someone who has just recommended a large new investment in his or her country will present an unbiased evaluation of the political risks associated with it. (2) The range of contacts of most country managers is often limited, whether they are local nationals or not. Even if they push beyond the normal circle of the expatriate community to local business people, or even government officials, it is rare for them to have a broad range of contacts within society. Interaction with labor leaders, students, and the political opposition is difficult, and in some cases may be illegal or dangerous. (3) Most country managers are not trained political analysts. While it is not necessary that they be political scientists to do the job, they do need some understanding of what to look for and how to find it.

One important internal source that is often ignored is other employees of the subsidiary. Staff managers or junior managerial employees may have a much broader range of contacts—and a very different view of local conditions—than top management. Yet, attempts to use that knowledge systematically are rare.

A second major internal source of information is *staff groups,* at all levels, who are assigned responsibilities for political risk analysis. These include formal political risk "units," others, such as strategic planners or treasury people, who have at least part time responsibilities in this area, economics staffs, and government or external affairs groups.

A number of *external* sources of information bear on political risks:

Banks. Most international firms consider banks to be an important information source. The large international banks may have considerable overseas experience and a presence in a large number of countries. They interact with a wide range of businesses and may have formal risk assessment systems in place. Sources of bias include banks' interests in host countries (concern about offending important clients or a need to be as positive as possible about major debtors) and a natural interest in building business with the firm as a customer.

Consultants. There are a large number of individuals and firms offering political risk consulting services. These include many established business consulting firms, some of the larger enterprises dealing in business information in general, specialized political risk consulting firms, and many individuals who have either a general background in international affairs, or regional or country expertise. As with any consultant, it is important to firmly establish credibility and expertise. It is also critically important to insure that the firm is buying estimates of political risks— potential impacts on the project in question—and not general country information that could be obtained more economically from any number of secondary sources. Groups such as APRA (The Association of Political Risk Analysts) can be useful sources of information about consultants.

Academics. Academics, who specialize in a region or country, can be valuable sources of information about potential political risks. There are two major problems in dealing with academics. The first is, simply, finding them and evaluating their capabilities. That requires access to the "network" or invisible college that forms in most specialties. The second is that academics are country experts who rarely know much about a business or its sources of vulnerability to political risk. Using academics effectively requires that considerable attention be paid to posing the right questions, a topic discussed in the section on analysis.

Government personnel. There are numerous people in government that have potentially valuable information about countries, regions, issues, and trends. These include people in the State Department, the intelligence community, Commerce, Treasury, and other agencies such as AID, OPIC (the Overseas Private Investment Corporation), the Export-Import Bank, and Agriculture. Others may be found in embassies and other agencies abroad. Another source, exploited by many international companies, is other governments that may have considerable expertise in certain areas of the world (e.g., the United Kingdom in its excolonies or France in central Africa) which can be accessed through subsidiaries in the relevant country.

The problems in using government people effectively are similar to those for academics. Competent and interested people are not always easy to find and official designations—such as "The Brazilian Desk"—are not always of much help. Government people tend to be area or issue experts, not political risk analysts. As with academics, tapping this potentially valuable information source requires access to the "network" and asking the right questions.

Other businesses.   A variety of external organizations can provide useful information, if exploited systematically, including: customers, suppliers, law and accounting firms, and businesses in other industries with experience in relevant areas. As information about political environments is rarely sensitive competitively and exchanges are usually a "two way street," firms usually are not reluctant to share their experience and knowledge.

Business organizations.   There are a variety of business organizations, both in the United States and in host countries, that can be of great help to the political risk analyst. Examples include both the American Chambers of Commerce abroad and local national industry groups. (In some countries, industry groups may bear a more "official" relationship to the government than is the norm in the United States.

Journalists.   Journalists, particularly those stationed abroad, can be an interesting source of information who may have a very different point of view than others normally contacted by businesses. They may also be able to provide suggestions of others in host countries who could supply valuable information.

In-country sources.   Developing a range of in-country sources representing divergent groups and points of view and who are willing to talk with foreign firms is difficult, but potentially rewarding. It requires both a concerted effort on the part of subsidiary management and some understanding of the task at hand.[6]

Other Sources

Political risk services.   There are a number of political risk rating services generally made available on a subscription basis. They are published at regular intervals and each use their own method to rate and/or rank countries. While these evaluations should certainly not be used as a sole basis for important decisions, they can be of value in allowing companies to follow a large number of countries regularly. Even the largest firms cannot devote the resources necessary to continually scan 70 or 80 countries, nor would it make sense to do so. The services can serve as "flags," alerting the reader that there may be changes or developments in a country that require further attention. Used properly, they can also provide one more outside source of information to compare against internal estimates to guard against bias and insularity.

While the reporting services are relatively inexpensive to purchase, they can be tremendously expensive if the information they provide is used improperly. Most provide quantitative "country scores" that readers may take to imply unwarranted accuracy. Managers should ask some hard questions before using any political risk reporting service:

1.   Where does the information come from? What are the ultimate sources of country data? Is information collected systematically? Are there multiple "experts"? Who are the "experts"? What are their sources of expertise?

2. What sorts of questions are asked of the experts? Does some underlying model or rough "theory" guide information gathering? Are there any explicit ideas about how political systems work and how they affect business firms?

3. Is any attempt made to insure that all the experts are really responding to the same question and that their answers are comparable? That is, can you be sure that one expert's ranking of 3 is really lower than another's 4?

4. How is the information aggregated and quantified? Is there really a sound basis for converting a great deal of country information into a precise score or rank? If someone else did the scoring, is there reason to believe that the numbers would look the same?

One major problem with the services remains: they provide general or aggregated information and find it difficult to differentiate between the impacts on different sorts of firms. The country score or rank may look very different if it is done for a bank, an oil firm, or an automobile manufacturer. At the least, the weighting scheme used to develop an aggregated score should be available so that users can modify it to reflect their own vulnerabilities and interests.

Again, political risk services can provide valuable sources of information at a reasonable price. They do have to be "taken with caution."

Country reports. Many political risk consultants, as well as others, offer in-depth reports on specific countries on a regular or occasional basis. These reports can provide very valuable sources of information oriented toward the business user, but all of the cautions noted above regarding the political risk services apply.

Government publications. There are numerous US government publications offered by federal agencies and departments such as State, Commerce, Treasury, and the CIA that are of use to the political risk analyst.

Other published sources. Any library contains a wealth of extremely useful regional and country information. While the quality certainly varies, there is a good deal available that should be used, at least on a preliminary basis. One gets the impression that, in some instances, firms pay outside consultants for information that may be readily available in many libraries.

Host country publications. One potentially valuable source of information that is widely ignored is host country newspapers and magazines. Reading several local newspapers that encompass a diversity of opinion should be required for anyone doing business in a country. In most countries, there are a variety of general news magazines and business publications that are also of value.

The media. Last, while the quality of international reporting varies in the U.S. general and business press—and it may well vary by area in the same publication—the major newspapers, business publications, and specialized trade publications all carry potentially relevant information. Country clippings files that are well maintained can be a valuable source for a review of recent events or a quick update.

ANALYSIS. The focus of political risk analysis is the project, not the political environment. It is concerned with evaluating *impacts* on assets, strategy, and operations, not with political analysis per se. To be clear, accurate political analysis is an absolute requisite for the effective analysis of political risks. However, it is far from sufficient; political analysis in itself is no more than data or information. The concern of the analyst is *what can happen to the business.*

Project Vulnerability.   Political risks result from the interaction of a firm—or project—and its environment. That has two important implications for analysis: (1) it is impossible to forecast political risks without knowing a good deal about the business; such as its strategy, technology, organization, managerial culture, asset base; and (2) what can happen to a project—its vulnerability—may well be limited by the characteristics of that project.

A thorough understanding of the political environment is not enough to evaluate political risks. The analyst also needs good grounding in all aspects of the business and its technology. He or she needs to be able to relate one to the other—to understand how a given political environment can affect a given project.

In some instances, the project rather than the environment may be the critical limiting factor. That is, only certain aspects of the project may be vulnerable, regardless of what happens in the host country. For example, a construction firm engaged for a limited period (e.g., say two years), on a project judged vital by every domestic interest group (perhaps a critical bridge), that is backed by external guarantees (AID) faces only limited risks. It is concerned with short term factors that could delay timely completion or increase costs. It faces little asset exposure (equipment), and changes in government that are not physically disruptive are unlikely to affect its work.

On the other hand, an automobile manufacturer spending hundreds of millions of dollars to build a plant as a long term investment is subject to a wide range of risks—potential loss of assets, constraints on implementation of strategy, or limits on operations. There is little that could take place in the host country over a very long period that would not be of interest.

In many instances, the most efficient place to begin political risk analysis is the project, not the environment. Asking "what could happen to us that would cause a significant problem—where are we vulnerable?" may limit the scope of necessary political analysis. While every firm needs a broad understanding of each country in which they operate, they do not need in-depth analyses of all aspects of the environment. That part of the environment which is relevant may be illuminated by project evaluation. It may be a good deal more efficient to go out and get information about relevant aspects of the environment than to try to get everything available about a country and then decide what is significant. More important, if you start by asking what can happen to a project, you are much more likely to end up answering that question than if you begin with extensive general political analysis.

Asking the Right Questions.   That leads to a question raised above, but deferred: What do you ask of the sources that you have carefully identified? Most, whether they are academics, government people, local officials, or labor leaders are of interest because they are country experts. If you ask them about the country, you are likely to get back volumes of interesting information that may be of limited use. On the other hand, few of them have the knowledge of your business needed to assess potential impacts and it is generally not very efficient to try to impart that knowledge to a large number of outside sources.

The analyst is presented with a dilemma: few individuals have both the extensive country knowledge and understanding of the business needed to do political risk analysis. The solution requires very careful attention to the questions asked of the "experts." The political risk analyst *must* begin with a solid understanding where a project is vulnerable and what sorts of political events, at least in a general sense, are likely to affect the firm. He or she can then solicit information about relevant aspects of the political environment in a way that will allow estimates of potential impacts.

In a very real sense, the job of the political risk analyst is to act as a *translator,* to know enough about both the business and the external environment to integrate information provided by outside experts with that generated internally. That requires very careful formulation of the questions asked as part of a systematic effort to evaluate political risk.

SYSTEMATIC ANALYSIS.   All firms operating abroad do some sort of political risk analysis. It is often very informal and implicit, reflected in statements such as, "you can't do business in Zork." Managers' interest in countries is affected by their impressions, what they hear from their colleagues, and what they read in the papers and hear on television. The danger of this sort of "informal" analysis is that subjective impressions may simply be wrong and, perhaps more important, what you hear about a country may have little to do with risks to your business.

While it is important that political risk analysis be explicit and formal, that does not mean complex or highly quantitative. It does mean that political risk analysis should be structured and systematic; it should be based on some "model" or idea of how politics works and how and why political events affect a firm, and it should be *explicit* in the sense that the procedure the analyst uses to arrive at his or her results is clear to all.

That does not require complex or elegant analysis. Careful consideration of where a project is vulnerable, what host government actions are likely to affect it, and why those actions are likely to occur, resulting in a *checklist* of critical questions to be asked, would go a long way toward formal and explicit analysis. What is important is that all involved understand what the assumptions are and exactly how the final conclusion was reached.

This sort of structured and systematic analysis provides two critical advantages. First, it allows companies to compare countries—to look at risks in a number of very different environments. Second, it allows comparison and integration of information from a variety of sources. It makes sure everyone starts from the same place and is asking the same kinds of questions. It also makes it much easier to answer the critical question, "what is likely to happen to the business."[7]

Quantitative versus Qualitative Analysis.   Quantitative analysis offers a number of advantages: it allows the analyst to handle large amounts of data and complex relationships; it results in a precise answer to a question (or at least the appearance of precision); it facilitates comparison between alternatives since the evaluations take the form or numbers or scores; and in a business context, it presents results in a "language" familiar to many managers, the language of capital budgeting and strategic planning.

The very strength of quantitative analysis—its precision—is the source of its major problem. The apparent neatness and preciseness of the solution can obscure the impreciseness of the data and assumptions about process. Formal mathematical analysis has limited value for political risk analysis. The problem is not so much the data, but rather that we simply do not know enough about either the political proess, or more important, how politics affects the firm, to formally specify and quantify relationships.

That does not mean that quantitative techniques have no place in political risk analysis. As noted above, our ability to evaluate and compare large amounts of qualitative data is very limited. How many two-page country reports can top management really keep straight at any given time? Numbers are important aids to both comparison and communication.

It does mean that formal modeling will be of limited use, and that the analyst has to be very careful to be explicit about how he or she "scores" the data, how final results are arrived at, and what they really mean. Again, what is important is that the analysis is systematic: that the assumptions, concepts, and methods are all made explicitly clear.

Techniques.   The purpose here is to provide some example of techniques—of varying sophistication and elegance—that facilitate systematic political risk analysis. The discussion of methods of analysis is far from complete and the reader is referred to books and articles cited in the bibliography for more detailed information.

It is important to note that more sophisticated—or more complicated—analytical techniques *do not* imply automatically better results. The analyst should look for a fit between the firm, its problems, capabilities, and the available techniques. There are many instances when a company may be much better off with a very simple method than a complex one. It should also be clear that no technique can improve the quality of the data collected or insure that the results are used intelligently.

Country Reports.   In many firms, political risk analysis takes the form of qualitative analysis modeled after the country reports done in government. The analyst relies on a variety of information sources including the media, specialized journals, and, most frequently, interviews with a range of people in and out of the target country. The reports may target a specific issue (e.g., protectionism), a project, or a country or region.

The advantages of country reports are simplicity and flexibility; their quality obviously depends on the capability of the analyst. Their very simplicity poses problems. The quality and reliability of the information sources are not always clear. The assumptions of the analyst, and the chain of logic that led to the ultimate conclusions, may not be explicit or obvious. The major problem with country reports is that their lack of specificity may limit usefulness. The report may tell you a great deal about a country or issue, but it may be difficult to use it as a basis for forecasting impacts on a given project. The unstructured nature of most country reports makes it very difficult to either compare risks across countries or to present a large number of countries to management in this form.

A number of the problems of country reports can be overcome if they are based on an outline or checklist that is carefully constructed to take account of project vulnerabilities. A basic outline, that can be modified as necessary, can also provide a reasonable degree of comparability across countries and make it easier to read a large number of them at one time. It also allows for a range of input into the political assessment process and provides a means of combining business and political expertise.

Checklists.   Checklists or outlines can be used by themselves as a basis for political risk analysis. They can be very specific or general and lengthy or brief as needed. It is important that they reflect careful consideration about the nature of political risks: which external events and processes are significant, when and how they may affect the business, and where a given project is vulnerable.

Checklists can markedly improve the comparability of reporting and allow thought about political risks before an urgent crisis. They can be used to decide what information is needed and where to get it, serve as a basis for interviewing respondents (as a vehicle to "translate" general country knowledge into political risk assessments), and as a guide for the eventual report. In addition to outlining the information needed, they can provide instructions for information gathering and preparation of the final report.

Rating Systems. Several of the political risk reporting services and a number of companies use scoring or rating systems to evaluate countries. While reports based on numerical scores exhibit ease of understanding, comparability, and they facilitate communication, they present all of the disadvantages of quantitative analysis discussed above. Their value depends on the validity of the model of political risk on which the system is based (are the right questions asked?), the accuracy of the information gathered, the logic of the weighting scheme used to aggregate, and the ultimate use to which results are put. Everyone who uses a numerical country rating scheme must understand all of the assumptions on which it based and exactly how it is put together.

General Motors, for example, has used a model to formulate a political risk index which assigns countries to one of four risk categories. Data are collected from a wide variety of sources and is generally qualitative. Judgments are made to score nine variables under three major headings: politics, policy, and regulation. Weights are assigned and the final score, which ranges from 0 to 100, is used to assign the country to one of four categories: low risk (81–100), medium low (61–80), medium high (41–60), and high (0–40).[8]

Other firms and services numerical rating systems are based on expert judgment and entail varying degrees of complexity in terms of the underlying model of politics and political risk and the methods used to calculate scores. Country scores are of most value in a rough or preliminary comparison of countries and certainly should not be the sole basis of any business decision.

Issue Analysis. The primary focus of issue analysis is not the country or region, but rather trends, ideas, regulations, and the like that could affect the business. Examples of issues include: protectionism, the control of transborder data flows, the debt crisis, local ownership regulations, control over transfers of technology for security purposes, export controls, local content regulations or development policy in general, regional integration European Economic Community (EEC), and terrorism.

The analysis of issues can take place globally, in a region, or a country, or at all three levels. While a variety of techniques are used in issue analysis, all involve identification of critical issues—those that can affect the business significantly and their analysis. The obvious advantage of issue analysis is that it is specific: The analyst concentrates on identifying trends, events, or processes that can affect the business. Furthermore, the identification of issues should not be left to specialists; it is an exercise in which general management can participate profitably. It involves comparing business vulnerabilities with knowledge of the external environment and often entails broad scanning of a variety of sources to identify emerging trends.

The value of issue analysis depends on correct identification of critical issues—those that can affect assets, strategy, or operations. Once critical issues are specified, a variety of techniques, including scenario analysis, can be utilized.

Scenario Analysis.   Given the degree of uncertainty that exists in most business situations where political risk is present, it may make more sense to try to understand the future—or alternative futures—than to try to predict it. Scenario analysis assumes that it is difficult and not particularly useful to develop a prediction of one specific future. Given that the probability of it occurring is usually well under one, there are a lot of probable, if less likely, alternatives that are ignored. Scenario analysis attempts to fix outer bounds about the uncertainty the firm faces—to limit it—and then to understand the more important alternatives that might occur. Scenarios are then, ". . . simply techniques for mapping the principal roads through the uncertainty."[9]

While there are a number of techniques used in developing scenarios, their basic objectives are all the same: ". . . to develop a story about how the future might evolve, with the critical criteria that all the elements of the scenario hold together and that there is a plausible sequence of events for 'getting from here to there.' If there are several plausible paths and configurations of elements, then several different scenarios are in order."[10]

Good scenarios should be rooted in history so as to understand the evolution of the current situation, sufficiently detailed to allow analysis of the important forces at work, clear enough to allow the analyst to see the major theme of the scenario, and numerous enough to cover the basic options but not so numerous as to be unmanageable.[11]

Scenarios are typically built around major themes. These range from *most likely, optimistic,* and *pessimistic* to those based on assumptions such *as decreasing oil prices, inflation,* or *flat economic growth.* An analyst preparing scenarios for South Africa, for example, might choose themes such as "increasing and unresolved violence, maintenance of the status quo, or peaceful and evolutionary change." Some analysts assign probabilities to scenarios while others do not.

It is important that scenarios capture the important "alternative futures" and then develop them as rigorously and as systematically as possible. The primary advantage of the technique is that it allows the firm to explore a variety of contingencies and plan for them in advance. The major disadvantage is the amount of work entailed. Given the degree of uncertainty firms face and the state of development of the art of political risk, scenarios have considerable attraction. A number of the techniques just described, such as numerical scoring and issue analysis, can be used to develop scenarios.

Summary.   Political risk analysis can focus on issues or geography and it can be undertaken globally, or in a region, a group of countries, or in a single country. There are numerous techniques available, each with their own benefits and costs. The approach of the firm, however, is much more important than the choice of technique. At the end of the day, political risk analysis is business analysis—it involves determining possible impacts on assets, strategy, or operations and their potential costs. That requires a knowledge of the business combined with an understanding of the external political environment and the ways in which it affects projects. The most important criteria for political risk analysis are that it (1) focuses on what can happen to the business, and (2) it is done explicitly and systematically.

ORGANIZING TO ASSESS POLITICAL RISK

The surge of interest in political risk analysis that peaked after the fall of the Shah in Iran raised questions in many firms about how to handle this new function organizationally. All sorts of vehicles have been tried including "mini State Departments" reporting to top management, lodging analysts in staff groups such as planning or treasury, and in many firms, handling analysis on an ad hoc basis as the need arises.

There is clearly a need to think carefully about how the company is going to handle the political risk analysis function. The brief history of the field is replete with examples of companies reacting to a political trauma (such as a major unexpected nationalization) by hiring very competent political analysts from State, the intelligence community, or universities and forming a "unit," which then encounters increasing frustration in trying to penetrate planning and decision making and is disbanded when the first economic downturn provides an excuse for personnel cuts.

It is equally clear, however, that there is no single correct organizational solution that is appropriate for all firms. More complex and formal structures are not necessarily better and sometimes simple and informal approaches may be optimal. How the political risk analysis function should be organized depends on the specific characteristics of a company.

GENERAL ORGANIZING PRINCIPLES.   There are some general principles or objectives that apply to any firm's attempt to organize the political risk assessment function. The organization should facilitate, and not hinder, the systematic and structured evaluation of political risks. It should allow the firm to combine, as effectively and efficiently as possible, assessments of the external political environment with knowledge of the industry, company, and project, to allow assessment of the probability and costs of a specific impact on an operation.

The function should be organized in a way that facilitates *effective and efficient use of the internal and external resources* that are available. That requires access to a wide range of sources including all levels of subsidiary people, diverse host country nationals, other foreign firms in the country, and a range of experts throughout the world.

However, providing access is not sufficient. As noted earlier, consensus is unlikely in this area and some means must be found to reconcile diverse opinions and insure that valuable information is not lost in aggregation. Assessing political risk requires a *focal point* within the firm where information, coming from very diverse sources, can be channeled and compared.

The system must also provide for *validity checks*. One of the most important tasks to be performed is the continuing education of managers in this area, both specialists and general management. This requires that individuals at all levels who are involved with international operations have a regular opportunity to compare their views of a country, and their concerns about potential impacts on a project, with those of others, including "outside experts." That does not imply a face-to-face confrontation, but rather some mechanism for sharing information on a regular basis.

The political risk assessment function must be organized in a way that clearly reflects the *interest and support of top management*. The function is often a new one that may be perceived as a threat by other elements within the firm. Legitimization by top management is an absolute requisite of success.

The organizational structure must facilitate frequent and open formal and informal *two-way communication* within the firm. In many instances, communication is limited to the analysts sending reports up the line of command with little interaction between them and the ultimate users of the information. That limits the usefulness of the analyses. Users really never understand what political risk analysis is all about and, as important, the analysts never really learn how their product is used. Without some understanding of strategic planning and capital budgeting within the firm, political risk analysts are unlikely to be able to produce useful reports.

In summary, political risk analysis must be organized so that it becomes an integral part of the organization. Political analysis is a new function and the background of analysts is likely to be different from that of other managers. In too many firms, political risk analysts are perceived as somewhat arcane specialists who have an office in the building but are not really part of the company.

If political risk analysis is to be integrated effectively into planning and decision making, the analysts must become part of the core organization and their product part of the firm's business information system. How that is to be done depends on the strategy, organizational structure, and characteristics of a specific company.

MODES OF ORGANIZING

Informal.   In some firms, political risk analysis can be handled most efficiently on an informal or ad hoc basis. In these—typically smaller—companies, top operating managers are directly and continuously involved in the process and may "do" the political risk analyses themselves, assigning specific tasks when necessary. The advantages of this approach are direct involvement and low cost. The problems are obvious: It is very difficult to do any sort of systematic analyses and all too often personal biases and opinions are substituted for rigorous evaluation.

Despite the problems, there may still be situations when this "lack" of organization is most effective. Most often this would be with a smaller firm heavily involved in one, or perhaps a very few, countries where political risk analysis is part of the ongoing responsibilities of many managers.

Part-Time Assignment.   In many firms, political risk assessment responsibilities are assigned to an individual—or group of individuals—who are part of a staff group such as treasury or strategic planning. Their primary tasks are their mainline staff responsibilities, but they may do political risk analysis on an ongoing basis part-time, or when the need arises (e.g., because of a new investment proposal).

The advantages of this sort of approach are relatively low cost, and more important, integration of political and business analysis. The political risk analysis is being done by people whose primary orientation is finance or planning. It is unlikely, however, that this sort of arrangement would allow for systematic scanning of a wide range of internal or external sources or provide a real focal point within the firm. It also makes it difficult to hire specialists, as the primary role of the individuals involved is their staff function.

Political Assessment Units.   Last, the firm can set up formal and full-time political assessment units devoted entirely to all of the aspects of political risk analysis. These have the disadvantage of a relatively high cost, but also may offer the greatest return in terms of effective performance. Organization of these units entails two major questions: Should they be staffed by specialists or managers drawn from the existing pool within the firm? Should they stand alone, or be part of another staff group?

Specialists—individuals with backgrounds in political analysis as a result of government experience or academic training—offer a number of advantages. The most obvious is their own store of knowledge. They may be experts in one or more regions or know a great deal about the structure and functioning of political systems. They also may have advantages when it comes to accessing a broad range of external sources. First, they may understand how universities and government agencies (in a number of countries) are organized and be able to find appropriate people quickly. Second, they may be part of one or more "networks" of country experts or political analysts that facilitate the exchange of information. Last, they may have more in common with sources than others managers—they may be able to "talk their language"—and their contacts with them may be more productive.

The disadvantages are that they probably know little about the business—or business in general—when hired. They do not understand the industry, the technology, perhaps the corporate "culture," nor are they likely to have had much in the way of business education or training. It will be hard for them to understand the uses to which their analyses are put and they may not "fit into" the organization as well as they might. Analytically, they will have a hard time applying political analysis to the business, and personally, they may have a hard time becoming part of the organization.

While the issue is complex, both political and business knowledge is needed to do effective political risk analysis. There is a strong argument for specialists, but it is critical that efforts be made to integrate them into the firm. That may require special training programs or even temporary assignment in other functions.

A separate unit is less likely to be biased by other organizational issues and may find it easier to access sources and remain part of critical networks. However, it is also much more likely to remain on the periphery of the firm than one that is part of another staff group and it will have difficulty ever becoming part of the capital budgeting or strategic planning process. Given the importance of the latter, there are strong arguments for attaching full time political risk assessment units to other staff groups such as strategic planning. That however, has to be done in a way that maintains independence and allows the group to bring its political expertise to bear effectively.[12]

THE MANAGEMENT OF POLITICAL RISK

All too often, management of political risk means crisis response. An effective program requires more than the occasional government relations effort or the purchasing of insurance after the investment decision is reached in "risky" countries. It requires an ongoing effort that integrates political risk assessment and strategic management. Managing political risks means taking full account of political factors in making strategic and operating decisions. It need not be said that effective management assumes effective assessment and evaluation.

AVOIDANCE. The easiest means of managing political risk is to avoid situations where the probability of costly impacts on projects is high. In some situations, that may well be the only viable response. There are times when it would not be prudent for any firm to engage in business in a country in any conceivable manner. The only reasonable course of action is to withdraw or to forego investment.

There are, however, a large number of situations that entail large opportunities as well as large risks. In many, it is possible to manage the risks, to reduce them to the point where the return justifies their acceptance, through a variety of vehicles available to the firm. This topic is complex and all that can be attempted here is a review of the major issues.[13]

LEGAL MEASURES. While the firm-government nature of the relationship in which most political risks arise may limit the scope of legal protection, there is much that can be done in this area. Many disputes can be avoided, or foreseen, if proper attention is paid to the initial contract when the firm first embarks on a project. The legal framework is not simply a means for pursuing salvage should a loss occur. Rather, "The existence of key legal rights can be an important deterrent to improper host government action. In this connection . . . the ability to obtain effective adjudication and enforcement rights is at least as important as the substantive rights created."[14]

It is possible to establish dispute resolution mechanisms, such as third party arbitration, that can prevent risks from materializing. An investor's ability to do that, however, varies by country. The Latin American countries generally refuse to accept external arbitration of investor-host government disputes as legitimate.

FINANCING. Financing can be used as a means for risk management. First, it can provide a vehicle for sharing the risk, for transferring some of the potential loss to another. Joint equity arrangements reduce the capital invested, and the substitution of debt for equity may facilitate transfer, to local sources or third parties such as international banks.

Debt financing also may increase the firm's leverage to help prevent the undesired event from occurring. That is especially true if the lender is a third party that is important to the host country for other reasons. The best examples are the major international banks and institutions such as the World Bank. Host countries may be reluctant to impose constraints on foreign investors if doing so raises the risk of compromising, often critical, relationships with international lenders.

INVOLVING LOCAL GROUPS. Influential host country groups can be brought into the project. The most obvious means is through a joint venture with local investors. Host country nationals can be appointed to the subsidiary's—or possibly, the parent's—board of directors. Many firms have formed local advisory boards, partially as a source of information and advice, but partially to involve influential individuals with the firm.

While the involvement of local nationals can be an effective means of managing risks, there are also a number of potential problems with this approach. First, a joint venture has strategic implications other than risk management, many of which may be negative. Second, an individual's true level of influence is difficult to judge, especially for a foreigner. All influence peddlers are not influential. Third, influence is far from permanent. Events such as the fall of the Shah of Iran or Marcos in the Philippines can quickly put the firm on the wrong side of the fence. Last, influence works both ways and the firm may find itself subject to local pressures rather than controlling them.

STRATEGY. Strategy can often be modified to respond to potential political risks. First, if equity investment is too dangerous, other entry vehicles can be utilized. Various forms of contractual arrangements, such as licensing or management contracts, allow a firm to take advantage of opportunities while reducing risks to levels that may be acceptable.

Second, vertical integration is often an effective means of risk management. If a plant is dependent on other subsidiaries (located in other countries) for essential inputs or for the disposal of output, its vulnerability may be limited. It has little value as a unit in itself. The dangers of this approach lie in the fact that host country concerns about dependency and minimal transfer of resources and capabilities may underlie the problems in the first place. Integration may be effective in the short run, but may well exacerbate longer term concerns.

Third, projects can be managed in ways that allow a menu of responses to government concerns. New products and processes, advanced technology, and increased exports are all objectives of many host governments and serve as sources of bargaining power for the firm. A company may be able to counter a government request for increased local ownership or other undesired impacts with a proposal for additional exports or local manufacture of new products.

Last, diversification is a time honored means of risk reduction. Whether that is possible, however, depends on firm specific factors.

INSURANCE.   There are a number of public and private sources of political risk insurance available. National schemes such as the Overseas Private Investment Corporation (OPIC) and the Federal Credit Insurance Association (FCIA) in the United States, and their counterparts in other countries, provide insurance against a variety of risks encountered in investment, trade, and contractual contexts. A number of private market underwriters, primarily in the United States and London, offer political risk coverages.

Policies are available to cover: confiscation, expropriation, and nationalization; currency inconvertibility; war, revolution, insurrection, and civil strife; contract repudiation; export license cancellation; unfair calling of guarantees; and other risks. Premium, rates, terms and coverages vary considerably.

OPIC coverage is available for a 20-year term and has the advantage of being issued by a government agency. However, it can only be issued at the time an investment is first made and is subject to a variety of public policy constraints (such as the income level of the country, the development impact of the project, and company size) that limit eligibility. Private coverages are much more flexible, involve few limits—other than risks—for countries or projects, and can cover existing as well as new investments. Private policies, however, are generally limited to three years duration and few private underwriters offer land based war coverages. Furthermore, inconvertibility insurance can be difficult to place in the private sector. In general private policies have much lower capacity limits than OPICs.

Insurance can be a very valuable means of transferring risk and is used widely. In some instances, the availability of insurance may be the deciding factor in a firm's willingness to take the risk of investment in a country. Insurance, however, is generally a means for damage control after the event. Much more can be done to manage potential political risks that allow a firm to continue to operate profitably in a country.

NOTES

1. Vikram S. Mehta, "Political Risk: An Oil Company's Perspective." Presented at the Association of Political Risk Analysts Conference, Princeton University, October 19, 1983.

2. Well publicized cases include Ford and Worthington in Canada in the late 1950s and Freuhauf in France in 1964.
3. Stephen J. Kobrin, "Expropriation as an Attempt to Control Foreign Firms in LDCs: 1960–1979." *International Studies Quarterly,* September 1984.
4. Kobrin, "Expropriation as an Attempt to Control."
5. The best recent example is IBM in Mexico in 1985. That company was able to bargain for 100 percent ownership when requirements call for 51 percent local equity by offering increased technological development and a high level of exports.
6. James S. Conway, "The Use of In-Country Sources in Corporate Political Risk Analysis." Paper presented at the APRA Conference, Princeton University, October 19, 1983.
7. Stephen J. Kobrin, *Managing Political Risk Assessment.* Berkeley: University of California Press, 1982. See also Appendix C for a more detailed discussion of assessment methods.
8. Gordon Rayfield, "Comparative Politics Applied: Theory and Practice in the Business Environment." Paper presented at the APRA Conference, Princeton University, October 19, 1983.
9. William H. Overholt, "The Scenario Technique." *Political Risks in International Business,* Thomas L. Brewer (ed.). New York: Praeger, 1985, 152.
10. William Ascher and William Overholt, *Strategic Planning and Forecasting.* New York: John Wiley & Sons, 1983, 88.
11. Overholt, "The Scenario Technique." p. 155.
12. Kobrin, *Managing Political Risk Assessment,* for an extended discussion of organizing the political risk assessment function.
13. For a more extensive review of this topic, see Fariborz Ghadar, Stephen J. Kobrin, and Theodore H. Moran (eds.), *Managing International Political Risk: Strategies and Techniques.* Washington: Bond Publishing Company, 1983.
14. Richard Stern, "Comments." *Managing International Political Risk,* Ghadar, Kobrin, and Moran (eds.), p. 92.

SOURCES AND SUGGESTED REFERENCES

Ascher William and William H. Overholt. *Strategic Planning and Forecasting.* New York: John Wiley & Sons, 1983.

Brewer, Thomas (ed.). *Political Risks in International Business.* New York: Praeger, 1985.

Ghadar, Fariborz, Stephen J. Kobrin, and Theodore Moran (eds.). *Managing International Political Risks: Strategies and Techniques.* Washington, D.C.: Bond Publishing, 1983.

Ghadar, Fariborz and Theodore H. Moran (eds.). *International Political Management: New Dimensions.* Washington, D.C.: Bond Publishing, 1984.

Kobrin, Stephen J. *Managing Political Risk Assessment.* Berkeley: University of California Press, 1982.

Rogers, Jerry (ed.). *Global Risk Assessments: Issues, Concepts, and Applications.* Riverside, CA: Global Risk Assessment, Inc., 1983.

Simon, Jeffrey. "Political Risk Assessment: Past Trends and Future Prospects." *Columbia Journal of World Business* 17, Fall 1982, pp. 62–71.

FORECASTING EXCHANGE RATES

CONTENTS

FORECASTING EXCHANGE RATES

Clas Wihlborg

Professional investment may be likened to those newspaper competitions in which the competitors have to pick out the six prettiest faces from a hundred photographs, the prize being awarded to the competitor whose choice most nearly corresponds to the average preferences of the competitors as a whole; so that each competitor has to pick, not those faces which he himself finds prettiest, but those which he thinks likeliest to catch the fancy of the other competitors.

(JOHN MAYNARD KEYNES, *The General Theory of Employment, Interest and Money*, p. 156)

The quote from the British economist John Maynard Keynes illustrates well the difficulties of forecasting exchange rates and making profits on the choice of currency denomination of investments and borrowing. Keynes was very successful in financial markets by applying his principle. However, its application demands an in-depth understanding of the determinants of future prices and the functioning of the markets. For each market participant earning above-average profits, there must be another market participant earning below-average profits, or losses.

This chapter should provide guidance for *what* to forecast, *when* to forecast, and *how* to forecast for a firm with foreign projects, foreign trade, or foreign borrowing.

The question of *what* to forecast is raised, because the exchange rate itself is irrelevant for the firm under certain conditions. Instead the exchange rate's deviation from the value it would have achieved under those conditions is the interesting variable. Also, estimates of the market's expectation of the future rate can often be observed in the market, in which case future deviations from this value are of interest.

The question of *when* to forecast is related to the quality of the observable estimate of the future rate. The forecaster must be able to do better than this estimate in order to invest resources in forecasting. Before investing in forecasting ability, the forecaster must be able to evaluate the benefits and costs of alternative forecasting methods. In other words, it is necessary to know *how* to obtain a forecast.

The first part of this section describes the conditions under which the exchange rate is irrelevant and illustrates the relevant variables to forecast over the long run, the short run, and the very short run. The long run is defined as above one or two years, the short run ranges from three months to one or two years, and the very short run ranges from the day-to-day horizon up to three months.

"Determinants of the Exchange Rate—Elementary Theory" summarizes modern theories of exchange-rate determination over the different time horizons and "Forecasting Methods" describes and compares alternative methods for obtaining forecasts with respect to cost and quality.

"Sources of Information" lists different sources of historical information about the variables of relevance for exchange-rate determination.

Finally, "Management Considerations" draws some conclusions with respect to forecasting and financial management under uncertainty about the future exchange rate.

No distinction is drawn between more-or-less flexible or fixed exchange rates. Most of the arguments are valid under any regime. A separate section in "The Role of Governments" contains a discussion about how government behavior in foreign-exchange and other markets could affect the forecasting of exchange rates by making the "long run" shorter or the "short run" longer.

The references at the end include books or articles that contain valuable summaries of the topics discussed.

IS EXCHANGE-RATE FORECASTING NEEDED?

It is not obvious that exchange rates should or need be forecast, even when a firm is heavily involved in international operations. The exchange rate simply does not matter under certain conditions in international goods and financial markets. The understanding of these conditions, even if unrealistic, provides insight into what variables need to be forecast.

There are two conditions under which the exchange-rate forecast is superfluous. First, when goods markets are in equilibrium with purchasing-power parity (PPP), the exchange rate is irrelevant. Second, when the interest-rate differential reflects the best-available information on the expected rate of change of the exchange rate, no gain can be made by forecasting, even if the exchange rate is of relevance. We shall explore the two conditions in greater detail.

GOODS MARKETS AND THE IRRELEVANCE OF THE EXCHANGE RATE.   Since the exchange rate formally is a price of one kind of money in terms of another, it is intuitively reasonable that changes in the exchange rate *need* not matter economically—in real terms. This is in fact the case when PPP holds. Then the exchange rate's movements offset movements in two countries' relative price levels. In other words, the exchange rate only translates one unit of account into another.

The implications of PPP are far reaching. If PPP holds, the firm need not worry about exchange-rate changes, since any unanticipated fluctuations would correspond to changes in at least one country's price level. *Exchange risk* would *not exist,* only uncertainty about inflation rates. Also, *exchange rates need not be forecast.*

PPP is not sufficient to make currency denominations of contracts irrelevant, however, because the firm may suffer losses on assets or liabilities in a currency when there are unanticipated changes in the *price level* in the contract currency. Thus the firm needs to be concerned about inflation in contract currencies when contracts are set in *nominal terms.* Naturally this is true whether the currency denomination is domestic or foreign.

Inflation is also irrelevant under certain conditions. Changes in a country's price level are irrelevant for the firm when *contracts* are specified in *real terms* and when *inflation is independent of relative prices* among commodities. Assets on which the return is indexed to the price level are perfect examples. The returns on physical assets such as buildings or machinery in a country are also independent of inflation, when prices (in terms of other goods) of the services or products that are produced by the assets are independent of inflation.

The arguments above illustrate the conditions under which *inflation and exchange rates* are of no economic consequence—when the firm need forecast only future *relative prices* among commodities when evaluating a project in any country. Thus only conventional business risk matters.

It is important to note that the conditions above are fairly strict. It was mentioned that inflation must be independent of relative prices and that the exchange-rate changes must reflect relative inflation rates. In addition, tax payments in real terms must be independent of the inflation rate. This is *not* true in countries where depreciation allowances are based on historical costs (Hong, 1977). Naturally the firm's concern must be the real value of the firm's profit stream as opposed to nominal profits. The fact that accounting is performed in nominal prices may cause "money-illusion" in the stock market. Firms could then be induced to be more concerned with accounting numbers than with economic values.

FINANCIAL MARKETS AND THE IRRELEVANCE OF FORECASTING. Explicit forecasting of the future exchange rate is naturally only profitable if there is no easily available market price that incorporates the best-possible forecast. Many economists argue that relative interest rates and the forward rate reflect all available information about the future. Then firms or investors need only study the interest rate differential on identical assets in two currencies in order to obtain the optimal forecast. Alternatively, the forward exchange rate provides the same information.

Note that forecasting can be irrelevant even if the exchange rate matters for the profit of the firm. The irrelevance implies only that the firm cannot hope to gain anything by investing or borrowing in one currency instead of another. Sales or purchases of goods may still be more profitable in one country than another as a result of deviations from PPP.

The conditions under which there are no gains to be made by attempting to forecast the exchange rate in order to obtain a favorable currency position are strict. For all available information to be incorporated in interest rates and forward rates, the small part of the market participants that have access to the best information must have *unlimited* access to arbitrage funds and they must *not* be *averse to risk* for the arbitrage process to function perfectly. There are profit opportunities for individuals or firms with good information and with little risk aversion, if one of the above conditions does not hold.

EMPIRICAL EVIDENCE ON ARBITRAGE. Exhibits 1 through 4 show nominal and real effective exchange rates for the United States, West Germany, Japan, and the United Kingdom, 1970–1984. Real exchange rates are deviations from PPP. The term *effective* implies that each rate is a (trade-) weighted average of the exchange rate of one country relative to a large number of trading partners. Real rates are calculated from manufactured goods prices. The underlying data can be found in *World Financial Markets,* published monthly by Morgan Guarantee Trust Company, New York.

The four countries show different patterns. For the United States, real and nominal exchange rates follow each other closely in long swings around the PPP-mark (100). Deviations seem long-lasting (2–4 years) and large. Note that a 25 percent real exchange rate change for an effective rate may hide much larger real exchange rate changes toward particular currencies.

The pattern for Germany is more consistent with PPP theory. The nominal exchange rate shows an upward trend, that is, the German mark appreciates. However, in real terms, the mark fluctuates closer to PPP than the U.S. dollar. The Japanese yen shows a pattern more similar to the dollar in the sense that nominal exchange rate changes correspond closely to real. However, there is also an upward trend in the yen offsetting inflation differentials. Finally, the pound depreciated drastically during the 1970s without a large change in the real rate. During the 1980s, when the inflation rate in the United Kingdom was similar to that in the rest of the world, real and nominal rates followed each other closely. Note also that up to 1979, PPP for the UK may be represented by the index 80. In 1979, there seems to be a shift in the long run equilibrium rate for the UK. This shift is most likely explained by oil exports. The composition of the U.K.'s exports and production shifted in 1979, while the composition of the statistical measures of the price level remained constant.

It is clear from the exhibits that real exchange rate changes can be substantial and long-lasting for manufactured goods prices. Consumer price indexes reveal even larger deviations, since they contain a larger share of nontraded goods. The figures affirm, however, a tendency toward PPP in the longer run although statistical measures of price indexes are very unreliable over long time horizons. Over the long term, relative price changes in countries with different taste patterns will cause deviations from PPP in a statistical sense. The economic conditions for the irrelevance of the exchange rate and the inflation rates is only that identical goods cost the same in two countries and that relative price changes are independent of the exchange rate and the inflation rate. At some point, the statistical errors in the estimates of PPP—increasing with time—will dominate the economic deviations—decreasing with time.

The very short-term deviations from PPP may also be exaggerated because prices on many goods with fixed list prices fluctuate in the short term in the form of rebates, credit terms, and the like. Nevertheless, there is little doubt that nontraded goods and imperfect international competition may cause substantial deviations from PPP over periods of up to four years.

Empirical evidence on any interdependence between inflation rates and relative price changes within countries is harder to come by. There are increasing indications that the volatility of relative prices increases with inflation (Wachtel and Cukierman, 1980) but this need not imply any correlation.

We turn now to empirical evidence on arbitrage conditions in international financial markets. The first important observation is that *interest-rate parity holds in forward markets among the major currencies represented in Euromarkets* (Frenkel and Levich, 1975; Kohlhagen, 1978). The forward markets in other currencies are not sufficiently well developed to test, but it is safe to assume that temporary deviations occur. This is the case, for example, for Sweden, where parity relative to the Eurodollar is violated for periods up to a couple of months (see Sveriges Riksbanks *Förvaltningsberättelse,* the yearly report by the Swedish Central Bank). The implications for forecasting is first that forward rates *or* interest rates are not unbiased estimates of the future spot rate among most minor currencies. In fact,

**EXHIBIT 1 NOMINAL AND REAL EFFECTIVE EXCHANGE RATES,
USA, 1970–84, 1980 = 100**

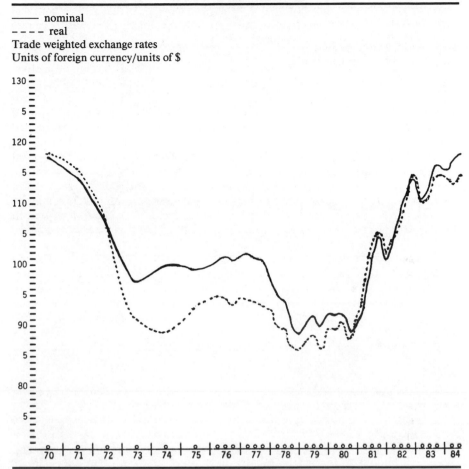

——— nominal
– – – – real
Trade weighted exchange rates
Units of foreign currency/units of $

Source. World Financial Markets, Morgan Guaranty Trust Company, various issues.

it is most likely that neither of the two is unbiased. Second, forward rates *and* interest rates *may* be, but *need not* be, unbiased estimates for the major currencies. Interest-rate parity is not a sufficient condition for perfect arbitrage in international financial markets.

It is naturally difficult to test whether the forward rate or the interest-rate differential is equal to the best-available forecast of the exchange rate. Measures of the expectations of the most well informed market participants are necessary. A number of indirect tests have been performed, however. First, Giddy and Dufey (1975), Levich (1979), Poole (1967), and others have studied whether daily fluctuations are serially correlated, since this may imply profit opportunities. The tests show mixed evidence for the random-walk hypothesis—that the spot exchange rate is the best forecast of the future exchange rate. These tests are typically very short run, because

EXHIBIT 2 NOMINAL AND REAL EFFECTIVE EXCHANGE RATES, WEST GERMANY, 1970–84, 1980 = 100

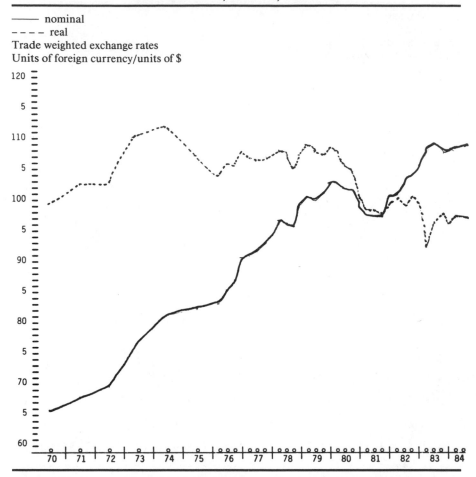

——— nominal
– – – – real
Trade weighted exchange rates
Units of foreign currency/units of $

Source. World Financial Markets, Morgan Guaranty Trust Company, various issues.

they cannot be performed over time horizons, when fundamental determinants are likely to change, without a detailed model.

Levich (1980 and in annual follow up studies published in *Euromoney,* 1981–1983) conducted another kind of indirect study of profit opportunities over different periods by tracing the performance of the forecasts of foreign-exchange advisory services relative to the forward rate. There is evidence that some services are able to outperform the forward rate consistently, indicating profit opportunities of having access to superior information (or judgment). However, it still remains to show that *one* foreign-exchange advisory service can outperform the forward rates among the major currencies consistently over long periods. If not, the firm or individual must know when to substitute one advisory service for another. Naturally this presumes the access to superior information by the firm itself.

**EXHIBIT 3   NOMINAL AND REAL EFFECTIVE EXCHANGE RATES,
JAPAN, 1970–84, 1980 = 100**

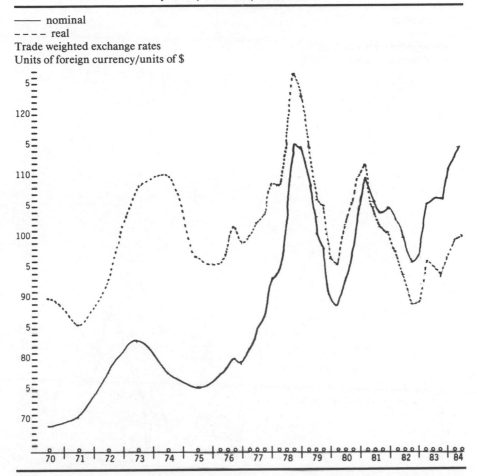

—— nominal
– – – – real
Trade weighted exchange rates
Units of foreign currency/units of $

Source.   World Financial Markets, Morgan Guaranty Trust Company, various issues.

Under some conditions it is possible to make predictions that are superior to the forward rate even without access to superior information. Specifically, it was mentioned above that arbitrageurs will not necessarily push the forward rate to the expected future spot rate when they are risk averse and/or when the supply of arbitrage funds is limited.

The latter violation of market efficiency is likely to hold for most minor currencies in countries with less developed financial markets. The evidence with respect to risk-premia is mixed. There is no strong evidence of the existence of risk-premia per se, though a number of recent studies show that the forecast error of the forward rate is not purely random. Wihlborg (1982) shows that relative inflation variances among countries have a weak influence on relative interest rates. Bailey et al. (1984), Sweeney (1985), and others provide evidence that there exist *either* time varying

**EXHIBIT 4 NOMINAL AND REAL EFFECTIVE EXCHANGE RATES,
UK, 1970–84, 1980 = 100**

nominal
– – – – real
Trade weighted exchange rates
Units of foreign currency/units of $

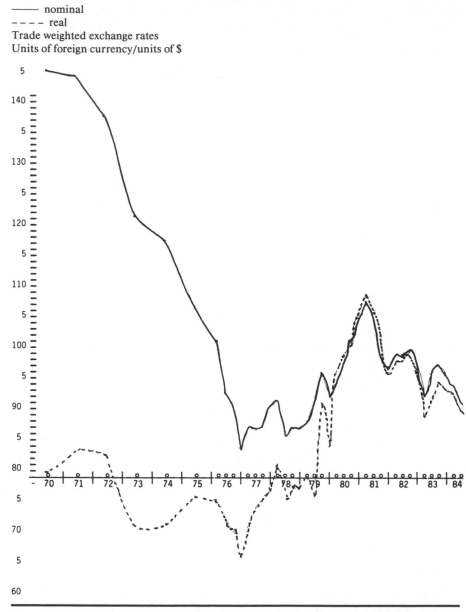

Source. *World Financial Markets,* Morgan Guaranty Trust Company, various issues.

risk-premia *or* market inefficiencies in foreign exchange markets even among major currencies. The magnitude of explicit or implicit risk-premia seem small, however, and their pattern is hard to explain. It cannot be ruled out that learning processes after, for example, shifts in central bank behavior explain a large part of what may seem to be a risk-premium or market inefficiency. During the 1980s when the dollar was strong for several years, the forward rate consistently underestimated the dollar's strength as did most forecast services. Thus, forward rates may have reflected expectations though forecast errors of these rates have been nonrandom.

CONCLUSIONS: WHAT SHOULD BE FORECAST. The discussion of the relevance of the exchange rate can now be summarized as follows:

1. Exchange-rate changes may have real effects on the firm, independent of inflation rates, up to at least periods of 2 to 4 years.
2. Inflation or deflation in the currency of denomination of a fixed-price contract (accompanied by exchange-rate changes) leads to gains or losses on contracts that are fixed in nominal terms. This consideration gains in importance with the length of the contract periods.
3. Inflation affects the real return on physical assets when the tax liability of the firm depends on historical costs, and when some relative prices depend on the rate of inflation.

These conclusions imply that the firm needs estimates of *future deviations from purchasing-power parity* and *inflation rates* to be able to forecast the real value of cash flows that are fixed in nominal terms. In other words, exchange rates *and* price levels need to be forecast. *Forecasts of the deviations from PPP suffice* when nominally fixed contracts play minor roles. Forecasts of *levels* of exchange rates and price levels *may be unnecessary* if deviations from PPP can be forecast directly.

The conclusions of the discussion of arbitrage conditions in financial markets are as follows:

1. The forward rate and the interest-rate differential for *major currencies* can normally be outperformed only by the forecaster who holds *superior information or judgment* about future determinants of the exchange rate.
2. The investors or borrowers with *less* risk aversion than those that last entered the market (the marginal market participant) may gain by forecasting even when their available information is not superior to the information held by the marginal market participant.
3. Exchange rate expectations for currencies without well-developed financial markets are less well reflected in relative interest rates and forward rates. This increases the value of separate forecasts.

Forecasting Needs for the Long Run. Forecasting needs for the long run (above two years) would mostly be needed for long-term project analysis and long-term financing. Purchasing-power parity is usually a reasonable approximation for periods above two years. Only *inflation forecasts* are then needed, and only for fixed-price contacts. Naturally, the exchange rate may deviate temporarily from parity in both directions, but such deviations are likely to cancel out over long periods for major currencies.

Therefore, it is only the firm with a relatively short pay-off period (high cost of capital) that needs to be concerned about possible deviations over the short term when making cash-flow estimates.

We have also seen that inflation does not affect the real value of the firm if its market prices *relative to other prices are independent* of the average price level and if depreciation allowances based on historical costs play a minor role. The firm can evaluate cash flows at a constant price level under these circumstances and need only forecast how its input and output prices are going to develop relative to each other and substitutable commodities. Heavy disturbances and government actions may slow down the adjustment process. This seems to have happened during 1977 and 1978, when the dollar remained undervalued relative to other major currencies for longer than two years, and between 1980 and 1984, when the dollar remained strong. We shall discuss this further in "The Role of Government." Similarly, central banks defend a disequilibrium exchange rate much longer during a pegged system than during a flexible regime. This happened during the late 1960s and the early 1970s while the Bretton Woods system was breaking down. Accordingly, the validity of the long-term relationship could differ among countries with different degrees of commitment to an exchange rate.

Forecasting Needs for the Short Run.   The short run here means periods from a quarter of a year up to one or two years, or the period over which long-run relationships should hold for a particular pair of countries.

It follows from the discussion above that the firm should *concentrate on the forecasting of deviations from PPP* (the real exchange rate) over the short run. The reason is not only that this is the variable that is of real significance but that the deviations may many times be easier to forecast. The long-run relationship (PPP) can be described as a trend line, describing the *scale* of nominal magnitudes (the relative units of account), whereas the short-run forecasting problem involves the estimation of deviations from the trend. Such deviations can be viewed as temporary *overvaluations and undervaluations* of an exchange rate due to factors that will be discussed below.

The firm that faces decisions about the currency in which to borrow or about whether to cover a foreign currency position must evaluate effective interest costs, including exchange rate changes. The main concern in these situations is to evaluate whether the interest rate differential over- or underestimates the expected rate of change of the exchange rate, and whether the forward rate is higher or lower than the expected future spot rate. The actual rate of change of the exchange rate does not matter for these financial decisions, assuming that the firm wishes to borrow at the lower cost.

The deviations from PPP or the real exchange rate can be forecast as the difference between the expected rate of change of the exchange rate and the change in relative price levels. This may be the most practical procedure when the forward rate provides a reasonably unbiased forecast. However, when the forward rate is biased or does not exist, and when inflation forecasts are uncertain, it may be easier to forecast deviations from purchasing-power parity directly from economic and political observations, since the variables that determine the deviations are likely to be separable from those that determine the trend (compare "Determinents of the Exchange Rate—Elementary Theory").

Statistical problems provide another reason for forecasting deviations from PPP rather than the levels of exchange rates and inflation rates. More specifically, consumer and wholesale price indexes that can be used for forecasting are often not the most-relevant measures of price-level developments. It is *economic* deviations rather than the often-exaggerated statistical deviations that are of interest to the firm. These economic deviations may be more correctly forecast directly rather than by using forecasts of price indices that could misrepresent inflationary developments. Similarly, it could be easier to forecast whether interest rates and forward rate overestimates or underestimates the future exchange rate in order to obtain exact numerical forecasts. Government policies with respect to interest rates could provide important insight, for example.

Forecasting Needs for the Very Short Run. The very short run is defined as any time horizon between a day and a quarter. Shorter periods are hardly relevant for firms and individuals except those directly involved in market making.

The very short run is characterized by negligible changes in the price levels and large fluctuations in the exchange rate (measured as annual rates of change). Accordingly, the changes in the exchange rates correspond almost perfectly to changes in the *real* exchange rate—deviations from PPP. The exception occurs for or between countries with hyperinflation like many Latin American countries in the 1970s. The long-term and short-term relationships can be expected to hold over much shorter time periods for these countries (Frenkel, 1977, provides empirical evidence for this hypothesis with reference to the German hyperinflation in the 1920s).

The volatility of the exchange rate over the very short run under flexible exchange rates has induced a number of tests of the random-walk hypothesis (compare section below) and of the forward rate as the best available predictor. The empirical evidence referred to above suggested that the forward rate may often, but need not be, the best-available forecast. In any case, the major concern for the forecaster should again be *the development of the exchange rate relative to the forward rate rather than relative to the current spot rate*. Even though it may many times suffices to *forecast the bias of the forward rate* in its prediction of the future spot rate, it does not follow that this forecasting task is an easy one. However, Levich's (1980) empirical evidence suggests that many foreign-exchange advisory services have been able to predict the bias sufficiently consistently for the user of the forecasts to make profits although the mean square error of the actual forecasts was larger than the forward rate's.

DETERMINANTS OF THE EXCHANGE RATE— ELEMENTARY THEORY

The exchange rate is a price of one currency (money) in terms of another. Thus we would expect that relative supplies and demands for money in two countries would be important building blocks in a model of exchange rate determination. It is true that this view gives us substantial insight into the factors determining the exchange rate. For example, the exchange rate is a relative price of financial assets, like prices of equity in stock markets, and depends therefore on *expectations* about the future. However, the supplies and demands for money are determined by a number of factors some of which are stock variables—they can be defined at a certain point in time, like wealth—whereas others are flow variables—they must be defined over a certain time horizon, like yearly production. Moreover, an individual's demand for a stock of money at an instant is certainly related to the flow of, for example, consumption over some period in addition to expectations about the future rate of return or loss on holdings of money. Thus the demands and supplies of money—and the exchange rate—depend on a combination of interrelated stock, flow, and expectations variables. The relative importance of different variables must be related to the time horizon over which we are looking. With this introduction, we shall look briefly at modern theories of exchange-rate determination over different time periods.

THE LONG-RUN PURCHASING-POWER PARITY.   The PPP theory of the exchange rate exists in a multitude of formulations. The *absolute* version considers the relationship between price levels at points in time. Taxes, tariffs, transport costs, and the like, make it difficult to implement tests of this version of the theory. Instead we shall be concerned with the *relative* PPP theory which says that the *rate of change* of the exchange rate reflects different inflation rates in two countries.

The PPP theory has also been developed for different kinds of price levels. There are consumer price levels, wholesale price levels, producer price levels, factor price levels, and price levels referring to parts of different aggregates. Since the demand for money should be related to the level of prices on the purchased bundle of goods and services, we shall discuss the theory for *consumer price levels.* We would ideally like price levels that correctly reflect changes in people's welfare at a certain nominal income, but such "economic" price levels cannot be constructed.

The PPP theory in its relative version for consumer price levels says simply that the *rate of change of the exchange rate is equal to the percentage change in the ratio of price indexes.* One explanation is that commodity arbitrage among countries will make the exchange rate adjust in this way, provided that the exchange rate is the less rigid variable. Although all goods are not in international trade, PPP should hold, because the prices of nontraded goods must follow traded goods prices as long as taste and production patterns do not change.

The above explanation of the theory indicates that the exchange rate need *not* reflect PPP, if taste and technology induce different developments of the relative price between traded and nontraded goods in two countries. Empirical evidence substantiates this. Isard (1978) showed that there were deviations from consumer price-index parity over the period 1950–1970 for most industrialized countries. For example, the ratio of the exchange rate to the relative price index for United States and Germany was .72 in 1950 and .87 in 1970. Other countries show similar, though smaller, deviations.

The conclusion from this is that the *PPP theory does not hold perfectly for available price indexes.* Thus, the forecasting of exchange rates by the forecasting of relative inflation rates is likely to be misleading. Still, PPP in an *economic sense* may hold for an individual, when comparing exchange rate developments with the development of the relative price level in terms of *the individual's own* consumption bundle. Thus, the long-run neutrality of the exchange rate may hold better for an individual or a firm than the available data actually shows.

The factor-price version of the PPP theory should also be mentioned here. It says that the exchange rate should move so as to offset changes in the ratio of factor prices. If factor costs (estimated in a common currency) grow faster in one country than another, the first country's competitive position deteriorates. This may be reflected in the current account and unemployed resources—market disequilibria.

Most often the factor-cost version is expressed in terms of labor costs. Unit labor costs expressed in terms of a common currency should move together for labor markets to be in equilibrium. This theory suffers from a number of difficulties, as it presumes identical capital-labor ratios in all countries for a certain sector. Also, when we aggregate over all sectors, the average unit labor cost depends on the relative sizes of different sectors in each country. Thus changing structures may account for statistical deviations from parity even when there is cost parity for each sector.

The unit-labor-cost parity is probably a weaker long-run condition than consumer-price parity, because labor markets adjust slower than commodity markets. It is well known that countries have suffered from substantial labor-market disequilibria over much longer periods.

An additional weakness of the purchasing-power parity theory for forecasting purposes should be mentioned. The economic reason for the exchange rate to adjust to prices and factor costs rests on the presumption that exchange rates are more flexible. However, central banks rarely allow complete flexibility but peg the exchange rate or manage the float (dirty float). Then the market pressures could work to restore parity by adjustments of prices and factor costs instead. In this case, the exchange rate must be used to forecast these other variables. Evidently government behavior is crucial for the direction of causality and the forecast. We shall return to this point later.

The conclusion of this section is that purchasing-power parity for consumer price indexes is probably the best forecast for the long run without detailed forecasts of consumption patterns and relative price changes. This is a qualitative forecast, however. The *statistical problems* of measuring actual price levels indicate that it may be better to estimate future cash flows for long-term projects at constant price levels and simply neglect inflation. Then it suffices to forecast real exchange-rate changes— deviations from PPP. Again, it should be mentioned that this is only valid when contracts are not fixed in nominal magnitudes and when the effects of inflation are negligible. Also it is important to obtain an estimate of the *time horizon* over which commodity and labor-market disequilibriums correct themselves. Government behavior and the magnitude of disturbances are important for this consideration.

THE SHORT RUN: REAL EXCHANGE-RATE CHANGES. Theories of exchange rate determinations over the short run are generally concerned with deviations from PPP—the real exchange rate. The exceptions are monetarist models that are based on PPP. The models that are summarized here refer solely to recently developed explanations of "real" exchange rate changes. Thus, any forecast of the actual exchange rate would have to be based on the above long-term models in addition to those presented below.

Two papers, Kouri (1976) and Dornbusch (1976), formulate the main ingredients of modern exchange rate theory. Many other authors have developed the models further, but these two articles provide the basis for this section.

Recent exchange rate theory stresses the distinction between flow and stock equilibria. Flow equilibrium holds in the long run and implies that goods and wealth are not reallocated among countries. It is characterized by current-account balance and PPP. Stock equilibrium holds in asset markets in the short run and determines relative interest rates and the exchange rate.

A common story of adjustments after a shift in demands or supplies for a country's financial assets is as follows. At *constant nominal rates of interest and expectations,* an increased supply or decreased demand for domestic money or bonds leads to a sudden *depreciation* of the real exchange rate until outstanding supplies are willingly held. The depreciation will slowly induce a current-account surplus. This corresponds to increased holdings of foreign-currency assets by domestic residents. The exchange rate *appreciates* over time with the accumulation of foreign-currency assets, since these will not be willingly held unless the foreign currency depreciates. The process goes on until the current account is in balance at the original exchange rate and the initially desired portfolio shift has occurred.

The above model illustrates that an expansive monetary policy and an expansive fiscal policy both lead to a depreciation at *constant interest rates*. However, interest rates need not be pegged by the central bank. Then the expansive fiscal policy would lead to a higher interest rate that could increase the demand for domestic currency assets so that the sudden depreciation would not occur. The expansive fiscal policy is likely to increase aggregate demand so that the current account goes into a deficit. This deficit and a corresponding capital account surplus may be accommodated by an appreciation of the exchange rate and a higher interest rate. Over time the current account deficit would cause a depreciation as foreigners accumulate domestic assets and demand an increasingly large incentive to absorb more assets.

The exchange rate effect of a particular disturbance depends on its impact in money, financial, and goods markets, as well as on the central bank's response to the disturbance. Without going into great detail of tracing these effects, Exhibit 5 lists the likely impact on the *real* exchange rate of common types of disturbances. These impact effects are based on common exchange rate models. They are not indisputable but seem to accord with empirical regularities.

The impact effect on the real exchange rate is merely the beginning of a dynamic process as noted above. Thus, as the relative asset position of countries change, when the current account is not balanced, secondary exchange rate effects occur. In general, the real exchange rate tends to return over time to its previous equilibrium position unless substantial relative price shifts have occurred among traded and nontraded goods.

Increased expenditure and consumption, and/or investments may similarly push the current account into a deficit and the capital account into a surplus.

Expectations have hardly been mentioned so far. They have been assumed to be stationary. In other words, the developments above take place only when the disturbances are *unanticipated*. The view of the exchange rate as a financial variable makes it clear, however, that the demands for assets of different currency denominations depends crucially on *expectations about the future exchange rate*. Thus, a depreciation occurs not only when the above disturbances take place but *starts when the disturbances are anticipated* and only obtains the full effect at the time the actual disturbances occur. Modeling exchange rate determination involves, therefore, the modeling of expectations formation to a very large extent.

The implications of the role of expectations for forecasting are fundamental. *Forecasting the exchange rate involves not only forecasting the actual disturbances. Information must be obtained on other market participants' expectations about future disturbances.* The observed exchange rate at a point in time incorporates the average market expectations about future economic disturbances and the effect they will have on the exchange rate.

In Exhibit 5, it is assumed that foreign variables remain constant. Naturally, foreign disturbances of the same kinds and domestic disturbances with the opposite signs induce the opposite effects.

THE ROLE OF GOVERNMENTS.   Government and central-bank policies are of great relevance for the modeling and the forecasting of exchange rates and deserve separate

EXHIBIT 5   REAL EXCHANGE RATE EFFECTS OF COMMON DISTURBANCES

Disturbance (Unanticipated)	Exchange Rate Effect
Monetary expansion	Depreciation
Fiscal expansion at constant interest rates (monetary accommodation)	Depreciation
Fiscal expansion without monetary accommodation	Appreciation
Portfolio shift out of domestic assets	Depreciation
Increased aggregate demand at constant interest rates (monetary accommodation)	Depreciation
Increased aggregate demand without monetary accommodation	Appreciation
Increased aggregate domestic supply at constant interest rates (wage drop or productivity increase)	(Possibly small) Appreciation
Increased aggregate domestic supply without monetary accommodation	Appreciation
Domestic demand shift in favor of non-traded goods	Appreciation

treatment, although the above theories should, in principle, hold under any exchange-rate regime. The reason for stressing the role of governments is that their monetary and fiscal policies and anticipations about these are among the major determinants of the exchange rate. Thus predicting government behavior is crucial for forecasting the exchange rate. More interesting is that governments can affect the *adjustment process* in financial, commodity, and labor markets by their policies. They may do this by holding policy targets for monetary and fiscal policies that differ from the tendencies of the market. Also, they may impose quantitative controls that affect the functioning of the market and therefore the relevance of the above models. These two issues will be addressed here.

We shall first note that the forecasting of government behavior is as superfluous as the forecasting of other determinants of the exchange rate when markets are so efficient that unbiased forward rates exist for all time horizons.

Government-policy targets that differ from the tendencies of the market could be extremely important for the forecasting of exchange rates over the short run. Intervention in foreign-exchange markets provides the most obvious example. It is common that central banks stick to a pegged rate, although it has become clear to most market participants that the rate is not viable. At the same time, nominal rates may be pegged so that the forward rate becomes "locked in" at a level far apart from the forecasts of most observers. These conditions characterized long periods during the late 1960s and early 1970s, when large adjustments were made at times. The adjustments were often made months or quarters after it had become a safe bet to forecast an adjustment. In other words, forecasts that were different from the forward rate were highly successful. In fact, forward markets nearly disappeared for some currencies. Private arbitrageurs could move funds aggressively into, for example, deutsche marks, with central banks purchasing the weak currencies. Once the adjustments were made, central banks realized losses and private market participants realized gains.

There is little doubt that the adjustments toward the long-run equilibrium were delayed for years by the central-bank policies during the late 1960s. Thus, real exchange rates went far out of line and the most important forecasting task was how long central banks would keep on intervening to sustain an unrealistically pegged rate.

Black (1980) showed that the management of the dirty float during the 1970s has been characterized by similar behavior, though to a lesser extent. Many times, when substantial exchange-rate changes would have occurred during a clean float, central banks have intervened to hold on to an exchange-rate target only to let go of it after some time. At the same time, nominal interest rates have not been allowed to adjust to reflect exchange-rate expectations, with the consequence that forward rates at times could have been biased predictors. It seems, however, as if central banks' policies have changed during the late 1970s. Specifically, money-supply targets have been substituted for exchange-rate and interest-rate targets in many countries.

The second area in which governments' price targets may prolong the adjustment process is labor-market policies. For example, a government may pursue a full-employment policy, when nominal wage increases or a fall in productivity otherwise would have caused unemployment and an adjustment of wages. A depreciation and price inflation could follow, but if the government's employment commitment is strong, labor can obtain compensation for the fall in real wages. Thus real-wage flexibility becomes low, so that adjustments of relative unit labor costs becomes extremely slow. The country may find itself with continuing and increasing inflation and depreciation of its currency without any substantial impact on the real disequilibrium. England has found itself in this situation during large parts of the 1970s.

The other kind of government policies of importance for the adjustment process is *direct regulation.* Most obvious in this connection is exchange controls on financial-capital flows, but import licensing and price and wage controls are also important.

Most countries impose controls on the private activity in foreign-exchange markets. The measures may range from "voluntary" agreements on limits to banks' foreign-exchange exposures to direct regulation of exports and imports. All these measures have in common that quantity adjustments to incentives are slowed down. The financial-arbitrage activities become less efficient, with the result that there is more room for relative interest rates and the forward rate to deviate from the expected future spot rate.

Controls on trade flows, as in many developing countries, may also have the effect of prolonging market adjustments in commodity markets, with the result that deviations from the long-run equilibrium could be sustained longer than otherwise.

Domestic price and wage controls often go hand in hand with labor-market policies in countries with substantial inflation. Their effects in this context could be that exchange-rate changes take longer to be reflected in domestic prices. Thus demand and supply adjustments after exchange-rate changes take time with the result that deviations from the long-run equilibria are prolonged.

In conclusion, government behavior is important for exchange-rate modeling and forecasting, not only because monetary and fiscal policies contribute to exchange-rate changes, but also *for assessing the values of the different kinds of exchange-rate models and the value of forecasting over different horizons.* Price targets with respect to the exchange rate, commodity prices, and wages prolong the period over which there are large deviations from PPP and make forecasts of deviations from PPP more important. Government activities in the form of direct regulations may have the same impact, but could also hamper the functioning of international financial markets. The consequence of this is that forward rates become less-effective predictors of the future spot rate. The value of forecasting increases over the very short run (weeks) as well as over periods of several years in extreme cases.

FORECASTING METHODS

This section deals with different kinds of forecasting methods that are available to a firm. The relative accuracy and costs are discussed. The following alternatives are treated here:

1. The forward rate and relative interest rates.
2. Time-series analysis of historical developments.
3. Econometric modeling.
4. Leading variables.
5. Advisory services.

Before discussing the forecasting methods, different kinds of forecasts and the evaluation of forecasts will be described.

DESCRIPTION AND EVALUATION OF FORECASTS.   Forecasts may take many different forms depending on the method of forecasting. Naturally, the desired form of a forecast depends on the purpose of it as well as on costs of obtaining it.

A *point forecast* for a certain date is a forecast of an actual price at a future date (e.g., $3.00/£ for January 1, 1984). It gives the impression of exactness though the uncertainty usually is considerable. Accordingly, a point forecast can be accompanied by a likely *range* or a *standard deviation* for the same date in the future. A range is a simple measure of uncertainty and describes subjectively evaluated maxima and minima (e.g., $2.90/£–$3.10/£ for January 1, 1984).

A standard deviation is a somewhat more sophisticated measure of uncertainty and describes a band within which the exchange rate is going to fall with a probability of, for example, 95 percent according to the forecasters (e.g., a standard deviation of $.10/£ in the above example implies that the 95 percent probability range is $2.95/£–$3.05/£).

A point forecast can be useful for making financial, purchasing, or sales decisions with respect to a specific future date.

The quality of a borrowing or covering decision depends on the outcome of the exchange rate *relative to* the forward rate or the interest rate differential rather than the exact outcome. It may therefore be more desirable to limit the forecast to *the future spot rate relative to the forward rate or relative to the expected rate implied by the interest rate differential.* Such forecasts could be cheaper to form. The range or the standard deviation of a point forecast may contain the forward rate and therefore offer little guidance for a financial decision. However, a point forecast combined with a standard deviation contains implicitly the probability that the future spot rate will exceed the forward rate.

An even simpler forecast can be stated in the form of *direction of change.* However, such a forecast is not useful for financial decisions unless the forward rate is equal to the spot rate at the time the forecast is made. On the other hand, this is the easiest forecast to make by judgment alone.

Many forecasting methods cannot produce forecasts for specific dates but only for *averages over periods.* For example, a point forecast of $3.00/£ could be the expected average rate during the month of January 1984, the first quarter of 1984, or even the expected average for the entire year. It is nonsensical to make a forecast for a specific date far into the future. Most forecasting models are based on averages of historical data over months or quarters and can produce forecasts only in the form of such averages. Nevertheless, the forecast may be presented in the form of a point forecast for a specific date. It is impossible to produce meaningful average forecasts for periods that are shorter than a month. Even this may be overly optimistic. The impression of exactness of a point forecast should not fool the user. It is unnecessary to have specific date forecasts for many purposes, such as for cash flow analysis of foreign projects.

The *evaluation* of forecasts depends naturally on the form that they take. Directional forecasts relative to the spot rate as well as relative to the forward rate can be evaluated by the *proportion of forecasts showing the correct direction.* Alternatively, one can measure the *profits that would have resulted from relying on the forecast relative to the profits of alternative strategies.*

Point forecasts make it possible to estimate the *mean squared error* of the forecast. This is a good measure of the degree of exactness of the forecasts but it need not be a good measure of the profitability of relying on the forecasts since the point forecast can be near the outcome but still on the wrong side of the forward rate. Levich (1980) shows that the forward rate is better than most advisory services in terms of mean squared errors; however, he also shows that relying on the forward rate would have been less profitable over certain periods than relying on some of the advisory services for covering decisions.

THE FORWARD RATE AND RELATIVE INTEREST RATES.   The forward rate is naturally the cheapest available forecast of the exchange rate. Its accuracy relative to other forecasting methods was discussed above. It was argued that the forward rate does not represent the ideal forecast for all countries and all time horizons. First, forward markets are well developed only for the major currencies. Second, they tend to become thin for periods longer than a year for all currencies. Third, there is limited evidence that forward rates can be outperformed for considerable lengths of time even for the major currencies. It should be stressed again, however, that an alternative forecast in cases where well-developed forward markets exist presumes either superior information or judgment about future disturbances and their effects or less risk aversion than the marginal participant in the forward markets.

The forecast contained in the forward rate for relatively long periods, say from six months to two years, is not necessarily the most interesting from a firm's perspective, since many times it is changes in the *real* exchange rate (deviations from PPP) that are of concern. Then inflation rates must be forecast in addition to the future exchange rate.

In conclusion, the forward rate is hard to beat and is a cheap forecast of the future exchange rate as well as of deviations from PPP for the major currencies for the very short run or for periods when the price level is stable.

TIME-SERIES ANALYSIS.   Many economic variables develop over time in such a way that the historic development provides a guide to the future course. The exchange rate between two countries could behave in this way over time when inflation rates differ. A trend forecast would in this case only concern nominal exchange-rate changes and not deviations from PPP. A more interesting issue is whether the real changes—changes in the very short run or the short run—show any such "autocorrelation" over time. Roll (1979) and Pigott and Sweeney (1985) have analyzed the time pattern of deviations from PPP. In both cases, deviations follow a near random walk process (i.e., the random walk cannot be rejected). In light of exchange rate theory and Exhibits 1–4, these results are surprising since we expect the process to be mean-reverting, that is, PPP should hold in the long run. The results may be accounted for by the short time horizon of the analysis in the articles referred to.

Turning to time-series analysis of nominal exchange rate changes (which in the short run approximate real exchange rate changes for most countries), Meese and Rogoff (1983) show that over certain periods auto-regressive processes predict better than both structural models and the forward rate. It is a sign of market inefficiency or the existence of a risk-premium if time series analyses consistently outperform the forward rate. The results so far indicate only that over some periods and some currencies such a result is possible. In order for time series analysis to be truly useful one must also predict for which periods and currencies the forward rate can be outperformed in this way.

Giddy and Dufey (1975) conducted time-series tests on the daily exchange rates of Canada, France, and the United Kingdom relative to the dollar. The tests were performed on data for the flexible period up to October 1974. The results showed that there is *some* autocorrelation of daily exchange rates, but the predictive power of the tests is extremely low.

Time-series forecasts were also compared to other forecasts for different time horizons up to 90 days. The time-series forecasts in this study were consistently worse than those provided by so-called martingales or submartingales. The former implies a pure random walk, whereas the submartingale is a random walk around the forecast implied by relative interest rates. When interest-rate parity holds, this is equivalent to the forward rate.

These mixed results for the time-series forecast do not rule out their use at all times. They may be valuable, for example, when substantial government intervention is suspected because government targets may make the autocorrelation of exchange rates relatively high. The time series forecast could also be more valid for longer-term inflationary developments and, therefore, for *long run* exchange-rate changes. There is no empirical evidence to substantiate these hypotheses, however.

The techniques of time-series forecasting should be commented upon. It is a relatively cheap econometric method. A regression on historical data with different weights is run. Forecasts are updated as new data are observed. A major problem is naturally to assign the weights to data of different ages. Fairly sophisticated models, *ARMA* and *ARIMA,* have been designed for this purpose. Most major textbooks on econometrics describe these methods. The *Box-Jenkins* technique for regression analysis, also described in most textbooks, is a popular and powerful technique that can be applied on ARIMA models. Naturally, simpler time-series models like moving averages and exponential smoothing can be used for forecasting purposes, though these models are less powerful than ARIMA.

ECONOMETRIC MODELS. Econometric modeling of exchange rates range from large simultaneous multiequation interdependent structures to simple one-equation systems. The largest model heretofore has been developed at the Federal Reserve Board. It is a quarterly five-country model (plus the rest of the world) with about 30 equations for each county, including commodity, labor, and financial markets (see Berner et al., 1976). Naturally, the building of such a model is extremely costly, and the continuous use of it for forecasting purposes involves updating not only of data but of essential parts as well.

On the other extreme are simple monetarist one-equation models. Since these models are based on the assumption that PPP holds and that financial markets are efficient; they do not provide an alternative to the forward rate. These models are estimated for the purpose of explaining, but not necessarily forecasting, exchange rates.

In between these extremes, there are a number of efforts at econometric modeling of exchange rates. Helliwell (1969), Herring and Marston (1977), and Artus (1976) provide examples.

Most of the models referred to are structural models, that is, their main purpose is *not* to obtain efficient forecasts but to test exchange-rate theories. The main problem for forecasting purposes is to describe expectation formation and government behavior. Many of these models treat the latter as exogenous, whereas a forecasting model must include a formulation for the government's reaction to different disturbances. It is naturally a very difficult task to achieve general formulations for government behavior as well as for expectations formation. Meese and Rogoff (1983) show that simple structural model specifications tend to be unstable over time and inferior in predictive ability to forward rates and time series analysis.

Econometric models explicitly for forecasting purposes have been developed by a number of advisory services. These models need not be structurally correct, but it is instead important that they capture variables that systematically lead exchange-rate changes. The task of developing, changing, and running large models is naturally enormous and can only be worthwhile if they consistently outperform the forward rate or other more simplistic forecasting methods. The empirical evidence for these forecasting services is mixed (see section on forecasting services), but it is clear that it is a formidable and expensive task with an uncertain outcome for an individual firm to attempt to construct its own large-scale model.

LEADING VARIABLES. A simple and inexpensive method that can be used to complement and evaluate the forward rate and relative interest rates as predictors, is to study variables that tend to indicate changes in exchange rates before they occur (leading variables). Naturally this implies that the observer has some more-or-less-explicit exchange-rate model in the background. This kind of forecasting is probably done in more or less sophisticated a manner by all forecasters.

A large number of variables can be thought of as leading variables for different time horizons. For example, the theory in "Determinants of the Exchange Rate" suggests that long-lasting deviations from PPP cannot be sustained—the exchange rate must adjust. Similarly, relatively fast increases in unit labor costs often proceed adjustments of pegged rates. Over shorter time periods the forecaster could ask: How have monetary aggregates developed, and does it seem as if the exchange rate has not adjusted sufficiently? Current-account developments and changes in exchange reserves are also variables that often are mentioned as leading variables. It is necessary to be very careful with the use of these indicators, because the exchange rate and the mentioned variables may be interdependent and the order of changes that occur depend on a number of economic circumstances. Therefore, it takes a trained eye with an overview of economic developments and a good grasp of exchange-rate determination to use this forecasting technique successfully.

Forecasting by leading variables can, of course, be performed by econometric techniques as well. The forecaster who attempts to obtain exact estimates of the future rate can use regression equations of the conventional kind. *Factor* and *discriminant analyses* have also been attempted. These methods—explained in econometric textbooks—involve the search for the variables that take on certain values at the time the exchange rate changes in certain ways.

Discriminant analysis is used for prediction by classifying observations into groups, such as depreciation or appreciation. Then one studies the "classificatory power" of different variables—the extent to which other variables take on certain values when the target variable falls in the different classifications. Folks and Stansell (1975) used this method successfully to predict large exchange-rate movements for a number of countries in 1971–1972. They developed a discriminant function on observations drawn on an earlier period. The variables that were most powerful in discriminating between countries with more than 5 percent depreciation over a two-year period and those outside this group were the change in the price index, the growth of reserves, a variable indicating the debt-service burden, the ratio of exports to imports, and the central bank's discount rate.

There are naturally serious drawbacks to discriminant analysis. It cannot be used to obtain exact and continuous forecasts, and it is not based on structural relationships. Therefore, the classificatory power that is found during one period could be coincidental.

Leading-variables observation in general may be a valuable complement to other forecasts. Especially with respect to deviations from PPP in different versions, and for forecasting changes in pegged rates, this technique could be successful.

FOREIGN-EXCHANGE ADVISORY SERVICES.   There are now a large number of firms specializing in forecasting and a number of large banks and brokerage firms in the United States have set up departments for the forecasting of exchange rates. Most of these firms and banks sell not only forecasts but a whole range of advisory services for the international firm.

The subscription fee for obtaining the full services of a forecasting firm ranges between $10,000 and $20,000 per year. This may sound like a high figure, but it is small for the firm that is heavily involved in international trade. The service need not beat the forward rate by many points continuously for the fee to pay off.

Most forecasting services provide biweekly or monthly direct forecasts horizons ranging from a month up to one or two years, normally for 11 major currencies. Judgmental evaluations of economic developments with respect to the exchange rate can be obtained for shorter and longer terms. It is possible to purchase regular forecasts for 40 countries.

The techniques used by forecasting services can be all combinations of the highly intuitive and the technically sophisticated models. Some services rely on large-scale econometric models and others rely only on the observation and evaluation of economic developments.

The quality of the forecasts supplied by private forecasting services is very low in absolute terms (all forecasts are), and some services have been able to predict better than the forward rate consistently over several years. However, there is not one service that has been clearly and consistently superior over all time horizons or for all currencies (Levich, 1980). There is no doubt, however, that many services are able to say whether the forward rate will exaggerate or underestimate the future spot rate and be right more than 50 percent of the time. The problem for the customer is to evaluate when and for which currency to employ a particular forecasting service, or whether to purchase several forecasts and employ a weighted average. In summary, it takes expertise to derive benefits that exceed the costs of forecasting services.

SOURCES OF INFORMATION

International Financial Statistics, published by the International Monetary Fund is a monthly publication with historical *monthly, quarterly,* and *yearly* data on nearly all relevant financial and real variables of relevance for forecasting.

Main Economic Indicators, published by the OECD (Organization for Economic Cooperation and Development) contains similar data for the OECD countries.

Many banks publish limited financial data for many countries coupled with analysis in the form of biweekly or monthly newsletters as part of their foreign-exchange advisory services. Harris Bank in Chicago collects and makes available for subscription a very complete set of *weekly* financial data, covering spot exchange rates, forward rates, and Euromarket interest rates over different maturities for nine currencies. The Morgan Guarantee Trust Company in New York publishes *World Financial Markets.* This contains monthly data and analysis of developments in the international money and bond markets in North America, Europe, and Asia.

The central banks of most countries publish annual reports containing statistics and often English summaries. The U.S. Federal Reserve Board also has a quarterly journal, the *Federal Reserve Bulletin,* with a statistical appendix on a large amount of national and international financial and banking data. The *Bank of England Quarterly* is the corresponding British publication, and the German Central Bank (Deutsche Bundesbank) prints quarterly, largely statistical publications. Data on international trade can be found in the *United Nations' Monthly Bulletin of Statistics* and *Directions of Trade.* Detailed national-accounts-data for the United States is published in the *Survey of Current Business* by the Department of Commerce. The *U.S. Treasury Bulletin* (quarterly) and publications by the regional Federal Reserve Banks are additional sources of national and international financial data.

Finally, *Annual Report on Exchange Arrangements and Exchange Restrictions* lists and describes all exchange controls imposed by members of the International Monetary Fund. It is published by this organization.

MANAGEMENT CONSIDERATIONS

GENERAL CONCLUSIONS FOR FORECASTING.   It is obviously impossible to summarize the whole discussion about the forecasting of exchange rates by a simple recommendation on how to go about it and what sources to use. It is clear that the forward rate and relative interest rates can be outperformed as predictors of the exchange rate, but the manager must ask: At what costs and what can be gained? It takes the continuous use of substantial human resources to predict better than the forward rate consistently. Forecasts by foreign-exchange advisory services are certainly cheaper and seem to perform well for many currencies, but the optimal use of these services also demands additional time for evaluation and choice. Naturally the more time and resources a firm spends and the more alternative methods for forecasting that are compared, the better a forecast could become. However, most of the fluctuations in exchange rates during the flexible regime have been unanticipated. In other words, *all* forecasts have been *bad* forecasts, and the gains that can be made relative to the forward rate are marginal for the major currencies. Nevertheless, such marginal improvements may be worthwhile for large firms with large international transactions.

It should also be noted that even if the exchange rate could be forecast well by the forward rate, the firm may need additional forecast capability for price levels in order to be able to assess the "real exchange rate"—deviations from PPP—over different time horizons. This is the variable that matters for the return on foreign projects, equity, and other investments that are not defined in nominal terms.

TREATMENT OF UNCERTAINTY—HEDGING AND COVERING. Once a forecast of the future development has been obtained, there is still considerable uncertainty about the forecasts. What should the firm do in face of this uncertainty? The answer to this question depends on the risk attitude of the firm, the time horizon of the cash flow, and on the forecast rate itself.

The *time horizon* is important because uncertainty about the exchange rate need not be of any major concern if it is believed that prices at home or abroad can be adjusted or will adjust in the market. This has been discussed in connection with the relevance of the exchange rate. A few examples could add clarity to the argument. First, a firm with a production subsidiary in Brazil need not worry about long-term depreciations of the *cruzeiro,* if it can raise its output prices there correspondingly. Second, a firm that has borrowed long term in Swiss *francs* need not worry about long-term appreciations of the currency if this appreciation depends on inflation in the United States, because the larger amount of dollars that are needed to pay back the loan is worth less in terms of purchasing power. Third, the importer with trade credits need not worry about exchange-rate developments *if* the goods are held in inventories and the sale prices in the United States can be adjusted to compensate for exchange-rate changes. The implication of this discussion is again that it is mainly "real" exchange-rate uncertainty against which the firm potentially needs to cover. This kind of uncertainty is of major importance in the short run (up to 2 to 4 years). Thus, the fact that forward markets do not exist for the long maturities is of no real concern. Locking in the exchange rate for the long term would expose firms to other risks, such as inflation uncertainty in the domestic currency.

Uncertainty about the inflation rate could, of course, be a major consideration for long-term financial loans or investments. However, this kind of uncertainty exists for domestic as well as for foreign loans and could be decreased by shortening the loan periods or by making the interest rate flexible or renegotiable.

The *risk attitude* of the firm should depend on whether the stock market puts a premium on the firm with a low variance in its profits. There is some dispute about this, which we cannot cover here. The risk-*neutral* firm strives to maximize the *expected return* on investments without considering the variance. (The expected return naturally contains an evaluation of the probabilities of different exchange-rate changes. Once the expected return is estimated, the decisions are based *only* on this value.)

The behavior of the risk-neutral firm would be characterized by a reluctance to pay transactions costs for reducing uncertainty. Therefore, such a firm would *never hedge* or *cover* accounts payable or receivables when the forward rate is equal to the expected future spot rate, because no gain can be expected by such a transaction. The risk-*averse* firm, on the other hand, would *always cover* short-term payables and receivables when the forward rate is equal to the expected future spot rate (unless the transactions costs are so high that the firm's risk aversion does not motivate the outlays).

The argument above is, of course, valid also for covers and hedges taken in money markets (a loan is taken in the currency with an expected positive cash flow, transferred to the home currency and invested in the money market) as long as interest-rate parity holds, that is, when the forward rate reflects the interest-rate differential.

The simple rules above, always cover or never cover, cannot be recommended when financial and exchange markets are less efficient. The firm can then obtain forecasts of the future exchange rate that deviates from the forward rate or relative interest rates. The deviation from interest-rate parity for the forward rate is less interesting, since it only affects the choice of forward cover versus money-market cover. When the expected future spot rate is not equal to the forward rate it may pay for the risk-neutral firm to use the forward markets (though we should not call it cover or hedge) because the value of a future payable in a foreign currency may be worth more translated at the forward rate than at the expected future spot rate. The risk-neutral firm would naturally always choose the most advantageous rate.

The risk-averse firm may choose *not* to cover when the forward rate is such that the firm expects a higher domestic currency value when the payable is translated at the future spot rate. Naturally the degree of risk aversion and the difference between the forward rate and the expected future spot rate will determine whether to cover or whether to take the risk of leaving a foreign-currency position open.

The terms *hedging* and *covering* are often used interchangeably. However, cover should refer to the taking of a position in forward or money markets that makes the value of a *future cash flow* certain in terms of the domestic currency. In other words, cash flows are covered. Hedging, on the other hand, refers to the taking of a position in forward or money markets in order to offset potential gains or losses on foreign-currency assets or liabilities. Thus hedging implies that the firm may realize a gain (loss) on the forward contract against an unrealized loss (gain) in the value of an asset. Accordingly, balance-sheet or translation exposures are hedged. Hedging of translation exposures has been used with two different meanings in the literature. Sometimes (and correctly) it stands for the *locking in* of the firm's accounting value at a certain date (see, e.g., the introductory chapter in Levich and Wihlborg, 1980). The locked-in value includes translation losses/gains *and* the realized gain/loss on the forward contract. This kind of hedging would naturally only be done by the risk-averse firm that is concerned about fluctuations in its accounting net worth.

The second use of the term *hedging* is used in some textbooks like Aliber (1979) and Rodriguez and Carter (1976); firms can take positions in the forward markets on which they expect to realize gains that are equal in size to expected translation losses. This operation presumes a forecast of the future exchange rate to calculate the expected translation loss. Also, the forward rate must differ from the expected future spot rate for the operation to be feasible. Otherwise it is impossible to make a gain on the forward market transaction. Naturally, this kind of hedging is highly speculative and may expose the firm substantially to potential economic losses. The closer the expected future rate is to the forward rate, the larger the forward transaction must be to obtain an expected gain of a certain size. No risk-averse firm would undertake such "hedging" operations unless the forward-rate bias is expected to be substantial. The risk-neutral firm could be willing to undertake such risky operations, but there is no economic reason to limit the forward contract to the implied size if the firm has trust in its forecast.

SOURCES AND SUGGESTED REFERENCES

Aliber, R.Z. *Exchange Risk and Corporate International Finance.* London: Macmillan, 1978.

Artus, J.R. "Exchange Rate Stability and Managed Floating: The German Experience," International Monetary Fund, *Staff Papers,* Vol. XXIV (1976), pp. 312–33.

Artus, J.R. and J.H. Young. "Fixed and Flexible Rates: A Renewal of the Debate," International Monetary Fund, *Staff Papers,* Vol. XXVI (1978), pp. 324–55.

Bailey, R.W., R. Baillee, and P.C. McMuhun. "Interpreting Econometric Evidence in the Foreign Exchange Market," *Oxford Economic Papers* 36 (1984), pp. 67–85.

Berner, R., P. Clark, H. Howe, S. Kwack, and G. Stevens. *Modeling the International Influences on the U.S. Economy: A Multi-Country Approach,* International Finance Division, Discussion Paper No. 93. Washington, D.C.: Federal Reserve Board.

Black, S.W. *Flexible Exchange Rates and National Economic Policies.* New Haven, CT: Yale University Press, 1977.

———. "Central Bank Intervention and the Stability of Exchange Rates," *Exchange Risk and Exposure,* R.M. Levich and C.G. Wihlborg (eds.). Lexington, MA: Lexington Books, D.C. Heath, 1980.

Dornbusch, R. "Expectations and Exchange Rate Dynamics," *Journal of Political Economy* 84 (1976), pp. 1161–76.

Eiteman, D.K. and A.I. Stonehill. *Multinational Business Finance.* Reading, MA: Addison-Wesley, 1979.

Folks, W.R. and S.R. Stansell. "The Use of Discriminant Analysis in Forecasting Exchange Rate Movements," *Journal of International Business Studies* 6 (Spring 1975), pp. 32–50.

Frenkel, J.A. "The Forward Exchange Rate, Expectations and the Demand for Money: The German Hyperinflation," *American Economic Review* 67 (September 1977), pp. 653–70.

Frenkel, J.A. and R.M. Levich. "Covered Interest Arbitrage: Unexploited Profits?" *Journal of Political Economy* 83 (April 1975), pp. 325–38.

Giddy, I.M. and G. Dufey. "The Random Behavior of Flexible Exchange Rates: Implications for Forecasting," *Journal of International Business Studies* 6 (Spring 1975), pp. 1–31.

Helliwell, J. "A Structural Model of the Foreign Exchange Market," *Canadian Journal of Economics* 17 (1969), pp. 90–105.

Herin, J., A. Lindbeck, and J. Myhrman. *Flexible Exchange Rates and Stabilization Policies.* London: Macmillan, 1977.

Herring, R.J. and R.C. Marston. *National Monetary Policies and International Financial Markets.* Amsterdam: North Holland, 1977.

Hong, H. "Inflation and the Market Value of the Firm: Theory and Tests," *Journal of Finance* 32 (1977), pp. 1031–48.

Isard, P. *Exchange Rate Determination: A Survey of Popular Views and Recent Models,* Princeton Study in International Finance, No. 42 (1978).

Jacque, L.L. *Management of Foreign Exchange Risk.* Lexington, MA: Lexington Books, D.C. Heath, 1978.

Kohlhagen, S.W. *The Behavior of Foreign Exchange Markets—A Critical Survey of the Empirical Literature,* Monograph Series in Finance and Economics, No. 3. New York: New York University, 1978.

Kouri, P.J.K. "The Exchange Rate and the Balance of Payments in the Short Run and the Long Run," *Scandinavian Journal of Economics* 78, No. 2 (1976), pp. 148–70.

Levich, R.M. "Further Results on the Efficiency of Markets for Foreign Exchange," *Management Exchange Rate Flexibility,* Federal Reserve Bank of Boston, No. 20 (1979).

————. "Analyzing the Accuracy of Foreign Exchange Advisory Services: Theory and Evidence," *Exchange Risk and Exposure,* R.M. Levich and C.G. Wihlborg (eds.). Lexington, MA: Lexington Books, D.C. Heath, 1980.

————. "An Examination of Overshooting Behavior in the Foreign Exchange Market," Occasional Paper, Study Group on the Foreign Exchange Markets of the Group of Thirty (May 1981).

Levich, R.M. and C.G. Wihlborg. *Exchange Risk and Exposure.* Lexington, MA: Lexington Books, D.C. Heath, 1980.

McKinnon, R. *Money in International Exchange, The Convertible Currency System.* Oxford: Oxford University Press, 1979.

Meese, R.A. and K. Rogoff. "Empirical Exchange Rate Models of the Seventies—Do They Fit Out of Sample?" *Journal of International Economics* 14 (1983), pp. 3–24.

Officer, L.M. "The Purchasing Power Parity Theory of Exchange Rates: A Review Article," International Monetary Fund, *Staff Papers,* Vol. XXIII (1976), pp. 1–60.

Piggott, H.C. and R.J. Sweeney. "Purchasing Power Parity and Exchange Rate Dynamics," *Exchange Rates, Trade, and the U.S. Economy,* S.W. Arndt, R.J. Sweeney, and T.D. Willet (eds.). Cambridge, MA: Ballinger, 1985.

Poole, W. "Speculative Prices as Random Walks: An Analysis of Ten Time Series of Flexible Exchange Rates," *Southern Economic Journal* 43 (1976), pp. 468–78.

Rodriguez, R.M. and E.E. Carter. *International Financial Management,* 1st ed. Englewood Cliffs, NJ: Prentice-Hall, 1976.

Roll, R. "Violations of Purchasing Power Parity and Their Implications for Efficient International Commodity Markets," *International Finance and Trade,* M. Sarnat and G.P. Szego (eds.). Cambridge, MA: Ballinger, 1985.

Schadler, S. "Sources of Exchange Rate Variability: Theory and Empirical Evidence," International Monetary Fund, *Staff Papers,* Vol. XXV (1977), pp. 253–96.

Sveriges Riksbank. *Förvaltningsberättelse.* Stockholm, 1980.

Sweeney, R.J. "Stabilizing or Destabilizing Speculation? Evidence from the Foreign Exchange Markets, *Exchange Rates, Trade, and the U.S. Economy,* S.W. Arndt, R.J. Sweeney, and T.D. Willett (eds.). Cambridge, MA: Ballinger, 1985.

Wachtel, P. and A. Cukierman. "Differential Inflationary Expectations and the Variability of the Rate of Inflation: Some Theory and Evidence," *American Economic Review* 69 (1979), pp. 595–609.

Wihlborg, C.G. *Currency Risks in International Financial Markets,* Princeton Study in International Finance, No. 44 (1978).

————. "Currency Exposure Taxonomy and Theory," *Exchange Risk and Exposure,* R.M. Levich and C.G. Wihlborg (eds.). Lexington, MA: Lexington Books, D.C. Heath, 1980.

————. "Interest Rates, Exchange Rate Adjustments and Currency Risks," *Journal of Money Credit and Banking* 14 (February 1982), pp. 58–74.

CONFLICT MANAGEMENT IN INTERNATIONAL BUSINESS

CONTENTS

CONFLICT MANAGEMENT IN INTERNATIONAL BUSINESS

Thomas N. Gladwin

THE CHALLENGE OF CONFLICT MANAGEMENT

CONFLICT AND THE MULTINATIONAL CORPORATION. *The Economist* (1978) has captured "it" well:

> It fiddles its accounts. It avoids or evades its taxes. It rigs its intracompany transfer prices. It is run by foreigners, from decision centers thousands of miles away. It imports foreign labor practices. It overpays. It underpays. It competes unfairly with local firms. It is in cahoots with local firms. It exports jobs from rich countries. It is an instrument of rich countries' imperialism. The technologies it brings to the third world are old fashioned. No, they are too modern. It meddles. It bribes. Nobody can control it. It wrecks balance of payments. It overturns economic policies. It plays off governments against each other to get the biggest investment incentives. Won't it please come and invest? Let it bloody well go home.

"It," of course, is the multinational corporation (MNC)—which from a multiplicity of quarters has found itself under heavy fire. No other institution in history has ever been so pervasively unloved and misunderstood throughout the world. The fact of conflict—of somehow being involved with opposing forces—has surely come to be a dominant connotation attached to the very phrase *multinational corporation*. The causes, course, and consequences of conflict involving the MNC have been persistent and major themes in the international business literature, as reflected in works, for example, by Barnet and Muller (1974); Bergsten, Horst, and Moran (1978); Gilpin (1975); Sauvant and Lavipour (1976); and Vernon (1977).

Gladwin and Walter, in *Multinationals Under Fire* (1980), have summarized the challenge of conflict confronting multinationals as follows. They see multinational corporate conflict as *inevitable,* given that MNCs operate in an environment of multiple interest groups that place conflicting demands on them. Such conflict is *different,* both in kind and degree, from that which is purely domestic because of unique features both of the MNC itself and of the interdependent global system in which conflicts occur. As a result, the disputes are often far more *complex.* And given that the world is moving deeper into an era of growing demands and diminishing resources, it's quite likely that the frequency and intensity of conflicts involving

MNCs will be *increasing*. The challenge of conflict is truly *diverse* and *pervasive* with respect to the kinds of issues, opponents, tactics, and areas involved. The structure or focus of conflict, in addition, is growing increasingly *transnational* through time. Finally, the conflicts can be *consequential*, in both destructive and constructive ways, and have often been *mismanaged*. Let's explore this "arena of conflict" in a bit more detail before turning our attention to a new contingency-based approach to conflict management appropriate for use within it.

THE NATURE OF MULTINATIONAL CORPORATE CONFLICT

CONFLICT ISSUES.   Myriad issues give rise to multinational corporate conflict. Exhibit 1 organizes them into nine subject areas: terrorism, human rights, politics, questionable payments, marketing, labor relations, environment, technology, and economics/finance. Case examples from all of these areas are highlighted below. But following from Gladwin and Walter (1980), the diverse and pervasive nature of conflict confronting multinational corporations can be quickly appreciated by considering a typical issue or question associated with each area, as follows:

> **Terrorism.**   Should MNCs be allowed to pay ransom and publish revolutionary manifestos of terrorist groups in order to gain the release of kidnapped employees?
>
> **Human Rights.**   Should MNCs be allowed to expand present investments or make new investments in nations where human civil and political rights are violated?
>
> **Politics.**   Should MNCs be allowed to decline doing any business in Israel in order to avoid being blacklisted by Arab League nations?
>
> **Questionable Payments.**   Should MNCs be allowed to offer or give a bribe in order to obtain or retain business in nations where bribery and corruption are the way of life?
>
> **Marketing.**   Should MNCs be allowed to advertise and promote in developing nations the sale of infant-formula products that substitute for breast milk?
>
> **Labor Relations.**   Should MNCs be allowed to threaten to transfer the whole or part of an operating unit from a country in order to influence the results of collective bargaining?
>
> **Environment.**   Should MNCs be allowed to circumvent restrictive environmental or occupational health laws at home by shifting "dirty" facilities to poor developing nations?
>
> **Technology.**   Should MNCs be allowed to concentrate most of their R&D activities at home rather than dispersing them widely around the globe?
>
> **Economics/Finance.**   Should MNCs be allowed to use transfer pricing between subsidiaries that does not conform to an arm's length standard for purposes of reducing taxes in nations with high tax rates?

CONFLICT LOCUS.   Multinational corporate conflict is of course nothing new, as business historians such as Wilkins have extensively documented (1970 and 1974). The composition of issues at stake in the conflicts has naturally varied over time, reflecting the influence of social and political movements, fads, contagion, and domino effects. Most MNCs' disputes over ecology and bribery, for example, emerged only after 1975.

Conflicts involving multinationals undoubtedly occur in every society in which they operate, but they vary widely in terms of content, frequency, intensity, forms of expression, and duration. This variation is perhaps largely attributable to the diverse economic, social, political, and institutional contexts in which MNC operations take place. Disputes over ownership and kidnapping, for example, have emerged most frequently in developing nations, whereas issues involving labor relations and consumerism have largely occurred in the developed economies.

A valuable locational perspective emerges when MNC conflicts are classified according to "issue locus," that is, whether the conflict emerges in a home nation over a purely domestic matter, in the home nation over a foreign matter, in a host nation over a domestic matter, or in a host or third nation over a foreign matter. Conflicts can be deemed to be over "foreign matters" when the overseas behavior of the multinational corporation is at issue or when foreign transactions, opponents, or reactions are significantly involved. Church-group protests in the United States regarding labor practices of U.S. firms in South Africa, for example, represent home-nation disputes over foreign matters.

Gladwin and Walter (1980) have found that the content of the issues in MNC conflict has been growing increasingly international or transnational over time. This is probably the result of growing economic interdependence, improved global communications, intergovernmental coordination, and a greatly increased propensity on the part of citizen lobbies, politicians, and regulators to concern themselves with events and conditions in foreign lands. The veil that used to insulate MNCs from attacks in one nation for their behavior in others has thus progressively been lifted. The challenges posed by such interdependence and transnationalism have been surveyed by Keohane and Nye (1977); Nye (1974); and Vogel (1978).

CONFLICT OPPONENTS.   Who seeks to hinder, compel, or injure the activities of multinationals? The answer, it seems, is just about everybody. Some of the opponents are small and others very large; some are novices and others old pros at waging conflict; some are poor and others rich; some are ad hoc and unorganized, whereas others are long established and highly structured; some are obsessed with a single issue, whereas others dally in multiple issues; some have entire armies at their disposal, whereas others only have typewriters; some are out for a little fun and excitement, whereas others are willing to die for their causes.

The opponents of MNCs can be classified into four general categories: citizen lobby, regulatory, political, and commercial. *Citizen lobbies* (e.g., environmental, religious, human rights, social action, consumer, community, university) tend to have deep-seated and ideological convictions, thus often producing greater rigidity in their conflict behavior and transforming conflicts with MNCs into eternal struggles over fundamental "truths." *Regulatory agencies* (e.g., antitrust, finance, welfare, environment, natural resources, commerce) are generally empowered to carry out mandates entrusted to them from either legislative or executive branches of government. *Politicians* (e.g., heads of state, political parties, legislative bodies, international bodies, nationalist/separatist groups, terrorist groups), wherever they are, are constantly striving to remain in, or get into, power. Politicians in power are often motivated to extract additional benefits from MNCs, whereas those out of power often tend to fix blame on MNCs for undesirable states of affairs. Finally, *commercial bodies* (e.g.,

EXHIBIT 1 ISSUES IN MULTINATIONAL CORPORATE CONFLICT

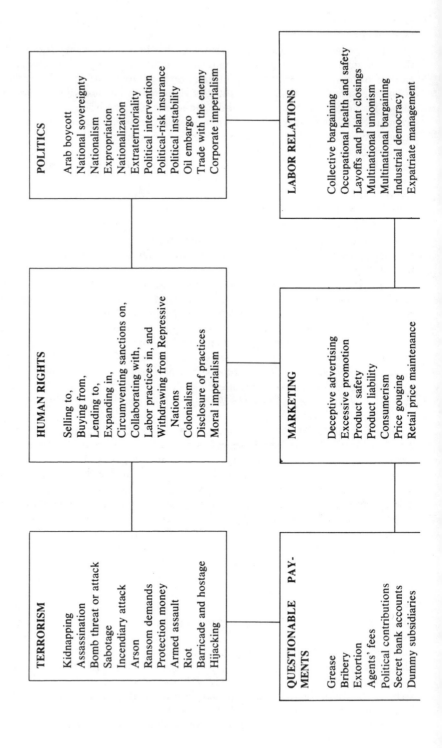

TERRORISM

Kidnapping
Assassination
Bomb threat or attack
Sabotage
Incendiary attack
Arson
Ransom demands
Protection money
Armed assault
Riot
Barricade and hostage
Hijacking

HUMAN RIGHTS

Selling to,
Buying from,
Lending to,
Expanding in,
Circumventing sanctions on,
Collaborating with,
Labor practices in, and
Withdrawing from Repressive
Nations
Colonialism
Disclosure of practices
Moral imperialism

POLITICS

Arab boycott
National sovereignty
Nationalism
Expropriation
Nationalization
Extraterritoriality
Political intervention
Political-risk insurance
Political instability
Oil embargo
Trade with the enemy
Corporate imperialism

QUESTIONABLE PAY-MENTS

Grease
Bribery
Extortion
Agents' fees
Political contributions
Secret bank accounts
Dummy subsidiaries

MARKETING

Deceptive advertising
Excessive promotion
Product safety
Product liability
Consumerism
Price gouging
Retail price maintenance

LABOR RELATIONS

Collective bargaining
Occupational health and safety
Layoffs and plant closings
Multinational unionism
Multinational bargaining
Industrial democracy
Expatriate management

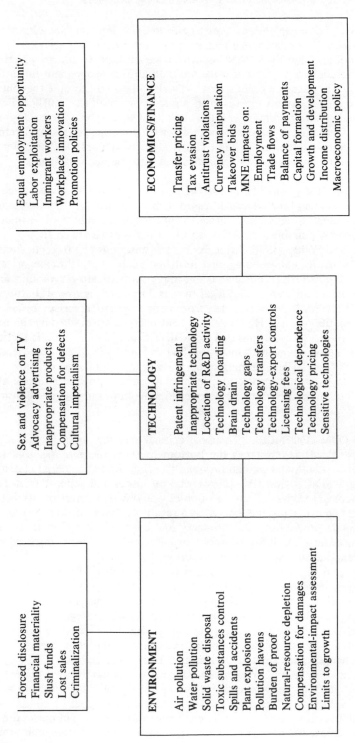

Forced disclosure
Financial materiality
Slush funds
Lost sales
Criminalization

ENVIRONMENT

Air pollution
Water pollution
Solid waste disposal
Toxic substances control
Spills and accidents
Plant explosions
Pollution havens
Burden of proof
Natural-resource depletion
Compensation for damages
Environmental-impact assessment
Limits to growth

Sex and violence on TV
Advocacy advertising
Inappropriate products
Compensation for defects
Cultural imperialism

TECHNOLOGY

Patent infringement
Inappropriate technology
Location of R&D activity
Technology hoarding
Brain drain
Technology gaps
Technology transfers
Technology-export controls
Licensing fees
Technological dependence
Technology pricing
Sensitive technologies

Equal employment opportunity
Labor exploitation
Immigrant workers
Workplace innovation
Promotion policies

ECONOMICS/FINANCE

Transfer pricing
Tax evasion
Antitrust violations
Currency manipulation
Takeover bids
MNE impacts on:
  Employment
  Trade flows
  Balance of payments
  Capital formation
  Growth and development
  Income distribution
  Macroeconomic policy

Source. Gladwin and Walter, *Multinationals Under Fire* (1980).

corporations, labor organizations, press), tend to come into conflict with MNCs almost exclusively when matters of direct economic self-interest are at stake.

We should note that many MNC conflicts are multiparty affairs, which means that MNCs often have to contend with radically different opponent-incentive systems in regard to the same general issue. It's also important to note that audiences and/or third parties are also involved in a good portion of the conflicts involving multinationals. Third parties enter into conflicts in several broad role categories: as possessors of superior powers to impose a settlement (e.g., judges, arbitrators), as reconcilers of disparate interests (e.g., fact finders, mediators), and as expert assistants to one or the other contending parties (e.g., attorneys, consultants).

CONFLICT TACTICS.   The tactics used against multinationals are as varied as the groups using them and the issues addressed. Opponent arsenals include means that range from violent to nonviolent, direct to indirect, legitimate to illegitimate, persuasive to coercive, simple to complex, and inexpensive to quite costly.

Gladwin and Walter (1980), after examining hundreds of MNC conflicts, have classified the tactics employed against multinationals into eight categories: legal, legislative, administrative, financial, economic, communicative, symbolic, and violent. Although administrative and legal tactics dominate the overall battleground, the kinds of tactics utilized vary widely from issue to issue. Terrorism, by definition, exclusively entails violence. Human-rights controversies are marked by communicative, financial (proxy resolutions and stock divestitures), and symbolic tactics. Administrative interventions mark most political and marketing disputes, whereas economic tactics (e.g., strikes) dominate the labor scene. Conflicts over questionable payments, environmental protection, technology, and economics/finance all have strong legal-administrative flavors. We should note, however, that a wide variety of tactics are brought to bear on most issues.

CONFLICT CONSEQUENCES.   The most critical question about MNC conflict is, of course, so what? Just what is the bottom line? At the extreme, that line for multinationals is nothing less than survival. Conflict has the potential of disrupting or reducing a MNC's vital flow of essential resources and support from relevant interest groups in a variety of ways. Examples would include investments lost due to government takeovers, production lost as a result of strikes, markets lost after bans are imposed on production, and property and executive lives lost from terrorist attacks. The acquisition of future resources can also be seriously impaired by conflict that translates into delays and obstruction.

Conflicts can be costly in still other ways. They can result in badly tarnished public images, consume disproportionate amounts of top-management time and attention, entail skyrocketing legal fees, sink employee morale, and induce role stress within executives. But all is not negative. Conflict can also be legitimate, productive, and desirable for both individuals and organizations. It can serve to foster internal cohesiveness, prevent stagnation, help clarify objectives, direct managerial attention to needed changes, and stimulate adjustment to new conditions. Conflict in MNC operations can thus be functional, dysfunctional, or both at the same time.

The appropriate objective of conflict management should therefore not be that of avoiding or resolving all external conflicts. Since some types of conflict can be detrimental and others beneficial, the goal must rather be one of optimal balance. This can be achieved by constructive management actions that serve to minimize the negative effects and enhance the positive effects of any given dispute. The key is not to misread the "true" nature of a conflict situation, for example, underestimating or overestimating the amount of power at the MNC's disposal, misconceiving the real stakes riding on the conflict outcome, falsely defining occasions that might permit mutual gain as situations of pure "zero-sum" conflict, misinterpreting the quality of the firm's relationship with an opposing party, thereby missing useful communication opportunities, and so forth. The multinational must also strive to avoid a wide variety of other destructive processes: narrowing of vision, heavy-handed power tactics, overreactions, biased perceptions, excessive loyalties, over-sensitivity to differences, stereotypic thinking, impoverished communications, failures to adapt to changing circumstances, and so on.

There are of course no simple cookbook approaches to dealing with conflict in MNC operations—no panaceas, no foolproof strategies, no one best answer. There are a wide variety of strategies and tactics potentially available for use in constructively managing conflicts, and the appropriateness of any given strategy or tactic will naturally depend upon the particular circumstances found in a specific conflict situation. Let's turn now to a general model for managing conflicts in international business that embodies this "contingency" perspective.

THE MANAGEMENT OF MULTINATIONAL CORPORATE CONFLICT

STRATEGIES FOR DEALING WITH CONFLICT.   In dealing with any given external conflict, MNC management must primarily concentrate on obtaining a satisfactory outcome rather than resolving the conflict itself, although the latter is, of course, often preferable if feasible. In addition, management must also be concerned with its relationship with the parties who constitute its opposition. Depending on the emphasis placed on these two factors of assertiveness and cooperativeness, one of five styles of conflict management may be chosen as noted by Thomas (1976) and as indicated in Exhibit 2. Management may choose to *compete* tooth and nail (assertive/uncooperative) in an attempt to overcome the opposition. It may opt to *avoid* (unassertive/uncooperative) conflict and withdraw from the fray or to *accommodate* (unassertive/cooperative) the opposition. It may actively *collaborate* (assertive/cooperative), hoping to satisfy both sides of the issue, and, finally, there is always the option of *compromise*, which "splits the difference" in a bargaining context and represents an intermediate position in terms of both assertiveness and cooperativeness. For an in-depth examination of the nature of each of these modes or styles see Gladwin and Walter (1980).

The differences between these conflict strategies are well illustrated by the reactions of Sperry Rand Corporation, and Dresser Industries to the export controls instituted by the Carter administration during the summer of 1978 to express displeasure with the Soviet trials of political dissidents and American journalists. Sperry was denied an export license to ship a $6.8 million computer system to Tass, the official Soviet press agency. Dresser, a diversified energy-industry supplier, was affected when all American exports of oil-field technology to the Soviets were placed under governmental control. J. Paul Lyet, Sperry's chairman, reportedly greeted the license denial with, "Bah, humbug," but added that the company had always complied with the wishes of the U.S. government on "where and with whom" the company traded and would "continue to follow that policy." Dresser's reaction was almost the opposite

EXHIBIT 2   MODES OF CONFLICT MANAGEMENT

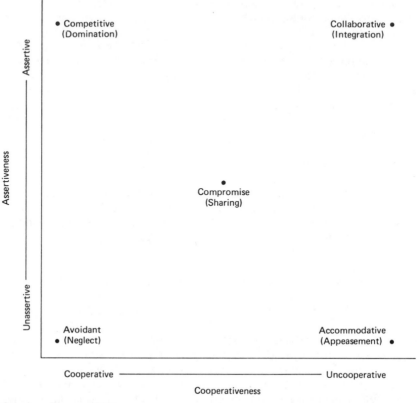

Source.   Thomas, 1976.

of Sperry's relatively unassertive and cooperative stance of accommodation. Carter's oil decision was labeled "sheer idiocy," and John V. James, Dresser's chairman, speedily and bluntly attacked efforts by the President's senior advisers and a special review panel convened at Defense Secretary Harold Brown's request to stop the firm's $150 million contract to build a drill-bit plant in the Soviet Union. The highly competitive approach helped produce a go-ahead for the Dresser sale. The Carter administration flip-flopped 2 years later and revoked Dresser's license. By this time, however, the bulk of all equipment and technology for the plant had already been shipped. The White House also eventually reversed its decision on the Sperry sale, but unfortunately for the company, the Russians in the meantime had found a new supplier, CII-Honeywell-Bull of France.

There are, of course, many possible combinations of cooperativeness and assertiveness, but most are combinations or variations of the five "polar" positions depicted in Exhibit 2. It should be emphasized that these options are ways of *coping* with conflict and not necessarily ways of *resolving* conflict, that is, only collaboration and compromise involve conflict resolution in the sense that both opposing parties obtain satisfaction. Thus crushing an attempt by unions in Europe to bargain on a multinational basis, terminating business payoff-prone regions such as the Middle East, or temporarily halting bank loans to the South African government may enable the firm to suppress or bypass the open expression of conflict, but do not really resolve the underlying issues.

DECIDING ON A CONFLICT-MANAGEMENT STRATEGY. Suppose there are demands to get out of South Africa, stop the marketing of infant formula in Haiti, or cut the price of tranquilizers in Great Britain. How should MNC management go about deciding how assertive to be in such situations? That is, what factors ought to determine the levels and kinds of resources that should be invested in an attempt to obtain a favorable outcome? In general, the answer depends on the *stakes* management places on that outcome along with the relative *power* or leverage of the enterprise in the conflict situation.

The Role of Stakes.   Stakes can typically be assessed subjectively, but are difficult to pin down rigorously. A great deal naturally depends on management's own perceptions. It was relatively painless, for example, for Proctor & Gamble (Folger's coffee) and General Foods (Maxwell House) to end their U.S. importation of Ugandan coffee in 1978 in response to pressure from human-rights groups and U.S. congressmen to end America's business connection with Idi Amin's regime, as Ugandan supplies amounted to only 6 percent of U.S. coffee imports. The story certainly would have been different had the supplier in question been Brazil. Tough competition rather than accommodation surely would have been the result.

The most important factor in determining a multinational's stakes in a particular conflict is usually management's own global strategy. Thus conflict outcomes that weaken the heart of that strategy—damaging the firm's distinctive competence, degree of control, or unique capabilities—are likely to be those that management wants most to avoid. And although multinationals often pursue multiple strategies in different product or geographic divisions, it is possible to distinguish between different kinds of strategies, as has been done by Fayerweather (1978), and show how the stakes in any particular conflict depend on them. For example, firms such as IBM that concentrate on exploiting technological leads in a few product areas normally consider it essential to maintain an exceptionally strong R&D program, high product-quality standards, tight control of technological skills, and close supervision of marketing strategy. The need for tight reins on production and marketing, however, is not as critical to those multinationals that are comparatively efficient in the development of innovative leads in a wider range of product lines and markets. Thus companies like Honeywell, Westinghouse, ITT, and L.M. Ericsson have been relatively calm when faced with pressures for local ownership participation in countries like France or Brazil, whereas IBM has fought the same pressures every step of the way.

In contrast, multinationals in the oil, copper, aluminum, and chemical industries as explored by Vernon in *Storm Over the Multinationals* (1977) tend to pursue strategies resting on the advantages of large scale, and view barriers to entry, coordination of decisions at various stages of production, security of raw materials supply, and stability in product demand as their particular "jugular veins." A serious threat to any of these factors would probably evoke strong reactions. On the other hand, multinationals in the food and pharmaceutical industries rely on strategies based on advanced managerial and marketing skills, proprietary knowhow, strong trade names, or massive promotional expenditures. Tight control of marketing programs is usually viewed as absolutely essential, and conflicts that affect such programs are usually assigned high stakes. There are still other strategies that rest on the multinational's global scanning capability and well-integrated, efficient logistical system. In the automobile and electronics industries, for example, where returns depend on low-cost production locations and effective global marketing, tight internal control is needed to tie together the multinational network, and threats to that network involve high stakes.

Besides such strategic factors, stakes are affected by the firm's financial condition. If the enterprise in very well off, it may be prepared to offer greater concessions to its opponents than if it is close to collapse. During the winter of 1975–1976, for example, Chrysler, as noted by Young and Hood in *Chrysler U.K.* (1977), was able to translate its financial weakness into what some observers labeled a "triumph of negotiations" in the United Kingdom. Specifically, Chrysler's threats to liquidate its failing British subsidiary enabled management to squeeze an aid package of $360 million out of the Labour government—five times the amount the government first proposed.

Other determinants of stakes include sunk costs, precedents, and accountability to third parties such as joint-venture partners, industry associations, suppliers, customers, and government regulators. At the same time, perceived stakes may be reduced in various ways. One is insurance, such as that provided to U.S. companies by the Overseas Private Investment Corporation against seizure of overseas property by foreign governments, inability to repatriate profits, or acts of war. Another is the existence of options such as the availability of alternate markets or sources of supply. A third is the joint ownership of capital-intensive facilities, such as aluminum smelters, copper mines, oil fields, natural-gas pipelines, and petrochemical complexes, which tend to create a common cost structure and common exposure to risk for the firms involved. Thus if a consortium facility is impaired or expropriated, competitive relationships may remain more or less intact, and losing a conflict does not necessarily set one firm back relative to its rivals. Such stakes-reducing and risk-management techniques are examined in works by the Congressional Research Service (1973); Franko (1971); Haendel and West (1975); Lloyd (1976); Moran (1973); and Robinson (1978).

In trying to ascertain its stakes in a conflict outcome, management also has to consider carefully the time element. For example, as time pressures increase, the perceived need to obtain the most desirable outcome may fade. Urgency tends to increase "decision costs," promoting management to soften its demands, reduce its aspirations, or increase its concessions. Such was the case in Standard Oil Company of Ohio's (52 percent owned by British Petroleum) ill-fated attempt to construct a tanker terminal in Long Beach, California, and pump Alaskan crude oil to Texas refineries. The urgency of servicing the company's huge debt associated with the Trans-Alaska Pipeline and finding a way of getting petroleum products to its Midwest markets cheaply caused Sohio to become an "environmental Santa Claus." The company even agreed to spend $78 million to reduce pollution at a Southern California Edison generating plant as part of a pollution offset arrangement in the hope of gaining a quick green light for the project. Five years of delay, however, eroded the $1 billion project's once-attractive economics, and it was abandoned in 1979.

Whether the stakes are attributable to strategic requirements, financial condition, precedent, available options, or urgency, management should usually try to be assertive in conflict situations in which those stakes are perceived to be high. Among other things, this means that considerable time and energy should be spent to either steamroller the opposition or pursue avenues of collaboration. In contrast, when the stakes are low, major outlays of corporate financial and human resources usually do not make sense.

The Role of Power.   Although stakes succeed in defining much of management's motivation in social conflict, they don't go very far toward suggesting appropriate levels of assertiveness without reference to the firm's relative influence or power position. This depends on both the multinational's own characteristics and the situation in which it finds itself, and can differ enormously from one conflict situation to another. For our purposes, power can be defined as suggested by Raven and Kruglanski (1970); Swingle (1976); and Wrong (1979) in terms of the range of conflict outcomes through which one party can push another in a conflict situation, with greater power corresponding to a greater range of outcomes. It should be noted that relative power positions can change rapidly, as demonstrated by the rapid and dramatic decline in the leverage of most multinationals operating in Iran following the overthrow of the Shah.

What are the sources of a multinational's power? Generally, the ingredients of power include a firm's size, financial base, human resources, expertise, leadership quality, prestige, communication and persuasion skills, access to the media, cohesiveness, prior experience in dealing with conflicts, intensity of commitment, degree of trust and legitimacy, and risk-taking ability. For example, management may be able to convince the other party that it has superior knowledge or abilities, and may hold out the promise of benefits such as new investment or job creation, whereby it is clear that the reward depends on a conflict outcome that is favorable to the enterprise. Alternatively, management may be able to convince the opposition that the firm is justified in making a particular demand on grounds of precedent, reciprocity, or fair play.

Another important ingredient of relative power in multinational corporate conflict is the formation of coalitions with protagonists having complementary objectives. One example of such a coalition was the joining together of 63 major U.S. multinationals and banks in the early 1970s to form the Emergency Committee for American Trade in order to aggressively lobby against the highly protectionist AFL-CIO-backed Hartke-Burke bill. Similarly, more than 100 U.S. firms agreed to endorse the principles on the Rev. Leon Sullivan aimed at eroding apartheid and promoting fair employment practices in South Africa; 170 U.S. firms represented on the Business Roundtable joined together to bargain with African Jewish groups on the Arab boycott issue; and 9 major companies and 30 industry associations jointly went to court in West Germany during 1977 in an attempt to get that country's codetermination law overturned on constitutional grounds.

The site of a conflict may also affect relative power. Multinationals play most of their conflicts "away" rather than "at home," and usually have to contend with opponents on their own territories, where those parties are more familiar with the local environments and often enjoy the ability to control or influence them. Moreover, the multinational enterprise, as a guest, may be constrained in its assertiveness by a need for caution in an unfamiliar setting—although it can occasionally obtain assistance from its home government. The lack of options is also a power-limiting factor. A classic case that illustrates this point occurred in the early 1970s, when some of the richest oil fields in the North Sea were discovered in the Shetland basin by multinational oil firms including Shell, British Petroleum, Conoco, Burmah, Exxon, and Total. As reported by Baldwin and Baldwin (1975), it became evident to the residents of the Shetland Islands, which lie about 100 miles due west of the field, that the companies would be seeking permission to pipe the oil ashore at Shetland, the nearest possible landing point. But very few of the islands' 19,000 inhabitants wanted oil development encroaching on their way of life. Seizing the initiative, in 1974 the Shetland Island Council pushed an unprecedented piece of private legislation through the British Parliament that gave the council extensive rights to control and participate in oil-related development. With the Shetland landfall and tanker terminal vital to the economic exploitation of the fields, the oil companies were in no position to argue, and yielded at almost every turn to the council's demands on siting, facility design, and inflation-hedged royalties.

The existence of options, on the other hand, naturally enhances the multinational's power. One example is dispersion of production. Enterprises that rely on well-diversified supply sources are less vulnerable to embargoes and nationalizations, and are perhaps more resilient in conflicts in general than firms that rely on more-concentrated sources. They gain in leverage from limitations in the ability of governments or other opponents to reach out for alternative sources of technology or capital. In manufacturing industries, power can derive from breaking down the production process so finely that threats to the firm become meaningless—a government's expropriation of a screwdriver-type electronics-components-assembly operation that puts together imported inputs for export would yield little. Finally, multinationals attain power through a degree of indispensibility, that is, by possessing something unique to offer or withhold when a conflict arises. For discussions of these and other power factors in relation to a firm's vulnerability to expropriation see Jodice (1980); Kobrin (1980); and Truitt (1974).

Although the ingredients of power may be complex, they are also usually the primary determinants of the feasibility of different types of conflict behavior. Thus a clearly superior power position is likely to favor relatively assertive behavior in conflict situations. This can take the form of either a straightforward competitive stance or one of active collaboration, where the firm's problem-solving resources imply a position of strength and low risk. By contrast, an inferior power position normally inhibits management's ability to compel the other side to negotiate or make concessions, and unassertive behavior (avoidance or accommodation) may be most appropriate.

The Role of Interests.   Besides deciding how assertive it should be, management must also decide how cooperative to be. This decision will depend on the interdependence of *interests* between the multinational and its opponent and the ability to translate the need to cooperate into action given the quality of *relations* between the two parties.

The convergence or divergence of interests in conflict situations can arise from interdependence of both "goals" and "means," as noted theoretically by Deutsch (1973), and Rubin and Brown (1975). For example, a cooperative goal situation is one in which the various parties sink or swim together, whereas in a purely competitive situation, if one swims, the other must sink. Means interdependence, in contrast, exists when the methods that one party needs to reach its goal affect those available to the other. The management often finds that even though both itself and the opposition are in general agreement on a common goal, there is basic disagreement on how it should be accomplished. Mining companies like AMAX, Rio-Tinto Zinc, and International Nickel, for instance, have often found that even though they are in general agreement with governmental agencies and citizen groups on the desirability of exploiting a particular mineral resource, they still have serious differences on how to go about it—fast or slow, small or large scale, one extractive method or another, and so on.

Goal and means incompatibility often arise because multinationals inevitably affect a wide range of politically sensitive areas in the countries where they operate. As noted in works by Hawkins (1979); Hood and Young (1979); and Walter (1975), these range from economic growth, employment, prices, technical change, income distribution, and taxation to human rights, pollution control, balance of payments, and even national security. Consequently, any actions that they take that are perceived to threaten these interests are likely to represent points of incompatibility with host governments or various local interest groups. This is especially likely when matters of national identity or autonomy are involved. Thus in 1976, Dow Chemical found itself the target of severe criticism from Italian Communist Party economist Eugenio Peggio for "dismantling" the research and sales operations of its 70-percent-owned Italian pharmaceutical subsidiary, Gruppo Leptit S.A., and placing them under the Dow umbrella. The result, according to Peggio, was that "if Dow decides to leave, what is Italy left with?" In his view, those multinationals that "devoured and dismembered Italian companies for their own benefit" had to be opposed.

One of the most fundamental sources of diverging interests, according to observers such as Barnet and Muller (1974); Behrman (1970); Bergsten, Horst, and Moran (1978); and Vernon (1971), is incompatibility between the *global* views of management and the essentially *national* perspective of most of the institutions with which it comes into conflict. Macroeconomic policy at the national level has traditionally been viewed as setting the conditions within which the microeconomic functions of the firm are carried out. With multinationals, however, we have the global microeconomics of the firm often influencing the parameters of macroeconomic policy at the national level. And although the multinational has interests that extend beyond the border of any single country, its managers worry about the problems that arise from overlapping national jurisdictions, particularly with regard to their affiliates being used as political tools, conduits, and hostages by competing sovereign states.

In general, management is likely to be best able and most highly motivated to behave in a collaborative or accommodative manner in situations where both goals and means are positively interdependent. Some multinationals, for example, have chosen to meet the Third World call for "appropriate technologies" by engaging in product innovation designed specifically for the special conditions and needs of developing nations, as Ford Motor did with the "developing nations tractor" and GM with its "basic transportation vehicle." Value conflicts in the transfer of technology have been explored by Goulet (1977).

The Role of Relations. Conflicts, however, may still occur even when there is no perceived or actual divergence in goals or means among the parties. When this happens, it usually results from poor prior relations and attitudes. A positive relationship will generally serve to foster mutual trust, recognition of the legitimacy of the other party's interests, open communications, and an increased willingness to respond helpfully to the other party's needs. Hostility, on the other hand, tends to feed upon itself and is triggered by factors like isolation, stereotypes, failure or disillusionment in prior conflicts, mutual ignorance, racial differences, distorted perceptions, and institutional barriers. In some instances, local ideologies and values may even reject the multinational enterprise as an institution. For example, in those countries with socialism as a basic commitment, the Marxist concepts of capitalist exploitation, imperialism, and class struggle will naturally place a burden on constructive conflict resolution. Similar problems are caused by anti-American, anti-German, or anti-Japanese paranoia, as well as by questionable behavior on the part of a handful of multinationals, such as ITT in Chile.

The primary sources of negative relations between multinationals and local institutions, however, are probably ethnocentricism and nationalism, which have been studied by Fayerweather (1975); Johnson (1965); and LaPalombara and Blank (1976). Ethnocentrism reflects an inability to appreciate the viewpoint of others whose cultures have, for example, a different morality, religion, or language, and leads to an unwillingness to see the common problems that lie beneath differences in social and cultural traditions. Nationalism, as an extension of ethnocentrism, adds a strong chauvinistic and emotional component to many conflicts involving multinationals. For instance, surges of nationalist sentiment have, from time to time, spurred Canadian governments to impose protectionist measures aimed at reducing the flow of U.S. influence into that economy. One industry particularly affected has been publishing, with classic battles erupting over the government's attempts to drive *Time* and *Reader's Digest* out of the country.

The annals of multinational corporate conflict contain plenty of examples of hostility—Nestlé and the Third World Action Group over infant-formula promotion in developing nations; Firestone and the Young Americans for Freedom over plans for a synthetic-rubber plant in Rumania; Mobil and the Center for Social Action of the United Church of Christ over alleged petroleum supplies to Rhodesia; and ITT and the Senate Foreign Relations Subcommittee on Multinational Corporations over its Chilean activities are just a few of these. Case histories of these "classic" battles can be found in Gladwin and Walter, *Multinationals Under Fire* (1980). Positive relationships, however, are possible, and the factors that can lead to them include experience of successful prior interactions, perceived similarity in beliefs, common values and attitudes, good communications, and the concern of the parties about their ability to work together in the future. In general, management is most likely to exhibit a high degree of cooperativeness (collaboration or accommodation) when relations are open, friendly, and trusting.

Putting It All Together.   Our framework suggests that in any given conflict situation, the appropriate combination of assertiveness and cooperativeness ought to be a product of the interaction of four situational variables—*outcome stakes, relative power, interest interdependence,* and *relationship quality* (see Exhibit 3). Multinationals regularly encounter conflict situations of a relatively pure form in which the variables combine to unambiguously suggest a corporate conflict-management position. These four factors are seldom of equal importance, however. Instead, in most situations, the "motivational structure" of conflict (stakes and interest interdependence) is probably a more-important determinant of conflict behavior than the "capability structure" (power and relationship quality). This is because capabilities are more readily changeable than underlying motives. Also there are often linkages among the situational factors themselves—parties who dislike one another, for example, are apt to emphasize or develop incompatible goals. Thus, it's not hard to

EXHIBIT 3   DETERMINANTS OF APPROPRIATE
CONFLICT BEHAVIOR

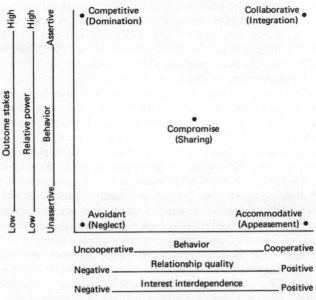

Source.   Gladwin and Walter, *Multinationals Under Fire*, 1980.

understand why most multinationals have been unwilling to engage in a dialogue with representatives of the World Council of Churches: the WCC declared its vehement opposition to multinationals in 1977 on the grounds that they are accomplices of "repressive states, predatory local elites, and racism" and thus pillars of a system that "oppresses, excludes, and exploits" (*The Economist,* 1977). And as the stakes in a conflict outcome increase, so does the incentive to utilize every source of power that may be available to each side.

SELECTING THE APPROPRIATE STRATEGY.   External conflicts in multinational corporate operations emerge in many shapes, sizes, intensities, and complexions. Selecting an appropriate conflict management thus critically depends on an accurate diagnosis of the motivational and capability structures at hand. In some conflict situations, a strategy of using one conflict-handling mode alone will suffice, whereas other situations may recommend the use of two or modes simultaneously. And dynamic situations will naturally necessitate the utilization of different modes at different stages of the conflict. Let's examine these single-, simultaneous-, and sequential-mode strategies in more detail.

Single-Mode Strategies.   A *competitive* (assertive, uncooperative) response to conflict is appropriate when a multinational's stakes and power are relatively high, and when interest interdependence and relations are relatively negative. The objective is domination. Such is the case in the uranium-cartel dispute involving two Pittsburgh neighbors—Westinghouse Electric and Gulf Oil—along with 28 other uranium producers, with Westinghouse charging Gulf and the others with creating an international cartel that forced the price of uranium from $8 a pound to more than $40 a pound over a two-year period. This thorny legal imbroglio—dubbed the "lawyers full-employment case" by a federal judge—began trial in late 1980. The direct dispute between Westinghouse and Gulf was settled in 1981 when Gulf agreed to pay Westinghouse $25 million and to supply six of Westinghouse's utility customers with uranium valued at about $350 million.

An *avoidant* (unassertive, uncooperative) approach to handling conflict is useful when the firm's stakes and power are relatively low, and when interest interdependence and relations are relatively negative. The objective is to throw in the towel or move on to greener pastures at lowest possible costs. A clear example would be the quiet withdrawal of the U.S. executives of GM, Exxon, Ford, Coca-Cola, and other firms from Argentina in 1973–1974 when the executive-kidnap rate in that country reached 10 per month. Other cases of responding to terrorism in this manner are reported in Clutterbuck (1978). Avoidance can be useful in many kinds of situations, such as when alternate projects or markets are readily available, when the issues in conflict are trivial and represent only minor annoyances, or when potential disruption and negative publicity seem to outweigh the benefits of conflict resolution.

A *collaborative* (assertive, cooperative) approach to handling conflict is likely to be best when the multinational's stakes and power are relatively high, and when interest interdependence and relations with the opposition are relatively positive. The widely publicized experiment in workplace innovation in the Volvo assembly plant at Kalmar, Sweden, represents a case in point. The goals of that experiment, not yet fully achieved, are to upgrade workers' tasks into ones that are more creative and satisfying for the individual, thereby leading to a higher level of worker motivation, greater productivity, reduced absenteeism, and reduced strike activity. Collaboration is especially effective when both sides want to achieve the same objective, but differ over the means.

An *accommodative* (unassertive, cooperative) response to conflict is suitable when stakes and power are relatively low, and when interest interdependence and relations are relatively positive. The objective is appeasement, and this makes sense when issues are more important to others than to the firm itself, when the firm finds that it has been wrong on matters of substance, and when organizational energy is needed for other conflicts where the stakes are higher. How else can one explain the unprecedented "orgy of self-flagellation" noted by Gladwin and Walter (1977) during which some 400 American-based multinationals voluntarily disclosed to the Securities and Exchange Commission that they had made a total of almost $1 billion in questionable payments abroad?

Finally, a *compromise* (moderately assertive and cooperative) mode tends to be useful when the firm's stakes are moderate and power advantage or disadvantage is slight, and when interest interdependence and relations are mixes of positive and negative elements. The objective is to "split the difference," especially when conflicts involve differences in goals, attitudes, and values, and when many issues are involved that are given different priorities by the various parties in conflict. During 1976–1977, for instance, the American Jewish Congress (AJC) negotiated agreements with a number of major U.S.-based multinationals regarding the Arab boycott of Israel, a subject investigated by Chill (1976) and Turck (1977). Gulf Oil, Bethlehem Steel, Goodyear Tire & Rubber, Standard Oil of California, and Tenneco were among those who agreed to provide requested information about boycott practices and/or to revise corporate policies in return for the AJC's withdrawing its share-holder resolutions on the matter. Compromise makes sense when goals are important but not worth the effort or potential delays associated with more-assertive kinds of behavior. It can produce expedient solutions under time pressure as well as temporary settlements to complex issues. And it can be a primary backup strategy when collaboration or competition are unsuccessful.

Simultaneous-Mode Strategies.   Let's turn to more-complex conflict situations. One of the reasons multinational corporate disputes often become so protracted is that the bones of contention become fused into a monolithic whole that is not easily broken apart. Each side comes to view the issues as so interconnected and the resulting complex so overwhelming that the give-and-take process of compromise and concession appears impossible. The likelihood of reaching a satisfactory solution to a conflict can often be increased, according to Fisher (1964), by separating or "fractionating" the large issues involved into smaller and more-workable ones. The issues can often be manipulated—sized up or down, hooked together, broken apart, or stated in different language. They can be differentiated in terms of importance and relatedness, and different conflict-management techniques applied to each at the same time. Some questions can be avoided, others compromised, and still others subjected to intensely assertive behavior on the part of management. Fractionation of issues in conflict can help alleviate the stultifying effects of excessive commitment often associated with attempts to deal with large and complicated conflicts.

Opponents can also be divided, a procedure that is especially useful when the opponents themselves have divergent interests. For instance, Enka Glanzstoff, the fiber subsidiary of the Dutch chemical firm AKZO, announced plans in 1975 to close fiber operations in three countries and eliminate 6000 jobs by 1977 in an effort to regain profitability. AKZO's two major Dutch and German unions, inspired by the International Federation of Chemical, Energy, and General Workers Unions, called for discussions with the company to be held only an international basis, hoping to set a precedent in multinational labor cooperation against multinationals. Dutch Prime Minister Joop den Uyl publicly supported the union demands. But AKZO steadfastly refused to talk on a multinational basis and successfully shattered the front orchestrated by Charles Levinson of the international federation by appealing to the desires of small Dutch unions that did not want an all-out confrontation during a recession. AKZO was thus able to negotiate the plant closings with its labor unions in each country separately. For studies of multinational unionism and bargaining see Hershfield (1975); Kujawa (1979); and Northrup and Rowen (1974).

Certainly unique to conflicts facing multinational companies are issues involving parties in different nations, and the multinational can easily become the "monkey in the middle." Because of its "double identity" and questions of overlapping and conflicting jurisdiction, management often finds itself wedged between the hauling and pulling of parties in several countries whose interests point in fundamentally different directions. Consider Fruehauf's majority-owned subsidiary in France, sandwiched between conflicting U.S. and French government positions in 1965 regarding shipment of truck trailers to China; or Volkswagen angering the Brazilian government during the 1975 recession when the company reassigned an export production order from its Brazilian subsidiary back to Germany to appease workers at home; or Gulf Oil confronting incompatible demands with respect to disbursement of royalty payments from its Angolan operations in 1975 exerted by the Ford administration and the three factions vying for control during the Angolan revolution; or British Petroleum losing its assets in Nigeria to nationalization in 1979 when it got caught in the middle of a dispute over the African policies of the government of Prime Minister Margaret Thatcher.

Even in single-country conflicts, management may find it advantageous to use different conflict-handling strategies simultaneously to block the formation of powerful opposing alliances, encourage counter-coalitions, or promote division or contention among weaker parties. Boeing, for example, found it useful to collaborate with the State Department while competing with the SEC on disclosure of the names of its agents and consultants abroad who had received more than $70 million in questionable payments. The company refused to comply with the SEC demands, claiming that the disclosure of "proprietary and confidential information" could cause "substantial, irreparable harm." This position was supported by the State Department, which on Boeing's behalf told the U.S. Appeals Court that disclosure "could reasonably be expected to cause damage to the foreign relations of the United States."

Sequential-Mode Strategies. Conflicts, in addition to often being complex, are generally also dynamic. They usually do not appear suddenly, but rather pass through a series of progressive stages during which the degree of conflict may either escalate or abate as described and modeled in works by Gulliver (1979), Lockhart (1979), Schelling (1960), and Zartman (1977). Moreover, conditions related to stakes, power, interest interdependence, and relations with opponents often shift significantly from one time period to the next. Consequently, a firm's conflict-management strategy should be adapted accordingly. The saga of IBM in India, which followed a path of collaboration → competition → compromise → avoidance illustrates this point quite well. The company responded positively to an invitation of Jawaharlal Nehru to establish an accounting-machine plant in Bombay in 1951 (*collaboration*). IBM went on to dominate the Indian computer industry, and eventually the Indian government pressed the firm both to reduce its 100 percent ownership to 40 percent and to extend its computer design and manufacturing operations in India for the domestic as well as export markets. IBM was initially highly reluctant to consider any deviation from its traditional global policy of keeping all of its foreign affiliates under 100 percent IBM ownership (*competition*). However, an equally rigid position on the part of the Indian government forced IBM to propose a range of concessions in the hope of *compromise*. These concessions were not enough for the Indians, though, and IBM's proposals were rejected. Finally, IBM concluded that the equity dilution demanded by the Indian government "would seriously impair [IBM's] ability to manage an international high technology company requiring sharing of resources and know-how across national borders," and it subsequently announced its withdrawal from the nation on November 15, 1977 (*avoidance*).

It is not sufficient for a conflict strategy to be adaptive, however. It should also be proactive at times, for the various elements that determine the nature and intensity of conflict management can be consciously altered as time goes by. Values, beliefs, and perceptions of the opponents, for example, can be changed through communication and persuasion. In short, the quality of relations can be improved, as noted by Behrman, Boddewyn, and Kapoor (1975); Blake (1977); and Dunn, Cahill, and Boddewyn (1979) through skilled public affairs. Likewise, the power balance may be shifted by working on the firm's leverage points or the effectiveness with which they are used. Coalitions, for instance, can be formed to offset an initial power disadvantage. The perceptions of the stakes involved in a conflict can also be changed dramatically by restricting or expanding the options available to oneself or one's opponents. Similarly, perceptions of interest interdependence can be altered by substitute goals, third-party intervention, reformulating the issues involved, or introducing "superordinate" goals or threats that outweigh the existing hostility and divergent objectives.

There may also be changes in conflict circumstances beyond the control of the parties concerned. This is perhaps best illustrated by the inevitable cycles that appear in the bargaining strength of multinationals and governments of developing countries in the natural-resource industries, where the initial contractual arrangements between these firms and governments tend to obsolesce over time. Such agreements are normally reached in order to facilitate development of the country's natural resources. However, once the capital has been sunk and the initial risks have been taken, attitudes often change. In these circumstances, management almost always perceives the project as offering even more promise than before. But the government—with the project now "captured"—often comes to view at least some of the original terms of the agreement as unreasonable. And knowing that the terms needed to retain the essential benefits or the project are much less now than those needed to attract it in the first place, it typically presses for renegotiation. The ingredients of conflict management for both sides have thus changed. Examples of this "obsolescing bargain" phenomenon are legend and have been explored in efforts by Mikdashi (1976); Mikesell (1975); Moran (1974); and Smith and Wells, Jr. (1975). The government of Papua New Guinea, for example, demanded a renegotiation of the terms of the Bougainville copper-mining agreement with Bougainville Copper Ltd. (Rio-Tinto-Zinc) just one year after the world's fourth-largest copper mine had been in operation—partly a consequence of extraordinarily large profits earned during the first year.

As follows from above, Exhibit 4 illustrates 16 potential paths of change in a multinational's conflict behavior. Several of these paths may be used during the course of one particular conflict. Even in such circumstances, however, the "opening moves" in the form of offers, gestures, and actions are often critical in the creation of the psychological setting that may prevail throughout, since it is at this early stage that rules and norms are first implanted, the issues such as trust and toughness are considered for the first time, and each party's preferences, intentions, and perceptions are first exposed.

Collaborative Paths. In general, initial use of the *collaboration* mode is recommended whenever possible. This is because outcomes of such behavior are likely to come close to outcomes that are viewed as substantively "fair" or in the "public interest." The assumption here is that, over the long term, the interests of the enterprises will best be safeguarded if they coincide with perceptions of public interest in home and host nations. But joint problem-solving efforts are fragile and may break down. And so the collaborate → compromise shift (*path 1*) may be needed to resolve remaining issues. Moreover, if the breakdown is severe enough, and if management finds itself in a weak bargaining position, then the collaborate → accommodate route (*path 2*) may be necessary to maintain a positive working relationship with the opposition. However, if the multinational's power base is sufficiently strong and the relationship is viewed as expendable, then the collaborate → compete path (*path 3*) may be a viable last resort should irreconcilable differences emerge.

**EXHIBIT 4   SEQUENTIAL PATTERNS OF MODE
UTILIZATION**

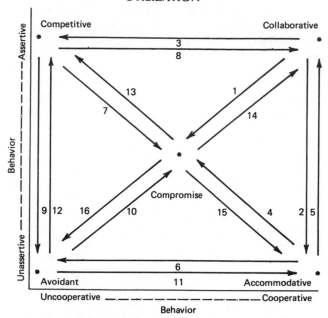

Source.   Gladwin and Walter, *Multinationals Under Fire*, 1980.

Accommodative Paths.   When a multinational confronts an issue that generates intense and aggressive feelings, however, *accommodation* may be more useful than collaboration as a starting point. In particular, if management can fully understand and
empathize with the other side, the accommodative approach may establish a relationship that can eventually employ either compromise (*path 4*) or possibly even collaboration (*path 5*). Accommodation may also facilitate influence by gradations—the "foot
in the door" technique—or even induce guilt or obligation in the other party, making
that party less likely to resist the more assertive and/or uncooperative behavior that
follows. Nevertheless, a shift from accommodation to avoidance (*path 6*) may be necessary if the enterprise is pushed too far or if things just don't work out. Polaroid's
experience in South Africa, chronicled by O'Connell (1973), is an example of the latter
situation. In this case, demonstrations, sit-ins, and an attempted product boycott in the
United States in 1971 led management to acquiesce to some of the demands of the
Polaroid Workers Revolutionary Movement. In particular, the company, as part of a
widely publicized "experiment," required its independent distributor in South Africa
to improve the wages and job opportunities for blacks and banned sales of its products
to the South African government. Unfortunately, Polaroid was forced to pull out of the
country altogether in 1977 when it confirmed reports from exiled black activists that its
local distributor had sold film to the South African government in violation of the
earlier understanding.

Competitive Paths.   Initial collaboration or accommodation should be avoided
whenever such early cooperation could lead to a superficial or unstable agreement

before the underlying issues in the situation were really worked through. In such circumstances, competition, even with its threat of losses to both sides, may be necessary in order to motivate the parties to approach the negotiation process in a mature fashion. By starting out tough, management can systematically soften its position by making positive concessions, either as part of a compromise (*path 7*) or as an attempt for full collaboration (*path 8*). One illustration of this approach was observed in the head-on clash between Hoffmann-LaRoche and the U.K. Monopolies Commission and Department of Health and Social Services over the pricing of librium and valium. Roche chose to get involved in a battle of "epic proportions" in order to prevent the spread of price-cutting demands in a dozen other nations. But the stakes declined as Roche's patents in these tranquilizers expired, and the Swiss firm compromised not long afterward. And, as with all other modes, the enterprise always has the option to throw in the towel (avoidance) should the going get too rough or too costly (*path 9*). Three examples of this sequence are Coca-Cola's withdrawal from India in the face of that government's demands that it disclose its secret formula; Firestone's termination of a Rumanian rubber-plant deal as a result of the protest orchestrated by the Young Americans for Freedom; and the Shell Oil Company's departure from the state of Delaware after a bitter "To Hell With Shell" campaign by environmentalists fighting the firm's local refinery-construction plans.

Avoidance Paths.   When the firm's stakes or power are low, where a zero-sum game is involved, or where there is a great deal of hostility, avoidance-oriented behavior often makes sense for openers. Management can let it be known that it won't touch the issue with the proverbial "10-foot pole." Yet if it backs off and lets the situation cool down, it is possible that a basis may later emerge for meaningful dialogue and negotiation (*path 10*). For example, in 1976 it became known that Coca-Cola's independent bottler in Guatemala had engaged in repressive actions against employees exercising their right to union representation. Faced with church groups demands that it terminate the franchise agreement, Coca-Cola argued that it was not the owner of the plant and had no control over its labor practices, and thus tried to disassociate itself from the conflict. The pressure of a shareholder resolution eventually led the company to agree to investigate the charges in exchange for a withdrawal of the church action. Church sponsors even visited Guatemala in 1978 and witnessed the signing of an agreement between the bottler and the workers. But murders, the use of riot squads, and abductions reportedly continued, and this led church groups to again press Coca-Cola into adopting a "code of minimum labor standards" that would be required of its franchisees around the globe. The company then returned to an uncooperative stance, restating that allegations involving independent bottlers were none of its business. In other circumstances, a transition from avoidance to accommodation may be appropriate (*path 11*), should the relationship improve or interests converge. Or if the stakes go up or the power balance reverses, a switch to competition (*path 12*) may become the logical course of action.

Compromise Paths.   As noted earlier, *compromise* is an appropriate initial course of action when stakes are relatively moderate, power is about equally distributed, and when interests and relations are mixed in character. However, it occasionally makes sense to move away from the compromise model. Thus when negotiations are moving slowly or when additional leverage is needed, the enterprise may find it expedient to introduce some threats into the picture (*path 13*). Goodrich in 1976, for instance, was attempting to reorganize the profitless non-tire section of Rubberfabriek Vredestein N.V. of Holland, which it had acquired in a bitter takeover battle with Goodyear in 1971. The unions protested the proposed reorganization, which would have meant layoffs of 762 of 4700 employees. This brought the Dutch government into the dispute. Negotiations ambled along until Goodrich, fed up with the slow pace, delivered an ultimatum—it offered to sell Vredestein to the government in June 1976 and announced it would sell off or close down if no agreement could be reached. The pace then quickened with negotiating teams flying back and forth between Akron and The Hague, and a fade-out agreement was reached in October 1976.

In other cases, the very experience of "good faith" bargaining and the development of mutual trust between the multinational and another party may allow compromise to evolve into collaboration (*path 14*). For example, when faced with intensifying nationalistic pressures in Guyana in the 1960s, Booker Sugar Estates, a subsidiary of Britain's Booker McConnell Ltd., embarked upon a comprehensive program, as reported by Litvak and Maule (1975) to win Guyanese acceptance by drastically increasing its contribution to the local economy. Working closely with government departments, the company promoted the formation of new business ventures, encouraged the expansion of independent cane farming, helped develop a local economic infrastructure, sought local equity participation in its own operations, progressively "Guyanized" its management, and generally attempted to reduce the industry's traditional paternalism. In sum, Booker's efforts to embody Guyanese goals in its corporate strategy allowed the company to operate unscathed until 1976, when a government takeover was negotiated. Other multinationals, such as Alcan, which had not engaged in such efforts in Guyana, were nationalized a number of years earlier.

In other circumstances, especially when the firm faces a decline in power or has a strong desire to maintain a particular relationship, a movement toward accommodation (*path 15*) may be called for. Perhaps the most classic case of this approach involves the relationship between the oil majors and OPEC examined in Vernon, *The Oil Crisis* (1976). In that instance, the entry of lean and hungry independent oil companies into the Middle East caused the leading "Seven Sisters" to lose their ability to set the terms of doing business. As a result, decisions that were the product of compromise in the 1950s and 1960s became products of accommodation in the 1970s and 1980s.

Finally, if bargaining fails to produce an acceptable agreement and competition or accommodation are inappropriate, management always has the option of pulling out (*path 16*). In early 1979, for example, the Swiss banking subsidiaries of Citicorp and Dow Chemical withdrew at the last minute from a syndicate that was floating a $33 million loan to Algeria. The eleventh-hour exit was prompted by a complaint made public by a manager of Banque Rothschild of Paris that his bank had been excluded from the syndicate because of its Jewish connections. Withdrawal was the only way in which the two American firms could comply with U.S. antiboycott laws that outlaw discrimination in the underwriting of loans.

In sum, since conflicts are not static, conflict management cannot be either. The 16 two-point incremental sequences above show some of the possibilities for change. Even more extreme changes in behavior, say from competition directly to accommodation (bypassing compromise), or collaboration to avoidance, and vice versa, may be appropriate when stakes, power, interests, or relations change abruptly and radically. The point is that multipoint sequences are compelled by the dynamics of conflict, and in many cases the pattern of emergent behavior must "track" all over the grid that has been presented.

THE IMPLEMENTATION OF CONFLICT MANAGEMENT

INCENTIVE SYSTEMS. Accepting the logic and value of the above contingency approach to constructive conflict management is one thing; executing such an approach effectively and efficiently on the part of MNC management is another. How can implementation of the approach best be encouraged or facilitated? The answer, according to Gladwin and Walter (*Multinationals Under Fire,* 1980) lies in creating a conducive management environment *within* the MNC. This, in turn, depends vitally on two systems—the *incentive system* under which MNC managers operate, and the *task system* necessary for carrying out conflict management itself. Some of the more important "points of leverage" bearing upon the organizational climate for constructive conflict management are shown in Exhibit 5.

The outer ring of Exhibit 5 shows various elements of the corporatewide incentive system that can be shaped by senior management. Constructive conflict management

EXHIBIT 5   INCENTIVES AND TASK SYSTEMS FOR CONSTRUCTIVE CONFLICT MANAGEMENT

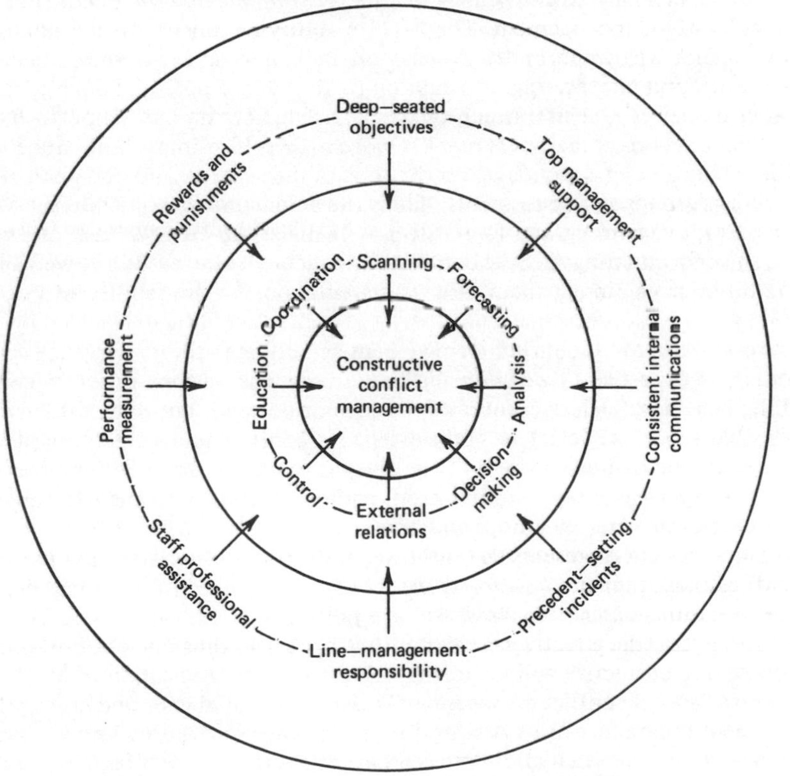

Source.   Gladwin and Walter, *Multinationals Under Fire,* 1980.

must be a deeply ingrained facet of the MNC's corporate personality—shared in, believed in, and acted upon at every level. To become an integral part of the normal planning and decision-making process, conflict management must gain strong and consistent support at the highest levels of management. Senior managers need to communicate clearly and forcefully how much constructive conflict management means to the firm—one effective way of doing this is to creatively use a conspicuous incident (e.g., an investment project that has been blocked because of obviously poor conflict management) as a corporate learning experience in order to send a strong message to the middle managers who are most directly involved in managing such conflict.

Conflict management should be primarily a "line" function; a sure route to disaster is to leave conflict-management strategies and tactics totally in the hands of staff specialists and then issue them to line managers as directives. Staff professionals can, of course, play a useful support role to the line organization, but responsibility and authority should clearly rest in line-management hands. This is because conflict management will only be effective if it is a continuous and major element in the line manager's decision system. As such, the function of conflict management should be tested by periodic measures of performance and organizational "carrots and sticks" used to reinforce desired managerial behavior.

TASK SYSTEMS.   Attention can now shift to the inner ring of Exhibit 5, which identifies the primary tasks essential to effective *implementation* of conflict management by MNC management. The MNC's ability to constructively manage external conflict will importantly depend on its expertise in *scanning*, selecting, transmitting, and interpreting information related to the potential emergence and actual character of conflict. Much of the scanning activity can be performed by staff "boundary-spanning" personnel. *Forecasting* is also important, since astute conflict management depends on predictions of the potency and demands of various interests groups and assessments of how the demands may constrain the MNC's actions. Proper scanning and forecasting will make the creative task of *analysis* easier, since formulating specific conflict-management alternatives as well as evaluating differences among them largely depends on the availability of cognitive resources.

The essence of MNC conflict management according to the contingency scheme, of course, is expertise in *decision making* among the various types of conflict-handling behavior. Such decision making cannot be rigid, but must rather be fast and flexible; timing will often be of the essence in conflict management. Implementing the decisions that are made will typically involve *external relations;* the MNC thus needs expertise in representing itself, communicating with and exerting influence over relevant external groups and organizations.

A control system represents an important adjunct to the decision-making system in conflict management. *Control* is essential mainly because external demands change over time—as noted above, stakes, power, relations, and interests are dynamic variables—the effectiveness of conflict behaviors thus must be continuously monitored and corrective actions taken when necessary. *Education* of MNC managers in the "art" of conflict management is also an essential task, and management-development programs can be designed to bridge gaps in required knowledge, attitudes, and skills. The final and most critical task is that of *coordination;* "unity of effort" must be brought about in the performance of all of the tasks described above.

CONFLICT MANAGEMENT IN THE YEARS AHEAD

A FUTURE OF CONTRADICTIONS. What general trends seem to be shaping the challenge of conflict management as it will confront multinationals in the years ahead? Gladwin and Walter, in *Multinationals Under Fire* (1980), have forecast a "future of contradictions"—a global environment facing MNCs that will be characterized by often-incompatible factors bearing upon corporate objectives and policies. They see many trends that may work in almost dramatically opposed directions.

Some examples include the following. The importance of nationalism may continue to grow, but so will world economic and political interdependence. The power balance between MNCs and host nations may continue to shift in favor of host nations, but at the same time, home countries may increasingly assert their powers in the form of political controls over outward technology transfer, investment, and trade. And most developing nations appear steadfast in their desire for a "new international economic order," but their demands for a more "equitable" share of global prosperity are coming at a time when they need the MNC as much as ever and when developed nations are in no mood to make concessions as a result of unemployment, inflation, and energy problems.

The contradictions continue. The push of technology in telecommunications, computers, and travel will continue to shrink time and space, and will produce increasingly universal standards of behavior, but cultural homogenization appears to be increasingly resisted by groups seeking ethnic, religious, and cultural identity. The new importance given to maintaining local values may translate into more-frequent charges of "cultural imperialism" against MNCs in host nations—yet pressure groups at home seem intent on forcing MNCs to carry homegrown values abroad, particularly regarding ethical and moral dimensions of corporate policy. And employees will continue to demand a greater say in how their companies are run, but at the same time, myriad outside interest groups are bound to continue their struggle to have a say in corporate governance.

MANAGING THE CONTRADICTIONS. We could go on, but the fact that MNCs will in part create, collide with, and be victimized by contradictions in the 1980s and beyond should be clear. The central task of conflict management on the part of multinationals will be to cope with such contradictions. The opposing trends imply that tensions surrounding the MNC will remain and perhaps intensify. We may increasingly find MNCs being used as political tools, hostages, and bargaining chips by competing sovereignties; the risks of being caught between conflicting parties may thus grow more serious.

Many of the trends also imply that MNCs may experience a loss of autonomy and discretion—the mixture of emerging law, regulation, government intervention, trade-union/employee power, and citizen-lobby pressure can only translate into increased external control. The trends also signal increasing turbulence, with the key factor here being interdependence. Shifts in the external environment are increasingly going to come from anywhere without notice, to produce consequences unanticipated by those initiating the changes and those experiencing the results. In sum, multinationals will have to show far more political-social savvy in the years ahead in order to ensure survival and success. Under fire, the multinational must approach conflict management in a more proactive, contingency-based, and strategic manner.

SOURCES AND SUGGESTED REFERENCES

Baldwin, P.L. and M.F. Baldwin. *Onshore Planning for Offshore Oil: Lessons from Scotland.* Washington, D.C.: The Conservation Foundation, 1975.

Barnet, R.J. and R.E. Muller. *Global Reach: The Power of the Multinational Corporations.* New York: Simon and Schuster, 1974.

Behrman, J.N. *National Interests and the Multinational Enterprise: Tensions Among the North Atlantic Countries.* Englewood Cliffs, NJ: Prentice-Hall, 1970.

Behrman, J.N., J. Boddewyn, and A. Kapoor. *International Business —Government Communications.* Lexington, MA: D.C. Heath, 1975.

Bergsten, C.F., T. Horst, and T.H. Moran. *American Multinationals and American Interests.* Washington, D.C.: Brookings Institution, 1978.

Blake, D.H. *Managing the External Relations of Multinational Corporations.* New York: Fund for Multinational Management Education, 1977.

Chill, D.S. *The Arab Boycott of Israel.* New York: Praeger, 1976.

Clutterbuck, R. *Kidnap and Ransom: The Response.* London: Faber and Faber, 1978.

Congressional Research Service. *The Overseas Private Investment Corporation: A Critical Analysis.* Prepared for the House Committee on Foreign Affairs. Washington, D.C.: U.S. Government Printing Office, 1973.

"Controlling the Multinationals," *The Economist* (January 1978), pp. 68–69.

Deutsch, M. *The Resolution of Conflict: Constructive and Destructive Processes.* New Haven, CT: Yale University Press, 1973.

Dunn, S., M.F. Cahill, and J.J. Boddewyn. *How Fifteen Transnational Corporations Manage Public Affairs.* Chicago: Crain Communications, 1979.

Fayerweather, J. "A Conceptual Scheme of the Interaction of the Multinational Firm and Nationalism," *Journal of Business Administration,* Vol. VII (1975), pp. 67–89.

Fayerweather, J. *International Business Strategy and Administration.* Cambridge, MA: Ballinger, 1978.

Fisher, F. "Fractionating Conflict," *Daedalus,* Vol. XCII (1964), pp. 920–41.

Franko, L.G. *Joint Venture Survival in Multinational Corporations.* New York: Praeger, 1971.

Gilpin, R. *U.S. Power and the Multinational Corporation: The Political Economy of Foreign Direct Investment.* New York: Basic Books, 1975.

Gladwin, T.N. *Environment, Planning and the Multinational Corporation.* Greenwich, CT: JAI Press, 1977.

Gladwin, T.N. "Environmental Policy Trends Facing Multinationals," *California Management Review,* Vol. XX (1977), pp. 81–93.

Gladwin, T.N. and I. Walter. "How Multinationals Can Manage Social and Political Forces," *The Journal of Business Strategy,* Vol. I (1980), pp. 54–68.

Gladwin, T.N. and I. Walter. "Multinational Enterprise, Social Responsiveness, and Pollution Control," *Journal of International Business Studies,* Vol. VII (1976), pp. 57–74.

Gladwin, T.N. and I. Walter. *Multinationals Under Fire: Lessons in the Management of Conflict.* New York: John Wiley & Sons, 1980.

Gladwin, T.N. and I. Walter. "The Shadowy Underside of International Trade," *Saturday Review,* Vol. IV (1977), pp. 16–59.

Goulet, D. *The Uncertain Promise: Value Conflicts in Technology Transfer.* New York: IDOC/ North America, 1977.

Gulliver, P.H. *Disputes and Negotiations: A Cross Cultural Perspective.* New York: Academic Press, 1979.

Haendel, D. and G.T. West. *Overseas Investment and Political Risk.* Philadelphia: Foreign Policy Research Institute, 1975.

Hawkins, R.G., ed. *The Economic Effects of Multinational Corporations.* Greenwich, CT: JAI Press, 1979.

Hershfield. D.C. *The Multinational Union Faces the Multinational Company.* New York: The Conference Board, 1975.

Hood, N. and S. Young. *The Economics of Multinational Enterprise.* London: Longman, 1979.
"In hoc Signo," *The Economist* (August 13, 1977), p. 13.

Jodice, D.A. "Sources of Change in Third World Regimes For Foreign Direct Investment, 1968–1976," *International Organization,* Vol. XXXIV (1980), pp. 177–206.

Johnson, H.G. "A Theoretical Model of Nationalism in New and Developing States," *Political Science Quarterly,* Vol. LXXX (1965), pp. 169–185.

Keohane, R.O. and Nye, J.S. *Power and Interdependence: World Politics in Transition.* Boston: Little, Brown, 1977.

Kobrin, S.J. "Foreign Enterprise and Forced Divestment in the LDCs," *International Organization,* Vol. XXXIV (1980), pp. 65–88.

Kujawa, D. "Collective Bargaining and Labor Relations in Multinational Enterprises: A U.S. Public Policy Perspective," in R.G. Hawkins, ed. *The Economics of Multinational Corporations.* Greenwich, CT: JAI Press, 1979.

LaPalombara, J. and S. Blank. *Multinational Corporations and National Elites: A Study in Tensions.* New York: The Conference Board, 1976.

Litvak, I.A. and C.J. Maule. "Foreign Corporate Social Responsibility in Less Developed Economies," *Journal of World Trade Law,* Vol. IX (1975), pp. 121–135.

Lloyd, B. *Political Risk Management.* London: Keith Shipton Developments, 1976.

Lockhart, C. *Bargaining in International Conflicts.* New York: Columbia University Press, 1979.

Moran, T.H. *Multinational Corporations and the Politics of Dependence.* Princeton: Princeton University Press, 1974.

Moran, T.H. "Transnational Strategies of Protection and Defense by Multinational Corporations: Spreading the Risk and Raising the Cost for Nationalization in Natural Resources," *International Organization,* Vol. XXVII (1973), pp. 273–287.

Mikdashi, Z. *The International Politics of Natural Resources.* Ithaca: Cornell University Press, 1976.

Mikesell, R.F. *Foreign Investment in Copper Mining: Case Studies in Peru and Papua New Guinea.* Baltimore: John Hopkins University Press for Resources for the Future, 1975.

Northrup, H.R. and R. Rowen. "Multinational Collective Bargaining Activity: The Factual Record in Chemical, Glass and Rubber Tires," *Columbia Journal of World Business,* Vol. IX (1974), pp. 49–63.

Nye, J.S. "Multinational Corporations in World Politics," *Foreign Affairs,* Vol. LIII (1974), pp. 153–175.

O'Connell, J.J. "Polaroid Corporation Case," in C.E. Summer and J.J. O'Connell, eds. *The Managerial Mind,* 3rd ed. Homewood, IL.: Richard D. Irwin, 1973.

Raven, B.H. and A.W. Kruglanski. "Conflict and Power," in Paul G. Swingle, ed. *The Structure of Conflict.* New York: Academic Press, 1970.

Robinson, R.D. *International Business Management: A Guide to Decision Making,* 2nd ed. Hinsdale, IL: Dryden Press, 1978.

Rubin, J.Z. and B.R. Brown. *The Social Psychology of Bargaining and Negotiation.* New York: Academic Press, 1975.

Sauvant, K.P. and F.G. Lavipour. *Controlling Multinational Enterprises.* Boulder: Westview Press, 1976.

Schelling, T.C. *The Strategy of Conflict.* New York: Oxford University Press, 1960.

Smith, D.N. and L.T. Wells, Jr. *Negotiating Third World Mineral Agreements.* Cambridge, MA: Ballinger, 1975.

Swingle, P.G. *The Management of Power.* Hillsdale, NJ: Lawrence Erlbaum Associates, 1976.

Thomas, K.W. "Conflict and Conflict Management," in M.D. Dunnette, ed. *Handbook of Industrial and Organizational Psychology.* Chicago: Rand-McNally, 1976.

Truitt, J.F. *Expropriation of Private Foreign Investment.* Bloomington: Division of Research, Graduate School of Business, Indiana University, 1974.

Truck, N. "The Arab Boycott of Israel," *Foreign Affairs,* Vol. LVV (1977), pp. 472–439.

Vernon, R. *Sovereignty at Bay.* New York: Basic Books, 1971.

Vernon, R. *Storm Over the Multinationals: The Real Issues.* Cambridge, MA: Harvard University Press, 1977.

Vernon, R. ed. *The Oil Crisis.* New York: W.W. Norton, 1976.

Vogel, D. *Lobbying the Corporation: Citizen Challenges to Business Authority.* New York: Basic Books, 1978.

Walter, I. "A Guide to Social Responsibility of the Multinational Enterprise," in J. Backman, ed. *Social Responsibility and Accountability.* New York: New York University Press, 1975.

Wilkins, M. *The Emergence of Multinational Enterprise.* Cambridge, MA: Harvard University Press, 1970.

Wilkins, M. *The Maturing of Multinational Enterprise: American Business Abroad from 1914 to 1970.* Cambridge, MA: Harvard University Press, 1974.

Wrong, D.H. *Power: Its Forms, Bases and Uses.* New York: Harper and Row, 1979.

Young, S. and N. Hood. *Chrysler U.K.: A Corporation in Transition.* New York: Praeger, 1977.

Zartman, I.W. *The 50% Solution.* Garden City, NY: Anchor Books, 1977.

INTERNATIONAL LABOR RELATIONS

CONTENTS

INTERNATIONAL LABOR RELATIONS

Duane Kujawa

THE IMPORTANCE OF INDUSTRIAL RELATIONS. No manager would deny the importance of industrial relations to the success formula of the company. Collective employee-employer relationships implemented within a union-management under-standing determine costs (wages, fringe benefits, etc.) per unit of labor input, man-agement's rights (or lack of unilateral discretion) in deciding the work flow, defining the job, assigning personnel, altering production methods, and fixing work sched-ules and quality standards, and the procedure for resolving questions of rights granted to the parties by the labor contract. In addition, most union agreements confirm a production commitment through no-strike/no-lockout provisions. Suc-cessful industrial-relations management involves the maintenance of competitive labor costs and production continuity and the protection of management's right to initiate changes in work force organization and to innovate in production technology and work methods.

Industrial relations is no less important to the multinational firm. It is, however, much more complex.

THE IMPORTANCE OF INTERNATIONAL INDUSTRIAL RELATIONS. Managers lo-cated at the operating subsidiary level are invariably responsible for the conduct of industrial relations. Nonetheless, parent-company, or headquarters, management is vitally concerned with the subsidiary's industrial relations. Part of this concern is based upon the stewardship function of the headquarters group and the need to assess and evaluate local management's performance. The parent is concerned too since subsidiary-level production costs, flexibility in staffing and work assignments, prospects regarding industrial peace, and so forth are all key ingredients in planning processes and important strategic decisions at the multinational enterprise (MNE) level. Relevant topics here include production location and reallocation decisions, intraenterprise production-integration networks, plant closings, and major equip-ment purchases. Additionally, the control function at the MNE level utilizes produc-tion, financial, and other data generated by subsidiary operations. Significant vari-ances between budgeted, anticipated events and actual events can result because of industrial-relations problems at a subsidiary. Such problems must be appraised in terms of their cost and schedule impacts on anticipated performance. Operations elsewhere within the MNE system may well be affected.

These and other management-related issues will be discussed later in this chapter. But first some of the institutional foundations affecting international labor-relations management will be identified and clarified. These include the various, usually country-bound, industrial-relations systems within which subsidiaries operate, as well as the international structures and activities of unions (and governments) that are distinctive and unique to industrial relations at an MNE level.

COMPARATIVE INDUSTRIAL-RELATIONS SYSTEMS

WHAT IS AN INDUSTRIAL-RELATIONS SYSTEM?   Labor-relations issues and practices can vary considerably among countries, and even within countries across industries or geographic regions. Diversity among systems can be immense. Unions may or may not exist. Management or government may dictate terms and conditions of employment. Labor agreements may or may not be contractual obligations. Management may conclude agreements with unions that have little or no membership in the plant, or with nonunion groups that wield more bargaining power than the established unions. Some principles and issues are relevant in some contexts but not in others (e.g., seniority in layoff decisions, or even the concept of the layoff).

Such diversity in experiences provides fertile ground for analysis, especially regarding causes and effects, and for speculating on the potential impact of (proposed) changes. (e.g., in France, this happened. But why? Could it happen here?) However, such diversity also makes understanding systems and comparing across systems more difficult. Yet understanding industrial-relations systems is fundamental to successful management practice. Fortunately, the conceptual framework used in the analysis of industrial-relations systems is straightforward and simple, yet universal and insightful.

Dunlop (1958) characterizes an industrial-relations system as one comprising actors and contexts, a body of rules and an ideology (unifying or destabilizing). The actors encompass supervisors and management hierarchies, workers and their representatives, and (relevant) government agencies. Any single actor, or set of actors, may dominate decision making, may be irrelevant, or may accommodate others in the decision-making process. Different actors, across or within these three key groups, may conflict or collaborate with one another. One actor may participate in several ways, depending on the times and the issues. Government, for example, may legislate (or dictate) terms and conditions of employment, abstain from influencing labor-management relations, and/or structure union-company processes such as union recognition and collective bargaining either by law or administrative behavior.

The contexts are the givens of the environment of the system. Dunlop (1958) notes that they are determined exogenously by the larger society and consist of the following:

1. Technological characteristics—as they affect product configuration, workforce size and deployment, management organization, supervisory problems, skill-level and skill-mix requirements of the workers, potential for public regulation, profit potential, safety requirements, and so forth.

2. Market, or budget, constraints—as they include the extent or lack of competition, the ability of a firm to afford higher wages and/or to administer prices to pass along wage increases, ease of entry among suppliers of labor, and so forth.

3. The locus and distribution of power (in the larger society)—as it reflects and determines power relationships among the actors and circumscribes or influences the control of each over rule setting.

The body of rules is the output of the system and is universal to all systems. It includes procedures for setting up the rules, the substantive rules themselves, and procedures for the administering of rules. For example, the body of rules might include union recognition, the duty to bargain in "good faith," the job-classification scheme, wages, overtime and shift premiums, fringe benefits, seniority rights in promotions and layoffs, the grievance procedure, and so forth. The determining of these processes and rules is the core of the industrial-relations system (Dunlop, 1958). Certain actors may dominate in setting certain rules. Specific rules may reflect technical or market constraints (such as safety rules in bituminous-coal mining and seniority as a preference determinant in work assignments among airline pilots). Rules, in a sense, are the dependent variables that are explainable in light of the other factors.

Ideology is what holds the system together by defining acceptable roles of behavior by the actors, including the common recognition of the limits of the system and the acceptable use of power. For example, the concept of private property militates against the occupation of a plant by workers as a bargaining tactic.

As a final note, industrial-relations systems are *systemic* in nature, not *systematic,* or preplanned. Industrial-relations systems are interactive processes in which individuals or groups seek to optimize a position at a point in time, and do so in light of constraints and power relationships. The behavior rationale is time- and place-bound, and perhaps opportunistic. It is pragmatic in stable systems, revolutionary in unstable systems.

SELECTED INDUSTRIAL-RELATIONS SYSTEMS. To illustrate variations among systems and the usefulness of Dunlop's systems model to facilitate inquiry, brief commentaries on different country-level systems follow. The United States is included as a familiar base point, West Germany and the United Kingdom since they have been significant donors and recipients of MNEs' direct investments, and Japan since it provides rich contrasts to the others and is, to some observers, superior to the other systems in terms of productivity and harmony.

United States. Government's role in industrial relations in the United States has traditionally been concerned with supporting free, decentralized collective bargaining, and at the same time defining certain practices as contrary to the national interest. Such illegal practices include recognition strikes, the closed shop (where workers must belong to the union before being hired), and secondary boycotts. Other employment-related practices are legally mandated, such as those in the areas of equal employment opportunity, safety and health, social security (retirement and disability insurance), and unemployment compensation. U.S. law acknowledges the labor agreement as a contractual obligation of the parties, with performance deliberately contrary to the contract enjoinable in U.S. courts and with employees surrendering individual employment rights (generally) in favor of those set forth in the contract. The government is a direct party to the union-management relationship in several ways: for example, in determining the appropriate bargaining unit, conducting and certifying union-recognition elections, and requiring "good faith" bargaining limited to terms and conditions of employment. Federal and state governments have also established legally prescribed minimum wages, maximum hours to be worked per day and per week at regular pay, amounts of overtime and holiday premium pay, and so forth.

A core concept in U.S. industrial relations is *exclusive jurisdiction:* Only one union represents and bargains collectively on behalf of the workers in the bargaining unit. This is legally required and is certainly compatible with the *business unionism* (as contrasted with *political unionism*) culture in the United States. The in-plant administration of the labor contract, involving company management and union members and officers exclusively, displays similar roots. Notwithstanding what the law requires of the parties, the body of rules is substantially determined, or altered through time, through collective bargaining between management and union. Power, implemented mainly through the strike and lockout weapons, is essential to collective bargaining, and a balance in power between the parties promotes mutual respect and a need for mutual accommodation. U.S. labor law supports this balance of power as being in the national interest.

Typically, collective bargaining is conducted at company-specific, local, and national levels with industrial or trade-oriented unions. Some industrywide bargaining also occurs, most notably in the steel industry on a national basis, and in the building trades and trucking on a regional basis. In the auto industry, binational (Canada and the United States) collective bargaining is conducted on a company basis. Usually only a single union participates in company-specific negotiations. An exception arises, however, in conglomerated or multidivisional firms with bargaining units represented by different unions, and where "coordinated bargaining" occurs.

Labor contracts in the United States are for fixed periods of time. Contents invariably cover union recognition and security, management rights, job classifications and wages, wage premiums, standard work periods, holidays, vacations, medical and retirement insurance, seniority rights, grievance handling (frequently culminating in binding arbitration), and no-strike/no-lockout commitments.

In the U.S. system, the right to strike is limited legally to issues germane to terms and conditions of employment, and is usually prohibited during the contract period. Strikes then invariably relate to disputes over interests of the parties as proposed contractual relationships are under consideration (as contrasted with disputes over rights of the parties granted through an existing contract or agreement). "Wildcat," or spontaneous, strikes do occur but are more frequently over local (adverse) conditions, are brief (half-day or so) and are not union initiated or sanctioned. If an impasse in collective bargaining is reached and a strike appears imminent, the parties may agree to call in outsiders to mediate the dispute. Such outsiders may be private individuals or representatives from either federal or state mediation and conciliation agencies. With the notable and recent exception in steel, interest arbitration is not evident.

West Germany. Similar to the situation in the United States, labor law in West Germany is quite influential and extensive. Gunter and Laminsky (1978) observe that the state originally conceived of itself as a guarantor of security and order and an intervenor, "in a compensatory way, to prevent economic and social disruptions." Lately, however, the state has become more active, especially regarding social security, full employment maintenance, and worker participation in management.

Fundamental legislation includes two types of laws: those relating to collective bargaining between unions and employers, and those relating to workers' rights and interests at plant and company levels. The Collective Agreements Act of 1949 guarantees the independence of employers and unions, circumscribes the use of strikes and lockouts, and acknowledges the validity of collective agreements. The Works Constitution Act of 1952 mandates employee-elected works councils in larger firms to conclude enterprise-level agreements covering local practices, such as the typical secondary conditions of employment (e.g., start and quit times, vacation schedules, etc.), and periodically to receive information on the firm's economic/commercial situation (present and anticipated). In addition, laws passed in 1972 and in 1976 responded to workers' interests to be on companies' boards of supervision and share in decision making at the very top with the shareholders' representatives. Together, works-council and supervisory-board participation constitute the German experience characterized as *codetermination.*

Collective agreements are fixed-period, legally binding contracts spelling out the mutual obligations of the parties. The works council is responsible for handling employee grievances, but, since the collective agreement is seen as an addendum to an individual's employment contract, a worker also has access to the Labor Court regarding a grievance. Usually collective bargaining occurs at the industry and state levels between the union for that industry and the relevant employer's association. The agreement applies to all employers who are members of the contracting association, and to all employees of such employers whether they are union members or not. Nonfederated firms may apply the terms and conditions of (relevant—i.e., by industry and state) association agreements to their employees if they wish. In some situations, the Ministry of Labor may extend obligations under collective agreements to all firms in the industry (Seyarth, et al., 1969).

Typically, several agreements (which are not necessarily coterminous) together define terms and conditions of employment. For example, in metalworking, Kujawa (1971) has noted four contracts:

1. The wage- and salary-structure agreement—covering wage and salary grades, percentage compensation differential between grades, remuneration systems, and special allowances.
2. The wage (tariff) agreement—covering minimum-wage and salary rates.
3. The general-employment-conditions agreement—covering working time, dismissals and personal leave, short-time work, vacation and overtime pay, and vacation periods.
4. The agreement protecting employees against the effects of rationalization—covering special compensation, redundancy payments (for dismissals), and retraining allowances for employees displaced by technological change.

Other, specialty types of agreements occur from time to time and have, for example, related to conciliation and arbitration, and the recognition and rights of "union men of confidence," shop stewards appointed at the firm level and functioning parallel to the works council (Gunter and Laminsky, 1978). In metalworking, the four agreements noted above were negotiated on behalf of both hourly and salaried workers by the industry union Industriegewerkschaft Metall (IG-Metall) and the salaried-employees union Deutsche Angestellten Gewerkschaft (DAG).

Association-level wage agreements set minimum rates, reflecting perhaps a history of employer cooperation within industries not unlike that typified in cartel-type models. Actual wages, that is, incorporating increments above the minimum required, are set at the company or plant level in response to labor-market, union and/or works-council pressures. Holidays are designated by law (at the state level) and are not usually supplemented by additional holidays defined in collective agreements. Unemployment compensation for laid-off workers is publicly provided, as are disability insurance and pension benefits.

Use of the strike and lockout weapons is constrained by German law, which imposes a peace obligation on both management and labor. Strikes and lockouts may only occur over an issue related to collective bargaining and only when the issue is not covered by an agreement currently in effect. Since various agreements with varying termination dates are usually evident, these limitations on strikes and lockouts greatly diminish the potential for confusion over important issues. Wildcat strikes, once rare in the German system, have been occurring more frequently recently—especially as inflation has offset wage increases called for in fixed-term contracts (Gunter and Laminsky, 1978). As in the U.S. case, strikes are overwhelmingly interest related (not rights related). Interest arbitration is absent, but mediation and conciliation may be required by collective agreement or may be voluntarily utilized.

United Kingdom. In contrast to the situation in the United States and West Germany, British industrial relations is characterized by the relative absence of legal constraints and structuring. Trade unions are voluntary associations and not legal persons; collective agreements are understandings and not contracts. Neither has legal status. Thomson and Hunter (1978) have noted, however, that the state is becoming increasingly involved in industrial relations and is searching for ways to control or substantially influence the system. For example, the Employment Protection Act of 1975 accords unions rights to certain information and to consult with management over redundancies (i.e., workforce reductions or layoffs). It established arbitration, mediation, and conciliation agencies to implement and secure individuals' and unions' rights granted by the act. It also allows unions to claim, as a right, comparable levels of pay for their constituents in line with industry or district norms. Experience to date on this aspect of the law has been quite limited however (Thomson and Hunter, 1978). Government involvement has also been seen in its income policies, which have been various schemes and attempts, since the early 1960s, to limit pay increases outright or link them to productivity gains and to restructure, in some cases, the employment patterns in manufacturing and service industries.

Collective bargaining is conducted at both industry levels between groups of employers and unions, and at company or plant levels with a union or group of unions identified at a district (regional) level. Fixed-term agreements are becoming more evident, but the stable sections refer to procedural matters. Negotiations on substantive issues, such as wages, are frequently reopened. The concept of the agreement is that it reflects the understanding between the parties, given present underlying conditions. If these conditions change, a new understanding is required. Agreements typically cover wages (or minimum piece rates), the job classification, pay for overtime and shift work, the standard work week, starting times, work breaks, and procedures for settling disputes and changing the agreement. In some industries, agreements also cover job or machine-manning levels and schedules, job demarcations, work-sharing and redundancy rules and apprenticeship programs (Thomson and Hunter, 1978).

Industrial relations in the United Kingdom, however, cannot be so handily characterized in terms of union-management relations and collective bargaining. There is a dual system of industrial relations. As Sturmthal (1972) noted:

> Britain [has] . . . not one but two industrial relations systems . . . often in conflict . . . [one] based on . . . collective agreements; the [other] . . . derived from understandings on the factory floor between management and individual work-place groups . . . This conflict expresses itself in a gap between contract and effective wages, in chaotic forms of grievance handling, and in a disturbing number of "unofficial strikes."

The shop steward is as much evident in rule making and in administering rules as is the union, if not more so. He is especially concerned with the application of the labor agreement, its interpretation on the shop floor, the changing needs and interests of the workers as times change, and the reestablishment of acceptable compensation, working conditions, and so forth. The situation can be delicate in several ways. The steward, elected by the workers, channels company or plant-specific issues and problems to management for attention and resolution. He must be acknowledged. Yet there is no organic link between stewards and union negotiating committees, which conduct (more formal) collective bargaining (Roberts and Rothwell, 1974). Ad hoc arrangements to accommodate stewards during company-level (union) bargaining have been attempted, but one must still admit the potential for steward-union rivalries and conflict remains high. (For an example involving the Fort Motor Company, see Kujawa, 1971.)

Voluntarism, a social philosophy characterized by undisputed self-pursuit of self-interests, is a hallmark of industrial relations in the United Kingdom. Thus there are few, if any, limitations on the right to strike (or the use of the lockout, for that matter). Frequently, strikes are thus also unanticipated (when compared to the expectation of a strike that occurs during a collective-bargaining impasse at the termination date of a labor contract, as in the United States or West Germany). They are more disruptive, therefore, to supplier relationships and are generally viewed as having a more destructive, adverse industrial impact than those in the United States (for instance). In the early 1970s, workdays in the United Kingdom lost per 1000 employed averaged two to three times the French experience, but total workdays lost per year were considerably less than in West Germany.

Japan. Government involvement in industrial relations in Japan works toward three objectives: delivering tangible, financial-welfare benefits to workers, establishing minimum standards for wages, hours, overtime, and so forth, and securing workers' rights to engage in collective bargaining. Social security legislation is fairly extensive and mandates employer/employee-supported funds for health, welfare, accident, pension, and employment insurance. Company-provided welfare benefits are generally regarded as more extensive than those covered by social security and include housing, medical and health care, daily-living support (e.g., company-provided meals, barber shops, laundries, commuting tickets, day nurseries, etc.), mutual-aid credit facilities, and cultural, recreational, and sports activities and facilities.

The 1947 Labor Standards Law and subsequent amendments prescribe minimums for wages, hours, overtime, rest periods, vacations, sick leave, sanitary and safety conditions, and discharge notice; these are as high as those of other advanced, industrial societies (Shirai and Shimada, 1978). Unions in Japan have special committees for shop-floor inspection to identify, document, and report violations of legally required labor standards.

Regarding unions, Article 28 of Japan's constitution stipulates workers have a "right to organize, to bargain and to act collectively," and that (as noted in Article 12) this right is "eternal and inviolable" (Hanami, 1979). In addition, the Trade Union Law also spells out workers' rights to organize, to bargain collectively, and to engage in strike action. Patterned after the U.S. labor legislation, the Japanese law identifies (employer) unfair labor practices and, to protect unions, establishes tripartite (i.e., with labor, management, and public representatives) labor-relations commissions to examine and prohibit unfair labor practices and to provide mediation, conciliation, and arbitration services upon request (Shirai and Shimada, 1978).

There is little, if any, direct government participation in collective bargaining. The policy is one of "noninterference," even in the event of a strike. Nonetheless, a labor-relations commission can require collective bargaining in good faith if an employer refuses to bargain with a union. The union-management agreement is an enforceable contract and it supersedes individual labor contracts that do not meet its standards.

The predominant form of union organization in Japan is the enterprise union, which usually includes both hourly and salaried employees (except managerial). Over 90 percent of union members belong to enterprise unions, about 5 percent to industrial unions, and the remainder to craft unions and others (Hanami, 1979). The enterprise unions are company-, branch-, or plant-specific and, as may be expected, are fairly numerous—over 70,000 were in existence in the latter 1970s (Hanami, 1979). If a union is recognized, all workers are included in the bargaining unit.

Collective bargaining in Japan can be conducted at both enterprise and industry levels. With the former, joint labor-management negotiations (company-specific) cover contract revisions concerning wages, bonuses, working conditions, grievances, personnel affairs, and welfare issues. The latter level involves *shunto,* or the annual spring offensive, and is more evidenced in oligopolistic industries where firms have the capability of passing on industrywide wage increases to their customers. Enterprise unions affiliate with industry federations, which in turn negotiate with employer associations. Wages are the subject matter of *shunto.* Unions not affiliated with those involved in the spring offensive often conduct simultaneous, but independent, wage negotiations with their employers.

The extent of strike activity in Japan is relatively low compared to Western experiences. Moreover, about half the strikes are less than four hours long. About half are coordinated with and supportive of *shunto.* About two thirds of all labor disputes are usually over economic issues. As mentioned before, a labor-relations commission can, upon request, participate in resolving strike issues, and typically does so in about 10 percent of the cases.

Several key characteristics of Japanese industrial relations have developed fairly independently of union pressure, but should be mentioned. One is the permanent employment commitment to certain classes of employees at the larger firms. Another is the *ringi* system of consensus-building in decision making, which rises from the bottom up. There is also the group identification of the workers and the absence of narrowly defined job classifications. Last, but not least, is the quality circle, which embraces the worker's commitment to error-free performance and his willingness to participate in defining and improving products and production processes. Quality circles, as with many things in Japan, are adaptations of practices imported from the West, especially the United States.

COMPARING THE SYSTEMS.   Although the preceding country-level descriptions of industrial-relations systems were hardly detailed, they do illustrate how the roles of the actors vary (among unions, workers, stewards, governments—legislators and administrators—and management). Think of how the extremes might be characterized if a country governed by a totalitarian regime were included. Cultural influences are evident too—note the orderly, almost regimented logic of the German system and the classic liberalism in the United Kingdom. Contrast these to the paternalism evident in Japan, and the influence of the U.S. occupation of Japan following World War II. Note too how each country's economy is broadly market based and how this supports decentralization in industrial-relations decision making. For contrast within market-based systems, compare the grouping of industrial-relations experiences by industry in Germany, where historically cartels have been a hallmark of industrial organization, to the company-oriented business unionism predominant in America's more competitive, free-enterprise industrial society. These are all rational—that is, intrinsically logical—observations.

It would appear almost obvious that the different systems exhibit certain features that are of critical importance to management. Such features would include the nature and frequency of strikes and the nature and incidence of other modes of worker resistance (ranging from "work-to-rule," as may likely be experienced in Great Britain, to worker occupation of the factory, which would appear more likely in more-communist or socialist-oriented societies, such as France or Italy). They would also include the ability of industrial relations to accommodate technological change. When a production process is improved in the United Kingdom, management may indeed be confronted immediately with a "gain-sharing" demand by the workers (who operate within a representative and legal structure that allows for such). Contrast this to the Japanese environment, where it's not the production improvement, per se, that enhances workers' incomes, but the demonstrated success of the improvement in terms of profit impact and experience that (later) enhances workers' periodic bonus and wage levels.

Obviously the questions and concerns become quite real and detailed. The more-crucial concerns certainly require on-site investigation and analysis beyond the country level to industry, regional, and company (or plant) levels. The more detailed the analysis required, the more relevant and useful is Dunlop's systems approach, which allows for cause-effect relationships to be identified and the rationale of each system (at the different levels) to be understood. This should be the starting point for further management inquiry and analysis.

INTERNATIONAL LABOR ACTIVITIES

IDENTIFYING THE SPECTRUM.   International labor activities can perhaps be best categorized in terms of the identity of the predominant actor or influence—which, in turn, fairly well determines the constituency of issues and interests confronted by the actor or organization at that level. Broadly speaking, three such groupings come to mind.

Some international organizations that involve national governments as members are concerned with workers' and unions' interests. Examples include the International Labor Office (ILO) and the Organization for Economic Cooperation and Development (OECD). These organizations are not directly involved in collective bargaining (with one notable case experience—to be discussed later), but are more likely concerned (more or less) with public-policy formulation (usually within their member countries) related to workers and unions, the evaluation of national policies affecting workers and unions, and the construction and publication of relevant data bases.

Several kinds of union associations function at the international level. They range from those involving national union confederations concerned with the more broad, political issues (either among or within countries or among union/worker movements and philosophies) to those involving workers and unions at different national locations of a single multinational enterprise. Perhaps the most influential of these types of organizations have been the different industry-based international trade secretariats, especially relative to MNE activities, and the regionally identified groups of unions, especially those active in Western Europe, seeking to influence public policy and industrial relations in important industrial sectors.

The third category is identified with activities of U.S. unions and the AFL-CIO, which are international in scope and involve collective bargaining directly, the international extension of a free-trade-union philosophy, or practices aimed at constraining the international activities of U.S. MNEs or offsetting the allegedly onerous domestic-employment and industrial-relations effects of MNEs' activities.

INTERGOVERNMENTAL ORGANIZATIONS.   The ILO is undoubtedly the most important intergovernmental organization concerned with worker and union-related issues. Its origins trace back to the League of Nations period, and its membership consists of governments, trade-union organizations, and employer associations. One major focus of the ILO has been directed toward establishing and promulgating fair labor standards covering working conditions (including safety and health standards) and workers' rights (including freedom of association). Another relates to its gathering and publishing of data bases (covering, for example, wages and working conditions by country and industry) and the presentation and analysis of empirical data and other firsthand information useful in modeling future trends (for example, such as employment and income concerns and effects associated with the oncoming shakeout in the world semiconductor industry).

The ILO has completed three major projects of special relevance to MNEs. The first was a broad inquiry in the early 1970s involving testimony and the presentation of evidence, positions, and so forth, from the parties directly concerned (mainly MNE and trade-union representatives), seeking to ascertain the social-policy implications of multinational enterprise. This was followed in the latter 1970s by a series of empirical studies on MNEs' activities in Western Europe, covering, for example, social and labor policies and practices of both U.S.- and non-U.S.-owned MNEs in selected industrial sectors, wages, and working conditions in MNEs, and so forth. In 1980–1981, the ILO published a series of country studies on the employment effects of MNEs. Specific attempts were made to quantify these effects both in terms of job numbers and job quality in some of these studies.

The International Institute for Labor Studies was established by the ILO in 1960 to promote a better understanding of labor problems in all countries through education, discussion, and research. Like the ILO itself, the institute covers a broad spectrum of issues and interests, including those related to MNEs.

The U.N. Centre on Transnational Corporations, its Committee for Trade and Development, and so forth certainly touch on labor- and MNE-related issues, but these are not their main concerns. They defer, in many instances, to their U.N. affiliate, the ILO, for inquiry and expertise on these issues.

The member countries of the OECD agreed in 1976 on a set of "guidelines for multinational enterprises." The guidelines are voluntary, but are felt to be morally binding and sanctioned by public opinion and government action (Blainpain, 1977). They espouse the principle of national treatment by member countries to all MNEs in their territories and an MNE obligation to respect laws, regulations, and administrative practices in member countries. Trade unions and business and industry associations were very active in the preparation of the guidelines and there is no doubt that the direction of the guidelines is toward employment and worker-related social-policy issues, as well as toward tax treatment, financial subsidies, and other policies affecting MNEs' investment decisions.

A landmark case involving the application of the guidelines to an MNE and an interpretation of "national treatment" occurred in 1976. At issue was the inability of the Belgian subsidiary of the Badger Company, Inc., which is in turn owned by the (U.S.) Raytheon Corporation, to compensate discharged Belgian workers at the legally required indemnification limit as it was closing down. The Belgian operation had been marginally profitable and had a positive net worth when abandoned. The Belgian unions pressed the point with the Belgian government and the other OECD members that the parent company intentionally bled the Belgian operation of its finances, that it was the parent's responsibility to cover the shortfall in indemnification funds, and that a national firm would not behave in such fashion. The Badger Company denied the allegation, but settled nolo contendere when several OECD governments pledged not to award engineering contracts to Badger until the indemnification issue was settled (Blainpain, 1977).

The fundamental question in this case is important. Do subsidiaries enjoy the limited liability granted them when they are incorporated, or is there a contingency liability on the parent's part? (Notwithstanding fraudulent or other criminal behavior, the liability of an individual person as a stockholder is certainly limited.) In Badger's case, the market vulnerability of the company to the government's actions tipped the balance of power in favor of the unions' interests. The basic issue, however, of "national behavior/national treatment" as a counterpoint to limited liability remains unanswered.

INTERNATIONAL ASSOCIATIONS INVOLVING UNIONS. Windmuller (1967) identifies four categories of international trade unionism with reasonably distinctive jurisdictions and functions: global internationals, regional internationals, specialized internationals, and industrial internationals.

Global Internationals. The global internationals comprise the International Confederation of Free Trade Unions (ICFTU), the World Federation of Trade Unions (WFTU), and the International Federation of Christian Trade Unions (CISC). Windmuller notes they are global internationals because they claim constituencies in nearly every country, and their vertical structures include industrial, regional, and specialized internationals. The global internationals tend to emphasize representation (i.e., present union views to international organizations such as the U.N., ILO, etc., and pressure governments on union rights violations) and missionary activities (Windmuller, 1969).

From an MNE viewpoint, the ICFTU is the most important global international. It claims nearly exclusive jurisdiction in North America and Western Europe, heavy representation in Latin America and the Caribbean, and affiliates in Africa and Asia. The spread of its constituency and its locus of power generally (geographically) parallel that of the MNE (exclusive of Japan). The WFTU monopolizes representation from communist countries and communist unions in noncommunist countries. The CISC is the smallest of the three, is European oriented, and relates to Christian trade unionism (centered mainly in France, Belgium and the Netherlands).

Regional and Specialized Internationals.   Most of the regional internationals are geographically defined subdivisions of the ICFTU and CISC. Those of the ICFTU operate in Europe (ERO), the Americas (ORIT), Africa (AFRO), and Asia (ARO); the CISC has a Latin American subdivision (CLASC). Regional internationals that are not affiliated with global internationals include the African Trade Union Confederation (ATUC) and the All-African Trade Union Federation (AATUF). The activities of these organizations parallel those of the global internationals with ERO and ORIT, with their greater financial and organizational resources, operating comparatively more independently of ICFTU direction than their sister organization (Windmuller, 1967).

Specialized internationals focus on intergovernmental agencies to function as a component of such agencies or to lobby them. The Worker Group in the ILO, the Trade Union Advisory Committee in the OECD, and the European Trade Unions Congress, which provides worker representation in the European Economic Community (EEC), are examples of specialized internationals. These organizations are important to MNEs in that the larger bodies (e.g., ILO, OECD, and EEC) to which they relate are very involved in public-policy issues impinging on MNEs' interests. They are not, however, directly involved in multinational collective-bargaining attempts.

Industrial Internationals.   The membership of the industrial internationals consists of national trade unions that share a common industrial identification. The industrial internationals themselves are affiliates of the global internationals, that is, the International Trade Union Secretariats (ITSs) in the ICFTU, the Trade Union Internationals (TUIs) in the WFTU, and the Trade Internationals (TIs) in the CISC. From an MNE perspective, the most important are the ITSs, which are fairly independent of ICFTU influence on industrial issues (but acknowledge ICFTU leadership on major political and economic issues—Windmuller, 1967).

Northrup and Rowan (1979) report 17 ITSs active as of 1979. These include those especially concerned with MNEs, for example, the International Metalworkers' Federation (IMF) and the International Federation of Chemical, Energy and General Workers' Unions (ICF).

To illustrate how an ITS responds structurally to implement its interests, the IMF, for example, consists of departments, such as the automotive department, and worldwide company councils, such as the Ford Motor Council, the General Motors

Council, and so forth. The identification of these councils relative to MNEs' concerns appears intuitively obvious. The membership of the councils consists of representatives of unions that relate to an MNE in its different national subsidiaries or at the parent company. The activities of the councils can be categorized conceptually into four rather distinctive types: information, intervention, involvement, and intimidation (Kujawa, 1978).

The "information" function represents union interests in providing adequate data and knowledge of MNE management structures to member (country-bound) unions in support of existing collective-bargaining relationships. It has been implemented rather successfully within the world company-council concept. Data are exchanged among council members that cover contract surveys as well as legally required benefits (by country) and on-line experiences (e.g., safety practices). Unions use this information offensively, to push for concessions in collective bargaining to equal conditions elsewhere in the global MNE structure, and defensively, to attempt to balance the power equation in (national) collective bargaining by providing the union (concerned) with specific information on company operations, profits, and decision-making structures.

The "intervention" function has also been implemented rather successfully. It involves direct contact between union representatives and parent-company management to identify and resolve specific labor-relations problems or eliminate onerous management practices at the subsidiary level. Union claims to success in interventions are often difficult to substantiate, but in many cases parent companies have responded responsively to unions' complaints on behalf of other unions in other countries. These complaints ranged from the lack of advance notice by a General Motors subsidiary in Switzerland regarding a plant closing to the discharge of workers at Chrysler Corporation's Spanish subsidiary (Kujawa, 1971). Parent-company management has acknowledged, off the record, that information such as that provided by unions through their intervention activities can often be quite welcome.

The "involvement" function means multinationally coordinated and conducted collective bargaining involving unions in different countries and a single MNE. Notwithstanding some ITSs' claims to the contrary, substantial transnational collective bargaining has yet to be experienced, except in very few instances (Northrup and Rowan, 1979, and Kujawa, 1978). The reasons for this are several, and include legal, structural, cultural, and economic barriers (Kujawa, 1975).

The "intimidation" function relates to the manipulation of the press by certain ITSs (most notably the ICF) to create an image of transnational union activity eminently more successful than the facts imply. The message here, of course, is to get at the facts of each reported instance of union success.

Aside from the ITSs, industrial regional internationals exist, such as the European Metalworkers' Federation, which support the work of regional internationals, such as the ETUC vis-á-vis the EEC, as well as seeking to coordinate transnational collective bargaining at international and regional levels, for example in the case of Philips (Dronkers, 1975).

The bottom line for management regarding transnational collective-bargaining attempts by ITSs (or others) is that much of the content and process of collective bargaining is place-bound and not really open to transnational influence. Moreover, organized labor has little power to bring to bear on such bargaining.

INTERNATIONAL ACTIVITIES OF U.S. UNIONS AND THE AFL-CIO

A Special Case—Canada.   Aside from their participation in ITSs activities, U.S. unions are directly involved with MNEs in several other ways. Many U.S. unions (e.g., the United Auto Workers and United Steel Workers) are distinctly binational regarding the United States and Canada—the latter is often one of several geographic regions comprising the "international union." The binational unionism on the labor side, combined with many technical, market, and cultural similarities within industries that span the two countries (indeed, including many firms that operate in both countries), has resulted in binational collective bargaining, coordination in collective bargaining between firms and subsidiaries and union representatives from the United States and Canada, and assistance from union and management personnel from one country involving issues, at impasse, perhaps, in the other country.

Following the implementation of the 1965 free-trade agreement in automobiles and automotive parts and accessories, Chrysler, Ford, and General Motors (separately) negotiated wage-parity agreements with the UAW to equalize wage structures and levels and other employment practices between their U.S. and Canadian operations (Kujawa, 1971). Other examples and evidence on the extensiveness of U.S.-Canada binationalism in industrial relations can be found in a special report on the topic by The Conference Board (Hershfield, 1975). Both U.S. and Canadian companies have also experienced situations in which a contract settlement in one country set a pattern for subsequent negotiations in the other country, and, albeit on a much less frequent basis, union and company representatives from a Canadian parent (for example) sometimes seek to mediate a dispute at a U.S. subsidiary.

Coordinated Bargaining Attempts.   In their U.S. collective bargaining, American unions have attempted to confront MNE-related issues through coordinated bargaining and contract control over information disclosure on international operations and allocation of production to foreign subsidiaries. Neither approach has been particularly successful from a union perspective. The lead experience in coordinated bargaining developed by a U.S. union and involving a U.S. MNE is the General Electric (GE) case with the International Union of Electrical Workers (IUE). In conjunction with the 1969 and 1973 meetings of the GE world council (an ITS activity), representatives of unions at GE's foreign plants were invited to attend and observe subsequent contract negotiations between GE and the IUE. Notwithstanding those in attendance, there has never been any collective bargaining during U.S. negotiations on conditions or interests of workers at foreign plants. Northrup and Rowan contend, moreover, that IUE pressure to do so would be contrary to the (U.S.) court order allowing the IUE to select attendees to U.S. bargaining sessions so long as only matters pertaining to the IUE bargaining unit are bargained over, and thus likely considered a "refusal to bargain in good faith" (Northrup and Rowan, 1979).

Attempts to Limit Foreign Sourcing.   Two cases involving attempts by U.S. unions to bargain collectively over MNEs' foreign-sourcing decisions have been reported (Kujawa, 1972). One involved a UAW challenge to the decision by Ford Motor to produce engines and gear boxes at England and German subsidiaries for car assembly operations in the United States and Canada. The union contended that this practice transferred work traditionally done by U.S. UAW members to foreign plants and could lead to U.S. employment losses, production interruptions, and so forth. The company denied these contentions, and the UAW pressed no further (Kujawa, 1972). The other case involved GE and the IUE. During the negotiations on the 1969–1972 contract, the union proposed a clause forbidding GE to transfer work from U.S. to foreign operations or to establish an overseas plant to perform work customarily done by U.S. (unit) employees. In support of this proposal, the IUE requested a substantial amount of information from GE on its foreign operations. The company refused this request, and the union filed an unfair-labor-practice charge. The general counsel of the National Labor Relations Board denied the charge, noting that the detailed information was not needed to bargain over a broad prohibition covering foreign-production transfers, and that the union had not substantiated its claim that such transfers were even occurring (Kujawa, 1972).

AFL-CIO Activities. The AFL-CIO is involved in MNE issues mainly in its attempts to influence U.S. public policies affecting MNE activities. Kujawa (1981) notes that the AFL-CIO, with its social-movement orientation and concern, contends that society's interests supercede those of MNEs and that MNEs are therefore subject to social control. In promoting this perspective, the AFL-CIO has conducted and supported positions and research concluding that U.S. MNEs export employment, sell high-technology expertise (developed often with U.S. government funding support) to overseas affiliates and other customers, contribute to balance-of-payments problems and foreign-exchange crises, and so forth. Moreover, it contends the U.S. government grants MNEs substantial tax benefits supportive of multinational expansion at the expense of (U.S.) domestic growth, and that the deterioration of key U.S. industries occasioned by MNEs' activities contributes to the demise of urban areas and U.S. defense capabilities (Jager, 1975). This is certainly a substantial set of allegations and should be understood by MNE management personnel.

Beginning with its support of the proposed Foreign Trade and Investment Act of 1972 (the Burke-Hartke bill), which called for import quotas, government approval of licensing technology abroad, and so forth, the AFL-CIO has been noticeably active in promoting its public-policy objectives. With few exceptions, it has not been as successful as it would like, however.

Regarding multinational collective bargaining, the industrial union department of the AFL-CIO has been especially supportive. The action, nonetheless, has involved mostly certain key unions and firms, as already discussed in the GE/IUE situation.

Internationally, especially in Latin America, the AFL-CIO cosponsors organizations to promote the development of free trade unionism, such as the American Institute for Free Labor Development. In these instances, some MNEs have joined with the AFL-CIO through direct support.

INTERNATIONAL MANAGEMENT OF INDUSTRIAL RELATIONS

LOCUS OF DECISION MAKING. Labor relations is a very place-bound activity. Issues, actors, structure and method may change considerably from one industry and country to the next. With but few exceptions, industrial relations decision-making is taken at the local, subsidiary level. For example, Robert Copp the overseas liaison manager, labor relations staff, at Ford Motor Company's world headquarters, notes (Copp, 1977):

> Every Ford subsidiary has . . . an appropriate staff . . . to develop and administer an industrial relations program appropriate to the national setting. Indeed, this staff, along with the managing director and the board of the subsidiary, is the principal management decision maker in industrial relations matters.

Supportive of Copp's view, Frank Angle, director of industrial relations in General Motors' overseas operations division, states (Angle, 1975):

> Management in General Motors has always been based on the line-and-staff principle. Line executives, whether based in the United States, Canada, or overseas, have full operating responsibility and authority . . . to ensure the flexibility necessary to adapt individual operations to local conditions.

Similarly, Jack Belford, Massey-Ferguson's vice-president of personnel and industrial relations, states (Belford, 1977):

> . . . it would be a brash corporate management that would substitute its judgement of an industrial relations situation for the judgement of the local management. If they do, they are asking for trouble. There is no substitute for local judgement. In this regard I feel strongly about the importance of senior industrial relations managers in every location being national and indigenous.

Exxon's George McCullough, the manager of employee relations, reports that industrial-relations management is highly decentralized (McCullough, 1977):

> My company operates in 131 countries. The variations in our labor relations processes, the manner in which we go about collective bargaining, and the differences in items included in collective agreements are staggering. Even in two countries like Holland and Belgium, where the proximity between Rotterdam and Antwerp has caused us to consolidate some management functions, the labor relations processes are totally independent of each other and the contracts bear little resemblance.

More broadly based studies (involving groups of multinationals) confirm these management statements (Walker, 1972, and Roberts and May, 1974).

Behavioral dimensions of collective bargaining also support the concept of decentralized decision making. Tradeoffs among objectives are made during negotiations, and these reflect specific local priorities. Complete agreements, incorporating the outcome of this process, are either accepted or rejected by local worker constituencies. Management that participate in this process had better be well aware of what will "work" in these give-and-take exchanges.

A few limited exceptions involving parent-company management in subsidiary-level labor relations have been noted, however (Kujawa, 1972). These include the example of a parent's participation in setting an overall industrial-relations strategy at the subsidiary to restructure labor relations away from plant-level agreements and piece rates to a multiplant agreement pattern and time-measured day rates accompanied by a substantial infusion of funds by the parent to modernize production processes. Another situation more commonly evidenced involves a parent's participation in negotiations over pensions when the parent's staff includes actuarial expertise not available locally (to management) and where the pension commitment itself is viewed as a potential liability of the parent company.

THE HEADQUARTERS-STAFF ROLE. Since labor relations is so localized, there is no line responsibility or function for it at the headquarters level. There is frequently a staff function, however, and it is concerned with effectiveness in industrial relations at the subsidiaries and in operations at the multinational level, and in implementing the stewardship role of the MNE management.

The Advising Function. An MNE's labor-relations staff usually embraces considerable industrial-relations expertise, especially in terms of the firm's technology and its work-force-management requirements and the corporate philosophy regarding the role and handling of workers, unions, and other aspects of employee relations. This capability at the MNE staff level is not used to intimidate local industrial-relations managers or to impose a unified approach to labor-management relations. Rather, it is made available to local management (frequently only at the request of local management) to respond to ideas and/or to suggest alternatives. The frequency of this parent-company supportive participation increases when an impasse and strike occurs at the subsidiary level, but even then, decisions on both contract substance and management tactics are invariably locally taken. (Of course, if a strike occurs during industrywide negotiations, as may be evidenced, for example, in either Germany or France, any kind of participation by MNE staff is far removed from what may or may not be effective in securing an agreement.)

In most MNEs, the parent-company labor-relations staff monitors subsidiaries' labor relations to ensure that agreements do not compromise the integrity of the local labor market and determines what is required to secure a local agreement. This is done to prevent the establishment of a global company-specific pattern in local collective agreements. The role of the MNE staff in this regard is not one of dictating to subsidiary managers, but rather one of information gathering on local conditions and situations and the sharing of this information with all the subsidiaries. The monitoring function is useful in developing data, not in imposing conditions and bargaining positions. It is becoming increasingly important as unions in different countries are themselves becoming increasingly knowledgeable about contract settlements and employment conditions in other subsidiaries (of the same MNE) and identify and/or press for similar treatment or concessions during local bargaining.

As a side note, what may first appear as exceptions to this MNE objective of localizing wages, benefits, and other employment conditions are the labor agreements in the auto industry to include U.S. and Canadian UAW members in a single wage- and job-classification system. This was accomplished in the initial contracts by bringing Canadian workers' wages up to parity ($1 Canadian = $1 U.S.) with those of U.S. workers. Exchange rates (over time) reflect productivity differentials and money-supply changes between countries. As these have changed between the United States and Canada since wage parity in the auto industry was established, the real purchasing power and the U.S. dollar cost of the wages paid Canadian workers have declined substantially. Nonetheless, the U.S.-dollar-Canadian-dollar parity in the auto industry remains. The foreign-exchange market has effectively matched local labor-market and other economic conditions between the United States and Canada and factored the contractually determined parity condition by whatever differentials found. The integrity of local markets, as they relate to wage payments, remains intact!

The Interpretive Function.   Being aware of labor issues and conditions at the subsidiary level, the MNE labor-relations staff performs a very important interpretive role to staff with other functions at the parent-company levels. It provides others with data and other information necessary to their planning activities and to their understanding and assessments of local situations. Production, of course, is affected by strikes at the subsidiaries, and, depending on the extent of intersubsidiary production integration, contingency plans to maintain production elsewhere and to supply market needs must be developed. Or, in the event of multiple production capabilities among subsidiaries, production elsewhere may need to be expanded. The MNE staff's interpretation of the local strike situation as it affects production continuity is essential to these contingency plans.

Budgeting at the headquarters level is also related to the MNE labor-relations staff's functions. What may be required to secure a labor agreement at a subsidiary will likely affect overall production costs and necessitate new cost forecasts. These in turn may affect product prices and sales and revenues forecasts. It is quite common for the MNE's labor-relations staff to be called upon to give estimates (developed with local input) of anticipated labor-cost changes to both the corporate finance and marketing functions.

A third interpretive activity follows from the need of the senior line management that deals with subsidiary management at the parent-company level to be knowledgeable about local labor conditions and problems. This allows them to respond intelligently, responsibly, and responsively to the line-management decisions.

The Stewardship Function.   Stewardship is often equated to control. Regarding subsidiary-level labor relations and the role of the MNE staff, stewardship is implemented through indirect control, that is, through input on the selection of industrial-relations executives at the local level, the professional development of these executives, and, in some cases, the influencing of the compensation paid local executives and the staff capabilities evidenced at the subsidiary level. In nearly every case, the line management controls the appointment of management personnel to key positions. This means the managing director at the subsidiary selects the (local) senior labor-relations officer and that person selects his subordinates. The management level above that identified with the selection decision most frequently concurs with the decision, or, sometimes, takes exception to it (invariably prior to the announcement of a final decision). The MNE staff usually advises the MNE line management (invariably on a continuous basis) on the advancement potential of labor-relations executives at the different subsidiaries and offers specific inputs when specific personnel are nominated by subsidiary management for the (local) senior industrial-relations position. It must be emphasized, however, that both initiative and ultimate control are at the subsidiary level. The MNE-level line management and staff would rarely, if ever, impose the appointment of a certain manager on the subsidiary management. Likewise, the appointment of (subsidiary) managers below the level of the senior industrial-relations executive is commonly totally contained at the local level—including the nomination, selection, and approval decisions.

In larger firms, professional development and career-tracking of executives at subsidiary levels are frequently evidenced at the parent level. Training (aside from that locally provided) is often accomplished through intersubsidiary meetings of industrial-relations personnel (on either a regional or global basis) at which information and experiences are shared and ideas tested. Sometimes parent-company personnel may perform (usually informal) functional audits of local industrial-relations management and offer ideas for improvement. Quite commonly, the parent-company labor-relations staff follows the development of local industrial-relations personnel and assesses their promotion potential. This may or may not lead to specific promotional opportunities, and the procedure and interest is not unlike that accorded subsidiary executives in other functional areas.

Occasionally (definitely not frequently), the MNE staff advises line management on compensation levels for subsidiary industrial-relations executives and on the general functions and capabilities necessary to support the conduct of labor relations locally. This is more often than not done on an exceptions basis and then (most likely) only to promote minimum performance levels. The MNE staff is most likely performing an advocacy role to convince local management to upgrade salaries or local competencies.

INTERNATIONAL BUSINESS STRATEGY AND INTERNATIONAL AND COMPARATIVE INDUSTRIAL RELATIONS

Most MNEs confront a variety of strategic decisions on a fairly routine basis. These decisions might encompass product design, product-market identification, long-term financing, research and development support, political involvement, and so forth. Regarding industrial-relations consideration, and limiting our inquiry to include only MNEs in manufacturing or processing, three such decisions appear particularly relevant: the foreign direct-investment decision, decisions on the allocation of production among parent and subsidiaries, and the disinvestment decision. Care should be taken in making these decisions, both to weigh industrial-relations effects as elements in the decision process and, once the decision is made, as expectations of what may ensue as labor-management opportunities or problems.

THE FOREIGN-DIRECT-INVESTMENT DECISION. Most direct investments by MNEs are defensive in nature; that is, to protect or maintain what had been export sales to foreign markets, usually in advanced, industrialized economies, or to protect or enhance domestic (U.S.) market shares by production cost cutting derived from the location of production facilities in low-labor-cost, developing countries. In other words, foreign direct investments are made to serve foreign markets with local (foreign) production, or domestic (home) or third-country markets with foreign ("offshore") production.

In the former case, the MNE had most likely been serving foreign markets with U.S. exports, but as foreign-based firms have cut into these markets, the premium return on the product's sales has declined, and distant and (local) less market-responsive operations are no longer economically optimum (or justified). What's required is an actual production presence in the foreign market that is sensitive to and likely adjusted to specific market needs and the actions of competitors. Success in this type of venture also requires a competitive edge in terms of product or process uniqueness, or financial or marketing strength enjoyed by the MNE. In most cases, product, process, or managerial technological superiority is the key. The foreign industrial-relations environment where the prospective direct investment is sited, must be accommodative to the implementation of these competitive strengths. This implies that a production environment characterized by shop-floor militancy and social-class cleavages would be less desirable to the MNE than one in which in-plant labor-management relations were more harmonious and less strike prone. Likewise, an environment in which management is able to capture the economic benefits of improved technologies, at least for the first few years, is preferred to one in which nearly immediate "gain-sharing" with the workers is required. Both considerations point to West Germany or perhaps Spain as preferred plant location sites compared with the United Kingdom, for example. Production continuity, either because of transnational production integration or the inability to stockpile finished product may also be a key factor. A plant site prone to wildcat strikes (including strikes at key local suppliers) would not be satisfactory. Unit labor costs are also important, as are the distance from the production location to the consumers, tariff barriers, and so forth. Analysis of the entire situation lends itself to probabilistic modeling with alternative outcomes and expected costs (e.g., foregone sales, reduced profits, etc.) delineated.

In the offshore production situation, the direct-investment motivation is essentially production cost cutting. The product is likely to be a mature product and the profit margin likely to be thin. Import competition (including that generated by other U.S.-based firms) is heavy. The economics of the situation compels the export of labor-intensive production to low-wage foreign production sites. The quality of the offshore work force, as well as the potential for demand changes in the (U.S.) product market, may well necessitate segmentation in the production process—for example, with garments, where design and cutting are done in the U.S. plant and sewing in the offshore facility. Labor quality, labor cost, and production continuity are likely the key industrial-relations considerations in deciding on a location for offshore production. Most low-wage countries that can respond to this type of direct-investment opportunity (e.g., because of proximity to the United States) have commercial- and economic-development agencies and production "free zones" that will gladly work with a U.S. firm in establishing an offshore facility.

If the firm bargains with a U.S. union whose unit members will be affected by the location of production to the offshore facility, the company is clearly obliged by U.S. labor law to consult with the U.S. union over the effects of that decision on unit members. Enlightened management would also consult with the union before a final decision was made to see if the economic rationale favoring the offshore location could be reversed, for example, by changing U.S. work practices, foregoing wage and benefit increases, and so forth (Kujawa, 1972).

THE PRODUCTION-ALLOCATION DECISION.   If production allocation affects U.S. employment of bargaining unit members and is essentially a reallocation situation, the economics of the decision should be addressed within the legal context and union-consultation suggestion discussed above. If production involves new products, then the pertinent industrial-relations considerations are likely to be similar to those discussed already in the foreign direct investment to serve the foreign market situation.

As multinationals themselves have matured, they have expanded product lines in foreign markets and have continued to rationalize production of more mature lines through interplant (including transnational) production integration. The MNE is thus diversifying regarding product-market risk, but becoming less diversified regarding labor-resource risk. This is occurring while product profit margins are becoming increasingly thin because of growing worldwide resource competition and producer cartelization (especially in financial and energy markets) and increasing (especially international) product-market competition. This means that the production-allocation decision is more important than ever (no product-market staying power) and that it may well turn on narrow differentials in comparative unit labor costs, or on the firm's ability to negotiate with governments over location incentives (e.g., financial subsidies, tax holidays, etc.) that might reverse the direction of these differentials. Firms should be careful to investigate alternatives in detail and to base decisions on present value expectations that factor comparative trends in the growth of unit labor costs and the potential for future successful negotiations with governments in their cash-flow analyses. (Unit labor costs, incidentally, include costs of production stoppages, legally required fringes, etc., and changes in unit labor costs would include workweek and holiday/vacation trends, etc. Anticipated foreign-exchange-rate changes would also be relevant to trend analyses in comparative unit labor costs. Changes in productivity in the specific industry the MNE operates in must be evaluated with expected overall country-level productivity changes that in turn affect exchange rates and the comparative competitiveness of the firm's production in foreign markets, especially in the shorter time periods. In the long run, exchange rates move with productivity changes, and unit money costs of production are not as important to the comparative analysis required.)

THE DISINVESTMENT DECISION. Disinvestment is not an unusual event for an MNE. Indeed, Vernon (1977) has observed that

> . . . between 1968 and 1974, 180 U.S. based multinational enterprises sold or liquidated 717 manufacturing subsidiaries located in foreign countries . . . out of a total population of about 6,500 such subsidiaries, . . . suggesting the existence of an entropic process in the multinational enterprise.

As noted earlier, many products and industries have matured with little prospect for substantially altering product or process technology. In these cases, profit margins are likely not sufficient to cover the extra costs associated with internationally distributed management. Disinvestment, or even abandonment of a market, is the result, and in many cases should even be anticipated.

Anticipation may be the key to handling disinvestment successfully regarding industrial relations. Selling off an operation while it is still profitable may entail some foregone benefits, but these should be measured against the potential of not selling the operation once it is unprofitable, or of having the facility occupied (and perhaps run) by irate workers who do not want to lose their jobs. Plant closings in Western European countries (England excepted) usually involve an indemnification payment to the discharged workers—which (as discussed earlier in the Badger Company case in Belgium) can amount to several thousand dollars per employee (Blainpain, 1977). The amount of this payment should be the first ingredient used by an MNE in determining the discount applied to the selling price of the subsidiary!

Planning for disinvestment is also important. In countries where employee works councils are legally franchised to receive economic and financial data and forecasts, a surprise disinvestment decision could hardly be expected. Planning the disinvestment beforehand, allowing workers time to adjust to the pending closure (maybe by finding alternative employment early on), and offering workers employment elsewhere (within the MNE system) are all sensible activities.

Country policies on required indemnification payments have raised some interesting problems (for countries) and opportunities (for MNEs). Some companies (with dual production capabilities) have been known to cut back employment more in the country with the less-costly indemnification requirement. This saves the firm money (all else being equal). The problem is then that the country with the less-onerous requirement receives a disproportionate share of the unemployment. The countries of the EEC are presently investigating the need for harmonizing social policy on this issue. Finally, there is the case of the U.S. MNE that traded a "no-layoff" commitment in local collective bargaining for some union concessions. The company's actions were based upon detailed analysis of the severance payments due the work force in the event of layoffs factored by the probability of such layoffs occurring during the 3-year life of the contract, and then balancing of this expected cost against the expected gains resulting from the concessions.

SOURCES AND SUGGESTED REFERENCES

Sources

Angle, F. "The Conduct of Labor Relations in General Motors Overseas Operations," in D. Kujawa, ed. *International Labor and the Multinational Enterprise.* New York: Praeger, 1975.

Belford, J. "Comment," in R.F. Banks and J. Stieber, eds. *Multinationals, Unions and Labor Relations in Industrialized Countries.* Ithaca: New York State School of Industrial and Labor Relations, Cornell University, 1977.

Blainpain, R.G. *The Badger Case and the OECD Guidelines for Multinational Enterprises.* Deventer, The Netherlands: Kluwer, 1977.

Copp, R. "Locus of Industrial Relations Decision Making in Multinationals," in R.F. Banks and J. Stieber, eds. *Multinationals, Unions and Labor Relations in Industrialized Countries.* Ithaca: New York State School of Industrial and Labor Relations, Cornell University, 1977.

Dronkers, P.L. "A Multinational Organization and Industrial Relations: The Philips' Case," in D. Kujawa, ed. *International Labor and the Multinational Enterprise.* New York: Praeger, 1975.

Dunlop, J.T. *Industrial Relations Systems.* New York: Henry Holt, 1958.

Gunter, H. and Laminsky, G. "The Federal Republic of Germany," in J.T. Dunlop and W. Galenson, eds. *Labor in the Twentieth Century.* New York: Academic Press, 1978.

Hanami, T. *Labor Relations in Japan Today.* Tokyo: Kodansha International, 1979.

Hershfield, D. *The Multinational Union Challenges the Multinational Company.* New York: The Conference Board, 1975.

Jager, E. "U.S. Labor and Multinationals," in D. Kujawa, ed. *International Labor and the Multinational Enterprise.* New York: Praeger, 1975.

Kujawa, D. "Foreign Sourcing Decisions and the Duty to Bargain Under the NLRA," *Law and Policy in International Business,* Vol. IV, No. 3 (1972), pp. 41–66.

Kujawa, D. *International Labor Relations Management in the Automotive Industry: A Comparative Study of Chrysler, Ford and General Motors.* New York: Praeger, 1971.

Kujawa, D. "Transnational Industrial Relations and the Multinational Enterprise," *Journal of Business Administration,* Vol. VII, No. 1 (1975), pp. 23–37.

Kujawa, D. "U.S. Labor, Multinational Enterprise and the National Interest," *Law and Policy in International Business,* Vol. X, No. 3 (1978), pp. 192–206.

Kujawa, D. "U.S. Manufacturing Investment in the Developing Countries: American Labour's Concerns and the Enterprise Environment in the Decade Ahead," *British Journal of Industrial Relations,* Vol. XIX, No. 1 (1981), pp. 74–91.

McCullough, G.B. "Comment," in R.F. Banks and J. Stieber, eds. *Multinationals, Unions and Labor Relations in Industrialized Countries.* Ithaca: New York State School of Industrial and Labor Relations, Cornell University, 1977.

Northrup, H.R. and Rowan, R.L. *Multinational Collective Bargaining Attempts.* Philadelphia: Industrial Research Unit, The Wharton School, University of Pennsylvania, 1979.

Roberts, B.C. and May, J. "The Responses of Multinational Enterprises to International Trade Union Pressures," *British Journal of Industrial Relations,* Vol. XII, No. 3 (1974), 34–70.

Roberts, B.C. and Rothwell, S. "Recent Trends in Collective Bargaining in the United Kingdom," in *Collective Bargaining in Industrialized Market Economies.* Geneva: International Labour Office, 1974.

Seyfarth, Shaw, Fairweather, and Geraldson. *Labor Relations and the Law in West Germany and the United States.* Ann Arbor: Bureau of Business Research, Graduate School of Business Administration, University of Michigan, 1969.

Shirai, T. and Shimada, H. "Japan," in J.T. Dunlop and W. Galenson, eds. *Labor in the Twentieth Century.* New York: Academic Press, 1978.

Sturmthal, A. *Comparative Labor Movements: Ideological Roots and Institutional Development.* Belmont, CA.: Wadsworth Publishing, 1972.

Thomson, A.W.J. and Hunter, L.C. "Great Britain," in J.T. Dunlop and W. Galenson, eds. *Labor in the Twentieth Century.* New York: Academic Press, 1978.

Vernon, R. *Storm over the Multinationals: The Real Issues.* Cambridge, MA: Harvard University Press, 1977.

Walker, Kenneth F. *Labor Problems in Multinational Firms.* Report on a Meeting of Management Experts, Paris, June 21–23, 1972. Paris: Organization for Economic Cooperation and Development, 1972.

Windmuller, J. "International Trade Union Organizations: Structure, Function, Limitations," in S. Barkin, *et al,* eds. *International Labor.* New York: Harper and Row, 1967.

Additional Suggested References

Bomers, G.B.J. *Multinational Corporations and Industrial Relations: A Comparative Study of West Germany and the Netherlands.* Assen/Amsterdam: Van Gorcum, 1977.

Dore, R. *British Factory/Japanese Factory: The Origins of National Diversity in Industrial Relations.* Berkeley/Los Angeles: University of California Press, 1973.

Gennard, J. *Multinational Corporations and British Labour: A Review of Attitudes and Responses.* London: British-North American Committee, 1972.

Jacobs, E. et al. *The Approach to Industrial Change in Britain and West Germany.* London: Anglo-German Foundation for the Study of Industrial Society, 1978.

Kennedy, T. *European Labor Relations.* Lexington, MA: D.C. Heath, 1980.

Kujawa, D., ed. *American Labor and the Multinational Corporation.* New York: Praeger, 1973.

Kujawa, D. *Employment Effects of Multinational Enterprises: A United States Case Study.* Working Paper No. 12. Geneva: International Labour Office, 1980.

Kujawa, D. *The Labour Relations of United States Multinationals Abroad: Comparative and Prospective Views.* Research Series, No. 60. Geneva: International Institute for Labour Studies, 1980.

Martin, B. and Kassalow, E.M., eds. *Labor Relations in Advanced Industrial Societies.* Washington, D.C.: Carnegie Endowment for International Peace, 1980.

Multinational Enterprises and Social Policy. Geneva: International Labour Office, 1973.

Spalding, H.A. *Organized Labor in Latin America.* New York: New York University Press, 1977.

INTERNATIONAL PUBLIC AFFAIRS

CONTENTS

INTERNATIONAL PUBLIC AFFAIRS

Jean J. Boddewyn

WHY PUBLIC AFFAIRS?

There are three basic ways of making money in business. One is through *operational efficiency,* by minimizing inputs and maximizing outputs in any given activity and for the whole firm. Such savings and higher productivity translate into greater profits. The second profit-generating way rests on *market effectiveness* in buying and selling. The old principle of "buy cheap, sell dear" applies here, although nowadays it takes rather sophisticated forms in developing sourcing, marketing, and corporate strategies.

This leaves us with *public affairs*—the third way of making money. A firm may be efficient and well positioned in the market, but what if it is boycotted because of its union-busting and environment-polluting activities? In such a case, the profits resulting from efficiency and market effectiveness will be jeopardized. Conversely, a company can secure favorable legislation, obtain a relaxation of onerous regulations, and gain the goodwill of actual and potential consumers, and thereby achieve greater profits.

To put it more generally, public affairs is about obtaining and retaining *legitimacy* and *power* vis-à-vis the firm's "publics." A "legitimate" business is one that not only acts legally but also according to local customs and in tune with current expectations of good behavior vis-à-vis its own employees, the communities where it operates, and the society it serves. Such legitimacy protects the profits made by the company as a producer and marketer. It also opens new avenues for gain through the creation of a better operating environment and the reaping of more immediate benefits such as tax concessions and greater patronage. A "powerful" business is more likely to affect both its market and nonmarket environments. This is the domain of public affairs—also called external affairs, social affairs, public relations, issues management and other names.

Public Affairs (PA) is concerned with enlisting the support and negating the opposition of significant nonmarket units (public institutions and private organizations, looser collectivities, and individuals) in the firm's environment. Its targets (constituencies, publics, stakeholders) consist of (1) government in its multiple roles of legitimizer, regulator, and promoter; (2) business, trade, labor, and professional associations as well as other firms in their pressure-group, private-regulator, and legitimizing roles; (3) the intellectual, moral, and scientific communities as legitimizers and opinion makers; (4) public opinion at large as voter and general legitimizer; and (5) the firm's stockholders and employees as legitimizers. These targets constitute the "nonmarket environment" of the firm as distinguished from the "markets" for its commercial inputs and outputs.

Some people scoff at such profit protecting and making through public-affairs activities. They feel that business has no business meddling in politics and government, and in manipulating public opinion. This view, however, denies business the right to speak up, to petition, and to avail itself of political and economic benefits open to all private and corporate citizens. Exhibit 1 presents an overall description of the public-affairs function and emphasizes "good conduct" as the basis of all PA activities. It also stresses the continuous feedback that should inform them.

WHY INTERNATIONAL PUBLIC AFFAIRS?

The legitimacy issue looms even larger in international business, because a foreign firm is generally perceived as a "foreign body" whose contributions and loyalty are questionable.

For one thing, headquarters personnel and managers sent abroad are relatively ignorant of host-country policies, laws, legal traditions, local notions of what is considered "fair" business behavior, attitudes, customs, and so on. To make matters even worse, many expatriate managers prove impatient or ethnocentrically intolerant in the face of such differences—"Why are they not like us?"

Some home-based and expatriate managers go even further and flatly refuse to accept local traditions and expectations. This may be caused by sheer intolerance of foreign ways, or it may simply reflect the human desire to simplify life and continue operating as at home. It may also be the product of corporate policy and of its bias toward standardized operating procedures, since multinational corporations need some global vision and uniform approach in order to maximize their advantages over local firms that will always know their milieus better.

Consequently, the legitimacy of foreign-owned and controlled companies is frequently challenged by host nations, which then translate their fears and suspicions into special entry, operating, and exit requirements, often stricter than those applying to local firms (see previous sections: The Political Environment of International Business, International Codes of Conduct, and Managing Conflicts). The home country also presents PA challenges, since the multinational character of a firm may be perceived as detrimental to that country's welfare by exporting jobs, capital, and technology, among other things.

KEY IPA FACTORS

Identifying targets as well as developing, implementing, and evaluating the appropriate programs to reach and influence them constitute the tasks of international public affairs (IPA). Before analyzing these classical elements of planning, organizing, staffing, directing, and controlling, it is well to focus on some of the key factors that affect the conduct of the IPA functions.

TYPE OF INDUSTRY.   Clearly, some industries have more IPA problems than others. Mining and extracting, for example, raise a host of sensitive issues because many countries view their natural resources as a sacred patrimony that is out of bounds for foreigners, who should not own or exploit the "soil"—the national territory—that embodies the concept of sovereignty.

Other industries are vulnerable because they are polluters (e.g., refining and chemicals), or because of some priority assigned to them as a source of export earnings (many commodities, for example), as the basis for economic development (e.g., steel and banks), as necessary for national defense (e.g., transportation, armaments, communications), as the guarantor of low national-health costs (e.g., pharmaceuticals), as the basis for modernization (e.g., machine tools, computers, biochemistry), or simply because they are prestigious and have caught the fancy of some key political leader. Consequently one finds that firms like Exxon (petroleum), Pfizer (pharmaceuticals), IBM (electronics), Citicorp (banking), and Ford (automobiles) have a well-developed IPA function.

On the other hand, some industries are practically invisible and stir very little concern. Eaton, which makes a large number of intermediary products that find their way into better-known ones, could advertise at one time that: "We probably are the largest multinational company that you have never heard of!" A particular company, of course, may have many different product lines and thus face varying public-affairs situations. Westinghouse sells both air conditioners and nuclear reactors, but the former line generates far fewer problems than the latter.

Conversely, some economic activities suffer from "benign neglect" and do not generate enough public support because they are taken for granted or considered to be of minor importance. Pure marketing organizations such as department stores and supermarkets often have to clamor for government attention and incentives because economic-development authorities often assume that distribution will take care of itself, or because they consider it to be a parasitic activity.

SIZE, GROWTH, AND EVOLUTION. Large size—absolute or relative to local firms—usually makes for visibility, greater impact on the local economy and society, and vulnerability to the criticisms addressed to monopolistic and oligopolistic companies. This calls for more public affairs to justify the firm's size in terms of economies of scale and as part of a multinational organization that can draw on the resources and experiences of its many parts.

The company that grows internally or through acquisitions also creates problems as local firms feel crowded out, and as the specter of foreign domination raises its ugly head. J.J. Servan-Schreiber made *The American Challenge* a common fear in Europe, but Latin Americans resent *dependencia*, and Africans and Asians reject new forms of imperialism and colonialism.

Other changes can be equally bothersome. The multinational that closes a plant in one country and opens another elsewhere is frequently branded as irresponsible and profit thirsty. Expanding here rather than there also rankles the feelings of the neglected governments—especially if several nations competed vigorously for the new plant or expansion.

The *entry* stage poses different problems from those of later stages. There are typically active and multiple contacts with the authorities and various experts to ascertain the overall investment climate, to get the necessary permits and guarantees, and to obtain investment incentives (tax holidays, training allowances, cheap loans, free grants, etc.) if available. At this point, relations with government and the public are often smooth and cordial when the foreign investor has been invited or welcomed by the host country, although some local interests may object.

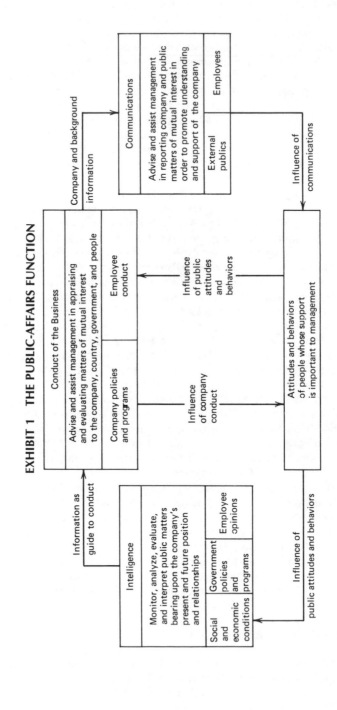

EXHIBIT 1   THE PUBLIC-AFFAIRS FUNCTION

After the honeymoon period is over and the *ongoing-operations stage* sets in, public affairs may settle into a placid routine, although constant vigilance is necessary in order to avoid being ignored and even harmed as later investors now get new benefits. Governments policies and priorities do change over time; the cost/benefit ratio tends to look less favorable to government which now sees foreign companies paying fees and royalties to their parent and repatriating profits while the subsidiary's contributions in terms of jobs, exports, taxes, and so forth tend to be taken for granted.

At *exit*—forced or voluntary—time, new public-affairs problems emerge as both the government and public opinion oppose layoffs and the loss of productive capacity unless local ownership and management can take over. Even when forced out, the multinational must negotiate for compensation and try to maintain good relations with its constituencies in order to protect its other investments in the host country and elsewhere, and to prepare for its possible return at a later date.

CORPORATE CULTURE AND INDIVIDUAL ATTITUDES.   Some companies have no significant PA experience at home and are thus unaware of such problems abroad and unprepared to cope with them on an international scale. For example, IBM's European subsidiaries were at one point more sophisticated in public affairs than their parent company because they had first faced, in the United Kingdom, France, and Germany, public policies designed to favor local computer companies through government purchases and subsidies. Hence there was little that the corporate headquarters could provide in the way of PA assistance. Conversely, a multinational such as Caterpillar, which has a well-developed corporate public-affairs philosophy at home, is more likely to implement it in host countries.

The implementation of company policy depends on people, but some managers are not temperamentally or professionally suited to be active in public affairs. They may resent the publicity, abuse, and even injuries (kidnapping, kneecap shooting, assassination) associated with visibility and outspokenness. Others object to the required politicking and public-relationing because of their engineering, production, or marketing background, which has oriented them to other forms of profit making.

Executives experienced in legal and financial matters, on the other hand, are more inclined to recognize opportunities in this area and to minimize the concomitant risks, since their regular work requires much contact with government anyway. As the financial director of a multinational in Belgium put it: "The more interesting part of my job is not financial statements and cash flows—I have able assistants to do that—but interacting with numerous bureaucracies to obtain permission to increase prices, to get favorable customs valuations, to repatriate dividends, and so on."

Over time, even managers with little inclination toward public affairs do learn from experience; and strong admonitions from higher corporate levels ("We don't want problems with host governments!") help move reluctant converts in that direction.

IPA INTELLIGENCE AND PLANNING

INSTITUTIONALIZING THE PLANNING FUNCTION.   Setting goals and action plans for tomorrow requires good intelligence today. A major problem here is that public-affairs issues vary greatly from country to country, product to product, and function to function. One obvious solution is to fully decentralize public affairs among the multinational company's units regions, countries, divisions, and departments.

This approach, however, leaves unattended the central headquarters' tasks of (1) identifying common issues around the world, (2) collecting and sharing worthwhile knowledge and experiences, (3) centralizing those monitoring activities that are best done once and for all, and (4) appraising the units' planning performances so that the latter may be ultimately upgraded. How do multinationals cope with this classical problem?

Ultimately, all solutions require the appointment of one or more people at headquarters—the question is who and where? A relatively simple answer consists of expanding the role of the *market-research and/or corporate-planning staff* beyond their traditional economic analyses of the world environment to include IPA matters. Since these staffs' resources are limited in terms of time and expertise, this solution ultimately requires the addition of one or more IPA specialists—often someone with a liberal-arts and/or social-science background, although engineers and scientists are also included when technical problems loom large (e.g., environmental protection).

Alternatively, the chief executive officer may appoint a *special assistant* operating outside of the corporate planning staff in order to emphasize the chief executive officer's concern with these matters, and as the possible nucleus for a full-fledged IPA department. A few multinationals (e.g., Exxon) assign a member of the *board of directors* to the surveillance of IPA matters.

A more elaborate solution consists of placing such intelligence gathering and planning *within the corporate public-affairs department*, whose role is thus extended to encompass international developments. This is a more advanced approach because it signifies that the multinational corporation has seen it fit to create a separate public-affairs function that provides inputs and generates favorable outcomes just like the other major units of the firm (marketing, production, finance, product divisions, geographic areas, etc.).

ESTABLISHING PRIORITIES AND TARGETS.   A perusal of any list of topics on the agendas of the U.S. government, foreign governments, and the United Nations reveals scores of long-term issues and immediate problems with which a multinational can concern itself. (See also Gladwin and Walter, 1980.) Exhibit 2 illustrates the major topics with which they have to cope to one degree or another.

Can such public-affairs issues be tracked down so that management may take adequate initiatives in time? Several think-tank and consulting organizations are in the process of developing the technology that a small but growing number of multinational corporations are beginning to use and improve. (Molitor, 1977; LaPalombara and Blank, 1977; Kobrin, 1979; Terry, 1977; Haendel, 1979; Kraar, 1980). The techniques and their validity remain crude, but multinationals are undoubtedly expanding and refining their monitoring of the relevant environments (Kobrin et al., 1980, Fahey et al., 1981, and the Kobrin chapter on Political Risk Evaluation).

In any case, some sorting out is essential in terms of *specificity* to the firm, *urgency*, and *danger/opportunity* significance. Besides, both *short-term* and *long-term implications* must be considered—for example, immediate compliance with a new ill-designed regulation on consumer protection *and* prevention of its spreading to other countries through more-effective monitoring and lobbying. (For an excellent treatment of the monitoring function, see Brown, 1979.)

Ultimately, issues translate into specific *targets* that embody problems and opportunities:

EXHIBIT 2 PUBLIC-AFFAIRS ISSUES

Main Issues	Subissues
Multinationalism (pressures on multinational companies)	Protectionism (tariff and nontariff barriers); foreign ownership; indigenization of personnel; exporting jobs; local research and sourcing; import substitution and controls; joint ventures; expropriation and nationalization; choice of appropriate technology; patent/trademark/licensing restrictions; codes of conduct (UN, OECD, EEC, UNCTAD, ICC, ILO, national, industry, etc.); bribery and other corrupt practices; Arab boycott; South Africa; human rights; transborder data flows; multinational unions; foreign divestment; disclosure of information to governments, unions, employees, and stockholders; accounting standards; multinational unions, terrorism.
Labor relations	General industrial relations climate; theory and practice of participation through works councils, trade unions, staff associations, etc.; codetermination; cooperatives; attitudes of employers and employees; layoffs; plant closures; unemployment; motivation; automation; international comparisons and differentials; legislation and regulations; employee health and safety.
Environmental pollution	Air, land, water; noise; resource conservation; resource allocation; recycling; new technologies; legislation and regulations (local, national, EEC, UN, etc.).
Individual and organization	Alienation; pressure groups; power groups; role of women; trade unions; civil rights; women, immigrants; participation in planning; consumer protection; legislation and regulations.
Consumer affairs	Pressure groups; fair trading; customer service; product liability; subsidies; shortages; substitutes; misleading advertising; consumer redress.
Business and society	Ownership; profit; disclosure; big vs. small business; entrepreneurship; licensure; marketing concept; government intervention; capitalism vs. socialism; mergers, monopolies; social responsibility; social audit; centralized control; move to service economy; inflation; prices and incomes; investment and jobs; company legislation and regulations.
Government	State of politics; political parties; democracy; nationalization; devolution; sovereignty; internationalization; defense; direct intervention; civil-service practices; legislature vs. executive and judiciary.
Technological change	New technologies; technological impact; mass communications; rate of change; investment in research; responsibilities of technologists and scientists; technology transfer; scientific entrepreneurs; social impact/technology assessment; appropriate technology; education for a world of change.

EXHIBIT 2 *(Continued)*

Main Issues	Subissues
Changing values/social trends	Materialism vs. quality of life; growth vs. no growth vs. balanced growth; desire for participation; leisure; crime, security; health (physical, mental); drugs; sex; alienation; elitism; invasion of privacy; morals, ethics, religion; attitudes toward business, government; role of youth; home, family; education; demand for information; racism; sexism; minorities.
Urban affairs	Inner-city slums; infrastructure; decision making, participation; transportation; education; housing; social services; local government finance; minorities.
The third world	North vs. South; power blocs; East vs. West; role of private enterprise; role of EEC, UN, OECD, etc.; foreign aid; population; natural disasters; education; training; pollution; technology; use of power by resource-rich less developed countries (oil, tin, cobalt, etc.).
Resources	Energy; raw materials; basic foodstuffs; fresh water; conservation; recycling; new sources; oceans; man-made substitutes; legislation and regulations (national, regional, international).
International affairs	EEC; East-West relations; Europe-U.S. relations; Far East; Middle East; trends in nation states; GATT, trade bodies; OECD; United Nations and its agencies; Commonwealth; monetary situation; global inflation; expropriation; war; security.

Source. InterMatrix, Greenwich, CT.

1. Who are the people, institutions, and organizations who can cause us trouble or assist us?
2. How do they operate, and what are they likely to do?
3. What do we want them to do or not to do?

These targets are not all external to the firm but include shareholders and employees. Customers and suppliers are also important elements in public affairs, because they represent potential or actual allies and enemies. Without such a target list, no definite action plans can be effectively developed.

SOURCES OF INFORMATION. The intelligence gathered should be related to the company's main problems around the world. Otherwise, too much unnecessary information clutters the whole process and ultimately dooms the project to failure, since it is not perceived as being sufficiently action oriented. Still, more-sophisticated multinationals allow for the monitoring of "horizon" issues still dimly understood in terms of their corporate implications (Molitor, 1977).

Internal Sources.   The plans and reports produced by subsidiaries are being progressively expanded to include public-affairs issues and actions. However, this takes time, pressure, and education because the natural inclination of operations managers is to focus on more-traditional quantitative issues (market trends, operating costs, etc.). Much information is also gathered through visits to and from foreign subsidiaries, meeting of public-affairs officers from various countries, the debriefing of returnees, and regular intracorporate communications through letters, telephone calls, telex messages, and so on.

External Sources.   There is an increasing number of good information sources, ranging from the regular reading of *The New York Times*, the *Wall Street Journal*, the *Economist*, and the *Financial Times*, to subscribing to more-specialized country and issues reports generated by such outfits as the Economist Intelligence Unit, the Conference Board, the InterMatrix Group, Rundt, Business International, International Business-Government Counsellors (Washington, D.C.), The Global Business Forum (New York), the United States Council for International Business, and the International Advertising Association. Companies are now able to buy computerized services from Public Affairs Information, Inc. (PAI) and from Commerce Clearing House, Inc. (CCH). Additionally, conferences provide settings where experiences and current knowledge can be more interactively shared (e.g., the meetings of the Public Affairs Council and the International Public Relations Association).

A major principle here is that multiple sources of information and interpretation should be used, because no single person or department has the necessary expertise, and because several heads are better than one when it comes to analyzing complex issues. This suggests the elaboration of alternative scenarios rather than simple black-and-white diagnoses and prognoses.

Besides, one gets information by sharing one's own, since some topics are too delicate to be put in writing. This requires identifying the people (including experts, government officials, and critics) and associations that have the necessary information and cultivating them regularly through visits and by attending conferences in which they participate.

Coordination.   Although some centralized information keeping is necessary, most data remain with the subsidiaries and divisions. This suggests developing a system comparable to British Oxygen Company's "ring and main" approach. The units are conceived of as in a circle, and the corporate planning "center" is only one of the groups on the circle. Each unit has access through requests to information in any other unit, but this requires that the units be made cognizant of each other's store of knowledge through the circulation of master lists (Who keeps track of what?) and periodic meetings of information officers.

The Chief Executive Officer's Special Problems.   The chief executive officer's information problems are unique, because much of it comes to him filtered, and because subsidiaries are reluctant to communicate bad news or draw attention to new problems on which they will be queried and prodded. Consequently, he must complement the organization's monitoring system by his own sources: peers in other firms, government officials at home and abroad, membership in key associations (e.g., the Business Roundtable), board members (including foreigners) specially appointed for that purpose, advisory boards, contacts with experts and critics, the commissioning of special studies, and so on.

INVENTORYING RESOURCES.   This step is crucial for deciding what changes are needed in organization structure, staff, activities, and controls after identifying what the firm can already do by itself with its present resources. Additionally, external potential sources of assistance must be identified and evaluated. Questions include:

1. How much *information* already exists in the firm: Who knows what?
2. Who knows whom, in terms of the necessary *contacts* with the main targets?
3. How good is the *communication system* for collecting, interpreting, storing, retrieving, and sharing public-affairs information?
4. What *budgets* are available and how are they spent?
5. What *outsiders* (consultants, associations, information services) are good at what and at what cost to complement the firm's own resources?

SETTING GOALS, TIMETABLES, AND BUDGETS.   Public-affairs goals cannot simply be *general philosophy statements* of the type: "We will behave as good citizens of the countries where we operate." They have to be translated into specific tasks linked to desired outcomes, and with a timetable—for example, to hire a former U.S. government official of subcabinet rank to head the firm's Washington office within 6 months ; to postpone for at least two years the enactment of regulations barring the use of certain food ingredients in France; or to increase the proportion of Brazilian people who think favorably of the company from 15 to 25 percent within one year.

Headquarters must also issue *policies and guidelines* within which the subsidiaries' public-affairs plans will be developed. Some brook no exceptions (such as the proscription of bribing officials) whereas others simply set broad parameters—for example, representation on the board of major business associations is highly desirable, but the choice of associations and the timetable for obtaining representation is left flexible.

Whenever possible, *financial budgets* must be related to the achievement of particular goals—for example, how much it will cost to conduct a public-relation campaign designed to convey certain messages to a specific target audience within a defined time period. On the other hand, slush funds must be avoided, because they falsify the budgetary process and complicate the assessment of results—not to mention possible legal and legitimacy problems.

Time budgets are also important, since it is estimated that anywhere from 5 to 70 percent of the top managers' time is spent on public-affairs matters. Should new goals require more time, these executives must receive special assistance or delegate some of their other tasks.

As in all other forms of planning, flexibility is essential, because situations and conditions change. Hence it is essential to maintain a constant monitoring of the environment, to develop alternative contingency plans ("If this happens, we do that instead") and to have versatile resources that can be shifted from old to new problems.

STRUCTURING THE IPA FUNCTION

Proper organizing of the IPA function is not easy, because of the multiple factors bearing on it (e.g., type of industry, size of the multinational and its foreign subsidiaries, corporate tradition, personal attitudes, etc.). Besides multinational corporate experience in this area is still relatively meager, so that one finds a variety of patterns further complicated by the numerous organizational changes undergone by many multinationals in recent years.

Indeed, the public-affairs function must largely adapt itself to whatever global organizational form (international division, geographic, product, matrix) has been adopted by a multinational. In particular, the move toward a worldwide product-division basis has created problems to the extent that this organizational form complicates the conduct of public affairs at all levels, because product divisions operating in a single country are not typically organized to coordinate their PA activities on a national or regional basis.

A key principle here is that *PA policies and implementing decisions that have major implications for the entire company have to be made at higher levels.* The higher levels are also involved if only they possess the credibility and weight to make corporate policies believable by others—for example, to increase R&D expenditures abroad as a sign of the multinational's commitment to its host nations.

Yet it is desirable to involve those lower levels that have relevant information and/or will have to live with the new policies. A company spokesman should not be inadvertently caught lying because he did not know that the firm had a particular policy or was engaging in certain practices (e.g., bribery).

It is not unusual to find that the different levels in the firm—global (corporate), regional (e.g., Europe), national, and local (community)—are unevenly developed, and similar variations are found among product divisions and geographic areas. When the field is more active in public affairs than the center, headquarters has problems assisting and supervising the subsidiaries.

The facts that public affairs itself is made up of many parts (public relations, government relations, consumer relations, employee relations, etc.) and that some of them are lodged in other departments (personnel, marketing, finance, legal, etc.) also complicate the design of an effective IPA structure.

Exhibit 3 presents the respective ideal roles of the corporate, regional, and national levels. Such a division of labor is only approximated in a few multinationals such as Caterpillar Tractor Company, which has a definitely centralized headquarters-oriented approach to international public affairs. Standard Oil Company of California, on the other hand, uses a decentralized approach because a large number of countries is involved, and they believe that it is impossible for a small corporate staff to stay abreast of foreign and international developments. Other companies are learning, and several other patterns are evident besides such an "advanced" one.

BEGINNING STEPS: THE MINIMAL PATTERN. One finds here firms with no significant public-affairs problems, those with no awareness of, or interest in, such problems, those not quite knowing what to do about them, and those that have taken a few preliminary, tentative, partial steps to develop a PA function within their organizations.

At the *national level*, the minimal response consists of assigning to some manager or staffer whatever PA tasks have become necessary, besides what the chief executive himself shoulders in this area. Typically, it will be a second- or third-level manager whose function already involves relations with government and other nonmarket groups. The personnel manager is, therefore, frequently assigned the nascent PA activities, but the chief financial officer or the legal counsel are also common choices, since they already deal with labor ministries, tax authorities,

EXHIBIT 3   THE IDEAL ROLES OF THE CORPORATE, REGIONAL, AND NATIONAL LEVELS IN INTERNATIONAL PUBLIC AFFAIRS

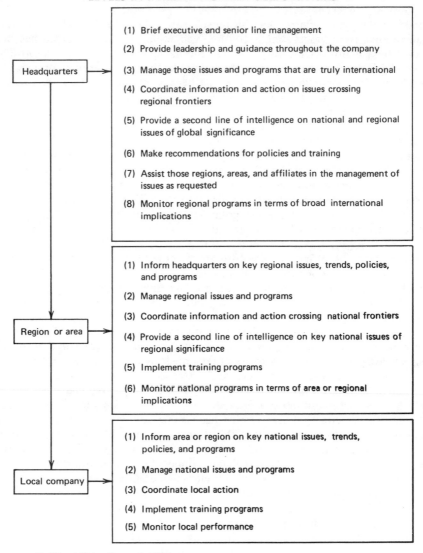

Source.   Public Affairs Council, 1980.

foreign-exchange matters, price-controls, and so forth. Lower-level professionals such as engineers and accountants are brought in whenever their expertise is needed to study issues, prepare reports, and make presentations.

This pattern, by the way, is the one generally found at the *plant* or *community level,* even when the national subsidiary has a more fully developed public-affairs function: The plant manager or his personnel officer carry out whatever community relations are necessary on a part-time basis, sometimes with the assistance of a public-relations man.

At this early stage, outsiders such as bankers and lawyers are frequently used to supplement the firm's meager resources, and some firms use the service of the American Chamber of Commerce (and similar bicountry associations) and of their embassy (see below).

The simplicity of such light arrangements should not obscure the real problems connected with the lack of in-depth expertise and full-time attention, and the difficulty of coordinating all sorts of piecemeal and diffuse efforts. Such problems can be remedied up to a point through training programs and exchanges of information among affiliates. Sooner or later, however, this set-up proves too awkward and ineffective.

ON THE WAY: THE INTERMEDIATE PATTERN.   Most multinational firms are at the intermediate stage—aware of the growing public-affairs problems facing their type of company, curious to find out what others are doing, discussing the problems at various levels within the organization, and building some of the major components of a full-fledged PA function. Major factors prompting greater involvement and the development of a more elaborate structure are the successful examples of other firms active in this area, some crisis (e.g., a negotiation poorly handled or a major attack on multinationals), pressure from higher hierarchical levels, and/or the interest and initiatives of the general manager or of some staffer—for example, the legal counsel or the public-relations officer.

The major characteristic of this intermediate stage is the existence of some formal external-affairs position *somewhere* in the international organization—frequently at the regional (e.g., European) level as far as U.S. firms are concerned—but going beyond whatever public-relations activities the firm may already be engaging in. It may be nothing more than the general manager getting a special assistant to deal with public affairs, or some functional manager having his position formally extended and upgraded to include government relations and other PA matters as a way of learning more about what should be done and how.

ALL THE WAY: THE ADVANCED PATTERN.   At the advanced stage, all four levels—local, national, regional, and world—have well-developed public-affairs objectives, structures, and personnel (including the involvement of top executives), although some locations, countries, and regions typically are less grown and sophisticated than others.

These are companies in industries where government relations are crucial, as in petroleum, pharmaceuticals, computers, chemicals, and automobile manufacturing. They are large, or at least affect the country's economy significantly; they are continuously in the process of expanding, contracting, and rationalizing their production, marketing, and financial operations in a number of countries—with concomitant changing impacts on home and host countries.

They are usually organized on a geographic basis, but those with worldwide product divisions or of a conglomerate nature (such as ITT) have regional and/or national coordinating and assisting units. Exhibit 4 presents a simplified organizational chart for such arrangements.

National Line Executives.   These executives concentrate on four major tasks:

1. Identifying problem areas, indoctrinating their managers and employees about them, and assigning accountability for them to various subordinates and staff while remaining ultimately responsible for the PA function.

2. Assisting in the gathering of information about nonmarket developments through meetings with various elites in economy and society—on a personal basis and in the context of associations, conferences, and select gatherings of executives.

3. Obtaining support for the firm's actions from decision makers (mainly legislators and government officials), opinion makers (the press, academics, financial analysts, etc.), and other significant influencers and public-opinion segments.

4. Negotiating with other decision makers when power and protocol considerations make national line executives the only valid spokesmen for the company.

Lower-level line managers are of course also active in relations with government and the public when their counterparts are of commensurate rank and when these managers' technical expertise is crucial in supporting roles. Here, top executives and officials often initiate contacts and negotiations and then leave them to their subordinates to pursue until they have to be formally concluded or some impasse has been reached.

National Public-Affairs Staff.   The public-relations function is typically very developed at this advanced stage and includes personnel specializing in such activities as receptions and visits, the production of various publications, press relations, and academic/scientific relations. This staff advises top executives as well as other departments.

However, sophisticated companies do not stop at these more-traditional PR activities (often assisted by the regional and world levels, which have relevant expertise to communicate) designed to project a company's image. They also conduct such activities as consumer-complaint handling, charitable contributions, beautification and safety programs, developing community facilities such as swimming pools, and making free computer time available to worthy causes. Hence PR titles are often upgraded to "public affairs" or "external affairs," and a separate government-relations officer may be appointed.

A few companies include advertising and sales promotion in public affairs, but this is exceptional—as is the full inclusion of the legal department. Similarly, some PA staffs handle employee relations (elsewhere handled by the personnel department), customer relations (elsewhere handled by the marketing department), and/or trade/technical/professional relations (elsewhere handled by the manufacturing department). Thus the U.K. subsidiary of IBM at one time combined under "communications" the following activities:

Civic affairs (general involvement as a corporate citizen).

Academic and scientific relations.

Press relations.

Employee relations.

Technical and professional relations.

Customer relations.

Community relations.

Government relations.

EXHIBIT 4   ADVANCED PATTERN IN INTERNATIONAL PUBLIC AFFAIRS

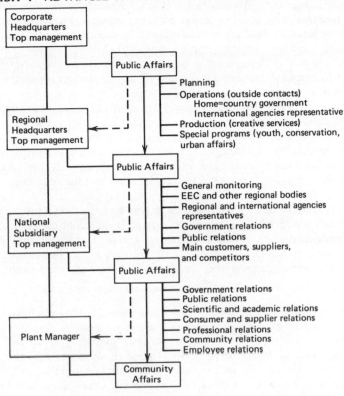

——————— Line authority   — — — — — Staff or functional authority

Source.   Business International, 1975.

Some companies organized on a product basis have found it desirable to form national councils for the various product subsidiaries in the same country so as to develop and share information on common environmental concerns, and provide a single voice for the firm. Otherwise, host governments ask: "Who speaks for the company in this country?"

Local Community Level.   Although some public-affairs matters are conducted from the center, distance and the need for close and sustained relationships usually bring about the appointment of at least one local PR-type officer. However, this responsibility may simply be given to the local plant manager or personnel manager.

Regional Level.   This level represents a half-way point between: (1) the national level, where needs and resources may be too limited to warrant the formal appointment of a public-affairs man; and (2) the world level, where the task is largely unmanageable on a global scale (see below).

As a fairly typical example of this development, one U.S. firm has a public-affairs director at the European level whose task it is to (1) oversee the creation and upgrading of this function in national subsidiaries; (2) coordinate the sharing of national experiences with other subsidiaries in the region; (3) monitor and influence developments in public and international organizations (EEC, OECD, UN, International Chamber of Commerce) through secondary sources and personal contacts; (4) relay information from and to the world level; and (5) advise the top regional managing director as well as national managers and PA staffs.

The latter task reveals that the regional PA executive has no direct supervisory role over the national subsidiaries but can only exercise influence through his own boss—with the affiliates remaining responsible for PA activities in their countries, as should be the case. Since a number of these regional executives have had national experience during some prior assignment, their advise is typically well accepted— particularly since they are themselves aware of the fact that they can only "sell" but not "tell."

This role is more complex when the company is organized on a product basis— especially when product headquarters are located in different countries (e.g., the European chemical division is based in London, and the textiles division in Rotterdam). One company handles this problem by having a more "philosophically oriented" PA man loosely capping the "day-to-day" staffers attached to the product divisions.

The World/Corporate/Global Level.   Few international companies have a distinct staff for public affairs at this level and it is likely to be a one-person unit. Instead, most do it on a part-time basis or in association with something else—with existing staffs such as legal and corporate planning brought in whenever necessary to plan new investments, to review the performance of subsidiaries in public affairs, and to provide occasional assistance to foreign subsidiaries. One also witnesses the appointment of international specialists such as an international governmental affairs and/or international public relations director—usually under the corporate vice-president for public affairs. Exhibit 5 profiles such positions in two major European multinationals.

Internal communication is important in terms of diffusing relevant experiences within the multinational company among all countries and regions. It is also essential for foreign-subsidiary executives and staffers to know those corporate-headquarters people that handle public affairs so that communications may be based on more personal relations. This leads to frequent visits in both directions, as well as to the regular convening of PA staffers from all over the world, so that the company philosophy may be better understood, problems may be aired, new policies and plans may be discussed, fellow practitioners may get to know each other better, and the attitudes and practices of the more-effective subsidiaries and levels may influence others.

A few companies practice a fair amount of "industrial diplomacy" through their top corporate officers. The better-known practitioners have been David Rockefeller (of Chase Manhattan) and Henry Ford II, who traveled widely and met visibly (and sometimes loudly) with foreign elites of various kinds. Other firms choose to do it less flamboyantly, if only because the company name and that of their chief executive are not well known. Such visits provide these travelers with prime sources of key information about investment climates and government policies, but this

EXHIBIT 5 INTERNATIONAL PUBLIC-AFFAIRS JOB DESCRIPTIONS

Volvo: Director, International Affairs

1. Responsible for International Affairs, subdepartment of Corporate Affairs (including Public Affairs, Market Relations, and International Press Relations).
2. Continuously follow worldwide developments concerning trade and industrial-policy issues with relevance to Group activities (countries and international organizations).
3. Report on a regular basis to top management on the economic-political development worldwide.
4. Coordinate information and policies toward international organizations and authorities and to foreign subsidiaries.
5. Representative and coordinator toward Swedish authorities and organizations in matters concerning trade policies.
6. Under Head of Corporate Affairs, responsible for contents and logistics in connection with yearly international PR-conference.
7. Develop contacts toward international organizations.
8. Follow-up of foreign subsidiaries concerning PR and Public Affairs matters.
9. Report and draft documents (lectures, letters, etc.).
10. Responsible for updating of files (on international organizations, issues, countries, etc.).

Alfa-Laval: Director, Public Affairs and Communications

Objective

To create an understanding of, and favorable attitudes toward the Alfa-Laval Group, inside and outside the Group. The ultimate goal is to maintain and enhance the Group's competitive strength in a broad sense of the term.

Authorities and responsibilities

Develop, Maintain and Promote:

• Policies, rules and recommendations to ascertain a company profile program, and to uphold it through training and corrective measures.

• Methods and systems to coordinate Group communications and to improve personal proficiency.

Participate in:

• Establishing "Public Affairs and Communications" units in the major Alfa-Laval markets in order to carry out an effective and efficient communications activity Group-wise. This also comprises the selection of professional communicators to serve Group companies as staff members or as consultants.

Perform:

• Function as the primary communications channel of the Executive Group Management (company spokesman, press officer, etc.).

• Conduct research on the attitudes of important groups toward Alfa-Laval, and develop programs to increase company awareness.

• Function as a general-purpose information bureau to deal with "company questions," and to channel requests to appropriate sources.

• Function as an opinion maker by participating in various debates, etc., to present and represent Alfa-Laval.

• Develop and carry out short- and long-term information programs with the aim of broadening public knowledge and acceptance of Alfa-Laval.

Render Services:

• "Trouble-shooting" within the entire field of communications of the Group. Other Group units may thus occasionally utilize central resources to solve communications problems of an unusual or infrequent nature.

Source. Conference Board, 1985.

information appears to be poorly diffused within the organization for lack of good debriefing processes. The major benefit of such visits is symbolic, as they manifest the international commitment of the firm. The visits also open up channels of communication for lower-level executives and staffers who engage in the actual negotiations and routine contacts.

SPECIAL PATTERNS.   When one part of a company has more experience and influence than another on account of size, age, type of industry, and so forth, it is not uncommon to have it assume responsibility for conducting all or most of the public affairs of the other. A classical example here is the oil company assisting its petrochemical affiliate within the same country and/or region.

A parallel arrangement exists when one product division is more experienced and carries out the PA function for the others. Thus the computer division of one U.S. firm in Italy services the office-equipment, industrial-equipment, and consumer-products parts of the subsidiary. This special pattern, however, requires close physical proximity of the related parts.

Similarly, the head of the major Belgian subsidiary of a highly diversified firm has been appointed "senior officer" and is charged with the government relations of the other subsidiaries—largely because the electronics-equipment firm he heads has a long experience in this area, and because he is considered to be most effective. This approach is particularly indicated when the various parts of the conglomerate firm cannot be brought under a single national holding company because of the desire to make some of the affiliates look national rather than American, when the latter image could hurt sales and other external relations.

CONCLUDING REMARK.   About one third of international firms may be said to have a fairly well developed public-affairs function or to be moving in that direction, with some building blocks already in place. Thus, a recent Conference Board Report (Lusterman, 1985) reveals that IPA professionals are employed on the corporate staff of 29 of the 82 multinationals queried; in more than half of them, the IPA function was created only within the last ten years. Even for them, however, the stage of development is uneven, particularly at the world level.

Yet there is often more here than meets the eye. In many firms, one looks in vain for a vice-president for international public affairs and/or for a supporting staff in these areas. At the same time, however, one is struck by the fact that all sorts of people have part of the necessary information, the indispensable contacts, the appropriate awareness, and the essential determination to cope with problems in the nonmarket environment of the firm. Indeed, a growing number of these people have been stationed abroad, travel frequently to visit subsidiaries, attend regional and worldwide company seminars and working committees, and communicate regularly and even incessantly with other company executives and staffers at home and abroad by mail, telephone, and telex.

One may well prefer to find something neater and more clearly understandable; one is aware of gaps and weak links; and one wishes that even more attention and resources would be devoted to this area of great and increasing importance. But for most of these companies, such informal arrangements do work until a major crisis makes it evident that something more formal and explicit as well as better endowed is necessary.

IPA STAFFING

International public affairs requires a variety of skills and, therefore, persons—both insiders and outsiders.

RANK AND STATUS.   The more-sophisticated multinationals recognize that their chief executives have to be involved in public affairs for symbolic power and protocol reasons. In the first place, the chief executive officer is the only valid *spokesman* of his organization in matters dealing with the nonmarket environment of the firm (including government). Symbolically, only the person who is perceived as able to *represent* and *commit* the entire organization is believable and trustworthy in formal contacts and negotiations. It is also a matter of protocol to the extent that outside of the United States, people tend to delegate much less authority to their subordinates, so that only the top executive is thought to have the necessary knowledge and power.

Lower-level executives and specialists (treasurer, accountant, personnel manager, legal counsel, etc.) are regularly involved in more routine and more technical contacts and negotiations. Their symbolic role is small or nil, however, unless their participation has been preceded by formal introductions and a meeting of the principals involved, who then retire until the detailed negotiations are over and the official agreement is ready to be ratified and the ribbons cut.

BACKGROUND, NATIONALITY, AND ROTATION.   Public-relations experience—particularly in press relations and speech writing—is commonly found in public-affairs staffers, although people with a technical background are increasingly brought in to provide the expertise needed for dealing with technological and environmental problems. It is felt by some companies that they also need "thinkers" as PA staffers as well as executive trainees in the process of rounding their exposure to the firm's functions. The pure print-oriented PR man seems to be declining in importance.

Government-relations people are seldom hired directly. Instead, they are started in other parts of the company in order to familiarize them with its operations. They are then progressively given more government-relations responsibilities until their task becomes full-time.

There is a presumption in favor of the local national, based on his greater familiarity with the local environment, his knowledge of the native language, his greater loyalty toward the host nation (his country), and the notion that his appointment proves the foreign corporation's ability to train and promote its native employees. These are very valid arguments, but they should not be exaggerated, because local nationals are often unaware of, and insensitive to, major factors and trends in their own countries. After all, how many U.S. managers paid much attention to the nascent civil rights, ecology, women's liberation, and consumerist movements?

Knowledge of the local language is, of course, a major advantage for the native manager, although less so in multilingual countries (e.g., Switzerland, Belgium, and the Philippines), where English is often the preferred second language. A major handicap for Americans lies in the fact that trade associations conduct their business meetings in the native language(s) without simultaneous translation, thereby discouraging U.S. managers from participating in important discussions and acquiring influence within such groups. Some U.S. managers send a lower-ranking native to represent them, but this move can be misinterpreted because foreigners do not believe that a number-two or number-three man knows as much as his boss, and because of the symbolic and protocol importance of having the number-one man present.

Language aside, the fact of being a foreigner is not necessarily a handicap for the general manager, because local officials believe that a foreigner is more likely than a native to be heard and heeded at the corporate level. Besides, expatriates are often seen as carriers of such desirable values as efficiency, technology, and entrepreneurship, and thus derive much legitimacy from this perception. In any case, governments usually accept that Americans and other expatriates predominate at the regional and world levels as a recognition of where the ownership and control of the company really lie.

A reverse problem exists as far as relations with home-country embassies are concerned, to the extent that the ambassador and foreign-service officers are more at ease with their compatriots than with native managers in terms of language, the common background that facilitates discussions, and trust in the loyalty and discretion of the managers when sensitive information is being communicated. This problem promises to increase as more local nationals become managing directors.

The reassignment of foreign executives certainly poses a problem in terms of developing and maintaining effective rapports with government officials and industrial elites. Frequent rotation, for one thing, prevents the development of language fluency unless the executive is transferred to a country with the same language or to the regional headquarters. Reassignments also discourage government officials faced with the endless task of getting to know the foreign executive and "educating" him about the government's policies and concerns.

FORMAL AND INFORMAL PA ROLES.   At least six types of PA men are evident in sophisticated multinationals.

The Monitor/Analyst/Thinker.   This kind of specialist is used to "scan the environment," to keep track of relevant developments such as regulatory proposals, public-opinion changes, and initiatives by important interest groups. He interprets them for line managers and other departments, and prepares recommendations for action— frequently in consultation with other knowledgeable people inside and outside the firm. To him is also assigned the task of preparing position papers as well as reports to higher levels within the multinational.

Typically, this kind of PA man has a liberal-arts or social-science background, although a growing number of firms are appointing engineers and line managers as a way of broadening their training in anticipation of higher-level assignments, or in order to draw on their expert knowledge (e.g., of pollution controls if environmental protection is a key issue).

Few subsidiaries have such a monitor/analyst/thinker but rely instead on an economist within the firm, their legal counsel, or some outside firm specializing in monitoring and reporting environmental developments.

The Contact Man/Door Opener/Introducer.   When there is frequent rotation of foreigners at the head of the subsidiary so that they never have the chance to develop personal relationships with key outsiders, intermediaries are used on a permanent or occasional basis. Some of them wear another hat within the organization as in the case of the personnel manager who has an aristocratic background and is well introduced in political and economic circles.

Others sit on the board of directors on account of their political, economic, and social connections. Men of this caliber not only provide introductions, but they also help legitimize the foreign subsidiary for whose "seriousness" they vouch. The problems with such appointments are that some big names lose their usefulness once away from power or do little to stir themselves, and it is very difficult to get rid of them on account of their important symbolic roles. Changes in political regimes can also make them useless if not embarrassing.

There are, however, plenty of less well known contact men who are useful on account of their social (nobility, upper bourgeoisie), educational (elite schools), and professional (former high-level government bureaucrats) background, or because of family and personal connections.

When the subsidiary is a joint venture with a local firm of some standing, this intermediary role frequently devolves to the partner. Practically always, these "introducers" are local nationals, because they require extensive familiarity with national elites, which only a native can acquire.

The Adviser/Consultant/Trusted Confidant.   This group is typically made up of outsiders, but some of them have a more permanent relationship with the subsidiary, and have the title of assistant to the president or a position on the board of directors. This category often overlaps with the contact-man category, since the knowledge these people possess is based on the significant relations that they have with various elites. Thus a former prime minister advised a U.S. manufacturer about the timing and manner of its announcement to the host government of a major acquisition to which the latter was bound to object.

Local bankers and well-known lawyers often serve in this advisory capacity on the board of directors, or simply as consultants, because of their knowledge and contacts. Here again, local nationals predominate, although a variety of nationalities are used when it comes to dealing with supranational authorities such as the European Community (but even here, the tendency is to use an Italian to advise about approaching Italian Eurocrats).

The Negotiator.   This kind of PA person is rare because the crucial role of the line executive in high-level bargaining and because lower-level managers and staffers conduct most of it at their respective levels. The chief executive and other managers may have been appointed precisely because of the excellence of their negotiating skills if the subsidiary is involved in some critical dealings with government. However, outsiders, such as lawyers, are used here when the foreign investor must remain anonymous at an early exploratory stage and when negotiating skills are missing within the firm.

The Communications Specialist.   This category is clearly linked to public relations and its emphasis on mass communication. Typically, such persons write speeches, testimonies, and presentations to officials, commissions, and legislators, and prepare various brochures about the company. Thus a couple of U.S. electronics firms in the United Kingdom have special newsletters designed to acquaint parliamentarians with the development of the computer industry so that they will be better informed when dealing with protectionist U.K. policy in this regard.

The Program Man.   He frequently overlaps with the public-relations expert, but his expertise lies more in running special programs—for example, charitable contributions, aids to universities, community-action endeavors, and projects (e.g., plant openings).

Concluding Remark.   These six roles overlap to some extent, although the same person is rarely effective in more than a couple of them. Besides, roles can be combined with other assignments within the organization, as when the personnel manager has excellent social connections and can serve as a door opener for others. Furthermore, the higher regional and world levels can assist or replace lower-level ones.

In all cases, the line managers cannot abdicate their responsibilities to the PA staff or part-time participants because the latter two types are only specialists in detecting and appraising external conditions, in suggesting certain responses, and in carrying some of them out. They are "early-warning and bag men," but it is management's responsibility to determine the need for some response, to give the go-ahead signal, and to carry out key negotiations.

OUTSIDERS.   Not even the largest firm can handle all of its public affairs by itself, and this is particularly true in international matters. *First,* many foreign laws and regulations as well as customs simply require that such outsiders as lawyers and notaries be used to incorporate, organize, and run a subsidiary, to apply and report to government agencies, to negotiate taxes, and so on. *Second,* the sheer number of regulatory and policy developments in a large number of countries and the great variety of PA roles usually preclude a company (even a large one) from having the full capacity to follow up and influence these developments at all geographic levels (local, national, regional, world). This forces them to rely on external and shared resources. *Third,* some expert assistance may be only sporadically needed and not warrant the full employment of a qualified person. *Fourth,* some PA expertise is scarce (e.g., about crucial public policies or the likely reaction of a host government to a major investment); and the few experts available have to be shared by several firms, which employ them as consultants, agents, or board members. *Fifth,* it is usually indicated to validate and/or double-check internally generated information through outsiders—either to improve the accuracy of the company's decisions or to appraise the effectiveness of lower hierarchical levels in performing various aspects of the PA function. *Sixth,* some government relations require anonymity, as when a multinational wants to test the host country's reaction to some of its initiatives but without being identified as the inquirer so that intermediaries are indispensable. *Seventh,* some intermediaries are able to obtain more-accurate and faster information than a single company can because of special relationships (some consultants and lawyers are very well introduced) or because they can legitimately insist on receiving it (for example, the U.S. embassy can easily inquire about the discriminatory treatment of U.S. subsidiaries in violation of a bilateral treaty of establishment).

Exhibit 6 outlines the major forms of outside PA assistance used and received by multinationals.

COLLECTIVE ACTION.   Working with and through American chambers of commerce, business and trade associations, as well as partners offers the classical advantages of economies of scale and a bigger and more effective voice.

However, collective action is costly in money and executive resources, since many benefits can be obtained only through active participation in associations—possibly in a large number of them. Besides, some associations abroad remain indifferent or hostile to foreign firms considered upstarts, lacking industrial statemanship, and dangerous rivals for leadership. The antitrust problems connected with collective action are real even though often exaggerated.

Still, the principles guiding the choice between single and collective action are fairly clear. As the experienced managing director of a diversified firm put it: "We approach government alone when it is the only way to do it—for example, to apply for some permission, when we have been singled out by some bureaucratic action, when we need an exemption from some general rule, and when one of our subsidiaries is clearly the leader in its industry—when we are the industry in fact! On the other hand, working through a trade association makes a lot of sense when it makes you more credible that way, when it gives you more clout, and when delicate issues have to be explored or novel situations clarified without revealing who is asking and who stands exactly for what!"

IPA ACTION

Previous sections have already dealt with the multiple interactions between multinationals and their environments, and with the various tasks required to achieve effectiveness in international affairs (information gathering, negotiation, etc.). It remains to comment on the response mode, style, and philosophy connected with such actions.

MODES OF RESPONSE.   Multinational firms differ in their responses to nonmarket environmental challenges. Some still exhibit sheer *inactivism* or avoidance (see comments about the low profile below). Most common is *reaction,* that is, adaptation or accommodation on a *post-factum* basis. A few enlightened firms are moving toward *proaction* through monitoring, anticipation, and manipulation in order to deflect or kill emerging issues before they harden and can only be reacted to (Arrington and Sawaya, 1984; Brown, 1981). *Interaction* remains largely an ideal, and would consist of a fairly simultaneous combination of environmental and organizational change designed to narrow the gap between social expectations and corporate performance. (See Post, 1978 and Sethi, 1975 and 1982.)

More concretely, the major operational problem in public affairs remains that of making the *entire organization responsive and committed to its nonmarket environment.* This would roughly correspond to Phase 4 in Exhibit 7.

PROFILING THE MULTINATIONAL CORPORATION.   Different MNCs obtain or choose various profiles or images about (1) their contributions to home and host countries and (2) the clout they carry with government and other target groups.

A particular profile may be inevitable because the firm is too small to be noticed or too important to be ignored by government. Clearly, IBM has a *high profile* in most foreign countries because of its size, dominance of the industry, technological significance, multinational character, U.S. ownership and control, and connection with such hot issues as privacy and transborder data flows.

On the other hand, some MNCs try to achieve a *low profile* because it apparently presents fewer risks, requires less justification, and is usually advised by those

EXHIBIT 5   TYPES OF OUTSIDE ASSISTANCE

	Influential Elites	International Law Offices and Local Lawyers	International and Local Financial Institutions	International and Local Public-Relations Firms
General information, interpretation and advice about the country		X	X	X
Specific information and advice about an investment	X	X	X	X
Introductions to government people	X	X	X	X
Presentation of company and industry views and demands to government	X	X		
Negotiation	X	X	X	
Compliance with local laws and regulations		X	X	
Mass communication				X
Public-affairs programs (plant openings, philanthropy, etc.)				X

[a]Denotes a particularly significant role on the part of that type of outsider.

intermediaries whose forte consists precisely in quiet face-to-face negotiations (e.g., lawyers). Besides, many executives fear public exposure and the wear and tear of the hostile confrontations that are more readily encountered in high-profile situations.

Ultimately, the *right profile* must be chosen in terms of its effectiveness in helping achieve PA goals. This may require a mixture of high and low profiles. For that matter, a firm is—by definition—always visible to its PA targets, so that a low profile really means: "By whom do we *not* want to be seen as doing certain things?" This perspective raises interesting questions about the preference for such invisibility, since it suggests illegal or unethical practices (Boddewyn and Marton, 1978).

Exhibit 8 outlines the major situations and strategies connected with the various stages in the international firm's investment life cycle. Thus where the profile is typically high at entry, a low profile may be needed if the country is going through an antiforeign phase. Besides, the height of the profile varies with the target involved— for example, high with government, but low with the general public; the respective roles of the national and higher levels depend on who has more credibility *and* bargaining strength.

PHILOSOPHY.   The effective performance of international public affairs requires certain attitudes (whether or not translated into official company policy) to inform and dynamize this function.

SOUGHT AND OF TYPES OF HELP AVAILABLE[a]

International and Local Media	Home-Country Embassy	American (and Similar) Chambers of Commerce	International and National Business and Industry Associations	Host-Government Bureaus and Departments	Local Partners (Joint Ventures)
X	X	X	X	X	X
				X	X
	X		X	X	X
	X		X		X
			X		X
			X		
		X	X		

Public Affairs Is Important and Inevitable. Unfortunately, too many executives are still ill at ease handling the increasing involvement with government and other constituencies required in today's economic world—either for lack of experience or on account of prejudices and misinformation. Others fear the cost (in terms of time and money) and the obligations entailed by closer involvement with target groups, since such relationships normally involve quid pro quos.

Journalistic exposés of firms like ITT as well as business associations, lobbyists, and "superlawyers" make it appear that large firms are very proficient at government relations and are routinely "walking the corridors of power" and manipulating public opinion. Reality, however, presents a much less flattering or threatening portrait. The first order of business for many multinationals remains one of greater awareness about the importance and magnitude of this function.

Public Affairs Is a Proper and Legitimate Function. What must be extirpated is the false notion that government relations is "not nice," irrational, and unbusiness like, or that it can be "tolerated" only when the company needs to be protected or rescued by government or must defend itself against some unconscionable action on the part of the authorities. This view is akin to considering the government a "partner of last resort" and viewing government affairs as a "necessary evil" type of practice best left to some remote Washington representative—some mysterious special assistant to the President, or some hidden "department of dirty tricks"—a deplorable way of tainting this function from the start.

EXHIBIT 7   THE FOUR PHASES OF PUBLIC-AFFAIRS INVOLVEMENT

	Phase 1 Emerging and Diffuse Concern	Phase 2 Early Leadership	Phase 3 Public-Affairs Institutionalization	Phase 4 Public-Affairs Commitment
Policy issue	Are there significant PA problems?	Should the firm concern itself with them?	What responses are appropriate	How is the response to be managed and disseminated throughout the organization?
Requirements	Individual interest	Individual commitment Information	Corporate policy Information and analysis	Corporate policy Information and analysis Organizational concern and commitment
Organizational involvement, structure, and staffing	Minimal, diffuse, sporadic	Chief executive or some other executive Heavy reliance on part-timers and outsiders	Chief executive PA specialists Part-timers and outsiders	Chief executive PA specialists Operating managers Part-timers and outsiders Collective action
Reporting system	None	Reporting conspicuous incidents	Fuller reporting but without action implications	Systematic and action-oriented reporting
Performance evaluation and reward system	None	None	Criticism for specific and blatant errors	Appraisal and approval based on a systematic review against plans

Source.   Adapted from Ackerman (1974).

EXHIBIT 8   THE INVESTMENT LIFE CYCLE AND APPROPRIATE PROFILES

Stage	Bargaining Strength	Publicity (Profile)	Role of Geographic Levels
Entry	Higher	High (about terms)	World, regional
Expansion		High (about terms)	National, regional
Implementation		High	National, regional, world
Ongoing operations		Low or medium	National
Acquisitions		High (about terms)	National, regional
Stagnation, decline		Low	National
Disinvestment		Low (preferably)	World, regional, national
Expropriation, renegotiation		High (about terms)	World, regional, national
Reentry after withdrawal	Lower	Medium (about terms)	World, regional

Actually, the notion of "corporate citizenship" that is so highly recommended nowadays includes by definition both the *duty* to serve society (the part usually stressed) and the *right* to be heard (and preferably heeded). This right of petition is guaranteed by the First Amendment to the U.S. Constitution, whereas in Europe, many planning and concertation schemes make such relations with government a matter of routine if not of obligation (e.g., in the context of the mandatory "consultative bodies" of countries like Belgium). Hence it is perfectly proper for multinational firms to contact and try to influence governments at home and abroad.

Obviously there are socially acceptable and unacceptable ways of monitoring and influencing governments and other elites, but occasional improprieties do not invalidate the legitimacy of this function any more than shady advertising claims or "yellow" labor contracts obliterate the fundamental need for marketing and industrial relations or the societal contributions that these functions make. Of course public affairs is more likely to be accepted as legitimate if it is seen as being related to the broad concerns of society, which governments everywhere make explicit and attempt to satisfy, rather than being only concerned with manipulating the state and society for purely selfish personal and corporate interests.

Public Affairs Is an Earning Function.   Politics has a negative connotation for many business executives, as is evident in the contrasting of "political *risks*" with "market *opportunities*" in studies of foreign countries. Because of this negative view of politics, there is a tendency to view government relations in a defensive manner and as a protective device against the machinations of political demagogues and power-hungry bureaucrats. The latter certainly exist, and guarding one's firm against unfavorable developments is certainly a critical component of the public-affairs function, even if it costs time and money to engage in such purely defensive moves.

Beyond this elementary observation lies the more profitable realization that modern governments control all sorts of scarce and valuable goods in their capacities as creditors through state financial institutions, as regulators, suppliers and/or partners through state enterprises, customers through their purchases, grantors of partial or complete monopolies through their selective distributions of permissions to invest, subsidizers of research and training programs, providers of public utilities and "law and order," and so on. There are real political *opportunities* here—not just risks.

Public affairs is much more than a "spending" function on the order of a night watchman who protects a firm's real sources of profits. It has, instead, real *earning* potential; it deserves as much executive attention as the other two pillars of profitability, namely, efficient management within the company and business effectiveness in the marketplace.

This emphasis on earnings, of course, should not obscure the fact that the effectiveness of public affairs can seldom be immediately measured in terms of its impact on sales, profits, or return on investment, since so many things contribute to corporate performance, and on account of the special difficulties connected with measuring results in this area. Government relations is no panacea and by itself is usually insufficient to insure a firm's prosperity or survival even though the Lockheed and Chrysler cases illustrate the life-saving contribution of this function.

Still, many PA initiatives have delayed and/or indirect effects. In the United States, for example, pressures from business against excessive environmental-protection requirements were not as effective as the energy crisis in getting them reviewed, but they certainly prepared the groundwork for such a review.

Public Affairs Must Be Managed.   The test of good management is explicit goals, clear assignments of responsibility, good forecasting, timely action, and relevant reporting. Moreover, effective management of the PA function requires that the chief executive be actively involved in its planning, conduct, and supervision because representing the firm to the outside world is an intrinsic and fundamental part of top management's job, which cannot be delegated downward even a variety of subordinates can assist. On the other hand, top management should not be overexposed nor its "shock value" spent over minor matters.

A key principle in this respect is that informed commitment is more important than any particular organizational structure or technique. Moreover, simply imitating some competitor's move, coping with problems on an ad hoc and crisis basis, or succumbing to the entreaties of a consultant are poor ways of getting started in or conducting public affairs. PA should rest instead on an understanding of the function's importance and an appraisal of risks and opportunities in this area. This awareness and commitment must then pervade the entire organization instead of being relegated to some specialized niche and personnel.

Public Affairs Works Best as a Two-Way Process.   The relation between business firms and governments in the mixed economies of today is increasingly one of symbiosis: They have to rely on each other in order to achieve their respective objectives. The correct perspective is thus not one of a "zero-sum game," where public power grows only at the expense of private enterprise, but rather a frequent "positive-sum game," where both benefit from the relationship. On the other hand, a very uneven relationship, where one party can dictate to the other, is seldom fruitful in the longer run because it leads to ill feelings, recriminations, renegotiations, nationalizations, suits (for example, the problems of Union Carbide in India and the United States, following the tragic chemical accident in Bhopal), stagnation of investment, and/or divestment.

Instead, the best gains are those that leave the other party satisfied too—now and for the foreseeable future. Hence it is essential for firms to consider the problems and goals of governments and to couch their own approaches in terms of what they will contribute to the satisfaction and achievement of public objectives. As one executive put it: "We must talk of 'participating in economic development' rather than of 'coping with the environment'; and we must talk of 'sharing in change' rather than of 'dealing with change.'" Conversely, opposition to government policies must stress how they may be self-defeating or inferior in terms of what a country needs and wants.

Many firms find it hard to adopt such a posture because of the nearly irresistible attractiveness of high profits and of getting something for nothing (or cheaply), and because companies prefer to compensate for high overseas risks through quick and handsome returns. Still, getting all one can get with no thought for the morrow and the other party is inviting trouble overseas just like at home. We can expect an increased emphasis on the criteria of fairness and equity in the division of burdens and benefits among countries and companies; firms should, therefore, try to understand this increasingly important requirement for mutually beneficial solutions.

Public Affairs Is an Inside Job, Too.   Few companies effectively apply the principle that "external affairs begins at home." There may be various employee newsletters and other publications dealing with the firm's foreign affiliates, international involvement, and contributions to host economies and societies. However, they suffer from the well-known shortcomings of such endeavors—particularly their low credibility.

For that matter, many firms do not even make the effort to report on pending legislation detrimental to the company, public-opinion attitudes unfavorable to foreign direct investment, or the firm's contributions to its home and host countries. This is in contrast to national and international unions and consumerist organizations, which are increasingly propagandizing their members, the public, and international organizations about the dangers and problems associated with multinational companies. In Europe, the growing importance of works councils and of other forms of worker representation and participation is, of course, forcing firms to reveal much more about their operations to labor representatives. However, much of this communication is still marked by distrust and undercandidness.

Still, a few companies are improving their efforts in this area, being particularly careful to tailor their communications to the various audiences they address, since a worker's interests are different from those of a stockholder and even of a union leader. British Oxygen, for example, publishes a monthly tabloid widely distributed at the workplace. It has gained considerable credibility among its readers by refusing to gild the lily and reporting company shortcomings. A second quarterly magazine is written for middle and top management, with think pieces on various environmental and internal (e.g., reorganization) topics.

Obviously, multinational firms will have to do much more and much better in this area. As one executive put it: "Having 10,000 employees say good things about the company amounts to both a low profile and a lot of speaking out, and is well worth the effort!"

IPA REPORTING AND CONTROLLING

Performance must be measured in public affairs as in any other business function, but there are special problems connected with the transfer of information and the reporting of activities in this area.

CHANNELS. National PA staffs formally report to the line management of the subsidiary rather than to the corresponding PA staff at the regional and/or world levels. This adds time and a filter to the reporting of information and action; in many firms, this official/formal channel is supplemented by frequent communications (mail, telephone, telex), visits from line executives and PA staffers, regional and worldwide meetings (for example, ITT-Europe meetings in Brussels and the regular convening of public-affairs managers from all over the world by Pfizer), and by board-of-directors meetings in Europe and other operating areas (Caterpillar, IBM, Dow).

Locational factors also affect the allocation of PA reporting responsibility, as when the Belgian subsidiary is charged with following up EEC developments, since the EEC Commission is located in that country. Places like London and New York are very important listening posts regarding financial controls everywhere, because major international banks are located there and keep abreast of relevant regulations and financial conditions all over the world.

INTERACTION AMONG LEVELS. The general principle that decision should be made where the facts are available and understood militates against much reporting to higher levels when the latter do not possess such information. However, international companies qualify this principle in a number of ways.

First, *higher levels have to be kept informed of locally made decisions, even if they did not participate in them* in order to (1) appraise the effectiveness of public affairs at lower levels ("We are particularly interested in finding out what subsidiaries were surprised by political and regulatory changes that might have been anticipated"), (2) evaluate the adequacy of the budgets requested and obtained for that function, and (3) form an impression about trends in policies and regulations in the regions or in the world at large—something for which national subsidiaries usually lack perspective.

Second, *reporting systems vary according to the types of external events covered and the types of required company responses*. Some governmental policies are beyond the control of higher levels and are only *ultimately* reported to them for information's sake and/or to justify certain actions and performances of the affiliates (e.g., to explain why the subsidiary could not avoid a price freeze in a foreign country). Promptness in reporting such a new regulation is not crucial, because the appropriate response can usually be decided by the local management.

Other local policy developments, however, have more serious implications for the rest of the international company, and therefore require *immediate reporting*. An example would be stricter controls on capital movements in and out of a foreign country. When the financial function is centralized, the regional and world levels want to know of such a regulation or of its imminence right away, because they have to shift funds around, alter financial plans, and make other decisions. It is also a kind of development in which international treaties and special agreements between the parent company and the host government may be relevant and therefore invite representation by the firm or the U.S. government if some violation or discrimination is involved.

Some regulatory or public-opinion developments may be of purely local import, whereas others may interest *other affiliates*. Thus the EEC directive allowing manufactured goods from underdeveloped nations to enter member countries duty free (up to a certain volume) made it possible for the Brazilian subsidiary of a U.S. international company to export more parts to EEC countries at a lower cost.

This example involves a tactical response, but the parent company may also need to know of regulatory developments for *strategic* purposes. For example, the banning of phosphates in detergents is a type of policy change quickly reported because it may require dropping an entire line of products and stepping up research efforts to come up with substitutes. It is also a regulation likely to be adopted by other countries, since concern with protecting the environment is widespread. Consequently, a firm may want to stop using such an ingredient in other countries even before it is obliged to do so.

The distinction made above is between (1) what is urgent and must be immediately reported, (2) what must be ultimately known, and (3) what is of marginal or no interest to higher levels and should be left out of intelligence channels that may already be overburdened. This sorting out process is not always obvious but must be inculcated and implemented through company directives, conferences, reviews, and other means.

Strangely enough, it appears that good news often does not travel as readily as bad news, because overseas subsidiaries are not eager to be asked to do more or to change procedures because some regulation has been removed or modified. Bad news, on the other hand, provides a handy excuse for not meeting some assigned goals. In addition, perceiving new opportunities requires thinking changes through, but few subsidiaries have been staffed with that kind of managerial and staff talent.

Still, *crisis developments* tend to move very quickly up the organizational hierarchy. This is a reflection of the fundamental principle that higher levels concern themselves with "exceptional" problems—especially when the amounts involved and the possible implications for other parts of the international company are significant and assume policy dimensions. Furthermore, difficult transactions with foreign governments bring about escalation to higher levels in order to impress foreign governments with the fact that the international company has alternatives in other countries and must reconcile its national obligations and opportunities with foreign and international ones. Finally, higher levels are usually brought in to remove the pressure from the national manager—especially if the affiliate is small and its manager a native of the country, because local managers are much more vulnerable to governmental pressures (including physical ones), whereas foreigners at least are somewhat protected by their embassies and bilateral treaties of establishment.

Third, *the assessment of intelligence varies according to the prevalent authority structure*. Multinationals with loosely connected foreign affiliates are much more likely to let them process their own intelligence, decide accordingly, and simply keep the parent company informed, than centralized firms bent on controlling their subsidiaries rather tightly.

Fourth, *the respective competences of field and headquarters affect the reporting system*. National subsidiaries, through their closer association with operations, are more attuned to local developments and better aware of obstacles and unpredictable developments. However, they are also susceptible to that complacency of those who feel that they are doing the right thing simply because they are the local experts. Headquarters, on the other hand, is often better at detecting the uncommon, which may be more clearly perceived from a distance, but it may be deficient at understanding the proper importance of such exceptional developments. Therefore, there are normal disagreements between national and regional subsidiaries and the corporate headquarters about the meaning and magnitude of overseas environmental developments. For example, Italy is always a difficult country to evaluate from a distance because it seems so unstable and messed up, although, on the spot, the same events may look "normal" and manageable. Such a divergence obviously requires a lot of mutual "education" so that reports and plans may be more intelligible and acceptable to all levels concerned.

FORMAT, TIMING, AND CONTINGENCY PLANNING. National-level reports about government and public affairs have to be condensed and integrated with other subjects in the short summaries prepared for higher levels. What may have started as a 20-page analysis written by the PA director in Germany ends up a 1–2 page component in the more general report of the German general manager to the European headquarters, which itself condenses Germany to a paragraph or two in the European report going to New York, where the worldwide analysis finally reduces it to a couple of lines! *It is then extremely difficult for anyone at that level to interpret and act meaningfully on such scanty information.*

Besides, the *timing* of intelligence is frequently faulty. Most overseas subsidiaries do not catch problems at the incipient stage. Later on, they remain optimistic that things will work out, because they have in the past. Therefore, they usually fail to communicate detailed information and forecasts about such developments. When events finally become unmanageable, they provide handy excuses for no longer performing satisfactorily. However, the matter of urgency should not be overstated, because in fact major policy developments are few and slow in coming, and there is usually time to obtain the necessary information.

Poor timing is compounded by the fact that *there is little contingency planning embodied in most PA reports.* That is, affiliates very seldom report developments in a form outlining what is likely to happen (with various probabilities) and what alternative courses of action are open regarding each possible outcome. Instead, their reports typically present some overall appraisal of the state of the environment and aim at reassuring the parent company that the situation is being carefully followed up. Still, a small but increasing number of international companies are insisting that their foreign affiliates develop flexible responses and build a system for government relations so that channels may be available and in working order when crises develop.

LOCUS OF CONTROL. Public-affairs action gets harder to appraise as one moves away from the locus of their performance. Still, the increasing number of executives and staffers at the regional and world levels who have served in foreign countries is helping to improve the review process, since they can ask better questions and even double-check with former business and government contacts in those countries. A few companies also ask international public-relations firms and consultants to audit the subsidiaries' resources and performance in this area.

In general, higher-level PA staffs monitor the performance of lower-level ones in the process of advising their own superiors about the supervision of the regional and national subsidiaries. A few large companies with complex organizational structures have appointed a member of the corporate committee or of the board of directors to act as the contact man for international public affairs.

CRITERIA OF EFFECTIVENESS. "The collection, interpretation, and diffusion of information as well as those relations with the authorities and public opinion conducted for the corporate purposes of acquiring legitimacy, of influencing the contents of public policy, and of obtaining and retaining favorable treatment." This definition of public affairs makes it obvious that most of it is of an intangible nature and difficult to measure for control purposes.

Control is undoubtedly easier when careful PA planning has resulted in specific goals matched with specific budgetary allocations. More companies now specify in their PA plans such concrete tasks as getting to know certain politicians and officials, improving by five percentage points the proportion of people who think favorably of the company, getting the subsidiary's general manager elected an officer of a key trade association, and so on. These are valuable and even necessary targets, but there is a danger that their use may degenerate into pointless nose counting of favorable press clippings, bureaucrats visited, industry citations received, and so forth.

More important still, such measurements (preferably of the before-and-after kind) are only loosely and vaguely linked to the achievement of overall corporate objectives of the "hard" kind: return on investment, share of the market, rate of growth, and so on. It is well to stress such hard goals at this point, because many executives still believe that they are the only ones worth considering. Even those firms that take "social responsibilities" into explicit consideration have the disconcerting habit of becoming hard-nosed about "soft" goals and the corresponding budgetary allocations when profits decline or growth slows down. Hence a solid rationale for public affairs as well as concrete goals (and their commensurate achievement) are most important. This is certainly the way the more reflective PA officers feel, because they have seen axes fall in their areas and in other such soft areas as training and research after the recessions of the early 1980s and the movement toward deregulation in quite a few countries.

In any case, *some result-measurement problems cannot be eliminated.* The fundamental reason for this situation is that a good part of public affairs is of a defensive or "reserve power" nature, designed to prevent undesirable outcomes (e.g., unfavorable legislation and poor image). The public-affairs function here resembles that of the armed forces in a peace-loving nation, that is, to *prevent* attacks and other destructive actions. However, if the country is never attacked on account of this effective military posture, outsiders have a tendency to ask: "Why do we need an army? They never do anything!" In the same vein, a government-relations officer remarked: "It takes a lot of effort to build good connections in government, but you may never need to use them, and you may never have to pick up that phone for something very important. You need it 'just in case,' but that 'case' may never materialize. However, other people only see those fancy luncheons you had with government people, and they think you wasted a lot of good money and company time in the process!"

Besides, *it is hard to isolate the credit owed PA efforts for some favorable outcome* because other companies, trade associations, foreign embassies, and so forth may have worked at it too. Consequently, reviews and evaluations must also encompass processes and causes:

1. Were the goals well set in the first place?
2. How were they achieved, and how effective was each of the means used?
3. Why were they effective or not?

As one astute observer put it: "Was this a battle we really could have won if our people had been wise enough to talk to the press at the right moment? Or were we really beaten before we started, and did the public-affairs people do the best they could? Did they give away too much in the compromise, or did they do a pretty hard nosed job of negotiating? Did their predictions as to who would do what hold up pretty well, or did they misanalyze the picture from the start? Were there some relationships they should have built earlier?" (Fenn, 1979).

Similarly, the quality of the reports must be appraised in terms of the following questions:

1. How timely were they?
2. How understandable were they in terms of why certain things happened or not?
3. Were they action-oriented in clearly identifying revised goals and contingency actions?

REWARD AND PENALTIES.   Individual performance review must be geared to better results next time. This will depend, to a considerable extent, on whether people were properly rewarded and/or punished for what they did in managing the public affairs under their control.

International public affairs is an endless task, never completed and never performed perfectly, so expectations should not be higher than in the case of other functions. After all, 9 out of 10 new products fail in the marketplace, and all financial schemes are not profitable. Still, the stakes are high and deserve the best management that the state of the art allows.

SOCIOECONOMIC REPORTING.   The emphasis on this section has been reporting for *managerial* purposes. Multinationals, however, are being increasingly asked to report to such *external constituencies* as governments, international organizations, national and international pressure groups, and public-interest monitors about their contributions to a variety of physical (e.g., environmental protection, safety), economic (e.g., development), social (e.g., training and education), political (e.g., emancipation of minority or downtrodden groups), and cultural (e.g., respect of local traditions and support of local arts) goals.

These demands take various forms, ranging from the mandatory *bilan social* (social balance sheet) in France to requests for information from concerned groups (e.g., about MNC action vis-à-vis the apartheid situation in South Africa). The reports themselves vary in size, scope, and sophistication from brief references in annual reports to jobs created and exports generated, to such lengthy analyses as the Nestlé reports on their compliance with infant-formula marketing regulations.

This is a complex topic in itself, which cannot be investigated here. For a recent discussion of the disclosure issue and of various concrete responses to it by multinationals, see the handbook written by the Public Affairs Council and the InterMatrix Group (1980).

PROGRESS REPORT.   IPA is still a fairly young function, and only 15 percent of the participants in a Conference Board study (Lusterman, 1985) expected any marked improvement toward better-managed IPA programs between 1985 and 1990. The future, therefore, is a mixed bag. On the one hand, there has been a decline in the IPA efforts of a few companies—particularly in the oil industry—due to decreasing pressure from various stakeholders. Conversely, the IPA function is much more needed now that multinational companies have been recognized as significant actors on the world economic scene as the nonmarket environment is more volatile than ever, requiring well-managed proactive IPA departments and staffs.

There is a trend toward selecting more public-issue oriented people at top management. At Bank of America, a major criterion for promotion is a manager's sensitivity to the firm's environments; at General Electric, lack of sensitivity tends to block promotions.

The need for greater awareness of the importance of the IPA function has already been mentioned. Other key weaknesses include: (1) a lack of truly international perspective or global thinking by top managers; (2) a shortage of adequate staffing, which means that too much time is spent fighting fires rather than preventing them; (3) frustration with the performance of line managers and their failure to develop appropriate plans after the company provides a system to identify and prioritize issues, and (4) insufficient integration of decentralized efforts. While public affairs are handled locally, there is still need for communication and coordination at the corporate level which must motivate subsidiary managers and provide policy guidance. Local managers must believe that they are better off working with the parent company, and that it is in their interest to keep the IPA regional and corporate staffs informed.

CONCLUSION

The multinationals have been challenged, and the contest can no longer be avoided. The task of international public affairs consists precisely of presenting a true picture of these firms' contributions and fitting them into the economic, political, and social mechanisms of the societies in which they operate. This is why the IPA function is needed so much now that multinationals have definitely been recognized as significant actors on the world economic scene and have been seriously challenged by some governments and other segments in their home and host societies.

However, there are also profit opportunities in being perceived as legitimate and powerful partners in the development of home and host countries. This positive perspective should dominate the further growth, elaboration, and perfecting of this relatively new function.

SOURCES AND SUGGESTED REFERENCES

Ackerman, R.W. "Putting Social Concern into Practice," *European Business,* Vol. VIII (1974), pp. 33–44.

Ackerman, R.W. *The Social Challenge To Business,* Cambridge, MA: Harvard University Press, 1975.

Arrington, C. and R. Sawaya. "Managing Public Affairs: Issues Management in An Uncertain Environment," *California Management Review,* Vol. IV (Summer 1984), pp. 148–60.

Behrman, J.N., J.J. Boddewyn, and A. Kapoor. *International Business-Government Communications: U.S. Structures, Actors and Issues.* Lexington, MA: D.C. Heath, 1975.

Blake, D.H. and V. Toros. "The Global Image Makers," *Public Relations Journal,* Vol. V (June 1976), pp. 10–12.

Blake, D.H. *International Public Affairs: Programs for the 1980s.* Washington, D.C.: Foundation for Public Affairs/Public Affairs Council, 1978.

Blake, D.H. *Managing the External Relations of Multinational Corporations.* New York: Fund for Multinational Management Education, 1977.

Boddewyn, J.J. and K. Marton. "Corporate Profiles: Low, High and Right," *IPRA (International Public Relations Association) Review,* Vol. VII (September 1978), pp. 9–12.

Boddewyn, J.J. "The External Affairs of Transnational Firms: A Research Note," *Management International Review,* Vol. XIX (1976/3) pp. 47–57.

Boddewyn, J.J. "Western European Policies Toward U.S. Investors," *The Bulletin,* No. 93–95. New York University, Graduate School of Business Administration, Institute of Finance (1974), pp. 1–95.

Brown, J.K. *Guidelines for Managing Corporate Issues Programs.* New York: Conference Board, 1981.

Business International. *Corporate External Affairs.* New York and Geneva: B.I. 1975. (J.J. Boddewyn, main reporter.)

Carson, J.J. and G.A. Steiner. *Measuring Business Social Performance: The Corporate Social Audit.* New York: Committee for Economic Development, 1974.

Channon, D.F. and M. Jalland. *Multinational Strategic Planning.* New York: American Management Association, 1978.

Dunn, S.W., M.F. Cahill, and J.J. Boddewyn. *How Fifteen Transnational Corporations Manage Public Affairs.* Chicago: Crain Books, 1979.

Fahey, L., W.R. King, and V.K. Narayann. "Environmental Scanning and Forecasting in Strategic Planning—The State of the Art," *Long Range Planning,* Vol. XIV (February 1981), pp. 32–39.

Fayerweather, J. (ed.). *International Business-Government Affairs: Toward an Era of Accommodation.* Cambridge. MA: Ballinger, 1973.

Fenn, D.H. "Finding Where the Power Lies in Government," *Harvard Business Review,* Vol. XXII (September-October 1979), pp. 144–53.

Gladwin, T.N. and I. Walter. *Multinationals Under Fire: Lessons in the Management of Conflict.* New York: John Wiley & Sons, 1980.

Haendel, D. *Foreign Investments and the Management of Political Risk,* Boulder, CO: Westview Press, 1979.

Hargreaves, J. and J. Dauman. *Business Survival and Social Change.* New York: John Wiley & Sons, 1975.

International Business-Government Counsellors. *Multinational Government Relations.* Washington, D.C.: IBGC 1977. (J.J. Boddewyn, main reporter.)

Jackson, R.A. (ed.). *The Multinational Corporation and Social Policy; With Special Reference to General Motors in South Africa.* New York: Praeger, 1974.

Josephs, R. "A Global Approach to Public Relations," *Columbia Journal of World Business,* Vol. VII (Fall 1973), pp. 93–98.

Kobrin, S.J. "Political Risk: A Review and Reconsideration," *Journal of International Business Studies,* Vol. X (Spring-Summer 1979), pp. 67–80.

Kobrin, S.J. et al. "The Assessment and Evaluation of Noneconomic Environments by American Firms: A Preliminary Report," *Journal of International Business Studies,* Vol. XI (Spring-Summer 1980), pp. 32–47.

Kraar, L. "The Multinationals Get Smarter About Political Risks," *Fortune,* Vol. XXIV (24 March 1980), pp. 86–93.

LaPalombara, J. and S. Blank. *Multinational Corporations and National Elites: A Study in Tensions.* New York: Conference Board, 1976.

———. *Multinational Corporations in Comparative Perspective.* New York: Conference Board, 1977.

Lusterman, S. *Managing International Public Affairs.* New York: Conference Board, 1985.

MacMillan, K. "Managing Public Affairs in British Industry," *Journal of General Management,* Vol. IX (Winter 1983–84), pp. 74–90.

McGrath, Ph. S. *Managing Corporate External Relations.* New York: Conference Board, 1976.

Molitor, G.T.T. "The Hatching of Public Opinion," *Planning Review,* Vol. V (July 1977), pp. 3–7.

Negandhi, A.R. and B.R. Baliga. *Quest for Survival and Growth: A Comparative Study of American, European and Japanese Multinationals.* New York: Praeger, 1979.

Post, J.E. *Corporate Behavior and Social Change.* Reston, VA: Reston Publishing, 1978.

Public Affairs Council. *Guidelines on Integrating International Public Affairs Perspectives* newsletter, April 1984.

Public Affairs Council. *Managing International Public Affairs Perspectives,* newsletter, 1979, p. 2.

Public Affairs Council Handbook. Washington, D.C.: Public Affairs Council, 1983.

Public Affairs Council and the InterMatrix Group. *Handbook on Socioeconomic Activity and Performance Reporting on Overseas Operations.* Washington, D.C.: Public Affairs Council, 1980.

Sethi, S.P. "Dimensions of Corporate Social Performance: An Analytical Framework." *California Management Review,* Vol. XVII (Spring 1975), pp. 58–64.

Sethi, S.P. "Corporate Political Activism," *California Management Review,* Vol. XXIV (Spring 1982), pp. 32–42.

Terry, P.T. "Mechanisms for Environmental Scanning," *Long Range Planning,* June 1977, pp. 2–9.

Traverse-Healy, T. "Public Affairs Activity by Multinationals in Europe," *IPRA (International Public Relations Association) Review,* Vol. IV (September 1977), pp. 28–35.

U.S. Department of Commerce. *Corporate Social Reporting in the United States and Western Europe,* Report of the Task Force on Corporate Social Performance. Washington D.C.: U.S. Government Printing Office, 1979.

Wells, L.T. "Social Cost/Benefit Analysis," *Harvard Business Review,* Vol. XXII (March-April 1974), pp. 40–56.

ORGANIZATION DESIGN

CONTENTS

ORGANIZATION DESIGN

Stanley M. Davis

Methods of organizing and managing multinational industrial corporations have matured considerably in the last 15 years, and the basic rules are now rather well understood. Changes in the external environment, however, together with new complexities that arise from corporate responses to these changes, continually reduce the effectiveness of these basic structures and practices. The result is that new methods and forms are evolving in response to the new exigencies. My purpose in this chapter is to chart and explain these recent trends in the evolving patterns of global organization among U.S.-based corporations.

We will examine the problems arising from the well-recognized patterns, and the refinements that are being made to cope with them. Basic design involves three different ways of organizing units: by *functions,* by *product,* and by *geography.* Neat distinctions between the three, however, have been found inadequate because they only optimize along one of these dimensions. Here are some of the trends:

Worldwide functional structures show definite instabilities.

Corporations organized by country are exploring how and where to place product management more adequately in their frameworks.

Firms with worldwide product groups require better coordination within countries and regions than their structures provide.

Corporate planning and development activities have led some companies to organize around markets, not geography.

Some companies experiment with global matrix management and structure.

These developments all point to a trend of learning to integrate and manage diversity in ways that were not possible with the early generations of multinational organization design. This chapter is intended as a guide to those who are seeking innovative adjustments to organizing the complexities of global corporations.

THE INTERNATIONAL DIVISION

Whereas domestic organization emphasize functional and product bases of structure, international growth introduces the area element for dividing the structure.

The transition from a domestic organization to a worldwide organization involves a number of phases in which foreign activities begin as a minor and peripheral part of the firm and end up being so central as to change the geographic basis for organization to global parameters. The strategic changes that led to the development of new organizational forms are understandable in terms of the product-life-cycle concept as it applies to international trade. According to this concept, there are four phases in the life history of any product: introduction, growth, maturity, and decline.[1]

During the early phase of the product's manufacture and sale there is a low price elasticity for aggregate demand and for the individual firm. The nature of demand is not yet well understood. Only a small number of firms are involved, and they rely heavily on R&D, skilled labor, and short production runs. All manufacture is domestic, and exports are limited to developed countries with high GNPs. This phase, historically, was characteristic of the early twentieth century, when U.S. firms found that their strategic shift to product diversification stimulated the growth of exports, and this frequently became an important source of revenue for the domestic companies. Organizationally, however, this seldom meant more than the creation of an export office.

In the growth phase, as the technology and the development of the new products come to be understood, methods of mass production are introduced, firms' price elasticity increases, and price competition begins. There are a large number of firms manufacturing the same product line and production starts in other high-GNP countries. The early investment in direct foreign manufacture generally has been in defensive response to this threat to export markets by local manufacture. The foreign subsidiaries created in the early phases of domestic firm's move abroad are generally quite independent from the managerial and administrative control of the parent. This initial period of subsidiary autonomy, however, is rather short-lived. Sixty percent of the 170 companies studied in the Harvard Multinational Enterprise Project historically grouped their subsidiaries under an international division after the acquisition of only their fourth foreign unit.[2]

There are many variations in organizational design of an international business, but the general tendency is quite clear (see Exhibit 1). Whereas the structure of the domestic company is laid out along product and/or functional lines, the international division is organized around geographic interests. The head of the international division is on a hierarchical par with the heads of the domestic product groups, and all report directly to the president. General managers of each foreign unit report to the boss of the international division, and the units themselves reflect the same functional organization as exists in the domestic product divisions. With an increase in the number of foreign manufacturing units in any one geographic area, an intermediary level of regional direction (e.g., vice-president Europe) is usually created between the subsidiaries or affiliates and the head of the international division. During the early period of its existence, the international division has little staff of its own, and what staff does exist frequently is more closely tied to its functional department at the corporate level than to the international area division.

The initial impetus for the creation of an international division is to congregate the activities whose specialized character is that they occur outside the borders of the home country. For the parent corporation, the locus of foreign expertise comes to be here, and the coordination of functions and products is still largely in the international division. Coordination between the domestic and foreign sides of the enterprise is very loose and is not paid much attention except at the top of the corporate hierarchy. From

EXHIBIT 1   ORGANIZATION STRUCTURED BY DOMESTIC PRODUCT DIVISIONS AND INTERNATIONAL (AREA) DIVISION[a]

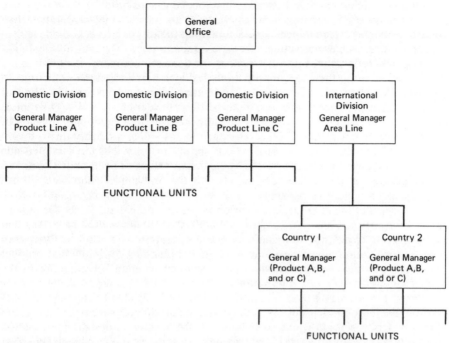

[a]Shows line positions only, not staff.

the corporate perspective, the formation of an international unit gives legitimacy to a policy of multinational expansion not formally recognized and explicitly stated before, and it provides an organizational base from which to develop. In its infancy, the division most generally turns its attention inward and develops under an umbrella of the benign neglect of the domestic company. Although the initiative for foreign expansion begins with the international division, which is strategically distinct from plans for domestic growth, the management of the foreign subsidiaries is now linked more closely with the parent. Thus the symbiotic reality becomes more apparent. For the foreign subsidiaries and affiliates, the international division provides guidance and support, but its creation also increases the control of the center over the periphery and reduces some of their previously enjoyed autonomy.

The creation of an international unit enables the firm to balance the self-interests of individual subsidiaries for the benefit of the company's total international performance. This can only be done by standardizing information and controlling some aspects of the subsidiaries' activities. Once this is done, taxes, for example, are minimized through the transfer price established for goods and services that move between sister subsidiaries in different countries. Central coordination of international activities also enables the company to make more-secure and more-economic decisions about where to purchase raw materials, where to locate new manufacturing facilities, and from where to supply world customers with products. Also, when the financial functions of the international division are coordinated, investment decisions can be made on a global basis and overseas development can turn to international capital markets, instead of just local ones, for funds.

The benefits of coordinating some activities on an international basis, rather than country by country, lead to centralized control at the division level and above. But other activities, such as marketing, often must remain local. The international division begins to reflect the same dual needs as the domestic company: to maintain the specialized inputs at their appropriate levels and locations and, at the same time, to coordinate them to maximize the total utilization of common resources. The two pressures are experienced, however, with a different order of priorities. The typical domestic side of an enterprise is specialized according to a functional division of labor; it coordinates primarily by product groupings and secondarily through centralized staff functions. Area considerations are low priority. The international side of the organization, in contrast, marks its particular expertise by its ability to differentiate geographic areas. It is then faced with the problem of coordinating both products and functions across areas.

The success of the international division provides rationalization for the organization of a company's activities abroad, but it also creates a dual structure that ultimately works against the benefit of the corporation as a whole. "Even with superb coordination at the corporate level, global planning for individual product lines is carried out at best awkwardly by two 'semi-autonomous' organizations—the domestic company and the international division. To add a series of country (or area) management makes the problem more difficult."[3] By creating an international division, the joint problems of specialization and coordination are raised to the top of the corporate hierarchy, but, as is found in the functional design, coordination also has to occur at lower levels in the organization and cannot all be bottlenecked in the president's office. Although the general tendency is to view structure as a static phenomenon, we see its dynamic in the dialectical effect that the success of an international division has on its own potential for survival. Once the international division has grown large enough to rival the largest domestic product division in size, the pressures for reorganization on an integrated worldwide basis become irresistible.[4] The next question becomes: What should be that basis? The two dominant choices involve maximizing either the product or the geographic element.

PRODUCT VERSUS GEOGRAPHY

In the global product structure, the international division is carved up, and its products are fed back into other parts of the organization, whereas domestic units become worldwide product groups. Products that require different technologies and that have dissimilar end-users are logically grouped into separate categories, and the transfer of products into various world markets is best managed within each distinctive product classification. Product diversification may be in related or unrelated lines. A strategy of global product diversification requires heavy investment in R&D, and the global product structure facilitates the transfer and control of technology and new products between domestic and foreign divisions.

To create a global structure based on geography, the domestic business is labeled the North American area and the regional pieces in the international division are elevated to similar status. In contrast to the product-structured firms, with their diversity and renewing growth phases, companies that elect an area mold tend to have a mature product line that serves common end-user markets. They generally place great reliance on lowering manufacturing costs by concentrating and specializing production through long runs in large plants, using stable technology. They also emphasize marketing techniques as the competitive basis for price and product differentiation. Industries with these characteristics that favor the area structure include food, beverage, container, automotive, farm-equipment, pharmaceuticals, and cosmetics industries.

The worldwide area structure is highly suited to mature businesses with narrow product lines because their growth potential is greater abroad than in the domestic market, where the products and brands are in later phases of their life cycles. Since they derive a high proportion of their total sales from abroad,[5] intimate knowledge of local conditions, constraints, and preferences is essential. Many of these firms rely heavily on advertising and benefit from standardizing their marketing as well as production techniques worldwide. But standardization and area differences are sometimes incompatible. In one classical gaffe, for example, advertisement for a major U.S.-based banking firm used a picture of a squirrel hoarding nuts. The idea was to convey an image of thrift, preparedness, and security. When the same advertisement appeared in Caracas, however, it brought a derisive reaction, since Venezuela has neither winters nor squirrels as we know them. Instead, the image evoked a thieving and destructive rat. The major advantage of a worldwide area structure, then, is its ability to differentiate regional and local markets and determine variations in each appropriate market mix. Its disadvantage is its inability to coordinate different product lines and their logistics of flow from source to markets across areas.

Alternative global organizations include a mixture of product and area structures, and in some cases the use of function as the defining element in the macrodesign. All designs, however, represent tradeoffs. The one that is ultimately selected appears to have the greatest advantages. But what about the advantages that are lost by not having chosen the other designs? In the following sections we will see how global corporations are attempting to answer this question and achieve the advantages of several designs simultaneously. We will look at how various industrial corporations have juggled the functional, product, and geographic dimensions in their attempts to get the best global organization design. The first step generally involves elimination of the international division.

ELIMINATING THE INTERNATIONAL DIVISION

Through time, the disjunction between a corporation's product structure in its domestic divisions and geographic structure in its overseas activities creates difficulty. Ironically, the more successful the international division, the more rapidly these difficulties occur. Strategically, the posture shifts from that of a domestic firm with international activities to that of a global corporation. Structurally, the pressures build to reflect this new unity. Although the emergent design is rather predictable in rational economic terms, the speed, clarity, and success with which it is accomplished depends mainly on history, power, and personalities in the firm. As Stopford has pointed out,[6] the major players are bound to have different structural priorities as follows:

Domestic Priorities	International Priorities
Products	Areas
Functions	Products
Areas	Functions

Central staff may compound the conflict by their predominantly functional orientation. While managers are looking for ways to maximize the advantages of all three dimensions simultaneously, resolution is delayed by this need to defend their interests and perspectives. In the process, the existing organization lags behind the evolving strategy, usually catching up in a large quantum jump known as a shake-up, only to begin lagging behind again.

The detailed study by Beer and Davis,[7] gives an example of the conflict and cost experienced during the phase when the international division is dismantled. The process generally takes years, and even then the international division may survive for political and quasi-rational reasons.

Clark Equipment is a company that has been in the process of shifting to a global organization and reducing the scope of its international division for several years. Clark is a highly integrated manufacturer and distributor of industrial end-user products that are sold through a global network of independent dealers. It has sales of over $1 billion, and international sales represent about a third of this amount. In 1970 the company operated with seven domestic product divisions and an international division. At that time there were many discussions about U.S. versus European sourcing and facilities expansion, and about the need for continent-wide product planning. Clark needed a global perspective for its various product lines, but lacked information systems and a formal structure with which to realize this goal. As part of a rationalization program to realize these needs, they separated marketing and operations as independent "profit" centers functioning worldwide. They rationalized manufacturing facilities to eliminate multiproduct plants and to develop product-centered operating subsidiaries. Next the domestic divisions assumed worldwide profit responsibility, and the European headquarters lost its profit-and-loss responsibility.

Still, in 1976 the international division has survived. Within Clark it is seen as a group of "area-based, entrepreneurial generalists." Their job is to enter new markets and to develop global dealer networks; they are not expected to have functional or product expertise. They play a staff role with regard to established operations, yet they maintain operating and profit responsibility for Clark's Latin American and Asian activities. Two continuing questions for the firm are the following:

Organizationally, when is the right time to shift responsibility to the worldwide product divisions?

Strategically, is there sufficient reason to maintain the international division rather than fold it into corporate planning?

In the world of organization theory, the pure answer to the second question is probably no, but historical and political conditions are compelling.

Many international divisions such as the one at Clark and the ones examined by Beer and Davis continue to exist, some as useful anomalies and some as mere anachronisms. The general model assumes that the international division will be replaced by regional or product divisions, whereas in practice international divisions die hard and often linger on in residual roles, sometimes continuing to play important, though reduced, roles. In all cases, the transformation is a struggle to piece together the dimensions of a new global structure. Even firms as sophisticated as IBM have been very slow to break up their international divisions. Although there are no quantitative data to prove it conclusively, it appears that firms that diversify their products before they diversify the countries they operate in attempt to disband their international divisions sooner but may have more difficulty doing so. Corporations that expand globally without or before becoming multiproduct, on the other hand, seem to retain the international divisions longer but are able to make the transition more smoothly, as the IBM and Pfizer examples in the next section will show.

The moral of the tale is that firms assuming a global strategy would do well to adopt a global structure. When they don't, it is likely to be because of the firm's history, politics, and personalities. Companies that want to avoid domestic-international splits in management should avoid the same in structure.

Given: Geographic Organization

Needed: Global Product Management

The international division and the extension of the geographic basis to a worldwide area structure improve the coordination of all product lines within each zone, but at the expense of reduced coordination between areas for any one product line. The unwillingness to make this tradeoff leads corporations with a geographic structure to introduce global-product-line management into their organization design. Narrow product line companies that embark on a diversification strategy, for example, have drifted away from earlier typical methods of integrating the new lines into the existing geographic setup. These new lines, generally small when considered as a proportion of the whole, tend to drift upward in the geographic hierarchy, gathering product/management identity and independence as they become more centralized. IBM's office-products division and Pfizer's international-diversification efforts are examples of this phenomenon.

IBM.   IBM was one of the last holdouts for the international-division (IBM World Trade Corporation) structure long after its international sales suggested that a dichotomous structure of "here and abroad" was inadequate. Shortly after it broke up its international division and created a worldwide area structure, it began to differentiate the global structure for its office-products (OP) business. The OP operations are substantially different from the very large data-processing (DP) operations, and the head of the OP division wanted it to be one profit center, independent of the geographic profit centers for data processing. In less than three years, between 1972 and 1975, the locus of OP in the IBM hierarchy moved upward from a position subordinate to DP in each country unit to that of a product division with worldwide responsibility.

Until 1972 there was a single composite sales-and-profit objective at the country level for both DP and OP. Since as much as 90 percent of a country's business was DP, OP would usually be slighted in any tradeoff. Also, staff at World Trade Headquarters were shared, and on critical decisions like pricing, OP did not get the support it needed. Steps were taken to correct this problem in 1972, when the country manager was no longer allowed to make OP-DP tradeoff decisions; they were to be made at the group (Europe, Americas/Far East) level. For a brief while the OP country managers reported to the OP group managers, but then the reporting line was further centralized and they reported directly to World Trade Headquarters. Under that arrangement OP became a separate profit center within the international side of IBM, and the reporting lines effectively bypassed the area and country levels of the old structure. In what must have been read as a moderate challenge to the hegemony of the country managers, who were generally DP types, the OP country manager then had to rely on him only for nonmarketing staff support on a dotted-line basis.

The third structural change in three years took place in mid-1975, when OP was centralized once again. It was taken out of the two geographic groups (United States and Americas/Far East) and set up with the new minicomputers and software as part of a worldwide General Business Group. The General Business Group, an almost $4 billion unit, then set up its own international division based on country management units.

Pfizer.   Pfizer, one of the world's leading pharmaceutical companies, has followed a similar path. With about half of its sales and more of its earnings coming from abroad, it has still held onto its international division rather than shift to a global area design. Beginning in the early 1960s it embarked on a diversification program to counter the decline in new drugs due to the harsh regulatory climate and severe technological obstacles. Its program was both ambitious and haphazard. The company made about 60 acquisitions in 12 years and strayed far afield of its basic business: drugs and health-care products in a science-based company. Organizationally, most of these new product lines were fit into the existing geographic structure of country management. During the period from acquisition through adjustment and often to divestiture, these units would be moved up and down the geographic hierarchy looking for the appropriate way of pitting diversified product lines into a geographically differentiated structure. Many, of course, were dumped along the way, including pesticides, plastics, protein fish meal, door-to-door cosmetics, and baby foods. Those fitting into the more traditional Pfizer product groups finally survived within the international division. Significantly, the more distinct businesses were ultimately organized as separate worldwide product divisions, bypassing the international-domestic split and reporting directly to corporate headquarters. These included Quigley refractories, Howmedia orthopedic supplies, and Coty consumer products.

The reasons and conditions for pulling a product line out of its geographic moorings are similar to the reasons for creating a global structure based on product lines in general. Among the most important are the following:

Sharp differences in marketing or production and supply.

Little or no interdependence between the main line and the new one.

Currently small, but potentially large, growth of the separated product.

Avoidance of rivalry and hostility among managers in different product groups. The lessons of IBM and Pfizer are repeated in other firms that move outside their original, narrow product base. These lessons are as follows:

Pure geographic structures do not permit sufficient integration of any one different product line.

The more differentiated a new product line is from the main business, the more centrally (globally) it should be managed.

The need to introduce product differentiation into a geographically specialized hierarchy increases the managerial and the structural complexity by geometric proportions.

Given: Global Product Management

Needed: Geographic Coordination

Global corporations that are organized along product lines have the opposite problem: how to coordinate their diverse business activities within any one geographic area. When they have made the strategic choices to carry a diversity of products to new areas, their structures reflect the need to maximize technological linkages among the farflung plants in each business unit. This has been done, however, at the cost of duplicating management and organization in each area. To cope with problems of coordinating and simplifying these parallel managements, firms must reach through their existing product structure and weave an additional dimension across the organizational pattern. In the language of this metaphor, those who do it successfully will have a blend rather than a plaid fabric as the result. Eaton Corporation offers one example of a global firm that has successfully woven a few threads across the straight grain.

Eaton.   Eaton is a highly diversified company in the capital goods and automotive industries. It has sales of over $1.5 billion, employs over 50,000 people, and operates over 140 facilities in more than 20 countries. In 1974 each of its four worldwide product groups had a managing director for European operations. Each of the firm's 29 manufacturing facilities and 6 associate companies in Europe reported to one of these four people. In addition, 18 service operations, a finance operation, and an R&D center in Europe reported to their functional counterparts in the parent company. Senior management was concerned about how well it was coordinating these activities in Europe.

It was important for Eaton to be able to evaluate and respond to significant trends and developments in European countries, such as tariffs, tax matters, duties, government legislation, currency fluctuations, environmental controls and energy conservation, codetermination and industrial democracy, labor matters, nationalization, and government participation in ownership. Its current organization structure did not provide a regular and convenient means of communication among its European units, either for exchanging information, for building a positive corporate identity, or for assessing corporate needs and coordinating programs and procedures to meet them.

Rejecting the notion of country managers and/or one vice-president for Europe, they instituted a European Coordinating Committee (ECC) together with coordinating committees in each country where they had a major involvement. The four European managing directors were permanent members of the ECC and each served as a coordinator for one or more of the country committees; Europeans representing various functions were appointed to one-year terms; and the firm's executive vice-presidents and group vice-presidents were all made *ex officio* members, with one present at each ECC meeting on a rotating basis. Meetings are now held monthly, midway between the monthly meetings of the corporate operating committee, and minutes were sent to world headquarters within five working days. Attendance is required, the chair rotated periodically, and the location rotated among the major facilities. The president and the four group vice-presidents fly to Europe to formally launch the new coordinating committees, and the corporate newsletter devotes an entire issue to the new developments.

Six months after launching the coordinating committees, Eaton formed a Latin American Coordinating Committee, and about a year after that they created a U.S. and Canadian Division Manager's Council using the same model. The same attention was paid to details of the committee's operations and to their implementation. The European committee, then, served as a model for realizing better coordination across business lines in each of the firm's major geographic areas, and it is probable that the capstone in the future will be a council of councils that will take the form of annual or semiannual worldwide coordinating meetings.

This example illustrates a moderate step, in structural terms, toward complementing the warp of a traditional product-line organization with the woof of geographic coordinates. The fabric of the organization is not significantly altered, rather it is reinforced. Little is done to increase the complexity of the global design or management practices. Success depends on thorough implementing of a plan that least disturbs the existing managerial style and corporate culture. The change is supplementary, rather than radical, and it has the desired effect of managing *both* product and country diversity.

Firms that are organized along global product lines will probably experience similar needs to coordinate their activities within a foreign country when they have at least two significant but organizationally independent business units there; there are economies to be gained from pooled information; there are benefits derivable from a more unified corporate identity; or there is a discernible need for assessing and coordinating corporate programs and their implementation.

THE FUNCTIONAL DIMENSION IN GLOBAL TERMS

The product and area structures, and any combinations, all treat the functional dimension in tertiary fashion, locating it in the various parts of the structure after the deck has already been cut twice. The extractive raw-materials ventures are an exception to this rule.

Functional activities play a critical role in, for example, the petroleum industry because of the scale required for economy, the technological complexity involved, and the importance of captive markets for the sale of crude. All major petroleum companies carry out exploration, crude production, tanker and pipeline transportation, manufacturing (refining), and marketing, in addition to the logistics of worldwide supply and distribution at each step in these process and product flows. These flows may be managed directly through centralized functional departments acting with worldwide line responsibility and supplemented by corporate staff who coordinate the functions within areas; or, conversely, through area management, with staff coordination for the functions. In any one petroleum company, the structure is either a mixture of the two or else it shifts back and forth. Conoco, for example, dropped its area division and returned to a functional structure. It reasoned that environmental changes, such as the oil import program and the Arab oil embargo, no longer made it feasible to think of domestic and foreign markets separately.

Most oil companies have a petrochemical products division reporting directly to the president, and since they have diversified into other energy sources, they also have a unit for that at the top of the hierarchy. The result is usually a three-dimensional mixture of parallel hierarchies: Some functions, some regions, and some products all report directly to the chief executive. Each of the hierarchies then has its own particular structural sequence: for example, a functional division will be subdivided by regions, whereas a region division reporting directly to the top would subdivide by functions; a product division might subdivide by functions or by regions. The result is a complex array of different hierarchies (Exhibit 2).

Whichever dimension is chosen as the organizing principle for a corporate division, that unit will confront problems integrating the other dimension(s) in its lower levels. Also, the corporation as a whole faces the problems of integrating each dimension as it is variously located in different countries, different hierarchical levels, and different divisions. By varying the primary building blocks, rather than using only one as the basis, the coordinating dilemmas are compounded rather than resolved, no matter how intelligent the choice of mix is. It is an open question whether management is ultimately backing into structural diseconomies; each structural choice is rational, but the totality nevertheless creates complexities that often negate the gained advantages. The structural choice at these macrolevels of design is also motivated by whether they are politically more or less vulnerable to dissection by the government in the event of moves to break up the big oil companies.

The aluminum industry is another example of an industry in which functional activities continue to play a primary role in fixing the structure. Alcan, for example, organized its activities in 1970 around the three major steps in the making and selling of their single-product line. Reporting directly to the president were three executive vice-presidents for raw materials, smelting, and fabricating sales. Within each of these functional divisions, foreign subsidiaries then grouped around area managers. Where a national subsidiary is itself vertically integrated, as in Brazil and India, it reports up the fabricating line. A worldwide functional structure, however, is not very stable, and in 1973 Alcan subsumed its ore activities under the executive vice-president smelting. Its concern was with the vulnerability of its sources of supply. This left the company with a global dichotomy between production and sales

EXHIBIT 2   STRUCTURAL SEQUENCE OF VARIOUS
HIERARCHIES

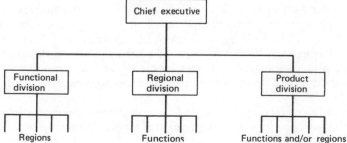

in line operations, which continue to drift to an area format with problems of integration for supply and distribution on a global basis.

The lesson is, do not organize global structures around business functions unless you are in extractive raw-materials industries, and even then you will find that these structures are unstable and will have to share primacy with geographic factors and, in some instances, with product differences. For global industrial corporations, basic functions such as manufacturing and marketing are and should be subsumed under product or geographic units. Even European-based companies, which have tended to emphasize functional structures in their domestic activities far more than U.S.-based ones, give this dimension less importance in their multinational design.[8]

ORGANIZING AROUND MARKETS, NOT GEOGRAPHY

Although the basic organizing dimensions for multinational corporations are functions, products, and geographic areas, some firms have begun to think in terms of market differences as a more important basis for determining their global structures. A market is conceived of as an identifiable and homogenous group that has similar patterns of need, purchasing behavior, and product use. Taking this definition and applying it to the nations of the world, companies are less likely to divide the globe on the basis of physical proximity than on the basis of needs and abilities to satisfy them. The traditional categories of Latin America, the Far East, Europe, and the like lose their power, and the new categorization is derived from development economies. Here the oversimplified dichotomy between developed and less developed has yielded to the current preference for dividing the globe into five "worlds." The first world includes the familiar capitalist economies of the industrialized world, and the second world includes the 1.3 billion people in the centrally planned communist economies. The third world comprises developing countries that have a modern infrastructure and/or have exceptional wealth in natural resources. Able to attract foreign investment and borrow on commercial terms, they need time and technology more than foreign aid. They include OPEC members, Brazil, Mexico, South Korea, Taiwan, and Turkey. The fourth-world countries have similar characteristics but in much less generous amounts and therefore need injections of both trade and aid. The fifth-world countries are the complete have-nots, without resources or the likelihood of ever improving their lot.

Business planners and marketers have taken these distinctions and, together with their own companies' historical records, have redrawn their organizational lines. One firm began with Stanford Research Institute's economic projections for 1975–1990 and planned a growth-market group around 10 countries that are expected to have annual growth rates averaging 6 percent or more: Brazil, Iran, Taiwan, Korea, Indonesia, Mexico, Venezuela, Japan, Turkey, and Spain.

Before divesting Merrill Labs, Richardson-Merrill, another multinational, maintained its Latin America/Far East unit, but reorganized the country groupings within it to reflect the same market differentiation as follows:

Group 1.   Andean Group, Southeast Asia, Philippines, and the Caribbean represent small, noncomplex, and underdeveloped markets for their products in places they have chosen to operate.

Group 2. India, Indonesia, and Iran represent large, noncomplex, and high-potential growth markets.

Group 3. Mexico, Brazil, and Australia represent large, complex markets to them, with proven records for their company as well as satellite markets in neighboring countries.

Group 4. Japan stands by itself as another large, complex, and mature market that requires specialized attention.

Ingersoll Rand distinguishes between offensive and defensive strategies when establishing manufacturing plants abroad: "Offensive" plants are to be used for exports as well as for sales in that country, whereas "defensive" location decisions are mainly made to protect against erosion of market share in that country. Other firms are finding it useful to define area managements in terms of a composite scale of key factors: examples include labor-capital intensity of the technology employed, the level of anticipated competition, the character of government (e.g., a socialist-bloc group), the cost of energy, and the availability of skilled personnel.

Market-centered thinking is making deeper inroads into planning and development than into operations, but the evolutionary trend is clear nonetheless. General Electric carries the idea into its planning around "strategic business units," which easily translate into families of businesses laid out on a product/geography grid. Again, the older and already tested structure acts as a supportive framework while new strategies evolve some kinds of metastructures as overlays. As the new language developed in central staffs gets absorbed, and as the future orientation becomes operating reality, it is not unlikely that we will witness a new generation of structural form in global corporations.

The basic principle in this approach is that geography is an obfuscation for conceptualizing global growth strategy and for organizing and managing the multinational corporations' responses. Market segmentation for domestic activities is far from new. A common differentiation in a domestic structure, for example, is between a government sector, an industrial sector, and a consumer sector. Organizing around markets, rather than geography, is recent, however, as applied to worldwide corporate structuring. The country, or nation-state, is kept as the basic unit of analysis, but the grouping together of countries is done on the basis of a different set of questions and assumptions: not on the assumption that understanding management in Mexico helps to start a business next door in Guatemala, but that demographic, income, natural-resource data, and the like are more relevant criteria, and are also ones that lend themselves to country-cluster analysis and hence to market-determined organization design.

The patterns and problems discussed above for the global industrial corporations are also reflected in the multinational spread of service corporations. Here market segmentation around clients and services is analogous to the product dimension in a manufacturing firm, and management searches for ways to integrate this dimension with the familiar geographic design.

The market-center concept is useful to all firms, though few thus far have actually structured their worldwide activities around it. Companies might want to do so when operations in neighboring countries are totally independent of each other; communication networks are good, and the technology for processing information rapidly and accurately is present or is not important; a marketing orientation already exists within the parent company; a set of markets can be identified that have more managerial validity than do sets of countries with geographic regions; the concept is already familiar to managers through the planning process; management is not locked into defense of territories.

GLOBAL MATRIX ORGANIZATION

The trends in organization that we have discussed all start with a primary structural dimension—either functions, products, or geography—and then try to compensate for the benefits lost by not choosing another of these dimensions as the major organizing theme. All of them involve tradeoffs. When a company shifts from organization form A to form B, many benefits of the old form linger on, because they have been deeply ingrained. At some imaginary fleeting moment, there is a balance of benefits, but over time the advantages of the abandoned form are bound to atrophy. This imbalance frequently worsens until there is a sense that the tradeoff has gone too far. Companies then either swing back to the earlier form, as in the familiar centralization/decentralization/recentralization cycles, or else they introduce subordinate coordination schemes such as the ones described in the sections above.

In other words, when companies face multiple goals, they often deal with them in sequence rather than simultaneously. Or else different parts of the company organize around the different subgoals. Translated into structural terms, there is an implicit assumption that the entire organization cannot specialize by two or three dimensions simultaneously. It is this assumption that some firms are rejecting. In doing so, they must reject a pattern of organization based on a hierarchy of power and a unity of command, and they must replace it with a dual or plural model that involves a balance of interest and power. One structural design is not overlaid with elements of another; rather, the two are blended and given coequal weight. The general manager of a French subsidiary, for example, will report to a vice-president for Europe. This is the essence of global matrix organization (Exhibit 3).

Dow Chemical Company is perhaps one of the first industrial corporations to use the matrix form in its global macrostructure. Although Dow does not publish organization charts for internal or external consumption, its 1968 annual report nevertheless did publish a matrix diagram of sorts in the form of a photo cube. Along each dimension of the cube were photos of the key managers for the various functions, product groups, and geographic areas in the Dow organization. At that time the Dow organizational philosophy was that they managed with a three-dimensional matrix. Shortly after that, in fact, one of Dow's senior managers, William Goggin, became president of Dow Corning and introduced there what he called a four-dimensional matrix, by adding "time" into the sense of structure.

EXHIBIT 3   GLOBAL MATRIX ORGANIZATION

Although these ambitious notions of multidimensional structuring grappled with managing global complexities simultaneously, they proved exceedingly difficult to keep in balance. By 1970 it was apparent that Dow Chemical's matrix was effectively two-dimensional, a worldwide grid of product and geography with functions variously located at different levels in the grid hierarchies. In 1972 the matrix became further imbalanced when the product dimension lost line authority and was kicked upstairs in the form of three business group managers who reported to the corporate product development division. They were to be separate channels of communication for their product groups across the areas, and their clout came from their control over capital expenditures. Life sciences was the only product division that maintained worldwide reporting control.

Around 1974 Dow Chemical held a meeting of its senior managers worldwide. During an anonymous question-and-answer period with the chairman, Carl Gerstaker, the question was asked: "Which dimension of the matrix do you consider to be most important?" The very fact that the question was asked demonstrates that the matrix had deteriorated significantly. Gerstaker's answer was to the point: The most important dimension in a matrix organization is the weakest and/or the most threatened. Despite the chairman's understanding of multidimensional structures, however, the matrix continued to decompose. In 1975 the life sciences division lost its worldwide reporting line and was subsumed under each of the geographic "operating units." Whereas each product used to have an identifiable team linking its business through the area, the basic locus of these teams now exists within each area. Today Dow Chemical would be described more appropriately as using a geographically based structure. In retrospect, it should be noted that, with the exception of the life sciences division, only the areas ever had their own letterhead stationery. Although the ideology of global matrix management still exists in some corners of Dow, the ethos and spirit of it is not to be found.

The example of Dow is not to be read as a failure. As Peter Drucker says, the matrix structure "will never be a preferred form of organization; it is fiendishly difficult."[9] He concludes, nevertheless, that ". . . any manager in a multi-national business will have to learn to understand it if he wants to function effectively himself."[10] Dow's global matrix was a valiant and creative effort, a radical approach to structuring a multinational corporation. Some European firms, such as Phillips, have operated with a matrix organization for years, and some U.S.-based nonindustrial corporations have also relied on the matrix form. Global construction and engineering firms, such as Bechtel Corporation, and one bank, Citibank, are examples that have been more successful than Dow Chemical.

Dow Corning, a twentieth the size of Dow Chemical, had been more successful in maintaining its global matrix. A relatively smaller size may be one reason, but far more important is that Dow Corning pays great attention to the behavioral requirements of matrix management in addition to the structural ones. The chairman is an overt enthusiast of the matrix, amiably stressing to his managers that they will be democratic and share power. The balance of power and shared decision making are translated into nonconcrete form, for example, by the elimination of walls and corridors in favor of office landscaping around family groupings. Since Dow is purposefully built around a paradox of competing claims, stability rests in managers' behavior more than in structural form. Matrix is a verb.

Corporations need not organize their domestic activities around a matrix in order for the form to be used in their global frameworks. But if they are going to attempt to implement a matrix design, they should only do so when there is diversification of both products and markets requiring balanced and simultaneous attention; the opportunities lost and difficulties experienced by favoring either a product or geographic unity of command cannot be ignored; environmental pressure to secure international economies of scale require the shared use of scarce human resources; there is a need for enriched information-processing capacity because of uncertain, complex, and interdependent tasks; information, planning, and control systems operate along the different dimensions of the structure simultaneously; as much attention is paid to managerial behavior as to the structure.

The corporate culture and ethos must actively support and believe in negotiated management. They have to think matrix.

The increasingly common response during the past five years is to turn to some form of matrix design. As author of a recent book on the subject,[11] I have watched the growth of matrix usage closely. A strange and paradoxical, though understandable, phenomenon is occurring. There is parallel increase in the *usage* of and *dissatisfaction* with the matrix. By now, the structural requirements are rather clear; it is the behavioral changes that are resisted and resented. Little wonder! In common usage, the form is only a few decades old. After centuries of a one-boss model, based around principles of the unity of command, the shift to a two-boss model, based on a balance of power, will take many more years before it is legitimated and accepted.

For the purpose of brevity, two examples of major world corporations will suffice. Only five years ago only a few of General Electric's strategic business units were organized around some form of matrix. By 1977, 25 percent reported using a matrix, and only one year later as many as 40 percent of the strategic business units were employing it in one way or another. Whereas the matrix is found at middle levels in GE, it has been used as an organizing principle for the entire institution at Citibank, the second-largest bank in the world. The results are mixed, and senior management is searching for a way to get "beyond the matrix" without returning to the either/or world of the already existing models.

The two examples are instructive for another reason. The principal organization models are ones that have been developed by industrial firms in an industrial economy. The United States, however, has a postindustrial or service economy. This has received scant attention for the most part, and few observers or practitioners have understood the implications of this major historical shift for both the strategy and organization of world corporations. IBM, for example, is much less than 20 percent manufacturing-based with the rest service-based, yet the firm is considered an industrial corporation. Corporations in the service sector of the economy have used organization models developed in and for the industrial sector. It is my hunch and prediction that the major breakthroughs in organization design will occur in the now-dominant service sector. It is only a logical extension that if and when there is a major advance in the organization of multinational corporations, it will come from multinational *service* corporations.

CONCLUSION

In summary, the basic patterns of organization for global corporations are rather standard by this time. While the posture of a firm is domestic with only some foreign activities, the latter are generally grouped into an international division. Once a global orientation is assumed by the firm, either a worldwide product structure or worldwide geographic divisions are the most-common alternatives. Functional specialization is seldom used as the organizing basis for a global structure; natural-resource industries are sometimes the exception to this rule.

When organizations experience significant diversification in both their products/services and markets, the singular structure based on *either* global product divisions *or* geographic area divisions becomes inadequate. Diversification has led to experiments in global organization design that simultaneously structures a corporation by product/service *and* by geography. This occurs through a variety of forms, although the principles of design are the same in each.

In the simpler form of this new design, corporations develop an overlay of the second organizing dimension across the basic dimension used in the global structuring. Examples include using area-coordinating committees in a product-structured firm; shifting the level of product-line reporting, according to the unique requirements of each, between country, region, zone, and worldwide, in a geographical-structured firm; and using the corporate planning function to negotiate product-market interdependencies.

In the more complex form of the new design, corporations are using global matrix management and matrix structures. These involve some manner of dual reporting lines between the product/service and market dimensions; dual accounting and planning; and a sense of shared responsibilities in which tradeoffs have to be negotiated at the point of interface, rather than sent up to a common boss for resolution. Global matrices are structurally unstable, as are their domestic counterparts. Conflict is inherent in the design, and is managed as an acceptable cost of having the best of both forms of organization.

The general trend is clear. Traditional structures, with their simple choice of functional, product, or geographical design, are relied on less and less by global industrial corporations because they optimize along only one dimension. Changes in the external environment and the strategic responses to these changes, however, led global corporations to develop and manage more-complex organization designs than were possible only a decade ago. The new designs attempt to integrate and manage competing needs simultaneously. As the new patterns are understood more clearly, it becomes evident that their success does not lie in having made the most rational choice of structure in any given case. Instead, success with the new patterns depends more on managerial ability to live with a paradox.

NOTES

1. For the application of the product-life-cycle concept to international trade, see Wells of *Business Administration, Harvard University,* (1972).
2. The Harvard Multinational Enterprise Project is a large-scale study that has been going on since 1965, under the direction of Raymond Vernon. The 60 percent figure comes from one of the study's volumes. (Stopford and Wells, 1972, p. 21).
3. Clee and Sachtjen (1964, p. 60).
4. Of the 170 firms examined by Stopford and Wells (1972, p. 51), 90 had an international division in 1968, but the international division was the largest in only 4 of the 90.
5. Stopford and Wells (1972, p. 64) report that when foreign sales reach 40 percent of the total, most firms turn to some form of direct area coordination.

6. Stopford and Wells (1972, p. 77).
7. Davis (1976, pp. 35–47).
8. Franko, (1977).
9. Drucker, (1978, p. 598).
10. Drucker, (1978).
11. Davis and Lawrence (1977).

SOURCES AND SUGGESTED REFERENCES

Clee, G.H. and W.M. Sachtjen. "Organizing a Worldwide Business," *Harvard Business Review,* Vol. XIV, No. 6 (1964), pp. 60–78.

Davis, S.M. "Creating a Global Organization," *Columbia Journal of World Business,* Vol. VII, No. 2 (1976), pp. 35–47.

Davis, S.M. and P.B. Lawrence. *Matrix,* Reading, MA: Addison-Wesley, 1977.

Drucker, P. *Management: Tasks, Responsibilities, Practices,* New York: Harper and Row, 1978.

Franko, L.G. "The Move Toward a Multidimensional Structure in European Organizations," *Administrative Science Quarterly,* Vol. XVIII, No 4 (1977), pp. 493–506.

Stopford, M.J. and L.T. Wells, Jr. *Managing the Multinational Enterprise,* New York: Basic Books, 1972.

Wells, L.T., Jr. ed. *The Product Life Cycle and International Trade,* Boston: Division of Research, Graduate School of Business Administration, Harvard University, 1972.

INTERNATIONAL CORPORATE PLANNING

CONTENTS

INTERNATIONAL CORPORATE PLANNING

Michael Z. Brooke

THE PURPOSES

A BRIDGE BETWEEN THE COMPANY AND ITS ENVIRONMENT. Corporate planning provides a company with a sense of direction and a means of coping with opportunities and problems. The activity is one in which every executive engages in some form: The dream as a result of which the company was founded was itself a pioneer corporate plan. Statements to the contrary, like "this company started planning in 1974," are commonly heard at executive seminars, but reflect a limited view of the subject. Such sayings refer to the introduction of a *formal* system of corporate planning, whereas the exercise has its informal side as well. In the formal sense, as it happens, many companies stopped planning in 1974, at least temporarily. They became disillusioned with an expensive activity that, in many instances, failed to make provision for a steep rise in fuel prices. Normally a company that operates across frontiers does come to see the sense in moving toward some formal planning even if the price seems high. Issues that are straightforward at home develop unexpected complications abroad, and the first reason for developing formal procedures is to provide a bridge between the company and its environment. A few examples will illustrate the point.

The *mining company's* decision about where to locate a mine is mainly determined on geological grounds in its own country. Naturally there is local opposition to contend with, possibly also central government policy, and certainly the fluctuations in the commodity markets during the long period that elapses between the decision to go ahead and the production of salable material. That period is much longer when the exercise is outside the home country, and political, legal, economic, and other considerations external to the company become critical.

The *machinery manufacturer* may well have a protected market at home. Where there are tariff barriers, local specifications, established relations with customers, or other impediments to trade, the full impact of competition is not met until the company starts to sell abroad. Then the environment becomes very competitive indeed; the strategies of the opposition have to be understood along with local laws and customs.

The *food-processing company* is not, at first sight, an obvious candidate for international operations. The technology is not among the most advanced, the materials are relatively simple, and the market is local. But a second impression reveals that a large part of this industry is in fact international. Staple foods—bread, cereals, fruit juices, preserves, butter, margarine—are manufactured or packed by a limited number of companies with plants in numerous countries. The production of cattle fodder is even more concentrated. The wide range (spread) of multinational food manufacturers argues for a subtle international strategy, including the necessity of understanding the local environment at its most mysterious—eating habits and farming methods—and determining where standardization is possible and where variety is required.

Service industries, like banks, advertising agencies, and insurance companies, start abroad in order to retain existing customers and to relate to the customers' international strategies. Once industries seek local customers thereof as well and develop their own foreign policies.

Each sector has its own route and its own planning requirements. Difficulties occur if the environment is not understood, and opportunities arise if it is. The lure into international business comes from higher profits to be made abroad, wider sales from the same expenditure on product development, and the opportunity of transferring to other markets the knowledge acquired at home. The task of international corporate planning is to ensure that the potential is realized and the traps avoided.

A TOOL FOR ALL SEASONS.   International corporate planning steers the company through a host of pressures and attractions. It is not intended to be a straitjacket restricting the ability to maneuver. One of the problems in 1973–1974 was that over-rigid planning systems had been adopted. Not only was the first oil crisis not foreseen by many—it *was* by some—but the plans were not flexible enough to make the necessary adaptations. Companies have now learned what some were practicing in the 1960s, that corporate planning exists to provide a choice of routes that will enable rapid adjustment to opportunities and problems as they arise. The word *contingency* summarizes the planning outlook that underlies these pages.

Contingency Planning.   Broad objectives are set, and the piloting of the company toward those objectives is carried out, by a series of criteria and guidelines for responding to changes and difficulties as they arise. This is contingency planning, and it provides a business with the flexibility to switch from one route to another as conditions change instead of being stymied when the chosen path is closed. The intention is that the destination becomes more important than the means of getting there.

The building of a factory in Nigeria, for instance, will absorb much of the resources of a small company; but even so, provision is required for achieving the proportion of income expected from the plant if there is another revolution in that country and foreign property is expropriated. The planning will ensure that such major disasters, as well as smaller inconveniences, will not prevent the income and growth targets from being reached. The problems can be offset by restricting the extent of the exposure, by hedging and by insurance; a company with sufficient staying power can, indeed, turn an apparent disaster to good effect—a time of instability is often followed by a period of postwar reconstruction when funds are freely available, especially for capital equipment and consulting services. Alongside this approach goes the more difficult issue of central and local participation in the planning.

Centralization and Decentralization.   The international planner is often accused of assuming a kind of imperialist role by disposing of the world from his ivory tower in the corporate headquarters. The alternative is then seen as the drafting of plans in the local units, with the headquarters approving or amending. The phrases *top down* and *bottom up* are used of these approaches. The former can be insensitive to the local situation, whereas the bottom-up approach can easily sacrifice the advantages of being international. The benefit of the part does not necessarily aid the well-being of the whole. In the example mentioned in the last paragraph, the Nigerian subsidiary might wish to plan for the reinvestment of all its income in its own operation. The parent company, on the other hand, would want to draw as much revenue out of the Nigerian affiliate as possible once an optimum size had been reached. The money could be used to boost dividends and to finance a project elsewhere to provide a hedge against any setbacks in Nigeria. For this reason the central planning department would see a different purpose for the Nigerian revenue and recognize that the subsidiary needed a skilled finance manager able to gain government agreement to remitting the surplus funds abroad. This is a typical case of a clash of interest between the local operation and the center.

Most companies need a strong central sense of direction, but this has to exist with the consent and cooperation of the local units. Insensitivity at the center is best overcome by fixing formal procedures for local participation—and this participation should not just consist of meetings of professional planners. One company has regular meetings of national chief executives in each region in which it operates as a part of the planning process. Such procedures highlight the third aspect of the purpose: the special nature of *international* planning.

The International Dimension.   A domestic company does not have to concern itself with transferring money across frontiers, and this consideration symbolizes the special requirements of international planning. A chief executive officer has declared that "it is totally wrong to distinguish between planning for our domestic business and for that abroad." It is unlikely that a company adopting his view will make the most effective use of its foreign operations, but naturally only large companies can afford specialized and full-time international planners. At a rough estimate, annual sales of $40 million are required to support a full-time planning department, so the specialization will usually have to be carried part time.

Similar techniques as were used before the company thought in such terms may well be employed to design global plans, but much more complex data will be incorporated into the equations, and the resultant strategies will have the geographic as a prominent dimension. Both the resemblances and the differences between countries have to be noted, but the differences are harder to identify. Many a well-ordered plan has been wrecked because insufficient account was taken of the legal system, the accounting conventions, the local prejudices against a particular marketing ploy, or any of the other factors such as customs and immigration procedures that scarcely have to be considered in domestic planning.

The impact of the planning on both the company and the country is another vital consideration. As a company grows abroad, its management system is going to change. There will come a stage—20 percent of the business outside the home country has been suggested—when the organization will have been altered completely and many of the staff with it. The figure of 20 percent is arbitrary, the proportion will vary according to the industry sector, but the process is inevitable.

So international planning is concerned with the response at home as well as the development abroad. Part of that development will have impact on national economies. One of the reasons for the growing political opposition to the international firm is precisely that planners in one country are effectively, if unconsciously, vitiating the carefully considered plans of another. The word *sensitivity* must be placed alongside the word *flexibility* as a hallmark of international planning.

In sum, the company can expect of the international planner that he will provide an understanding of the conditions that favor and constrain the international business, and that he will mark out a path to make the most profitable use of any favorable circumstances and to overcome the risks. With this understanding of the aims and objects as a background, it is possible to summarize the contents of the global strategy.

THE CONTENT—STRATEGY FORMULATION

DIVERSIFICATION.   There are a number of options for corporate development, including making more profitable use of existing resources, but if *expansion* is the selected strategy, it will not be long before *diversification* is considered in addition to the organic growth of existing business. There are two ways to diversify:

1. *By geography.* This is the international route. The planner prepares the evidence for and against developing foreign markets and works out the implications once the decision has been made.
2. *By product.* The move into new businesses may be an alternative to going abroad or may by itself lead into foreign markets. A company finds itself purchasing another that already has foreign operations.

Geography.   In the discussion on diversification, there are many arguments for an international strategy. Moving into other countries, for instance, brings the company under the influence of different national economies. Since these are unlikely to go through the cycles of boom and slump at the same time, the company achieves some leveling out of its business, which is one of the objectives of diversification. The more even flow of orders and income that results is especially important for concerns that are much affected by the ups and downs of national economies or by seasonal variations. On the other hand, naturally, an international strategy has its problems, and there are numerous traps to guard against. Compiling a list of these traps is another task of the planner. For instance, a small manufacturer of fancy goods in the United States developed a substantial market in Germany. The growth of sales there encouraged the manufacturer to appoint a local agent. The appointment was made without adequate planning or investigation of the snags. When the U.S. company gave the agent notice, it was discovered that considerable compensation was owed. There was no mention of this in the contract, but German law includes a clause protecting local firms that act as agents to foreign companies. This is a typical trap because no such law exists in the United States, whereas it does exist in all European community countries except Britain and Belgium—who may soon fall into line.

The international planner, then, has to signal the traps. In addition to the need to operate under different legal systems, a selection of common pitfalls includes the following:

1. *Different accounting systems.* One company was nearly bankrupted because the controller's department at head office failed to see the signs of trouble soon enough as a result of a misreading of the accounts.

2. *Appointing insensitive managers to sensitive parts of the world.* One company lost much business after putting a racially prejudiced manager in charge of a subsidiary in a newly independent African country. The promotion of the wrong local manager can be equally disastrous in some countries.

3. *Less-obvious traps.* Some of the traps, such as the failure to adapt to local conditions, are obvious; others, like the offense that can be caused by over-adaptation, are less so. More than one writer has commented on the ability to alienate customers abroad shown by companies which possess a reputation for being market conscious at home. Their patronizing efforts to acquire local colour are not appreciated.

International diversification may, then, produce difficulties; but a high proportion of companies also express reservations about product diversification.

Product Diversification. An apparent advantage of emphasizing diversification by product is that existing skills are employed. The routes available can, indeed, be classified by the skills employed—the *marketing* route, whereby different businesses that require similar marketing abilities are acquired, and the *technical* route, in which industry sectors that employ similar technologies are entered.

Another means of diversification is *financial,* the conglomerate, where acquisitions are made for their financial logic. The companies acquired fit specifications the planner has identified, such as return on investment and asset growth potential. Yet another route is *vertical integration,* when a supplier or customer is purchased.

All the methods can have international implications and are to be considered, along with further international developments, as part of the strategic decision-making process. Vertical integration, for instance, is a common route abroad as a company sets out to ensure its supply network as well as its outlets. Every method of diversification has been described as a spread of risk that carries its own risk, and the planner is interested in reducing the uncertainties. For this a set of criteria are required, and these include some simple and arbitrary, but very common, guidelines like: "This company will place half of its new investment each year outside the home country." A more subtle guideline arises from listing the strengths of the company and determining in which parts of the world they are most likely to be profitably employed. The initial decision to move abroad comes from answers to questions about the strengths and resources already possessed by the company; the answers to other questions determine the route to be followed.

THE ROUTE. A distinctively international decision is about the method of entering the foreign market. There are three main routes: the sale of knowledge (technical, marketing, or general management); the sale of goods; foreign investment (which may include the other two). Each, of course, has many subdivisions.

A prevailing view is that the most profitable route is through foreign investment, and that the sale of knowledge is only for risky markets or companies that cannot afford any other means. This view, repeated in many textbooks, underestimates the opportunities available to the international planner. His object is to make money abroad, and in a form in which it can be brought home. This may mean adopting different strategies from those suggested by a straightforward pursuit of profit. A company does not need one general strategy for the thrust abroad; it requires separate routes for each product and each market. The different approaches need to fit together, and the way they match is obviously an important consideration. Each main strategy will be identified in the following sections.

Sale of Knowledge.   This route to foreign markets includes a wide variety of activities, beginning with licensing and franchising. In their simplest form, these involve planning in one specialist function only—the technical for licensing and the marketing for franchising. But strategic decisions are never that simple. The licensing department is selling the company's skills, but is itself a branch of marketing, with which it has to be integrated. If this does not occur, a spread of manufacture by licensing, with each case considered purely on its merits, will restrict a company's strategies for years ahead. Then again, the licensing contract cannot always be regarded just as a means for making more money out of research and development without any implications for other functions. The licensee, for example, may have inadequate marketing or financial skills, and so a more complicated arrangement will be required to compensate for the deficiencies of the foreign operator. The same applies to franchising, a sale of marketing knowledge that becomes a total corporate strategy.

There is a spectrum of agreements that gradually grow more complex, with the pure licensing agreement at one end and the management contract at the other. Along the line other functions become involved. The management contract includes, on principle, the management of a company in its entirety but without ownership. Originally developed as a means of using surplus management capacity among transport concerns (a management structure required to operate 10 ships, aircraft, or buses can also operate 100) and expropriated firms in tropical agriculture, this method is now being used in a widening selection of businesses. The various forms of knowledge agreement are shown in Exhibit 1, which demonstrates the range available to the strategist and some of the considerations that apply.

It is characteristic of all knowledge arrangements that

1.   Little capital is required for the foreign operation, but expenditure is required at home to ensure that the company remains at the front in research; otherwise the knowledge may soon become unsalable.

EXHIBIT 1   KNOWLEDGE AGREEMENTS AND THEIR STRATEGIC RELATIONSHIPS

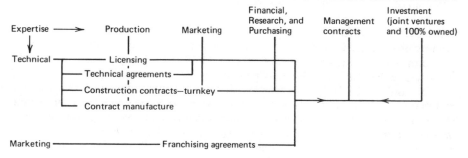

2. The risks of loss are minimized in the short term, but safeguards are needed for the longer term to prevent the foreign partner from becoming a competitor. The only real safeguard against this and other problems that arise is in the business relationship, which is, therefore, the planner's main concern. The legal contract is usually irrelevant except when the relationship breaks down.

3. The knowledge arrangement is determined as a result of a conscious decision that this is the company's most salable asset.

4. From most countries it is easier to bring money home as payment for know-how (royalties) or for management assistance (fees). The tax position is also more favorable. Until the mid-1970s, both these statements were normally true. More recently, however, suspicions of overcharging for technology have produced changes in some tax systems as well as stricter control of money transfers. The assumption that there are universally applicable tax and remittance rules must now be added to the list of traps for which the planner has to be on the watch.

The amount of money passing through knowledge agreements as a whole has increased but, contrary to most expectations, not as rapidly as other forms of international business. The total is estimated at not much more than 10 percent of world trade payments, although some forms (especially those which involve management or a little equity involvement) have expanded more rapidly than others. It seems that international firms are slow to discover the possibilities of additional income by this route, but small, dynamic high technology companies are likely to use it increasingly.

The Sale of Goods and Services.   Export is the traditional means of making money abroad, and the traditions themselves frequently increase the expenses. Methods that were appropriate when labor was cheap and technology primitive have survived in the transport, dock-handling, revenue service, and other sectors. The total costs of distribution—packing, transport, insurance, clearance across frontiers, and documentation—can add over 100 percent to the cost of a product that is bulky and inexpensive. On the other hand, export is favored by governments concerned with balance-of-payments problems, so assistance to offset the expenses may be available.

The planner is naturally interested in examining the special opportunities for the company's goods and the adaptations, if any, required for the foreign market. He is also concerned that export shall be seen as a strategic option that can be adapted in numerous ways to capture the greatest-possible commercial advantage. For instance, part assembly may ensure orders in some markets, even where it is not legally required, and the advantages that could have been gained by part assembly will eventually be lost if a policy of promoting finished goods is rigidly maintained. The part assembly may be carried out under contract or through a local subsidiary. The assembler sometimes provides after-sales servicing and the stocking of spare parts; both these will improve the sales pitch against competitors. It is, indeed, the competitive pressures that are changing the approach to export planning and ensuring that this is seen as part of a selection of strategies.

Investment.   Most studies of international business in the last 20 years have stressed the growth of foreign investment. In fact, all the routes have been increasingly used in spite of floating currencies, import restrictions, and numerous measures that were once said to be disruptive of trade. Foreign investment has had the most public discussion, because it is the most visible and controversial route, with its political and social implications. There have also been spectacular successes along this route, but these have been accompanied by notable, even if less publicized, failures. The number of withdrawals has been increasing, and one challenge to the planner is to make sure that withdrawal is also an orderly process when it becomes necessary.

This review has been concerned with the planning of two major international strategies—diversification and the route. A profitable, and therefore compatible, package is required when reviewing the plans. Attention is now turned to the part the planner plays in the decision-making process.

THE STAGES—FROM FORMULATION TO IMPLEMENTATION

Planning starts from a question. It may be a general query: "Where is this company going?" In practice it is likely to take a more specific form: "Would it not be a good idea to move into product X?" Or perhaps: "What would be the implications of opening up a business in country Y?" Whatever the starting point, a number of stages occur between the first statement of an idea and its profitable operation. Some of these stages are for the planner, some for the decision maker. In the small company the two will be the same person; where professional planners are employed, their work will be a useless expense unless they cooperate closely with the appropriate decision maker at each stage.

LONG-TERM PLANNING.   The planner picks up a question, or the germ of an idea, and works out some ways in which it can be answered. This stage is usually called decision preparation.

Decision Preparation.   The planning process begins when the planner develops a number of options in the light of the question or statement that forms his brief, and with the corporate objectives in mind. His aim is to provide a reasoned view of where the company could hope to be within 5–10 years, and then to support the findings with some glimpses into the longer term. The exact time horizon will depend upon the industry sector and the type of decision. For a fashion-conscious industry like clothing, five years will be long term for product decisions but not for diversification planning. For an industry like mining, five years is very short term indeed—perhaps only the time taken to get permission to sink a mine and the initial decision will be looking more than 20 years ahead.

The Tools of Long-Range Planning.   The methods used are mainly qualitative, but this does not mean that price tags with the most exact figures possible are not required. No decision will be made without an estimated return on investment and some quantitative forecasting techniques will be used to assist with this. Increasingly used is scenario-writing, describing the likely situations in which the company may find itself in relation to various changes in the environment. Different companies adapt the technique to their own circumstances, but a typical engineering or chemical concern is likely to start with a look at the prospects for technical change over the next 10–15 years. For this, the planners are dependent on the research-and-development department. Changes in the market are also considered in the countries in which the company already operates, together with the prospects in other countries. The report includes long-term possibilities for new manufacturing or selling facilities, and the rationalization of the old. Desirable lifetimes for the company's assets are considered. Each scenario, although drafted in general terms, contains a general statement of funding requirements and expected income. Even at this stage the income may be stated in terms of the expected, the best-possible, and the worst-conceivable, requirements and results. The scenarios are constructed from information much of which is external to the company—changes in technical, commercial, economic, social, political, and other factors that are likely to affect the business. Each scenario is then considered in the light of the company's strengths and weaknesses and those of the principal competitors. The story of business in the last 30 years has been full of incidents in which a number of manufacturers have seen a coming gap in the market that they have all moved in to fill. Industry sectors such as basic chemicals and steel have suffered from heavy overcapacity and the resultant losses for individual companies. Hence the planner asks himself how the competitors are likely to react, and who is best placed to win if a commercial war breaks out. Among the techniques for company and competition analysis internationally is the use of a matrix diagram that relates the strengths and weaknesses of the company being analyzed to the opportunities and threats in the environment. Exhibit 2 gives a simplified example of how such a diagram can be designed. In this case a small selection of issues is included for illustrative purposes, and pluses and minuses show the advantages and disadvantages. In actual use, the selection and ordering of the factors would be more systematic, and a number of symbols would be used to identify the most- and the least-advantageous situations and a range in between. From this exercise a list of eligible strategies can be brought together concerning *what* the company is most likely to achieve, to be followed by other strategies suggesting *how* these can be carried out. The resultant report with its recommendations is summarized and handed to the corporate decision-making body. Once this body has decided among the proposals, the next stage of the planning can follow.

The Advantages.   The long-term planning exercise is expected to provide the following:

1. A stimulus to a more detached view about the company's future, since wishful thinking can be a poor adviser.
2. A guide to routine decisions, since the unguided acceptance of opportunities can mean disaster later.
3. An indication of the timing for further decisions and preparations, since delay can destroy a chosen policy.
4. The ability, even for the smallest company, to ensure that corporate resources are used to the greatest possible advantage.
5. A framework for assessing the information constantly becoming available both from inside and outside the company.

PLANNING FOR THE MEDIUM TERM.   Basic decisions have now been made about the strategy, and its transition into tactics is being undertaken.

Translation.   General schemes for the future of the company have to be turned into programs for operating departments, and a decision to enter a particular market

EXHIBIT 2 STRATEGY-FORMULATION MATRIX[a]

Opportunities and Threats in the Environment	Company Strengths and Weaknesses					
	Successful Contracts in Middle East	Limited Sources of Funds	Strong Research and Development	Weak Presence in Europe	Much-Improved Distribution System	Spare Management Resources
Middle East market increasing	+ +					
Steep increase in funding requirements anticipated		– –				
Technological change becoming less important			– +			
Competitors' products unsuccessful in Europe				+ –		
Fast deliveries required					+ +	
Diversification opportunities						+ +

[a]A similar chart, elaborated to any degree required, can be drafted for the company itself and for its competitors.

must be translated into requirements for facilities and finance. Firm recommendations are made that will determine priorities for a long time to come. The route to a market may be through export, licensing, or investment. Each of the three routes has many subroutes and numerous related decisions. The decisions themselves have different time scales. For instance, investment through starting a new subsidiary from scratch has one set of planning implications. Such an exercise begins with the choice of a site; whereas, if an existing company is to be purchased, a lengthy and painstaking search for a suitable candidate may be involved. If the financing requirements of a project mean a new equity issue, to take a different kind of example, another long wait may be necessary before the money market is ready for the placement on suitable terms. In the process of working out the tactics, all the implications of the decision are considered and systematically turned into medium-term plans for each of the departments concerned.

The Tools of Translation Planning.   The methods used are a mixture of the quantitative and nonquantitative; there is a special emphasis on capital requirements supported by income forecasts, market-share proposals (and the costs of achieving them), and timing. In some companies the timing is specified in a policy statement containing preferred timings for each major activity from two to five years ahead. Every year the plans are moved further ahead while the current year, or whatever period of time is determined, moves into the sphere of operational planning and budgeting. A number of techniques are available to the medium-term planner, and these will be more quantitative than those used by his long-term colleague and will include econometric models, but the figures will be accompanied by general appraisals of the situations under discussion. The techniques include simulation and decision models, in which computer programs are used to show the financial outcomes of the various options. Contingency models are employed in conjunction with the simulations to keep in view the various factors that can affect the outcomes, and criteria are drafted to ensure that the decisions taken are in line with the objectives.

The Advantages.   The company derives a number of benefits from medium-term planning, including the following:

1. A systematic list of deadlines for the progress of a project for both general and departmental decisions and actions.
2. A set of guidelines for appraising opportunities as they arise together with approaches from would be collaborators.
3. Further guidelines for coping with problems that might otherwise deflect the company from its objects.
4. Tactics to meet reactions on the part of competitors.
5. A means of undertaking complicated international logistic exercises with manufacturing units that purchase their supplies from a number of countries and then dispatch their products to numerous other countries. Some of the suppliers and some of the customers may be within the same company, and all the countries may have restrictions on the free movement of goods across their frontiers.
6. Formulas for bringing together the resources of the company into a common decision system.

In general the translation is more complex and specialized than the earlier or the later stages, and it is here that the advantage of employing professional corporate planners is first likely to become obvious.

SHORT-TERM PLANNING.   The final stage is to turn tactical decisions into plans that can be carried out in each operational unit of the firm. This stage is that of implementation.

Implementation.   Precise lead times are now required for the ordering and the delivery of equipment or components and the completion of buildings, renovations, market research, and selling plans, as well as numerous other related activities. The deadlines are carried as far forward in time as such accuracy is possible, but the first year's plans are turned into budgets according to a regular annual procedure. The proposals for the route abroad, determined by the medium-term planners, are turned into courses of action for the selection and appointment of agents or licensees, or for the formation of subsidiaries. Naturally not all the intentions are carried out within the time scales of short-term planning, and some are labeled "search," with contingency plans ready if some decision has to be postponed for lack of a suitable collaborator in the chosen market.

The Techniques.   The short-term planner has a battery of techniques at his disposal, most of them quantitative. Included are short-term forecasting methods that enable him to identify supply and financing opportunities in detail. Similar techniques enable the operations to be geared to seasonal changes and to those of the trade cycle. Market research, which is also used in the earlier stages for more general purposes, is used at this stage for final decisions about the presentation of the product. One of several forms of network analysis (diagrams designed to show accurately how different activities interrelate) and other scheduling techniques are used to determine precise deadlines for deliveries, funding, establishing facilities, preparing the market, and the launch of the product.

The Advantages.   At this stage of the planning, unlike the two earlier stages, few doubt that the advantages are self-evident. Money can be saved by ensuring that purchases are not made too soon and loans are not acquired (with the interest attached) before they are needed; there is the equal necessity of avoiding expensive delays when some part of the program is late. Any argument at this stage is about the techniques rather than about the purposes of the planning. The small company should take advice, as the wrong technique or a misinterpretation of facts can be expensive. The larger company is likely to possess its own experts on these subjects.

The advantages of individual elements in the planning process have been suggested, the next section looks at the benefits the company can expect from the planning process as a whole.

THE ROLE

THE PROVISION OF CRITERIA.   The arrival of opportunities cannot be planned, but it can be foreseen, and a reception prepared. A set of guidelines can be formulated to assist in making a judgment about whether a particular opportunity is to be welcomed or whether it is to be regarded as a trap—a short-term advantage that would hinder longer-term developments. The guidelines should be as detailed as possible. Even so, no proposal can be expected to fit all the criteria, but a decision can be taken according to the importance of those that are not met.

Principal factors on the list are the following:

1. *Income.* If accepted, the income (discounted over the life of the project) has to fit the profit objectives of the company.

2. *Growth.* Similarly, some statement of anticipated growth is required.

3. *Synergy.* The proposal needs to fit with the company's existing business. The word *synergy* is often used by planners to indicate the degree of mutual advantage to be found between the suggested operation and the existing activities of the company. In developing the detailed criteria, the synergy heading should be subdivided into the relationship between the project under consideration and each subsidiary, division, and specialist department. Although prospective income is seldom ignored, a proposal that is only marginally adequate by return-on-investment forecasts may be worthwhile if it contributes to the profits of an existing part of the business. A high-technology company may set up a subsidiary in a country where relevant expertise exists without the hope of making much impact in that country; the intention is to derive benefits that will be put to profitable use in other markets.

4. *Market.* A calculation has to be made about market share, sector, and segment to ensure that the new product matches existing capabilities and new opportunities.

5. *Industry sector.* Another group of criteria limits the industry sectors and types of technology.

6. *Time scales.* Preferred time scales are stipulated to ensure that a mixture of long- and short-term projects are made available as required.

7. *Size.* The size of the project is fixed to some extent. This is determined in the light of a decision about whether it is more opportune, in the current state of a company's development, to spread the corporate risk among a number of small undertakings or to concentrate on a few larger ones.

8. *Resources.* Another group of criteria ensure that existing resources, including the staff, will be used to their best advantage.

9. *Nature.* The detailed nature of the project is specified. If, for instance, there is a proposal to buy a company, then another set of criteria is required specifying the minimum requirements for a company that is to be purchased.

Numerous other factors will be listed among the criteria; their systematic consideration before a proposal is accepted is essential and the planning department is well-placed to carry this out. The next element in the role provides a reason why it is so well placed.

THE OBJECTIVE VIEW. Presenting a detached view of a firm's prospects is a function of the planner. Already mentioned in connection with long-term planning, this is required at the other stages as well. Naturally the detachment is more easily achieved when the planner is full time. If he is also a member of line management, he will find it harder to step out of the biases and the vested interests that are part of his life to take an objective view of his company's prospects. Even the full-time planner often finds himself immersed in corporate politics, or in considerations of personal advancement, that make detachment difficult. Nevertheless, there are obvious advantages to the company in possessing an ability to look at the situation as a whole, as if from the outside, and the use of techniques that resist manipulation will aid such a look. This is one reason for the search for greater quantification in forecasting, but the doubtfulness of the figures and the weakness of some of the gimmicks employed make them liable to manipulation when long-term considerations are at stake. In the end, and when all the aids have been recognized and adopted, objectivity depends on the professional conscience of the planner.

THE LINKING.   The planner is able to take an overview of the company's business and point out the weaknesses in the structure. Managers all the way up the hierarchy hold appointments that limit them to certain aspects of the business. The appointments may concern a corporate function, like marketing, or the management of a specific product, or operations in a particular part of the world. The managers are intended to champion their own departments, and are judged according to their successes. This is the time-honored means of managing any organization, and the allocation of responsibilities entailed is usually regarded as essential. But such an allocation does contain divisive pressures. Strong leadership in one unit may advance the interests of that unit against the well-being of the whole company. This is a special difficulty in an international firm, where the contribution that the many parts make to the whole may be obscure, as well as dependent on a number of assumptions about longer-term advantages. The planning department can be expected to provide an overview of all operations so that more rational decisions can be taken about where the company will place its resources.

THE BALANCING.   The twin activity to linking is balancing. The international firm has a variety of facilities and markets, and therefore has numerous logistic questions to answer. There is always scope for improving the supply-and-distribution systems. The balancing of other systems, already mentioned under "Implementation," is of special importance but many other operations have to be balanced as well. Already mentioned under implementation, this is important at all the stages of planning, but balancing includes other issues as well. For instance, rationalization across frontiers is frequently a profitable option but one that is hard to carry out. A concentration of manufacture for a particular product in one country can be desirable on economic grounds but difficult to implement when the closure of a plant in another produces a politically explosive situation. The planner can first determine the measure of rationalization that is desirable, to ensure that the opposition is worth provoking. After that, steps can be worked out to minimize and meet any problems that may arise. One large electrical manufacturer spent years on the careful planning of an international rationalization program. The plans included consultation with the relevant interests, thus ensuring that opposition which could have caused costly delays later was reduced to a minimum.

In order to provide balancing, linking, objectivity, and criteria, the planner requires a considerable amount of information. One aspect of his job is that of determining how to collect and process the necessary data.

THE INFORMATION

THE FLOW, THE SPASM, AND THE SIGNAL.   The tools of corporate planning require facts, sometimes in large quantities. A principal objective is to reduce the mass of information to a limited number of indicators that can be used as guides to decision making. The word *flow* is used to suggest that a continuous supply of information is being poured into the planner. In practice this is not the way things happen. The data arrive in *spasms,* snowstorms they have been called, since the searches are spasmodic, not continuous. It is not usually possible to maintain a general system of monitoring the environment. Such a system is frequently proposed, but is found to be too expensive; most companies have sufficient difficulty coping with the information required for a particular decision. The planner converts this limited information into signals for action.

The most efficient exercise would be that which could detect the signals in the first place without collecting the information. This may occur sometimes, but usually data have to be collected and sifted to produce a convincing case.

The Cost of Information.   The first requirement in determining the information to be collected for corporate planning purposes is a policy about the cost. The common arrangement whereby this fluctuates according to the prosperity of the company is wasteful when all is well and unreliable at other times. A satisfactory arrangement is one that ensures a minimum supply of information related to the size of the firm, with a full-time specialist appointed as soon as growth warrants. The person appointed should be briefed to observe signs rather than to assess data. Whatever the size of the information budget, this should be increased to match the needs of specific projects. There is a formula for determining the viable cost of information in relation to a particular project. The calculations are made in the light of the amounts at stake. If the risks are low (say a maximum loss of $1 million if the project fails) but the rewards are high (an income of $10 million in the first three years of operation), then an estimate of 1–2 percent of the project budget for information costs would be reasonable. If the rewards are less and the risks greater, then a smaller information cost would be all that could be justified. If, on the other hand, the rewards are higher (say $100 million income over three years) and to fail would carry the risk of bankruptcy, then 5–6 percent of the project budget would be allocated to information collection. These figures are, of course, only broad indications. The actual figures used in a particular company must depend upon its size. The possibility of overwhelming success or disaster is the factor for determining the viable cost of information, not the desirability of knowledge. The purpose is to reduce the gambling element; the information available can never ensure certainty.

Indications of Change.   For the international planner, the cheapest and most reliable information is that which signals change: one market beginning to improve, another to decline; one product at last showing greater potential, and other such general indications. More specifically, the armaments manufacturer watches the national budget while the producer of educational equipment looks out for changes in the birth rate or the law on the school-leaving age. Such indicators often produce little response because they do not signal urgently enough. Attention may be concentrated on current crises while important trends are overlooked. By the time the signs are noticed, they are also obvious to competitors, and any response has become more difficult and less profitable. The search for the early warning is a vital and frequently inexpensive element in the data-collection system.

THE QUESTIONS TO BE ANSWERED.   The purpose of the information is to answer questions, and these will be of a number of kinds:

1.   What evidence is coming to light that offers fresh opportunities or threatens disaster? The difficulty, as has just been suggested, is to receive this information—especially when it comes from abroad and may therefore seem less urgent than it is. Guidelines can be issued and duties allocated, but perhaps the most-effective means of overcoming the difficulty is to ensure that there is always time at meetings, always space on agendas, and always some listening time available. A few minutes wasted is better than ignoring important messages.

2.   What evidence is available for a particular long-term project? How reliable, or how available, is the evidence? Can it be employed in connection with the techniques being used? The answers to these questions enable some calculations of costs related to the issues at stake to be made.

3.   What information is required for the tactical and operational planning of the project? This question can be broken down into general and departmental issues. The markets and the competition will have been identified and will now require a closer look. The general view of the prospects will have to be broken down into the following:

   a.   *Financial statements,* detailed presentations of the way the new product or national market can be expected to contribute. The financial planning will include the measures to be taken to ensure, as far as possible, that the expected amount of money can be remitted home at minimum cost in delays or tax deductions. If a new subsidiary is to be founded, decisions about its financial structure will depend on knowledge about the local money market, the banking system, relevant legislation and the possibility as well as the desirability of moving funds within the company.

   b.   *Marketing requirements* in addition to those that have already been assessed, like the size of the market and the state of the competition. A more detailed market study will be required to demonstrate the changes, if any, that are needed in the presentation of the product and its promotion. Knowledge about the distribution system in the country and how the customer is usually serviced will also be sought.

   c.   *Technical information* will be needed if local manufacture is anticipated, and the extent to which the subsidiary will fit into local industry has to be assessed. The equipment available locally and its sophistication will also be studied. The production manager will require information on the availability of staff at all levels and the state of labor relations.

SOURCES OF INFORMATION.   There are two sources of information available to a company, the *internal* and the *external,* and both can be provided *orally,* by *documentation* or through a data base. Studies have shown that most corporate decision making is based on facts generated internally, and that for external information, oral sources are preferred. Keegan (1974) states: "Businessmen clearly rely very much on information that is not contained in the literature and must have, to be effective, a network of human . . . sources." The construction of such a network by the international corporate planner enables questions to be answered by phone, and can reduce considerably the time taken in documentary searches—even if some additional information from documents is required. The personal sources can be tested, their reliability gauged, and replacements made if necessary. They can also be cross-questioned. Nevertheless, biases and prejudices influence the advice given, particularly when the nuances of foreign markets or the characteristics of local labor are being discussed.

The internal documentary sources, which can also be cross-questioned since they originate from foreign employees of the firm, are derived mainly from the control system. The planner, as well as the accountant, helps to decide the items on which reports are required. To the financial data are added items of market information, especially on sales and market share. Figures for production—including machine utilization and delays, labor quality and turnover rates, training requirements, and other relevant facts—can also be demanded.

Some problems of using the control information as the basis of the planning information do have to be recognized. One is that data from this source relate to the past and may be misleading in considering the future. At the least a trend, such as the increasing success of a particular product, should be carefully examined before resources are committed. Another problem is the influence on the subsidiary of pressure to collect information not required for its own business. This can imperil its efficiency.

External documentary information is another source, and is provided in a variety of ways—customers, banks, suppliers, and general contacts perhaps operating on a reciprocal basis. The criteria are the ability to meet the requirements suggested earlier in this chapter to provide adequate signals for action at a viable cost, ability to provide an objective check against the information received through the internal and oral routes, and accuracy and costs within fixed limits.

Some of the most useful literature comes either free or at a trivial expense from sources like banks, embassies, trade associations, and the International Monetary Fund. In the next rank come a few indispensable reference books like the *United Nations Yearbook* (beware the dating of the information) and the publications of the World Bank, the International Monetary Fund and the Organization for Economic Cooperation and Development. Finally, there are the commercial reference books—the *Europa Handbooks* are among the most reliable—and the news services, of which the various publications of Business International are the most useful for the professional corporate planner. An indexing system is required to make the best use of the information and to record where it can be found when required again. Advice on appropriate systems, which should be stored on a computer, is easily obtainable, but the arrangements finally made should be personal to the company. Increasingly, the information can be bought in machine-readable form, and the costs are often far less than the labor costs of library searches.

THE PLANNING DEPARTMENT

FUNCTION. "Planning may be as old as thinking man, but as a recognized part of the equipment of the business firm and with its own organization it is relatively new"

(Brooke and van Beusekom 1979, p. 211). A number of approaches to the role have already been discussed. The place of the planning department itself may be understood in relation to its *level* in, and its *degree* of involvement with, the management system of the company. *Level* refers to the position at which the planning department is slotted into the organization. This may be near the top, as an advisory service to the chief executive; at the divisional level; at the subsidiary level; or at any combination of the three. Once the planning function develops, departments emerge at many levels with or without a common organization. The degree of involvement, or the amount of detachment, is likely to be related to the level. The advisory service to top management is mainly objective: The planners are not expected to be concerned with implementation. The lower-level service, which is usually introduced first, is concerned with implementation—ensuring that the implications of longer-term commercial decisions are carried out systematically—and with conducting a search for acquisitions. This last, often a specific duty given to the planning department, is a wasteful confusion of role in an international context. The planner is best employed performing the other activities already outlined—providing the objective standpoint, the linking, and the balancing—while the search for acquisitions is carried out by line management within the framework of whatever international organization the company possesses. The planner provides guidelines and lead times to assist the line manager, and he determines the criteria for purchase, not the companies to be bought. Some aspects of the work of the international planner emerge in a simple example. Assume that an agreed-upon strategy includes developing two products extensively in Latin America, on the grounds that the income objectives for those two products are most likely to be achieved on that continent. Assume also that the company already has extensive business in six of the Latin American countries, this business is in other products as well as the two selected, and it is being conducted at present through a large number of licensees, agents, sales offices, and other outlets. Assume finally that tactical guidelines are developed that include a rationalization of the various outlets and the purchase of an existing company that can manufacture the products in the area and undertake a major thrust into its own national market, to be extended to other countries later. As soon as word of this policy gets around, the company is going to be inundated by agents, licensees, and others proposing that they become the subsidiary and with plans for the rationalization. In the end, the company may appoint consultants to advise on a suitable firm, after first determining which is the preferred country, or may use an internal team for the purpose. This is a task that is not suitable for the corporate planning department. If it does become involved, there will be no unit that is not subject to the immediate pressures, for and against a particular acquisition or agency, and that is able to ensure that objectives and tactics are fulfilled. The decisions will be made in any case; but the profit contribution from Latin America is likely to be watered down if the planning department does not retain its ability to judge objectively, to balance, and to link. The department plans the implementation and provides the criteria for the final decisions, but leaves the actual selection of units for sale or development to others.

The second element in the department's function is complementary to the first; it is to involve the implementer in the global planning. The planning process internationally consists of much travel and many meetings, so that the benefit of the local unit and its specialized knowledge is fully considered and makes the greatest possible contribution to the well-being of the whole concern.

Other activities vary with the stage of the planning process. In the early stages, the long-range planner stands by the central decision maker with his overarching view of the corporation, while the implementation planner provides a service to the operating managers. At every stage some equilibrium has to be achieved between a planning system that destroys local initiative and that which fails to realize the international potential. If this task is found to be easy, then it is probably not being fulfilled.

ORGANIZATION.   There are a number of ways of integrating the planning department with the rest of the organization. Essential is that the department be treated as an independent unit answerable to general management at the relevant level.

The most-useful services of international planning will not be provided if the planners report to marketing executives. Among companies with separate planning functions, there are two main forms of organization. In Exhibit 3 these are called *integrated* and *group*. The relationships of planning with the other departments are shown in the diagrams, and the main characteristics of each type are discussed in the following sections.

Integrated.   This is an arrangement whereby the planning department is organized as a whole throughout the company, with a section attached to the head office and

EXHIBIT 3   THE PLACE OF THE PLANNING DEPARTMENT IN THE CORPORATE SYSTEM: (a) INTEGRATED (ONLY P₁ IS INVOLVED IN LONG-TERM PLANNING; P₂ IS MAINLY IMPLEMENTATION.) (b) GROUP (P₁ AND P₂ ARE BOTH INVOLVED IN ALL TYPES OF PLANNING AS RELEVANT TO THEIR UNIT. THE CONTACT BETWEEN THEM IS INFORMAL.)

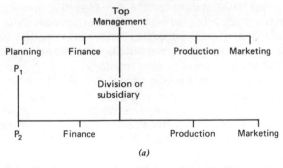

(a)

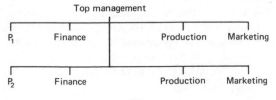

(b)

one to each of the divisions and subsidiaries. The department is integrated in that the manager in charge at the head office is also in charge for the whole of the company; there will be considerable division of labor between the units; each will play a different part in the stages of planning and may have special product and geographic interests as well. The actual relationship to the subsidiary management will vary from company to company, but usually the local chief executive will be in charge with a strong link to the center, as is shown in Exhibit 3.

Group.   The other method is for each unit to have its own planning organization, which is unspecialized and performs any functions the local management may require. Links with the center are weak.

SELECTION OF ORGANIZATION TYPE.   The type of organization chosen by a particular company depends on many factors unrelated to planning—industry sector, background, management style, and so on. From the point of view of the professional planner, the integrated form has many advantages. There are also dangers. One is that the planning can become overcentralized. Just as the resources of an international group are wasted if there is no strong center taking a global view of resources, so the opportunities will be frittered away if the dialogue with the subsidiaries is weak. The danger then is that planning will develop along esoteric lines remote from the needs of the business. The form of organization needs to avoid this danger, to keep the planners closely in touch with day-to-day management but without damaging their objectivity. Their recruitment and training will be required to serve the same objectives.

RECRUITMENT AND TRAINING.   The professional planner has to earn the right to be heard, demonstrate his skills in a convincing manner, and achieve both the detachment and the involvement demanded of him. As soon as the size of the department justifies it, corporate planning can be divided into two groups—the longer term (strategic and tactical) and the short term (operational). Recruits for the former group will need some business experience and to have demonstrated their ability at making judgments and choosing between options under conditions of uncertainty, with evidence that seldom seems adequate. The job also requires imagination. The recruit may well come from line management and perhaps may expect to return there. He may even be on temporary secondment.

The short-term planner, on the other hand, is likely to have a mathematical background and to intend a career in planning. He will be involved in simple day-to-day practicalities and at the same time with complex corporate models. An ability to handle sustained routine activities is required. For the operational planner, qualifications are more important and personal characteristics less so than for his longer-term colleague.

Part of the training program needs to make the planner more familiar with the other aspects of the business, and a joint program to bring together planners and other representatives of both staff and line management is useful. Other aspects of a planning course include the nature of planning, its uses and phases, forecasting, scheduling and other means of fixing deadlines, planning in functional departments, organization, demand analysis, inventory control, the role of the planner and the skills required, the production of planning cycles, and the collection and use of information.

THE CONTROL OF THE PLANNING FUNCTION. There is no known productivity measurement for the planning department, and planners have no difficulty in resisting attempts to find one. Nevertheless, thorough checks are required in an activity that influences so much of a company's most sensitive activity and brings together action and knowledge throughout the most far-flung operations. Significant objectives of appraisal of planning are the following:

1. To determine the size of the department and what resources can be allocated with a reasonable hope of a satisfactory return. A rough and ready calculation of what a company could *afford,* a full-time planner for $40 million dollars' worth of sales, has already been suggested. The object here is to decide what a company *needs.* For the purposes of determining the optimum size, the department must be considered both as an advisory service and as an insurance. Contingency planning provides some hedges against disaster that would be more expensive if paid for in any other way. The cost of the planning department can be compared with the cost of providing the services by other means.

2. To determine whether appropriate techniques are being used and used effectively. To do this, a checklist of available techniques is drafted, as well as an inventory of those used in the company. Then members of staff are asked to answer two questions:

   a. Why are certain techniques being used and others not?

   b. Why does a particular mixture of techniques exist in the company itself?

   These questions check the planner's knowledge of new developments outside the firm and of what is going on inside. The point of the questions is to make such a check, not to question the planner's professional expertise.

3. To examine the detailed results, this is mainly applicable to the short-term planner in whose case some attempt can be made to ensure that the scheduling techniques have given the correct signals to line management and their suppliers. For the longer-term planner, such an attempt is undesirable; it may affect his objectivity by concentrating his attention too much on the obvious and the predictable. Some list of probable reactions to corporate proposals from different parts of the world can be expected of the tactical planner.

4. To ensure that the role of the department is in accordance with corporate policies and management styles—to ensure, for instance, that the planners are not exercising a centralizing influence when the company is attempting to decentralize.

None of these control objectives provide simple quantitative checks, but together they come as near as is possible to an appraisal of the work being undertaken without damaging the objectivity and detachment of the department. Naturally individual planners will also be subject to any personal evaluation schemes employed by the company. The purpose of appraising the planning function as such is to make judgments on its relevance and expertise. The checks will be carried out on the basis of reasonable assumptions about the contribution the planner can make. The department does not exist to provide some magical insight into the future; it exists to provide a sense of direction for steering through the global opportunities for success and failure.

THE FUTURE

NEW EMPHASES.   The last decade has seen an increase in the funds committed to international trade; the increase proves steep even after allowing for inflation. This growth has occurred in spite of obstacles that were previously considered fatal. Floating exchange rates alone were once confidently said to be enough to destroy a large sector of commerce; but their effect has hardly been noticed even though accompanied by growing national restrictions and escalating fuel prices. The response of business to national economic problems and growing competition has been to seek every available advantage by selling in more markets, seeking supplies from more sources, and funding from as many centers as possible. It must be said that the fact that world trade has increased, in real terms, in every year since 1972 apart from a modest setback is a tribute to the skill of planners, exporters, importers and financial services—the later for devising fresh instruments (including financial futures) to overcome exchange rate problems.

Such developments have increased the need for international corporate planning in spite of the damage to its reputation caused by the first energy crisis. The changing emphasis already noted is likely to continue with more stress on targets and on keeping options open—with carefully calculated deadlines at which particular options have to be jettisoned—and less on detailed routes. This trend will be accelerated by increasing costs. Even with the mechanization of data storage and of the techniques for employing the data, corporate planning will remain labor intensive and will be used with discretion. There is likely to be more effort devoted to reducing uncertainties and less to global scanning. Indeed this latter activity, much recommended in the past, is likely to go out of fashion except where some easily recognizable indicator is being sought in order to forecast changes in a particular market.

One activity that is likely to increase is the use of scenarios, and since this requires specialist skills, some degree of professionalism will be needed. The skills are most appropriately developed inside the company, even on a part-time basis, by an executive trained for the purpose but retaining other duties. If no suitable insider can be seconded, outside assistance may be required. In either case an intimate knowledge of the company is essential. The scenarios will identify the pitfalls likely to be encountered and will enable a number of options to be considered at whatever depth is desired or can be afforded. They will also be as comprehensive as possible in including all the issues that can affect the future of the business, from changing technologies through consumer fashions to government intervention.

Many commentators are preoccupied with discontinuities in the environment—both over time, where new technology has wiped out well-established industries, and over space, where many markets remain bound into established cultural patterns. This preoccupation is likely to grow, and international planners will need to devise new tools to identify where discontinuities are likely to arise for particular products. The competitive advantage will rest with adaptability rather than dramatic innovation, and the ability to adapt will be the subject of increasing pressure.

INTERNATIONAL PLANNING AT THE SERVICE OF THE COMPANY.   The changing emphasis will clearly lead to changing demands on planning services. Questions couched in the form "What will happen if . . ." are likely to be the stock in trade, but the planner will often have to frame the question as well as the answer. He will also provide sets of criteria in the light of which the questions can be answered by others. The place of formal planning in the management system will be partly determined by the size of the company. At any size, companies are increasingly likely to be conducting business across frontiers, but naturally the small (under $100 million a year sales) and the very small (under $10 million sales) will not be able to hire specialized planners for the international operations. Such companies will need to second one executive part time to learn how to devise systems that can greatly simplify the activities abroad and make them more profitable. As the company grows toward the $100 million sales, more resources can be allocated for providing a stimulus and a warning to those units that operate abroad. The ability to set up guidelines for the avoidance of common errors can be a profitable skill. Even before a company is large enough to hire a full-time planner for the international operations, a period in this field may be regarded as a necessary part of the training program for a senior manager. Thus it is possible to appoint a full-time planner for a limited period. During that time the person appointed will devise the guidelines for international management, and the experience gained will still be available to the company when he moves on to a more senior post. Middle-size companies (sales under $1,000 million) will also be concerned with adequate indicators of the problems and opportunities to be met abroad, but will be able to go further in using linking and balancing activities. The planners will spend more time than is usual at present watching the different markets and assessing the effectiveness of the agents, the licensees, and the other foreign collaborators. In the larger companies, much of the international planning will be delegated to the divisions, but training, recruitment, and the development of new methods will be retained at the center.

The tenor of these concluding remarks is that international planning is both necessary and profitable if used correctly. The proper use is not as a supplement to general management, to perform jobs like seeking acquisitions, which no one else wants. Rather the planner should be encouraged to retain his neutral status and provide, if only part time, an advisory service on how the company can fulfill its objects and where it can avoid the pitfalls. In helping to steer the firm, the planner can often be more effective than the outside consultant.

A final word concerns a strategy for the planning itself. The phased introduction of the more-formal services begins by improving the implementation and moves gradually backward to the tactics and the strategy formation. There are, as already suggested, a number of ways of building international planning into the management system. The executive on secondment in the small company, or operating full time in the large one, constructs a network of contacts for the rapid collection of facts when national markets are being assessed or reappraised. He will then ensure that there is some system of assembling and sifting the data; after this, targets for market entry, expansion, or change can be determined. When the whole process has been organized, the balancing and linking functions can be inserted. This chapter has listed the main provisions. With them a company can accumulate the benefits of international corporate planning without undue disruption or expense.

SOURCES AND SUGGESTED REFERENCES

The following is a list of some of the more readable works published since 1976 that are relevant to the international corporate planner.

Brooke, M.Z. and H.L. Remmers. *International Management and Business Policy.* Boston: Houghton-Mifflin, 1978a.

Brooke, M.Z. and H.L. Remmers. *The Strategy of Multinational Enterprise,* 2nd ed. London: Pitman, 1978b.

Brooke, M.Z. and M. van Beusekom. *International Corporate Planning.* London: Pitman, 1979.

Buckley, P.J. and M. Casson. *The Future of the Multinational Company.* London: Macmillan, 1976.

Channon, D.F. and M. Jalland. *Multinational Strategic Planning.* New York: American Management Association, 1979.

Eitemann, D.K. and A.I. Stonehill. *Multinational Business Finance,* 2nd ed. Reading, MA: Addison-Wesley, 1979.

Keegan, W.J. "Multinational Scanning: A study of the Information Sources Utilized by Headquarters Executives in Multinational Companies," *Administrative Science Quarterly,* Vol. XIX, No. 4 (1974), pp. 411–421.

Leroy, G. *Multinational Product Strategies.* New York: Praeger, 1976.

Naylor, T.H. and D.R. Gattis. "Corporate Planning Models," *California Management Review,* Vol. XVII, No. 4, (1976), pp. 69–78.

Steiner, G.A. *Strategic Planning: What Every Manager Must Know.* New York: The Free Press, 1979.

Vancil, R.F. "Strategy Formulation in Complex Organizations," *Sloan Management Review,* Vol. XVII, No. 2, (1976), pp. 1–18.

Vernon, R. and L.T. Wells. *Manager in the International Economy,* 3rd ed. Englewood Cliffs, NJ: Prentice-Hall, 1976.

INVESTMENT INCENTIVES AND PERFORMANCE REQUIREMENTS

CONTENTS

INVESTMENT INCENTIVES AND PERFORMANCE REQUIREMENTS

Micheál Ó Súilleabháin

Since the early 1970s, industrial policy has emerged as an ad hoc grouping of economic policy instruments to take its place beside the traditional and more readily identifiable areas of fiscal, monetary, and trade policies. Because of the frequent switch of its emphasis from industry in general to specific sectors or regions, and because it draws upon policy instruments from all areas, industrial policy proves an elusive concept especially when one follows its development across national boundaries or over time. A common feature, however, is the significant role which industrial policy assigns to investment incentives and performance requirements. In practice, one can find incentives and disincentives (performance requirements) applied singly or in combination. The range and nature of the measures most frequently encountered can be summarized as follows:

	All Industry	Specific Industries	Specific Regions
Disincentives	Trade-related	Trade-related	
	Non-trade-related	Non-trade-related	
Incentives	Fiscal	Fiscal	Fiscal
	Financial	Financial	Financial
	Nonfinancial	Nonfinancial	Nonfinancial
	Trade-related	Trade-related	Trade-related

In general it appears that industrial policy instruments affect both indigenous and foreign firms indiscriminately. This certainly applies to the vast majority of the 24 member countries of the OECD (Organization for Economic Cooperation and Development), comprising Western Europe, North America, Japan, Australia, and New Zealand. Nevertheless, because it is almost inevitably foreign direct investing firms which express resentment of those interventionist measures, the available documentation is predominantly concerned with their evaluation of the situation. That evaluation comprises the following three points:

- the overall effect of incentives and disincentives on investments is quite weak;
- in specific cases, however, their impact can be very substantial;

- international trade and investment would be better off without a system of investment incentives and disincentives.

Whether or not industrial policy intervention is, in principle, justifiable, is a question that does not belong on our agenda. Neither does the question as to whether industrial policy in practice has as yet been adequately assessed in order to form a definitive opinion on its impact. Nevertheless, one seems to be on firm ground in pointing out that

- the motives of emulation and retaliation provide a fertile breeding ground for such interventionist measures;
- their practical administration relies on a combination of rules and discretion that tend to be applied arbitrarily and yield inconsistent results; and
- accountability for such interventions is generally a dead letter.

INCENTIVES AND DISINCENTIVES IN DEVELOPING COUNTRIES

Because the source material on incentives and disincentives (a term which, in the present context, is interchangeable with performance requirements) has been mainly generated in conjunction with investment and trade flows between developed countries, it would seem expedient to clear the ground for a more comprehensive treatment of that material by first adverting to conditions in the developing countries.

The developing countries seem to operate a combination of carrot-and-stick approach in relation to foreign direct investment (FDI) to an extent not commonly found in the developed countries. In a recent survey, Balasubramanyam (1984) has suggested that the incentives offered by the developing countries have been largely ineffective in attracting FDI, while their complex web of controls and regulations may have proved a substantial deterrent. Among these disincentives he has listed entry regulations specifying the sectors and industries in which foreign firms are not allowed to operate; stipulations concerning the extent of foreign equity participation; requirements that existing foreign firms should "dilute" their equity in favor of local nationals; performance requirements covering inter alia export obligations, utilization and processing of domestic raw materials, employment generation and the setting up of domestic R&D facilities; requirements that local nationals should be appointed to managerial positions; and imposition of ceilings on rates of royalty and duration of technology licensing agreements.

In order to give a rough approximation of the proliferation of fairly common incentive and disincentive measures among selected developing countries, and thereby provide an opportunity for more detailed comment on some of the measures, we present, in Exhibits 1 and 2, two tabulations compiled by the OECD from a variety of outside sources. In both cases, it will be noted, we are concerned with trade-related measures only.

INVESTMENT IN EXPORT PROCESSING ZONES (EPZ)

The exhibit is useful as a first approximation of the nature and extent of trade-related incentives, but it cannot dispense with the necessity to probe more deeply if one is to

EXHIBIT 1   TRADE-RELATED INVESTMENT INCENTIVES OF SELECTED DEVELOPING COUNTRIES

	Exemption or Reduction of Import Duties	Tax Exemption or Reduction Exports	Export Processing Zones
Egypt[a]			X
Nigeria			X
Mexico	X	X	
Argentina	X	X	
Brazil	X	X	
Colombia		X	
India[a]	X		
Indonesia	X	X	
Philippines	X	X	X
Singapore	X	X	X
South Korea	X		X
Taiwan		X	X

Source.   OECD utilizing source material dated 1981–82

[a] Egypt and India also offer incentives in the form of favorable foreign exchange treatment

EXHIBIT 2   TRADE-RELATED INVESTMENT DISINCENTIVES OF SELECTED DEVELOPING COUNTRIES

	Local Content Requirements	Limitations on Imports	Minimum Export Requirements	Technology Transfer Requirements
Algeria	X	X		
Argentina	X	X	X	
Brazil	X	X	X	X
Colombia	X		X	
Egypt	X	X	X	
India	X	X	X	X
Indonesia	X	X		
Malaysia	X	X	X	
Mexico	X	X	X	X
Nigeria	X	X		
Philippines	X		X	
Singapore	X	X	X	
South Korea	X	X	X	
Taiwan	X	X	X	

Source.   OECD utilizing outside source material dated 1981–82.

get a more adequate perception of what individual measures really signify on the ground. For this reason, we shall pick out Export Processing Zones (EPZ) and throw some additional light on them and the environments within which they function.

The first EPZ was set up at Shannon in Ireland in 1960, following the realization that the commercial development of long-range jet aircraft across the North Atlantic was leading to a 20 percent annual drop in the number of transit passengers using the airport. Fifteen years later nearly as many countries had followed Ireland's example and established EPZs (Barbados, Columbia, the Dominican Republic, El Salvador, India, Malaysia, Mexico, Mauritius, the Philippines, Singapore, South Korea, the Syrian Arab Republic, and Taiwan). In the same year, plans were afoot for EPZs in fourteen further countries (Cyprus, Egypt, Gambia, Guatemala, Haiti, Indonesia, Ivory Coast, Jamaica, Liberia, Morocco, Nicaragua, Senegal, Thailand, and Tonga).

What may be broadly termed the standard package of incentives offered to foreign investors in EPZs, in addition to infrastructure facilities and exemption from customs duties and quotas, comprises:

- tax exemption of more than 10 years (corporate income tax and dividend tax);
- exemption from foreign exchange controls (free repatriation of profits) often up to 20 years;
- deferral of depreciation charges until the end of the tax holding period;
- investment allowances (increase of asset costs for tax purposes);
- preferential financing (subsidized interest rates) for the initial establishment;
- preferential transportation between the zone and the seaport or airport; and
- preferential utility rates, rents, general service charges, etc.

Surveying the position that had been reached by the mid-1970s, Wall (1976) reported that the predominant types of industries found on EPZs were concerned with electronic components, sophisticated metal products (such as jigs and dies), optical instruments, electrical appliances, garments, diamond processing, toys, handicrafts, and food processing. The available evidence tended to confirm the hypothesis that it was the availability of cheap low-skilled workers in high value/low weight products which attracted foreign investors to the EPZs. Balasubramanyam and Rothschild (1985) have put their finger on a related incentive, which characterizes a number of locations. Firms on the Massan Zone in South Korea, for example, receive an official guarantee that their work force will not be allowed to unionize, while absence of wage legislation is a feature of zones in Hong Kong.

This is far from giving the whole story, however, for one must also take account of the 'push' exerted by their home countries on many of those inward investing firms. Pointing out that Japanese firms almost monopolized the Massan EPZ operations in 1973 while, at the same time, they represented the largest group of firms in the Kaohsiung EPZ in Taiwan, Wall (1976) associated this development with the policy of the Japanese government to persuade such firms to move out of Japan and into neighboring, low labor-cost countries in order to maintain international competitiveness, and reduce pressure on labor supplies and consumer prices in Japan. It was a moot point, he added, as to how much of the Japanese investment in these EPZs was attributable to the incentive package and how much would have gone there anyway.

The more general form of home country 'push' is the "offshore assembly provisions" (OAPs) granted by industrialized countries such as the U.S., Germany, and the Netherlands, a convenient survey of which will be found in Finger (1976, 1977). The essence of the OAP is to confine the incidence of tariffs in the industrialized importing country to the value added in the off-shore location to components that originated in the country granting the OAP. McCulloch (1985) has pointed out that even foreign subsidiaries operating in the OAP granting country (e.g., Japanese firms in the United States) can avail of these facilities.

Local content requirements specify that a given percentage of the value of final output must be obtained from local sources or produced locally by the foreign investor. The measures limiting imports, on the other hand, apply equally to indigenous and foreign firms. Performance requirements relating to exports are also very widespread and are occasionally (e.g., in South Korea) linked to international product mandate requirements. In contrast to the preceding measures, the technology transfer requirements are apparently reserved for the three countries (Brazil, India, and Mexico) characterized by very large domestic markets. With a view to putting this measure in its relevant overall context, we now take a closer look at the case of India.

TECHNOLOGY TRANSFER CONSTRAINTS IN INDIA.   India's technology transfer policy tries to strike a balance between the conservation of scarce foreign exchange resources and the promotion of the country's industrial potential. In order to achieve this objective, the Indian government has identified lines of production for which an import of foreign technology appears to be desirable. It has also named those industries where technological cooperation is deemed unnecessary.

Following the recession which affected India in the mid-1960s, the government introduced two important pieces of legislation. In 1969, the Monopolies and Restrictive Trade Practices (MRTP) Act was introduced, which decreed stricter licensing procedures for large companies and foreign enterprises. A few years later, the Foreign Exchange and Regulation Act (FERA) of 1973 exempted foreign equity participation of less than 40 percent from the MRTP Act, while at the same time foreign companies were requested to reduce their equity participation to 40 percent or less. Exemptions were granted for companies with highly sophisticated technology or with a high export share. For instance, a company which exports 100 percent of its sales is also allowed 100 percent equity participation.

Once the preliminary administrative procedures (licensing, etc.) have been complied with, a technology transfer agreement for an approved duration of usually eight years can be entered into. There is a limit for royalty payments in the case of domestic sales (5 percent) and export sales (7 percent), respectively. Lump-sum payments, royalties, and dividends can be freely transferred after they have been taxed (20 percent for lump-sum payments, 40 percent for royalties, and 25 percent for dividends).

In a 1984 evaluation of European experience with India's transfer policy, it was urged that an extension of the duration of technological cooperation and easier royalty terms for suppliers would facilitate a more substantial transfer. The Indian observers, for their part, were inclined to look beyond the transfer agreement terms for a more basic explanation of the limited technology flows. They suggested that if foreign firms exporting technology to India could be given a greater stake in the sale of the goods produced with their technology, a much-improved performance could result. Accordingly, the Indian government might need to take a more neutral role in regulating domestic competition and replace restrictions on the expansion of firms by more positive incentives to firms favored by the policy. In addition, it was felt that initiatives which linked changes in technology import policy to export growth would have a better chance of success (Hoffmann et al.; Alam; Desai, 1985).

A more general argument along these lines was spelled out a number of years previously by Baranson (1978), when he pointed out that the bargaining position of technology importing enterprises in the developing world depends on:

- the economic environment in the country (including the size of the internal market and access to third-country markets);
- the financial position of the enterprise and the economy to fund technology acquisition without foreign equity;
- the role of government in screening and controlling foreign investment, licensing, and so forth; and
- the technical absorptive capabilities at enterprise and sector levels.

The propensity of developing countries like Brazil, India, and Mexico to avail of their exceptionally large market size in order to control the terms of technology transfer agreements was remarked upon at the outset of our discussion of disincentives. In the light of what has been said in the meantime, it should be clear that in pursuing further policy objectives such as the regulation of competition, these countries may well throw up impediments to technology transfers which eclipse the specific disincentives upon which one would otherwise focus.

THE FOREIGN INVESTMENT ENVIRONMENT OF THE DEVELOPED COUNTRIES

Since the latter half of the 1970s, the international environment for direct investment flows from and to the major industrialized countries has undergone a radical change. As Exhibit 3 shows, by the first half of the 1980s, the role of the U.S. in particular had undergone a dramatic transformation. The United States changed from being the predominant source of outflows in 1977–80, when it eclipsed the combined performance of the other five countries shown, to being the most significant host country in 1981–84.

Broadly speaking, the other major countries moved in the opposite direction. They managed to maintain or even increase their already substantial outflows, while their inflows fell without exception. A conspicuously low level of inflows characterized Japan even in the early 1980s, while the inflows to Canada were negatived by an unprecedented degree of disinvestment in 1982 in contrast to which there was a no less

EXHIBIT 3   ANNUAL AVERAGE DIRECT INVESTMENT FLOWS 1977–84 ($ Million)

	Inflow		Outflow	
	1977–80	1981–84	1977–80	1981–84
United States	10,098	18,370	18,098	3,776
Canada	472	−664*	1,901	2,994
Japan	136	258	2,325	4,685
France	2,565	1,954	2,026	2,911
Germany	1,191	986	3,596	3,160
United Kingdom	3,581	2,608	5,692	5,169

Source.   OECD.

* negative flow-back on foreign investments in Canada (disinvestment).

remarkable upsurge in outward investment. In a world recessionary context, international cooperation conducive to a more liberal investment climate was proving more difficult to achieve and, at the same time, more necessary than every before.

The extent to which investment incentives and disincentives tended to operate to the detriment of U.S. firms was already being documented at the beginning of the period just reviewed. A survey undertaken by the U.S. Department of Commerce showed that in 1977 about 14 percent of U.S. affiliates worldwide were subject to performance requirements, while nearly twice that percentage were encountering investment incentives. Tariff incentives tended to be used more frequently by developing countries, while tax incentives were a measure commonly used in all intervening countries. The performance impositions ranged from minimum local labor and local input requirements to minimum required exports and maximum permitted imports.

The incidence of intervention measures in 1977 varied substantially from one industry to another. Transportation equipment proved a particularly conspicuous target for attention: over 40 percent of the U.S. firms surveyed in this industry were affected by incentives, while 27 percent were subject to disincentives. In other industries such as food products, electrical engineering, and mining the incidence of intervention measures was also high. At a later stage, we shall look at the current situation regarding industry-specific measures. Our immediate task, however, must be to identify and evaluate the incidence of incentives and performance requirements across-the-board in the industrialized countries, which in the present context can be equated with the member countries of the OECD.

With a view to documenting the importance of incentives and disincentives in the major industrialized countries, the OECD has adopted the following working definition of these terms: An incentive (disincentive) represents any government measure which influences an investment decision by increasing (decreasing) the prospective profit accruing to the project or decreasing (increasing) the prospective risk attaching to it. As we have seen at the outset, it is usual to classify the incentive (disincentive) measures under the broad headings of trade-related, fiscal, and financial/nonfinancial measures. Given the need to be selective in our discussion of these measures, it is as well to start with performance requirements, for that is where the shoe appears to pinch most.

PERFORMANCE REQUIREMENTS IN OECD COUNTRIES. Expressed in simple terms, the strength of a government or administrative agency facing inward investors can be looked upon as a function of its market size, its proximity to markets competing for similar investment projects, and the emphasis it chooses to give to a regional dimension within its industrial policy. A quick application of this criterion leads us to expect a "give-and-take" arrangement in European Economic Community (EEC) member countries such as the United Kingdom and Italy, in contrast to a "take" arrangement imposed by governments in, for instance, Australia or Canada.

It must be added, however, that the more incisive intervention characterizing countries such as Australia and Canada is viewed by them as an exercise, not of hostile, but of countervailing power. They justify their performance requirements on the grounds that they are necessary in order to frustrate what they look upon as an abuse of oligopolistic power by the inward investors. This means counteracting transfer pricing, licensing and franchising terms, closed procurement arrangements, formal export restrictions, product mandating, and restrictions on the location of certain activities or functions such as R&D. Countries in this class may go so far as to impose conditions relating to technology transfer and international product mandates.

Following accepted practice, one usually distinguishes between trade-related and nontrade-related performance requirements, although the dividing line is quite loosely defined. The three most commonly encountered trade-related measures in the OECD countries comprise local content requirements, relative or absolute export requirements, and in the case of the oil and gas exploration and production industries, bidding procedures. The nontrade-related measures to be singled out here comprise employment requirements, energy use requirements, and commitments in relation to the protection of the environment.

At the level of the enterprise affected, performance requirements, in contrast to incentive measures of a fiscal or financial nature, tend to have an indirect effect on the profits expected to accrue but a direct effect on the related risk. In conditions where technological leadership is more quickly eroded than was previously the case among the world's leading industrial nations, but where world markets are in recession, the potential of performance requirements to deter or divert international investments takes on added significance.

There are two reasons which render the performance requirements more formidable in this case. Otherwise favorable cost opportunities abroad are adversely affected when local content requirements impact on material input costs, while the labor-capital mix is directly influenced by employment and technology transfer commitments. In the intensified competitive conditions of a recession, this occurs at a time when it is not capacity constraints, but rather acute cost constraints, that prompt enterprises to invest abroad in the first place. At the same time inward investors face magnified risks in fulfilling their employment and export requirements under circumstances where control over important macroeconomic variables, such as exchange, interest, and inflation rates, is beyond the capacity of the governments in the host countries.

Let us now single out the nontraded-related disincentives before dealing in greater detail with the trade-related measures. Employment requirements have been reported in respect to Canada, France, Ireland, Italy, Spain, and the U.K. They also occur in Belgium and are usually imposed by the regional authorities. In Sweden, they include commitments to training of the labor force and the protection of employees in addition to employment creation. Conditions conducive to the protection of the environment are found in many countries including Belgium, Finland, Sweden, and the U.S. Finally, there is a variety of conditions imposed in individual countries, such as those relating to energy use in Finland, or technology transfer and R&D expenditures in Austria.

The trade-related measures most commonly encountered are set out in Exhibit 4. The four countries which have special bidding procedures in relation to gas and oil exploration and production seek to ensure equal opportunity for local firms to provide goods and services on a competitive basis and develop this sector of their economies.

In at least five of the countries which impose local content requirements (Australia, Austria, Canada, Greece, and Spain), there appeared to be almost mandatory application of the requirements to the automobile industry. The limited role of local content requirements in European countries is due, to a large extent, to the fact that discrimination among the member countries of the EEC is incompatible with the Treaty of Rome. The provisions of that Treaty will have to be upheld by Greece, Portugal, and Spain when they become full members of the Community.

EXHIBIT 4   TRADE-RELATED PERFORMANCE REQUIREMENTS IN OECD COUNTRIES

Performance Requirements	Reporting OECD Countries
Bidding procedures	Canada, Denmark, United Kingdom, Norway
Export requirements	Australia, France, Greece, New Zealand, Portugal, Spain
Local content requirements	Australia, Austria, Canada, Greece, New Zealand, Portugal, Spain, Turkey.

Source.   OECD.

If one leaves aside specific countries like Canada, and specific industries like automobile manufacture, both of which attract adverse comment by the investing countries affected, it becomes practically impossible to identify a consensus view regarding the degree to which the imposed conditions adversely affect the economies of the OECD member countries as a whole. The United States, for example, is apparently not in a position to evaluate the effects of measures taken by other OECD partners because of a lack of empirical data. Germany also reserves its position, while showing an awareness that individual enterprises may be considerably affected and that a few cases may tend to influence general opinion on the negative aspects of the investment climate in a particular country.

In order to highlight the inherent difficulties that beset attempts to evaluate the effect of performance requirements, it is perhaps useful to single out the operations of Canada's Foreign Investment Review Agency (FIRA). The United States has expressed the view that FIRA-approved proposals from 1975–79 resulted in 50,000 Canadian jobs and $4 billion in investment, and asserted the likelihood that some of these jobs were shifted from the American workforce to the Canadian workforce because investors felt compelled to make larger investments than originally planned in order to establish a larger level of production or additional investment in order to meet their local content or export commitment. This kind of evaluation is difficult to accept at face value not simply because FIRA's side of the story remains untold—it never publishes details of the commitments undertaken by foreign investors. A no less formidable impediment arises when one tries to establish the counterfactual position, namely, what would have happened in the absence of some or all of FIRA's performance requirements.

INVESTMENT INCENTIVES IN THE OECD MEMBER COUNTRIES.   In the present section we shall leave trade-related incentives aside on the grounds that they are generally considered to play a very subordinate role in the OECD member countries and have not been recorded systematically. This leaves us free to focus on fiscal, financial, and nonfinancial incentives.

One can study these incentives either from the perspective of the home or host country involved, or from that of the investing enterprise. In the first case, one is trying to quantify the determinants of investment, of whatever origin, in the medium term. Key roles are generally attributed to expected market growth, relative factor prices, and cash flow. The predominant influence seems to be exerted by demand expectations and this factor, of all the three considered, is reckoned to be least sensitive to the stimulating (retarding) effect of investment incentives (disincentives).

The alternative and more fruitful perspective comprises the medium- to long-term growth prospects of the enterprise. Here the focus is on the option of "going international," while the overall decision-making process is visualized in terms of the following five stages, which, as a first and crude approximation, may be considered distinct and sequential:

- the choice of strictly international versus domestic activities;
- the form of the international activities (i.e. direct investment or licensing as against exporting);
- the particular location of the direct investment;
- the size of the investment; and
- the timing of the investment.

There seems to be widespread acceptance of the view that incentives and disincentives do not enter into the calculations in a significant way until the initial "go international" decision has been taken. In deciding upon the form of the foreign investment, there are undoubtedly preconditions and performance requirements in many cases which have to be averted to. In general, however, it is in relation to the location, size, and timing of the foreign direct investment that an important role is assigned to incentives and disincentives. Most sensitive of all is apparently the location decision.

The first step in tackling the location decision consists in differentiating between world regions, which, for this purpose, may often be coterminous with the continents. These broad regions represent noncompeting groups in the sense that one region is a weak substitute for any other one as far as a given investment project is concerned. Prospective developments of exchange rates of currencies most closely identified with those regions serve to reinforce their noncompeting role accordingly as one region's strength reflects another region's weakness.

The second step consists of distinguishing between countries within these regions in terms of market size, taking income as well as population into account. Here one is separating Japan, for example, from small Southeast Asian countries, or Germany and France from smaller countries on the periphery of Europe.

Viewing the "world horizon" of foreign investing enterprises in this way prompts the idea that incentives are most likely to influence the choice of location within regions of a country or among countries in a given world region which are in relatively close proximity to one another and whose markets are of roughly the same order of magnitude. This broad classification does not rule out cases where firms take more than one world region into their calculations when the scale of the planned capacity exceeds the requirements of any one region or when it is a question of bulk-processing raw materials from developing countries for ultimate sale in developed countries.

Incentive Types and Investor Preferences. A detailed table showing the occurrence of the main types of fiscal, financial, and nonfinancial incentives used for across-the-board promotion of domestic and inward investments in the OECD countries in the early 1980s is shown in Exhibit 5. Space constraints have forced the omission of a number of less important fiscal incentives (e.g., tax free reserves and reduced social security contributions) and financial incentives (mainly subsidies on interest rates).

EXHIBIT 5   FISCAL, FINANCIAL AND NONFINANCIAL INVESTMENT INCENTIVES FOR OVERALL INDUSTRIAL DEVELOPMENT IN OECD COUNTRIES

	Fiscal		Financial		Nonfinancial
	Accelerated Depreciation	Preferential Tax Rates, Exemption, Tax Credits	Grants	Loans at Preferential Terms	
Australia	X	X	X		X
Austria	X	X		X	
Belgium		X	X		
Canada	X	X	X	X	X
Denmark		X	X	X	
Finland		X	X		
France	X	X	X	X	
Germany		X	X	X	X
Greece	X	X	X		X
Ireland	X		X		X
Italy	X	X	X	X	
Japan	X	X	X	X	X
Luxembourg		X	X	X	X
Netherlands		X	X		
New Zealand	X	X	X	X	X
Norway		X	X	X	
Portugal	X	X	X		X
Spain		X		X	X
Sweden	X		X	X	
Switzerland			X		X
Turkey		X		X	X
United Kingdom	X	X	X		X
United States	X	X		X	X

Source.   OECD.

Among the fiscal incentives, accelerated depreciation is used in over one-half of the OECD countries, while nearly all of them offer preferential tax rates, exemptions, or tax credits. The financial incentives tend to differ systematically from the fiscal measures in that they are often linked to specific sectors, such as "sunrise" or "sunset" industries, special classes of enterprises (e.g. small or medium-sized enterprises), or specific activities (export promotion, R&D activities, etc.). The preferred instruments are: grants in respect of investment projects, labor training, relocation costs, etc. In addition to these, one finds loans at preferential rates and loan guarantees. Finally, the heading of nonfinancial incentives includes a diverse range of measures extending from specific physical amenities to training and advisory services and government contrasts.

Judging by the views expressed by, or on behalf of, business interests, it appears that grants or other similar financial incentives, which frequently come on-stream with start-ups, have a greater effect than fiscal incentives, the benefits of which begin to accrue only if and when taxable profits are earned.

A second criterion used in evaluating incentives relates to their visibility and/or predictability. Here, the cost of information-gathering will weigh differently with firms, depending on their size and their experience of the incentive system in question. A relatively small, inexperienced firm may favor cut-and-dried, cost item-related incentives to discretionary, project-related measures. The opposite may hold true of firms which are equipped, by experience or consultant advice, to know what kind of deal is "in the cards" as far as they are concerned.

We may note, before concluding this section, that advantages and disadvantages also attach to the different incentives as viewed from the perspective of the host country government. For example, the take-up of automatic incentives such as cost-related cash grants can easily run foul of government expenditure plans. The host country may prefer to offer profit-related incentives but, if only because their practical worth is difficult to evaluate, these incentives may prove less attractive to potential investors, especially when the carrot of tangible up-front benefits is offered to them in alternative but broadly similar markets.

In the light of the evidence available to it, the OECD tends to equate the principal impact of investment incentives and disincentives with an influence on intraregional investment location. More precisely, they are calculated to influence the choice of location within a set of relatively homogeneous and neighboring countries. Also, the economic conditions prevailing since the early 1970s may have rendered firms more sensitive to cost and risk factors, which in turn may imply an enhanced impact for incentives and disincentives.

Industrial Policy Incentives in the Electronics Industry.   In recent decades, the electronics industry has been a conspicuous candidate for government support, particularly in the OECD countries. Its candidature has been based on its significance as a core technology for other industries and its key role in defense and space programs. In the 1950s and 1960s, tariff barriers, controls on foreign investment, procurement practices, and reorganization measures were the preferred instruments used to promote the industry. The semiconductor and computer industries benefitted from large protected home markets in Japan (due to tariff protection) and in the U.S. (due to government procurement). Most trade protection was removed in the 1970s and, thereafter, procurement, investment, and organizational policies decreased in importance. In the present decade, tax incentives and R&D assistance are the preferred policy instruments in this industry. At the same time there has been a considerable degree of direct government intervention for the purpose of achieving mergers or break-ups or making substantial changes in the extent of state participation. In this latter context, conflicts are frequently encountered between industrial and competition policy and the balance between the two is frequently tilted one way or the other by ideological preferences regarding the role of the state vis-à-vis private enterprise.

In the semiconductor industry, conspicuously rapid progress has been made by Japanese firms during the past decade. In the 1960s and up to the mid-1970s, the Japanese industry was protected by closing the domestic market to foreign investment and by imposing import quotas. Thereafter, inward investment was permitted and the degree of trade protection reduced. Joint research activities were begun in 1975 by the leading Japanese computer producers under the auspices of MITI (the Ministry of International Trade and Industry) and NTT (Nippon Telegraph and Telephone). The five major companies were formed into two cooperative associations (NEC-Toshiba and Fujitsu-Mitsubishi-Hitachi) with the objectives of developing VLSI (very large-scale integrated) circuits.

The design effort and capital outlay required by developments in semiconductor production are expected to rise very substantially during the present decade. In the case of VLSI circuits, for example, it has been estimated that the design effort in man-years will, by 1990, have reached seven times the 1980 level, while the cost of a chip-fabrication facility will have risen from $40 million to $100 million. By 1985, as Exhibit 6 shows, the top ten producers of semiconductors, half of which were the Japanese firms we have just mentioned, accounted for over 60 percent of world production. In this field, European firms are distinctly backward and they have sought to hitch on to progress elsewhere by direct investment in the United States, and by joint ventures and licensing agreements with U.S. and, to a lesser degree, Japanese firms in their own European markets.

In the telecommunications equipment industry the top ten producers account for 85 percent of world sales, but in this case there is a notably wider geographical dispersion of the leading companies. Among the top five, for example, one finds a German (Siemens), a Canadian (Northern Telecom), and a Swedish (Ericsson) company. This reflects a situation in which, in Europe in particular, public telecommunications agencies not only control the network infrastructure but exercise a monopoly over permits and design standards. It must be noted, however, that the United Kingdom, France, and Germany have been working to open their telecommunications markets to each other's manufacturers and standardize their products throughout the European Community.

The computer industry shows the highest degree of concentration of all, due mainly to the exceptionally dominant position of IBM. At the other end of the top ten, is one European (Siemens) and two Japanese firms (Fujitsu in the sixth, and NEC in the ninth place). The Japanese industry divides its attention between data-processing equipment and the manufacture of peripheral equipment such as monitors, diskdrives, keyboards, and printers. The former sector divides its attention, in turn, between a home demand which emphasizes large office computer systems and an export demand for large OEM computer systems. Fujitsu, for example, supplies Siemens (Germany) and ICL (U.K.) with mainframe computers, while Hitachi has similar arrangements with BASF (Germany) and Olivetti (Italy). Meanwhile, 80 percent of the peripheral sales are oriented toward the American market.

In general, it is worth noting that recent years have seen both a considerably escalated merger activity and a rapid growth of international linkages in the world electronics industry. A recent OECD study listed a total of 56 reported technology exchange, cross-license, second-source, and joint venture agreements at the international level in the semiconductor industry alone between 1980 and 1984. About a dozen second-source agreements were listed. Present trends favor a further extension of this kind of agreement to transfer product technology and thus allow one firm to make an exact copy of another firm's product.

While tariff barriers to international trade in electronics products have been reduced by some of the major industrial countries in recent years, their example has not been matched by the member countries of the European Community. Thus, as a result of the Tokyo Round and subsequent negotiations, Japan and the U.S. agreed to tariff reductions on semiconductors, computers, and other electronic products. The European Community, however, still levies a 17 percent tariff on semiconductors and there is, in fact, talk of increasing the protection currently granted to microelectronics and telecommunications.

Nontariff barriers, especially national technical standards and regulations, still persist and European countries tend to avail of that shelter to foster their own "national champions" such as ICL (U.K.), CII-HB (France), and Siemens (Germany). In addition to import protection, measures to promote exports have been undertaken

EXHIBIT 6 PRODUCTION SHARES OF THE 10 LARGEST PRODUCERS OF SEMICONDUCTORS, TELECOMMUNICATIONS EQUIPMENT & COMPUTERS 1984/85 ($BN)

	Semiconductors		Telecommunications		Computers	
	Company	Revenue	Company	Sales	Company	Sales
1.	NEC (Japan)	1.95	AT&T (US)	10.2	IBM (US)	43.0
2.	Texas Instruments (US)	1.82	ITT (US)	4.7	Digital Equipment (US)	6.2
3.	Hitachi (Japan)	1.75	Siemens (Germany)	3.4	Burroughs (US)	4.5
4.	Motorola (US)	1.65	Northern Telecom (Canada)	3.3	Control Data (US)	3.7
5.	Toshiba (Japan)	1.37	Ericsson (Sweden)	3.2	NCR (US)	3.7
6.	Fujitsu (Japan)	0.95	IBM (US)	3.0	Fujitsu (Japan)	3.5
7.	Intel (US)	0.90	Motorola (US)	2.9	Sperry (US)	3.4
8.	National Semiconductor (US)	0.89	NEC (Japan)	2.7	Hewlett-Packard	3.4
9.	Matsushita (Japan)	0.87	Alcatel (France)	2.6	NEC (Japan)	2.8
10.	Philips (Netherlands)	0.85	GTE (US)	2.3	Siemens (Germany)	2.8
	Total ($bn)	13.0		38.3		77.0
	Percentage of World Production	61.3		84.9		90.1

Source. OECD, drawing on data from Integrated Circuit Engineering (Semiconductors); Arthur D. Little (Telecommunications Equipment) and Datamation (Computers), OECD estimate of world production.

in recent years. This tends, of course, to spark off retaliation, as when the export financing arrangements of the French firms Thompson and Bull were matched by similar U.S. Export-Import Bank facilities to buyers of U.S. equipment.

The Effect of Incentives and Disincentives in the Computer Industry.   Far from displaying a monolithic structure with a representative growth rate, the international computer industry is characterized by a high degree of diversification under both headings. At the upper end of the market, a highly-concentrated effort is being directed at the production of a supercomputer, while in the middle range, considerable uncertainty has spilled over from the office technology and telecommunications sectors. The most dynamic changes have been located in the lower cost computer range according as semiconductor firms integrated forward, consumer electronics firms switched markets and completely new firms sprang up in the face of relatively low entry barriers (minimum requirements in terms of capital and overall expertise). To these trends was added 'competition from above' as IBM entered the microcomputer market.

The rapid extension of the market for computers and the adaptability of supply resulted in growth rates of exceptional magnitude. Forbes magazine (January 4, 1982), for example, pointed out that over the preceding five-year period a median annual growth rate of 23 percent had been achieved by thirteen prominent firms in the U.S. computer industry, compared to an all-industry median rate of 14 percent. The average growth rate of sales by firms such as Wang, Data General, and Digital Equipment lay in the range of 36 to 46 percent annually during the same period. The front-runners among more recent entrants to the industry, it can be added, were frequently firms that depended to an unprecedented degree on outside vendors while building their own corporate profile on their systems and software superiority.

As we already pointed out, foreign direct investment in the computer industry is predominantly in the hands of American firms when it comes to operating wholly-owned facilities abroad. The Japanese firms have tended, at least up to now, to either expand abroad at an upstream level or to sell downstream products to OEM manufacturers in Europe. One can isolate three key questions that have to be addressed in either case:

- Shall I engage in offensive or defensive direct investment?
- To what extent shall my foreign facilities be joined by trade links with (a) my home base and/or (b) with one another?
- Shall I forge logistic trade links at the interregional level without direct investments at the end of one or more of those links?

Since the answers to these questions have important implications for the assessment of incentives and disincentives in individual markets, it is worthwhile looking a little more closely at them. The term offensive investment means the pursuit of increasing market shares in both the host country and beyond. It is looked upon as a first-best option, undertaken in the expectation of yielding satisfactory profits. Defensive investment, on the other hand, represents the reluctant acceptance of a relatively unfavorable situation in order to keep open an option that may otherwise be jeopardized. It may take the form of the preemptive staking of a claim vis-à-vis rival firms or a move which anticipates a heightening of entry barriers vis-à-vis all inward investors on the part of the host country.

On the question of trade flows that link the foreign facilities with the home base and/or with one another, this is a matter upon which incentives and performance requirements impinge directly. Considering, for the moment, the U.S. home base and foreign affiliates in Europe and Southeast Asia respectively, one gets a triangle, the sides of which can represent one-way or two-way, one-stop or two-stop flows. An affiliate operating in a host country which imposes severe performance requirements would generally be expected to display an antitrade bias.

The third question contemplates the prospect of linking foreign affiliates in one region with up stream vendors in another region. In practice, one is talking here of intermediate imports, not of an intrafirm nature, from Southeast Asia to Europe. In short, it is a question of the extent to which global logistics are planned with a more limited degree of global investments than might emerge in the answer to the preceding question.

To what kind of international investment pattern has the answering of these questions given rise? Miller's contribution on the computer industry to the recent World Bank study on Investment Incentives and Performance Requirements (Stephen E. Guisinger and Associates, 1985) throws valuable light on this point. About half of the eight U.S. companies interviewed by Miller articulated a viewpoint vis-à-vis Mexico and Brazil, which would seem to justify describing their actual or proposed investments in these host countries as defensive. This applies more clearly in the case of Mexico, where a "now or never" issue of timing seems to have been critical. The prospective "infant industry" status of Mexico contrasts with that of Brazil, which for many years has fostered an infant industry that is not in any hurry to grow.

The U.S. presence in Brazil's computer industry is restricted to main-frame computers, for the minicomputer industry, tightly constrained by government policy, has never proved attractive enough to U.S. investors. While the tariff-boosted prices in Brazil are favorable to investors, prevailing performance requirements effectively preclude state of the art technology and the realization of expansion opportunities. At best, it appears that the management of U.S. subsidiaries try to come to terms with an increasingly difficult policy environment in the hope that, in the course of time, a more favorable business climate for foreign investors may be induced.

Europe is the second main region covered by Miller's survey, while Southeast Asia emerges as a kind of optional extra, whether one is contemplating the European context or even pushing on to consider Japan as a host country. Within Europe, a particularly keen contest is fought between Scotland, as a favored region within the U.K., and the Republic of Ireland as potential host countries. While the number of cases on record is quite limited, it does seem true to say that in most of them, whether they relate to U.S. or Japanese firms, the European investments go hand in hand with Southeast Asian investments. As already pointed out, the Japanese investments in this context are of an upstream nature. In other words, investments in world regions (Europe and Southeast Asia, respectively) tend to be complementary while investments within regions (e.g., Taiwan or Singapore, Scotland or Ireland) tend to be substitutable. It is in the latter case that government incentives acquire substantial significance but whether they manage to eclipse market incentives (e.g., the superior discipline and skills of Singapore workers or the size of the U.K. market and its added bonus of government procurement) remains an open question. Company-specific imponderables can tilt a fine balance one way or the other.

**INVESTMENT INCENTIVES AND PERFORMANCE REQUIREMENTS IN THE AUTO-
MOTIVE INDUSTRY.**   In common with the electronics industry, the automotive
industry is dominated by a relatively small number of large firms; it is estimated that
the top ten car manufacturers account for about 80 percent of world car production.
The leadership structure has changed dramatically in recent decades, however, with
the unprecedented advance of the Japanese cars on the world markets. At the same
time the outstanding characteristic of the Japanese presence has been its concentration of integrated production in Japan itself with a logistics strategy emphasizing
"just in time" flows that minimize locking resources into stock holdings. The exceptional mobility of the Japanese exports would tend to make outward direct investment redundant. However, so-called voluntary export restraints and implicit threats
of import impediments in potential host countries have caused the foreign investment option to be reexamined and this point must be borne in mind in assessing the
impact on Japanese investments of the conventional incentives and disincentives.

The principal U.S. firms, on the other hand, have been international in their activities for many decades, partly for historical reasons (government intervention in major
markets and differences in tastes) and, more recently, as part of a conscious strategy to
rationalize and integrate global production, modifying their strategy where necessary,
to take account of incentives and performance requirements.

In order to make clear what the integration of a transnational car production
process entails and how it may give rise to coordinated investments in a number of
countries, the underlying options may be outlined briefly. There are four activities
to be considered. The *first* of these combines the foundry operations, where the
engine and transmission components are cast, with the subsequent machining operations from which emerge the complete engines, gearboxes, and axles. The *second*
activity, characterized by its capital-intensity and durability, is the stamping operation, linked to which is the costly activity of designing and developing the car body.
The *third* set of operations consists of the acquisition of bought-out components. The
production of the latter, which may comprise more than half of the total cost of the
finished vehicle, is distinctly labor-intensive. For example, if one considers the division of labor exhibited by the British car industry in the mid-1970s, for every one-
hundred workers engaged directly in car manufacture, there were sixty workers
employed in other supply and component sectors. This propensity of the car industry to generate jobs in the manufacture of components makes it particularly attractive to countries which aim, whether by incentive or otherwise, to promote inward
investment by car manufacturers. The *fourth* activity, which has traditionally been
labor-intensive, consists in the assembly operation.

If we leave aside the acquisition of components and concentrate on the car manufacture proper, we find that, unless multiple sourcing is desired for security reasons, an
optimum scale of one to two million units can be handled by a single press and stampings plant. Scale economies would suggest the utilization of two engine and transmission plants to provide the same range of output units. In the case of the assembly
operation, however, the number could vary from four to eight plants, depending on
whether one had a throughput of one or two million vehicles (Bhaskar, 1979).

In the case of truck manufacture the order of magnitude of optimum production
levels is a fraction of that which applies to cars. Rhys (1984) has suggested that the
minimum volumes comprise about 40,000 or more for chassis frames and axles,
200,000 or more for cabs and engines, and 100,000 or more for final assembly. The
Daimler-Benz factory at Woerth, West Germany, for example, manufactures vehicle

cabs and complete vehicles in volumes that exceed 100,000 units in a year. The investment of over $400 million that this facility required brought car production assembly techniques to heavy vehicle construction and assembly. For instance, the vehicle cabs were built on a unitary principle in which the same basic parts could be built in a variety of final forms.

The possible location combinations for the major production and assembly sectors yield quite a contrasting pattern, as one contemplates, for instance, the European community or the United States, on one hand, or Latin American and Southeast Asia, on the other hand. Import restrictions and local content and export requirements have impeded the integration of the latter locations into the global logistic systems of the foreign investing companies. What these options look like in practice is perhaps best illustrated by the example of Ford's pioneering moves to establish a complex international division of labor within its corporate organization.

One of the first manifestations of this policy meant a clear shift of emphasis to continental Europe and away from the United Kingdom, which had traditionally been the largest manufacturer of Ford cars, trucks, and tractors outside the United States. At the time of the British accession (1973) to the European community, the assembly capacity and the nature of specialization of the six Ford car plants in Europe was described by contemporary observers as follows:

United Kingdom	Dagenham	300,000 Cortinas and engines for Detroit
	Halewood	250,000 Escorts and parts for Genk and Saarlouis
Germany	Cologne	400,000 Tanus engines for Detroit and parts for Genk
(Franco-German Border)	Saarlouis	250,000 Escorts
Belgium	Genk	250,000 Escorts
France	Bordeaux	Automatic gearboxes and components for the above car plants

During the 1970s, a number of important investment decisions figured on Ford's agenda. The first of these related to an eventual need to produce about one million engines, to be supplied on an absolutely dependable basis to assembly plants in about a dozen developing countries. As the *Financial Times* motoring correspondent pointed out at the time (February 25, 1971), the project was estimated to cost about $100 million, and six sites in continental Europe, Australia, South America, and the U.K. were taken into consideration. The latter country was soon dropped, because regularity of supply was as important a factor in assessing the appropriate location as were wage costs or investment incentives.

The second Ford decision, taken in the late 1970s, also related to engine production but, in stark contrast to the preceding case, the preferred location was actually the United Kingdom. The plant, which was commissioned at Bridgend in South Wales, was required to make the new front wheel drive Escort engine for the whole of Europe. Bhaskar (1979) explains this reversal in Ford policy by relating the 1971 criticism to Ford's experience with British assembly plants, pointing out that industrial relations on the components manufacturing side had always been better, but also adding that the new plant would be highly automated and employ about 2,500 workers, compared to the Dagenham engine plant, then due to be scaled down and switched to diesel engines, which at the time employed 5,500 workers.

In the mid-1970s, Ford decided to venture into small-car production with the Fiesta. Ford had made little impact on the Spanish, French, and Italian markets, and it was hoped that the Fiesta would provide an opportunity to establish a strong marketing base in these and other areas. In order to be in a position to invest heavily in Europe, Ford cut back on model developments in the relatively sluggish American market. How the corresponding location decision was made, along with the two preceding decisions, has been analyzed in the contribution by Hood and Young to the World Bank study (Guisinger and Associates, 1985). It must be pointed out that the contributors to the World Bank study went to some lengths to avoid disclosure of the precise locations chosen. Any implications which we draw regarding the location decisions are based solely on outside evidence.

Hood and Young discussed a total of twelve investment decisions taken by eight manufacturers (three American, three European, and two Japanese). Eight of the decisions were made in 1978 or later, three in the years 1975–77, and one in the period 1974–76. If we leave aside, for the moment, some apparent differences between the Japanese companies and their American or European counterparts, which were observed in other industries also in the World Bank study, a start can be made with some general observations on investments in the automotive industry. According to Hood and Young:

- decision making tended to focus on the continent or region rather than spread over the global horizon;
- within the region a strong pull was exerted by countries with a large market potential but in which the company did not already have a marketing presence;
- where countries of the latter kind were located in developing regions, investing companies were prepared to take a very long-term view in which security of market share outweighed short-term performance prospects; and finally
- at the international level, labor cost differentials did not appear to have any substantial impact on investment decisions.

The Japanese car manufacturers, granted that their experience of alternative arrangements was exceptionally limited, seem to have had little, if any, doubt about the superiority of integrated production in Japan, so that for them investment abroad was at best a necessary evil, undertaken for defensive purposes. This prompts the idea that a large economy, like that of Japan, that resists inward investment, may also tend to generate relatively little outward investment. Rhys (1984), for example, seems to suggest that future expansion by the four giant Japanese truck manufacturers will be based upon Japanese buying-in from an efficient supply infrastructure that has very long production runs, thanks to supplying assembly plants which enjoy a monopoly of their home market. In any case, the three Japanese car industry investments in Southeast Asia/Oceania, the destination of which may be tentatively identified as Australia and Indonesia, were chiefly a consequence of performance requirements. In the first case, these consisted of severe import restrictions and local content requirements; in addition, some unspecified export requirements seem to have applied. While the requirements in the second case were quite vague, they seem to have related mainly to output level and local content. In both cases, certain offsetting incentives were availed of. It is worth noting that in neither case did the Japanese investors consider an alternative destination.

The three investments in Latin America (specifically, it would appear, in Mexico and Brazil) which are analyzed in the World Bank study, cover two engine production facilities and a project involving truck manufacture. The German and American firms, which opted to engage in engine production, were "sitting ducks" in the sense that they felt constrained to justify their continued presence in Mexico and, accordingly, did not contemplate any alternative locations in Latin America. The elements of stick and carrot applied in both cases were similar. The performance requirements provided for imports of materials to be balanced by exports, minimum local content of around 50 to 60 percent, and price controls, to list only the major elements. On the other hand, the incentives comprised 100 percent exemption from duties on imports not produced in Mexico; an export subsidy (15% f.o.b.); subsidized export financing; free land and services free up to site, etc. The European truck maker who opted for Brazil found that his exports could not be internationally competitive despite the incentives, the benefit of which was eroded by high local content suppliers' costs. In general, Hood and Young reported that companies which had experience of conditions in both countries tended to favor Mexico against Brazil. Domestic price controls tended to squeeze profitability more in Brazil than in Mexico; the latter country allowed a choice between increased exports and increased local content, while the former's local content requirement, by including stampings, forced companies to keep the product in existence longer to get adequate volume. Here we may note that a comparison of the alternative investment locations turned not on the categories of the disincentives but rather on the incidence of the differential emphasis placed on those categories. We shall advert briefly at a later point to the implications of nonfulfillment of the performance requirements.

Perhaps the most striking difference between the foregoing decisions and those relating to European locations—we shall leave aside two cases of investments in the United States—was the wide range of location options scanned by the American investors (apparently Ford and General Motors). In fact, the keen competition between the would-be host countries resulted in a bidding process that is probably specific to Europe. Upon closer inspection, the pacemakers in the bidding process seem to have been countries which, like the United Kingdom, wished to salvage some viable operations in its orderly scaling down of the national involvement in the automotive industry, or countries like Portugal, Spain, and Austria, which were still virgin soil as far as the investing companies were concerned. Italy seems to have been disfavored because of labor problems, political violence, and corruption, while France seemed rather xenophobic, inflexible regarding the allocation of sites, and disadvantaged by reason of differences in its engineering technology.

The United Kingdom had played host to both Ford and General Motors (through the latter's Vauxhall subsidiary), but while it had ranked first as a Ford location, the primary emphasis of GM's European operation lay in Germany with Opel. Ford's British workforce was twice that of GM in 1973. Faced with Ford's expansion and rationalization program, GM had, as Bhaskhar (1979) pointed out, three major options:

- to follow Ford into a high-growth area (e.g., Spain). This, however, was thwarted by the Spanish government's veto on GM's efforts to purchase British Leyland's Spanish plant;
- to concentrate on expansion of its Opel operations in Germany and Belgium; or
- to enhance and expand its Vauxhall operations in the United Kingdom.

The third option was discarded, apparently because of the United Kingdom's bad industrial relations and the company's unhappy experience with Vauxhall. Instead, Vauxhall was assigned a stronger role in commercial vehicle production and two components plants were added in the United Kingdom. Expansion in Germany proved difficult in a tight labor supply situation. A second attempt to follow Ford to Spain resulted in the setting up of a major plant in Valencia and a minor one in Cadiz. At about the same time, car engine and transmission manufacture was begun in Austria.

The latter project was looked upon by the government of the host country as a milestone toward establishing a strong Austrian presence in the international automotive industry, although Bayer in his contribution to the Handbook of Austrian Economic Policy (1982) argued persuasively that the costs to Austria exceeded the benefits. The quantifiable Austrian incentive corresponded to about 42 percent of the GM investment, while among the additional unquantifiable incentives were such things as free use of the site for 99 years, tax reductions, worker training costs, etc. The circumstances under which the deal with GM was made cannot be adequately grasped without taking account of the preceding years of fruitless negotiations conducted by the Austrian government with Volkswagen, Chrysler, Lada, and Lancia in the years 1976–77, when Austria was attempting to lay the foundations for a genuine Austrian car manufacture. Thereafter, two years of negotiations followed with Ford, with a view to establishing an assembly plant giving direct employment to about 8,000 workers. When, at the beginning of April 1979, Ford announced the suspension of further greenfield investments in Europe, the Austrian government ended its two years of discussions with that company, and rounded off a little more than two months of discussions with GM with an agreement on the powertrain project in Vienna.

In their World Bank study, Hood and Young confessed some difficulty in accepting GM's ranking of the factors which influenced its Austrian investment decision, namely (1) Market size and growth (country and continent); (2) Intangibles (labor stability, work ethic, political, and government stability), and (3) Incentives. They considered that the incentives were more important than shown, bearing in mind that another multinational enterprise had rejected the country because, in total, the return expected (even with incentives) was well below the alternative return arising from the expansion of an existing plant. To this one can add the point that the entire output of the Vienna plant was dedicated to supplying the GM facility in Spain.

Summing up the factor rankings submitted by the two American companies, Hood and Young report that market access emerged as the crucial factor in most of the non-EC European investments, although, in the case of GM's investment in Austria, the factor was expressed in terms of European market access, which they saw as a reason for investing in Europe and not in any one country specifically. Since the same qualification applies in the case of Ford's engine factory investment in the United Kingdom, the general conclusion would seem to be that market access carried priority in car assembly investments, while incentives took precedence over immediate market size in determining the engine plant locations.

INCENTIVES (DISINCENTIVES) VIEWED BY JAPANESE AND AMERICAN FIRMS RESPECTIVELY

The attitudes of Japanese and American governments and firms to international trade and foreign direct investment (FDI) and, accordingly, their reaction to trade and investment impediments, differ quite substantially. Writing about ten years ago, Kobayashi (1976) pointed out that, at a time when American multinational enterprises were under attack for having exported advanced technologies and even job opportunities, the Japanese were gearing themselves to restructure their industry by purposely transplanting manufacturing facilities abroad. This strategy, which was deemed to serve the mutual interests of Japan and the potential host countries, was directed in the first instance at resource-rich and labor-rich (developing) countries respectively. But, as a position paper of the Japanese Ministry of International Trade and Industry (MITI), quoted by Kobayashi, remarked: "If we are successful in developing new innovative technologies, our investments in technology-oriented industries in developed countries will expand. We find it necessary to do so in order to meet the requirements of, and to realize, an appropriate division of labor between Japan and the Western countries" (Kobayashi, 1976 p. 179).

Reviewing the situations a few years later, Kojima (1978) pointed out that most Japanese FDIs consist of joint ventures, where typically, 20 to 30 percent of the equity is held by a manufacturer, 15 to 25 percent by a trading company, and the remainder by local interests of the host country. Japanese manufacturing enterprises considered themselves inadequately equipped with the management, technological, and informational resources needed to emulate the American multinationals. For important sectors of Japanese industry, such as automotive products, the time to "go international" has apparently not yet come. For example, the Japanese car makers surveyed in the World Bank study were adamant that their investments in Southeast Asia, Oceania, and the United States would not have gone ahead were it not for host country intervention. Their American counterparts, while agreeing that performance requirements were an evil, conceded that increased competition from the Japanese in the absence of such performance requirements was an even greater evil.

In the electronics industry, while Japanese export sales of mainframe computers to OEM outlets in various European countries continue, Japanese FDI frequently moves in step with non-Japanese investments in those markets in the context of either downstream linkages or joint ventures. Japanese pharmaceutical companies, for their part, although world pacemakers in certain fields of biotechnology, have yet to develop an exporting role, not to mention an FDI role. Thus, given the low profile of several important Japanese industrial sectors in FDI, it is not surprising that most attention should continue to be devoted to the American response to incentives and performance requirements and to host country responses to the problems and opportunities represented by the American firms.

Even if, aside from the additional complications arising from performance requirements, one could quantify the relationship between direct investment flows and some weighted aggregate index of the many different incentives that impinge on those flows, one would still be begging the question as to the magnitude of the flows in the absence of incentives. The question and its answer, if such could be found, are cast in such general terms, however, as to deprive them of prescriptive power in relation to any particular country or firm. The more modest exercise, at national level, of a project appraisal such as that undertaken by Bayer in the case of the Austrian car engine project, could not but be more fruitful. As we said at the outset of this discussion, however, accountability of industrial policy measures is a virtue more honored in the breach than in the observance.

SOURCES AND SUGGESTED REFERENCES

Alam, G. "The Nature of Technology Imports in India—A Study of the Main Characteristics and Trends," paper presented at the conference on Technology Transfer and Investment, European Community-India. Berlin, November 26–27, 1984.

Adam, K.F. and L.W.T. Stafford. "Tax Incentives and Investment Policy: A Survey Report on the United Kingdom Manufacturing Industry," *Management and Decision Economics,* Vol 6 (1) (March 1985), pp. 27–32.

Balasubramanyam, V.N. "Incentives and Disincentives for Foreign Direct Investment in Less Developed Countries," *Weltwirtschaftliches Archiv,* Vol. 120 (4) (1984), pp. 720–35.

Balasubramanyam, V.N. and R. Rothschild. "Free Port Zones in the United Kingdom," *Lloyds Bank Review,* No. 158 (October 1985), pp. 20–31.

Baranson, J. *Technology and the Multinationals.* Lexington, MA: Lexington Books, 1978.

Bayer, K. "General Motors in Aspern: Grundstein einer neuen oesterreichischen Industriepolitik?," *Handbuch der oesterreichischen Wirtschaftspolitik,* H. Abele, E. Nowotny, S. Schleicher, and G. Winckler (eds). Vienna: Manzsche Verlags- und Universitaetsbuchhandlung, 1982, pp. 427–40.

Bergsten, C.F., T. Horst, and T.H. Moran. *American Multinationals and American Interests.* Washington, D.C.: Brookings Institution, 1978.

Bhaskar, K. *The Future of the UK Motor Industry.* London: Kogan Page, 1979.

Desai, A.V. Technology Imports and Indian Industrialisation. Paper presented at the conference on Technology Transfer and Investment, European Community-India. Berlin, November 26–27, 1984.

Directory of Incentives for Business Investment and Development in the United States. A State-By-State Guide. National Association of State Development Agencies; National Council for Urban Economic Development, and The Urban Institute. Washington, D.C.: The Urban Institute Press, 1983.

Doz, Y.L., C.A. Bartlett, and C.K. Prahalad. "Global Competitive Pressures and Host Country Demands: Managing Tensions in MNCs." *California Management Review,* Vol 23 (3) (Spring 1981), pp. 63–74.

Finger, J.M. "Trade and Domestic Effects of the Offshore Assembly Provision in the US Tariff," *American Economic Review,* Vol. 66 (4) (1976), pp. 598–611.

——— "Offshore Assembly Provisions in the West German and Netherlands Tariffs: Trade and Domestic Effects," *Weltwirtschaftliches Archiv,* Vol. 113 (2) (1977), pp. 237–49.

Friebe, K.P. and A. Gerybadze (eds.). *Microelectronics in Western Europe: The Medium Term Perspective 1983–1987.* Berlin: Erich Schmidt Verlag, 1984.

Frisch, D.J. and D.G. Hartman. Taxation and the Location of U.S. Investment Abroad, NBER Working Paper No. 1241. Cambridge MA: National Bureau of Economic Research, November 1983.

Gladwin, T.N. and I. Walter. *Multinationals Under Fire: Lessons in the Management of Conflict.* New York: John Wiley & Sons, 1980.

Globerman, S. "The Consistency of Canada's Foreign Investment Review Process: A Temporal Analysis," *Journal of International Business Studies,* Spring–Summer 1984, pp. 119–29.

Guisinger, S.E. and Associates. *Investment Incentives and Performance Requirements. Patterns of International Trade, Production and Investment.* New York: Praeger, 1985.

Guisinger, S.E. "A Comparative Study of Country Policies," *Investment Incentives and Performance Requirements. Patterns of International Trade, Production and Investment,* S.E. Guisinger and Associates. New York: Praeger, 1985, pp. 1–55.

Hoffman, L., H. Reile, H. Sanders, and F. Vardag. Problems and Perspectives of the Transfer of Technology between the Countries of the European Community and India: A Survey of Firms in the F.R. of Germany, France, Italy and Denmark. Synthesized Report presented at the conference on Technology Transfer and Investment, European Community-India. Berlin, November 26–27, 1984.

Hindley, B. "Empty Economics in the Case for Industrial Policy," *The World Economy.* Vol. 7 (3) (September 1984), pp. 277–94.

Hood, N. and S. Young. "The Automobile Industry," *Investment Incentives and Performance Requirements. Patterns of International Trade, Production and Investment.* S.E. Guisinger and Associates. New York: Praeger, 1985, pp. 96–167.

"How Ford Has Invested in World Market Freedom," *Financial Times,* Thursday, February 25, 1971.

Humpage, O.F. "U.S. Taxation of Foreign-Source Corporate Income: A Survey of Issues," *Federal Reserve Bank of Cleveland Economic Review,* Winter 1980–81, pp. 1–18.

Johnson, C. (ed.). *The Industrial Policy Debate.* San Francisco: Institute for Contemporary Studies, 1984.

Kobayashi, N. "The Japanese Approach to 'Multinationalism,'" *Journal of World Trade Law,* Vol. 10 (2) (March–April 1976), pp. 177–85.

Kojima, K. *Direct Foreign Investment. A Japanese Model of Multinational Business Operations.* London: Croom Helm, 1978.

Leibfritz, W. *Steuerliche Investitionsfoerderung im internationalen Vergleich.* Munich: IFO Institute for Economic Research, 1985.

McCulloch, R. "US Direct Foreign Investment and Trade: Theories, Trends and Public-Policy Issues," *Multinationals as Mutual Invaders. Intra-Industry Direct Foreign Investment,* A. Erdilek (ed.). London: Croom Helm, 1985, pp. 129–51.

Miller, R.R. "Computers," *Investment Incentives and Performance Requirements. Patterns of International Trade, Production and Investment,* S.E. Guisinger and Associates. New York: Praeger, 1985, pp. 168–236.

OECD (Organization for Economic Cooperation and Development). *The Aims and Instruments of Industrial Policy.* Paris, 1975.

———. *Report on the Role of Industrial Incentives in Regional Development.* Paris, 1979.

———. *Controls and Impediments Affecting Inward Direct Investment in OECD Member Countries.* Paris, 1982.

———. *Investment Incentives and Disincentives and the International Investment Process.* Paris, 1983.

———. *The Pharmaceutical Industry. Trade-Related Issues.* Paris, 1985.

———. *The Semiconductor Industry. Trade-Related Issues.* Paris, 1985.

Pugel, T.A., Y. Kimura, and R.G. Hawkins. "Semiconductors and Computers: Emerging Competitive Battlegrounds in the Asia-Pacific Region," *Research in International Business and Finance,* Vol. 4 (Part B), pp. 231–86.

Relationship of Incentives and Disincentives to International Investment Decisions, Response of BIAC (Business and Industry Advisory Committee) to the OECD Committee on International Investment and Multinational Enterprises. Paris: BIAC, 1981.

Rhys, G. "Heavy Commercial Vehicles: A Decade of Change." *National Westminster Bank Quarterly Review,* August 1984, pp. 25–35.

Rugman, A.M. "The Regulation of Foreign Investment in Canada," *Journal of World Trade Law,* Vol. 11 (4) (July–August 1977), pp. 322–33.

UNIDO (United Nations Industrial Development Organization). "Export Processing Zones in Developing Countries." UNIDO Working Papers on Structural Changes, No. 19. Vienna, 1980. Mimeo.

U.S. Department of Commerce, Office of International Investment. *The Use of Incentives and Performance Requirements by Foreign Governments.* Washington, D.C.: October 1981.

Wall, D. "Export Processing Zones," *Journal of World Trade Law,* Vol. 10 (5) (1976), pp. 478–89.

Wiegner, K.K. "Computers," *Forbes,* January 4, 1982.

Yuill, D. and K. Allen. *European Regional Incentives.* Glasgow: Centre for the Study of Public Policy, 1986.

OFFSHORE SOURCING, SUBCONTRACTING, AND MANUFACTURING

CONTENTS

OFFSHORE SOURCING, SUBCONTRACTING, AND MANUFACTURING

Richard W. Moxon

One of the fastest-growing international activities of U.S. companies in recent years has been the importation of products formerly manufactured in the United States. Although imports have always been important in some sectors, companies in more and more industries find offshore sources of components and finished products a means of increasing their profitability. As offshore sourcing has spread across industries, it has also spread to countries in Asia, South America, and other developing areas that were not traditionally viewed as exporters of manufactured products. Offshore sourcing today is an important part of business for retailers, wholesalers, and manufacturers in industries as different as apparel and electronics. Grunwald and Flamm (1985) is a good review of offshore assembly, one form of offshore sourcing, with emphasis on electronics.

The motivations for offshore sourcing are usually to obtain lower-cost products. The degree of overseas involvement by the U.S. buyer varies widely. Some do no more than order products from a catalog, whereas others invest time and money in the establishment of their own offshore manufacturing subsidiaries. The main focus in this section is on sourcing in which the U.S. buyer has some substantial involvement abroad, either in subcontracting or in manufacturing. Furthermore, since developing countries have emerged as important sites for offshore sourcing and provide the most challenges for U.S. buyers, much of the discussion will focus on those countries. Finally, the discussion pertains only to manufactured products, not raw materials or agricultural goods.

SELECTING THE FORM OF OFFSHORE SOURCING

ALTERNATIVES. Although the specific forms of offshore sourcing arrangements vary widely, the basic distinction is the degree of control exercised by the U.S. buyer over the foreign source. Exhibit 1 diagrams the four major buyer-seller relationships.

Offshore Purchasing. This is a relationship between independent buyers and sellers in which goods are exchanged for money. The arrangement may vary in many

EXHIBIT 1   ALTERNATIVE OFFSHORE SOURCING RELATIONSHIPS

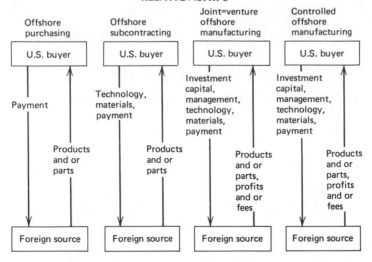

ways, including whether the transactions are directly between the buyer and seller or through one or more agents in the United States or overseas, whether the buyer and seller deal on a transaction-by-transaction basis or have some longer-term contract, and whether purchasing is undertaken by an individual enterprise or by a buying group. Choices among these variations are essentially not very different than they are for domestic transactions.

Offshore Subcontracting.   This term covers many different relationships between independent companies in which the buyer is more involved with the source than in a simple buyer-seller relationship. The buyer may provide detailed product specifications, technical assistance, raw materials or needed components, or even some financing to the foreign manufacturer. Again, such relationships vary as to their duration, the degree of involvement by the U.S. buyer, and whether intermediaries such as agents are involved.

Joint-Venture Offshore Manufacturing.   This relationship involves the joint ownership by a U.S. and a foreign company of an offshore manufacturing enterprise. These arrangements vary by the extent of ownership of each partner, the extent of control exercised by each, what resources each partner contributes, and the specific type of legal entity involved.

Controlled Offshore Manufacturing.   This relationship is that of a parent and a wholly owned foreign operation, generally a subsidiary corporation, that supplies the parent's needs for a product. Such foreign plants vary in how closely they are tied to the rest of the parent's world operations, whether they also serve outside customers, and the legal and financial arrangements.

SELECTION CRITERIA.   A company's decision regarding the form of offshore sourcing it chooses is strongly influenced by what forms other companies in its industry have selected. The needs of different industries vary, and so do their offshore sourcing patterns. In the apparel industry, offshore sourcing is done mainly through purchasing or subcontracting, whereas in electronics there is much more controlled manufacturing. But the needs of all companies in an industry are not the same, and it is important for a firm to look closely at what it is trying to achieve with offshore sourcing, and which form is most appropriate for that objective. Four important considerations are (1) company capabilities and resources, (2) availability and capabilities of suppliers or partners, (3) projected sourcing volumes and variability, and (4) degree of integration of offshore sourcing with other operations.

Company Capabilities and Resources. Different forms of offshore sourcing demand different abilities on the part of enterprises and vastly different commitments of resources. Simple offshore purchasing requires little experience or investment, whereas controlled offshore manufacturing requires a considerable commitment of investment capital and management time.

Investment capital requirements increase as a company chooses to have more control over its foreign sourcing. Even with minimal control, as in subcontracting, there may be a need to help finance working capital for the supplier; controlled offshore manufacturing requires investment in fixed assets as well. In many developing countries, there are methods for reducing these capital requirements, whether through leased, instead of purchased, plants, low-cost development loans, or even outright capital grants from the government. Nevertheless, some investment capital will be required, and the investment will often be in a country regarded as politically and economically less stable than the United States. Companies with limited financial resources or hesitant about "risky" foreign investments will find purchasing or subcontracting more attractive than alternatives involving more control.

Often as crucial as capital requirements is the necessary investment of management time. Again, the establishment of an offshore manufacturing facility normally will require more attention from management than the other alternatives. The actual time investment needed, however, will depend on the type of operation and on the company's previous experience. Time is invested both in establishing an operation and then in operating it. Setting up a simple purchasing agreement normally will require little time, whereas establishing a wholly owned offshore manufacturing plant will require considerable management attention. The time needed to maintain a relationship will depend mainly on the complexity of the interactions between the two parties. If the U.S. company is transferring a lot of technology to the foreign source, or if it owns all or part of the foreign source, the time devoted to managing the relationship is greater. The amount of management time needed to establish and maintain offshore ventures depends also on the company's previous experience with sourcing in general, with the particular form of sourcing, and with the region and particular country with which it is dealing. An experienced company needs to budget considerable time for solving unexpected problems, especially when setting up its own offshore plants.

Availability and Capabilities of Suppliers or Partners. An important determinant of how a company sets up offshore sourcing is whether or not acceptable partners or suppliers exist in the countries in which the U.S. company wants to locate a source. Suppliers with the needed production experience, technology, and management capabilities can be hard to find, as can partners with investment capital and other important inputs. Whether acceptable suppliers and/or partners are available

depends, of course, on the country, on the complexity of the production requirements, and on the size of the proposed operation. Small operations for relatively
simple products may have a wide choice of suppliers or partners, whereas larger
investments for more complex products will be more limited in this respect. This
partly explains why more controlled offshore manufacturing exists in electronics
than in the apparel industry.

Projected Sourcing Volume and Variability.   The size and variability of a company's offshore sourcing requirements will be a major determinant of which form of
offshore sourcing the company chooses. Companies needing large volumes of foreign
products can often justify a large fixed investment, as the fixed costs can be spread
over the high volume of output. For companies with smaller needs, an independent
supplier will be more attractive. The variability of a company's requirements is also
important. If the company establishes its own manufacturing plant, it will want to
keep it running steadily to cover its fixed costs. If the business is variable, the
company will be more likely to choose the purchasing or subcontracting alternatives.
These alternatives are often chosen for fashion-type products, where sales are difficult to project.

Degree of Integration of Offshore and Domestic Operations.   If a company wishes
to integrate its offshore sources tightly within the company's operations, it will need
considerable control over all sources. This will require controlled offshore manufacturing unless a very tight relationship with a foreign company can be established. A
closely controlled offshore operation will facilitate coordinated production scheduling, ease transfer of technology, and provide flexibility in financial decisions regarding transfer pricing of components and finished products, dividend payments, and
capital investments. Many companies that perform one stage (such as assembly)
offshore in a multistage manufacturing process find that they must establish their
own manufacturing facility in order to achieve sufficient coordination. But when a
company can tolerate a somewhat looser relationship with its sources, or when
requirements are so predictable that control is less important, foreign purchasing or
subcontracting is often preferable to controlled offshore manufacturing.

Summary.   The factors listed above are important for any company to consider
when deciding how to do its offshore sourcing. No one method is obviously best for
all companies; a careful balancing of the advantages and disadvantages of the various alternatives is necessary.

EVALUATING PRODUCTS FOR OFFSHORE SOURCING

MAIN COST TRADEOFFS.   Some products are sourced offshore because they are
not available domestically. In these cases there is no alternative to offshore sourcing.
But such cases are rare. In most cases offshore sourcing is chosen because it is
cheaper than domestic sourcing. Whether offshore sourcing is cheaper depends on a
product's manufacturing cost structure, that is, the mix of labor, material, and other
inputs needed in its fabrication. The relative costs of different inputs vary greatly
among countries; the differences are greatest between industrialized countries like
the United States and the developing countries of Asia, Latin America, and Africa.

Some costs are likely to be lower for offshore sources, but others are higher. The best products for offshore sourcing are those that use intensively the inputs that are cheaper abroad.

Labor.   Direct labor costs are often much lower outside the United States and provide the basic attraction of offshore sourcing. Some examples of relative labor costs are given in a later section. The differences are generally greater for lower-skilled production labor than for skilled workers, technicians, and managers, but significant differences exist in all categories.

Materials and Components.   Local and imported material inputs are often an important part of production costs. Whether they are cheaper or more expensive for an offshore source than for domestic production depends on the country; this varies widely among countries and products. In a few cases, cheap sources of materials may be an important attraction of offshore sourcing.

Factory Overhead.   Some indirect production costs will typically be lower overseas, especially those related to indirect labor or the provision of certain labor-intensive services. Other cost inputs, such as utilities or the amortized costs of construction may be higher or lower than in the United States. In the developing countries, net factory overheads are generally lower than in the United States.

Corporate Overhead.   Corporate overhead associated with offshore sourcing includes the cost of headquarters or domestic managers involved in supervising or coordinating offshore sourcing, and travel and communication costs between the offshore source and domestic operations. These can generally be expected to be higher for offshore sourcing. Distances are greater, so travel and communication costs increase. And offshore sources often need more attention in order to assure adequate performance. Communication difficulties occasioned by language and cultural differences may also increase costs.

Shipping and Duties.   Two major cost disadvantages of offshore production are shipping costs and import duties. Sometimes offshore sourcing involves sending materials and components abroad for assembly and shipment back to the United States. Such transport costs can be high, as can the costs of having capital invested in goods in transit. U.S. import duties can also be significant cost items for some products.

PRODUCTS SUITABLE FOR OFFSHORE SOURCING.   Products suitable for offshore sourcing generally are those for which savings in production costs are sufficient to offset higher costs of transportation, duties, and corporate overhead. Although each product must be evaluated individually, certain products are generally more suitable for offshore sourcing. Products that are labor intensive and standardized in product specifications and manufacturing technology, that have a predictable pattern of sales and a high ratio of value to weight, and that are not subject to high duties are the best candidates. These characteristics are discussed next.

Labor-Intensive Products.   Most products or components suitable for offshore sourcing have a significant labor input. Especially attractive are articles requiring large amounts of low-skilled labor, which is relatively expensive in the United States. Finding sufficient numbers of U.S. workers for such tedious jobs as sewing garments or assembling semiconductors has become increasingly difficult. Workers overseas can often be trained to perform such jobs well at costs dramatically lower than in the United States. Often a product can be produced in a series of steps, only some of which are labor intensive. In these cases it may be possible to perform only the labor-intensive operations—for example, assembly—overseas. For example, semiconductor chips are manufactured in the United States in a capital-intensive and technology-intensive process, shipped abroad for assembly, into finished products, and then reimported into the United States. There are many reasons why it may be undesirable to locate the capital-intensive parts of the process in developing countries. Maintenance of capital equipment is costly, exposure to political risk is increased, and it may not be consistent with the employment goals of the foreign government.

Standardized Products. Products whose design, specifications, and production technology do not rapidly change are likely to require less supervision by the U.S. buyer. Changes in product design or technology must be communicated to the source, and such communications are often difficult and expensive. With standard products, once the production technology is transferred, the foreign source can operate with little outside help. It is also likely that the manufacturing process can be routinized to the point where few skilled workers are required and where the number of supervisory personnel is minimized.

Products with a Predictable Sales Pattern. This topic is closely related to product standardization. Products with steady sales, or at least predictable sales, are more suitable for manufacturing than are products that face abrupt shifts in demand. Offshore sources can be given long production runs that can be programmed well in advance of required delivery dates. Little communication is needed between the U.S. buyer and the overseas source, whether they are independent companies or parts of the same enterprise. Likewise, disruptions in supply due to strikes or transportation problems can normally be overcome in time to meet delivery dates. Products subject to rapid changes in sales levels require sources that can rapidly vary production levels and delivery schedules. This is difficult for offshore sources, and disruptions in supply have very serious consequences. For these reasons, fashion products are less suitable for offshore sourcing than more-stable product lines.

Products That Are Easy to Ship and Face Low Import Duties. Products with high value relative to weight (and volume) will have low transportation costs relative to their total manufacturing costs and sales prices. They also may be shipped by air freight, allowing quicker responsiveness to the market. The import duties faced by different products and components also vary greatly. Also, some goods are eligible for special duty treatment, whereas others are not. These duty considerations are discussed in detail in the section on U.S. custom considerations.

TRENDS IN PRODUCT SELECTION FOR OFFSHORE SOURCING. Over the last few years of dramatic growth in offshore sourcing from developing countries, both U.S. companies and their offshore sources have increased their capabilities for managing this activity. Offshore sources have improved their technology, and have gained valuable manufacturing experience. Likewise, U.S. manufacturers and buyers have learned more about working with offshore sources. The result is that more complex products are being sourced offshore. Increasingly it is not just the most labor-intensive products that are made abroad, and smaller runs of less-standardized products have become feasible. Such upgrading to more-sophisticated technologies and to products with higher values is in the interest of the developing countries and the more experienced U.S. and foreign companies.

EVALUATING SOURCES AND PARTNERS

GENERAL CHARACTERISTICS.   Most criteria for selecting foreign companies as sources or as joint-venture partners are similar to those used for domestic business. It may be more difficult to evaluate foreign partners because of lack of information or cultural differences, but identifying partners with desired qualities is essential to successful offshore sourcing. Before selecting a source or a joint-venture partner, it is important to decide what capabilities are required of the foreign company and what kind of relationship is optimal. Many relationships have failed because these requirements were not clarified or because the objectives of the two parties were too divergent. Since many U.S. companies have little experience with subcontracting or joint-venture relationships before moving offshore, and since the opportunity for misunderstanding is greater when the parties are from different countries, it is especially important to clarify objectives before entering into such relationships.

EVALUATING INDEPENDENT SOURCES.   For a supplier or subcontractor, the most important selection criteria relate to the source's capabilities for manufacturing and delivering acceptable products on time at acceptable costs. It is important for the U.S. buyer to define explicitly for itself and the source its expectations in terms of quality, delivery schedules, and expected production volumes and their variability. Next it is necessary to evaluate the source's ability to meet these expectations. Here the company's record in serving other clients is important. A difficulty is that many of the best potential sources in developing countries are relatively young and inexperienced. They have capabilities that are growing and being refined with each job they do, but they may not have a long-established track record.

Sources should also be evaluated in terms of their willingness to be good long-term suppliers. Some firms with the best capabilities may not wish to tie themselves very tightly to a U.S. buyer, wishing instead to diversify customers or to eventually move out of subcontracting into producing and marketing their own products. They may consequently give little attention to the U.S. buyer's needs. It is important, therefore, to raise questions about a source's interest in an enduring relationship.

EVALUATING PARTNERS.   A joint-venture partner should be selected with considerable care, as the relationship is likely to be long term, and requires relatively complex interactions between the partners. First, it is important to clarify what a partner is expected to contribute and its capability to actually make such contributions. A partner is generally expected to bring to the venture considerable expertise in addition to its capital investment. Experience in managing operations in the local business environment is most important. Managing large groups of workers in a developing country demands management skills that local partners may already have developed, and which can be a very important contribution.

Important too may be the government and business connections that a foreign partner brings to a venture. Government relations is often a much more important part of management's job in developing countries than in the United States, and the right partner can provide valuable experience and contacts for smoothing such relations. Nevertheless, a local partner does not guarantee good government relations, and it is important to know how the partner views this function. Clearly it is desirable to obtain as much information as possible from objective sources on the prospective partner's connections and abilities in this regard.

Finally, it is crucial to understand whether the goals and expectations of the U.S. company and foreign partner are congruent. A joint-venture relationship implies joint decisions on matters such as capacity expansion, profit-layout policies, transfer prices, and product diversification, which can be quite controversial if the partners have different objectives. As discussed in Holton (1981), joint ventures contain both mutuality of interest and conflicts of interest, and these must be recognized and dealt with if the partnership is to be successful. Discussing such problems during the formation phase can reduce problems later.

NEGOTIATING WITH PROSPECTIVE SOURCES AND PARTNERS. Negotiating purchasing, subcontracting, and joint-venture agreements with foreign enterprises requires all the same negotiating skills that a domestic venture requires. In addition, however, cultural differences and differences in the role of the host-country government are important to recognize. Bargaining styles differ greatly across countries, and the best U.S. negotiator may not be effective in a foreign negotiation. The hard versus soft sell, the role of haggling over prices, the use of entertainment and social occasions in negotiating, and the value of personal relationships may differ from practices in the United States. Many errors can be avoided by getting advice from people with experience and by reading available material on cultural differences that cause problems in doing business abroad.

The foreign country's government is often part of any negotiation, especially for joint ventures. It may have to give its approval to any agreement that is negotiated, and often will have definite opinions on how the venture should be set up and run. It may also have views on the relative desirability of different local partners. Even if the government is not actively involved, it is important for the U.S. company to understand its views, as government incentives and controls may be crucial to the success of the venture.

EVALUATING PRODUCTION SITES

IMPORTANT CRITERIA. One of the most important decisions related to offshore sourcing is the choice of the country from which to source, especially if a firm contemplates the establishment of its own manufacturing facility. Many factors must be considered in evaluating the desirability of a site; they can be grouped into four categories as follows:

1. Labor factors.
2. Infrastructure factors.

3. Government policy factors.
4. Stability factors.

LABOR FACTORS.   Since labor-cost savings provide the major motivation for off-shore sourcing, choosing a country with low labor costs is obviously important. But low labor costs are of little help unless sufficient productive and reliable labor is available. In fact, since wage rates are so uniformly low throughout the developing world, other factors assume a larger importance.

Labor Costs.   Wages vary greatly throughout the world. Exhibit 2 presents some estimates of wage rates in different countries. Although the data are somewhat out of date, the basic relationships still hold. It must be remembered when making such estimates that the level of fringe benefits is often much higher abroad than in the United States, sometimes approaching the base wage itself. Also savings are often available in other job categories. Many companies find that technicians, engineers, accountants, and other professionals can be hired for relatively low wage rates in developing countries, and that their training is often very good.

Labor Availability.   Although unemployment rates are high in many developing countries, labor of the right kind is often scarce. People with skills may be in short supply, and turnover rates for such people may be high. A company locating in such an area must plan an extensive training program. In countries that have recently experienced rapid economic development skilled workers may be abundant, but it may be difficult to find workers willing to do tedious assembly work. Successful economic development increases worker skill levels; companies needing unskilled assembly workers may have to move to new locations.

Labor Productivity.   Labor costs are determined not only by wage rates but also by worker productivity. Low productivity has a number of undesirable side effects besides its direct effect of increasing unit labor costs. If productivity is low, more workers are required, thereby generating extra overhead and other problems associated with managing a larger work force. Low productivity also implies an increase in required investment in working capital as work-in-process inventory increases.

EXHIBIT 2   AVERAGE HOURLY WAGES IN MANUFACTURING IN SELECTED COUNTRIES (1980)

Country	Hourly Earnings in Dollars
Peoples Republic of China	1.13
South Korea	1.28
India	0.41
Philippines	0.38
Singapore	1.09
Taiwan	1.35
Japan	5.70
United States	7.27

Source.   Business International, Inc., *Investing Trading and Licensing Conditions Abroad,* 1985.

Labor productivity depends on the experience of the workers, the technology available to them, the scale of operators and the management of the enterprise. The value of experience depends on the type of job. Some jobs can be learned quickly, whereas others require months or years of training. But it is clear that technology and management are crucial. Workers with the right tools and equipment, organized and managed effectively, are much more productive than those who are poorly equipped and managed. Effective plant scheduling, worker training and supervision, and other aspects of good management are important determinants of productivity. Scale economies common in most manufacturing result in larger factories being more efficient than small ones.

It has generally been found in the overseas operations of U.S. firms, as well as by economists in comparative studies, that foreign workers can be just as productive as U.S. workers if they are given the same technology and management. A U.S. Tariff Commission study (1970) found that workers in offshore manufacturing plants can be trained rapidly for most jobs and they approach or exceed U.S. productivity levels.

Productivity is not just a function of management, however. Cultural and historical factors also play a role. The industrial experience of the country influences the extent to which workers have been exposed to modern technology and determines the number of technically oriented people available. Educational levels also influence productivity, especially for some types of jobs. Even nutrition may be an important influence in some of the poorest countries. And culture certainly influences attitudes toward work. The Protestant work ethic may be dying in the West, but many companies have found something comparable in countries of the Far East.

Labor Reliability and Unions.   In many offshore sourcing operations it is important to maintain a steady flow of production, as this output feeds into other parts of the company's operations. Disruptions due to strikes can be very serious. Rapid turnover or high rates of absenteeism are also of concern. Turnover in many offshore plants is high because a high proportion of workers are young women who are only temporarily in the labor force.

Strikes and other disruptions abroad have not been a major concern for most companies engaged in offshore sourcing, although U.S. dock strikes occasionally cause problems. In many countries where offshore plants are located, government policies and regulations sharply circumscribe the rights of labor to organize and/or strike, and in some cases these laws are even stricter for export operations than for companies serving the domestic market. Governments realize that export-oriented enterprises will move elsewhere if disruptions become common. But as economic development proceeds, governments may loosen such laws in response to democratic pressures, and labor relations may become more similar to those in the United States.

Whether or not unions are tightly controlled by the government, it is important to become familiar with the role and organization of unions in a prospective offshore manufacturing site. Often the role of unions is quite different than in the United States. In some countries unions are organized on a company basis, as opposed to a craft or industry basis. In others, unions are extensions of political parties, and a country may have communist, socialist, and other politically affiliated unions. In such cases, labor disputes often have more to do with the national political scene than with wages and working conditions.

INFRASTRUCTURE FACTORS.   Infrastructure includes a wide variety of facilities and services required by any offshore operation, ranging from utilities and plant sites to schools, shopping, and services for expatriate families. Among the factors to consider for offshore location decisions are the availability of industrial sites, communications, transportation services, and suppliers of needed goods and services.

Industrial Sites.   A determining factor in some location decisions is how fast a facility can be established and begin operations; construction delays can be extremely long. Some countries have industrial sites available to foreign investors on attractive terms and without legal complications involving the determination of title. Others may have standard industrial buildings available to buy or lease, which if appropriate to a company's needs, can save both time and investment capital. In virtually all developing countries, industrial parks of some type have been established, but these vary widely in terms of the types and reliability of services provided and kinds of facilities available.

Transportation and Communication.   Offshore sourcing is a relatively complex logistical operation, often involving imports, exports, and considerable international communication to coordinate plans and schedules. Efficient and reliable transportation and communication is therefore essential. Although these services are constantly improving elsewhere in the world, they still differ considerably among countries. International telephone and mail service, which are often taken for granted in the United States, are difficult in some places. Countries also vary in terms of the frequency of air and sea shipping connections to the United States and other countries.

Local Suppliers of Goods and Services.   An important ancillary advantage of some offshore sites is the availability of inexpensive supplies of component parts, raw materials, and needed services. If materials and components must be imported, costs are often higher, and problems such as bureaucratic delays or corruption may be encountered. If services are not available, the company will be forced to provide them itself. The negative side of this is that governments sometimes force companies to use local suppliers even if they provide goods or services of substandard quality, all in the name of local economic development. It is important, therefore, to investigate the capabilities of local suppliers as well as government policies regarding their use.

GOVERNMENT POLICY FACTORS.   In most developing countries where offshore sources are located, governments play a very active role in shaping economic development. It is important, therefore, to understand the current policies regarding foreign investment and offshore sourcing, as well as to develop a feeling for the government's general attitudes in these areas, so as to be able to anticipate possible changes. Governments can be both a help and a hindrance to foreign investors, and their general attitudes range from hostility to active support.

General Attitudes.   Most governments have had considerable experience with foreign investors, and this has conditioned current attitudes. Much of this experience may be considered by them negative, having colonial or neocolonial overtones of exploitation. In some countries there is a strong Marxist movement, either in power or exerting political and intellectual influence, which sees foreign investment as imperialistic. These critics often see offshore sourcing as having a very negative impact on their countries, interpreting it as exploitation of workers with little lasting benefit for the country. If such attitudes are prevalent, foreign-investment legislation may be, or may become, quite restrictive.

On the other hand, some countries see foreign investment in general, and export-oriented foreign investment in particular, as playing an important role in economic development. Such governments have a more positive view of foreign enterprise and see special benefits such as providing jobs, training, and foreign-exchange earnings. In such countries, the government may be quite supportive of offshore sourcing operations.

Government Regulations. In most developing countries new foreign investments need formal government approval, and the process differs widely among countries. And government rules and regulations often require constant management attention after operations are set up. Most governments have tried to simplify procedures for offshore sourcing in an effort to attract more of these export-oriented operations. Thus exporters are sometimes exempted from certain regulations, or the government sometimes sets up a free-trade zone or export-processing zone in which many of the normal rules don't apply. Good sources of information on export processing zones are the Economist Intelligence Unit reports (1984, 1985). Especially attractive are situations in which authority rests in the hands of an independent zone management, thereby reducing the need to deal with a large number of government offices. In most cases, however, a company needs to learn how to deal with the government and how to expedite needed government services or approvals.

Government Incentives. Various incentives are offered by many developing countries to companies establishing offshore manufacturing plants. These include favorable tax treatment, subsidized services, and freedom of movement of goods, people, and money in and out of the country. Many countries provide tax holidays or other favorable treatment such as rapid depreciation. The value of such treatment will vary among investors, however, based on their tax situations in their home countries. For example, a tax holiday abroad sometimes simply means that a U.S. investor pays more taxes in the United States, but in other cases U.S. taxes can be deferred. Government subsidies come in the form of low-cost sites, cheap loans for construction or importation of equipment, or provision of low-cost services. And of course tax regulations are often used to subsidize exports.

It is important for offshore sourcing that goods, people, and money be permitted to flow freely in and out of the foreign country. Although the degree of freedom differs, most countries have moved toward satisfying this need. On the imports of materials or components to be incorporated in exports generally duties are not paid (or duties are rebated upon export). Likewise, the paperwork and licenses required for imports are generally reduced for export operations. Finally, there are generally looser regulations for exporters than for other companies on employment of expatriates, remission of profits, and requirements for partial local ownership.

STABILITY FACTORS. Economic or political instability can cause unexpected problems for offshore sourcing operations. Inflation, currency fluctuations, civil disruptions, or changes in government all may have unfortunate consequences.

Economic stability is closely related to political stability. High inflation, for example, may lead to social disruption and political change. Likewise, political changes often lead to changes in economic policies.

Economic Instability.   The general economic health of a country is important to any investor, but since offshore sourcing plants serve export markets rather than the local market, inflation and currency changes are more relevant than other economic indicators such as growth rates. Inflation and currency depreciation often occur simultaneously. Inflation affects all local costs and could make some products non-competitive with those of other countries. But if the local currency is depreciating along with inflation, the cost in dollars of the goods may not change. The net effect on a company during a given time period will depend on the relative rates of inflation and currency depreciation, especially compared with competitive countries. Some exporting countries systematically devalue their currencies in line with inflation, in order to remain competitive, whereas in others there is sometimes a time lag between inflation and devaluation. The net effect also depends on the extent to which the company uses imported components and materials, which will increase in price as the currency depreciates.

Political Instability.   A major concern of foreign investors is political risk. With regard to offshore sourcing, investors should consider the potential risks posed by external threats, internal political disturbances that have the potential for disrupting normal operations, and drastic changes in government policies that could affect the success of a company's operations. Predicting political instability and analyzing political risk is a complex art and is covered elsewhere in this handbook. Approaches range from simple numerical rating schemes to an in-depth analysis of the political dynamics of a given country.

Various techniques can be used to reduce the political risks of offshore sourcing. The insurance programs available from government or private sources are covered in another section of this handbook. The best protection, however, is a backup source of supply. Many companies have either multiple offshore sources or a backup production facility available in the United States.

SOURCES OF INFORMATION ON PRODUCTION SITES.   Most countries that are potential sites for offshore sourcing have offices, often in the United States, to provide information and assistance to companies interested in investing in the country or finding partners or suppliers. These offices can be very valuable for obtaining basic information, sources of other information, and some feeling for government attitudes.

Another important source is the reports that describe various aspects of the political, economic, and regulatory climates in different countries. Some of the most useful ones are the following:

1. *Overseas Business Reports,* published by the U.S. Department of Commerce.
2. *Investing, Licensing and Trading Conditions Abroad,* published by Business International Corporation.
3. *Country Reports,* published for most countries by the Economist Intelligence Unit.

4. U.S. Department of State, *Background Notes,* a series of brief profiles of most countries in the world, with helpful advice for business executives.

5. Reports published by a number of banks and public accounting firms.

Many of these are available in good public or university libraries.

Finally, it is important to talk to other companies with experience in a given country. Valuable information on how the published information translates into reality can be obtained in such interviews. However, companies may have biases, either pro or con, on a given country based on their own experiences, so the opinions of several companies should be solicited.

U.S. CUSTOMS REGULATIONS

U.S. customs regulations on imports should be understood by companies engaged in offshore sourcing. Many products that are selected for offshore sourcing are subject to special treatment under U.S. laws. Some are eligible for favorable treatment because of their origin in developing countries, whereas others come under special restrictions because of the poor health of the competing U.S. industry. Still others make use of special features of the tariff laws that favor certain types of transactions. The purpose of this section is not to cover U.S. import regulations in any detail, but instead to outline some basic considerations that can be studied in more detail in other sections of this handbook and in publications of the U.S. Customs Service. The best source of basic information, itself having extensive references to other sources, is *Importing into the United States*, published by the U.S. Customs Service. The subjects covered here are (1) normal treatment of imported goods, (2) generalized system of preferences (GSP), covering some imports from developing countries, (3) special quotas on particular goods, and (4) tariff items 806.30 and 807.00, covering imports of products that are produced abroad using U.S. components or materials.

NORMAL TREATMENT OF IMPORTED GOODS. Most products imported to the United States pay duties based on the product's definition, its value, and its national origin.

Products are defined for customs valuation and assessment using the *Tariff Schedules of the United States*, published by the U.S. International Trade Commission. This document classifies each product into a special category based on one or more product characteristics. Often it is unclear from the tariff schedules exactly how an item should be classified, and seemingly minor product differences may result in a different classification and a widely different rate of duty. It is wise to verify the duty on an imported product by consulting with U.S. Customs Service officials; sometimes it will be necessary to request an official ruling on a controversial duty assessment.

Once the product is identified, the method of calculating the duty is specified in the tariff schedules, as is the applicable duty rate. For most products, duties are calculated on an *ad valorem* basis, that is, as a percentage of the value of the product. There are some products, however, whose duty is based on weight, and some that pay a given duty per unit. For products whose duty is based on value, the normal value used is the so-called export value, which corresponds to the free on board (f.o.b.)

price, that is, the price received by the exporter including the costs of transporting the goods to the port of exportation and loading the goods onto the export vessel.

The classification of the product and its country of origin determine the rate of duty that must be paid. In the *Tariff Schedules of the United States*, three applicable duty rates are found, corresponding to three different groups of countries. Imports from most countries is dutiable under the most-favored-nation (MFN) rates in Column 1 of the tariff schedules. Currently only a few communist countries do not enjoy most-favored-nation status, and imports from these countries are generally assessed the much higher duty shown in Column 2. A few of the least developed developing countries are granted lower rates, shown in the LDCC column.

GENERALIZED SYSTEM OF PREFERENCES.   A wide range of products qualify for duty-free entry into the United States if imported from a developing country. The products that qualify for GSP duty-free treatment and the eligible developing countries are identified in the *Tariff Schedules of the United States*. The GSP applies to roughly 150 developing countries in Latin America, Africa, and Asia. It covers mostly manufactured industrial goods, *excluding* textiles and apparel, footwear, and selected glass items, steel articles, electronics, watches, and miscellaneous other items. In addition, a "competitive-need criteria" denies GSP treatment for particular products when imported from especially competitive developing countries (these countries and products are identified in the *tariff schedules*). Finally, imports under the GSP must conform to a number of rules regarding origin of component parts and documentation to verify that the products are substantially transformed in an eligible developing country. Importers should consult with U.S. Customs for current regulations.

QUOTAS.   A number of products sourced offshore are subject to absolute quotas as well as duties. Quotas essentially limit the volume of imports into the United States and are normally administered on a product and country-of-origin basis. Such quotas have generally been imposed in response to U.S. industries that are threatened by excessive imports. Hence some of the imports that have enjoyed the most success in the U.S. market are subject to quotas. Some quotas are administered by the U.S. Customs Service itself, and others by foreign authorities under a so-called orderly marketing agreements or voluntary export restraints. In the latter cases, a quota level for particular products is negotiated with individual exporting nations, which in turn allocate the quota to individual exporters. Without the exporting government's stamp of approval, the product may not be imported into the United States. Needless to say, access to a country's quota may be very valuable, and the availability of a quota allocation may significantly affect a company's decision on where to source its imports.

ITEMS 806.30 AND 807.00.   Many products sourced abroad by U.S. companies enter the United States under the provision of items 806.30 and 807.00 of the *Tariff Schedules of the United States*. Item 806.30 provides that articles made of metal produced in the United States will upon importation into the United States be assessed duty only on the value of the processing done outside the United States. Item 807.00 provides that articles assembled abroad, in whole or in part, of components made in the United States will upon importation into the United States be assessed duty on the full value of the imported product less the value of the U.S.

fabricated components contained therein. These provisions are subject to many conditions, including elaborate accounting for the U.S. components incorporated in imports. Many companies have had problems in following U.S. customs regulations. Nevertheless, imports under these provisions have increased spectacularly in recent years. A good source of information on the use of Items 806.30 and 807.00 is U.S. International Trade Commission (1985).

LEGAL AND FINANCIAL CONSIDERATIONS

Offshore sourcing involves a number of legal and financial considerations that are covered in other sections of this handbook. The important factors will depend on which form the offshore sourcing takes. If it is simple purchasing or subcontracting, the concerns will relate to contractual considerations and trade financing. Information on these topics is available in publications of banks and public accounting firms. If offshore sourcing takes the form of a joint venture or a wholly owned manufacturing plant, the considerations will relate more to the relative advantages of different legal forms of establishment and the contracts necessary between joint-venture partners. Joint ventures and other such agreements with potential competitors may also lead to issues of U.S. antitrust law.

Of course some factors may be more important in offshore sourcing than in other forms of international business. Special tax incentives and sources of financing may be available from host-country governments. Foreign-exchange management assumes important proportions because of the extensive transfers of products across borders. And large amounts of intracorporate sales between a company's U.S. plants and its foreign subsidiaries mean that special attention must be given to the setting of transfer prices. But in the main, offshore sourcing involves similar financial and legal considerations as other forms of international trade and investment.

ORGANIZATION AND COORDINATION OF OFFSHORE SOURCING

COMMUNICATIONS PROBLEMS AND SOLUTIONS.   Communications with offshore sources, whether they are independent companies or a U.S. firm's own subsidiary, often run into problems common to most international business operations. Because they occur so often, and have such devastating effects, they are summarized briefly here, along with some possible approaches for resolving them.

Causes of Problems.   Time and distance are the most obvious causes of communication problems. The U.S. office and the foreign plant are typically in different time zones. Direct telephone contact is therefore limited to the small "window" in which the working day overlaps, or to situations in which one or the other party is making contact outside normal working hours. This can limit the quality of communication and encourages reliance on less-satisfactory forms of written communication, with attendant delays and mistakes. Communications over long distances, with no face-to-face contact and with time pressures due to the high costs involved, often lead to irritation, misunderstandings, and creation of distrust.

Language is another obvious problem area. Although the source managers may speak English, their language capabilities may be limited, which can be quite problematic in long-distance communications.

Problems of time and distance are exacerbated by the differences in cultural environment in which the two enterprises operate. The U.S. firm may not be able to understand why the local manager of a subsidiary finds it necessary to handle a problem in a certain way, whereas the local manager may feel that such a solution is only normal in the local business environment. The areas of labor relations and government relations are fertile fields for such misunderstandings.

These problems are made worse if the managers at either end of the communication channel have little international experience. This is an inevitable, but unfortunate, fact for many companies. Many firms have little experience overseas before beginning offshore sourcing, and do not have a reserve of experienced international managers to handle these communications. Most problems can be overcome quite easily, but a company should be aware of the opportunities for misunderstanding.

Solutions to Communication Problems.   Many of these communication problems can be solved by having the right people involved, by frequent visits between the U.S. offices and overseas sources, and by organizing communication channels properly. The right people can make a big difference. The ideal qualifications would include language capability, experience in the other party's operations, understanding and empathy for the other culture, plus the expected technical competence. Such people are hard to find, but fortunately, many people can effectively communicate internationally if they are patient and sympathetic to the position of those on the other side.

Frequent visits by U.S. managers to the foreign source, and by the foreign managers to the United States, are also important. Gaining a firsthand feeling for the foreign operation and its current situation helps put later communications in the proper context, and can reduce misunderstandings. Direct exposure to the U.S. market can also help a source understand the importance of its role in producing quality products. Face-to-face communications also can build trust and personal relationships that can help overcome subsequent problems.

Organizational relationships can also be structured to reduce communication difficulties. On the U.S. side it is often useful to have one person as liaison with the foreign source. This person can be responsible for insuring timely and effective communications and for clarifying and reducing misunderstandings. Independent foreign agents, appointed by a U.S. company to handle all dealings with foreign sources, can also perform such a function.

ORGANIZATION LINKS.   For many smaller companies the question of how to link a foreign subsidiary or independent source to the rest of the organization is not important. The link is through the sales, purchasing, production, or other functional department. But for larger organizations, a variety of possibilities present themselves.

Consider a multiproduct, multidivision U.S. company with a variety of foreign sources (assume they are controlled manufacturing plants), some of which serve more than one of the U.S. divisions. A simplified representation of such a situation, with the corresponding product flows, is given in Exhibit 3. Here it is assumed that the product divisions are responsible for U.S. production and sales, and the international division manages international operations. How should the foreign sources be linked to the

EXHIBIT 3   COMPLEX MULTISOURCE–MULTIDIVISION
SOURCING SITUATION

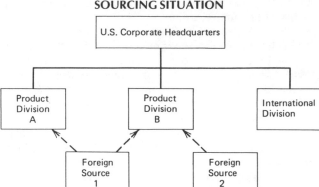

U.S. operations? Two major alternatives in this situation are to link sources organizationally to the product divisions that they serve, or link sources to the international division which manages other international operations. Neither alternative is without problems. Making source 2 a profit or cost center within product division B would not present problems, since all of its products go to the division. But for source 1, no such simple link is possible. Linking organizationally with either division may distort its relationship with the other.

Linking all sources to the international division would be consistent with the rest of the company's operations, and the international division is likely to have the experienced international managers for good communications. But these subsidiaries, whose primary mission is serving the U.S. divisions, are quite different from the normal subsidiaries that serve foreign customers. An immediate concern would be who was responsible for the success of these subsidiaries: the international division to which they report, or the product divisions that provide their entire market. This raises the question of the appropriate transfer price between divisions, a messy problem in any circumstances. Problems escalate if the example is extended to a greater number of divisions and sources.

The best advice is to choose the organization that seems most natural, probably the one where the bulk of the communication and coordination efforts will be, and then build in mechanisms to overcome difficulties in coordinating with the rest of the organization. In any case, the foreign source should have a clearly defined mission, whether it be a cost center or profit center, and should have the resources and authority necessary to accomplish this mission. The best performance of a foreign source will result when responsibilities and expectations are clearly defined.

SOURCES AND SUGGESTED REFERENCES

Business International Corporation. *Investing, Licensing and Trading Conditions Abroad.* New York: Business International Corporation. A continually updated looseleaf service covering most major countries.

Economist Intelligence Unit. *Country Reports.* A series of reports covering most countries.

Economist Intelligence Unit, *Export Processing Zones in the 1980s,* EIU special report no. 190, London, 1985.

Economist Intelligence Unit, *How to Make Offshore Manufacturing Pay,* EIU special report no. 171, London, 1984.

Grunwald, J. and Flamm, K.. *The Global Factory,* Washington, D.C.: Brookings Institution, 1985.

Holton, R.H.. "Making International Joint Ventures Work", in L. Otterbeck, ed., *The Management of Headquarters—Subsidiary Relationships in Multinational Corporations.* New York: St. Martin's, 1981.

U.S. Customs Service, Department of the Treasury. *Exporting to the United States.* Washington, D.C.: U.S. Government Printing Office, 1979.

U.S. Department of Commerce. *Overseas Business Reports.* A series of reports on different countries.

U.S. Department of State, *Background Notes.*

U.S. International Trade Commission, *Imports Under Items 806.30 and 807.00 of the Tariff Schedules of the United States, 1980–83.* USITC publication no. 1688, April 1985.

U.S. International Trade Commission. *Tariff Schedules of the United States.*

U.S. Tariff Commission. *Economic Factors Affecting the Use of Items 807.00 and 806.30 of the Tariff Schedules of the United States.* T.C. Publication 339. Washington, DC, 1970.

TECHNOLOGY TRANSFER

CONTENTS

TECHNOLOGY TRANSFER

Katherine Marton
Rana K. Singh

The application of innovative and improved technology has always constituted a critical element in the corporate strategy of business organizations, and the possession of proprietary technology and know-how has been an important determinant of a firm's competitive advantage in national and international markets. In recent decades, however, major new dimensions have been added to the role of technology, and the process of technology transfer between enterprises in various sectors and in different countries has assumed much greater significance. This has been due to several critical factors, including the fast pace of technological innovations, the rapid growth of technology licensing and other contractual arrangements, and the increasing importance accorded to technological growth and development in national policies of both industrialized and developing countries.

Technology can be embodied in machinery and equipment or can be in the form of patented and proprietary knowledge or unpatented know-how. In the case of equipment, technology transfer comprises the development of skills, initially in machinery operations and maintenance and, at a later stage, in replacement and manufacture of various capital goods. The concept of international transfer of technology, however, primarily relates to the transfer of nonembodied technology in the form of patented, proprietary, or specialized know-how. With rapid growth of technology transactions between enterprises in different countries, technology is increasingly emerging as a marketable commodity.

The last two decades have been a period of major technological development and, in several production sectors, there have been revolutionary changes in products and processes. The rapid pace of innovations in computers, microelectronics, genetic engineering, materials technology, and other high-technology fields has had considerable impact on product development and in manufacturing techniques, not only in these sectors but in most fields of production. Major developments in communications technologies and the electronic processing, storage, and transmission of data have resulted in the fast expansion of an information service sector. These technological innovations have mostly taken place in industrialized countries, especially in the United States, and have been accompanied by innovative technological adaptation, particularly in Japan and certain countries in Western Europe. The pace of technological absorption of industrial know-how has also increased significantly in several developing countries, particularly in parts of Asia and Latin America.

Though the technological gap between industrialized and developing countries has increased in high-technology areas, competitive production and technological capability has been developed in several production sectors including petroleum and mineral processing and equipment manufacture, apart from more traditional manufacturing fields such as textiles, shoes, and consumer products.

Historically, commercialization of technology took place within the process of foreign direct investments of transnational corporations. Financial returns from foreign operations included income from the supply of technology and technical services to subsidiaries and affiliates in different countries. Technology flow was closely linked to, and contingent on, foreign investment and supply of technology and know-how was limited to the technological needs of subsidiaries and affiliates. This pattern still continues and technology supply to foreign subsidiaries constitutes a major channel for technology transfer in several production sectors. However, in place of the informal arrangements regarding payments for technology that existed formerly between parents and their foreign subsidiaries, more formal agreements are increasingly being entered into. At the same time, technology licensing is increasingly utilized for technology transfer to nonaffiliated enterprises and in joint ventures involving minority foreign holdings. In fact, an important feature in international economic relationships has been the growth of technology licensing between enterprises across national boundaries. Licensing, cross-licensing, and other contractual arrangements relating to technology and technical services have provided companies with considerable access to knowledge and user rights regarding new products and processes in different fields; licensing of patented and proprietary technology and trade secrets and of unpatented know-how to nonaffiliated companies is becoming increasingly popular. The most marked and effective use of technology licensing has been by Japanese companies who have utilized this mechanism extensively over the last three decades.

An important feature of international technology transfer has been the greater availability of production technology and know-how, technical services from alternative sources, and increased knowledge and awareness regarding such alternatives. The process of technological diffusion through licensing and other contractual arrangements has brought about multiple sourcing of technology in most fields. The technology market continues to be highly imperfect and varies from sector to sector. In some areas, patented technology continues to be held by a single corporation and may not be available for licensing. In other fields, similar technology may be available from several sources in industrialized countries and also from certain developing countries. In high-technology areas also, the rapid pace of innovation has resulted in new technological developments and adaptations being achieved by a large number of enterprises, including small companies specializing in certain fields, such as biotechnology or microapplications. These developments necessitate greater knowledge regarding the potential and opportunities for technology trade and licensing on the part of both the suppliers and recipients of industrial technology.

GOVERNING FACTORS IN TRANSFER

Various factors govern corporate decisions as to the stage and form of transfer of proprietary technology and know-how. Considerable literature has developed around this subject, with respect to the stage and pattern of foreign production operations and licensing of proprietary technology.[1] Certain proprietary technologies have not been transferred at all, while others have been transferred only through wholly-owned subsidiaries if and when foreign production operations are undertaken. Licensing of technology to nonaffiliate companies in other countries has also emerged as an increasingly viable alternative in a number of situations.[2] These can be broadly considered in relation to the nature of the technology, the conditions of entry in foreign markets and the corporate strategy of the foreign firm. As for the first category, licensing can provide an appropriate source of additional income in the case of products and technologies which may be obsolete or on the verge of obsolescence in certain countries, yet have potential in other countries at different stages of development. These may include products with a short shelf life such as certain pharmaceuticals; technologies which may be fairly labor-intensive and which are gradually being replaced, as in the case of certain machine tools; or technologies whose patents are expiring in the near future. In several fields, competing technologies may have been developed and income from increased licensing could offset lower returns from sales. In certain sectors where technology is changing rapidly with innovative developments, as in minicomputers and semiconductors, licensing can be utilized to expand the usage of a particular product or technology in other countries. These situations can be either firm-specific or may relate to a production sector as a whole and they undoubtedly provide a wide range of situations where technology licensing may not only be practicable but necessary as a supplemental source of corporate income for owners of technology.

A separate set of considerations may govern the form of entry in foreign markets. There may be import restrictions and tariff barriers to protect local industry, and host country policies may require local production as a condition of entry. These may be accompanied by direct or indirect controls over foreign investments and the extent of foreign ownership. There may also be reluctance on the part of companies possessing proprietary technology to invest in certain countries because of risk factors. In many situations, licensing can provide a mechanism for entry into markets which may be growing rapidly, as in less-industrialized countries and which would otherwise be closed. Of these factors, perhaps the most significant in recent decades has been the constraint placed on foreign investments in a number of host countries. The most effective use of such restrictions was made by Japan since the 1950s. With foreign investments regulated by legislation and policies which only gradually eased over time, Japanese companies resorted extensively to licensing of technology from abroad, mainly from the United States. During the period from 1950 to 1978, 31,738 agreements were entered into for technology imports into Japan.[3] Even in subsequent years, the number of agreements for technology imports in Japan exceeded 2,000 per year, though this is partially offset by agreements for exports of Japanese technology. A similar pattern is emerging in countries such as Korea, India, Yugoslavia, and others, where considerable industrialization is taking place and where greater emphasis is being given to inflow of technology.

The corporate strategy for foreign production activities of firms possessing proprietary technology and know-how has varied considerably. In the automobile industry, for example, certain firms such as Ford (USA) effected considerable global integration through foreign subsidiaries in different countries while Fiat (Italy) has provided technology through licensing agreements to certain developing countries and in East Europe. In the manufacture of electrical and mechanical equipment, a number of firms have undertaken foreign operations only through wholly-owned subsidiaries while others have entered into joint ventures or licensing arrangements. In computers and semiconductors, most Japanese companies entered the field through licenses from U.S. corporations. With the growing availability of similar technology from alternative sources, most corporations are exercising much greater flexibility regarding their foreign production operations and are adjusting their investment and licensing strategy to the needs and policies of host countries in different regions.

CHANNELS AND FEATURES OF TRANSFER

The principal channels of technology transfer range from transnational corporations (TNCs) investing in other countries through subsidiaries and affiliates or supplying technology and know-how through licensing arrangements to foreign suppliers of machinery and equipment and foreign consulting engineering organizations performing specific technological functions. With respect to foreign direct investments, there has been a growing trend in several countries, mostly developing countries, to increase the proportion of national ownership in new, as well as in existing foreign-owned enterprises. This has led to the establishment of joint ventures, with minority equity holdings by foreign companies. There has also been a trend toward technology licensing without foreign equity holdings of technology suppliers. Trade in machinery and equipment has also increased significantly, especially to developing countries during successive stages of industrialization. The role of foreign consultants and engineering consultancy organizations expanded rapidly during the 1960s and 1970s, especially in countries undertaking large infrastructure projects such as electrical power plants and irrigation systems, or major industrial projects set up by national governments or through state-owned enterprises. The association of local consultants and personnel, in such consultancy arrangements, has been an important channel of transfer of planning, engineering, and construction skills. The nature of the technology package varies considerably from case to case and extends from supply of manufacturing drawings and production technology for relatively simple products to turnkey arrangements for the planning, installation, and initial management of major products. These functions can be performed either by a single foreign enterprise or the various elements of technology and know-how can be acquired from different sources, both domestic and foreign.

The use of alternative mechanisms for industrial technology transfer has depended on country-specific and industry-specific situations. Several factors are of significance, including the nature of the technology and the availability of alternatives, the use of foreign consultants, the level of industrial development, and host country policies on foreign investments and technology. In industrial branches, where production technology is largely embodied in industrial machinery and equipment, the channel of transfer has primarily been through suppliers of plant and equipment who also generally provide for training in operations and maintenance. In cases involving foreign investment, technology transfer has constituted a primary function of the parent transnational corporation, though the extent of transfer has largely depended on the role of the subsidiary or affiliate in the global operations of the parent corporation.

The nature and content of technology transfer can vary considerably, in the case of wholly-owned TNC subsidiaries and in joint ventures with minority TNC participation or license agreements with nonaffiliate enterprises. Wholly-owned subsidiaries continue to be preferred by most TNCs as this enables full control over the operations of subsidiaries and their effective integration with global manufacturing activities. In such cases, technology transfer by the TNC is full and complete to the extent of the technological requirements of the subsidiary. The limitations, however, arise from the local production activities of the TNC subsidiary being limited in scope, if viewed from the perspective of the host country. There is considerable technological dependence on the parent TNC and technological adaptation and enterprise-level R&D is extremely limited. The nature of the parent-subsidiary relationship places constraints on the growth of local technological capability in most cases, apart from various aspects of intrafirm resource transfers. Consequently, where foreign operations through TNC subsidiaries and affiliates have extended to most stages of production, because of large local markets, cheap labor, or other factor advantages or because of host country policies, the technology and know-how transferred by the parent corporation covers all such stages. In other instances, however, the activities of foreign subsidiaries may be limited to certain operations as in the mining of ore or the final stage of assembly of durable consumer products. Here the technology supplied is limited to the operations performed by the subsidiary. Technological decision making in both these instances is done by the parent corporation, which also determines the production function of its foreign subsidiaries.

The pattern of technology transfer differs considerably in the case of joint ventures with minority TNC participation and nonaffiliate licensing arrangements. In both cases, the nature and content of foreign technology and services to be supplied are detailed in the terms and conditions of the technology agreement. The technology agreement requires careful negotiation and should be based on the technological requirements of the recipient enterprise and related to its own program of manufacture, rather than on the global activities of the technology supplier.

The extent of technology transfer in the alternative forms of foreign participation just discussed can vary considerably. There have been several instances of effective technological absorption and adaptation by TNC subsidiaries not only in industrialized countries but also in certain developing countries, as Brazil and Mexico. Technology licensing without foreign equity is a common form of transfer between enterprises in developed economies, but has been successfully utilized by several domestically owned companies in Brazil, India, Korea, Mexico, and other developing countries. Joint ventures have taken place largely in developing countries, with foreign holdings ranging up to 49 percent. In most cases where foreign companies have holdings of 49 percent or thereabouts, control over use of technology generally rests with the foreign partner, particularly where local shareholdings are widely distributed. In some developing countries, national policies may require gradual divestment of foreign holdings over a period of time, but even in these cases, effective control over technology may continue to rest with the foreign partner for long periods.

Technology transfer in industrialized, developed countries has largely taken place either through the foreign investment process or through technology licensing arrangements. Since the 1950s in particular, a number of major U.S. companies began production activities in Western Europe. Such investments were welcomed and this pattern has continued in subsequent periods, with the major modification in more recent years, of increased European and Japanese investments in the United States. Foreign investment inflow in developed market economies increased from $8.1 billion in 1970–1971 to $27.1 billion in 1982 and $29 billion in 1983.[4] A significant feature has been the rise in global investment inflow in the United States as compared to market economies in Europe. During the period 1981–1983, foreign investment inflow in the United States amounted to $50.8 billion, as compared to $36.3 billion for European countries.[5] In terms of percentages, inflow in the United States rose from 8.6 percent of global investment inflow in 1970–1971 to 29 percent in 1983, as compared to 44.7 percent in 1970–1971 and 32.8 percent in 1983 for European market economies. With respect to outflows, foreign investments from the United States fell from $7.6 billion in 1970–1971 to $4.9 billion in 1983, while outflows from market-economy European countries increased from $4.2 billion in 1970–1971 to $15 billion in 1983. Foreign investment flows between industrialized market-economy countries may not, however, necessarily reflect transfer of industrial technology in all cases. In many instances, especially with respect to growing investments in the United States, such investments are primarily designed to participate in the expanding local markets for goods and services, though several elements and features of technology and management which are special to individual investing firms invariably accompany such investments. The extent of technology transfer between enterprises in industrialized market economies is better reflected in payments of fees and royalties for technology and services between these enterprises.

In the case of developing countries, there is a more direct relationship between foreign direct investments and inflow of foreign know-how and services, since most of such investments are in new fields and the accompanying technology inflow is an important factor governing such investments. Foreign investment inflow in developing market economies increased from $2.4 billion in 1970–1971 (average) to $14.6 billion in 1981 and to around $10 billion in 1983.[6] The severe foreign-debt situation facing several developing countries is likely to have significant impact on foreign direct investments in several of these countries, particularly in Latin America. National policies of foreign investments in these countries have also had, and will continue to have, considerable effect on the pattern and structure of such investments and their implications on technology transfer and development in these countries. In a number of developing market economies, ranging from Brazil to several Southeast Asian countries (Singapore, Hong Kong, the Republic of Korea, Thailand, and the Taiwan region of China), foreign investments and related technology inflow has taken place through subsidiaries and affiliates of transnational corporations, though technology licensing to nonaffiliate companies has also increased considerably in recent years. In India, Mexico, the Andean group, and several other developing countries, regulatory measures have been imposed on foreign direct investments and foreign technology agreements. Regulatory measures have sought to increase the extent of local capital ownership, including through phased divestment of existing foreign holdings and limitations on the extent of foreign ownership in new projects and enterprises. These policies have resulted in foreign technology being increasingly channeled through joint ventures and nonaffiliate licensing.

TRADE IN TECHNOLOGY

Trade in technology is measured primarily in terms of payments (1) for the use of certain patented rights by other enterprises, (2) for transfer of proprietary know-how, patented and unpatented, for production of specific products, and (3) for provision of specific technological services. In many instances, the transfer is a combination of these elements and payments may either be lumped together or shown separately.

Technology transactions still largely take place between enterprises in industrialized countries though the extent of payments from developing countries to technology suppliers from industrialized countries has increased in recent years. The total volume of technology transactions, measured in fees and royalties, amounted to about $25 billion in 1983.[7] Of this, technology transactions in five industrialized countries—the United States, United Kingdom, the Federal Republic of Germany, France, and Japan—accounted for about $18 billion.[8] With a large proportion of technological innovations taking place, the United States has been the principal exporter of industrial technology. Receipts from royalties and fees of U.S. companies rose from $2.5 billion in 1971 to $4.3 billion in 1978; $6.27 billion in 1983, and $6.5 billion in 1984.[9] Most of these receipts, including $5.07 billion and $5.39 billion respectively in 1983 and 1984, were from companies and enterprises in other industrialized and developed economies, especially Japan, Canada, and Western Europe.[10] As for other technology-exporting countries, receipts from technology fees and royalties in 1983 amounted to $992 million in the case of Great Britain; $489 million in France and $531 million in the Federal Republic of Germany.[11] The major importer of industrial technology has continued to be Japan since the 1950s. Despite spectacular industrial growth in recent decades, technology payments by Japanese enterprises have continued to rise from $800 million in 1976 to $1.6 billion in 1981 and over $2 billion in 1983, while technology receipts by Japanese companies amounted to about $600 million annually in 1982 and 1983.[12] Among Western Europe countries, technology payments by enterprises in the Federal Republic of Germany amounted to $982 million in 1982 and over $1 billion in 1983; in France to $978 million in 1982 and $945 million in 1983 and in Great Britain to $772 million and $786 million respectively in 1981 and 1982.[13]

Technology payments by developing countries in the form of fees and royalties increased from $270 million in 1965 to $1.4 billion in 1978 and to about $2 billion in the early 1980s.[14] This is expected to increase rapidly in the 1980s. While the proportion of such payments is still only about 15 percent of total trade in technology, and the magnitude of payments are fairly significant in the case of certain developing countries.

A large proportion of technology payments comprise receipts of parent transnational corporations from their subsidiaries and affiliates in various countries. In 1978, for example, about 80 percent of royalties and licensing fees in the manufacturing sector of transnational corporations from the United States was from their affiliates[15] and a similar pattern has been maintained in recent years. In the case of developing countries also, technology transactions are largely between subsidiaries and affiliated and foreign parent corporations, with a much higher degree of technological dependence on parent companies. Payments of fees for engineering and technical services to foreign companies also rose considerably in the 1960s and 1970s as a large number of major infrastructure and industrial projects were undertaken in several developing countries. During the 1970s and in the last few years, there has also been a marked increase in technology licensing to nonaffiliated enterprises in developing countries, largely because of the rapid growth of domestically owned industrial enterprises, both state-owned and in the private sector.

The nature of technological requirements are generally different for licensee enterprises from industrialized countries and those from developing economies. For enterprises in industrialized countries, a technology license mainly comprises user rights to a specific product or process, normally covered by patents, though also often accompanied by proprietary or specialized know-how with production conditions and the technological environment of licensor and licensee enterprises being at a fairly similar level. Developing country enterprises, however, often require a larger technology package, because of limitations in skills and in processed materials and technical services. Often, license agreements have been accompanied by, or been incorporated in, turnkey contracts for project implementation, or service agreements for specific functions in the postimplementation stage.

ROLE OF THE STATE

The role of the state is also assuming much greater importance in the process of technology transfer. In industrialized countries, while decisions regarding foreign investment and technology licensing are taken at enterprise level, considerable restrictions have been imposed in the United States on the transfer of latest technologies, especially in computers and other high technology areas, to certain countries. Though similar governmental restrictions have not been imposed in Western European countries and Japan, there is greater concern that the transfer of new and innovative technologies does not result in adverse impact on defense-related and other strategic industries nor lead to rapid growth of competitive production capability. These developments may have considerable impact on technology transfer in several fields where major innovative changes are taking place. The process of technology transfer to developing countries will also be affected particularly with regard to the latest technologies. However, most of the immediate technological requirements of these countries can still be met and is not likely to be unduly affected by restrictions in home countries, except in certain high technology areas.

In most developing countries, national governments play an important role in structuring the pattern of foreign investments and technology inflow. Partly for historical reasons and partly because of varying degrees of socioeconomic planning, proposals for foreign investment are screened by governmental agencies in many of these countries. During the last decade, however, in several developing countries, regulatory measures have also been extended to foreign technology proposals.

An important objective in developing countries is to achieve rapid technological growth and self-reliance through appropriate choice, absorption, and adaptation of foreign technology to local factor situations and innovative research and applications in national institutions and enterprises.[16] These involve the formulation and implementation of specific policies on technology and varying degrees of technology planning, extending from assessment of needs in critical production sectors and development of technological infrastructure to selection and acquisition of technology and its absorption and adaptation. They also require the institutional infrastructure for dealing with foreign technology and with the development of indigenous technological capability through specialized training and research programs. An essential aspect of technology policy is the choice of appropriate technology. The suitability of particular technology can only be judged in the context of given situations and requirements and has to be related to local factor conditions and availability of various materials and skills. What may be appropriate in one set of circumstances may be quite unsuitable in another, even in the same country. Development priorities may also be different together with the size of local markets and availability of various skills. In some cases, the latest technologies may be the most suitable as in export-oriented production, while in others, foreign technology may require considerable adaptation to meet local demand and conditions. The development of technological infrastructure involves specialized technical education and training programs, besides local facilities for technological services, including consultancy engineering and designs. The acquisition of required technology may necessitate measures for ensuring adequate foreign technology inflow but on acceptable terms and conditions and the development of facilities and incentives for increased use and application of indigenous technology. Increased technological absorption and adaptation may also require several measures designed to encourage such programs by national institutions and enterprises. Institutional facilities may also need to be created or developed for dealing with foreign technology or to provide closer links between national research institutions and production enterprises. A fairly well-defined package of technology policies, which are closely related to policies on foreign direct investment, require, therefore, implementation. The details of these policies may differ considerably from country to country and at various stages of time and economic development.

While various policies and measures for technological development have been introduced in several developing countries, considerable emphasis has been given to the regulation of foreign technology inflow and to the review of proposed agreements of foreign technology and services by governmental agencies. Governmental screening of technology agreements was undertaken in Japan in the 1950s and was also implemented in certain developing countries, particularly India, in the 1960s. In the 1970s, however, a number of Latin American and Asian countries enacted specific legislation. In other countries, such regulations formed part of foreign investment legislation as in Korea, or of measures relating to industrial properties as in Brazil.[17] Some other countries have adopted presidential or executive decrees, as in the Philippines and Spain, while some governments, as in India, have exercised considerable control through administrative measures and guidelines.

The regulatory provisions and related institutional arrangements are fairly similar in their coverage and procedures. They provide for compulsory registration of technology agreements, including those relating to services, franchise, etc. and governmental approval of the terms and conditions of such agreements is required before these can be considered valid. The procedure for registration, approval, and monitoring of such agreements is prescribed. Norms and guidelines are also set for various contractual provisions generally included in technology agreements. The objectives of these measures has primarily been to ensure that unruly, onerous or restrictive provisions imposed by licensors, which were inequitable for licensees or which adversely affected host economies, should not be permitted. Most of these guidelines were therefore intended to improve the bargaining position of licensee enterprise in these countries. Flexibility was sought by allowing exceptions to be made in particular cases.

The screening of foreign technology agreements by regulatory agencies in a number of developing countries, including Brazil, India, Mexico, the Andean Group countries, Korea, and the Philippines has inducted host country governments directly in the technology transfer process. It is difficult to accurately assess the impact of such regulatory measures on foreign technology inflow in any of these countries. While it can be argued that foreign technology flow through various channels would have been greater in some of these countries in the absence of regulatory control, this cannot be really determined. The substantial and continuing increase in technology payments by such countries indicates that regulatory measures have been applied on a fairly realistic basis, especially in more recent years. At the same time, as a result of such screening, the terms and conditions of foreign technology agreements in these countries have improved significantly from the viewpoint of licensees and have been more consistent with national policies and priorities in these countries. For foreign licensors, the terms of technology transfer may perhaps have been less favorable than they might have been, but a more lasting arrangement has been ensured, which would stand the test of time and would not be subject to pressures for modification during the period of agreement.

ISSUES FOR NEGOTIATIONS

Let us review the principal issues in technology transfer negotiations. Most of these have special relevance in developing countries, especially those where regulatory agencies and guidelines have been established. These aspects are not exclusive to developing countries; they also constitute issues for negotiations in large industrial projects in industrialized countries, particularly where governments of host countries become involved. They are especially applicable in negotiations for joint ventures and licensing in East European countries, though they also have relevance in negotiations between enterprises in industrialized, market-economy countries, especially proposed Japanese investments in other industrialized economies. These issues can be considered under two broad, though closely interrelated, categories. First, certain aspects can be characterized as general performance requirements for foreign subsidiaries and affiliates including, in certain cases, nonaffiliate licensees of foreign companies. Second, a number of issues relate specifically to terms and conditions which are generally incorporated in technology agreements.

PERFORMANCE REQUIREMENTS. These requirements vary considerably from country to country and from sector to sector. The employment of host country nationals, for example, has been an important requirement in most countries but is increasingly accepted as a matter of course. A linked aspect is that of training requirements and facilities, both in-plant and within the country, and training in the plant of the foreign partner or licensor. The need for this is also recognized, though details regarding fields of training, numbers to be trained, and duration of training require negotiation. Certain negotiations may prove to be difficult. These usually involve local content requirements, local research and development and development of export capability.

Local Content. This is an issue where the interests of foreign partners and licensors and those of host countries may diverge significantly. From a host country's viewpoint, technology should be transferred fully for a product or process and, subject to techno-economic viability, local content or value-added should be maximized. Foreign partners and licensors may, however, have a different approach and often prefer to participate in foreign manufacture and local content only to the extent that may be essential.[18] Thus in the processing of natural resources, production in developing countries was largely confined to mining and first-stage processing operations while, in the manufacturing sector, only the latter stages of assembly operations have been undertaken, with supply of intermediate products and components continuing for long periods from plants of the foreign partner or licensor. This pattern is changing as host countries increasingly press for maximum local content or integration in manufacture. In certain countries, such as Brazil and India, a phased program of integration and maximization of local content is viewed as an important prerequisite for foreign investment and technology proposals. In other host countries, including certain industrialized countries, there is a growing emphasis on full use of local inputs and maximum local content or integration in manufacture.

Research and Development.   With greater priority being given to technological absorption and adaptation, the development of R&D capability at enterprise level is becoming an important issue for negotiations with foreign investors and licensors. Research activities of TNCs are generally centralized in their host countries or in other industrialized economies and their foreign subsidiaries and affiliates are confined to limited product adaptation to local tastes and conditions, with little or no linkages with local R&D institutions and facilities.[19] The utilization of patents registered by TNCs in developing countries has also been very low, often falling below 1 percent of such registered patents.[20] In recent years, greater pressure is being exerted, particularly in developing countries, to intensify local research activities of TNC subsidiaries and affiliates. Provision for local research is also being made in licensing agreements though, in the case of nonaffiliate licensing, the extent of R&D is determined by local enterprises. In view of growing availability of technical manpower at lower cost in several countries, there is considerable potential for institutional and enterprise-level research. This aspect is likely to receive greater emphasis in negotiations in the future.

Export Capability.   A growing priority in technology transfer is the development of export capability through foreign technology. Technological diffusion and the availability of cheaper labor with marginal differences in productivity has already led to growth of competitive production capability and to increased production for exports in less industrialized economies in a number of fields. This shift has taken place through foreign investments and joint ventures in countries such as Ireland, Spain, and Portugal, and in Southeast Asia, which have been utilized as export platforms through export-processing zones (EPZs). Though EPZs have improved the export performance of these countries, the extent of technology transfer has been limited, since production activities have largely been comprised of repetitive, labor-intensive functions.[21] The operations of certain TNC subsidiaries and affiliates outside the EPZs have also been specifically geared to export-oriented production of a large variety of products, with the extent of technology transfer depending on the production activities undertaken. In most cases, foreign manufacturing activities, particularly in the larger developing countries, have been undertaken to meet the requirements of local markets. Certain changes have undoubtedly been brought about by host country pressure for increased exports, as with the exports of automobile parts and components from Brazil and Mexico. Host country policies have also provided for waiver from various regulatory guidelines in the case of export-oriented production by TNCs and these have also had some impact in increasing manufactured exports from these countries. However, in the case of technology licensing to nonaffiliate enterprises in these countries, the provisions relating to export rights are usually difficult to negotiate, with foreign licensors seeking to limit such rights and local licensees and regulatory agencies insisting on maximization of such rights, including provisions for specific export commitments wherever possible.

TECHNOLOGY CHOICE.   The selection of suitable technology in relation to local factor conditions is obviously a critical aspect of technology acquisition and transfer. The strategy of individual corporations is to bring about constant upgrading of existing technological knowledge and capability through research, licensing, or other means of obtaining access to improved products or processes. When foreign production operations are undertaken, the technology transferred to subsidiaries and affiliates is generally the same as the technology utilized by parent companies, though modifications may be made to suit local conditions or nonavailability of certain inputs, including specialized skills. In the case of joint ventures and licensing arrangements, however, the nature of details of the technology transferred is defined in the agreement and may relate either to the latest technologies in the particular field or to specific techniques, processes, and services which are agreed upon by the parties concerned.

The issue of appropriate technology has been a source of some controversy in the past with respect to technology transfer to developing countries. It has been argued that technologies transferred to these countries are based on techno-economic conditions prevailing in industrialized economies and are often inappropriate in relation to local objectives and priorities.[22] Cases have been cited of obsolescent technology on the one hand and highly capital-intensive techniques on the other. Other instances relate to a high degree of dependence on imports of intermediate products, parts, and components, often at unduly high transfer prices and for long periods of time. More appropriate technology has, in several situations, been identified with smaller scales of production and a higher degree of labor intensity; factors which are considered more suitable for developing countries. This is not, however, necessarily the case. In most industrial sectors, economies of scale are of vital importance and to the extent that such economies are possible with more capital-intensive techniques, these would be necessary for competitive production. At the same time, the need for substitution of labor by capital is much less in most developing countries and technology choice must take this factor into account. In the case of export-oriented production, the use of the latest, capital-intensive production techniques may be essential but may have to be combined with increasing levels of local content over a period of time. The technological needs of rural and semi-urban areas in developing countries may also be different and may necessitate the use of products and processes which are more geared to local demand and availability of investments and technology.

It is difficult to generalize on the question of technology choice, except to state that this has to be related to a given set of factors. With wide variations in factor conditions, priorities, and levels of development, the selection of technology by user enterprises must be made in the context of particular situations prevailing. As pointed out earlier, subsidiaries and affiliates of TNCs would, in general, use the technology available with the parent company. Local enterprises, however, can exercise greater choice if they have to acquire foreign technology through licensing or joint ventures, since there is considerable awareness of technological alternatives and different packages of investment can be negotiated.

Choice of technology must and can only be made by user institutions, enterprises, and individuals and that the role of governments should be very limited. Governmental agencies can undoubtedly prescribe certain broad parameters of technology choice in different fields and can set priorities in terms of local content, development of export potential, and the like, but final decisions on the nature and type of technology to be used must rest with the user.

CONTRACTUAL TERMS AND CONDITIONS.   The contractual provisions in technology agreements with licensees in different countries vary considerably, depending on the sector concerned, the nature of the technology, and the respective bargaining strength of the licensor and licensee. For process industries, for example, the technical details and warranties provided are generally much greater and more specific than in the case of semi-assembly industries. The technology package may range from an outright purchase of certain technology or a patent license entitling the licensee to use certain patented processes to turnkey projects covering various stages of project planning, implementation, and start-up. The bargaining position of the licensee differs considerably depending on the size of the market, availability of technological alternatives, and experience in negotiating such agreements. Contractual provisions between licensors and licensees may also be significantly affected by norms and guidelines prescribed by regulatory agencies in countries where technology contracts are reviewed by such agencies. However, while the detailed terms and conditions of such contracts may differ considerably, the various issues generally covered in these agreements tend to be similar.[23]

Definition of Technology.   The license agreement should clearly define (1) the products to be covered, (2) the production processes involved, including specific reference to production capacities where this may be relevant, and (3) the production and related documentation that may be necessary, such as blueprints, manufacturing drawings, etc., and essential features of such documentation. For example, the unit of measurement for engineering products may be different in the case of particular licensors, and may require modification to suit the licensee's production program. Drawings of certain parts and components may be required which are brought-out by the licensor but which may need to be manufactured by the developing-country licensee. The licensee may be required to use some locally manufactured materials or components which may necessitate modification in the manufacturing processes for a particular product. All such technological aspects need to be considered and incorporated in the agreement, in order to avoid subsequent misunderstandings and disputes. Similarly, technological services need to be specifically identified so that the scope of technical assistance is clearly defined by both parties from the start. This can include a number of services which a licensor would not normally be expected to provide to a licensee in a developed country, but which would be essential for a licensee in a developing economy. Technology agreements between TNC parents and their subsidiaries and affiliates should also define the nature and details of technology and technical services to be provided. The cost of technical services provided by technology suppliers should be comparable to costs for similar services from other sources, both foreign and domestic.

Training.   For the licensee, the provision of adequate training for local personnel is a critical issue. Contractual conditions usually provide for visits of a specified number of licensee's personnel to the licensor's plant for short, defined periods. The licensee needs to ensure that the number of such personnel and the time periods specified are adequate for technological absorption of the processes and techniques involved. An important element, particularly in contracts relating to machinery and engineering-goods production, relates to training in designs. While licensors may consider training in designs as outside the scope of licensing for manufacture, this aspect may be of crucial importance to the licensee for future adaptations and innovations. This may particularly need to be included in technology-supply arrangements between TNC parents and affiliates.

Technology Payments. Once the nature of technology and technical services has been defined, the remuneration for technology is among the most important elements to be negotiated. Where a license agreement is accompanied by capital participation, the extent of such participation may be closely related to the overall payment for technology. In certain developing countries, such as Brazil, India, and Mexico, no payments for technology are permitted by wholly-owned subsidiaries to their parent corporations. In other cases, technology payments are often sought to be reduced by regulatory agencies in joint ventures, where there is majority or substantial foreign equity participation. Consequently, remuneration for technology and know-how may be higher for a license agreement with no foreign equity participation than for one with, say, 40 percent capital ownership by the licensor.

Technology payments may take the form of a fixed fee or a running royalty or a combination of the two. Payments for specific technical services are considered separately for each service function. Where this is aggregated by the licensor as part of an overall technology package, it should be disaggregated by the licensees and considered independently. Lump-sum payments are usually made in cases where the know-how can be fully and completely transferred in the first instance. These usually relate to relatively simple manufacturing techniques or drawings, and may be negotiated by a licensee where no continuing support or assistance of the licensor is required. The more common form of payment is that of a percentage royalty, usually related to sales, though sometimes to production. In such cases, it is often provided that the landed value of imported intermediate products and components from the licensor is deducted from the sales figure for royalty computation, so that only the value-added is taken into account. It is essential for both the licensor and licensee to assess the payments involved against projected production and sales in arriving at the percentage rate. A rate of 4–5 percent may prove reasonable for tailormade items of high unit sales, but a much lower rate may prove unduly high for items produced in large quantities or for process industries.

Over the last decade, a fairly definitive pattern has gradually emerged in respect to license royalties paid in different production sectors, and licensees in developing countries are in a better position to compare payments made by other licensees for the same or similar know-how. While such information was formerly a closely guarded secret, it is now available. The fact that, in many countries, license agreements require approval of a governmental agency, also ensures that arbitrarily high royalty rates will not be accepted, particularly where similar technology has been acquired in the past, or where information from similar agencies in other countries can be obtained. In some countries, a ceiling limit is prescribed by regulatory agencies for royalty payments in different fields. This may, however, be rather arbitrary and may inhibit technology inflow.

In a number of license agreements, technology payments are a combination of lump-sum fees and a royalty percentage. The former is often treated either as a disclosure payment for basic documentation, while the royalty is linked with production know-how. Where there is a royalty ceiling or where the duration of the agreement is for a short period, the lump-sum fee insisted on by licensors tends to be correspondingly higher. Ultimately, in determining the technology payment, the overall figure has to be considered. It is not practicable to formulate any uniform principles as to the size of the lump-sum fee or the rate of royalty; this has to be considered on a case-by-case basis. What is necessary, however, is that these should fully take account of the implications and impact of such payments on the production structure of licensee enterprises and should bear relation to royalty payments in the same sector and for similar know-how from alternative technology suppliers.

Duration of Agreements. This issue is closely linked to that of technology payments. It is to the advantage of the licensor, including parent TNCs, to extend the duration as long as possible, as royalty income increases with increase in sales, while technological support tends to decline. For the licensee however, including TNC affiliates, the period should be linked to the time it takes for the licensee to fully absorb the know-how involved. Two other issues should also be considered in this context. First, where the technology is fast-changing, as in pharmaceuticals or microelectronics, and where the license agreement adequately provides for full access to all innovations and improvements effected by the licensor, it may be of advantage to the licensee to have a longer duration. Second, it is important that the life of the patents involved in any license agreement are taken into account. A licensee may face serious difficulty if the life of a critical patent extends beyond the duration of the technology agreement. While it is difficult to specify any duration period as being the most appropriate, it is generally accepted that where royalty payment is involved, the period of agreement should normally range from 5 to 10 years. Whatever the period negotiated, however, it is important that technological absorption is as full and complete as possible within such period.

Access to Improvements. This needs to be specifically provided for in technology agreements. It is also desirable to have a clear understanding between the parties on how such improvements are to be defined. In general, any innovations or improvements which are introduced in the plant of the licensor should be available to a licensee during the period of agreement.

Warranty. A license agreement should contain a warranty as to the results of its use. A technology should, for example, be capable of achieving a specified level of production in a process industry or a defined level of manufacturing integration in the licensee's plant over a period of time for engineering goods or assembly-type production. In any event, the contract should provide that the technology supplied is full and complete for the purposes defined in the agreement. Licensors can argue, with some justification, that the technology supplied cannot be more complete or better than that used in their own plant and that licensee enterprises should consequently take the same risks that the licensor takes in using particular processes and techniques. Whatever the warranty negotiated, it should provide for full and complete transfer of technological know-how as is used in the licensor's plant.

Territorial Sales Restrictions. A major difficulty in license negotiations relates to the exclusivity or otherwise, and to the territorial restrictions on sales by licensees. A technology license should normally be exclusive for a country and it is, of course, to the advantage of the licensee if it is made exclusive for a region. However, it is with respect to territorial restrictions in sales that negotiations tend to be difficult. Technology suppliers usually license their technology in several countries. Even where nonexclusive territorial rights are incorporated, the licensee enterprise may, and often does, prove a serious competitor over a period of time. At the same time, the imposition of undue restrictions on exports may prove to be a grave disadvantage for licensees. From a national viewpoint also, territorial sales restrictions can prove to be a major constraint in license agreements. In several developing countries, regulatory guidelines prohibit unreasonable territorial restrictions. One approach in this regard may be to provide for nonexclusive sales rights in countries, except where the licensor is legally precluded because of exclusive manufacturing rights given to other licensees.

Tie-in Provisions.   Contractual conditions relating to supply of intermediate products and components exclusively from the licensor have been the focus of considerable attention in relation to "transfer pricing." In general, tie-in clauses are not desirable and can constitute a serious disadvantage to the licensee in terms of component costs. Licensees should be free to obtain components and intermediate products from any source. However, in practical terms, a licensee usually does look upon the licensor for supply of intermediates and components. What has to be ensured is that the pricing of such components and intermediate products is not unreasonably high. This often presents considerable practical difficulty. It may be desirable to avoid any restrictive tie-in clauses and, in many developing countries, they are not permitted. Intermediates and components do have to be obtained and the licensee tends to rely on the licensor in this regard. From the host country's and the licensee's viewpoint, it may be necessary that domestic manufacture is undertaken to the maximum extent as is economically and commercially justified. This would reduce the magnitude of the problem and would avoid a common tendency on the part of licensors, to limit domestic manufacture in developing countries to assembly or semi-assembly operations for indefinitely long periods.

Even where a program of domestic integration is defined, the problem of pricing of imported components and materials still remains. Negotiations can center around certain aspects: (1) With respect to intermediate products bought and supplied by licensors, the price charged should be the cost to the licensor, plus any handling or other charges that may be involved. (2) Where components are manufactured by the licensor, the cost of such components should be on the basis of armslength transactions. In some cases, such costs can also be linked to the cost at which the components are priced in the next stage of production in the licensor's plant, plus any handling and other costs that may be involved. An alternative approach may also be for licensors to supply such products and components at internationally competitive prices and accord most favored licensee treatment to licensees from developing countries.

Patents.   In technology agreements, the first need is to provide user rights to the various patents that may be involved. It is through patents, that licensors hold the real bargaining strength and licensees must ensure that the patent provisions are carefully determined, including usage rights for patent-validity periods beyond the duration of an agreement. The license agreement should provide for transfer of user rights for any new patents registered by the licensor during the period of agreement. It is necessary to provide that, in the event of any alleged or actual infringement of third party patents by use of a particular technology licensed, responsibility remains with the technology supplier or is at least shared by the licensor and licensee.

Trademarks.   Trademarks are often considered of great importance by host countries and licensees in developing countries. Foreign brand names have a strong consumer preference and are necessary, especially in initial periods. At the same time, it is important that licensees should, over a period of time, develop their own brand names, as otherwise they would always be subject to royalty payments for the usage of foreign brand names. An approach which is being increasingly adopted in certain developing countries is that, for the period of agreement, the foreign brand name is used in conjunction with a local name so that, after the agreement terminates, the local name alone can continue to be utilized.

Postcontract Use of Technology. A contractual provision often included by licensors is that the technology licensed shall not be utilized by the licensee after the period of agreement. Where such technology is covered by a patent or patents, the situation has to be taken care of by the licensee. Where it relates to unpatented know-how, however, such a provision would not be permissible in most developing countries where technology agreements are screened by governmental agencies.

Arbitration and Governing Law. It is necessary to provide for the location and procedures for arbitration. Host countries and licensees prefer that arbitration should take place in the country of the licensee and that it is done by a group of three persons, two of whom would be appointed by the respective parties and the third person by mutual agreement. If the place of arbitration is outside the country, the licensee is placed at a great disadvantage and may have to incur considerable costs if arbitration becomes necessary. Most developing countries have prescribed that governing law shall be that of the licensee country.

Other Clauses. A number of other clauses relating to aspects such as assignability; confidentiality; sublicensing; language; currency of payment; inspection and reporting; and *force majeure* and the like, do not normally present undue difficulty in negotiations and can generally be satisfactorily resolved.

The finalization of a technology agreement and the related negotiating strategy can be a fairly complex process. Licensors, which are mostly transnational corporations, are much more experienced in the field of licensing than licensees in developing countries. Where technology regulation agencies have been set up, these agencies examine licensing proposals from a national viewpoint, and there may be several aspects where the approach of the licensee enterprises, particularly that of TNC subsidiaries and affiliates, and that of the regulatory institution may not necessarily be in consonance.

At the same time, it is important that the negotiations are left to the prospective licensee enterprise and should not be taken over by the regulatory institution except where TNC affiliates constitute the licensee enterprises. The success of a license agreement largely depends on the goodwill and close relationship between licensor and licensee enterprises. The process of negotiations is an essential element in developing adequate understanding of the problems involved in transfer of know-how. Close relationship and understanding is also necessary to ensure that the foreign processes and techniques acquired take local factor and material resources into full account. In many cases, this requires some adjustment of the foreign process and know-how and such modification may necessitate considerable time and effort on the part of the licensor. The intangible elements of technology are also such that, while developing-country licensees must ensure that contractual provisions are fair and equitable, a close and harmonious relationship is also built up with foreign licensors, so that transfer of foreign techniques and know-how is as complete and effective as possible.

It must be emphasized that the weak bargaining position of licensees from most developing countries necessitates governmental institutional support. The fact that foreign subsidiaries and affiliates control sizeable segments of manufacture in many of these countries, and operate primarily on a parent-affiliate rather than a licensor-licensee relationship, is an added reason for institutional control of technological aspects of their activities. It must, however, also be stressed that a positive and promotional approach to technology acquisition and transfer should be an integral feature of regulatory control.

It is likely that the exercise of greater selectivity in respect to foreign investments and technology and efforts to improve the bargaining position of recipient enterprises through regulatory control, will channel external investments and technology flow to priority sectors in host countries and improve the terms and conditions of technology transactions. While such inflow is undoubtedly necessary in several fields, it is also essential that local enterprises do not remain unduly dependent on foreign technology, with no effort towards indigenous research and for technological absorption and adaptation.

Experience of technology regulation in the last two decades has shown that regulatory measures can be adjusted fairly rapidly to changing technological requirements. This took place in Japan in the late 1960s when the review procedures were considerably eased. Similarly, in the Republic of Korea, regulatory requirements regarding foreign technology were considerably liberalized in 1979 and again in 1981–1982.[24] In India there was considerable relaxation in regulatory measures during 1985. The general approach in these countries has been that, as local industrial groups developed necessary capability for appropriate technology choice and negotiation of suitable terms of agreement within the framework of broad governmental policies, there was less need for a governmental agency to review foreign technology proposals in certain categories. This trend is likely to be extended in other developing countries where technology regulation is taking place.

While technology regulation has been useful in improving the terms and conditions of foreign technology agreements, the promotional aspect of ensuring adequate inflow of needed technology has been given relatively little attention in most developing countries. It may be necessary in the future to provide greater institutional assistance in locating alternative sources of technology and obtaining information regarding use and impact of alternative technologies in different conditions. While decisions regarding choice and application of particular technologies must necessarily rest with user enterprises, institutional support and assistance could be very useful in providing technological information, which is often lacking in most developing countries.

In the next decade, it is likely that regulatory guidelines will continue in several developing countries but, in view of the growing demand for industrial technology in these countries, it is likely that much greater flexibility and pragmatism will be exercised in dealing with foreign technology. As the negotiating capacity of developing-country enterprises improves, the role of regulatory agencies is likely to get reduced. Increasingly, the policy approach towards foreign technology is likely to become pragmatic, as these countries recognizes that they must function within the mainstream of international technological relationships. It is also possible to identify certain other trends that are likely. First, it can be expected that there would be much greater transparency and information on technology-supply arrangements in different countries, particularly regarding the commercial terms and conditions of technology transfer in various sectors and countries.[25] There is increasing exchange of information between different countries regarding licensing terms and conditions and regarding use of particular technologies in different conditions. Second, the technology market is getting increasingly competitive for a large range of products and services required in developing countries. There is greater knowledge of alternative sources of technology and their relationship with different factor endowments and conditions of application. Third, the policy approach on certain issues, particularly local content requirements and development of export capability, is fairly similar in a number of developing countries. The need for increased local integration in manufacture is particularly applicable to assembly-type industries, but can also be applied to resource-based industries such as minerals, pulp and paper, chemicals and fertilizers, and other process industries, where a greater degree of backward and forward linkages are sought. Foreign capital and technology is also particularly welcomed in developing countries if these contribute to greater exports of processed goods and guidelines relating to foreign capital ownership and other contractual terms are generally waived in the case of export-oriented enterprises. While there are obvious constraints in developing export capability, this factor is assuming a major role in negotiations on technology licensing.

NEGOTIATIONS AT THE INTERNATIONAL LEVEL

While national governments are playing an increasingly active role in technological development and in transfer of technology, considerable discussions and negotiations have also taken place at international level. These have largely centered around the need for closer cooperation between countries for scientific and technological development and the formulation of a code of conduct on technology transfer to developing countries.

Scientific and technological cooperation between countries was one of the aspects particularly stressed in the international conference on science and technology for development in Vienna in 1979. The need and potential for such cooperation was also emphasized in several other conferences at international and regional levels. Since the 1970s, there has been considerable increase in technical cooperation between developing countries. This has extended to industrial training programs and joint research activities; increased trade between these countries in manufactured products, including capital goods; greater use of consultancy engineering facilities between these countries; and the establishment of a large number of industrial projects, usually joint ventures, between enterprises in these countries. Certain developing countries, particularly oil-exporting countries, have emerged as important sources of foreign investment. Other countries such as Argentina, Brazil, India, the Republic of Korea, Mexico, the Philippines and Singapore have entered into arrangements for industrial investments and technology transfer, principally through joint ventures, in several projects in other developing countries.[26] At the same time, it must be recognized that transfer of industrial technology between developing countries is still very limited and that the flow of industrial technology is primarily taking place through foreign investors and licensors from industrialized, market-economy countries to enterprises in other countries.

The negotiations relating to a code of conduct on technology transfer, which have been conducted under the auspices of UNCTAD in Geneva, have continued for several years. The issues under negotiation relate largely to the terms and conditions of technology transfer between licensors from industrialized economies and licensees from developing countries, though they also extend to several policy aspects of technological development and foreign technology inflow in developing countries.[27] Though these issues have not been resolved and there has been no agreement on a code of conduct so far, the discussions and negotiations have highlighted several key aspects, which have been taken into consideration, to the extent considered necessary, in the formulation of policies, legislation, and administrative measures on foreign technology in a number of developing countries.

FUTURE TRENDS

It is against the above background of national policies and experience that future trends in transfer of industrial technology can be assessed. There is no doubt that, because of extensive diffusion of technology, there has been considerable increase in capability for technological absorption and adaptation in a much larger number of countries than a couple of decades ago. As a result, changes in comparative advantage are taking place in several industrial sectors which may necessitate varying degrees of international restructuring of production. At the same time, major technological innovations are bringing about significant transformation in products and processes in different fields which may require new initiatives for technology transfer and absorption. The availability of technology from an increasing number of sources, even in innovative, high-technology areas as minicomputers and biotechnology, certainly suggests that the pace of technology transfer will be further accelerated in the coming years.

The present trends in innovations and the high costs of research suggest that initial developments in high-technology areas will largely take place in the industrialized countries. Research expenditures in developed countries rose to over $195 billion by 1980, representing 94 percent of global expenditure on research and development.[28] R&D expenditure of corporations engaged in high-technology production was also very high, with expenditures in 1984 of IBM (USA) being of the order of $4.2 billion and that of General Electric $2.3 billion.[29] The ratio of research expenditures to sales in 1984 ranged from 9.1 percent for IBM (USA) to 8.3 percent for Siemens (Federal Republic of Germany); 8.2 percent for General Electric and 7.3 percent for Hitachi (Japan).[30] Research expenditure on this magnitude will not be practicable in the case of national governments and institutions in less developed economies or by industrial corporations in these countries. However, a considerable degree of blending of new and emerging technologies with more traditional technologies is possible and is partially reflected in the significant product developments being achieved by relatively small companies. There is substantial potential for such blending, not only in industrial applications, but in agricultural operations and agroprocessing in a number of developing countries. The process of technological adaptation in different industrial sectors is also resulting in modified technological processes being developed in several countries such as Brazil, India, and Southeast Asia, which may be more suitable in less developed economies in terms of scales of production and labor intensity but which would still enable internationally competitive production.

There can be little doubt that technology transfer will continue to increase rapidly in the next decade. It is projected that the total volume of such transactions will increase to $40 to $45 billion by the early 1990s. Most of these transactions will still take place between enterprises in industrialized countries, though the proportion of transactions with developing country enterprises may increase to around 20 percent of technology trade by the early 1990s. As for channels of transfer, it is expected that licensing to nonaffiliate companies will increase substantially, both in industrialized and developing countries and that technological linkages and contractual arrangements without foreign equity participation will become increasingly popular.

With respect to technology transfer to developing countries, further definitive trends can be identified. With growing industrialization, the demand for foreign industrial technology will continue to expand rapidly in these countries. While the technological lead of industrialized countries will undoubtedly be maintained, the absorptive and adaptive capacity in a number of developing countries is likely to create new demands for industrial technology and its transfer to these countries. At the same time, as locally owned enterprises including an increasing number of state-owned companies, grow and become increasingly diversified, technology licensing between unaffiliated companies is likely to become the most significant channel of transfer between enterprises in industrialized and developing countries. The rapid expansion of consultancy engineering capability in several developing countries is also likely to lead to increased contractual arrangements in the technological service sector. During the 1990s, it is expected that technology fees and payments for know-how and technical services by developing-country enterprises will increase to $6–8 billion annually and, of this amount, 60–70 percent may relate to technology transactions between unaffiliated companies. This aspect is further underscored by the growing importance of technology inflow as compared to foreign direct investment in several developing countries. While foreign investments will continue to be critical in certain countries, increased national participation in ownership may be sought and greater selectivity applied regarding the sectors in which such investments are permitted. Trends in the reduced flow of foreign direct investment to developing countries during 1982–1984 also suggest greater reluctance on the part of transnational corporations to invest heavily in a number of these countries. Consequently, the trend in the next decade would be increasingly for joint ventures and nonaffiliate licensing arrangements. This would enable local partners and shareholders to exercise more participation and control and would also ensure a greater degree of local autonomy for affiliates of transnational corporations. The continuing concern in developing countries regarding nonutilization of patents registered by foreign companies may create difficulties in certain countries with respect to industrial property rights. This also could lead to varying degrees of compulsory licensing, particularly in food, pharmaceuticals, and other priority production sectors in these countries. While technology licensing to developing countries will still continue to be a seller's market, conditions are changing rapidly and the negotiation process is likely to become more complex, with the added role of governmental regulatory bodies in several countries. However pragmatic and flexible the approach of these bodies may be, two-stage negotiations may often be necessary, initially with the local partner or license and subsequently in the light of governmental guidelines and response to particular proposals.

The next decade is likely to be a period of much greater trade in and exchange of industrial technology and know-how between enterprises in different countries. For those possessing or developing new products and technologies through research and adaptation, an important aspect of corporate strategy will be to maximize the returns from such developments on a global basis, including production and licensing in various countries. For these wishing to avail themselves of new techniques and processes, an increased number of sources and channels for transfer are likely to become available. With growing technological interdependence between enterprises in different countries in various sectors, the role of technology transfer will undoubtedly assume added and critical dimension in the coming years.

NOTES

1. Vernon, R. "International Investment and International Trade in the Product Cycle," *Quarterly Journal of Economics*, May 1966, pp. 190–207. Also see Magee, S.P. "Technology and the Appropriability Theory of the Multinational Corporation," in *The New International Economic Order*, edited by Bhagwati, J., Cambridge, MA: MIT Press, 1976, and Vernon R., "Enterprise Strategies: The Technology Factor," Chapter 3, pp. 39–58, from *Storm over the Multinationals*, Cambridge, MA.: Harvard University Press, 1977. For a literature review on the subject, also see Calvet, A.L. "A Synthesis of Foreign Direct Investment Theories and Theories of the Multinational Firm," *Journal of International Business Studies*, Spring/Summer 1981, pp. 43–59.
2. The need and rationale for licensing is analyzed by Contractor, F.J., "The Role of Licensing in International Strategy," *Columbia Journal of World Business*, No. 4, Winter 1981, pp. 73–83.
3. Yoshio Ohara: "Japanese Regulation of Technology Imports," *Journal of World Trade Law* Vol. 15 No: 1 (January 1981).
4. Sources for figures quoted in this paragraph are International Monetary Fund, *Balance of Payments Yearbooks* and U.S. Dept. of Commerce, *Survey of Current Business*, March 1985.
5. Ibid. The figures for Europe, however, exclude investments in Switzerland in 1981 and 1982.
6. UNCTC: *Trends and Issues in Foreign Direct Investment and Related Flow*, United Nations, New York, 1985. Figures based on IMF *Balance of Payments Yearbook* and data provided by OECD, Paris.
7. Technology transactions are calculated as the basis of technology receipts and payments of the countries. See for U.S.A.: Department of Commerce, *Survey of Current Business*, for Great Britain, Department of Industry, *Business Monitor—Overseas Transactions*, for Japan, Bank of Japan, *Balance of Payments Monthly*, for Federal Republic of Germany, Bundes Bank, *Monatsberichte der Deutsche Bundesbank*, for France, Ministere de l'Economie, des Finances et du Budget, *Statistiques et Etudes Financieres*.
8. Technology exports of the five countries 1983 amounted to $10,631 billion and technology imports to $7,481, billion, based on sources given under 7 above.
9. U.S. Department of Commerce, *Survey of Current Business*, various issues.
10. Ibid.
11. See for Great Britain; Department of Industry, *Business Monitor—Overseas Transactions*, and for the Federal Republic of Germany, Bundes Bank, *Monatsberichte der Deutsche Bundesbank*.
12. Bank of Japan, *Balance of Payments Monthly*, various issues.
13. See for Federal Republic of Germany, Bundes Bank, *Monatsberichte der Deutsche Bundesbank*, various issues, for France, Ministere de l'Economie, des Finances et du Budget,

Statistiques et Etudes Financieres, various issues and for Great Britain, Department of Industry, *Business Monitor—Overseas Transactions*, various issues.

14. Technology payments by developing countries in the 1960s and 1970s are based on estimates of UNCTAD, *Handbook of International Trade and Development Statistics*, 1979. For 1982 estimates, see, Singh, Rana K.D.N. "Long-term Needs and Expectations of Developing Countries in Technology Licensing," paper presented at the Seventh Annual Meeting of Licensing Executives Society, Atlanta, Sept. 1981.

15. Based on UNCTAD, *Legislation and Regulation on Technology Transfer: Empirical Analysis of their Effects in Selected Countries*, 28 August 1980.

16. The objective of technological self-reliance was the subject of the 24th Pubwash Symposium on "Self-reliance and Alternative Development Strategies," Dar-es-Salaam, June 1976. See also, Sagasti, F.R., "Technological Self-reliance and Co-operation among Third World Countries," *World Development*, 1976, Vol. 4, Nos. 10/11, Pergamon Press, pp. 939–946. For various aspects of technology policies in developing countries, see also Singh, Rana K.D.N. "Critical Issues of Technology Policy in Developing Countries" in Technology Management and Acquisition, Vol. 1, edited by Boger and Singh, ILI, Washington, 1984.

17. Such regulatory measures were promulgated, for example, in the Andean Group countries by Decision 84 and 85 of the Cartagena Agreement, in Argentina by Law N19231, in Mexico, by the Law on Registration and Transfer of Technology and the Use and Exploitation of Patents and Trade Marks and in Brazil, by 015/INPI. The issues in foreign technology regulation are discussed in Singh, Rana K.D.N.: "Institutional Regulation of Foreign Technology in Developing Countries," in Technology Management and Acquisition, Vol. II, edited by Boger and Singh, ILI, Washington, 1984.

18. For empirical, evidence on the high import-propensity of foreign subsidiaries see, Lall, S., "Transnationals, Domestic Enterprises: A Survey," in Lall, S. *The Multinational Corporations*, New York: Macmillan, 1980, Vaitsos, C.V. *Employment Problems and Transnational Enterprises in Developing Countries: Distortions and Inequality*, International Labour Office, Geneva, 1976. In the case of Brazilian heavy electrical equipment, see: Newfarmer, R.S. "International Oligopoly in the Electrical Industry," in Newfarmer, R.S. (ed.) *International Oligopoly and Development*, Notre Dame: Notre Dame University Press, 1984.

19. For R&D activities of U.S. based TNCs see Creamer, D., *Overseas Research and Development by United States Multinationals, 1966–1975: Estimated Expenditures and a Statistical Profile*, New York, The Conference Board, 1976. Also, Behrman, J.N. and Fisher, W.A. *Overseas R and D Activities of Transnational Companies*, Oelgenschlager, Gunn and Main Publishers, 1980. Exception from the general pattern of limited foreign R&D activity is presented by Ronstad, R. *Research and Development Abroad by U.S. Multinationals*, New York: Praeger, 1977.

20. For an analysis of this issue see Vaitsos, C.V., "Patents Revisited: Their Function in Developing Countries," *Journal of Development Studies*, Vol.9, No. 1, October 1972; Penrose, R., "International Patenting in the Less-developed Countries," *The Economic Journal*, Sept. 1973, pp. 768–787; United Nations, *The Role of the Patent System in the Transfer of Technology to Developing Countries*, New York, 1975.

21. A review of production activities in export-processing zones is presented in United Nations Development Organization, *Export Processing Zones in Developing Countries*, Working Paper on Structural Change, No. 19, 1980. Skill development in the case of two Asian countries is reviewed by Lim, L.Y.C., "Multinational Firms and Manufacturing for Export in Less Developed Countries: The Case of the Electronics Industry in Malaysia and Singapore," (unpublished Ph.D. dissertation), University of Michigan, Ann Arbor, 1978. Also see UNIDO "Reorientation of Industrial Strategy in Developing Countries and Selection and Application of Appropriate Industrial Technology," UNIDO paper, 1978, pp. 6–9, 13, 15–18, 20–28, in *Technology Management and Acquisition*, edited by Boger and Singh, Vol. II, ILI, Washington, 1984.

22. This argument is presented, for example, by Stewart, F. *Technology and Under-development*, Boulder: Westview Press, 1977; Bhalla, A.S., ed. Technology and Employment in Industry, International Labour Organisation, Geneva, 1975.

23. These contractual elements are discussed in detail by the United Nations Development Organisation, *Guide to the Acquisition of Foreign Technology in Developing Countries*, (ID/96), 1973 and *Guidelines for Evaluation of Transfer of Technology Agreements*, (ID/233), Vienna, 1980. Also see Singh, Rana K.D.N. "Contractual Provisions for Technology Transfer" in Technology Management and Acquisition, Vol. II, ILI, Washington, 1984.

24. Liberalization of foreign technology measures in the Republic of Korea is reviewed by the Technology Transfer Center, *The Comparative Studies of National Experience in Technology Policies—The Case of the Republic of Korea*, Korean Institute of Science and Technology, Seoul, 1981.

25. Recent trends in foreign technology regulation in developing countries is analyzed by Marton, K. *Technology, Multinationals and Industrialization*, Lexington Books, 1986 (forthcoming), Chapter 8.

26. UNCTC: *Salient Features and Trends in Foreign Direct Investment*, United Nations, New York, 1983, pp. 19–20 and Table 16.

27. Thompson, Dennis. "The UNCTAD Code on Transfer of Technology," *Journal of World Trade Law* Vol. 16, No. 4 (July-Aug. 1982) pp. 311–37.

28. UNESCO: *Estimated World Resources for Research and Development 1970–1980*, Paris, 1984.

29. *Annual Reports* of companies concerned.

30. Ibid.

INTERNATIONAL COMMERCIAL BANKING

CONTENTS

INTERNATIONAL COMMERCIAL BANKING

Francis A. Lees

The past three decades have witnessed the most extensive and penetrating expansion of international banking in world financial history. Although led by the overseas expansion of American banks, this growth has spread to the banks and banking systems of other countries as well. The development of international banking has contributed to the evolution of national financial markets in developing as well as industrial countries. More important, it has established firm linkages between the financial markets of all nations, and these linkages in turn have evolved into full-fledged international financial market sectors.

Whereas the early development of international banking was related primarily to the need to finance export-import trade and provide short-term credit facilities, subsequent stages of growth have witnessed the introduction of new international money-market instruments—dollar certificates of deposit (CDs) in London, revolving underwriting facilities (RUFs) in London and Singapore, floating rate CDs (FRCDs), and complex syndicated loans. The ability to arbitrage funds through the international money markets has been enhanced by the growing activities of international banks. Moreover, international banks have become more innovative in finding ways to borrow as well as lend internationally mobile funds.

GLOBAL ASPECTS

ROLE OF NATIONAL BANKING SYSTEMS. A discussion of the growth of international commercial banking inevitably begins with an examination of national banking systems and their banks, which furnish the basic building blocks. Several national banking systems have taken the lead in providing international commercial banking services, whereas other nations have been avid consumers. What makes a country prominent in international banking? Why are some countries more successful exporters of foreign banking representation, whereas others tend to attract foreign banking representation?

Although we do not yet have a definitive theory of international comparative advantage to explain why and how some countries export and others import international banking services, we can point to a number of factors that enter into determining how important any single country will be in providing international banking services. These include the importance of that country as a source of lendable funds, the strength of the country's currency, the size and importance of export-import trade, and the size and managerial efficiency of its banking institutions. In addition, a number of less tangible factors enter into the picture in influencing international banking leadership. These include the degree and type of cooperation provided by government agencies and the national attitude toward banking (liberal, tolerant, or populist).

Comparative statistics for the 10 leading countries in international banking are contained in Exhibit 1. At the top of the listing are the United States and the United Kingdom. These countries play a leading role in international banking because of their substantial position in world export-import trade, the prestige of their financial institutions, and their lead in foreign investment. New York and London have long enjoyed a special role as leading international financial and banking centers. The remaining eight countries play a somewhat different role in international banking.

West Germany has developed into a leading international banking country by means of its strong currency; rapid expansion in foreign trade; balance-of-payments surpluses, which permit foreign investment and foreign bond issue activity; and an inflow of foreign business investment. By contrast, Japan's status in international banking can be associated with extensive offshore borrowing by Japanese banks to finance rapid expansion in foreign trade. Moreover, Japan's capital market was closed to foreign borrowers until fairly recently. By contrast, Japan's status in international banking can be associated with extensive offshore borrowing by Japanese banks to finance rapid expansion in foreign trade. Moreover, Japan's capital market was closed to foreign borrowers until fairly recently. This has altered significantly. Japanese banks have increased their representation in key financial market centers and are able to absorb large amounts of loan funds via money and capital market securities issues (securitization). In turn the Japanese banks are playing a more prominent role as intermediators of funds and as lenders to major borrowers globally. Part of the success of Japan's international banks has been due to their support by government agencies and the central bank.

In contrast with Japan, the Canadian banks have built a substantial foreign-exchange and international-banking business based on their open economy (exports are 29 percent of GNP), substantial capital inflows from U.S. business investment and sale of bonds in New York, and development of a substantial organization of overseas branches and agencies. Canadian banks hold a large amount of foreign-currency assets as a reserve against foreign-currency liabilities.

Switzerland's status in international banking reflects a well-developed and efficiently managed financial market mechanism, a conservatively managed monetary system, and the stable value of the Swiss franc in world currency markets. The Swiss have attracted nonresident funds by their adroit and successful portfolio investments at home and overseas. Overseas representation of Swiss banks is moderate, but is directed along the lines of greatest efficiency.

The remaining four countries represented in Exhibit 1 also play an important role in international banking. This is based upon relatively open economies (column 1), substantial volumes of foreign trade (column 2), significant holdings of official reserves, and prominence of their banks in the Eurocurrency market. The currencies of seven of these countries accounted for over 85 percent of the official foreign exchange reserves of nations around the world in 1984 (Exhibit 2). The banks of the ten leading international banking countries account for 36 of the largest 100 banks in the world (Exhibit 3).

EXHIBIT 1 PRINCIPAL FACTORS RELATING TO INTERNATIONAL BANKING ROLE OF MAJOR COUNTRIES[a]

	Openness to International Trends[b]	Merchandise Exports[c]	Foreign Bond Issue[c]	Eurobonds by Currency[c]	Official Reserves[c]	International Bank Lending by Nationality of Ownership	
						$ Billions	Percent of Total
United States	8	220	5.5	63.6	23.8	614.5	28.1
United Kingdom	28	94	1.3	4.0	9.4	161.4	7.4
Germany	34	163	2.2	4.6	40.1	142.1	6.5
Japan	17	168	4.6	1.2	26.4	513.7	23.5
Switzerland	38	28	12.6	—	15.3	75.3	3.4
Canada	29	89	—	—	2.5	88.9	4.1
France	24	92	—	—	20.9	197.1	9.0
Italy	24	73	—	—	20.8	88.2	4.0
Netherlands	63	60	—	—	9.2	56.1	2.6
Belgium	71	46	—	—	4.6	38.5	1.8

Sources. IMF, International Financial Statistics; Bank of International Settlements, Annual Reports; Morgan Guaranty Trust Company, World Financial Markets.

[a] All data is for 1984.
[b] Exports divided by GNP.
[c] Data in billions of U.S. dollars.

EXHIBIT 2 SHARE OF NATIONAL CURRENCIES IN TOTAL OFFICIAL HOLDINGS OF FOREIGN EXCHANGE, END OF SELECTED YEARS IN PERCENT OF TOTAL

Currency Held	1977	1979	1982	1984
U.S. dollar	78.0	72.9	68.7	65.1
Pound sterling	1.8	2.0	2.4	2.9
Deutsche mark	9.1	12.5	12.3	12.0
French franc	1.2	1.3	1.3	1.1
Netherlands guilder	0.8	1.0	1.1	0.8
Swiss franc	2.2	2.5	2.7	2.0
Japanese yen	2.4	3.6	4.5	5.2
Unspecified currencies	4.4	4.2	7.0	11.0

Source. IMF, Annual Report 1985, p. 54.

WHAT IS INTERNATIONAL COMMERCIAL BANKING? International commercial banking has become a complex part of global financial relationships. Two decades ago it would have been possible to consider international commercial banking to include three essential activities: foreign-trade finance, overseas lending, and foreign-exchange trading. This relatively narrow definition is no longer valid. International commercial banking now functions as a separate system, in part operating above and beyond the national banking systems from which major international banks have evolved and grown. Using a Darwinian analogy, international commercial banking is a new species, with essential chromosome and genetic characteristics not to be found in its ancestors.

What are the unique genetic characteristics of modern-day international commercial banking that are not to be found in the large domestic banks of the older era of banking? Three distinct features characterize modern international commercial banking, as follows:

EXHIBIT 3 NUMBER OF BANKS IN TOP 100 IN WORLD BY NATIONALITY[a]

U.S.	14
U.K.	9
Germany	10
Japan	23
France	7
Switzerland	3
Canada	5
Italy	8
Netherlands	4
Belgium	3
Subtotal	86
All other	14
Total	100

Source. Moodys Bank and Finance Manual 1985.

[a] As of December 1983, ranked by total deposits.

1. International commercial banking has developed to a point where it now operates within international financial markets, which in turn depend on international banking activities for their sustenance. These include the Euro-currency, Eurobond, and global foreign-exchange markets.

2. International commercial banking services the multinational corporation. This has required that international banks develop special servicing for the multinational corporation, such as funds positioning and money transfer.

3. International commercial banking has extended itself into investment banking activities. For American banks this is a notable achievement in light of federal banking laws prohibiting the mix of commercial and investment banking. This separation is not characteristic in other national banking systems.

DEVELOPMENT OF U.S. INTERNATIONAL BANKING

STAGES OF DEVELOPMENT.   Analysis of the stages of development of international banking can focus on the long view or on a shorter time perspective. In the discussion that follows, we begin with a long view, and then shift our attention to shorter time periods.

Long View.   A long view of the development of international banking would focus on the hundred years prior to 1914 as an historical phase offering expanding opportunities, followed by a shorter three-decade period (1914–1945) in which international banking suffered retrogression. Following this retrogression period, international banking has enjoyed expanding opportunities for over 3½ decades (1945–1987).

The hundred years prior to 1914 witnessed rapid expansion of world trade, a gradual extension of the role of the international gold standard supported by a stable gold–pound-sterling relationship, and the acceleration of European investment into other parts of the world. As Herbert Feis (1930) has described so well in his study, Europe and particularly Britain had become the world's banker:

> Half a hundred types of financial institutions played a part in the process of investment of British capital. The huge commercial banks, where most checking accounts were kept, which financed commodity movements throughout the world, were the greatest source of credit, yet they played but an indirect part in the security issue business. Alongside of them stood the banks, public and private, of the British Dominions. These, growing to power, kept establishments in London to employ their funds, to share in the profits of trade financing, to handle governmental financial affairs.
>
> There were few governments in the world to which the English people did not make a loan, few corners in which some enterprise was not financed from London. The spread of English commerce, the almost universal range of the British-owned foreign banks, the huge extension of the colonial domain made it natural that British foreign investment should be widely scattered.

World War I and the currency disturbances that followed as an aftermath of hostilities brought an end to the expansion period of international banking. The pound-sterling–gold link was broken, foreign-investment flows were interrupted, and world-trade relationships were thrown out of balance. The world depression of the 1930s and World War II prevented any serious rebirth of international banking until the late 1940s and after. The third period, after 1945, brought with it a gradual expansion of international banking activity, but this expansion was largely confined to the trade financing aspect until the 1960s. Beginning around 1960 international commercial banking enjoyed a dynamic expansion.

Short View.   International commercial banking has not developed in a vacuum. Its expansion has been nurtured by its surroundings, and in turn by its own growth it has modified its own environment. Insofar as the postwar expansion of international banking is concerned, we can distinguish at least four distinct environmental periods, within which the pattern and pace of international banking expansion has varied according to the environment and conditions in the world economy. These periods may be described as follows:

1. *Dollar shortage, 1946–1957.* At the conclusion of the World War II, the United States was the only major country that could supply the rest of the world with virtually unlimited amounts of capital goods and consumer products for export. During the decade after 1945, the world was preoccupied with European reconstruction and reviving world trade. The dollar was much in demand because of the scarcity of merchandise for export outside the United States. Dollar credits were much in demand, since other countries had limited opportunities to earn dollars by exporting. By contrast these countries needed U.S. goods. As a result U.S. banks enjoyed a highly favored position in financing the U.S. export-import trade and in providing short-term dollar credits to overseas customers. There was little effective competition from banks outside the United States, since these institutions did not have ready access to hard currencies for loan and foreign-trade financing activities. A world dollar shortage persisted over much of this time period, which gave American banks a decided advantage in rebuilding and strengthening their international correspondent banking networks, and in competing in a growing market for financing export-import trade.

2. *Convertibility and early expansion, 1958–1963.* In 1958 virtually all of the Western European nations declared their currencies convertible for nonresident account. This signaled a return to normalcy insofar as international currency and foreign-exchange market conditions were concerned. Normalcy in foreign-exchange markets implied more stable conditions in the markets for goods and services, and the ability of many Western European countries to achieve reasonable balance-of-payments equilibrium. Foreign-trade financing became more competitive as European banks regained the ability to deal more freely in foreign-exchange markets. However, new opportunities for expansion were made available as the newly formed Common Market attracted massive American business investments requiring U.S. bank financing and servicing. Head-office lending to European and other borrowers provided additional opportunities for U.S. banks to expand their international & loan portfolios.

3. *U.S. capital controls, 1964–1973.* U.S. balance-of-payments problems in the early 1960s led to a series of controls over capital outflows. These were designed to achieve a strengthening of the U.S. balance of payments. Three types of controls were applied including (1) an Interest Equalization Tax (IET) on purchases of foreign securities by American investors, (2) restrictions on U.S.

direct-business investment outflows, and (3) restrictions on U.S. bank lending abroad. These controls accentuated the demand for funds outside the United States, leading to more rapid development of the Euromarkets. Moreover, they furnished incentives for American banks to establish offshore branches from which rising foreign loan demand could be fed. European banks responded to the challenge by establishing Eurocurrency operations and expanding their Eurobond-underwriting capacities. The international currency crises of 1971 and 1973 led to devaluation of the dollar and a floating-rate currency regime, basically altering the ground rules of international banking.

4. *Petrodollar and currency instability, 1974–1981.* The quadrupling of oil prices in 1973–1974 by the OPEC countries brought opportunities as well as challenges for international banks. U.S. authorities removed the capital controls to facilitate petrodollar recycling through U.S. financial markets. Sizeable payments surpluses of oil-exporting countries required deposit and investment management facilities, which international bankers were agreeable to provide. Competition for petrodollar deposits has been a watchword of international banking since 1974. At the same time international bankers were pressed to find profitable loan and investment outlets for these funds. As a result, the medium-term Eurocurrency lending market expanded, in large part related to the escalation in lending to nonoil developing countries. Bank regulatory agencies in the United States and other countries have maintained a close surveillance of this lending because of its pivotal position in world financial relationships, as well as its importance to the soundness of national banking systems whose banks are participants in their form of lending. In this period the expansion of American bank branches overseas slowed down. By contrast, this period witnessed a sharp growth in the representation of foreign banks in the United States.

5. *World debt crisis, 1982–1986.* The massive buildup in international bank lending, stimulated in part by petrodollar recycling needs, came to a halt in 1982 with a world recession and economic slowdown. Developing country borrowers were affected severely by this recession as world commodity prices weakened and LDC export revenues declined. This was followed closely by a slump in petroleum prices, causing the Mexican and Nigerian debt crises. These countries had based their large borrowings on an expectation that petroleum revenues would provide adequate debt servicing. This was not the case. Year after year (1982–1985) the number of required international loan restructurings has increased. International banks have not made any sizeable loan commitments to large debtor nations such as Brazil, Argentina, the Philippines, and Indonesia.

ORGANIZATIONAL STRUCTURES

ORGANIZATIONAL FORMS.   International banks developing their overseas activities have a range of organizational structures to choose from including correspondent bank relationships, representative offices, overseas branches, agencies or subsidiary companies. Most major banks maintain correspondent banking relationships with local banks in the countries in which they are developing business contacts. This reciprocal, or two-way, relationship includes placement of deposits as well as performance of services. A foreign correspondent is expected to accept drafts, honor letters of credit, provide credit information, and render other services for the U.S. bank at the other end of the relationship. The reciprocal nature of the relationship mandates "equivalent abilities and status," which must be broadly interpreted. Neither of the correspondent banks in a relationship maintains its own personnel in the other country. Therefore, direct costs are minimal. Benefits include access to banking services in a country in which the U.S. banks' own customers require good execution of banking and financial services. Correspondent relationships suffer from certain disadvantages, including the inability to control performance of services and transactions with certainty, the lack of status and prestige from direct representation in the country, and the inability to accept deposits in the country where correspondent banking relationships are used.

Often a bank relying heavily on foreign correspondents to render services in a given country will establish a representative office. Essentially, a representative office helps the parent bank to serve clients who conduct business in that country. A representative office is not a banking office as such, and cannot accept deposits, make loans, deal in drafts, or cash checks. Representative offices provide direct contacts in the country that can put parent-bank customers in contact with local government officials or local businessmen. In addition, they can provide credit information and analysis, and information concerning local business and economic trends. A representative office may be the first step toward establishing a full branch, or the only alternative in countries that prohibit general banking offices of nonresident banks.

The overseas branch is an integral part of the parent bank, backed up by the resources and lending power of the total organization. A branch does not have a separate corporate charter, does not issue ownership shares, and does not enjoy a separate legal status. Although it maintains its own accounts and sets of books, its financial policies are basically part of the parent organization. American banks have relied heavily on the branch form of organization in their postwar overseas expansion. This is due to the many advantages it provides, including the full-credit backing of the parent, the ability to attract corporate customers by use of the parent name and identity, and direct management control. Branches are usually simpler to organize than subsidiary companies. However, the profits of overseas branches are subject to immediate taxation in the home country.

In the period June 1972 to June 1985 the assets of foreign branches increased from $69.6 billion to $456.8 billion. At the later date 75 percent of these assets were denominated in U.S. dollars. Close to 35 percent of foreign-branch assets were located in branches in the United Kingdom. Foreign-branch assets represent close to 28 percent of the total assets in the U.S. banking system. Basic balance-sheet data for all overseas branches of U.S. banks are presented in Exhibit 4. In 1984 U.S. banks were operating close to 800 overseas branches.

Some local jurisdictions permit the representation of a foreign bank through an agency. The agency resembles a branch, with the exception that deposits cannot be accepted. New York State banking law provides for foreign-bank representation by agencies, and a number of these units carry out extensive trade-financing activities and money-market operations. California also provides for agency representation, and it is possible for these units to accept foreign-source but not domestic-source (U.S.) deposits.

EXHIBIT 4   AGGREGATE BALANCE SHEET OF FOREIGN BRANCHES OF U.S. BANKS, JUNE 1985 (BILLIONS OF U.S. DOLLARS)

Assets			Liabilities		
Claims on U.S.		121.3	Negotiable CDs		37.9
On parent bank	18.5		To U.S.		147.0
Claims on foreigners			Parent bank	79.4	
Other branches of parent bank		89.4	Other U.S. banks	19.4	
Banks		101.4	Nonbanks	48.1	
Public borrowers		22.7	To foreigners		250.7
Nonbank foreigners		101.3	Other branches of parent bank		90.3
Other assets		20.7	Banks		80.5
			Official institutions		21.7
			Nonbank foreigners		58.2
			Other liabilities		21.1
Total		456.8	Total		456.8

Source.   Board of Governors of the Federal Reserve System.

Subsidiary corporations are used extensively in international banking. At least three basic types can be isolated from the point of view of American banks: the Edge Act corporation, the foreign-incorporated bank, and the foreign-incorporated nonbank finance company.

Foreign banking subsidiaries provide direct, grass-roots representation. Often banking subsidiaries incorporated in the host country appear to be local in character, and can attract a base of resident clientele. Local management can give a foreign banking subsidiary greater access to the local business base. A special type of subsidiary bank, the consortium bank, has been utilized. Organized as a joint venture, generally three or more international banks hold ownership in consortium banks. Consortium banks are generally headquartered in London or Luxembourg and engage primarily in medium-term Eurocurrency lending.

Foreign nonbank subsidiaries are organized for two basic purposes. In countries that restrict or prohibit foreign ownership of banking institutions, nonbank companies permit the conduct of near-banking activities including loan, factoring, leasing, consumer-credit, and money-market operations. Where foreign-owned banking is permitted, it may be desirable to establish nonbank finance companies to take advantage of opportunities that are profit generators or that are better separated from the traditional banking operation.

Edge Act corporations are chartered in the United States by the federal government. They provide American banks with the opportunity to conduct international banking activities in locations other than the states in which the banks are organized to operate. For example, Chicago banks that cannot branch outside of the state of Illinois can operate Edge Act subsidiaries in New York, California, Miami, Houston, and other financial centers. In addition, they can operate as holding companies, owning the equity shares in foreign banks and finance companies that represent part of the global banking network of the parent bank. Parent banks are not able to own shares in foreign finance companies directly, but must acquire such ownership through their Edge Act subsidiaries. Finally, Edge Act corporations engage in specialty financing of offshore projects, taking long-term debt and other financing positions in these projects. Two types of Edge Act corporations have developed: the financing corporation and the banking corporation. Banking corporations are subject to lending limits and reserve requirements. Financing corporations can operate more freely with respect to lending and financing activities. Financial transactions of Edge Act corporations must be incidental to foreign or international business. The minimum capital investment in Edge Act corporations is $2 million. The International Banking Act of 1978 liberalized the reserve-requirement and liabilities limits so that Edge Act corporations could more competitively finance U.S. export trade.

FOREIGN BANKING IN THE UNITED STATES.   The decade of the 1970s witnessed a rapid expansion in the number of foreign banking offices in the United States—in the volume of banking assets and liabilities in the United States held by foreign banks. Over 140 foreign banks operate representative offices, agencies, branches, and subsidiaries in the United States. The range of operations of foreign banks has expanded in recent years, and includes lending in the domestic loan markets, money-market activities, retail banking, stock market transactions, securities underwriting, and servicing the needs of multinational corporations. Foreign banks now account for over 25 percent of the commercial and industrial loans made to borrowers in the United States.

Foreign banks have followed the inflow of foreign investment entering the United States. This foreign investment takes three principal forms: direct business investment, portfolio investment, and short-term investment in liquid assets. The growth of foreign banking is closely related to this inflow of foreign investment.

The following represent key aspects of foreign bank operations in the United States:

1. *Corporate services.* Foreign companies have accelerated their investment in the United States. Major foreign banks have followed their home-country corporate customers to retain their business. In addition, foreign banks have attempted to develop bank-service relationships with U.S. corporations. As a result, the foreign-bank share of commercial and industrial loans in the U.S. market has increased to over 25 percent.

2. *Money market.* New York offices of foreign banks have been important participants in the U.S. money markets. Canadian agencies in New York have been active in the call-loan and dealer-loan market sectors. Nearly all foreign banks operate in federal funds and certificates of deposit.

3. *Dollar sourcing.* A major consideration for foreign banks in establishing U.S. banking offices is the desire to have a base to secure dollar funds. Closely related is the fact that a U.S. office provides a clearing and deposit center for parent-bank operations. An office in New York may provide dollar funds to other units of the parent bank within prescribed limits. A dollar-based banking office can operate in the exchange market after European foreign-exchange markets have closed for the day.

4. *Retail banking.* A small number of foreign banking units in the United States have extended their operations beyond wholesale banking into retail activities. Often these have been banks with ethnic links such as the Puerto Rican and Israeli banks. In California foreign-owned subsidiary banks are heavily retail oriented.

5. *Securities-market linkages.* In the past, foreign banks have been prompted to extend their securities-trading and securities-underwriting activities in the United States. This activity has given foreign banks a competitive advantage, since domestic American banks are prohibited from simultaneously engaging in investment banking and commercial banking by the Glass-Steagall Act. With passage of the International Banking Act of 1978, foreign banks are prohibited from further developing investment-banking activities in the United States. Existing facilities have been grandfathered.

OPERATIONAL ASPECTS

International commercial banking has developed a diverse and complex set of operational activities. In our discussion five important operational areas are examined. The first four are discussed in this section. The fifth, international lending, is discussed in the following section. The five areas are:

1. Financing exports and imports.
2. Foreign exchange.
3. Money market.
4. Corporate services.
5. Lending and Eurocredits.

Export-import financing is the oldest operational aspect of international commercial banking. Traditionally, export-import finance has been the bread-and-butter business of commercial-bank international departments. In cases where the foreign trade of customers is facilitated by a letter of credit, the bank places its name behind the buyer. Time drafts drawn under letters of credit incorporate the financing of the transaction, and by accepting the draft the bank creates a bank acceptance, which tends to provide lower cost financing. U.S. banks open import letters of credit in favor of overseas sellers at the request of American buyers. Export letters of credit are advised by American banks on behalf of their foreign correspondent banks. In addition to issuing, confirming, endorsing, and paying against letters of credit, international departments of commercial banks provide loans and credits to support foreign trade. In addition to facilitating letter-of-credit transactions, banks process documents under standardized collection procedures. In such cases no bank obligation to honor drafts is involved.

International departments of major banks carry out a variety of foreign-exchange functions for customers and bank correspondents. These include buying and selling foreign exchange, providing advisory services to customers regarding management of foreign-exchange exposure, facilitating corporate-funds positioning to take advantage of currency and interest-rate relationships, and arranging for speedy money transfer and check collection on a global basis.

Money-market operations of international banks include dealing in different national money markets, international money markets, and facilitating arbitrage of funds across different money-market sectors. Eurocurrency dealing is a central aspect of money-market activities. Funding international loans by means of purchasing short-maturity Eurocurrency deposits is an extremely competitive aspect of money-market operations. Foreign banks with New York offices run a complete money-market operation in the United States dealing in federal funds, CDs, and commercial paper.

Corporate services provided by international banks have brought them closer to the field of investment banking. This is because many of the services they provide are investment-banking oriented. For example, long-term financing in the international capital markets requires an underwriting syndicate. It is interesting to note that many U.S. banks participate in such underwriting activities overseas, although the Glass-Steagall Act prohibits such activities domestically. Another important corporate service is locating and arranging mergers and acquisitions (and arranging divestments). Outside of the investment-banking area, international bankers provide valuable assistance to corporate management of working capital. This includes multicountry and multicurrency cash management, collections on receivables, inventory financing, general working-capital financing, fronting loans, provision of centralized depositories for more effective regional cash management, and provision of speedy money-transfer and funds-remittance facilities.

INTERNATIONAL LENDING AND EUROCREDITS

AMOUNT OF BANK LENDING. The international loan portfolios of American banks underwent dramatic increase in the period 1960–1980. This resulted from the interplay of several forces including (1) expansion of overseas activities of U.S. multinational corporations, (2) U.S. government restrictions on capital transactions, (3) the strategic needs of large American banks to achieve growth and diversification, (4) rising petroleum prices and the need of many countries to finance petroleum-payments deficits, (6) opportunities to recycle or intermediate petrodollars, and (7) the increased competitive efficiency of the enlarged Euromarkets compared with many domestic financial markets. The first three factors played a prominent role in the 1960s, whereas the remaining three were important in the 1970s.

The first half of the decade of the 1980s witnessed two different developments. In 1980–1981, the dramatic increase in international loan portfolios continued. But in 1982–1985, there was a virtual standstill in international lending as the developing country debt crisis came on the heels of a world recession. The debt crisis spread to oil exporting nations (Mexico and Nigeria), as well as to the nonoil developing countries. These developments are evident in the data in Exhibit 5 where international bank credits declined sharply between 1981 and 1983, only partly recovering in 1984. Exhibit 6 reflects the total outstanding claims resulting from international bank lending at year-end 1984.

We must distinguish between head-office lending by U.S. banks, which is essentially in the form of dollar credits, and foreign-branch lending, which is a combination of Eurocurrency and local currency lending. Data in Exhibit 7 provide insight into the rapid growth of claims on foreigners by U.S. banking offices. The slow growth in 1965–1970 reflects the U.S. capital-control program, which terminated early in 1974. The amounts in Exhibit 5 include various types of claims on foreign banks, corporations, and governments.

Claims on foreigners include direct loans, acceptances created by American banks for the account of foreign banks, claims of U.S. banks on foreign banks that are in the process of being collected, and other types of claims.

EXHIBIT 5   INTERNATIONAL BANK LENDING[1] (DOLLARS IN BILLIONS)

| | Changes in Outstanding Claims[2] | | | | Outstanding Claims at End 1984 |
| | 1983 | | 1984 | | |
	$	%	$	%	$
All banks[3]	170	6.8	190	7.2	2,749
Cross-border lending	108	5.3	130	6.2	2,176
Domestic lending[4]	62	12.3	60	11.0	573
U.S. banks[5]	4	1.1	−34	−9.5	323
Non-U.S. banks[6]	66	7.6	224	9.8	2,426
Memorandum[7]					
BIS-reporting banks	130	6.0	151	5.9	2,613
Cross-border lending	105	6.2	126	6.0	2,153
Domestic lending[4]	25	5.9	25	5.6	460

Source.   Morgan Guaranty Trust Company, World Financial Markets.

[1] Cross-border lending in all currencies plus foreign currency lending to residents. Based on unconsolidated data. Compiled by the Morgan Bank from various published sources.
[2] Changes are adjusted for the valuation effects of exchange rate movements.
[3] Bank offices in most industrial countries (Austria, Belgium, Canada, Denmark, Finland, France, Germany, Ireland, Italy, Japan, Luxembourg, Norway, Spain, Sweden, Switzerland, United Kingdom, and the United States) and in the major offshore market centers (Bahamas, Bahrain, Cayman Islands, Hong Kong, Netherlands Antilles, Panama, and Singapore).
[4] In foreign currency.
[5] Data for U.S. banks are on a consolidated basis and therefore not strictly comparable with the data for all banks.
[6] Data for non-U.S. banks are derived by subtracting the figures for U.S. banks from the totals for all banks.
[7] Differences between figures compiled by the Morgan Bank and those published by the BIS are explained as follows: Morgan Bank figures include and BIS figures exclude foreign currency lending to residents by banks located in offshore market center countries; also Morgan Bank figures treat the International Banking Facilities of banks in the United States as separate units engaged in Eurocurrency banking whereas the BIS treats them as an integral part of their parent institution.

EXHIBIT 6   CLAIMS ON FOREIGNERS REPORTED BY BANKS IN THE UNITED STATES 1955–1985 (BILLIONS OF DOLLARS)

	Short-Term	Long-Term	Total	% Short-Term
1955	1.5	0.7	2.2	70
1960	3.6	1.7	5.3	68
1965	7.7	4.5	12.2	63
1970	10.7	3.1	13.8	78
1975	50.2	9.6	59.8	84
1980	115.2	34.2	149.4	87
June 1985	158.6	73.1	231.7	69

Source.   Board of Governors of the Federal Reserve System.

EXHIBIT 7   NEW INTERNATIONAL BOND ISSUES AND BANK CREDIT COMMITMENTS (PUBLICLY ANNOUNCED, MEDIUM- AND LONG-TERM BILLIONS OF DOLLARS)

	1981	1982	1983	1984	Jan-Jun 1985
International bond issues	52.8	75.5	77.1	111.5	80.1
Floating rate notes and CDs	11.3	15.3	19.5	38.2	32.1
Fixed rate instruments	41.5	60.2	57.6	73.3	48.0
International bank credits	147.7	103.6	80.7	117.3	44.2
Syndicated loans	94.6	98.2	67.2	62.0	25.5
Involuntary new money loans	—	—	14.3	11.3	1.0
Voluntary loans	94.6	98.2	52.9	50.7	24.5
Other international credit facilities	53.1	5.4	13.5	55.3	18.7
Merger-related standbys	39.1	—	4.0	28.0	—
Other facilities[1]	14.0	5.4	9.5	27.3	18.7

Source.   OECD, and Morgan Guaranty Trust Company, World Financial Markets.

[1] Facilities extended by banks to back up the issuance of other financial instruments such as short-term Euronotes, certificates of deposit, bankers acceptances, and commercial paper.

Lending from the United States is conducted almost exclusively in dollars. Foreign claims of U.S. banks arise in connection with extension of commercial credits covering foreign trade, stabilization and standby credits, development credits, and medium-term credits to industrial borrowers to finance capital-equipment purchases.

Lending by foreign branches of U.S. banks is more diversified than lending by head offices. This lending varies based on differences in the national and international banking markets in which foreign branches operate. Lending is carried out in local currencies, mainly in cases of loans to local corporate and U.S. affiliated borrowers. Lending is carried in U.S. dollars in cases where the borrower has a need for dollar-denominated credits. A large part of the lending in primarily European and offshore-island (Nassau and Cayman Islands) branches is in Eurocurrencies. Branch systems, or networks, channel funds to bring together surplus and deficit money and loan markets. Multicurrency lending arrangements have developed in Europe, where credits can be transferred from branch to head office or in reverse, or can be participated among branches and head office in response to the needs of the borrower.

With the rapid escalation of international bank lending commencing in 1974 with the OPEC payments surpluses and need to finance payments deficits of oil-importing nations, the Bank for International Settlements undertook a comprehensive estimate of lending in the international markets. (This is published on a regular basis.)

RISK EVALUATION.   Although international lending offers significant rewards in the form of profit, the lending banks inevitably must assume a measure of risk over and beyond what is normally encountered in domestic lending. In practice these risks can be considered to include credit risk, country risk, currency risk, and funding risk.

In lending to private-sector business firms and multinational corporations, credit risks are always present. To evaluate the degree of credit risk assumed, we must consider the type of lending international bankers ordinarily undertake. International bankers ordinarily lend on a wholesale basis to large business firms in host countries where overseas branches may be located (Morgan Guaranty, Paris, to a large French company), or to multinational companies. In such cases credit risks often are well screened out, and only the more creditworthy and more substantial borrowers are approved. In addition, there is a considerable amount of interbank funds placement, either as part of the Eurocurrency trading activity or local money-market operation. Again, there is a tendency to deal mainly with good-quality Eurobanks or money-market institutions. As a result, credit risks are perceived to be relatively low, often lower than in the case of domestic loan portfolios.

Country risks relate to the exposure a bank has in its loans in a given country when events (economic or political) in that country could make it difficult or impossible for debtors to continue to make loan-servicing payments in the hard currency in which the loan was denominated. The event could be a business recession, a central-bank blockage of foreign exchange available for servicing commercial loans, or civil strife disrupting exports and foreign-exchange earnings. Excessive concentration of international loans in one country may leave an international bank lender in serious difficulties should economic or political conditions turn unfavorable in that country. A special type of country risk applies in cases where a bank lends to the central government, or an official agency created by the central government. This sovereign risk is an exposure that carries with it special problems for the commercial-bank lender. First, a sovereign entity may not be sued or brought to court for nonpayment in courts subject to its jurisdiction. Second, many countries, including those whose banks are actively engaged in international lending, will not support claims brought against sovereign entities in their own courts unless the sovereign entity was engaged in a commercial activity, or unless the sovereign gives permission to be sued.

Currency risk arises whenever a bank denominates loans in one currency but obtains borrowed funds or deposits in another currency. In general, international bankers try to avoid this type of risk. However, there are occasions where the interest differential between two currencies is highly conducive to currency-arbitrage activities.

Funding risk tends to be ever present, in domestic as well as international banking operations. Since international deposit funds are more competitively wholesale oriented and more responsive to interest-rate volatility than domestic funds, the international funding risk may be of a higher degree. Funding risk is considered to be an important factor whenever short-term deposit funds are utilized to fund medium-term loan portfolios. This is because rising interest rates may expose the bank to higher deposit-interest costs at a period when it is locked into relatively less attractive fixed interest rates on medium-term loans. International bankers have found a way out of this dilemma by use of floating-rate loans. The majority of medium-term Eurocurrency loans are made on a floating-interest-rate basis, where the borrower pays an interest rate equal to the London Interbank Offered Rate (LIBOR) plus a premium over LIBOR. LIBOR is the cost of funds of Eurocurrency-lending banks. This is the cost of short-term-deposit funds in the London wholesale interbank market. Periodically (3–6 months) the LIBOR rate is adjusted in the loan to reflect the changed level of interest costs of the lending banks. In addition to the LIBOR rate, other reference rates are used in international lending, such as MIBOR (Madrid Interbank Rate), HIBOR (Hong Kong Interbank Rate), and others.

PROBLEMS AND ISSUES. Several problem areas emerged in the late 1970s and early 1980s as a result of the escalation in international lending. These focused on possible excessive loan concentration and excessive country exposure of individual banks, the issue of developing-country debt-service capacity, and the locked-in effect experienced by bank lenders as borrowing nations find it not possible to service outstanding debt. Solutions to these problems are not easy. In the past two decades a number of international loan reschedulings have taken place, either on a multilateral or narrower basis. These reschedulings have involved stretch-out of principal repayments and temporary relief from interest payments. Such reschedulings have provided necessary relief, but do not get at fundamental issues such as the need for a more controlled expansion in international loans.

**EXHIBIT 8   INTERNATIONAL BANK LENDING TO DEVELOPING COUNTRIES[1]
(DOLLARS IN BILLIONS)**

| | | Changes in Outstanding Claims[2] | | | | Outstanding Claims at End- 1984 |
| | | 1983 | | 1984 | | |
		$	%	$	%	$
Latin America:	All banks	7.6	(3.9)	1.6	(0.7)	242.6
	U.S. banks	0.2	(0.2)	2.1	(2.5)	86.2
	Non-U.S. banks	7.4	(6.6)	−0.5	(−0.3)	156.4
Argentina:	All banks	0.5	(2.2)	−1.0	(−3.7)	25.9
	U.S. banks	−0.3	(−3.0)	−0.4	(−4.8)	8.4
	Non-U.S. banks	0.8	(5.9)	−0.6	(−3.3)	17.5
Brazil:	All banks	1.5	(2.7)	4.7	(6.5)	75.8
	U.S. banks	−0.4	(−1.6)	3.2	(14.9)	24.8
	Non-U.S. banks	1.9	(5.6)	1.5	(3.0)	51.0
Mexico:	All banks	4.1	(7.0)	0.7	(1.0)	72.8
	U.S. banks	1.1	(4.7)	0.4	(1.4)	25.8
	Non-U.S. banks	3.0	(8.6)	0.3	(0.6)	47.0
Venezuela:	All banks	−0.7	(−3.1)	−1.7	(−6.1)	26.2
	U.S. banks	−0.3	(−2.9)	−0.3	(−3.1)	10.6
	Non-U.S. banks	−0.4	(−3.5)	−1.4	(−8.2)	15.6
Asia:	All banks	4.4	(8.3)	5.2	(5.5)	98.4
	U.S. banks	1.0	(3.0)	−3.5	(−10.5)	29.9
	Non-U.S. banks	3.4	(16.6)	8.7	(14.2)	68.5
Korea:	All banks	0.7	(3.8)	1.8	(6.1)	30.8
	U.S. banks	0.0	(0.2)	−1.5	(−12.0)	10.9
	Non-U.S. banks	0.7	(10.8)	3.3	(19.5)	19.9
Middle East	All banks	6.5	(8.6)	1.9	(2.0)	93.9
and Africa	U.S. banks	0.8	(5.2)	−2.5	(−15.6)	14.7
	Non-U.S. banks	5.7	(9.4)	4.4	(5.5)	79.2
All LDCs:	All banks	21.5	(6.6)	8.5	(2.0)	434.9
	U.S. banks	2.0	(1.5)	−3.9	(−2.9)	129.8
	Non-U.S. banks	19.5	(10.0)	12.6	(4.2)	305.1

Source.   BIS and Bank of England.

[1] Lending by BIS-reporting banks to developing countries that are not offshore market centers.
[2] Adjusted for the valuation effects of exchange rate movements. Data for all banks and non-U.S. banks are affected by an enlargement of the BIS-reporting area at end- 1983.

Intense competition has developed in international banking and presents a real problem to American banks. In recent years non-U.S. banks have been expanding their international loans more rapidly than their U.S. counterparts (Exhibit 8). As a result, the U.S. share of international lending has declined, and at year-end 1984 represented 30 percent of the global total of loans to developing countries.

Another problem issue is the need for control over total international credit creation. Competitive financing of exports, loans to strengthen political alliances, and an overall lack of effective coordination between different credit-creating agencies and institutions represent basic problems to be dealt with. We return to these questions below in the section "Regulatory Aspects."

INTERNATIONAL BANKING AND THE THIRD WORLD

SERVING THE NEEDS OF DEVELOPING COUNTRIES. International commercial banking can contribute to the development efforts of the Third World in the following ways:

1. Assisting in the development of local financial institutions.
2. Supporting foreign trade.
3. Facilitating an inflow of capital and supplementing availability of foreign exchange.
4. Promoting thrift and savings habits.

A number of the developing countries have larger and more-sophisticated banking institutions of their own. In such cases some of the above-mentioned contributions are provided by local or indigenous banks.

ACCESS TO INTERNATIONAL CAPITAL. International commercial banking has assisted in channeling capital to developing nations. In general the developing nations have found it difficult to gain access to the international financial markets. Approximately three dozen (one out of four) developing nations have been able to tap the medium-term Eurocurrency loan market each year, and only a dozen developing nations have been able to issue bonds in the international bond markets. Inasmuch as developing nations have been able to obtain over half the funds made available in the medium-term Eurocurrency market in recent years, we can judge that the contribution here has been important.

Three factors influence the access of developing countries to international capital. These include the policies of industrial countries vis-à-vis the operation of their own capital markets, the stage of development of the borrowing country, and the ability of the borrower to maintain effective financial-management policies.

Financial-management policies followed by developing countries can influence the access they enjoy to international loan funds, as well as the loan terms they will be exposed to. For example, there is a close conformity between financial-management effectiveness of developing countries and LIBOR spreads paid by borrowing countries. Indicators reflecting central-government financial-management effectiveness include budget deficit as percentage of gross domestic product (GDP), increase in cost of living, growth of money supply, growth of real per capita GNP, growth or real gross domestic investment, current-account deficit as percentage of exports, debt-service ratio, official reserves as percentage of imports, and the percentage of compressible imports.

REGULATORY ASPECTS

International commercial banking has grown in relative importance in world financial markets to the point where it can affect credit flows and the safety and stability of national banking systems. The United States has had to make special provision for the ability of American banks to circumvent domestic credit controls, by imposing marginal reserve requirements on the Eurodollar borrowings of head offices from their foreign branches. One of the alleged reasons for support of the regulation of foreign banks in the United States was their ability to undermine domestic (Federal Reserve) credit controls by obtaining advances from their parent banks.

Intrepid central bankers have managed to erect hurdles around national banking markets, but international bankers have responded by taking up pole vaulting. At present the question of regulation of credit control over international banks has shifted to the Euromarkets and the prospects for applying credit controls to the international credit markets. Basic implementation problems relate to applying reserve requirements on Eurodeposits and forcing the market to shift to Far Eastern or Middle Eastern centers where no such reserve requirements apply.

In the United States, critics of the role of American banks in international banking have argued that the soundness and stability of the domestic banking system may be jeopardized by continued large-scale lending to high-risk developing countries. Alternately, critics may argue that country loan concentrations are too high. National bank examiners in the United States have reorganized their efforts to achieve a more effective and more uniform review and classification of international loans made by U.S. banks. Nevertheless, loan loss ratios on international loans remain considerably lower than those on domestic loans.

International banking has grown to the point where the quality and structure of American banking has changed and continues to change. The important question is: has international banking become large enough and important enough to warrant the application of special rules and regulations in light of these changes?

SOURCES AND SUGGESTED REFERENCES

Angelini, A., M. Eng, and F.A. Lees. *International Lending, Risk and the Euromarkets.* London: Macmillan, 1979.

Bank for International Settlements. *Annual Reports.* Basel.

Bitterman, H.J. *The Refunding of International Debt.* Durham, NC: Duke University Press, 1973.

Donaldson, T.H. *Lending in International Commercial Banking.* London: Macmillan, 1979.

Feis, H. *Europe the World's Banker: 1870–1914.* New Haven: Yale University Press, 1930.

International Monetary Fund. *Annual Reports.* Washington, DC: IMF.

Lees, F.A. *International Banking & Finance.* London: Macmillan, 1974.

———. *Foreign Banking and Investment in the U.S.* New York: Halsted, 1976.

SOURCES AND SUGGESTED REFERENCES   18 · 21

—— and M. Eng. *International Financial Markets.* New York: Praeger, 1975.

Mathis, F.J. ed. *Offshore Lending by U.S. Commercial Banks.* New York: Bankers Association for Foreign Trade, second edition, 1981.

Morgan Guaranty Trust Company. *World Financial Markets.* New York: Monthly.

Quinn, B.S. *The New Euromarkets.* New York: Halsted, 1975.

Walmsley, J. *The Foreign Exchange Handbook.* New York: John Wiley, 1983.

Walter, Ingo. *Global Competition in International Banking* (Cambridge, MA.: Ballinger, 1988).

Wellons, P.A. *Borrowing By Developing Countries on the Euro-Currency Market.* Paris: OECD, 1977.

World Bank. *World Development Report.* Washington, DC: World Bank, 1977–80.

INTERNATIONAL INVESTMENT BANKING

CONTENTS

INTERNATIONAL INVESTMENT BANKING

Edward B. Flowers

THE ORGANIZATION OF INTERNATIONAL INVESTMENT BANKING

EDGE ACT SUBSIDIARIES. Commercial banks in the United States engage in international investment banking through the incorporation of Edge Act subsidiaries. The law governing the establishment of Edge Act corporations (EACs) can be found in Title XXV of the Federal Reserve Act (12 USCS §§ 601–632). Enacted in 1919 and amended as late as 1978, the law authorizing Edge Act Corporations requires a minimum capital contribution of $2 million, which, under the 1978 amendment to the law, may now be paid in installments (see 12 USCS § 618). These EACs are federally chartered corporations not subject to state banking laws, and are regulated by the Federal Reserve Board. Before 1919 and the Edge Act, international investment banking was transacted through the use of "agreement corporations," which were also chartered by the Federal Reserve Board. These agreement corporations, however, were subject to the more-restrictive, day-to-day supervision of the Fed and required specific agreement with the Fed concerning participation in individual projects, and the law stated that only 10 percent of capital and surplus could be invested in any one international banking operation. The requirements of the 1919 Edge Act are much more liberal, and the 1978 amendments were enacted specifically to make the act more liberal, by extending its provisions more uniformly to banks across the United States, and to allow freer competition with foreign investment bankers.

OWNERSHIP PROVISIONS. The law on Edge Act corporations previously required that a majority of the shares be owned by U.S. citizens, but under the 1978 amendment (12 USCS § 619), a majority of the stock of a U.S. Edge Act subsidiary may be held by one or more foreign banks or institutions organized under the laws of foreign countries if the prior approval of the Fed is secured. This provision allows U.S. commercial banks to compete on a more even basis with, for instance, banks recently chartered in the United States using Saudi money, French banking expertise in Euromoney markets, and the U.S. capital markets, through a mixture of, say, six Saudi bank shareholders, one French Euromoney bank shareholder, and a number of U.S. banking shareholders.

BRANCHING UNDER THE EDGE ACT.   Edge Act investment banking operations are an exception to the rule that U.S. banks may not branch across state lines. Edge Act subsidiaries are often located outside the states of the parent U.S. banks. The principle Edge Act banking cities are New York, Houston, Miami, Chicago, Los Angeles, and San Francisco. This provision allows a very large bank to extend the source of its international investment-banking activities to the customers and capital markets located in all major cities and sections of the United States.

Under the amended Edge Act provisions, a U.S. commercial bank may engage in the following activities:

1. Accept deposits outside the United States.
2. Accept deposits in the United States if incidental to U.S. trade transactions.
3. Make loans (not more than 20 percent of capital and surplus to one borrower).
4. Make loans and advances to finance foreign trade.
5. Issue or confirm letters of credit.
6. Create bankers acceptances.
7. Receive items for collection.
8. Buy, sell, or hold securities.
9. Issue guarantees.
10. Act as paying agent for securities issued by foreign governments or foreign corporations.
11. Engage in spot and forward exchange transactions.
12. Purchase and sell coin or bullion.
13. Purchase and sell virtually any evidences of indebtedness.
14. Borrow and lend money.
15. Issue debentures, bonds, and promissory notes.
16. Engage in remittance of funds services.

The 1978 amendment to the Act (12 USCS § 615) liberalized the ability to accept deposits, deal in coin and bullion, make loans, and sell securities.

FINANCIAL VERSUS BANKING SUBSIDIARIES.   Edge Act banking activities fall into two broad categories: international commercial banking, and international "financing" activities. The financing activities of Edge Act corporations constitute the traditional range of investment-banking activities, and the rules for the Edge Act subsidiaries are different depending on which type of primary activity the subsidiary is engaged in. Since the 1963 Federal Reserve Board revision of Regulation K, the regulation by which the Fed governs Edge Act activity, however, this distinction has been dropped as a practical matter, although the EACs tend to still operate as if the original distinction continued (Baker and Bradford, 1974).

If the Edge Act subsidiary functions primarily as a banking subsidiary, it may hold shares of foreign banking subsidiaries and behave as a bank holding company. Foreign branch banks may not do this. The subsidiary may also act as a holding company for all or part of the parent bank's foreign commercial-banking subsidiaries, or may do this as a part of a joint venture with foreign or domestic banks or with other nonbanking institutions.

If the EAC functions primarily as a "financing" subsidiary, that is, as an investment bank, its activities are prescribed as follows:

1. It may hold portfolios of equity investments in foreign commercial and industrial firms

   a. Directly.

   b. Through an official or semiofficial development bank or corporation.

2. It may make direct investments in a wide variety of local businesses through the use of intermediate-term loans, purchase of shares of stock, or a combination of the above.

3. It may handle referrals of long-term development projects to the EAC by the parent bank (commitments from $100,000 to $1 million).

4. If engaged only in financing, it may invest up to 50 percent of its capital and surplus in a single venture (if engaged in general international commercial banking, the limit is 10 percent).

5. Profit derived from dividends (from equity participations), interest (on loans made), and capital gains (from the sale of equity participations), as well as interest paid on bonds, and various service fees.

EDGE ACT MANAGEMENT.   Although a commercial bank's international investment-banking activities are being channeled through an Edge Act subsidiary, and although the subsidiary may have foreign shareholders, the subsidiary is a U.S.-domiciled and U.S.-regulated corporation. This is, of course, a legal fiction to a certain extent, "the corporate veil" allowing the U.S. multinational commercial bank to participate in investment-banking activities everywhere except in the United States, where the Glass-Steagall Act prevents direct competition between banks and investment bankers. There has, however, been a great deal of commercial-bank lobbying in recent years to allow the commercial banks to compete with investment banks in the United States. Commercial banks anticipate that the 1980s will be an era of major refinancing for plant and equipment of U.S. industry, and this, coupled with the historically greater profit margins of the U.S. investment-banking industry, makes this market attractive domestically as well as internationally. Commercial banks, on the other hand, find their profits severely limited by federal controls, which often precipitate bank disintermediation, or the foreclosure of capital access during credit crunches, and, recently, by direct commercial-bank competition with savings banks' NOW accounts and the attempts of large investment houses to offer a "financial department store" of services virtually identical to (and more extensive than) those that commercial banks are legally able to offer. The one exception to this rule preventing commercial-bank competition with U.S. investment banks appears to be the rule that allows commercial banks to handle the underwriting of the debentures of state and local public corporations. Even here there is no direct competition, since investment houses are not allowed to underwrite these issues.

INTERNATIONAL INVESTMENT-BANKING COMPETITION.   The liberalized Edge Act allows U.S. commercial banks the option of competing in the lucrative *international* investment-banking market. It may be argued (Giddy, 1980) that the increasing activity of the multinational commercial banks in these markets has increased competition and has substantially changed the nature of the services offered. It is also likely that the passage of the International Banking Act of 1978 (12 USCS §§ 3101–3108), which governs the activities of *foreign* banks in the United States, will have some effect on the ability of U.S. banks to branch and compete with domestic investment bankers.

THE ACTIVITIES OF INVESTMENT BANKING.   In the case of domestic investment banking, it has been said that this industry does not engage in investment and neither does it involve banking. In the case of international investment banking, this is less true, because both international banks and investment houses participate side by side in their competition for international investment-banking markets. Unlike domestic investment banking, in the international arena, the device of the Edge Act corporation enables the commercial banker to hold and sell securities and to compete directly with the investment banker, pyramiding its international investment-banking activities atop its international commercial-banking activities in an operational, if not a legal, sense.

THE EMBELLISHMENTS OF INTERNATIONAL INVESTMENT BANKING.   In domestic investment banking, the primary business of the investment house is the secondary offerings of stocks and bonds and the arrangement of complicated financial packages, which are often used in connection with mergers and corporate takeovers. Since the primary business of domestic investment banking is the management of securities offerings, the "product" is the securities themselves. In international investment banking, the business is even more diverse and complex because the international networks of multinational commercial banks ar involved in merchant-banking activities across national boundaries and national and international capital markets in addition to the international and domestic merchant-banking activities of investment houses. Although the primary business of international merchant banking is still probably underwriting, mergers and acquisitions, and the sale of advisory functions, the breadth and scope of international investment-banking operations is so extensive that in order to grasp the protean nature of the potential of this industry, it is well to list the types of activities involved, as follows:

1. Securities issues
   a. Underwriting.
   b. Syndication.
   c. Management of issue.
   d. Private placements.
2. Arrangement of complex financing packages
   a. Syndicated loans.
   b. Mergers and acquisitions.
   c. Parallel lending, etc.
   d. Financial rescue operations.
   e. Project financing.
3. Trust management
   a. General.
   b. In relation to bond offerings.

4. Raising capital.
   a. Loans: Eurodollar primarily.
   b. Equity issues.
   c. Eurobond issues.
5. Financial adviser services
   a. Sources of capital.
   b. Assessing international capital markets.
   c. Selling financial deals: "feasibility."
   d. Negotiation of financial packages.
   e. Financial advisement to major projects.
   f. Advice in corporate reorganization.
   g. Advice on mergers and acquisitions.
   h. Energy-related financial advisement.
      (1) Government
      (2) Private
   i. Advice on corporate strategies.
   j. Advice on direct investments in the United States.
   k. Advice on any complex, or unusual financial problem needing international expertise, information, capital, or contacts.

KEY CHARACTERISTICS OF ACTIVITIES. One reason for the extensiveness and complexity of these international investment activities is the involvement of large multinational banks. These banks, in effect, market the expertise derived from their base in international commercial-banking operations. The information, expertise, contacts, market-monitoring networks, and international access to capital of the international commercial-banking operations can also be used to solve the more-unusual and more-complex problems arising in the merchant-banking field. The existence of the worldwide commercial-banking network of the multinational banks for use in the international investment-banking field tends to competitively extend the range and complexity of international investment-banking activities, at least qualitatively, far beyond the range of domestic investment banking. This is most readily noticed in the extensive range of advisory services offered through the financial operations of the Edge Act subsidiaries of the large multinational banks engaged in international investment banking. This range of services tends to extend beyond the traditional domestic investment-banking core activities of underwriting, mergers, and acquisitions.

INFORMATION NETWORKS. Although the end result of most international investment-banking operations is the provision of financing or capital, the activities of the Edge Act subsidiaries of the large multinational banks in this industry tend to shift the emphasis of the action more toward information access, rather than capital access. Another way of stating this is to say that a major function of international investment banking is now to define the range of the possible in international financing, based on the banks' information and expertise in international financial markets. Once the investment banking adviser has defined the possible, this is sold in the form of a feasibility study, which makes possible the securing of the financial package advised. It is much more likely that international capital-market access will be standardized in the future than will the process of organizing such access in investment banking. Thus based on its international banking and information network, an international investment-banking operation and its contacts act as a salesman who secures and certifies financial feasibility for complicated, novel projects that are generally very large and risky. A negative definition of international investment banking might be to say that aside from mergers, acquisitions, and underwriting, international investment banking involves only those projects that are unusual, or require unusual banking expertise.

MANAGEMENT OF SECURITIES ISSUES

One of the major parts of international investment banking is the underwriting, syndication, management, and private placement of both corporate equities and Eurobond issues. Because of the international nature of the distribution process, the large amounts of capital generally involved, and the fact that the regulations of no one nation determine the management of the issues, these activities vary considerably from the domestic underwriting activities of investment banks. Although the Edge Act subsidiaries of multinational banks and other investment houses often manage the issues of equity stock for large corporations, in the international investment-banking field, the management of equity issues is very much parallel to Eurobond issuing, which has, in terms of volume, tended to dominate the development of international investment banking in the field of securities issues since the late 1960s. For that reason this discussion will concentrate primarily on the methods for engaging in and competing with the investment bankers in the rapidly growing Eurobond market dominated by international investment bankers.

REASONS FOR THE GROWTH OF THE EUROBOND MARKET.   In the early 1960s, international money-market experts had expected a gradual integration of international capital markets because of the influence of massive direct foreign investment, which seemed to be tying together the international web of business communications. This integration did not take place, primarily because of national credit controls such as the voluntary and then mandatory controls on U.S. direct foreign investment. There were also other restrictions such as the Interest Equalization Tax, which restricted the foreign use of U.S. capital markets during the period of greatest U.S. capital outflow in the form of direct foreign investment. Such governmental regulation apparently interfered with international capital flows to an extent great enough to encourage the rapidly increasing rate of growth of international offshore funds markets—the Eurodollar and Eurobond markets.

In order to precisely understand international investment banking in the underwriting of equity and Eurobond issues, it is first necessary to be able to distinguish these activities from the more-traditional "international banking" activities of Eurodollar lending.

EURODOLLAR LENDING.   The dollar-denominated accounts in Europe that were funded by an excess outflow of U.S. funds during the post World War II years became a source of funds for international lending that was not regulated by any one national government. The lending consortiums (or syndicates) of multinational banks generally accessed these funds through the medium of one of their overseas branch banks located in a European money-market center, such as London. If the funds were sourced in London, the syndicate's lead bank would take down the funds by means of cable in London at the London Interbank Offered Rate (LIBOR) and lend them (under the proper legal loan documents) to a corporation or government anywhere in the world, by means of cable. The lending bank would then take its pro rata share of the spread of the lending rate over LIBOR and the lead syndicate bank would take its management fee for having arranged and managed the lending syndicate.

Such Eurodollar lending is *intermediated* lending, since the European banking system collects the dollars in the Eurodollar accounts and the banking syndicate arranges for the loaning out of this money. This source of some $350 to $800 billion is under the control of no government or central bank; it is an unregulated fund of international money governed only by market supply and demand.

THE EUROBOND MARKET.   Although capital from bonded indebtedness is often a substitute for a large, international, syndicated Eurodollar loan, the Eurobond funds are *nonintermediated* funding. The syndicate of international investment bankers who arrange the Eurobond issue merely facilitates the sale of Eurobonds, bonds denominated in any one of some 14 hard currencies, to the ultimate purchaser. The underwriting syndicate immediately provides the issuing corporation with the agreed amount of capital as the bonds are sold to the underwriting syndicate and then distributed by the managing syndicate to the underwriting syndicate (which is multinational in nature), which then *places* (see Giddy, 1975) the Eurobonds through its system of international bankers, brokers, and dealers in various countries.

Unlike domestic bond issues, most of a Eurobond issue will generally be placed outside of the country whose currency is used to denominate the issue. Thus the Securities and Exchange Commission (SEC) or the Fed or the other security and banking regulatory agencies in whose domicile the lead syndicating banker is located generally do not have a determinative regulatory interest in the issue. One important effect of this vacuum of regulatory authority is that generally Eurobond issues are not subject to withholding taxes generally paid on bond interest payments (see Giddy, 1975).

THE PLACEMENT OF EUROBOND ISSUES.   Another unique feature of Eurobond issues is that the bonds are not sold directly to the public as they might be if formally issued through a domestic underwriter and its network of brokers. A Eurobond issue generally works its way through a multilayered international distribution network that results in the bonds' being placed with a large number of buyers who have been presold on this issue before it takes place (see Giddy, 1975). Thus this business once again has the flavor of merchant banking in that it involves international connections between large, well-funded institutions that appear to be important in not only the distribution, but also the sale of Eurobond issues.

First the Eurobonds are bought by the managing syndicate of merchant bankers. This syndicate then distributes the bonds to a multinational group of bankers known as the underwriting syndicate. The syndicate members' organization of bankers, brokers, and dealers then place the bonds with their purchasers.

THE POPULARITY OF THE EUROBOND MARKET.   Giddy (1975) has outlined how this system results in a market that is able to provide large amounts of capital for often-complicated financing plans, at low cost, with great flexibility, anonymity, and safety. The placement market for Eurobonds is virtually worldwide, and the credit-worthiness of the leading syndicate banks is generally impeccable. All of this works for the safe provision of large amounts of capital funds. Since Eurobond issues generally bypass official authorizations, requirements for financial-disclosure queuing arrangements, and exchange-listing obligations, and are not under the regulation of the agencies of any one government, there is great flexibility in managing the issues. Interest costs have been competitive with other markets, and the management fees on these issues, about 3.5 percent of the face value of the issues, are low. It is often possible to avoid withholding taxes on the interest paid on the bonds, further reducing their cost (and increasing the yield of the issues). Corporations like the fact that they are able to rely on a sound and tightly knit institutional framework of investment bankers and their connections, and purchasers of the bonds like the fact that there is a vigorous market in "secondhand" Eurobonds, increasing the liquidity of their investment.

PROJECT FINANCING

Project financing has all of the earmarks of business in the area of merchant banking. Project financing is generally involved in extremely large, mining, energy, or raw-materials projects in remote locations and in countries of high political risk. Typically the sponsoring company could not, by itself, sustain the additional leverage it would have to incur to finance such a large project. This is especially true in the recent environment of high inflation rates, low depreciation rates, high costs of replacing capital equipment, high interest rates, and volatile prices in product and capital markets. Nonetheless, such projects generally offer great potential profits, both for the host country, sponsoring firm, and financiers. Thus the typical project is large, and requires special sources of capital, unique investment-analysis expertise, sharp negotiating skills, and the sort of financial-feasibility study that investment bankers often do best.

CHARACTERISTICS OF PROJECT FINANCING.   The characteristics of project financing as organized by an international investment banker would involve the following:

1.   The undertaking would be a separate financial entity from that of the sponsoring company.
2.   Heavy leverage would be involved; debt would typically represent 65–75 percent of capital.
3.   The recourse of borrowers would not be primarily to the sponsoring company, but would generally rely upon
     a. the assets of the project or
     b. the potential cash flow of the project.
4.   Supplier commitments would generally be a significant part of the credit support.
5.   The sponsoring firm's guarantees to lenders typically would not cover all the risks involved (called "laying off the risk").

6. The project debt would be differentiated from general debt on the sponsoring firm's balance sheet to avoid intolerable levels of leverage for the sponsoring firm.

This type of organization (see Wynant, 1980) allows the sponsoring firm to direct the operations of a development or mining project so large that the financing would overwhelm the firm itself. In one instance, the financing of a single project was equal to 70 percent of the capital of the sponsoring firm. Project financing also enables the prospective cash flows to be used to secure financing in a way that is not possible when many sponsoring firms act alone.

KEY ELEMENTS OF PROJECT FINANCING.   Key elements (these elements were gleaned from Wynant, 1980) in project financing are typically provided by the investment banker as follows:

1. The banker makes an assessment of start-up and operating risks that would lead to startup-cost overruns and quick failure of the venture before breakeven is achieved.
2. The banker identifies the major sources and terms for financing.
3. The banker develops a risk-analysis approach and may advocate methods for either avoiding or laying off some risks.
4. The banker may advocate unique ways for reaching leverage targets necessary to make the project viable:
    a. Special sources of financing: governmental or international agency sources.
    b. Support arrangements: governmental guarantees of loan arrangements.
5. The banker designs in flexibility to facilitate the availability of future financing.

THE CRITICAL START-UP PERIOD.   The investment banker is expected to anticipate start-up problems that can quickly knock out a project (Wynant, 1980). For example:

1. Problems in the recovery process (in a mining venture).
2. Poor engineering for product quality or product specifications.
3. Problems related to low labor productivity, especially in less developed countries.
4. High and inflated costs of replacement equipment, or supplies, possibly due to
    a. inflation in the host country or
    b. adverse movements in the exchange rate.
5. Effects of inflation, which may be quite significant in underdeveloped countries.
6. Problems involved with volatile prices in product markets upon which the project cash flows rely.

One method of anticipating the effects on the project of these diverse risks is to run a computer simulation of the project's start-up to assess project riskiness, and to judge the project's sensitivity to various operating and financial variables. These studies, combined with the banker's expertise and experience, provide a basis for entering the complex financial negotiations between governments, bankers, sponsoring firms, and other parties to the project.

LAYING OFF OF RISKS.   Various methods can be used to lay off some of the risks of the project. In the case of large mining operations, where the cash flows from the project depend on the export sale price of the ore, it is common to include a number of sponsoring firms from different countries in order to secure long-term contracts for the mine's output. This is one way of insulating the projected cash flows from the project from typically volatile raw-materials prices. The spread of nationalities in long-term contracting parties also tends to spread the risk of default as well as the anticipated project profits. It is in the interest of the contracting parties both to receive profits from the mine and to secure stable, long-term supplies of raw materials for their factories. The long-term contracts also take into account anticipated exchange-rate fluctuations that might have just as damaging an effect on project cash flow as falling raw-materials prices; thus the exchange rates for contract prices are often also agreed on.

SPREADING POLITICAL RISK.   Another benefit of securing participants of many nationalities in the project, both among financing parties and parties sponsoring and/or contracting for the project's output, is to bring the political clout of these large companies and banks into bargaining play during any threatened default or nationalization by a host-country government or a host-government joint-venture partner. An example of the use of such bargaining clout was when, in 1976, Peru sought $300 million in balance-of-payments financing from a group of U.S. money-market banks. The financing was conditioned upon Peru's satisfying the syndicate's demand for compensation to Newmont Mining Corporation for Peru's 1975 expropriation of the Marcona Mining Company, and for settlement of a back-tax dispute with Southern Peru Copper Company, owned by AMAX Inc.

FORECASTING AND PRENEGOTIATING POLITICAL RISK.   Eiteman and Stonehill (1979) recommended a technique of forecasting and negotiating away any excessive political risk before the project investment is made. The international investment banker would typically be a lead negotiator in such bargaining for a project-financed venture, because investment bankers are peculiarly well situated to pull together the interests involved. In fact, if the banker does not do this, the project will probably not receive the banker's approval, which is generally necessary in order to induce other sources of financing to participate.

The industries in which project financing is generally employed are transportation, power, chemicals, and agribusiness. All of these industries have a developmental flavor, and many recent project-financed ventures in these industries have been located in less developed countries. Thus negotiations with these host-country governments have often involved the host-country government or its development corporations or banks in some way in the venture as a partner in order to make the host's point of view more congruent with that of the venture.

Wynant (1980) has pointed out that in 1976, 200 projects of this type were project financed with capitalizations of over $200 million apiece. These projects could not have been made by the corporate sponsors alone because either the projects were too large, or the environmental constraints of high corporate leverage, high interest rates, and high inflation rates would have prevented it. Wynant believes that without the intervention of project financing, the world may experience a financial crisis of the type that was avoided by capital-market growth during the 1970s. If Wynant is right, this will be an important growth area for international investment.

PARALLEL LOANS

Parallel loans, currency swaps, and credit swaps are arranged by international investment bankers either to aid going concerns or to aid in project financing organizations, reorganizations, or other offbeat financial situations.

PARALLEL LOANS.   Parallel loans are a method of avoiding the risk that the exchange rate may change on the foreign currency denominating a loan before the loan matures. If, for instance, the exchange rate on a U.S. dollar loan made by a Belgian subsidiary of a U.S. company rises in favor of the dollar before the loan is repaid, then the Belgian subsidiary will book a loss upon repaying the loan because of the need to repay the loan in dollars that are now more expensive in terms of Belgian francs.

To avoid such a risk, Belgian subsidiary A might seek a parallel loan through the services of its investment banker. To do this, the investment banker would find Belgian subsidiary B, of an American firm, which was willing to loan the Belgian subsidiary A the francs that it needed. To complete the arrangement, the banker must have found a Belgian subsidiary B that had a U.S. parent corporation that *needed* a loan in dollars equal in value to the franc loan that its Belgian subsidiary B was making to Belgian subsidiary A.

It is easy to see why an investment banker is necessary to put together a deal like this. Since the foreign-exchange market is avoided, the banker's services are used to arrange a set of congruent loan needs that are simultaneously both equal and opposite in two countries. This loan arrangement literally takes one back to the days of barter. The advantage of the parallel or "back-to-back" loan is that it avoids, for both the parent companies and their subsidiaries, the need to enter the foreign-exchange market to pay back the loans. The parent of Belgian subsidiary B receives its loan repayment in dollars of local U.S. currency. Belgian subsidiary B receives its loan repayment in local Belgian francs. Thus there is no transaction risk on the repayment of the loans, and, since the loan to the Belgian subsidiary is in the local currency, there is no possibility of foreign-currency-denominated monetary assets getting out of balance with foreign-currency-denominated liabilities so as to cause foreign-exchange exposure on its balance sheet.

The investment banker obviously must demand a fee for arranging this type of transaction, but perhaps the fee is preferable to the foreign-exchange risk. The banker has sold his contracts and his peculiar knowledge of international corporate needs. Nonetheless, the difficulty of arranging such a transaction limits its use mainly to the facilitation of complicated financial deals negotiated by the investment banker.

CURRENCY SWAPS.   A currency swap involves the swap of equivalent amounts of two different currencies for a fixed period of time. These transactions are also arranged by investment bankers, but since these transactions closely resemble forward contracts in the foreign-exchange market (and are treated as such by U.S. accountants), they really do not accomplish much that cannot be accomplished more easily through the foreign-exchange market for a small brokerage fee.

CREDIT SWAPS. A credit swap is an exchange of foreign currencies between a business firm and a bank under an agreement to repay the currencies at a certain time. In this way, the business (and the bank) gets the use of the foreign exchange for a period of time without entering the foreign-exchange market and subjecting itself to foreign-exchange-transaction risk. Since, however, this device uses the deposit accounts of the foreign bank, it is often arranged through the offices of the branch bank, and is probably not generally considered to be international investment banking unless the transaction was in connection with a more-complicated financing that the Edge Act banking group was negotiating.

MERGERS, ACQUISITIONS, AND REORGANIZATIONS

MERGERS AND ACQUISITIONS. The Edge Act statutes under which international investment bankers operate is subtly rooted in the idea of mergers, because of the gradual reorientation of interpretation of the Edge Act from being considered a law stimulating short-term trade credit to being considered a law intended to encourage much-needed, long-term development financing. Originally the Edge Act had been sold to Congress as a bill to stimulate the financing of U.S. exports, which were perceived to be threatened. After World War I, however, the United States shifted from being a debtor nation to being a creditor nation, and the perception developed that the Edge Act, which was then in operation, could easily be interpreted as encouraging long-term financing of the kind that war-ravaged nations and less developed nations needed to develop and redevelop their natural resources (Baker, 1974). The provisions for "financing" Edge Act corporations and for equity participation in ventures and their financing especially aided this construction of the law. Thus the EACs began to move into large-scale financing of development projects such as those eventually represented by ADELA and PICA. Projects such as these often had governments as participating partners in the joint ventures, and this encouraged the scouting of many cosponsoring corporations in order to spread the risk of such large undertakings. This tradition in the use of Edge Act corporations has continued in the more-recent popularity of project financing for much the same reasons as those discussed above. Big development projects tend to encourage thoughts of joint venture, which naturally lead to the accumulation of the kind of information and expertise on the part of managing investment bankers that leads them to sell their expertise in financing and arranging mergers. The investment bankers have been in this type of business ever since the reinterpretation of the Edge Act in 1920.

SPINNING OFF EXPERTISE. It is in the international investment banker's financial interest to develop interest in mergers because mergers are a potential use for the type of expertise developed in other investment-banking ventures. Investment bankers find it natural to operate both offensively and defensively in the merger-acquisition field. The international merchant banker has access to funds outside of the country of the tender-offer issuance, which may provide a surprise defensive punch in the event that his bank is defending against an unfriendly takeover attempt. It is the business of investment bankers to have access to the large amounts of capital necessary for the purchase of a target company's stock in the open market, or in a tender-offer situation in which bidding competition sets off a price spiral in the target stock. Investment bankers, because of their constant need to make financial evaluations, are natural parties to advise about the critical effects on dividends, market price, and the qualitative factors affecting the finances of corporations, both during and after takeover.

SPOTTING MERGER PARTNERS.   The combined information network of multinational banks with Edge Act corporation investment-banking sections is probably unparalleled at screening and marrying merger partners with synergistic "fits." The evidence indicates (Weston, 1979) that none of the usual financial variables is good at predicting the success of merged firms, and this makes it likely that the qualitative factors involved in fitting together two or more firms with different resource strengths are the determinative factors in arranging good mergers. International investment bankers are well situated to aid in this process, firstly, because they are constant participants in the financing of the projects of the very large multinational corporations that tend to be corporate conglomerates that are constantly acquiring and selling subsidiaries. Secondly, the bankers are in on large development-financing projects and on project financings, which both tend to involve mixing corporate resources in a large-scale way. The skills involved in these activities (see Wynant, 1980) give the investment banker a set of experience and negotiating tools that are tailor-made for arranging mergers.

UNDERWRITING SKILLS.   The investment banker's practice in the marketing, placement, and management of large international equity and Eurobond financings provides the skills often needed in the arrangement and defense of mergers and take-overs. Mergers and takeovers often take place simply because they provide the way for growth to take place that, from both a financial and a resource-fit point of view, might not be possible otherwise. The size, diversification, and synergies of large firms make them often-superior competitors both in product markets and in capital markets. Large firms, because they are better diversified and better known, are often able to sell their stock at a lower required rate of return, and thus may be able to finance with cheaper debt and equity than would be available to a smaller firm. Moreover, there are often tax advantages in purchasing one company with the stock of another, since the owner of the target company will not have to pay capital-gains tax on the acceptance of the takeover company's tender offer of stock in the takeover company, rather than cash. This might mean that it would be cheaper for the takeover company to purchase a going concern with stock, rather than to purchase the assets and organize its own company subsidiary. High rates of inflation and the understated book values of many going concerns tend to make them good bargains. International investment bankers are peculiarly able to put together stock-swap packages for successful mergers and takeovers and to shepherd them through the intricacies of international capital markets in an optimal fashion.

FACTORS AFFECTING MERGER.   The banker should make a systematic assessment of the basic factors affecting merger possibilities:

1. Corporate earnings.
2. Rate of growth in earnings.
3. Dividends paid on stock.
4. Market values of stock.

5. Book values of corporations.
6. Net current assets of target corporations.
7. Qualitative factors affecting "fit."
8. Assessment of available legal complications for defense.

The availability of legal complications to impede a merger attempt might include securing legal advice about the following:

1. Federal Trade Commission approval requirements under the 1976 Hart-Scott-Rodino Act.
2. Relevant legal prohibitions under the Sherman Antitrust Act of 1890.
3. Available remedies under any applicable state law requiring notice before the issuance of a tender offer.
4. Any similar foreign laws applicable under the circumstances.

A survey of the legal environment surrounding any merger attempt suggests that the banker should formulate or aid in the formulation of a merger strategy. Some situations illustrative of the sorts of strategies that are available might be the following:

1. J. Ray McDermott Company outbid United Technologies in its tender-offer bid for control of the Babcock and Wilcox Company in 1977 because the initial tender offer of United Technologies was too low to preempt the stock.
2. In 1977 the stockholders of Kennecott Copper Company accused its managers of "squandering" its cash because it made a $66-per-share tender offer for the stock of the Carborundum Company, which was then selling for $33.25 per share. Kennecott argued that it had sought to defend itself from takeover by investing $1.2 billion from its forced divestment of the Peabody Coal Company in Carborundum at a price that would constitute a successful preemptive bid for controlling interest in Carborundum.
3. The Kern County Land Company was able to successfully defend itself from a $83.50 tender offer for its shares, which were then selling for $60 per share, by saying in print that its underlying assets were worth much more than the $83.50 offer of Occidental Petroleum indicated. Kern solicited higher offers from other, "friendly" tender bidders, and eventually accepted an offer from "friendly" Genneco Corporation, which of course, provided for continued tenure in office for Kern's management.

INTERNATIONAL BUSINESS NECESSARILY INVOLVES MERGERS. The international extension of the already complicated tactical and strategic considerations outlined above is a daunting proposition, but it is one that is inevitably involved in multinational-business management in today's world, and one that calls for the intervention, advice, intermediation, and negotiations skills of the international investment banker. *Multi*national business, by its nature, demands that corporations be large and have larger-than-average managerial, operational, and financial resources. This underscores merger as an important means of attaining these goals (aside from the previous list of theoretical, economic, and financial advantages). Many multinational corporations must merge in order to be able to successfully compete and survive. Large domestic size of a corporation does not guarantee its adequacy as an international competitor. One reason for this may be the fact that Europe has relatively few legal antitrust traditions. To the contrary, during the late 1960s the French government's program of "indicative planning" forced mergers in order to develop domestic corporations that were perceived to be large enough to thwart *le defi Americain*. International investment bankers will inevitably be involved in wave after wave of financially competitive international mergers. The era of such mergers is upon us, as indicated by studies such as that of Jean Boddewyn (1979) describing the standard patterns of retrenchment used currently as management tools of multinational corporations that may have overextended themselves during the direct-foreign-investment boom of the sixties and early seventies. These corporations appear to rationalize, cut back, and reorganize their worldwide multinational business. The international investment bankers who originally tagged along to service these multinationals may now be required to help manage their reorganization and merger problems.

REORGANIZATION, LIQUIDATION, AND BANKRUPTCY.   International investment bankers are most often involved in reorganization operations rather than either bankruptcy or liquidation proceedings. Bankruptcy is the toiling province of local legal and juridical specialists, and liquidations are generally handled through the auspices of the commercial-banking divisions of international banks. However, the investment banker is, more or less, constantly involved in reorganizations as he participates in project financings and mergers. The management of large-scale, risky international mining and development projects constantly involves negotiations to restructure, or "reorganize," the operations, the management, and/or the finances of these ventures. The spectrum of the reorganization activities ranges from the devising of methods to peacefully let out disenchanted investors to the over-the-weekend tactics for securing rescue capital for a coming insolvency crisis. Investment bankers are the doctors involved in saving the client. When the client dies, he is turned over to other specialists.

EXTENSION AND COMPOSITION.   Extension and composition are probably the investment banker's most-common approaches to the most severe reorganization problems his clients face. These methods avoid the legal technicalities and delays of bankruptcy or state common-law proceedings. Extensions postpone the dates of required payments of past-due obligations. In the case of Eurodollar loans, such permission is often directly within the power of the investment banker, and is commonly called "the management of financial default." In composition, some sort of negotiations must precede an agreement to reduce the creditors' claims on the debtor.

In presiding over, or advising upon, proceedings leading to either an extension or a composition, the banker must satisfy the presence of the prerequisites to a successful reorganization:

1. That the debtor is a good moral risk.
2. That the debtor has the ability to make a recovery.
3. That general business conditions are favorable to a recovery.

Upon the satisfaction of these criteria, there is generally a meeting of the debtors and creditors, the appointment of a committee of creditors, an exhaustive report by the committee, and an eventual meeting to work out the composition agreement.

REORGANIZATION.   The term *reorganization* as used in the context of bankruptcy or insolvency implies business failure. Actually, the investment banker is almost constantly involved in the reorganization of corporate financing, and if the reorganizations are well managed, failure is never directly an issue.

A business reorganization that is made to avoid business failure, however, generally involves the following:

1. Scaling down the company's fixed charges.
2. Converting short-term debt into long-term debt.
3. Securing new capital financing:
    a. to provide working capital and
    b. to rehabilitate assets.
4. Discovering the causes for failures:
    a. operational and
    b. managerial.

In order to successfully scale down the claims made upon the failing corporation, the banker must ensure that the reorganization agreement is fair to all parties. Reorganization is, after all, only another form of extension or composition. The feature of reorganization that most characterizes this approach to business failure is the issuance of new securities in return for the retirement of the old securities under whose terms the business appeared to be failing. A crucial issue in this exchange is: What is the market value of the old securities? Once this question is answered to the satisfaction of the parties and any relevant regulatory agencies (i.e., the SEC or the FTC), the exchange can be made. If the reorganization is successful, the corporation will have undergone a successful business analysis and corrected the operational, managerial, or financial problems that led to failure, and will have secured new capital to correct the problems, if necessary. This opens the possibility for the investment banker to profit from the anticipated cash flows of the reorganized business venture either through interest on loans, dividends on shares held, or the receipt of advisement fees.

TRENDS IN INTERNATIONAL INVESTMENT BANKING

LOWERED BARRIERS TO ENTRY.   The modern use of Edge Act corporations has only partially lowered the barriers to entering the international investment-banking industry. Foreign legal barriers still exist, as indicated by the recent study by the U.S. Treasury Department (1979) and by a similar study by the OECD (1978).

THE ADVANTAGES OF SIZE.   Aside from the legal barriers, the operational barriers to entry in the international investment-banking industry are formidable. If international investment banking is an industry composed of EACs selling firm aggregates of high-level banking expertise, the large multinational banks have a decided competitive advantage over traditional domestic investment-banking houses. The competitive advantages of size are evident in other areas as well. Giddy (1980) gives evidence that there are greater profits in the foreign-exchange operations of multinational banks with large branch-bank networks than in those with smaller networks of branch banks.

OPERATION IN A PROTECTED MARKET.   Once the operational and legal barriers to entry have been surmounted, an international investment-banking operation can expect to earn oligopolistic profits in a partially protected market (Giddy, 1980). And if the pattern in the United States extends to international banking, the profits in international *investment* banking will be higher than those in international *commercial* banking. This will encourage international investment bankers to further differentiate their services to sew up their markets. These investment banks' services are partially differentiated to begin with, because of the peculiar mix of international commercial-bank capabilities upon which the international investment-banking operations have been piggybacked. It should be easy enough to further differentiate the services using the appropriate advertising media mixed with word-of-mouth advertising.

PARALLEL DOMESTIC AND INTERNATIONAL COMPETITION.   An important question is whether or not the traditional domestic investment-banking houses can continue to compete with the piggybacked Edge Act corporations of large multinational banks. In the domestic (U.S.) investment-banking industry, investment-banking houses are attempting to integrate vertically. Wholesale houses are attempting to develop broad-based sales networks at the same time that retail houses are striving to develop sources of the "product"—original security issues (Hayes, 1979). In international banking the traditional investment-banking houses may feel the need to develop international commercial-banking capabilities in order to develop their own brand of vertical international integration. They may find it difficult to do this unless they can arrange appropriate mergers with other international commercial-banking networks.

SOURCES AND SUGGESTED REFERENCES

Aliber, R.Z. "International Banking: Growth and Regulation." *Columbia Journal of World Business,* Vol. X (1975), pp. 9–15.

Baker, J.C., and M.G. Bradford. *American Banks Abroad, Edge Act Companies and Multinational Banking.* New York: Praeger, 1974.

Battersby, M.E. "Avoiding Risks by 'Parallel Lending.'" *Finance Magazine,* Vol. XXI (1976), pp. 56–57.

Boddewyn, J. "Foreign Divestment: Magnitude and Factors." *Journal of International Business Studies,* Vol. X (1979), pp. 21–27.

Eiteman, D.K., and A.I. Stonehill. "Reacting to Foreign Exchange Risk," "International Capital Markets," and "International Banking," in *Multinational Business Finance,* 2nd ed. Reading, Addison-Wesley, 1979.

Federal Reserve Act (12 USCS §§ 601–632). Section 25(a)l.

Ganoe, C.S. "Foreign Banks: Reciprocity and Equality," *The Bankers Magazine,* Vol. CLVII (1974), pp. 28–30.

———. "International Banking Gets Stronger," *The Bankers Magazine,* Vol. CLVIII (1975), pp. 109–11.

Giddy, I.H. "The Blossoming of the Eurobond Market," *Columbia Journal of World Business,* Vol. IV (1975), pp. 66–76.

————. "Internationalization of Commercial and Merchant Banking: The Competitive Structure of the Industry." Paper presented at the Conference on Internationalization of Financial Markets and National Economic Policy, April 10–11, 1980, at New York University, Graduate School of Business Administration, sponsored by the Salomon Brothers Center for the Study of Financial Institutions.

Hayes, II, S.L. "The Transformation of Investment Banking," *Harvard Business Review,* Vol. LVII (1979), pp. 153–70.

Hutton, H.R. "The Regulation of Foreign Banks—A European Viewpoint," *Columbia Journal of World Business,* Vol. X (1975), pp. 115–19.

Logue, D.E., and J.R. Lindvall, "The Behavior of Investment Bankers: An Econometric Investigation," *Journal of Finance,* Vol. XXIX (1974), pp. 203–15.

Neukomm, H.A. "Risk and Error Minimization in Foreign Exchange Trading," *Columbia Journal of World Business,* Vol. X (1975), pp. 77–86.

Organization for Economic Co-operation and Development. *Regulations Affecting International Banking Operations of Banks and Nonbanks.* Paris: OECD, 1978.

Robinson, Jr. S.W. *Multinational Banking.* Leiden, the Netherlands: A. W. Sitjthoff, 1972.

Rudy, J.P. "Global Planning in Multinational Banking," *Columbia Journal of World Business,* Vol. X (1975), pp. 16–22.

Thoman, G. "International Banking Can Be Profitable for U.S. Regional Banks," *Columbia Journal of World Business,* Vol. X (1975), pp. 23–32.

United States Treasury Department. *Report to Congress on Foreign Government Treatment of U.S. Commercial Banking Organization.* Washington, DC: U.S. Government Printing Office, 1979.

Walter, Ingo. *Global Competition in International Banking* (Cambridge, MA.: Ballinger, 1988).

Weston, J.F. and E.F. Brigham. *Essentials of Managerial Finance,* 5th ed. Hinsdale, IL: Dryden Press, 1979.

Wolf, K. "The Impact of Rate Fluctuations on the Profitability of Swap Transactions," *Euromoney,* XXII (1975), pp. 26–29.

Wynant, L. "Essential Elements of Project Financing," *Harvard Business Review,* Vol. LVIII (1980), pp. 165–73.

SECTION **20**

LEGAL ASPECTS OF INTERNATIONAL LENDING

CONTENTS

LEGAL ASPECTS OF INTERNATIONAL LENDING

Michael Gruson

BASIC CONCEPTS OF A LOAN AGREEMENT

CONDITIONS OF LENDING

Need for Closing Conditions. A loan agreement between a bank and a borrower (the following assumes a loan agreement drafted in accordance with U.S. practice and governed by New York law) is usually signed by the parties well in advance of the actual making of the loan (the disbursement of funds). The loan agreement represents a legally binding obligation of the bank to make the loan, and if the bank refuses to advance funds after having signed the loan agreement, it may be liable to the borrower for damages. The bank can protect itself by specifying in the loan agreement conditions, so-called closing conditions, that must be satisfied before it is obligated to disburse funds. These conditions are intended to assure the bank that the factors that constitute the basis for the bank's credit decisions are true and that the legal aspects of the loan are in order not only at the time of signing the loan agreement, but also remain unchanged at the time of disbursement of funds. Most closing conditions are of a documentary nature, *i.e.,* their satisfaction must be evidenced by the presentation of specified documents, others are factual, *e.g.,* the absence of material adverse changes in the financial conditions of the borrower. If one of the conditions is not met, the bank has the legal right to refuse to make the loan. If all conditions are satisfied, the bank is normally legally obligated to make the requested advance even though there have been significant changes in the borrower's circumstances (unless, of course, the absence of material adverse changes was a closing condition). Customarily, most of these documentary closing conditions must be met only when the bank makes the first advance under the loan agreement and not also at the time of subsequent advances.

At a minimum, banks generally require as a closing condition evidence that the loan was and still is *duly authorized* by the appropriate governing body of the borrower (usually banks require resolutions of the borrower's board of directors authorizing the loan transaction and authorizing certain officers to execute and deliver the loan documents) and that the loan agreement was *duly executed* and delivered by an authorized officer.

Governmental Approvals; Exchange Control. It is customary to require the borrower to deliver copies of any necessary governmental approvals. Although the bank will require the borrower's representation and an opinion of borrower's counsel that all necessary governmental approvals have been obtained, it is advisable to receive copies of such approvals so that the bank and its counsel are able to verify for themselves that the transactions contemplated by the loan agreement have been approved. If it is known at the time of drafting the loan agreement which governmental approvals will be required, they should be specifically referred to in the loan agreement. This procedure helps counsel to focus early on the legal requirements.

A bank lending U.S. dollars or Eurodollars expects to be repaid in U.S. dollars; however, exchange-control laws of the country of the borrower may restrict availability, convertibility, or transferability of U.S. dollars. Accordingly, the bank should obtain the agreement or other assurance from the appropriate authorities that (1) U.S. dollars will be available to the borrower when needed to pay interest and principal and other amounts under the loan agreement, and (2) the convertibility of the borrower's currency into U.S. dollars and the transferability of U.S. dollars for purposes of the loan will not be restricted.

The International Monetary Fund (IMF) Articles of Agreement (the Bretton Woods Agreement) prohibit enforcement in any member country of an *exchange contract* involving the currency of any other member country that is in violation of the exchange-control laws of such other member country (assuming such laws are consistent with the IMF agreement). (Sec. 2(b) of article VIII.)

It has been suggested that loan agreements are exchange contracts for purposes of the IMF Agreement because they affect a country's exchange resources. However, the New York courts apparently have adopted the narrower view that "exchange contracts" include only transactions which have as their immediate object international media of payment and that a loan agreement calling for payment of U.S. dollar is not an exchange contract. [*J. Zeevi & Sons, Ltd. v. Grindlays Bank (Uganda) Ltd.,* 37 N.Y.2d 220, 333 N.E.2d 168, 371 N.Y.S.2d 892, cert. denied, 423 U.S. 866 (1975); *Libra Bank Ltd. v. Banco Nacional de Costa Rica, S.A.,* 570 F. Supp. 870 (S.D.N.Y. 1983).]

Legal Opinions. Most major loan agreements contain a closing condition that the bank obtain a favorable opinion of counsel. The purpose of this requirement is to obtain counsel's judgment that the legal assumptions upon which the credit decision has been made are correct. In addition, negotiating the scope of the opinion may bring into the open legal problems and uncertainties before the loan agreement is signed or the loan proceeds are disbursed. In some cases these problems can be solved, whereas in other cases the bank must decide whether it will accept these problems and uncertainties as a credit matter. The opinion of counsel has the additional function of helping to evidence the bank's prudence and good faith in making the loan.

Traditionally, banks require an opinion from borrower's counsel. This opinion usually covers the same subject matters as the representations made by the borrower in the loan agreement relating to legal matters, but does not cover the representations by the borrower relating to financial matters. The borrower's counsel is usually more familiar than the bank's counsel with the subject matters covered by the representations, and his opinion reinforces his client's representations. In many loan transactions the bank is satisfied with a legal opinion by the borrower's inside counsel. In more-difficult transactions where the opinion requires more-specialized expertise, or in unusually important transactions where the bank desires the safeguard of perhaps more-independent judgment, the bank may insist on a legal opinion from borrower's outside counsel. Even in the case where an opinion from borrower's outside counsel has been requested, the borrower's inside counsel may still be asked to render an opinion on legal issues relating to the internal affairs of the borrower, such as due incorporation, due authorization and execution, absence of litigation, etc.

In addition, some banks do regularly require an opinion of their *own* outside U.S. counsel about the validity and enforceability of the loan agreement or other matters. In the case of syndicated loans, the loan agreements usually provide for an opinion of special U.S. counsel selected by the lead manager who represents all members of the syndicate or the agent bank or both. This opinion is much more limited than the opinion of borrower's counsel and frequently is simply to the effect that the loan agreement and notes are legal, valid, binding, and enforceable against the borrower. In rendering his opinion, special bank's counsel must rely on the opinion of borrower's counsel with respect to those aspects of his opinion which relate to the internal affairs of the borrower, *e.g.,* authorization and due execution of the loan agreement by the borrower. Sometimes this opinion is to the effect that the legal documentation is "in substantially acceptable legal form" and that the closing documents are "substantially responsive to the requirements of the loan agreement." The "substantially responsive" opinion can only be given where the closing conditions are described with specificity in the loan agreement.

In the case of loans to foreign borrowers, the bank, because of its unfamiliarity with the foreign law, usually insists on an opinion by a foreign counsel of its own selection. Even where the bank retains local counsel in a foreign country, the bank usually expects its U.S. counsel to make a diligent effort to uncover problems that might arise under the relevant foreign law and to ascertain that these problems have been addressed and solved. In addition, U.S. counsel should ascertain that foreign counsel is familiar with the purpose and meaning of the proposed opinion. This requires close interaction between the bank's U.S. counsel and foreign counsel.

The opinion of foreign counsel and the opinion of U.S. counsel for the bank together must address all legal issues as to which the bank desires assurances. Some issues are governed by the foreign law of the country of the borrower and some issues are governed by the applicable U.S. state law and since each lawyer will opine only with respect to his own law, foreign counsel and U.S. counsel must understand what the proper scope of their respective opinions should be and which issues each should opine on. Traditionally, foreign counsel will be requested to state that the loan agreement which is governed by, *e.g.,* New York law "is legal, valid, binding and enforceable." The opinion on legality, validity and bindingness, if read together with the qualification that the opinion is rendered only under the foreign law, means (i) that the governing law clause, subjecting the loan agreement to New York law, is valid under the foreign law, and (ii) that none of the terms of the loan agreement violates the public policy (or similar principles) of the foreign jurisdiction. (Foreign counsel cannot be expected to opine that none of the rules of New York law applicable to the loan agreement violates a public policy of the foreign jurisdiction.) The opinion on enforceability means that, assuming the loan agreement is legal, valid and binding under New York law, in case of a breach of the loan agreement the courts of the foreign jurisdiction will provide some remedy to the injured party in accordance with the procedural rules of the foreign jurisdiction, the terms of the loan agreement and the applicable New York law.

Foreign borrowers, in particular foreign sovereign borrowers, have sometimes expressed annoyance at the requirement of an opinion of counsel. They do not understand why the opinion of a private attorney should determine whether or not the borrower obtains the loan. The answer is simply that a prudent bank will make a loan only if the loan agreement is legal, valid, and enforceable, and the legal opinion is a method of ascertaining whether the loan agreement meets these requirements.

Conditions for Each Disbursement.   If the loan is not disbursed in a lump sum but in a series of disbursements or advances, the loan agreement usually contains conditions designed to permit the bank to refuse to make advances if changes have occurred in the legal or financial assumptions underlying the credit decision. Normally the loan agreement will require as a condition of each advance that the representations and warranties remain true and accurate as of the date of the advance and that no event of default, or event that may become an event of default upon giving of notice or lapse of time, has occurred and is continuing at the time of the advance. If the loan agreement contains a representation that no material adverse change has occurred in the borrower's financial condition, operations or prospects since the date of the financial statements upon which the credit decision was based, this representation is repeated as of the date of each advance, and the bank could refuse to make an advance if there were a material adverse change. The requirement that no default has occurred picks up, through the provision making a breach of a covenant an event of default, all the covenants of the borrower, and again would permit the bank to refuse to make advances if the borrower were not in compliance with a covenant.

REPRESENTATIONS AND WARRANTIES

Purposes of Representations.   The representations and warranties set forth in the loan agreement state the legal and, to some extent, the factual and financial assumptions upon which the bank's credit decision is based. They serve several functions. If the loan agreement provides that it is a condition of the bank's obligation to make advances that the representations be correct on the date of each advance, the bank could refuse to make an advance if a representation were not correct on that date. If a material misrepresentation were to occur—either on the date of the loan agreement or on the date of an advance—it would constitute an event of default and would permit the bank to accelerate the loan. These rights are not conditioned upon a misrepresentation being the fault of the borrower. Rather, the representations operate to allocate the risk to the borrower for the matters covered by them. Borrowers unwilling to give a representation sometimes argue that they themselves are not certain whether the representation is correct; this argument is misdirected. The proper question is who should bear the risk if certain legal, factual or financial assumptions upon which the credit decision is based are not correct.

In addition, the representations serve as a disclosure device during the negotiations by requiring the borrower to disclose information inconsistent with the requested representations. Once the inconsistent information has been disclosed, the bank can decide whether to accept the new facts as a credit matter, to modify the representations accordingly and possibly to request additional protections or whether to ask the borrower to remedy the objectionable situation before the loan can be made. Finally, the representations may assist the bank in establishing that it acted in good faith in the transaction.

Typical Representations.   Representations relating to legal assumptions typically cover (1) the proper incorporation and good standing of the borrower in the jurisdiction of its incorporation; (2) the corporate power of the borrower to enter into the loan transaction; (3) the proper authorization of the loan transaction; (4) the absence of the need for obtaining authorizations or approvals from governmental entities for the loan or, if such authorizations or approvals are required, their validity and effectiveness; (5) the absence of violations of law, the charter or by-laws of the borrower or any contract binding on or affecting the borrower resulting from the loan (*e.g.,* the loan may violate other financing agreements of the borrower that limit the amount of indebtedness that the borrower is permitted to incur, and such violation could permit the other creditors either to declare defaults under their agreements or to bring suits against the bank for inducing a breach of contract); and (6) the fact that the loan agreement is a legal, valid, and binding obligation of the borrower, enforceable against the borrower.

In each loan, the bank must consider whether its credit decision is based on any particular assumptions that should be covered by representations. If, for example, the business of the borrower depends upon a particular contract or permit, it may be useful to have a representation of the borrower concerning it. If the credit decision is made on the basis of certain nonpublic information supplied by the borrower (for example, projections or cash-flow statements), the loan agreement may contain representations as to the accuracy of such information.

A loan agreement normally contains a representation as to the accuracy of the financial statements upon which the bank based its original decision to extend the credit. This representation usually refers to the latest audited financial statements as well as any more-recent interim financial statements.

The representations relating to financial assumptions reflect only the minimum assumptions as to financial matters; usually the borrower provides much more financial information to the bank than is set forth in the representations.

Absence of Material Adverse Change.   A common representation is that there has been no material adverse change in the financial condition, operations or prospects of the borrower since the date of the latest financial statements upon which the credit decision was based. Such change may or may not be reflected in the balance sheet or income statement of the borrower. This provision enables the bank to refuse to lend to a borrower whose financial situation has materially deteriorated. It does not permit the bank to declare outstanding loans due and payable unless the representation was materially false when made (at the time of signing or of any advance).

The *material adverse change* standard is designed to cover circumstances in which the borrower's ability to perform its obligations under the loan agreement has become doubtful. The standard lacks precision and the bank's refusal to make further advances to the borrower because of a material adverse change is likely to cause disagreement. The bank's position obviously would be more certain if it were able to point to a violation of a financial covenant or some other specific provision of the loan agreement. However, because of the difficulty in defining clearly all possible material adverse changes, having the ability to invoke this standard, however imprecise, remains very important. Even in cases where the bank and the borrower disagree on whether a material adverse change has occurred, the existence of the clause alone may improve the bank's negotiating position.

COVENANTS OF THE BORROWER

Functions of Covenants. The affirmative and negative covenants bind the borrower in the conduct of its business during the period of the commitment and for the duration of the loan. Covenants permit the bank to influence the future conduct of the borrower in a manner that will reduce the risk that the loan will not be repaid. Violations of covenants serve as warning signals of difficulties. Covenants accomplish this in several ways: by requiring the borrower to comply with applicable legal requirements, by restricting excessive leveraging (restrictions on debt and leases), by preventing the borrower from preferring other creditors (the negative pledge), by maintaining assets in the borrower (restrictions on dividends and the net-worth covenant), or by requiring the borrower to retain liquidity (working-capital covenant). Also typically included in the covenants is an agreement by the borrower to supply financial and other information so that the bank can monitor the condition of the borrower and take corrective action if the situation warrants such action. If the borrower has subsidiaries, the bank must decide whether to apply the covenants to the borrower alone, the borrower and its subsidiaries generally, or the borrower and a group of specified subsidiaries (frequently referred to as restricted subsidiaries).

A violation of these agreed-upon minimum standards for the borrower's future conduct should give the bank the right to refuse to make additional advances because such violation (in some cases upon notice and passage of an applicable grace period) creates an event of default, which should prevent the conditions of lending from being met and which should permit the bank to accelerate the loan and cancel its commitment.

Negative Covenants. The negative covenants may be more significant than the affirmative covenants, because they provide clear restrictions upon managerial decisions. These restrictions normally cover such areas as creation of liens, incurrence of indebtedness and lease obligations, payment of dividends, mergers, sale of assets, and investments.

The negative-pledge covenant usually prohibits the borrower from granting any security interest, lien, or mortgage on its property or its income to secure the payment of obligations to other lenders. The problem created by any such security interests, liens, or mortgages in favor of other creditors is that they subordinate the bank's loan to the borrower's obligations to other creditors in case of financial difficulty of the borrower. The purpose of a negative pledge is to provide a pool of assets that will be available for payment of the claims of unsecured creditors equally without any preference of one over the other; it does not create a security interest in favor of the bank. The negative-pledge covenant should apply to the borrower's right to receive income as well as its properties to prevent the use of devices that dedicate income streams to the payment of certain debts.

There is a great variety of possible positive and negative covenants. Which covenants the bank wishes to include in a loan agreement depends on the nature of the borrower's business, its financial condition, and the term of the loan. The covenants may be tied directly to detailed financial projections provided by the borrower if the credit risk is high, or may be limited to a few general financial benchmarks if the credit risk is low. In devising financial covenants for foreign borrowers, the bank should take into account the foreign accounting principles applicable to the borrower.

EVENTS OF DEFAULT.   Events of default are circumstances in which the bank has the right to declare the loan immediately payable and to terminate the bank's commitment to extend credit under the loan agreement.

Typical Events of Default.   Most loan agreements contain at least the following events of default: nonpayment of principal or interest, inaccuracy in the representations and warranties, violations of covenants, cross-default to other debt of the borrower, bankruptcy events, expropriation, and failure to pay a final judgment in excess of a certain amount.

A cross-default provision is important in circumstances in which the borrower has defaulted under another credit agreement, thus enabling other creditors to demand payment or negotiate improvements in their positions. The cross-default provision gives the bank the right to accelerate its loan in such event. The cross-default can be broadened to include events that have not yet become events of default under other credit agreements because notice requirements or cure (grace) periods are still applicable. This latter type of cross-default gives the bank the same opportunity to negotiate with the borrower as the other creditors prior to the occurrence of a formal event of default under their credit agreements.

In addition to the events of default mentioned above, the bank must consider whether, in the context of the particular loan transaction, there are other circumstances in which the bank should have the right to call the loan. However, many of these circumstances could more appropriately be located in other parts of the loan agreement. For example, if the purpose of the credit is to finance the construction of a hotel, the loan agreement could provide for mandatory prepayment rather than an event of default if the hotel is destroyed. If it is important for the bank that the borrower continues to be owned by its parent corporation, then instead of simply making the transfer of the borrower's stock an event of default, it might be preferable to have the parent corporation in a separate agreement covenant to continue to hold the stock of the borrower, and then make the violation of this covenant an event of default under the loan agreement. Structuring these circumstances as covenants or representations could be advantageous for the bank because a violation or breach of such covenants or representations would trigger a cross-default in many other credit agreements not immediately but only after the necessary notice under the loan agreement has been given and the applicable grace period had run. Furthermore, under proper circumstances, the bank may be able to obtain a court order enjoining the borrower or its parent corporation from violating a covenant or agreement.

Grace Periods and Notice Requirements.   Certain events of default may contain grace periods or notice provisions, whereas others are considered so significant that the mere occurrence of the event gives the bank the immediate right to accelerate. Grace periods are granted very infrequently in the case of a default for failure to make principal payments. Since the representations and warranties reflect the fundamental assumptions upon which the credit is extended, any material inaccuracy is considered serious and usually treated as an immediate event of default. Furthermore, a cure period is usually not provided for the curing of a misrepresentation because misrepresentations often are not susceptible to being remedied. Violations of covenants become events of default frequently after notice has been given by the bank to the borrower and a grace period has lapsed without the borrower having corrected the default. However, a loan agreement may create an immediate event of default upon violation of certain covenants, especially financial covenants, because they are fundamental to the basic credit decision or because the opportunity for correction is limited.

Immediate events of default may be disadvantageous to the bank because they may trigger cross-default provisions in credit agreements between the borrower and other creditors and may thereby introduce an element of instability in the borrower's financial affairs. This consideration would not be relevant, however, if another credit agreement contained a cross-default provision that was violated irrespective of notices and cure periods in the loan agreement or waivers by the bank.

Remedies.   Upon the occurrence and during the continuance of an event of default, the bank has the right to accelerate the loan and terminate its commitment. An event of default sometimes accelerates the loan automatically, especially the occurrence of bankruptcy or similar events, but automatic accelerations are unusual.

If the bank has accelerated the maturity of its loan, the bank might set off deposits of the borrower in the bank against the borrower's obligation to repay the loan. The right of set-off is the right of the bank to charge its deposit obligations to the borrower against the borrower's loan obligation to the bank. The right of set-off can be exercised in New York by the bank by virtue of a specific provision contained in the loan agreement, common law or statute [New York Debtor and Creditor Law § 151]. If the borrower is not in bankruptcy, the bank is normally able to obtain a judgment against the borrower for the amount of the debt due and then has available the remedies under the legal system for the enforcement of judgments. Furthermore, in appropriate cases the bank may be able to enforce a covenant or other term of the loan agreement in a suit for specific performance of that covenant or term. For example, the bank may be able to obtain a court order requiring the borrower to comply with a covenant or enjoining the borrower and third parties from violating a covenant.

In practice, banks rarely exercise the right to accelerate the loan, because an acceleration is likely to trigger acceleration by other creditors of the borrower and ultimately may cause a bankruptcy. The most frequent result of an event of default is a renegotiation by the bank and the borrower of the loan agreement together with a renegotiation of the borrower's other credit relationships. Even though rarely used, the right to accelerate is an essential remedy, because having this right substantially strengthens the bank's negotiating position with the borrower and other creditors. It also serves as a powerful incentive for the borrower to remain in compliance with the terms of the loan agreement. However, if bankruptcy appears inevitable, or if other creditors accelerate, or if there exists fraud or some other situation with which the bank cannot live, the bank may be forced to accelerate and set off deposits.

The enforcement by the bank of its rights under the loan agreement is subject to the general principles of equity and to principles of fairness and good faith. Courts generally strictly enforce agreements between sophisticated parties which were fully negotiated with the assistance of counsel. However, it is possible that in aggravated circumstances a court may look to equitable concepts and concepts of reasonableness to provide some relief to a borrower and thereby dilute the effect of the literal language of the loan agreement. [See K.M.C. Co., Inc. v. Irving Trust Company, 757 F.2d 752 (6th Cir. 1985), where the bank was held liable for its failure to make a requested advance under an uncommitted facility, on the ground that it had not acted reasonably and in good faith.]

EURODOLLAR LOANS

NATURE OF EUROCURRENCY.   Eurodollars are deposits of U.S. dollars with foreign banks or foreign branches of U.S. banks located outside the United States. Euro-Deutsche Marks are deposits of Deutsche Marks with banks located outside the Federal Republic of Germany. Thus a Eurocurrency is a bank deposit liability (or a claim against a bank) denominated in a currency other than the monetary unit of the country in which the bank is located. Eurodollars are created when a U.S. or foreign owner of a deposit with a bank in the United States transfers a U.S. dollar credit balance to a foreign bank (or to a foreign branch of a U.S. bank) located outside of the United States. The foreign bank assumes a deposit liability to the transferor owner payable in U.S. dollars, and itself has a corresponding claim in U.S. dollars against the bank in the United States (owns a deposit or credit balance with that bank). The foreign bank may transfer its U.S. dollar deposits to a second foreign bank, the second foreign bank may transfer the deposit to a third foreign bank, and so forth. In each case the transferee foreign bank becomes owner of the dollar deposit in the United States and assumes a deposit liability payable in U.S. dollars to the transferor foreign bank. The dollars originally deposited with a bank in the United States never leave the U.S. bank or the United States, so the total of bank deposits in the United States remains unchanged, but additional dollar deposits have been created abroad. When a bank, supported by such a U.S. dollar claim against a U.S. bank, transfers to a borrower a claim *against itself* for an equivalent amount of U.S. dollars, it makes a Eurodollar loan.

FUNDING.   The theory of a Eurodollar loan is that the lending bank acquires short-term Eurodollar deposits and lends the funds so borrowed by it to the borrower on a long-term basis. The interest rate on a Eurodollar loan is equal to the funding cost of the bank plus an agreed-upon *margin* or *spread*. The funding cost is expressed by reference to a specified Eurodollar interbank market (for instance, London) in which, theoretically, the bank expects to obtain the Eurodollars to lend. The loan agreements, however, do not restrict the funding of the loan to one market, and the bank may obtain the Eurodollars in any market it chooses. Because the bank passes the funding cost on to the borrower, the interest rate payable by the borrower remains fixed during the term of each U.S. dollar deposit acquired by the bank, but fluctuates during the term of the Eurodollar loan with the change of the funding cost of the successive U.S. dollar deposits acquired by the bank to fund the Eurodollar loan.

   The periods used for setting the interest rate payable by the borrower on the loan (interest periods) correspond, in theory, to the maturities of the U.S. dollar deposits acquired by the bank to fund the particular Eurodollar loan. At the end of any given term for a funding deposit the bank would, in theory, cause the maturity of such deposit to be extended, or would acquire another U.S. dollar deposit, for a term that similarly "matches" the next interest period (either selected by the borrower in accordance with the loan agreement or set by its terms). In practice, many large banks do not match deposits to interest periods of particular loans, but rather acquire an inventory of Eurodollar funds without consideration to any particular loan. In that case, the Eurodollar rate determined in accordance with the interest-period concept is a convenient and relatively verifiable way to establish a certain rate. Under normal market conditions longer interest periods will result in higher current rates but may be preferred by the borrower if he believes interest rates are rising.

Because in theory the term of each funding deposit matches the term of an interest period for the loan, the bank might suffer a loss if the borrower repaid or prepaid the loan or a portion thereof in the middle of an interest period. The bank would have to continue to pay interest on its funding deposit until the maturity of such deposit, but the borrower would not have to pay the corresponding interest on the "matching" loan. In addition, the bank may be unable to reinvest the funds at the interest rate previously paid by the borrower. To avoid this disadvantage for the bank, Eurodollar loan agreements provide that the interest periods (at least for an amount equal to the principal due) will end on each principal-repayment date, and that the borrower cannot prepay any portion of the loan except at the end of an interest period for such loan. If prepayment is allowed at some other time, the borrower should agree to reimburse the bank for any loss resulting from such prepayment.

LONDON INTERBANK OFFERED RATE (LIBOR).   Eurodollar loan agreements generally define the Eurodollar rate as the rate of interest at which U.S. dollar deposits (Eurodollars) are offered by the principal office of the bank to other banks in the specified interbank Eurodollar market (e.g., London) at a certain hour a certain number of days (usually two business days) before the first day of the applicable interest period for a period equal to such interest period (usually 1, 2, 3, or 6 months) and in an amount equal to the loan or advance to be made available during such interest period. Most agreements refer to the rate for U.S. dollar deposits *offered by* the bank in the specified interbank Eurodollar market to prime banks, the Eurodollar rate *posted* by the bank. In a syndicated loan the Eurodollar rate is determined by reference to an average (arithmetic mean) of the Eurodollar rates offered by specified reference banks. This averaging of rates takes into account both the relatively lower rates of the large dealer banks and the relatively higher rates of the non-dealer banks (which are more likely to "match" funding deposits to interest periods).

Eurodollar loan agreements in which dealer banks do not participate sometimes provide for a Eurodollar rate based on the rate *offered to* the bank or the reference banks in order to take the higher rate into account that such banks have to pay for U.S. dollar deposits.

YIELD PROTECTION

Increased Costs.   The Eurodollar interest rate consists of funding cost plus fixed spread, and customarily Eurodollar loan agreements guarantee this spread by providing that the borrower must indemnify the bank for *increased costs.* Increased costs could be incurred if because of a change in law (in the case of a loan through a London branch of a U.S. bank, U.S. law or English law) reserve or other monetary requirements were imposed on the bank or its branch. It is possible that U.S. or overseas monetary authorities will become concerned enough about the present lack of regulation in the Eurodollar markets that they will impose, or request "voluntary" compliance with, requirements intended to restrict, and make more costly, Eurodollar lending. Banks lending Eurodollars generally expect that the borrowers will assume the risk of such requirements and therefore will agree to pay the increased funding costs resulting from such requirements. If these additional costs unduly burden the borrower, Eurodollar loan agreements customarily permit the borrower to prepay the loan, at which time the bank's commitment terminates.

Regulation D.   Federal Reserve Board Regulation D provides that U.S. banks (including U.S. branches and agencies of foreign banks) are required to maintain reserves against certain types of deposits and other liabilities used to fund their loans. A bank will very often seek to pass on to its borrower the cost of the reserves the bank has to maintain against the deposits or other liabilities with which the loan is funded.

All banks subject to Regulation D will be required to maintain reserves thereunder with respect to funds obtained in the U.S. domestic market regardless of whether the loan being funded is extended to a U.S. or a foreign borrower. Such banks will also be required to maintain reserves under Regulation D with respect to funds obtained in the offshore market if the funds are advanced to a U.S. resident but will not be required to maintain reserves with respect to such funds if they are advanced by an offshore office of such a bank to a foreign affiliate of a U.S. corporation to finance its foreign operations. However, a foreign bank with U.S. branches or agencies will not be required to maintain reserves under Regulation D with respect to funds obtained in the offshore market if the funds are advanced to a U.S. resident by an offshore office of such bank, even if the funds are advanced to the U.S. resident for domestic use. All banks subject to Regulation D will be required to maintain reserves thereunder with respect to funds obtained in the offshore market if the funds are advanced to a foreign resident but will not be required to maintain reserves with respect to such funds if they are advanced to such foreign resident by an offshore office.

Tax Gross-Up.   As additional yield protection, banks generally require that all payments by the borrower must be made free and clear of withholding and all other foreign *taxes*. The borrower frequently argues that such provision is unjustified if the bank is entitled under its tax laws to a foreign-tax credit for the withholding taxes even if paid by the borrower. In addition, the loan agreement may provide that the borrower must indemnify the bank against income taxes imposed on the bank by its own country for imputed income attributable to withholding taxes paid on its behalf by the borrower (so-called gross-up provision). For example, under present U.S. tax law, if the interest due by the foreign borrower is $100, the withholding tax rate is 25 percent and the borrower pays to the U.S. bank $100 as required by the "free and clear" provision of the loan agreement, the U.S. bank is generally taxed in the United States on an income of $133 (*i.e.,* 75 percent of $133 ≈ $100) rather than $100.

FUNDING INTERRUPTION.   The determination of the Eurodollar rate is based on the assumption that the Eurodollar market will continue to exist substantially in its present form and Eurodollars will remain available, and Eurodollar loan agreements frequently provide that if this assumption (which may be expressed in different ways) is no longer true (e.g., because of a major dislocation of the specified Eurodollar market), the interest rate will be redetermined to reflect the cost to the bank of funding the loan. The procedure usually requires the bank and the borrower to negotiate with a view to agreeing on an alternative basis for the loan or for determining the rate. If no such agreement results after a specified period of time, then, many loan agreements provide, the bank is required to notify the borrower of the alternative rate at which the bank is prepared to lend. At that point the borrower has two choices: either to pay the alternative rate as determined by the bank or to prepay the loan. The borrower bears the risk that the Eurodollar market will not continue in its present form.

Frequently Eurodollar loan agreements cover the risk that it may become *unlawful* for the bank to continue to fund or to make its Eurodollar loans. This risk includes the possibility that the United States or the country of the lending office of the bank might prohibit, or permit on untenable conditions, transfers or purchases of U.S. dollar claims overseas or might regulate the volume or type of Eurodollar lending by banks. Loan agreements frequently (1) require that in such an event the borrower prepay the loan and (2) provide that the bank's commitment terminates.

PLACE OF PAYMENT.   Most Eurodollar loan agreements require the borrower to repay the loan at a bank located in the United States for account of the lender or, if the loan is made by a foreign branch of the U.S. bank, for account of such lending office. This requirement is important. First, the bank passes the *exchange control risk* to the borrower, for it is the borrower, not the bank, who is responsible for returning the U.S. dollar claims to the United States, where the claim becomes a currency in available funds. U.S. dollar credits overseas may not be worth as much as U.S. dollars in the United States if the uses to which such credits can be put are restricted or if exchange control laws restrict their transfer. Second, the bank minimizes the risk of something happening to the payment resulting from expropriation or other *adverse action* of the government of the foreign branch that acted as lending office or other overseas government.

LOANS TO SOVEREIGN BORROWERS

GENERAL CONSIDERATIONS.   Most major banks require even in the case of a government borrower a loan agreement that establishes a basis for effective enforcement proceedings. Such banks anticipate that a defaulting government may not always be motivated by a desire for continued access to the capital markets or may have access to alternative markets, that the banks would be in a weak negotiating position if the loan agreement provided for no legal action except that controlled by the government borrower, and that the bank's government may, for political reasons, be reluctant to intervene on behalf of the bank. Finally, the absence of provisions for effective legal action in one government-loan agreement creates a precedent for loan agreements with other government borrowers.

The legal protection of a bank should include a waiver of sovereign immunities by the government borrower, submission by the government to a neutral and commercially experienced forum, and the choice of a developed commercial law as governing law. A bank would not want its loan to a sovereign borrower to be governed by the law of the jurisdiction of the borrower. Such law is susceptible to being changed by and for the benefit of the sovereign borrower, and history has shown that a sovereign, when in trouble, tends to change its law to alleviate its troubles. If the law of the sovereign was specified as the governing law, courts may (and New York courts probably will) give effect to such changes in the specified law.

IMMUNITY FROM SUIT, ATTACHMENT, AND EXECUTION

Immunity.   Submission by the borrower to the jurisdiction of a court does not give much protection to a bank if the government borrower and its property are immune from suit, execution, and attachment. Under the U.S. Foreign Sovereign Immunities

Act of 1976 (28 U.S.C. §§ 1330, 1332, 1391, 1441, and 1602 et seq.), (1) a *foreign state* is immune from suit in federal and state courts in the United States, and (2) assets in the United States of a foreign state are immune from attachment, arrest, and execution, except in each case as otherwise specifically permitted by the immunities act. *Foreign state,* with minor exceptions, is defined to include a political subdivision of a foreign state and an agency or instrumentality of a foreign state; and *agency* or *instrumentality* is defined to include a separate legal person that is an organ of a foreign state or political subdivision thereof and a corporation organized under the laws of, and the majority of whose shares are owned by, a foreign state or political subdivision thereof. The exceptions from immunity from the jurisdiction of the federal or state courts in the United States are as follows:

1. A foreign state can explicitly or implicitly *waive* its *immunity from suit* in a federal or state court. Obviously, an explicit waiver is preferable over a waiver merely by implication.

2. A foreign state is *not immune from suit* in any case in which the action is based upon an activity of the foreign state that is *commercial* by its nature and that is carried on in the United States, or upon an act performed within, or having a direct effect within, the United States in connection with such foreign state's commercial activity elsewhere.

3. A foreign state can explicitly or implicitly *waive* its *immunity from attachment in aid of execution,* and its immunity from execution, upon a judgment entered by a federal or state court. Whereas a foreign state (that is not an agency or instrumentality) can waive immunity from attachment in aid of execution and from execution only for property used for a commercial activity in the United States, an agency or instrumentality of a foreign state engaged in commercial activity in the United States can waive these immunities for any property (whether commercially used or not) in the United States.

4. The property of a foreign state is *not immune from attachment in aid of execution* or from execution upon a judgment entered by a federal or state court if the commercially used property is or was used for the *commercial activity* upon which the claim was based, or if the property (whether commercially used or not) belongs to an agency or instrumentality of a foreign state engaged in commercial activity in the United States and the judgment relates to a claim based upon a commercial activity carried on in the United States or upon an act performed within, or having a direct effect within, the United States in connection with such agency's or instrumentality's commercial activity elsewhere (regardless of whether the property is or was used for the activity upon which the claim is based).

5. Commercially used property of a foreign state in the United States is *not immune from attachment prior to judgment* in any action brought in a federal or state court if the foreign state has explicitly waived its immunity from attachment prior to judgment *and* the purpose of the attachment is to secure satisfaction of a judgment that may ultimately be entered against the foreign state (and not to obtain jurisdiction).

6. Notwithstanding the above exceptions to immunity from attachment and execution, the property in the United States of a *foreign central bank* or monetary authority "held for its own account" is immune from any attachment and

execution whatsoever, unless such bank or authority, or its parent foreign government, has explicitly waived its immunity from attachment in aid of execution or from execution. But property of a foreign state of a *military character* or controlled by a foreign military authority and funds payable by certain *international organizations* to or on the order of a foreign state are absolutely immune from attachment or execution.

Each waiver of immunity is effective irrespective of any subsequent attempt to revoke it, unless the waiver is interpreted to be revocable.

The legislative history of the immunities act indicates that a foreign state's borrowing of money from U.S. commercial banks would be of a "commercial" nature and that a foreign state's incurring of indebtedness in the United States (if the loan agreement is negotiated and executed in the United States) would be a commercial activity carried on in the United States (House of Representatives, 94th Cong., 2d Sess. H. Rep. 1487 (1976) pp. 10 and 16). The courts, however, have a great deal of latitude in determining what is *commercial* and whether a particular commercial activity has been performed in the United States, and it is advisable to include in all loan agreements with foreign states an explicit waiver of all three immunities, that is, immunity from suit; immunity from attachment in aid of execution, and from execution, upon a judgment; and immunity from attachment prior to judgment.

Service of Process.   The immunities act specifies various ways for making service of process on a foreign state. However, if the potential plaintiff and the foreign state agree upon any special arrangement for delivery of summons and complaint, service must be made in accordance with such method. The immunities act intends to encourage potential plaintiffs and foreign states to agree on a procedure for service. A usual procedure is for the foreign state to appoint a process agent in the jurisdiction to which the foreign state submits. Such agent should accept the appointment, agree to forward all process to the foreign state and agree not to resign such appointment during the term of the loan. The consul of a foreign state in the United States may be appointed process agent, but may have its own diplomatic immunity from process; such immunity should be waived either by the consul itself or by the foreign state on behalf of the consul.

Representation.   A loan agreement with a governmental borrower often contains a representation to the effect that the borrower is not subject to sovereign immunity and that the execution, delivery, and performance of the loan agreement constitutes a commercial act. Such a representation may help to establish the commercial nature of the transaction.

SYNDICATION AND PARTICIPATION

SYNDICATED LOANS.   When a borrower's need for funds exceeds the amount that any single bank is able, willing or legally permitted to lend, several banks may join together in a syndicate to provide the required funds. A multibank syndicated loan represents an aggregate of commitments by the syndicate members, who agree to make the loan and to receive payments pro rata in accordance with the commitment of each. Each syndicate member is a party to the loan agreement and receives a separate note evidencing the portion of the loan made by it. The obligations of the syndicate members are separate, and one lender is not responsible for the commitment of another lender. In syndicated loans, one bank usually serves as *agent* for the syndicate in order to centralize the administration of the loan. An agreement between the agent bank and the syndicate members (which may, but need not, be part of the loan agreement) should clearly spell out the responsibilities and liabilities of the agent bank. Although loan agreements frequently state that the agent bank's function is limited to ministerial duties expressly set forth in the agreement, the agent may stand in a fiduciary relationship to the syndicate members. This relationship may, for instance, obligate the agent bank to disclose to the syndicate members inside information relating to the borrower and possibly even to keep itself informed about the borrower. An agent bank might find itself confronted with conflicting interests and duties due to other contractual and trust relationships with the borrower and its affiliates.

Frequently a syndicate is organized by a *manager* or a limited number of co-managers under the leadership of a *lead* manager (frequently the agent bank or one of its affiliates). Acting as manager involves responsibilities with the correspondent risk of liability. The lead manager has several roles that may conflict: The lead manager commits to the borrower to syndicate the credit; the borrower looks to the manager for informed advice; the syndicate participants rely on the manager to negotiate and structure the terms of the loan to their advantage; and in addition, in most cases the manager commits a substantial portion of the loan.

One of the most important provisions in a syndicated-loan agreement is the sharing-of-payments provision: To what extent must a bank that sets off a deposit maintained by the borrower with it against its portion of the loan share with the other banks? Sometimes a syndicated-loan agreement provides for a sharing among the banks of amounts set off and of other payments received with respect to the borrower's obligation to pay principal and interest. Such a provision prevents the borrower from favoring one bank in the syndicate when it is unable to satisfy all banks in full, and prevents any bank from receiving an advantage over the other banks because the borrower happens to maintain deposit accounts with that bank.

PARTICIPATIONS.   A bank (the lending or lead bank) may assign to another bank (the participant) not all of its rights under a promissory note or loan agreement, but only the right to receive part of the future payments of principal and interest (or both). In the latter case the lead bank retains the debtor-creditor relationship with the borrower. Such partial assignment is called a participation and it is generally permissible without the debtor's consent. The participant does not enter into any debtor-creditor relationship with the borrower and, therefore, may not exercise the common law right of setoff against the borrower [*In re Yale Express System, Inc.*, 245 F. Supp. 790 (S.D.N.Y. 1965)] and probably could not file a claim for its participation interest in the bankruptcy of the borrower. The loan agreement between the lead bank and the borrower may give the participant certain rights against the borrower, for instance, protection against withholding taxes, the benefits of indemnities, and possibly the right of setoff. However, in many cases the loan agreement makes no reference to the creation of participations in the loan.

The rights of the participant against the lead bank depend on the way their participation is characterized. The relationship between the lead bank and the participant is governed by a participation agreement or a participation certificate or both. Most participation agreements provide that the participant "purchases" from the lead bank and the lead bank "sells" to the participant an undivided partial or fractional interest in the lead bank's loan to the borrower (i.e., the lead bank's existing right to receive payment in respect of the debt owed by the borrower) upon payment to the lead bank of a commensurate percentage of the principal amount of the participated loan. [See *FDIC v. Mademoiselle of California,* 379 F.2d 660 (9th Cir. 1967)]. The participant owns an asset consisting of the right to receive the participated portion of future payments when, as and if made by the borrower. The participant's right to repayment arises only upon the receipt by the lead bank of payment from the borrower, and in case of a default by the borrower the participant shares in the loss pro rata with the lead bank. Thus, recourse against the lead bank is limited. Of course, the participation agreement may provide for a different relationship between the lead bank and the participant. For example, the participation agreement may provide that the participant will have full recourse against the lead bank irrespective of a default by the borrower.

A lead bank may wish to sell participations in a loan when the loan exceeds its lending limit or self-imposed country limit, when it desires to reduce its risk or to increase its liquidity or to raise the funds for the loan, or in order to promote its correspondent bank relationships. Selling participations may produce profits if there is a spread between the rate paid by the borrower to the lead bank and the rate participated by the lead bank to the participant; and by permitting the lead bank to take the participated portions of the underlying loan off its balance sheet as an asset increases the lead bank's return on assets.

The relation between the lead bank and the participant is governed by a participation agreement or a participation certificate or both.

LIABILITY OF MANAGER AND LEAD BANK. It is an open and much-debated question whether (1) a loan participation agreement or a participation certificate and (2) a note issued by a borrower to the bank, or even a noteless loan agreement, constitute *securities* in the meaning of the U.S. securities laws. [Compare *Union Planters National Bank v. Commercial Credit Business Loans, Inc.,* 651 F.2d 1174 (6th Cir.), *cert. denied,* 454 U.S. 1124 (1981) (loan participation is not a security) with *Commercial Discount Corporation v. Lincoln First Commercial Corporation,* 445 F. Supp. 1263 (S.D.N.Y. 1978) (loan participation is a security). See *Chemical Bank v. Arthur Andersen & Co.,* 726 F.2d 930 (2d Cir. 1984) (notes evidencing loans made by commercial banks to finance current operations of borrower are not "securities" within the meaning of the antifraud provisions of the securities laws).]

If a syndication of a loan involves a security, the manager may be liable to the syndicate members under the disclosure requirements of the antifraud provisions of the U.S. securities laws (especially Section 10(b) of the Securities Exchange Act of 1934). The manager would be liable if his written or oral communications to the prospective syndicate members (especially an information memorandum delivered by the manager) included any untrue statement of a material fact or omitted to state a material fact necessary in order to make the statements not misleading, and if the manager knew, or in the exercise of due diligence could have known, of such misstatements or omissions. The manager would be under an affirmative duty to disclose material "inside information" (information in the possession of the manager and known not to be available to the prospective syndicate members). It is still unsettled, however, whether or to what extent a manager would have to satisfy the requirement for a due diligence investigation of the borrower and other aspects of the syndicated credit. A manager's duty of due diligence could reasonably vary from one transaction to another in proportion to its role in the syndication. It is doubtful whether and to what extent a manager can avoid liability by disclaiming responsibility for, and by each syndicate member confirming that it has not relied on the manager for, the accuracy of statements made in connection with the loan agreement or the creditworthiness of the borrower.

If a participation involves a security, the same considerations would apply to the liability of the lead bank to the participant.

ACCOMMODATING ASSET SALES.   In recent years some money center banks have begun to sell to other banks advances made to borrowers under existing loan agreements for the duration of separate interest periods. One of the aims of the selling bank is to decrease the assets shown on its balance sheet during the interest period by the amount of the advance sold. Since under U.S. accounting rules an advance must be sold to maturity to achieve such off-balance sheet treatment, the loan agreement must provide that each advance will mature at the end of each interest period. The loan agreement must provide that on the last day of each interest period the borrower is required to repay the advance and then, subject to certain conditions of lending, can reborrow the funds. Thus, each advance has only one interest period and matures at the end of that period; each interest period is treated as a new and separate borrowing. Since each advance is required to be repaid at the end of each interest period, the loan agreement must reflect the bank's ongoing commitment to the borrower to lend, and that the borrowing and reborrowing continues to the final maturity of all advances at the expiration of the commitment. The borrower must reaffirm representations and warranties and the absence of defaults at each rollover date, not only at the occasion of each disbursement of new money.

GOVERNING LAW

NEED FOR GOVERNING-LAW CLAUSES.   Nearly every international loan agreement contains a *governing-law* or *choice-of-law* clause that sets forth the law that the parties intend to govern the agreement. It is important that the parties stipulate the applicable law because otherwise, under the principles set forth in the well-known case *Auten v. Auten* [308 N.Y. 155, 124 N.E. 2d 99 (1954)], the courts in the United States apply the law of the jurisdiction "which has the most significant contacts with the matter in dispute." Under the similar *governmental interest* approach, the courts apply the law of the jurisdiction having the most interest in the disputed issue. Under these approaches it is usually quite unpredictable which law the courts will apply to an agreement.

A bank usually insists on the law of the country or state in which it is located, because it prefers a familiar to an unfamiliar legal system, or on the law of a major commercial country or state, such as New York, on the theory that such jurisdiction has a well-developed commercial law that results in a relatively predictable interpretation and enforcement. In recent years, foreign borrowers, especially sovereign borrowers, have sometimes requested (or for internal or legal reasons insisted) that the law of their jurisdiction should govern the loan agreement. In the view of most banks this request is unjustified. After the bank has disbursed the loan, it is in a weak position, because it has performed its part of the bargain and has rights only under the agreement, primarily the right to receive payment of principal and interest. The borrower has only obligations, primary of which is the obligation of payment of the principal and interest. The bank alone bears a risk of loss. It would be unjustified to render the exercise of the bank's rights more difficult by asking it to enforce them under a law unknown to it. The borrower does not need the protection of a legal system familiar to it, because the obligation to pay principal and interest is very clear.

SCOPE OF GOVERNING-LAW CLAUSES.   In the United States, questions of validity and scope of a choice-of-law clause in a loan agreement are governed by state law. The court in which suit is brought to enforce a loan agreement analyzes under its own law (the law of the forum) the validity and scope of the governing-law clause, even if the clause stipulates the law of another jurisdiction as governing the agreement. If it finds the clause valid, it will apply the stipulated law. Therefore, it may be desirable for the bank to obtain legal opinions as to the validity of the governing-law clause from all jurisdictions in which it might seek to sue the borrower on the loan agreement.

If action to enforce a loan agreement is brought in the court of a country or state other than the country or state whose law is stipulated, the application of the validly stipulated law is limited in one respect: The stipulated law will not be applied by the court to the extent that a term of the loan agreement or a provision of the stipulated law applicable to the loan agreement violates a public policy or similar principle of the law of the forum or, according to some authorities, even to the extent that it violates a public policy of another jurisdiction that has a materially greater interest in the determination of the disputed issue than the country or state whose law was selected. New York limits the applications of the stipulated law only if a term of the loan agreement or a provision of the stipulated law applicable to the loan agreement violates an *important public policy* of New York.

As a general rule, a stipulation of the law of a country or state is a stipulation of the substantive rules of law of that country or state and not of the whole law, including the conflict-of-laws rules of that country or state. If the parties agree on New York law, they wish the substantive New York law to apply and not the law of that state that a New York court would apply under the New York conflict-of-laws rules absent a governing-law clause. However, even though a loan agreement stipulates the law of a particular jurisdiction as governing, questions relating to the "internal affairs" of the borrower, such as questions of the corporate power of the borrower to enter into the loan agreement, questions of authorization of the loan agreement by all appropriate corporate actions of the borrower, and questions of due execution and delivery of the loan agreement by appropriate officers of the borrower will be determined by a New York court under the law of the country or state of the borrower.

REASONABLE-RELATIONSHIP REQUIREMENT.   Most courts in the United States follow the rule that the parties to an agreement may choose any governing law so long as there is a reasonable relationship between the transaction and the country or state whose law was chosen. This concept is also expressed in Section 1–105(1) of the Uniform Commercial Code, which does not directly apply to loan agreements but, as one of the very few statutory expressions of a general principle of conflict of laws, carries great weight. This reasonable-relationship requirement should not create any problem if a loan agreement is governed by the law of the country or state where the bank's lending office or the head office of the borrower is located. New York used to follow the reasonable relationship rule, but in 1984 New York amended its law to facilitate the stipulation of New York law to govern large commercial transactions, including loan transactions. Section 5-1401 of the New York General Obligations Law now provides that the parties to any contract "in consideration of, or relating to any obligation arising out of a transaction covering in the aggregate" not less than $250,000 may agree that New York law shall govern their rights and duties in whole or in part, irrespective of whether such contract bears a reasonable relation to New York.

If the bank and the borrower wish to agree on the law of a country or state other than New York, the reasonable-relationship test remains important. A reasonable relationship between a transaction and a country or state is probably given, for instance, if the agreement is made or will be performed in that jurisdiction. It is helpful if substantial negotiation of the transaction took place in that jurisdiction. A U.S. dollar or Eurodollar loan agreement will probably be performed in the location in the United States where the loan must be repaid.

FOREIGN ACTS OF STATE.   Under certain circumstances the law of a foreign country (an "act of state") might affect a loan agreement even though the agreement is governed by a law other than the law of the foreign country. Courts have recently held that foreign exchange control regulations of a foreign country would be given effect in a suit by a U.S. lender or depositor against the foreign debtor if the debt is "located" ("has its situs") in that foreign country. Courts find the location of the debt in the country which has the most significant contacts with the loan transaction. [*Allied Bank International v Banco Credito Agricola de Cartago,* 757 F.2d 516 (2d Cir.), cert. dismissed, 106 S. Ct. 30 (1985) (debt located in New York, not Costa Rica); *Braka v. Bancomer, S.N.C.,* 762 F.2d 222 (2d Cir. 1985) (deposit obligation located in Mexico); *Callejo v. Bancomer, S.A.,* 764 F.2d 1101 (5th Cir. 1985) (deposit obligation located in Mexico).] It must be noted that none of the agreements involved in these cases contained an express governing law clause stipulating the law of a U.S. state. It is possible to argue that a foreign act of state does not overcome an express stipulation of New York law unless the foreign act of state represents an important public policy of the foreign state which the U.S. court gives effect in accordance with Sec. 187(2) Restatement (Second) of Conflict of Laws (1971).

STIPULATION OF JURISDICTION

SUBMISSION TO PERSONAL JURISDICTION.   Most international loan agreements contain a provision in which the borrower agrees to submit to the jurisdiction of the courts of one or more states or countries, frequently specifying the city in which suit may be brought. This facilitates enforcement by the bank of its rights under the loan agreement in case of a default by the borrower. Although there is no conceptual connection between this clause and the governing-law clause, it is usually preferable to litigate a dispute in the courts of the country or state the law of which governs the agreement, because proof of that law in the courts of another country or state can be difficult. At any rate, the selected forum should have a judiciary that has integrity and is experienced in commercial litigation. Another important consideration is whether a judgment by the selected courts would be enforced by the country in which the borrower has assets, that is, frequently the home country of the borrower.

Submission to the jurisdiction of a particular court by the borrower gives that court personal jurisdiction over the borrower (power of the court to render judgment binding on the defendant personally).

The parties to a loan agreement may stipulate that the agreed-upon forum be the exclusive forum for all litigation arising under their agreement. Thus, the borrower submits to the jurisdiction of the contractual forum, and the lender agrees not to bring an action in any other forum. On the other hand, the parties may agree that the provision in their agreement conferring jurisdiction on one forum does not exclude jurisdiction elsewhere. The lender remains free to bring an action in any forum which has personal jurisdiction over the defendant, and subject matter jurisdiction over the claims in dispute; but if the lender wishes to commence the action in the contractual forum, he is assured, by virtue of the borrower's consent to jurisdiction, of in personam jurisdiction over the borrower. If one party to an agreement which contains a forum-selection clause, whether exclusive or non-exclusive, brings an action in the forum selected by the agreement (the contractual forum), the court will look at the forum-selection clause as a submission to its jurisdiction. Forum-selection clauses whereby a party submits to the non-exclusive jurisdiction of the contractual forum, and the portions of exclusive forum-selection clauses whereby a party submits to the exclusive jurisdiction of the contractual forum, are often called "submission-to-jurisdiction clauses." Both federal courts and the New York state courts accept consent jurisdiction in the form of a contractual submission to their jurisdiction. [*National Equipment Rental, Ltd. v. Szukhent,* 375 U.S. 311 (1964)]. If, however, an action involving an agreement which contains an exclusive forum-selection clause is brought in a forum (the excluded forum) other than the exclusive contractual forum, the excluded forum will consider the forum-selection clause as excluding or "ousting" its jurisdiction. The question is whether the excluded forum will give effect to the clause by refusing to entertain the suit brought in violation of the clause, even though it has personal jurisdiction over the defendant and subject matter jurisdiction over the claim in litigation. Exclusive forum-selection clauses have been recognized in the United States since 1972. [*The Bremen v. Zapata Off-Shore Co.,* 407 U.S. 1 (1972) (the clause in that case selected English courts and thereby excluded U.S. courts).] The enforceability of forum selection clauses will be denied if the resisting party can "clearly show that enforcement would be unreasonable and unjust, or that the clause was invalid for such reasons as fraud or overreaching." [*Bremen*]

Valid submission by the borrower to the jurisdiction of a court does not dispense with the requirement of proper service of process on the borrower in accordance with the law of the country or state of such court or in accordance with the terms of the loan agreement. In many loan agreements, the borrower expressly appoints an agent located in the jurisdiction of the selected court on whom process may be served. It may be sufficient under applicable law if the borrower agrees to another manner of service of process, for example, being served by being sent by registered mail a copy of the process. [See *Bankers Trust Co. v. Kline,* 52 A.D. 2d 775, 776; 382, N.Y.S.2d. 795, 796 (1976).] If an agent for service of process has been appointed by the borrower, it is advisable to obtain the agent's formal acceptance of the appointment and his agreement to transmit to the borrower all process served upon him.

In the absence of the borrower's express consent to personal jurisdiction, personal jurisdiction of the forum over the borrower would have to be obtained under the forum's "long-arm" statutes, which require some contact between the defendant and the forum.

SUBJECT-MATTER JURISDICTION. A court must have not only jurisdiction over the person of the defendant, which can be created by a submission to its jurisdiction, but in addition subject-matter jurisdiction (power of the court to take cases of the kind in question), which cannot be conferred upon the court by the parties.

U.S. *federal courts* have subject-matter jurisdiction in actions involving loan agreements usually only if there is "diversity of citizenship" between the plaintiff and defendant (28 U.S.C. § 1332). Diversity of citizenship requires that one party to the litigation is a citizen of a state of the United States whereas the other party is a citizen of another state or of a foreign country. Thus diversity jurisdiction is not available where both parties are citizens of foreign countries, for example, in a suit by a foreign bank against a foreign borrower. In that case submission to jurisdiction by the borrower does not give the bank access to the U.S. federal courts. However, the U.S. Supreme Court has held [*Verlinden B.V. v. Central Bank of Nigeria,* 461 U.S. 480 (1983)] that the Foreign Sovereign Immunities Act of 1976 grants federal courts subject matter jurisdiction over certain civil actions by foreign plaintiffs against foreign sovereigns and that this statutory grant of jurisdiction is covered by the U.S. Constitution.

State courts, which are not subject to the above requirements, may be subject to other limitations relating to subject-matter jurisdiction. For example, Section 1314(b) of the New York Business Corporation Law permits actions by one foreign (*i.e.,* non-New York) corporation against another foreign corporation before New York state courts only in certain enumerated cases, the most important being actions brought to recover damages for the breach of a contract "made or to be performed" in New York. The New York Banking Law contains the same provision for actions involving foreign banks. Thus a New York court has subject-matter jurisdiction over an action for damages for breach of a loan agreement between a foreign bank and a foreign borrower only if the agreement was executed and delivered in New York or if disbursement and repayment of the loan is made through a New York bank account of the lender. The requirements of Section 1314(b) apply also to a federal court in New York sitting in a diversity action.

Section 5-1402 of the New York General Obligations Law, adopted in 1984, remedies this situation: Any person may sue a foreign corporation, non-resident or foreign state in the New York courts where the action arises out of or relates to a contract "in consideration of, or relating to any obligation arising out of a transaction covering in the aggregate" at least $1,000,000, if the contract contains a governing law clause stipulating New York law and a submission to New York jurisdiction. Section 5-1402 overrides the statutes which restrict actions by a foreign corporation against another foreign corporation.

FORUM NON CONVENIENS.   Even if a federal or state court has the power to hear a case, it may in its discretion still decline to hear the case on the ground of the doctrine of *forum non conveniens.* See 28 U.S.C. section 1404, N.Y. Civil Practice Law and Rules 327. Under this doctrine a court may dismiss or transfer an action over which it has jurisdiction if it is a seriously inconvenient forum for the trial, provided that a more appropriate forum is available to the plaintiff. It is an open question to what extent valid submission-to-jurisdiction clause precludes the borrower from asserting inconvenience of the contractural forum. However, Rule 327(b) of the N.Y. CPLR, as amended in 1984, provides that a court may not dismiss or stay any action on the ground of inconvenient forum, if the action arises out of or relates to a contract involving a transaction of at least $1,000,000, containing New York choice of law clause and a submission to the New York jurisdiction.

OUSTER OF JURISDICTION.   If a loan agreement selects the court of one jurisdiction, for example, England, as the exclusive forum for the litigation of disputes arising under the agreement, and an action is brought in that jurisdiction, the court will look at the forum-selection clause as a submission to its jurisdiction. However, if an action is brought in another jurisdiction, for example, New York, the courts of that jurisdiction will look at the forum-selection clause as an ousting of its jurisdiction. An exclusive-forum selection clause is both a submission to jurisdiction of a particular court and an ouster of all other jurisdictions. The U.S. Supreme Court in *The Bremen v. Zapata Off-Shore Co.* [407 U.S. 1 (1972)] upheld a forum-selection clause (the clause in that case selected English courts and thereby excluded U.S. courts) if the choice of forum was made in an arm's-length negotiation by experienced and sophisticated businessmen.

ARBITRATION.   Most banks are skeptical of arbitration. Arbitrators are apt to render a compromise award, and banks feel that the repayment of a defaulted loan is not susceptible to compromise or equitable considerations. The award, once given, is not subject to judicial review except on grounds of fraud or other extreme conduct on the part of the arbitrators. Further, if arbitration fees are based on the amount in dispute, costs of arbitration could be substantially higher than costs of a court proceeding.

SOURCES AND SUGGESTED REFERENCES

Effros, R.C. "The Whys and Wherefores of Eurodollars," *The Business Lawyer,* Vol. XXIII (1968), pp. 629–44.

Gruson, M. "Governing Law Clauses in Commercial Agreements—New York's Approach," *Columbia Journal of Transnational Law,* Vol. XVIII (1979), pp. 323–379.

———. "Forum—Selection Clauses in International and Interstate Commercial Agreements" *University of Illinois Law Review,* Vol. 1982, pp. 133-205.

———. "Contractual Choice of Law and Choice of Forum: Unresolved Issues," in Sasoon & Bradlow, eds., *Judicial Enforcement of International Debt Obligations.* Washington, D.C., International Law Institute, 1987.

———. and M. Kutschera, "Opinion of Counsel on Agreements Governed by Foreign Law," *Vanderbilt Journal of Transnational Law,* Vol. 17 (1986), pp. 515–531.

——— and M. Kutschera, *Legal Opinions in International Transactions—Foreign Lawyers' Response to U.S. Opinion Requests* (Report of the Subcommittee on Legal Opinions of the Committee on Banking Law of the International Bar Association) London: Graham & Trotman, 1987.

———. and R. Reisner, eds. *Sovereign Landing: Managing Legal Risk.* London: Euromoney Publications, 1984.

Rendell, R.S., ed. *International Financial Law: Lending, Capital Transfers and Institutions,* 2d ed. London: Euromoney Publications, 1983 (herein cited as "Rendell, *International Financial Law*).

Ryan, R.H. "Participations in Loans under New York Law," *International Financial Law Review,* Oct. 1984, pp. 40–47.

INTERNATIONAL FINANCIAL MANAGEMENT

CONTENTS

INTERNATIONAL FINANCIAL MANAGEMENT

James L. Burtle

Many of the requirements for operating a business overseas are not essentially different from the requirements for operating at home. Both foreign and domestic businesses are unlikely to succeed without strong overall management, an effective marketing strategy, and adequate cost controls. There are, however, special problems in an international business that are not usually found in a domestic business. The most important of these are (1) the risk of losses from exchange-rate changes, (2) the risk of losses as a result of tax management policies in either the home country or in the country of foreign investment, and (3) political risks including confiscation, wars, civil disturbances, restrictions on convertibility, debt repudiation, and types of discriminatory action in which a foreign business is treated less advantageously than a domestic business.

To put it another way, financial officers of international businesses, in addition to having the financial worries of any business, are typically concerned about the company's losing from exchange-rate changes, from paying taxes unnecessarily, and because of political actions of foreign governments. Each of these risks will be considered separately, and against this background, capital budgeting and the choice of investments abroad will be discussed for a multinational company.

THE EXPOSURE PROBLEM

With the advent of widespread floating of exchange rates in early 1973, a new and often formidable dimension was added to international business planning. Most companies became aware that success in production and marketing abroad does not necessarily guarantee profits for the parent company if earnings abroad are eroded because of exchange-rate changes. But although there is agreement that currency fluctuations have created a "problem," there have been wide variations in the policies that companies have followed to protect themselves. Company strategies differ with respect to (1) what is considered at risk under conditions of fluctuating exchange rates, (2) the extent that risks should be hedged, and (3) the appropriate hedging strategy.

The problem of what is at risk under conditions of variable exchange rates is known as the exposure problem. A great many definitions of exposure have been proposed.

From an analytical point of view, exposure can be broken down into three categories: transaction, translation, and operational exposure. *Transaction exposure* arises when one currency will be converted into another currency at a specific date in the future. For example, a U.S. importer may have ordered a shipment of glassware from Italy and agrees to pay in *lire* when the goods arrive. He thus runs a risk that the *lira* might rise in value in relation to the dollar. On the other hand, a U.S. exporter runs the risk that a foreign currency will depreciate before payment is received. In these and other cases of transaction exposure, there is an actual conversion of one currency into another.

In *translation exposure,* there is no currency conversion. Instead, assets and liabilities held abroad are adjusted in value for the changed exchange rate. In a simple case, a bank account in British pounds is worth less in dollars if the pound is depreciated. Thus the holder of the bank account suffers a translation loss. On the other hand, if the U.S. citizen owes British pounds, his debt is reduced by depreciation of sterling, and he shows a translation gain. In practice, the calculation of translation exposure is more complicated than indicated in the above examples because in the balance sheet of a company operating abroad, there is a wide range of different assets and liabilities, and accounting practices differ as to which of these items should be considered exposed, that is, adjusted for exchange-rate changes. In their financial statements, American companies are currently required to follow Financial Accounting Standards Board Bulletin 52 (F.A.S. 52), which specifies that all assets and liabilities are exposed. If companies overseas have greater assets than liabilities, exposure actually depends on the company's net worth, i.e., the difference between assets and liabilities abroad. Thus, a ten percent devaluation of the foreign currency reduces the company's net worth position abroad by ten percent. There is an exception, however, for companies that carry on operations in a foreign country but make almost all of their payments and receive almost all of their revenue in dollars. In these cases, the dollar may be declared the "functional currency" of the operation and there will be no foreign exchange exposure even though there is a foreign currency in the country of the operation. There are also special provisions in F.A.S. 52 for writing up the value of assets in countries with serious inflation and consequent currency depreciation. Otherwise, if assets were written down for currency depreciation and not written up for inflation, their values would be grossly understated. Rules governing translation exposure are subject, however, to widespread controversy. In actual management policies, many companies follow a variety of translation rules, although reported results are required to conform to F.A.S.B. 8. More recently, the FASB has asked for comments on a proposed new set of accounting rules that would consider all assets and liabilities exposed.

Operational exposure arises from the risk to company profits from the indirect effects of exchange-rate changes. For example, if a subsidiary of a U.S. company is exporting from England, there is an operational risk that a rise in the exchange rate of the pound will discourage export volume and thus lower profits. Likewise a company importing into the United Kingdom may be adversely affected if sterling depreciates and the price of imports rises.

Overall exposure encompassing transaction, translation, and operational exposure is known as *economic exposure.* In principle, economic exposure is defined as the difference between discounted cash flows of future earnings of a company with and without exchange-rate changes. In actual practice, however, most companies do not have the resources to calculate their overall economic exposure. Instead, there is a monitoring of the elements of translation, transaction, and operational exposure that appear to be of greatest significance to profits of the particular company. A firm engaged mainly in exporting and importing might emphasize transaction exposure. A company with an affiliate operating abroad might be concerned mainly with translation exposure. Operational and economic exposures are likely to be of special interest to a company that can afford a long-term planning apparatus.

HOW MUCH HEDGING?

Some companies, having defined exposure, attempt to avoid it entirely. In other words, they attempt to equalize exposed assets (sometimes known as long positions) and exposed liabilities (sometimes known as short positions) so that their P/L statement is unaffected by changes in exchange rates. Other companies are willing to leave exposed positions open if it is believed that the exchange rate is unlikely to move in an unfavorable direction or that the cost of protection (often known as *cover*) from foreign-exchange losses is excessive. Some observers would regard the latter viewpoint as speculative; a contrary view is that a company is speculating only when it takes foreign-exchange positions not related to the ordinary business of the company. Under this definition it would not be speculation if a company did not cover a Japanese *yen* exposure, but it would be speculation if a company took a position in *yen* even though it had no business connection with Japan. One simple rule, sometimes applied by companies that are willing to permit open positions, is that a company should not cover exposed positions unless the expected loss from an uncovered position is greater than the cost of cover.

HEDGING STRATEGIES

Companies that adopt a policy of not covering all exposed positions should organize a group that will monitor (1) changes in exchange rates, (2) changes in the costs of covering exposed positions, and (3) changes in the exposed position of the company. In an effective foreign-exchange management group, each of these three elements is forecast, and on the basis of the forecasts, it is decided whether or not to hedge an exposed position. A decision on whether or not to hedge the exposed position may depend on the cost of the hedge compared with the expected loss from not hedging.

If a company decides that it should cover an exposed position, a number of alternative hedging strategies are often available. The most frequently used strategies are (1) the forward market, (2) the money market, and (3) restructuring the company balance sheet. In the forward market, foreign-exchange contracts are traded with the requirement that foreign exchange be bought or sold at a specific time in the future. For example, if a foreign currency is sold forward, there is an agreement with someone to buy it at a specific rate at some period ahead. Usually foreign-exchange contracts are available for 1, 2, 3, 6, 9, and 12 months ahead. A currency may be at either a discount or a premium. At a discount, a currency sells forward for less than the spot rate. At a premium, the currency sells forward for more than the spot rate.

If a currency is expected to depreciate, a company in a long position can protect itself from losses from depreciation by selling the currency forward. However, this protection against foreign-exchange loss from depreciation will usually involve the cost of paying the discount on the forward contract. Likewise, a company in a net liability position in a particular currency can protect itself from exchange losses from appreciation by buying that currency forward, though again such protective action will usually involve paying the cost of a premium on the forward contract. A very large volume of foreign exchange contracts is traded between international banks in the *interbank market* which operates through telephone, telex and video screen contacts between bank traders. More recently, foreign exchange futures and options have also become an important part of the international money market. *Foreign exchange futures* are similar to futures on commodity markets. Under a futures agreement, a trader promises to either buy or make available a specific amount of a foreign currency on a given day (unlike interbank contracts which are always for a certain number of days ahead). Futures are often used by smaller businesses that want to cover amounts not large enough to be accepted by the interbank market. *Foreign exchange options* are widely traded on the Chicago Board of Trade (CBOE), the European Options Exchange in Amsterdam (EOE), the London exchange and the Philadelphia exchange. Options differ from interbank contracts and from futures since there is no obligation for an option holder to buy or sell the currency. The holder of an option has the right to buy or sell at a specified price but he or she is not required to do so. Thus many options are not activated. But, if there is a substantial change in an exchange rate, holders of options may be able to protect themselves from losses by buying (or selling) the currency at the exchange rate stated in the option. Before entering into contracts, futures or options, however, many companies will consider the possibility of losses on exposed positions against the costs of these arrangements. In some cases it may turn out that likely losses are significantly smaller than costs of covering so it may be preferable to leave exposes positions uncovered.

An alternative hedging strategy for protection against foreign-exchange losses is to use the money market. Money-market strategies involve borrowing a currency that is expected to depreciate or placing a currency that is expected to appreciate. If a currency has been borrowed and converted into dollars and there is a depreciation of the currency, repaying the loan in depreciated currency will offset most of the foreign-exchange loss on a net asset position. On the other hand, if funds are placed in a potentially appreciating currency—in the form of bank deposits or short-term government securities—a foreign-exchange loss on a net liability position can be offset by the gain from appreciation of the funds placed in the appreciating currency. As in the case of the foreign-exchange market, however, there is usually a cost connected with using the money market as protection against foreign-exchange losses. When a currency is expected to depreciate, interest rates are usually higher in the potentially devaluing currency compared with the home currency. Thus cover by borrowing means paying higher interest rates. On the other hand, for a currency likely to appreciate, interest rates are usually lower than in the home currency. Thus cover by placing money means earning less interest income. There is a tendency known as *interest arbitrage* for the costs of using the money market as a hedge against currency changes to be approximately the same as the costs of foreign-exchange contracts. Because of market imperfections, however, interest arbitrage does not always work out exactly, and it is worthwhile for the foreign-exchange manager to investigate carefully which method of coverage of exchange risks is likely to involve maximum protection at the least expense.

In many cases a company can avoid either a forward contract or a money-market hedge by eliminating the exposed position on the company balance sheet. A net asset may be reduced by remitting dividends, or by collecting receivables and placing the collected funds in nonexposed assets, or by allowing payables to rise. If inventories are not considered exposed, financial assets may be shifted into inventories. However, there may be costs connected with restructuring balance sheets. Profit remittances may be subject to withholding taxes. A company may lose customers if it sharply reduces accounts receivable. Lines of credit may be lost if accounts payable are allowed to become excessive.

TAXATION

It is convenient to begin the taxation section of this section with an oversimplified example of the calculation of foreign and U.S. taxes for both the foreign affiliate of a U.S. company and for the parent company. (U.S. firms operating in less developed countries calculate the tax somewhat differently, but the general methods are similar.)

Suppose that a subsidiary of a hypothetical U.S. company is operating abroad with pretax earnings of $1 million. These earnings are assumed to be subject to a foreign income tax of 25 percent and a foreign withholding tax on dividend remittances of 10 percent. The U.S. corporate income tax is taken at 48 percent (since reduced in the 1986 tax law). It is assumed that 50 percent of earnings abroad are remitted as dividends to the U.S. parent. Calculations of the foreign and U.S. taxes are shown in Exhibit 1.

From this exhibit it should be understood that a withholding tax is a misnomer; it is simply a tax paid on dividends that is not returned.

One principle of U.S. taxation is that double taxation should be avoided, that is, if a U.S. company has already paid taxes abroad, it should pay only enough taxes in the United States to bring the overall rate up to the U.S. rate. Thus foreign taxes

**EXHIBIT 1   CALCULATION OF FOREIGN AND U.S. TAXES ON
A U.S. SUBSIDIARY ABROAD ($ THOUSANDS)**

(1)	Pretax foreign earnings	1,000
(2)	Foreign income tax @ 25 %	250
(3)	Foreign aftertax earnings	750
(4)	Earnings remitted as dividends @ 50%	375
(5)	Withholding tax @ 10%	38
(6)	Net dividend received	337
	Foreign-Tax Credit	
(7)	Withholding tax	38
(8)	Deemed tax @ ½ × 250	125
(9)	Total tax credits	163
	U.S. Taxable Income	
(10)	Gross dividend (line 4)	375
(11)	Deemed tax (line 8)	125
(12)	Total	500
(13)	U.S. Tax @ 48%	240
(14)	Tax credit (line 9)	163
(15)	Net U.S. tax	77

already paid are subtracted from the U.S. tax as indicated in lines 7, 8, 9, and 14. However, the tax credit does not include all taxes paid abroad. It includes all of the withholding taxes but only a fraction of the total income tax abroad. The latter is known as the *deemed tax* and is calculated by multiplying the tax paid abroad by the proportion of aftertax income that is remitted as dividends. In the above example, the income tax abroad was $250,000, but since only half of the aftertax earnings were remitted as dividends, the deemed tax was $1/2 \times \$250,000 = \$125,000$. If a third of the aftertax earnings were remitted as dividends, the deemed tax would be equal to $1/3 \times \$250,000 = \$83,333$. (There is no tax credit for property taxes, excise taxes, value added taxes, and other nonincome taxes paid abroad.)

In a process known as the *gross-up* [the deemed tax (line 11)] is added to the gross dividend (line 10) to obtain the U.S. taxable income (line 12). The U.S. tax rate is applied to this sum (line 13), and tax credits for the deemed tax and the withholding tax are subtracted (line 14) to obtain the net U.S. tax (line 15). Note that in addition to the principle of *no double taxation,* the above calculation also involves the principle of *deferral of taxation* on earnings of foreign affiliates: no tax is levied on the parent company until dividends are actually remitted. The rule is different, however, if the foreign operation of a U.S. company is a *branch* of the parent company rather than a separate foreign *affiliate.* Then the earnings of the branch are consolidated with the earnings of the parent company and taxed on an annual basis.

When foreign affiliates' income taxes are lower than those in the parent country, there is a strong incentive for the parent company to attempt to shift profits to areas of lower taxes. This can be done in a number of ways including (1) charging overhead costs to the parent corporation, (2) selling to the affiliate below cost—sometimes called transfer pricing—and (3) setting up a separate company in areas of no income taxes and funneling profits to the so-called tax haven. To prevent each of these practices, special I.R.S. rules and statutes have been adopted as follows:

1. Section 1.861-8 of the *U.S. Treasury Regulations* requires an allocation of overhead costs of the parent to the affiliate. This has the effect of reducing the company's earnings abroad on which the tax credit is calculated.

2. Section 482 of the *U.S. Internal Revenue Code* requires that prices on transactions between the parent and an affiliate should be at the same price that would be charged a third party. Thus transfer pricing is, in effect, prohibited.

3. Subpart F of the tax code provides that when a foreign affiliate is set up in a tax-haven country as a "sham" to siphon income from a higher-tax area, that income in the tax-haven country should be considered "tainted" income. Tainted income may be treated as *deemed dividend* and is subject to U.S. taxes whether or not it is remitted to the United States. The proceeds from liquidating a tax-haven company may also be subject to deemed-dividend treatment and therefore subject to tax. This is sometimes called the "doomsday tax" (*Internal Revenue Code* 1248).

In earlier periods a company could reduce its taxes by switching from branch to affiliate status. Before the relevant legislation was adopted, a company might at a time of heavy start-up costs operate as a branch. Since branch losses are consolidated with the parent company earnings, the effect was to reduce overall taxes. When start-up costs were completed, however, and the foreign operation was earning profits, it would change to affiliate status. This practice is now limited because of a *recapture provision* in the Tax Reform Act of 1976 that provides that such tax savings may be claimed by the I.R.S.

U.S. tax law provides tax incentives for exporters under the 1984 tax reform act. To obtain these benefits, exporters must set up overseas a Foreign Sales Corporation (FSC). Some types of earnings of the exporter are permitted to be credited to the FSC and these earnings are subject to a lower income tax rate if the FSC meets rather stringent requirements. There may also be tax benefits from operating in Puerto Rico as a U.S. Possessions Corporation. To qualify in this category, 80% of the income of the corporation must be earned in the possession. However, U.S. Possession Corporations are exempt from U.S. taxes on income from overseas.

Although this section has attempted to give a bird's eye view of taxation of earnings abroad, the treatment is highly oversimplified. Solutions of actual tax problems should not be attempted without consultation with international tax attorneys. Also note that the above discussion concerns only U.S. taxation of foreign earnings. Problems of taxation by the government of the host country may be even more difficult, requiring assistance from tax experts within the country. It should be emphasized, however, that in some countries the levying of taxes may be less formal than in the U.S. Tax collectors will be expected to get a tax payment from a foreign company even though it may be making losses. Settlements are often reached through negotiations rather than through strict use of a tax code.

COUNTRY RISK

Country risk (see Section 7) covers a very broad area including political as well as economic risks. The essential element in country risk is, however, some form of government action preventing the fulfillment of an implicit or explicit contract or agreement. It would not be a country-risk problem if because of poor management, a foreign business failed and it could not pay for imports. It would be a case of country risk, however, if the company was prohibited from paying its bills by government exchange controls. The most frequently cited examples of country risk are expropriation, debt repudiation, and delays in payments for imports. However, there are many less-evident variants of these practices. Companies may not be confiscated but can be reduced to impotence by punitive taxation, lack of police protection, discriminatory labor regulations, and restrictions on remitting earnings. Debts that are not repudiated may be restructured with heavy losses to the lenders. Imports may be "paid for," but only after long delays and in depreciating local currencies.

Thus there is serious ambiguity in the definition of an unfavorable outcome of a country-risk gamble. Not only is there extreme difficulty in assessing and forecasting country risk; there is also difficulty in identifying when it turns unfavorable. Thus the country-risk problem can be compared to the uncertainties of rolling loaded dice in darkness. Nevertheless, the great importance of the subject led to a maximum effort, especially by banks, to analyze the problem in an effort to reduce potential losses to the greatest extent possible.

Earlier efforts at country-risk analysis were somewhat simplistic. Company officials would visit the country in question, or experts in the country would give subjective opinions. Sometimes these opinions were tested for internal consistency by probability-tree methods: The expert would be required to place probabilities on each step in a sequence of events leading to a favorable or unfavorable outcome. For example a joint probability might be formulated for the conditions of (1) a radical change in government, (2) confiscation, and (3) no compensation (see Stobaugh, 1969).

In a more advanced approach to country risk proposed by Haendel, West, and Meadow (1975), specific variables affecting country risk are identified and favorable or unfavorable points are assigned to each variable. Points for different variables are added. Typically a greater number of points means less country risk. Rated variables include GNP per capita, number of riots and demonstrations, number of government crises, size of internal security forces, and legislative effectiveness. There are, however, two basic difficulties with this method. First, because the models affecting country risk are complex, many of the variables may be Janus-faced, sometimes raising country risk and sometimes lowering it. As Knudsen (1974) has pointed out, rising GNP may lower country risk if it creates a level of welfare greater than the aspirations of the population. On the other hand, rising GNP may create an even greater rise in aspirations. Thus by widening the gap between aspirations and achievements, GNP may become negative for country risk. The second difficulty with a point-scoring method is that no system has been developed for testing whether or not a particular point system actually measures country risk. This is at a much lower stage of development than other forecasting models used in international finance. For example, no one would propose a model for forecasting exchange rates without first testing it out against past experience. In country-risk analysis, however, even past experience is foggy with respect to what events could be clearly identified as "succeeding" or "failing" as indicators of country risk. More recently, however, variables relating to country risk have begun to be tested. In these tests of the significance of variables affecting country risk, three definitions of success or failure have been developed.

1.   Success is identified with repayment of loans on schedule, whereas failure is identified with restructuring loans.
2.   Success is identified with a rise in U.S. direct investment in a country, whereas failure is identified with a decline.
3.   Success is identified with the payment of lower interest rates (usually in margins over the London Interbank Offered Rate), whereas failure is identified with higher interest rates.

The search for indicators that can give early warnings of debt rescheduling has usually applied variants of a statistical method known as discriminant analysis. This technique classifies the dependent variable categorically with respect to independent variables. Thus in a useful model, the independent variables will indicate whether the debt will be rescheduled or not rescheduled. In a successful test, "predicted" reschedulings will match actual reschedulings. On the other hand, there will be Type 1 error if reschedulings occur but are not predicted. Moreover, there will be Type 2 error if reschedulings are predicted but do not occur. Empirical attempts to "explain" debt rescheduling and other international debt problems are discussed by Walter (1980).

Another approach to testing for the impact of country risk involves direct investment as a dependent variable. To a considerable extent, U.S. foreign direct investment has been explained by regression analysis. One "simple" explanation relates foreign direct investment to a lagged value of investment itself and to changes in real GNP (see State Department, 1974). In another study, by Kobrin (1978), foreign direct investment was related to size of markets, market growth, previous export involvement, tariffs, and dummy variables for areas. Residuals from the regression may give indications of country risk, that is, indications of when investors, because of their risk outlook, put more or less into particular countries. Kobrin divided these residuals into low and high categories and, using a variant of the chi-square test, related the classified residuals to high and low cases of political variables that he calls turmoil, internal war, and conspiracy. No significant relationship was found between turmoil or internal war and the direct-investment residual. But a significant relationship was found between the residual and conspiracy, especially in cases of higher levels of economic development and governmental efficiency. The Kobrin analysis is important in its rejection of some political variables that on a common-sense basis might appear to affect perceived political risk.

A third attempt to quantify country risk relates country-risk indicators to interest rates on international loans. The hypothesis is that when a country pays a higher interest rate, it is being charged a risk premium. Walter (1980) found that there is a 0.81 Spearman rank correlation between interest-rate differentials and the risk rating of 93 countries provided in an *Institutional Investor* survey. Similar results appeared in a regression analysis by Angeloni and Short (1980).

One difficulty with relating residuals from explained investment and interest-rate differentials to risk variables is that the independent variables explain not actual risk but risk as perceived or believed by investors and bankers. But these perceptions may turn out to be wrong, as seems evident from investment in Iran and interest differentials on loans to Iran. Looking further back, the radicalization of Cuba was by no means widely expected. There is, however, the basic difficulty that the "sample" of truly revolutionary developments has been too small to be explained by any quantitatively rigorous methods. Thus situations, that were setbacks rather than disasters are used as dependent variables. This method is on methodologically stronger ground than purely subjective evaluations, but it may ignore the really key questions. More recently, the failure of much country risk analysis is evident from the appraisals of international debts by major banks, many using country risk evaluation methods. Clearly, these methods did not work for forecasting the serious debt crises of less developed countries. One of many problems in this analysis was that a financial crisis in one LDC may ignite a financial crisis in another LDC. For example, the crisis in Mexico, due in part to declining oil revenues, led to capital flight from Brazil that could not have been foreseen from simply looking at data on the Brazilian economy.

The Overseas Private Investment Corporation (OPIC), a government corporation in Washington, offers political risk insurance for U.S. companies making investment in an approved list of countries. Risks include expropriation, inconvertibility, war and losses from civil disturbances. Country risk insurance is also available from private companies. Again, the costs of insurance should be weighed against the actual political risk. One disadvantage of risk insurance—especially for losses from civil disturbances—is that it may cover what in any case might have been gained in compensation from the host government.

Sometimes restrictions on profit remittances may not be as onerous as might be supposed. Typically, in countries with balance of payments problems, interest rates tend to rise dramatically, thus offsetting in part the adverse effects of depreciation of the blocked funds. Also it may be possible to put blocked funds into assets, the appreciation of which may offset currency depreciation.

INTERNATIONAL CAPITAL BUDGETING

Against the background of unsteady exchange rates, internationally differing tax systems, and political risks, capital budgeting for an international firm becomes a complex process, though the basic procedures are not different in principle from capital budgeting for a purely domestic business.

Usually an international capital budget begins with a determination of the internal rate of return on the investment abroad, all in the local currency of the host country. The second step is to calculate the internal rate of return on the investment in the currency of the parent company, assuming that funds from the subsidiary are remitted to the parent. As discussed by Eiteman and Stonehill (1979), this involves considerations of exchange rates, taxes, exchange controls, and possible impacts of the foreign operation on the domestic business, as, for example, the impact of exports to the subsidiary from the parent company.

In calculating the internal rate of return on an investment abroad, there are two approaches for dealing with country risk. In the first approach, the cash flow is adjusted downward to reflect risk. In the second approach, the cost of capital, that is, the required rate of return on the project, is raised to account for country risk. The first approach has the advantage of greater flexibility, because projected cash flow can be allowed to vary over the life of the project if it is expected that risk will be concentrated in particular periods. The second approach is probably easier to manage if it is desired to take into account differences in risk between areas. Then it is easier to compare risk premiums rather than cash-flow streams.

One advantage of a capital budget in local currency for an investment abroad is that it gives an indication whether or not a direct investment in a country is reasonable. If the rate of return on an investment abroad is less than the return on government securities of the country, then the extra management effort of the project would be wasted. It would be simpler for the parent company to buy the government bonds of the host country. Likewise if the planned direct investment earns no more than publicly traded stocks, then it would be simpler to buy a security portfolio in the host country rather than to go ahead with the direct investment.

If funds can be transferred to the United States, a rate of return on the project can be calculated from the point of view of the parent company. This calculation becomes complicated when funds to be transferred are partially or fully blocked. Blocked funds are assumed to be reinvested in the host country. Thus losses from exchange-rate depreciation and inflation may be minimized. This procedure may, however, tend to understate the loss to the parent company, since there may be unfavorable psychological effects on financial markets from "bad news" abroad. The company in the United States may suffer from an overall higher cost of borrowed funds and a low price/earnings ratio for its securities as a result of perhaps distorted information relating to adversity in its foreign operations.

THE DECISION TO INVEST OVERSEAS

The previous section sketched out a very much oversimplified picture of international capital budgeting. Once there is agreement on capital budgeting methods, the decision to invest abroad may appear simple: Choose the area (including investment possibilities in the country of the parent company) where the internal rate of return is highest. One problem in applying such a rule—and this problem also arises in choosing investments on the domestic scene—is that opportunities do not all appear at the same time. If the firm expands by acquisition, a particular acquisition offer may expire in a few days and may have no realistic alternatives readily available. Thus it must be compared with projects that may turn up. But many executives with large cash positions or borrowing capabilities find this waiting process painful. Money is truly likely to burn holes in their pockets.

Aside from the problem that alternatives for investment may not be presented simultaneously, there are a number of special considerations that may lead a company to invest overseas even though the internal rate of return may be no higher abroad than in the home country. As has been fully developed in the so-called product-cycle literature (Vernon, 1976), an exporting company may face tariffs on its products. The only way to avoid serious losses may be to jump the tariff wall and manufacture abroad. (Analytically this may be forced into a capital budgeting mold with the choice between losing on an export business and holding the line, with an investment abroad.)

In other cases a company operating abroad may want to spread out its investments among several countries in order to spread country risk instead of facing the possibility of losing everything if all investments are in one country. (Again this choice might be manageable with capital-budgeting methods by raising the adjustment for risk—either in the projected cash flow or the discount rate, as discussed— in countries with a heavy concentration of the company's investment.)

Another special reason for overseas investment is the possibility of achieving economies of scale. In some cases, where it is important to spread fixed costs, an optimal scale in the country of the parent company may be impossible because of the small size of the country or, especially in the United States, because antitrust laws may limit the growth of the parent company.

As has been stressed by Knickerbocker (1973), a firm in a worldwide oligopolistic industry may establish itself abroad, even though the rate of return is lower, in order to prevent the growth of a competitor. This strategy might be handled by capital-budgeting methods, but in some cases the marketing strategy of an oligopolist has a horizon that extends far beyond the horizon of its financial strategy.

Finally, in literature stemming from Cyert and March (1963), the firm may not have a consistent overall maximization goal. Instead, the divisions of the company will attempt to apply some maximization rule to their own activity with no or very little concern for the rest of the company. Against this background, the foreign investment decision will arise out of the process of resolving intracompany conflicts. Certainly, in many such cases, conflict resolution will go a long way from the kind of rational decision implied by capital-budgeting methods. Instead, as has been suggested by Allison (1971), the conflict may be resolved by a compromise, perhaps involving logrolling agreements among company divisions. Another type of conflict resolution is the adoption of a rule or reference to precedent for determining the allocation of investment. By a type of pseudo-legal reasoning, past decisions are carried forward regardless of their validity for the overall operating results of the firm. For example, a rigid rule of one third of funds available for investment may be pushed (or pulled) overseas.

CONCLUSION

This chapter considered three major problems faced by companies operating abroad: foreign-exchange risk, tax-management risk, and the risk of political upheavals.

Many other problems of management abroad are basically the same as management problems in a domestic company. Nevertheless, exchange-rate changes, taxes, and political risks do complicate capital budgeting for an international company. It turns out, however, that business decisions to invest abroad are complex and cannot be fully explained by capital-budgeting considerations.

SOURCES AND SUGGESTED REFERENCES

Aliber, R.Z. *Exchange Risk and Corporate International Finance.* New York: Wiley, 1979.

Alison, G. *The Essence of Decision.* Boston: Little Brown, 1971.

Angeloni, I. and B.K. Short. "The Impact of Country Risk Assessment on Eurocurrency Interest Rate Spreads." International Monetary Fund, 1980, (unpublished).

Antl, B., ed. *Foreign Exchange Risk and the Multinational Corporation.* London: Euromoney Publications, 1981.

Cyert, R. and J.G. March. *The Behavior Theory of the Firm.* Englewood Cliffs, NJ: Prentice-Hall, 1963.

Eiteman, D.K. and A.I. Stonehill. *Multinational Business Finance,* 2nd ed. Reding, MA: Addison-Wesley, 1979.

Esnor, R. and B. Antel, ed. *The Management of Foreign Exchange Risk.* London: Euromoney Publications, 1978.

George, A. *Foreign Exchange Management of the International Corporation.* New York: Praeger, 1978.

Haendel, D., G.T. West, and R.G. Meadow. *Overseas Investment and Political Risk.* Philadelphia: Foreign Policy Research Institute, 1975.

Jacque, L.L. *Management of Foreign Exchange Risk.* Lexington, MA: Lexington Books, 1978.

Knickerbocker, F.T. *Oligopolistic Reaction and Multinational Enterprise.* Boston: Harvard Business School, 1973.

Knudsen, H. "Explaining the National Propensity to Expropriate: An Ecological Approach," *Journal of International Business Studies,* Vol. VII, No. 1 (1974), pp. 51–71.

Kobrin, S.J. "When Does Political Instability Result in Increased Investment Risk," *Columbia Journal of World Business,* Vol. XIII, No. 3 (1978), pp. 113–22.

––––––. "Political Risk, A Review and Reconsideration," *Journal of International Business Studies,* vol. X, No. 1 (1979), pp. 67–80.

Lessard, D.R., ed. *International Financial Management.* New York: Warren, Gorham and Lamont, 1979.

Levich, R.M. and C.G. Wihlborg, ed. *Exchange Risk and Exposure.* Lexington, MA: Lexington Books, 1980.

Nagy, P. *Country Risk.* London: Euromoney Publications, 1979.

Riehl, Heinz and Rita M. Rodriguez. *Foreign Exchange and Money Markets,* New York: McGraw-Hill, 1983.

Rodriguez, R.M. and E.E. Carter. *International Financial Management,* 2nd ed. Englewood Cliffs, NJ: Prentice-Hall, 1979.

Sargen, N. "Economic Indicators and Country Risk Appraisal," Federal Reserve Bank of San Francisco *Economic Review,* Fall, (1977), pp. 19–35.

Shapiro, Alan C. *Multinational Financial Management,* 2nd ed. Boston: Allyn and Bacon, 1986.

State Department Bureau of Public Affairs. *Factors Influencing Private Foreign Investment Among LDC's.* Washington, D.C.: State Department Bureau Intelligence Research, January 1974.

Stobaugh, Jr., R. "How to Analyze Foreign Investment Climates," *Harvard Business Review,* Vol. XLVII, No. 5 (1969), pp. 100–108.

Vernon, R. *Manager and the International Economy.* Englewood Cliffs, NJ: Prentice-Hall, 1976.

Walter, I. "International Capital Allocation," in R.G. Hawkins, R.M. Levich and C. Wihlborg, eds. *Internationalization of Capital Markets,* Greenwich, CT: JAI Press, 1982.

INTERNATIONAL FINANCIAL ACCOUNTING

CONTENTS

INTERNATIONAL FINANCIAL ACCOUNTING

Frederick D. S. Choi

Business and investment activities of multinational companies, which today encompass foreign operations as well as foreign trade, are exposing both financial managers and accountants to reporting problems not encountered when operating within the confines of a single country. In this chapter, I describe several important issues in the area of international financial accounting. These issues relate to currency translation, inflation, consolidation, transnational reporting and disclosure.

FOREIGN-CURRENCY TRANSLATION

REASONS FOR TRANSLATION. Foreign-currency translation, the restatement of account balances from one national-currency framework to another, is undertaken for several reasons, including the following:

1. Recording foreign-currency transactions in the financial statements of a reporting enterprise.
2. Preparing combined or consolidated financial statements coupled with accounting for foreign investments under the equity method.
3. Reporting the results of independent operations to foreign audiences of interest.

Item 3, convenience translation, is discussed in the section "Transnational Financial Reporting."

TERMINOLOGY. *Translation* is not synonymous with *conversion.* Conversion is the physical exchange of one currency for another. Thus a U.S. citizen vacationing in Japan would convert dollars into yen if he were interested in purchasing Japanese goods. Translation is simply a change in monetary *expression,* as when a balance sheet expressed in British pounds is restated in U.S. dollar equivalents. No physical exchange occurs, no accountable transaction takes place. Exhibit 1 defines other terms used in this section.

THE PROBLEM. The traditional medium for translating foreign currency is the foreign-exchange rate which denotes the price of a unit of foreign currency in terms

EXHIBIT 1   GLOSSARY OF FOREIGN-CURRENCY-TRANSLATION TERMS

Attribute   The quantifiable characteristic of an item that is measured for accounting purposes. For example, historical cost and replacement cost are attributes of an asset.

Conversion   The exchange of one currency for another.

Current Rate   The exchange rate in effect at the relevant-financial-statement date.

Discount   When the forward exchange rate is below the current spot rate.

Exposed Net Asset Position   The excess of assets that are measured or denominated in foreign currency and translated at the current rate over liabilities that are measured or denominated in foreign currency and translated at the current rate.

Foreign Currency   A currency other than the currency of the country being referred to; a currency other than the reporting currency of the enterprise being referred to.

Foreign-Currency Financial Statements   Financial statements that employ foreign currency as the unit of measure.

Foreign-Currency Transactions   Transactions (for example, sales or purchases of goods or services or loans payable or receivable) whose terms are stated in a currency other than the entity's functional currency.

Foreign-Currency Translation   The process of expressing amounts denominated or measured in one currency in terms of another currency by use of the exchange rate between the two currencies.

Foreign Operation   An operation whose financial statements are (1) combined or consolidated with or accounted for on an equity basis in the financial statements of the reporting enterprise and (2) prepared in a currency other than the reporting currency of the reporting enterprise.

Forward Exchange Contract   An agreement to exchange at a specified future date currencies of different countries at a specified rate (forward rate).

Functional Currency   The primary currency in which an entity conducts its operation and generates and expends cash. It is usually the currency of the country in which the entity is located and the currency in which the books of record are maintained.

Historical Rate   The foreign-exchange rate that prevailed when a foreign-currency asset or liability was first acquired or incurred.

Local Currency   Currency of a particular country being referred to; the reporting currency of a domestic or foreign operation being referred to.

Monetary Items   Obligations to pay or rights to receive a fixed number of currency units in the future.

Reporting Currency   The currency in which an enterprise prepares its financial statements.

Settlement Date   The date at which a payable is paid or a receivable is collected.

Spot Rate   The exchange rate for immediate exchange of currencies.

Transaction Date   The date at which a transaction (for example, a sale or purchase of merchandise or services) is recorded in a reporting entity's accounting records.

Translation Adjustments   Translation adjustments result from the process of translating financial statements from the entity's functional currency into the reporting currency.

Unit of Measure   The currency in which assets, liabilities, revenue, and expense are measured.

Source.   Adapted from Statement of Financial Accounting Standard No. 52, 1981.

of the domestic or reporting currency. If foreign-exchange rates were relatively stable, as they were prior to the early 1970s, the translation process would be as easy as translating inches or feet into their metric equivalents. However, exchange rates today are free to fluctuate in response to complex forces of supply and demand, creating difficulties in multinational companies' foreign exchange translation and conversion procedures.

FOREIGN-CURRENCY TRANSACTIONS. A foreign-currency transaction is one requiring settlement in a currency other than the primary currency in which an entity conducts its business. Examples include purchases and sales of goods and services whose prices are expressed in a foreign currency, borrowing or lending foreign currencies, and forward exchange contracts. The latter are agreements to purchase or sell a specified amount of foreign currency at a specified rate (the forward rate) on an agreed date in the future.

Three dates should be distinguished when accounting for foreign-currency transactions:

1. the *transaction date* = the date at which a foreign-currency transaction is initially recorded
2. the *settlement date* = the date at which a foreign-currency transaction is extinguished
3. the *financial statement date* – the date at which financial statements are prepared and which often intervenes between the transaction and settlement dates.

In October of 1975, the U.S. Financial Accounting Standards Board (FASB) issued Statement of Financial Accounting Standards No. 8 (F.A.S.B. 8) providing, for the first time, authoritative guidance on accounting for foreign-currency transactions and foreign-currency financial statements. Paragraph 7 of the statement (now superseded by paragraph 16 of F.A.S.B. 52) mandates the following:

1. At the *transaction date* [italics added], each asset, liability, revenue, or expense arising from the transaction shall be translated into (that is, measured in) dollars by use of the exchange rate (rate) in effect at that date, and shall be recorded at that dollar amount.
2. At each *balance sheet date* [italics added], recorded dollar balances representing cash and amounts owed by or to the enterprise that are denominated in foreign currency shall be adjusted to reflect the current rate.

On this basis, a foreign exchange adjustment (i.e., gain or loss on a settled transaction) is necessary whenever the exchange rate changes between the transaction and settlement dates of a foreign currency payable or receivable to reflect the difference between the amount originally recorded and the settlement amount. Should financial statements be prepared prior to settlement, the accounting adjustment (i.e., gain or loss on an unsettled transaction) will equal the difference between the amount originally recorded and the amount presented in the financial statements. These adjustments are depicted schematically below:

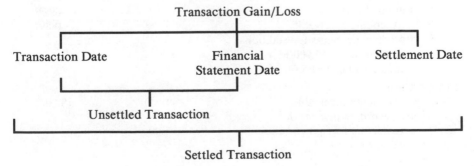

Two accounting issues arise with regard to the proper accounting disposition of the foregoing transaction adjustments. First, should the gain or loss of an unsettled transaction be treated differently than that of its settled counterpart? Second, should the latter be viewed as an adjustment of the original transaction's carrying value or as a "stand alone" gain or loss?

Regarding the former, the FASB rejected the view that a distinction should be drawn between gains and losses on settled and unsettled transactions arguing such distinctions to be incapable of practical application. It decided that gains or losses of unsettled transactions should be accounted for in the same manner as settled transactions. In the case of the latter, two accounting treatments are possible.

Single-Transaction Perspective.   Under a "single-transaction" perspective, an exchange adjustment would be treated as an adjustment to the original transaction accounts on the premise that a transaction and its subsequent settlement are a single event. This is illustrated next.

On December 1 of 19X1, a U.S. manufacturer sells, on account, goods to a French importer for $10,000 when the dollar/franc exchange rate is U.S.$1/FF4. The franc receivable is due in 60 days and the U.S. company operates on a calendar-year basis. Prior to collection of the receivable, the franc begins to depreciate. By year-end, the dollar/franc exchange rate is $1/FF4.5; on February 1, 19X2, it is $1/FF5.0.

U.S. Company's Record

		Foreign Currency (decrease)	U.S. Dollar Equivalent (decrease)
12/1/1	Accounts receivable	FF40,000	$10,000
	Sales		10,000
	(to record credit sale)		
12/31/1	Sales		(1,111)
	Accounts receivable		(1,111)
	(to adjust existing accounts for initial exchange-rate change; FF40,000/FF4 minus FF40,000/ FF4.5)		
2/1/2	Retained earnings		(889)
	Accounts receivable		(889)
	(to adjust accounts for additional rate change; FF40,000/FF4.5 minus FF40,000/FF5.0)		
2/1/2	Cash		8,000
	Accounts receivable	(40,000)	(8,000)
	(to record settlement of outstanding foreign-currency receivable.)		

In this illustration, the initial dollar amount recorded for both Accounts Receivable and Sales is considered an estimate until the account is collected. These accounts are subsequently adjusted for changes in the dollar/franc exchange rate. Further depreciation of the franc between the financial statement date (December 31) and the settlement date (February 1) would entail additional adjustments.

Two-Transaction Perspective. Under a "two-transaction" perspective, collection of the franc receivable is considered a separate event from the sale giving rise to it. Using the previous data, the export sale and related receivable would be recorded at the exchange rate in effect at that date. Depreciation of the franc between December 1 and December 31 would give rise to a *translation* loss (i.e., exchange loss on an unsettled transaction) and would leave unaffected the previously recorded revenue figure. Settlement of the foreign-currency receivable on February 1, 19X2, at the even-lower exchange rate would give rise to a *conversion* loss (i.e., exchange loss on a *settled* transaction).

U.S. Company's Record

	Foreign Currency (decrease)	U.S. Dollar Equivalent (decrease)
12/1/1 Accounts receivable	FF40,000	$10,000
Sales		10,000
(to record credit sale at 12/1/1 exchange rate)		
12/31/1 Foreign-exchange loss		1,111
Accounts receivable		(1,111)
(to record effect of initial rate change)		
2/1/2 Cash		8,000
Foreign-Exchange Loss		889
Accounts receivable	(40,000)	(8,889)
(to record settlement of foreign-currency receivable)		

To achieve uniformity, F.A.S.B. 52 (as did F.A.S.B. 8) requires the two-transaction method of accounting for foreign-currency transactions. This appears to be consistent with international practice. A Price Waterhouse International survey, cited here and subsequently (Fitzgerald *et al.,* 1979), suggests that this treatment is prescribed or the predominant practice in a majority of the 64 countries examined.

Forward Exchange Contracts. As mentioned earlier, a forward exchange contract is an agreement to purchase or sell a specified amount of foreign currency on an agreed future date at a fixed rate called the *forward rate.* Owing to differences in national interest rates, the forward rate will generally exceed or be less than the spot rate prevailing at the date of the forward contract. This gives rise to a *premium* or *discount* which, when multiplied by the amount of foreign currency to be received or delivered under the contract, produces a recognizable premium or discount on the forward contract. Being a special type of foreign-currency transaction, the forward contract will also give rise to transaction gains or losses whenever the exchange rate prevailing at the transaction date differs from those prevailing at interim financial statement dates or settlement dates. These adjustments might arise in the following manner.

On March 1, 19X1, a U.S. company enters into a contract to exchange one million Swedish krona (SEK) for U.S. dollars on June 1, 19X1. Exchange-rate information and related accounting adjustments appear below.

Amount of Forward Contract	SEK 1,000,000
Spot rate on 3/1/1	$0.24 = SEK 1
3-month forward contract rate on 3/1/1	$0.23 = SEK 1
Discount [($0.24 spot rate – $0.23 forward rate)	
× SEK 1,000,000]	$10,000

Amount of Forward Contract	SEK 1,000,000
Spot rate on 6/1/1	$0.21 = SEK
Gain [($0.24 spot rate – $0.21 future spot rate)	
× SEK 1,000,000]	$30,000

Forward exchange contracts may be secured to (1) hedge an unsettled foreign currency payable or receivable (the transaction has occurred; payment has not) (2) hedge a foreign currency commitment (both the transaction and payment has not yet occurred), (3) hedge an exposed asset (or liability) position, or (4) speculate in foreign currencies. The issue here is whether premiums, discounts, gains or losses on contracted forward exchange should receive similar or differing treatment for each of these categories. Under F.A.S.B. 52, each of the foregoing transactions requires a different accounting treatment for discounts, premiums, gains or losses.

The following matrix illustrates how these accounting adjustments would be reported following F.A.S.B. 52 dicta:

	Gains/Losses	Discount/Premium
Unsettled foreign-currency transaction	Recognize in current income	Recognize in current income
Identifiable foreign-currency commitment	Defer and include in dollar basis of foreign-currency transaction[a]	Same treatment as related gains/losses, or recognize in current income
Exposed net asset (liability) position[b]		
1. Foreign currency is functional currency (see "Features of Standard No. 52")	Disclose in separate component of consolidated equity	Same treatment as related gains/losses, or recognize in current income

(Continued)	Gains/Losses	Discount/Premium
2. Dollar is functional currency	Recognize in current income	Recognize in current income
Speculation	Recognize in current income[c]	Recognize in current income

[a] The amount deferred is limited to the amount of the related commitment, on an after-tax basis.

[b] Under F.A.S.B. 8, transaction gains or losses on forward contracts employed to hedge exposed asset or liability positions were recognized in current income.

[c] Gains/losses in this category are a function of the difference between the forward rate available for the remaining period of the contract and the contracted forward rate (or the forward rate last used to measure a gain or loss on that contract for an earlier period).

In addition to changing the accounting treatment accorded hedges of net asset or liability exposures, F.A.S.B. 52 also modified the conditions qualifying a forward contract as a hedge of an identifiable foreign currency commitment. The new conditions (less stringent) are contrasted with the old below:

F.A.S.B. 52	F.A.S.B. 8
Forward contract must be intended and designated as a hedge of a foreign currency commitment	Life of the forward contract must match that of the related foreign currency commitment
Forward contract need not commence at the commitment date	Forward contract must commence at the commitment date
Forward contract must be denominated in the same currency as the foreign currency commitment or in a currency that moves in tandem with it	Forward contract must be denominated in the same currency as the foreign currency commitment
Foreign currency commitment must be firm	Foreign currency commitment must be firm and uncancelable

FOREIGN-CURRENCY FINANCIAL STATEMENTS.   Financial statements of a multinational company's foreign branches and subsidiaries are translated for purposes of consolidation. Fluctuating exchange rates complicate this translation process by increasing the number of translation rates that may be employed: namely, historical rates, current rates, or averages of either (see Exhibit 1 for exchange-rate definitions). Choice of a translation rate, historical or current, is important, as each produces significantly different financial statement effects. Historical rates preserve the original cost of a foreign-currency item in the domestic-currency statements. If, for example, a German subsidiary of a U.S. parent company acquired a piece of equipment for DM 90,000 when the exchange rate was DM2/$1, this asset would have a U.S.$45,000 equivalent upon consolidation. Should the mark devalue to DM3/$1 by the next financial statement date, the dollar equivalent of the German asset would remain at $45,000, its historical cost in dollars, as long as it continued to be translated at the *historical* rate of DM2/$1. Thus historical rates shield financial statements from foreign-currency *translation gains* or *losses,* that is, increases or decreases in the dollar equivalents of foreign-currency balances due to fluctuations in the translation between reporting periods. The use of *current* rates produces translation gains or losses. In our previous example, translating the foreign currency asset at the new current rate would yield a translation loss of $15,000 (DM90,000 ÷ DM2 – DM90,000 ÷ 3).

Basic issues surrounding the translation of foreign currency financial statements thus include the following:

1. Which exchange rate should be applied to specific foreign currency financial statement accounts?
2. How should translation gains or losses be accounted for?

TRANSLATION METHODS. Varying exchange rates give rise to four major translation methods: current, current-noncurrent, monetary-nonmonetary, and temporal. Exhibit 2 summarizes the treatment of specific balance sheet items under each of the four methods.

These methods, in turn, are grouped into two categories. The first uses a single translation rate; the second, multiple rates. Each category, premised on different concepts of foreign operations and translation objectives, is useful.

Single-Rate Method. A single rate to translate foreign currency financial statements is appropriate when foreign entities are viewed from a *local,* as opposed to a parent-company perspective. This method recognizes a foreign-based operation as a separate unit doing business in a foreign currency, retaining the foreign currency as the appropriate unit of measure, and preserving the initial relationships (e.g., financial ratios) in

EXHIBIT 2 EXCHANGE RATES EMPLOYED IN DIFFERENT TRANSLATION METHODS FOR SPECIFIC BALANCE SHEET ITEMS

| | Single-Rate Method | Multiple-Rate Methods | | |
	Current-Rate	Current-Noncurrent	Monetary-Nonmonetary	Temporal
Cash	C[a]	C	C	C
Accounts receivable	C	C	C	C
Inventories				
Cost	C	C	H	H
Market	C	C	H	C
Investments				
Cost	C	H	H	H
Market	C	H	H	C
Fixed assets	C	H	H	H
Other assets	C	H	H	H
Accounts payable	C	C	C	C
Long-term debt	C	H	C	C
Common stock	H[b]	H	H	H
Retained earnings	*[c]	*	*	*

[a] C = Current rate.
[b] H = Historical rate.
[c] * = Residual, balancing figure representing a composite of successive current rates.

the foreign currency statements by translating all foreign currency items—assets, liabilities, revenues, and expenses—by a constant, namely, the current rate. Only the form, not the nature of the foreign accounts, is changed.

When a local-company perspective is maintained, reflection of any translation adjustments in current income would defeat the purpose of preserving relationships in foreign currency statements. Adjustments to Owners' Equity is preferable. (Choi and Mueller, 1984.)

The current-rate method was first supported by the Institute of Chartered Accountants in England and Wales (ICAEW) in their 1968 Statement N25. It is one of two methods recommended by the International Accounting Standards Committee in *IAS 21*, "Accounting for the Effects of Changes in Foreign Exchange Rates," and was popular in Europe and the Far East prior to its general acceptance in the Americas.

Multiple-Rate Methods. Multiple-rate methods utilize a combination of historical and current rates. Premised on a parent-company perspective, foreign-based operations are viewed as mere extensions of the parent company as opposed to independent entities. Hence, the objects of translation are to change the unit of measure for the financial statements of foreign subsidiaries from foreign currency to the parent company's reporting currency and to make foreign statements conform to accounting principles generally accepted in the country of the parent company. Thus if the historical cost principle is embraced by the parent, translation of a subsidiary's foreign currency denominated assets at the historical rate assures that they will also be reflected at cost in the consolidated statements. Translation at the current rate would restate foreign currency assets to a basis other than cost. Three historical-rate methods are discussed in turn.

Current-Noncurrent Method. Prior to F.A.S.B. 8, this was the most authoritative foreign-currency translation method in the United States. No longer permitted there, its use is still advocated in the authoritative literature outside the United States. It remains the predominant practice in countries such as West Germany, Iran, New Zealand, Pakistan, and South Africa.

Under the current-noncurrent method (described in Chapter 12 of *Accounting Research Bulletin No. 43* of the AICPA), a foreign subsidiary's current assets and current liabilities are translated into their domestic currency equivalents at the current rate. Noncurrent assets and liabilities are translated at historical rates.

Income statement items, with the exception of depreciation and amortization charges, are translated at average rates applicable to each month of operation or on the basis of weighted averages covering the whole period to be reported. Depreciation and amortization charges are translated at rates in effect when the related assets were acquired.

Monetary-Nonmonetary Method. Formally recognized in the United States with the issuance of Accounting Principles Board (APB) Opinion No. 6 (amending Accounting Research Bulletin No. 43), this method, like the current-noncurrent method, uses a balance sheet classification scheme to determine appropriate translation rates. *Monetary* assets and liabilities (see Exhibit 1) such as cash, receivables, and payables including long-term debt, are translated at the current rate. *Nonmonetary* items—fixed assets, long-term investments, and inventories—are translated at the historical rate.

Income statement items are translated under procedures similar to those described under the current-noncurrent framework. Although no longer permitted in the United States, the method is practiced extensively in Central America, the Philippines, Sweden, and Taiwan (PWI Survey).

Temporal Method.   Under this method, foreign currency assets and liabilities are translated in a manner that retains their original measurement bases. Cash, receivables, and payables are translated at the current rate. Assets carried in foreign financial statements at historical cost are translated at the historical rate. Assets carried at current values such as inventories, under the lower-of-cost-or-market rule, are translated at the current rate. Revenue and expense items are translated at rates prevailing when the underlying transactions take place, although average rates are suggested when revenue or expense transactions are voluminous.

Under a historical-cost valuation framework, the translation procedures resulting from the temporal principle are virtually identical to those resulting from the monetary-nonmonetary method. Translation procedures differ, however, if other asset-valuation bases, such as replacement cost, market values, or discounted cash flows, are adopted.

The temporal method of translation was introduced in the United States with the issuance of F.A.S.B. 8 and is one of the two translation methods recommended by the International Accounting Standards Committee.

Financial-Statement Effects.   Exhibit 3 highlights the financial-statement effects of the various translation methods described. The balance sheet of a hypothetical Swiss subsidiary of a U.S.-based multinational appears in the first two columns of the exhibit. The third column depicts the U.S. dollar equivalent of the Swiss franc (SF) balances when the exchange rate is $1/SF2. Should the franc appreciate by 33 1/3 percent in relation to the dollar (now $1/SF1.5), a number of different accounting results are possible. (Bracketed expressions in the exhibit identify those foreign currency balances affected by exchange-rate changes, giving rise to translation gains or losses.)

Under the current-rate method, exchange-rate changes affect the dollar equivalents of the Swiss subsidiary's *total* foreign currency assets (TA) and liabilities (TL) in the current period. Since their dollar values are affected by changes in the current rate, they are said to be *exposed,* in an accounting sense, to foreign exchange risk. Accordingly, under the current-rate method, an exposed net-asset position (TA > TL) would give rise to a translation loss should the Swiss franc depreciate in value and an exchange gain should the franc be revalued. An exposed net-liability position (TA < TL) would produce a translation gain in the event of a Swiss franc devaluation and conversely. In our example, current-rate translation yields a $300 translation gain, since the dollar equivalent of the Swiss subsidiary's net-asset position after the franc appreciation is $1200 ($3600 – $2400), whereas the dollar equivalent *before* the appreciation was $900 ($2700 – $1800).

Under the current-noncurrent method, the U.S. company's accounting exposure is measured by its net current asset or liability position, under the monetary-nonmonetary method, by its net monetary asset or liability position. Exposure under the temporal principle depends on whether the Swiss subsidiary's inventories or other assets are valued at historical cost or some other valuation basis.

EXHIBIT 3 TRANSLATION GAINS AND LOSSES UNDER DIFFERING METHODOLOGIES ASSUMING AN APPRECIATING FOREIGN CURRENCY[a]

Swiss Subsidiary Balance Sheet in Swiss Francs		U.S. Dollars Before Franc Appreciation ($1/SF2.0)	U.S. Dollar Equivalents After Swiss France Appreciation ($1/SF1.5)			
Amount	Item		Current Rate	Current-Noncurrent	Monetary-Nonmonetary	Temporal
	Assets					
SF 600	Cash	$ 300	$ 400	$ 400	$ 400	$ 400
600	Accounts receivable	300	400	400	400	400
	Inventories:					
	Cost (SF900)					
1200	Market	600	800	800	600[b]	800
3000	Fixed assets, net	1500	2000	1500	1500	1500
SF 5400		$2700	$3600	$3100	$2900	$3100
	Liabilities and *owners' equity*					
SF 1200	ST payables	$ 600	$ 800	$ 800	$ 800	$ 800
2400	LT debt	1200	1600	1200	1600	1600
1800	Owners' equity[c]	900	1200	1100	500	700
SF 5400		$2700	$3600	$3100	$2900	$3100
	Translation gain (loss)		$ 300	$ 200	$ (400)	$ (200)

[a]Note that if the exchange rate remained unchanged over time, the translated statements would be the same under all translation methods.

[b]Under some interpretations, this item would be reclassified as a monetary item and translated at the current rate.

[c]In the translated statements, Owners' Equity is a residual balancing figure.

ACCOUNTING FOR TRANSLATION GAINS AND LOSSES. Exhibit 3 reveals a wide array of accounting results—ranging from a $400 loss under the monetary-nonmonetary method to a $300 gain under the current-rate method. Yet each method presumably describes the same factual situation! This raises the issue of how to account for "translation gains or losses." While accountants in many countries continue to debate the issue, U.S. responses to the evolving translation problem are as indicative as those in any other country. To better understand recent developments on the U.S. translation accounting front, some background information is provided.

A distinction between conversion and translation gains or losses should be acknowledged at the outset. In the former case, there is an actual exchange of foreign currencies. Thus if a U.S. company borrows SF300,000 when the exchange rate is $1/SF2 and immediately converts the franc proceeds to dollars, it will receive $150,000. If, at the time of repayment, the franc appreciates to $1/SF1.5, the U.S. borrower will actually have to expend $200,000 to discharge its SF300,000 debt. A $50,000 conversion loss occurs. In accounting parlance, this loss has been *realized,* and accountants would generally agree that such losses (or gains) should be reflected immediately in period income.

In contrast, translation adjustments are "unrealized" gains or losses (i.e., bookkeeping entries) that result from the application of different translation rates to foreign-account balances. Under these circumstances the appropriate accounting disposition is less obvious.

Prior to 1976, the prevalent accounting treatment for translation adjustments under U.S. historical-translation methods was to net translation gains and losses incurred during the period. Excess translation losses were reflected in current income, excess translation gains were deferred in the balance sheet and used to absorb future translation losses. Consistent with practices outside the United States, some companies recognized gains and losses in current income, others reflected all gains and losses in consolidated equity, while a few deferred such gains and losses and amortized them to income over the remaining lives of the balance sheet items to which they related.

To end the practice diversity that existed, the F.A.S.B. issued in 1976 F.A.S.B. 8. In addition to mandating use of the temporal principle, this pronouncement required affected companies to include both translation gains and losses in operating results in the period of the rate change. Designed to assure accounting uniformity, this F.A.S.B. 8 feature proved more controversial than any other. In effect, F.A.S.B. 8 eliminated the use of balance sheet reserves to buffer current earnings from fluctuating exchange rates causing concern among executives of multinational companies that reported earnings of their companies would appear more volatile than those of purely domestic entities, and would depress their stock prices. Despite evidence to the contrary (Dukes, 1978), F.A.S.B. 8 had a significant effect on corporate-management practices. Studies on the economic impact of F.A.S.B. 8 by organizations such as the FASB (in 1978), Conference Board (in 1979), and Financial Executives Research Foundation (in 1980) found management incurring current and/or potential cash costs to minimize noncash (translation) adjustments, including the opportunity costs of management time diverted away from mainstream operating problems.

Dissatisfaction with F.A.S.B. 8 also centered around the unrealistic results often produced by specific translation provisions. In particular, the use of multiple rates as translation coefficients distorts both income-statement and balance sheet relationships (e.g., gross margins as a result of translating sales at current rates and cost of sales at historical rates) in the foreign currency statements. Similar distortions are produced when exchange gains or losses mask what has actually occurred. Furthermore, forward contracts and other hedging transactions were often not accounted for as such.

NEW TRANSLATION PRONOUNCEMENT. In May 1978, the FASB invited public comment on its first 12 pronouncements. Most respondents urged that F.A.S.B. 8 be changed. Accordingly, in December 1981, the FASB issued *Statement of Financial Accounting Standards No. 52*. It officially supersedes, in addition to F.A.S.B. 8, F.A.S.B. 20, *Accounting for Forward Exchange Contracts,* FAS Interpretation No. 15, Translation of Unamortized Policy Acquisition Costs by a Stock Life Insurance Company; and FAS Interpretation No. 17, *Applying the Lower of Cost or Market Rule in Translated Financial Statements.*

Foreign-Currency Transactions.   Foreign-currency transaction rules under F.A.S.B. 52 are similar to those under F.A.S.B. 8 with two major exceptions. Transaction adjustments—translation gains or losses on unsettled transactions as well as conversion gains or losses on settled transactions—are reported in a separate component of Stockholders' Equity in the following cases:

1.   When the foreign-currency transaction (including a forward exchange contract, discussed shortly) is intended as a hedge of a foreign operation's exposed net-asset or net-liability position.
2.   When the adjustment relates to transactions between a parent company and an affiliate that is combined, consolidated, or accounted for by the equity method in the parent's financial statements.

Transaction adjustments between two or more affiliates of the parent company, however, are reflected in current income.

Foreign Currency Financial Statements.   F.A.S.B. 52 also calls for major changes when translating foreign currency financial statements. Although retaining U.S. accounting principles as basic, the FASB adopts a situational approach and recognizes a local company perspective as a valid reporting framework. The new translation rules are designed to:

1.   Reflect in consolidated statements the financial results and relationships measured in the primary currency in which each consolidated entity conducts its business (its functional currency)
2.   Provide information that is generally compatible with the expected economic effects of an exchange rate change on an enterprise's cash flows and equity

These objectives are premised on the notion of a "functional currency," which mirrors the currency perspective adopted by management for consolidated entities. The functional currency of a particular foreign entity is defined as the currency of the primary economic environment in which it operates and generates cash flows. If a foreign entity's operations are relatively self-contained and integrated within a foreign country (i.e., an operation that is not an extension of the parent company) its functional currency would ordinarily be its local currency (e.g., pesos in the case of a Mexican subsidiary of a U.S. parent). If a foreign entity is merely an extension of a U.S. parent company, its functional currency would be the U.S. dollar. Exhibit 4 identifies circumstances justifying use of either the local or the U.S. currency as an entity's functional currency.

Determination of the functional currency is a key feature of F.A.S.B. 52 as it determines the choice of translation method and disposition of exchange gains and losses. If the foreign currency in which the foreign entity's records are maintained is deemed to be the functional currency, its financial statements are *translated* to dollars using the current rate method. Translation gains or losses arising therefrom are disclosed in a separate component of consolidated equity. This preserves the financial statement ratios as measured in the local currency statements. However, if the U.S. dollar is determined to be the functional currency, a foreign entity's financial statements are *remeasured* to a dollar perspective using the former temporal method prescribed by F.A.S.B. 8. Here all translation gains or losses arising from the translation process are included in determining current income.

In those instances where an entity has more than one distinct and "separable" operation (e.g., a branch or division) each operation may be considered an entity, each with a different functional currency designation. Thus, a U.S. parent might have a self-contained manufacturing operation in Ireland designed to serve the European market, as well as a separate sales outlet for the parent company's exported products. Under these circumstances, financial statements of the manufacturing operation would be translated to dollars using the current rate method. The pound statements of the sales outlet would be remeasured in dollars according to the temporal method.

EXHIBIT 4 FUNCTIONAL CURRENCY CRITERIA

Economic Factors	Circumstances Favoring Parent Currency as Functional Currency	Circumstances Favoring Local Currency as Functional Currency
Cash flows	Directly impact parent's cash flows and are currently remittable to the parent	Primarily in the local currency and do not impact parent's cash flows
Sales price	Responsive to changes in exchange rates and determined by worldwide competition	Largely irresponsive to exchange rate changes and governed primarily by local competition
Sales market	Largely in the parent country and denominated in parent currency	Largely in the host country and denominated in local currency
Expenses	Primarily related to productive factors imported from the parent company	Incurred primarily in the local environment
Financing	Primarily from the parent or reliance on parent company to meet debt obligations	Primarily denominated in local currency and serviced by local operations
Intercompany transactions	Frequent and extensive	Infrequent nor extensive

Source. Financial Accounting Standards Board. *Statement of Financial Accounting Standards No. 52* (Stamford, Conn.: FASB, 1981). Appendix A.

Once the functional currency for a foreign entity has been determined, F.A.S.B. 52 requires that it be used consistently unless changes in economic circumstances clearly indicate that the functional currency has changed. If a reporting enterprise can justify the change in conformity with Accounting Principles Board Opinion No. 20, "Accounting Changes," the accounting change need not be accounted for retroactively.

The purpose of translation is to restate foreign currency financial statements to a common reporting currency (e.g., the U.S. dollar). Under F.A.S.B. 52, procedures for translating foreign currency statements to dollars depend not only on the functional currency designation for a particular foreign entity but also on whether its records are originally maintained in its functional currency. Exhibit 5 flow charts alternate translation procedures.

Translation when local currency is the functional currency.   When the local currency of a foreign entity is its functional currency, and its records are maintained in that currency, the following current rate procedures are employed:

EXHIBIT 5

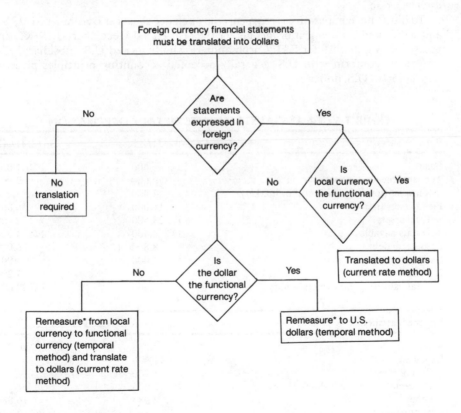

* The term *remeasure* means to translate so as to change the unit of measure from a foreign currency to the functional currency.

1. All foreign currency assets and liabilities are translated to dollars using the exchange rate prevailing as of the balance sheet date; capital accounts are translated at the historical rate.

2. Revenues and expenses are translated using the exchange rate prevailing on the transaction date, although weighted average rates can be used for expediency.

3. Translation gains and losses are reported in a separate component of consolidated stockholders' equity. These exchange adjustments bypass the income statement until the foreign operation is sold or the investment is perceived to have suffered a permanent diminution in value.

Translation adjustments under the current rate method arise whenever (a) year-end foreign currency balances are translated at a current rate that differs from that used to translate ending balances of the previous period, and (b) foreign currency financial statements are translated at a current rate that differs from exchange rates used during the period. The translation adjustment is calculated by (a) multiplying the beginning foreign currency net asset balance by the change in the current rate during the period and (b) multiplying the increase or decrease in net assets during the period by the difference between the average exchange rate and end of period exchange rate.

To illustrate, comparative foreign currency balance sheets at December 31, 19X1 and 19X2, and a statement of income for the year ended December 31, 19X2, are presented in Exhibit 6 for F&L Corporation, a wholly owned U.S. subsidiary. The statements conform with U.S. generally accepted accounting principles prior to translation to U.S. dollars.

EXHIBIT 6   FINANCIAL STATEMENTS OF F&L CORPORATION

Balance Sheet	12/31/X1	12/31/X2
Cash	FC 600	FC 1,000
Accounts receivable (net)	2,600	2,000
Inventories (lower of FIFO cost or market)	2,400	3,000
Fixed assets (net)	18,000	16,000
Total assets	FC 23,600	FC 22,000
Accounts payable	FC 4,400	FC 4,800
Long-term debt	8,800	6,000
Capital stock	4,000	4,000
Retained earnings	6,400	7,200
Total liabilities and owners' equity	FC 23,600	FC 22,000

Income Statement	Year Ended 12/31/X2	
Sales		FC 20,000
Expenses	11,900	
Cost of sales	11,900	
Depreciation (straight-line)	2,000	
Other	2,986	16,886
Operating income		FC 3,114
Income taxes		934
Net income		FC 2,180

Capital stock was issued and fixed assets acquired when the exchange rate was FC = $.17. Inventories at January 1, 19X2, were acquired during the fourth quarter of 19X1. Purchases (FC 12,500), sales, other expenses, and dividends (FC 1,380) occurred evenly during 19X2. Exchange rates for calendar 19X2 were as follows:

January 1, 19X2	FC 1 = $.23
December 31, 19X2	FC 1 = $.18
Average during 19X2	FC 1 = $.22
Average during fourth quarter 19X1	FC 1 = $.23
Average during fourth quarter 19X2	FC 1 = $.19

Application of the F.A.S.B. 52 translation process to the foregoing figures is depicted in Exhibit 7.

Translation when U.S. dollar is the functional currency.   When the U.S. dollar is a foreign entity's functional currency, its foreign currency financial statements are remeasured (translated) to dollars using the temporal method originally advocated by F.A.S.B. 8. Specifically:

1. Monetary assets and liabilities are translated using the rate prevailing as of the financial statement date; nonmonetary items including capital accounts are translated at historical rates.
2. Revenues and expenses are translated using average exchange rates for the period save those items related to nonmonetary items (e.g., cost of sales and depreciation expense), which are translated using historical rates.
3. Translation gains and losses are reflected in current income.

Exhibit 8 illustrates application of the F.A.S.B. 52 remeasurement process when the dollar is the functional currency.

Translation when foreign-currency is the functional currency.   If a foreign entity's records are not maintained in its functional currency, remeasurement into the functional currency is required prior to dollar translation. For example, if a Hong Kong subsidiary's functional currency is the British pound but it maintains its records in Hong Kong dollars, remeasurement would be necessary prior to dollar translation at the current rate. Remeasurement into the functional currency (e.g., British pounds) employs procedures identical to those enumerated in Exhibit 8.

THE CONTROVERSY CONTINUES.   While F.A.S.B. 52 is designed to still many of the criticisms leveled at F.A.S.B. 8, new issues stir new controversies; perhaps inevitable given the complexity of multinational operations and the many purposes of translation. Several basic issues are set forth below.

Concept of Income.   Under F.A.S.B. 52, adjustments arising from the translation of foreign currency financial statements and certain transactions are made directly to Shareholders' Equity, thus bypassing the income statement. The intention is to provide statement readers with more accurate and less confusing income numbers, that is, translated results that are "directionally sympathetic" with the economic

EXHIBIT 7 CURRENT RATE METHOD OF TRANSLATION (LOCAL CURRENCY IS FUNCTIONAL CURRENCY)

	Foreign Currency	Exchange Rate	Dollar Equivalent
Balance Sheet Accounts			
Assets			
Cash	FC 1,000	$.18	$ 180
Accounts receivable	2,000	.18	360
Inventories	3,000	.18	540
Fixed assets	16,000	.18	2,880
Total	FC 22,000		$3,960
Liabilities and Stockholders' Equity			
Accounts payable	FC 4,800	.18	$ 864
Long-term debt	6,000	.18	1,080
Capital stock	4,000	.17	680
Retained earnings	7,200	a	808
Cumulative translation adjustment		b	528
Total	FC 22,000		$3,960
Income Statement Accounts			
Sales	FC 20,000	.22	$4,400
Cost of Sales	11,900	.22	2,618
Depreciation	2,000	.22	440
Other expenses	2,986	.22	656
Income taxes	934	.22	206
Net income	FC 2,180		$ 480
Retained earnings 12/31/X1	6,400		632
Dividends	1,380	.22	304
Retained earnings	FC 7,200		$ 808

[a] See statement of income and retained earnings.

[b] The translation adjustment for the year can be derived as follows. Assuming calendar 19X2 is the first year in which the current rate method is adopted (previous translation method was a multiple rate method per F.A.S.B. 8) a one-time translation adjustment is calculated as of January 1, 19X2. This figure approximates the amount by which beginning stockholders' equity would differ in light of the translation switch. It is derived by translating F&L Corporation's January 1, 19X2 foreign currency net asset position at the current rate prevailing on that date. The beginning-of-period capital stock and retained earnings accounts retain their original translated amounts as of that date (i.e., carried over from the previous year's balance sheet). The resulting difference (calculated below) is F&L Corporation's beginning-of-period cumulative translation adjustment.

Net assets, 12/31/X1		FC 10,400
Exchange rate, 12/31/X1 (FC 1 = $.23)		× $.23
		$2,392
Less (as reported stockholders' equity, 12/31/X1):		
Capital stock	$680	
Retained earnings (per F.A.S.B. 8)	632	1,312
Cumulative translation adjustment, 1/1/X2		$1,080

EXHIBIT 7   (Continued)

Given this information, the following steps yield the translation adjustment for calendar 19X2:

1. Net assets, 12/31/X1	FC 1 = $.23	FC 10,400		
Change in current rate during year:				
Rate, 12/31/X1	FC 1 = $.23			
Rate, 12/31/X2	FC 1 = $.18	× $(.05)	$ (520)	
2. Change in net assets during year				
(net income less dividends)		FC 800		
Difference between average and year-end rate:				
Average rate	FC 1 = $.22			
Year-end rate	FC 1 = $.18	× ($(.04)	$ (32)	
Total			$ (552)	
3. Cumulative translation adjustment, 1/1/X2			1,080	
4. Cumulative translation adjustment, 12/31/X2			$ 528	

effect of exchange-rate movements. Some, however, dislike the idea of "burying" translation adjustments, heretofore disclosed. They fear possible reader confusion as to the effects of fluctuating exchange rates on a company's worth. Equity adjustments, moreover, violate the *all-inclusive concept of income* (APB Opinion No. 9, December 1966), which requires that companies disclose (1) operating revenues and expenses, and (2) all unusual, nonoperating, and infrequently occurring items in the computation of income, the latter category being reported separately in the income statement. This provision was designed to provide statement readers with all information bearing on a firm's "profitability." Which income concept is right?

Reporting Perspective.   In adopting the notion of a "functional currency," the FASB accommodates both a local as well as a parent-company reporting perspective in the consolidated financial statements. The first adopts the currency of the foreign operation's domicile as functional; the second, the U.S. dollar. As an example, a Mexican subsidiary might manufacture a component to be shipped to its U.S. parent for inclusion in a product resold in the United States. In this case, the Mexican subsidiary is merely an extension of the U.S. operation; its functional currency is the U.S. dollar. Should the Mexican entity maintain its records in pesos, its financial statements would be translated to U.S. dollars using the temporal method, and any translation adjustments would be included in current income (as per F.A.S.B. 8). However, several questions arise. First, are the translation adjustments just described any different from those resulting from use of a current-rate method (per F.A.S.B. 52)? If not, is any useful purpose served by disclosing some translation adjustments in income and others in Stockholders' Equity? Are financial statement readers better served by incorporating two different reporting perspectives and, therefore, two different currency frameworks in a single set of consolidated financial statements? The F.A.S.B. 8 concept of a single consolidated entity and a single unit of measure (the dollar) may prove the lesser of two evils.

To Smooth or Not to Smooth.   F.A.S.B. 8's treatment of exchange gains and losses was designed, among other things, to minimize a smoothing option permitted by the earlier use of balance sheet reserves to account for net translation gains. Ironically,

F.A.S.B. 52 reintroduces smoothing opportunities. Consider, once again, the notion of functional currencies. When a foreign entity's functional currency is not readily apparent, its determination is left to management. Once determined, the functional currency is expected to be used consistently, unless management ascertains a change in the underlying circumstances. Ernst & Whinney (1980) states that "a change in the functional currency would not be considered a change in accounting principle under APB Opinion No. 20, 'Accounting Changes.' We believe a change in the functional currency of a foreign entity would be viewed as a change to reflect new events or economic circumstances." This means that the cumulative effect of a functional currency change, computed for all prior periods to the beginning of the period in which the change is made, would not have to be disclosed.

As an example of a smoothing opportunity, assume that a U.S. parent company has a manufacturing subsidiary in Germany whose functional currency is the *U.S. dollar.* The U.S. parent wishes to borrow deutsche marks for use in its Frankfurt operations. If the parent were to take out the deutsche mark loan, an appreciation of the deutsche mark by the repayment date would be reflected in consolidated income. However, if the German *subsidiary* borrowed the funds and the deutsche mark were designated as its functional currency, an exchange adjustment, stemming from a rise in the deutsche mark's value, would bypass consolidated income and appear in Stockholders' Equity instead.

Assume now that the U.S. parent desired use of the deutsche mark loan proceeds. Again, borrowing deutsche marks through the German subsidiary would shield consolidated income from the effects of a fluctuating DM/$ exchange rate. Under F.A.S.B. 52 transactions between an investor and investee of a long-term nature are viewed as increases or decreases in a parent company's foreign investment. Accordingly, foreign-exchange adjustments, whether attributed to settled or unsettled transactions, are treated as adjustments to Stockholders' Equity. Alternatively, if the German subsidiary has a net exposed asset position, the U.S. parent could designate the deutsche mark borrowing as a hedge of the German subsidiary's positive exposure. In this instance, a transaction loss incurred on a rise in the mark's value vis-á-vis the dollar would flow to consolidated equity as an offset to the positive translation adjustment stemming from consolidation.

Foreign Currency Translation and Inflation.   An inverse relationship between a country's rate of inflation and its currency's external value has been empirically demonstrated. Consequently, use of the current rate to translate the cost of nonmonetary assets located in inflationary environments will eventually produce domestic currency equivalents far below their original measurement bases. At the same time, translated earnings will be greater because of correspondingly lower depreciation charges. Such translated results could easily mislead rather than inform. Lower dollar valuations would usually understate the actual earning power of foreign assets supported by local inflation and inflated return on investment ratios of foreign operations could create false expectations regarding future profitability. In light of these considerations, would some form of inflation adjustment be appropriate prior to translation?

Rather than address the foregoing issue, the FASB decided against inflation adjustments prior to translation believing such adjustments to be inconsistent with the historical cost valuation framework employed in basic U.S. statements. As a preliminary solution, F.A.S.B. 52 requires use of the U.S. dollar as the functional currency for foreign operations domiciled in hyperinflationary environments, that is, those countries in which the cumulative rate of inflation exceeds 100 percent over a three-year period. This procedure would hold constant the dollar equivalents of foreign currency assets as they would now be translated at the historical rate (per temporal method).

This accounting treatment, however, is not without limitations. To begin with, translation at the historical rate is meaningful only if differential rates of inflation between the subsidiary's host country and parent country are perfectly negatively correlated with exchange rates. Failing this, the dollar equivalents of foreign currency assets in inflationary environments will also be misleading. In addition, should inflation rates in the hyperinflationary economy subside in the future (e.g., fall below 100 percent), switching to the current rate method (local currency would now be the functional currency) could produce a significant translation adjustment to consolidated equity as exchange rates may have changed significantly during the interim. Under these circumstances, charging stockholders' equity with translation losses on foreign currency fixed assets could have a significant effect on financial ratios with stockholders' equity in the denominator. Indeed, the evidence suggests that some U.S. companies that adopted F.A.S.B. 52 early are worried about the reactions of investment analysts and especially the reactions of banks with which they have loan-covenant agreements on minimum debt to equity ratios (Business International, 1982). At issue is whether the equity impact of F.A.S.B. 52 will affect the evaluation of companies by creditors, shareholders, and credit-rating agencies. Given the nature of current exchange rates, the problem of foreign currency translation may very well be inseparable from the issue of accounting for inflation.

ACCOUNTING FOR INFLATION

THE PROBLEM.   Accepted accounting principles in most countries, including the United States, have traditionally assumed stable prices. As this assumption no longer squares with reality, the relevance of historical-cost accounting is being increasingly questioned. Thus matching revenues realized during an inflationary period against the historical costs of resources (notably inventories and property) acquired in the past generally result in overstated income, which may lead to the following:

1. Increases in proportionate taxation.
2. Demands by shareholders for more dividends.
3. Demands by labor for higher wages.
4. Unfavorable actions by home and/or host governments.
5. Unoptimal business decisions.

With inflation, there is always the danger that a firm may not preserve sufficient resources internally to replace higher priced assets. Also, failure to adjust corporate accounts for changes in the purchasing power of the monetary unit makes it difficult for statement readers to interpret and compare operating results both within and between countries. Conventional disregard for purchasing power gains and losses from holding monetary items further distorts business-performance comparisons during inflationary periods.

Many are cognizant of the need to consider price changes when interpreting historical cost based statements. Nevertheless, explicit recognition of inflation's effects in financial reports is useful for several reasons (FASB, 1979):

1. The effects of changing prices depend partially on the transactions and circumstances of an enterprise, and users do not have detailed information about those factors.
2. Alleviation of the problems caused by changing prices depends on a widespread understanding of the problems; a widespread understanding is unlikely to develop until business performance is discussed in terms of measures that explicitly allow for the effects of changing prices.
3. Statements by managers about the problems caused by changing prices will have greater credibility when enterprises publish financial information that addresses those problems.

TYPES OF INFLATION ADJUSTMENTS.   Accounting for inflation requires that a distinction be made between general and specific price movements. A *general price-level change* (inflation or deflation) refers to a movement in the prices of all goods and services in an economy on the average, that is, the purchasing power of the monetary unit changes in terms of its ability to command goods and services in general. A *specific price change* refers to a change in the price of a specific commodity, inventories and equipment, for example. General and specific price series seldom move in parallel fashion. Each differs in its financial statement effects; each is accounted for with different objectives in mind. Henceforth, accounting for the financial statement effects of general price-level changes is referred to as the *historical-cost/constant-dollar model*. Accounting for specific price changes is referred to as the *current cost model*.

General Price-Level Adjustments.   From a balance sheet perspective, income represents that portion of a firm's wealth (net asset) position that can be disposed of during an accounting period without decreasing its original net-asset position. To illustrate, assume a U.S. merchandiser starts the calendar year with $100,000 in cash (no debt), which is immediately converted into salable inventory. The entire inventory is sold on the last day of the year for $150,000 cash. Assuming stable prices, enterprise income would equal $50,000, measured as the difference between the ending and beginning net assets, or revenues minus expenses (cost of goods sold). In this case, a dividend distribution of $50,000 would indeed leave the firm with as much money capital at the end as it had at the beginning, namely, $100,000.

During periods of inflation, however, the $50,000 may no longer represent the amount of a firm's disposable wealth. General price-level adjustments take this into account by measuring enterprise income so that it represents the maximum amount of resources that could be distributed to various income claimants while preserving the firm's ability to command as many goods and services, in general, at the end of the period as it could at the beginning.

Assume now that the general level of prices, as measured by the consumer price index, increases from a level of 100 at the beginning of the period to 120 at the end. (It would take $120 at year-end to purchase what $100 would have purchased at the beginning.) Income, under the historical-cost/constant-dollar model, is thus measured by taking the difference between wealth at the end of the period ($150,000) and wealth at the beginning adjusted to its end-of-period purchasing-power equivalent ($100,000 × 120/100 = $130,000) or $30,000. Alternatively, historical-cost based expenses in the income statement could be restated to their end-of-period purchasing-power equivalents (constant dollars) and subtracted from period revenues, which are already stated in end-of-period dollars. In our example,

Revenues ($150,000 × 120/120)	$150,000
less Cost of goods sold ($100,000 × 120/100)	120,000
Price-level-adjusted income	$ 30,000

Disbursing no more than $30,000 would help assure that the company could command as many goods and services, in general, at the end of the period as it could at the beginning.

It is possible to convert measurements of historical cost to their beginning-of-period purchasing-power equivalents by multiplying the foregoing figures by the ratio of the general price-level index at the beginning of the period to the price index prevailing at the end. Either method, if used consistently, is satisfactory.

Current-Cost Adjustments.   The current-cost model views income as the amount of resources that could be distributed during a given period while maintaining a company's productive capacity or earning power. One way is to adjust a firm's original net-asset position using appropriate specific price indexes or direct pricing to reflect changes in an item's current-cost equivalent during the period. In our current example, if during the same period prices of the firm's inventories increased by 40 percent, income under the current-cost model would be measured as ($150,000 − $100,000 × 140/100) or $10,000. Again, the $150,000 figure could represent ending net assets or sales revenues and the $100,000 figure, beginning net assets or cost-of-goods-sold expense. In this case, distributing no more than $10,000 would help ensure that the firm would preserve sufficient resources internally to enable it to replace specific assets whose prices had risen during the period. Thus whereas the objective of general price-level adjustments is to preserve the general purchasing power of an enterprise's original money capital, the current-cost model attempts to preserve a firm's physical capital or earning power.

National accounting responses to inflation generally reflect the historical-cost/constant-dollar *or* current-cost models. Those favoring the former argue that the latter violates the historical-cost valuation framework, is too subjective, and is difficult to implement. It also ignores changes in the purchasing power of money and the resulting monetary gains or losses from holding monetary items such as debt. Those favoring current-cost adjustments argue that businesses are not affected by general inflation; they are affected instead by increases in specific operating costs and plant expenditures. Moreover, recording purchasing-power gains from holding debt during inflation could be misleading. Highly levered firms could show large monetary gains while on the brink of bankruptcy (Vancil, 1976).

Methods combining features of both current-cost and adjusted historical-cost models are also under limited experimentation in the United States. This financial information recognizes both changes in asset values and changes in the monetary-measuring unit.

THE U.S. RESPONSE. In September 1979, the FASB issued Statement of Financial Accounting Standards No. 33 (F.A.S.B. 33), *Financial Reporting and Changing Prices,* the result of intermittent efforts by the U.S. accounting profession to integrate inflation adjustments into U.S. annual reports.

Major Provisions. F.A.S.B. 33 required disclosure of both price-level adjusted historical-cost and current-cost information. The FASB concluded that preparers and users of financial reports should have further practical experience with inflation accounting. Hence the required disclosures *supplemented* rather than *replaced* historical cost as the basic measurement framework for primary financial statements.

The statement applies to public U.S. enterprises that had either

1. Inventories and property, plant, and equipment (before deducting accumulated depreciation) of more than $125 million, or
2. Total assets amounting to more than $1 billion (after deducting accumulated depreciation). Assets include those in foreign locations.

It also applied to publicly held non-U.S. companies that prepared their basic financial statements in U.S. dollars and in accordance with U.S. GAAP, such as the Royal Dutch-Shell Group when reporting to their U.S. shareholders.

Supplementary disclosure requirements of F.A.S.B. 33 are summarized below.

Information for the Current Year
Historical-Cost/Constant-Dollar Basis
Income from continuing operations.
Purchasing-power gain or loss on net monetary items.
Current-Cost Basis (beginning in 1980)
Income from continuing operations.
Current-cost amounts of inventory and property, plant, and equipment at year-end.
Increases or decreases in the current-cost amounts of inventory and property, plant, and equipment, net of inflation (general price-level changes).
Information for Each of the Five Most-Recent Years
Net Sales and Other Operating Revenues
Historical-Cost/Constant-Dollar Information
Income from continuing operations.
Income per common share from continuing operations.
Net assets at year-end.
Current-Cost Information (in constant dollars)
Income from continuing operations.
Income per common share from continuing operations.
Net assets at year-end.
Increases or decreases in the current cost amounts of inventory and property, plant, and equipment, net of inflation.
Other Information
Purchasing-power gain or loss on net monetary items.
Cash dividends declared per common share.
Market price per common share at year-end.

Level of the consumer price index used to measure income from continuing operations.

Explanations of the information disclosed and discussions of the significance of the information in the circumstances of the reporting enterprise.

In reviewing F.A.S.B. 33 after a five-year experimental period, the FASB issued F.A.S.B. 82 followed more recently by F.A.S.B. 89. In the former standard, the FASB eliminated the requirement for supplementary disclosure of historical-cost/constant-dollar information. Reasons underlying the decision were (a) elimination of confusion on the part of statement readers, (b) elimination of complexity, (c) reduction in the cost of compliance, and (d) the greater decision-utility of current-cost/constant-purchasing power information.

In its latest pronouncement, the FASB has decided to make the disclosure of changing prices information voluntary. Nevertheless, the Board encourages companies to account for changing prices owing to the distortive effects of inflation. A positive aspect of F.A.S.B. 89 is that it will enable reporting entities to account for changing prices in ways which best reflect their unique circumstances. ITT offers a useful reporting format for reporting changing prices information. It appears in Exhibit 9.

Foreign Operations.   Accounting for changing prices is especially relevant to foreign operations included in the consolidated statements of U.S. parent companies. In this regard, should the amounts of foreign subsidiaries and branches be adjusted for foreign inflation and then translated to U.S. dollars (restate-translate method)? Or, should they be translated to dollars and then adjusted for U.S. inflation (translate-restate method)?

The FASB considered the problem of consolidating the accounts of foreign subsidiaries domiciled in inflationary environments. At the time of its deliberations, F.A.S.B. 8, advocating the temporal method of foreign currency translation, was in effect. On this basis it concluded that the preferred method for achieving constant dollar measurements is first to translate foreign currency historical amounts into U.S. dollars in accordance with U.S. GAAP and then to restate the translated amounts for U.S. inflation. The translate-restate alternative was preferred because (*F.A.S.B. 33,* par. 192):

> The usefulness of constant dollar measurements is partly to provide information about the erosion of investors' purchasing power and the relevant measure of purchasing power for most investors in U.S. enterprises is the purchasing power of the U.S. dollar.

Current-cost measurements are to be translated to U.S. dollars at the current rate. Similar measurements presented in the five-year summary are to be presented in constant dollars (e.g., average-for-the-year constant dollars, end-of-year constant dollars or 1967 base-period dollars). These disclosure provisions are depicted schematically in Exhibit 10.

In light of F.A.S.B. 52, the FASB modified F.A.S.B. 33's reporting provisions to accommodate a local as well as a parent-company reporting perspective. These modifications are contained in F.A.S.B. 70.

To begin, F.A.S.B. 70 does not affect the reporting of supplementary inflation disclosures by enterprises adopting the U.S. dollar as functional for its foreign operations.

EXHIBIT 8 TEMPORAL METHOD OF TRANSLATION
(U.S. DOLLAR IS FUNCTIONAL CURRENCY)

	Foreign Currency	Exchange Rate	Dollar Equivalent
Balance Sheet Accounts			
Assets			
Cash	FC 1,000	$.18	$ 180
Accounts receivable	2,000	.18	360
Inventories	3,000	.19	570
Fixed assets	16,000	.17	2,720
Total	FC 22,000		$3,830
Liabilities and Stockholders' Equity			
Accounts payable	FC 4,800	.18	$ 864
Long-term debt	6,000	.18	1,080
Capital stock	4,000	.17	680
Retained earnings	7,200	a	1,206
Translation adjustment			
Total	FC 22,000		$3,830
Income Statement Accounts			
Sales	FC 20,000	.22	$4,400
Cost of Sales	11,900	c	2,732
Depreciation	2,000	.17	340
Other expenses	2,986	.22	656
Aggregate exchange gain (loss)		b	412
Income taxes	934	.22	206
Net income	FC 2,180		$ 878
Retained earnings 12/31/X1	6,400		632
Dividends	1,380	.22	304
Retained earnings, 12/31/X2	FC 7,200		$ 1,206

---

[a] See statement of income and retained earnings.

[b] 1. 12/31/X1 Monetary assets – monetary liabilities × change in current rate
    = FC 3,200 – FC 13,200 × (.18 – .23) = $500

2. Change in net monetary asset position:
   12/31/X1 FC (10,000)
   12/31/X2 FC (7,800)
   FC 2,200

Composition of change:
   Sources of monetary items × difference between year-end and average rate:
   Net earnings   FC 2,180
   Depreciation   FC 2,000
                   4,180 × (.18 – .22) = (168)
   Uses of monetary items × difference between year-end and average rate:
   Increase in inventories   FC 600
   Dividends   FC 1,380
                              1,980 × (.18 – .22) = $80
3. Aggregate translation adjustment: $500 – $168 + $80 = $412

[c] Beginning inventories   FC 2,400 at $.23 = $ 552
Purchases   FC 12,500 at $.22 = $2,750
Cost of goods available for sale $3,302
Ending inventories   FC 3,000 at $.19 = $ 570
Cost of sales $2,732

For these enterprises, the original provisions of F.A.S.B. 33 continue to apply. Firm's measuring a significant part of their operations in functional currencies other than the dollar are exempted from presenting historical-cost information measured in units of constant-purchasing power. Current-cost adjustments are to be measured in functional currencies (i.e., the foreign currency) while adjustments to current-cost data to reflect the effects of general inflation may be based on either the U.S. *or* foreign general price-level index. These provisions are summarized in Exhibit 11.

To illustrate the methodology that might be employed in calculating supplementary current cost information for a foreign subsidiary employing the local currency as its functional currency, comparative financial statements for Cruzado Corporation are presented in Exhibit 12. Relevant exchange rate and general price-level information appear in Exhibit 13. To simplify the illustration, Cruzado Corporation

EXHIBIT 9 ITTs INFLATION ACCOUNTING FORMAT
SUMMARY OF EFFECTS OF INFLATION (UNAUDITED)*

In Millions	Historic Cost (As reported)	Constant Purchasing Power	Current Cost	Current/ Constant
Reconciliation of Stockholders Equity December 31, 1982				
Inventories	$ 2,570	$ 2,693	$ 2,667	$ 2,724
Plant, property and equipment, net	5,172	8,321	8,507	8,690
Other assets (liabilities) less minority	(1,659)	(1,721)	(1,658)	(1,716)
Stockholders equity	6,083	9,293	9,516	9,698
Changes during 1983				
Income	675	290	209	209
Dividends declared	(408)	(408)	(408)	(408)
Other—including minority effect	46	44	44	47
Holding gains (losses)	—	509	460	(49)
Constant purchasing power adjustment	—	(509)	—	—
Purchasing power gain	—	106	—	106
Translation and parity adjustments	(290)	(380)	(455)	(414)
Total changes	23	(348)	(150)	(509)
December 31, 1983				
Inventories	2,322	2,329	2,440	2,386
Plant, property and equipment, net	5,022	7,790	8,151	7,973
Other assets (liabilities) less minority	(1,238)	(1,174)	(1,225)	(1,170)
Stockholders Equity	$ 6,106	$ 8,945	$ 9,366	$ 9,189
Results for 1983				
Sales and revenues	$20,249	$20,249	$20,249	
Cost of sales and services	10,221	10,330	10,274	
Depreciation	553	755	851	
Other costs and expenses	8,607	8,691	8,730	
Income taxes and minority equity	193	183	185	
Income	$ 675	$ 290	$ 209	

EXHIBIT 9 (*Continued*)

Comparative Data Adjusted for Inflation (Average 1983 dollars)	1983	1982	1981	1980	1979
Consumer price index—average for year	298.7	289.1	272.4	246.8	217.4
Sales and revenues—as reported	$20,249	$21,201	$22,386	$22,850	$21,215
—Constant purchasing power	20,249	21,905	24,547	27,655	29,149
Income**—as reported	675	572	685	668	608
—Constant purchasing power	290	103	247	76	495
—Current cost	209	97	264	277	488
Purchasing power gain on net monetary items	106	159	309	434	475
Holding gain net of inflation	(49)	(562)	(211)	(805)	(321)
Translation and parity adjustments					
—Constant purchasing power	(340)	(417)	(1,426)	(503)	153
—Current cost/constant purchasing power	(414)	(392)	(1,091)	(539)	77
Earnings per common equivalent share**					
—as reported	4.50	3.86	4.63	4.57	4.23
—Constant purchasing power	1.92	.67	1.65	.50	3.43
—Current cost	1.38	.64	1.76	1.88	3.37
Stockholders equity—as reported	6,106	6,083	6,084	6,324	6,015
—Constant purchasing power	8,945	9,333	9,812	11,313	10,908
—Current cost/constant purchasing power	9,189	9,698	10,804	12,208	12,136
Dividends declared per common share					
—as reported	2.76	2.70	2.62	2.45	2.25
—Constant purchasing power	2.76	2.79	2.87	2.97	3.09
Market price per common share at year end					
—as quoted	44.75	31.25	29.75	30.00	25.50
—Constant purchasing power	43.77	31.92	31.57	34.68	33.13

Source.

* As restated

** Exclusive of gain on sale of majority interest in U.K. subsidiary in 1982, Hartford tax settlement in 1981 (extraordinary item), and disposition of Canadian properties in 1980 and 1979.

EXHIBIT 10   RESTATEMENT METHODOLOGY FOR FOREIGN OPERATIONS

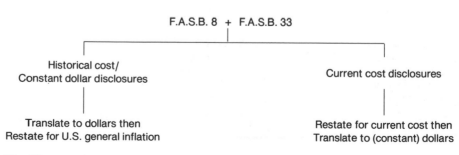

F.A.S.B. 8 + F.A.S.B. 33

Historical cost/
Constant dollar disclosures

Current cost disclosures

Translate to dollars then
Restate for U.S. general inflation

Restate for current cost then
Translate to (constant) dollars

EXHIBIT 11   RESTATEMENT METHODOLOGY FOR FOREIGN OPERATIONS

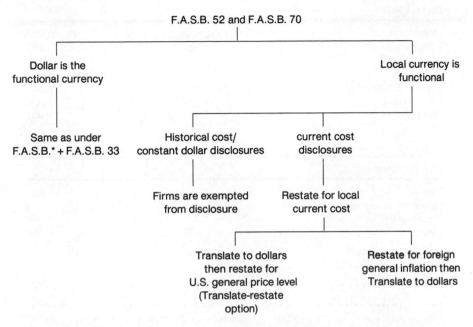

is assumed to have equipment but no inventory. The mechanics of calculating the current cost of inventory and goods sold are similar to that for equipment and depreciation.

Current-cost equity in nominal *cruzados* at the beginning and end of 19X7 is computed by adding net monetary items and equipment net of depreciation at current cost. Current-cost equity in nominal *dollars* is determined by translating the nominal cruzado balances by the average exchange rate. (See Exhibit 14.)

The Translate-Restate Method.   Under this method, amounts measured in current-cost nominal cruzados are first translated to dollars. These amounts are then restated for changes in the U.S. general price-level.

Current-cost depreciation for 19X7 may be calculated as follows:

Current cost—12/31/X6	Cr.	8,000
Current cost—12/31/X7		11,000
		19,000
		÷ 2
Average current cost, gross	Cr.	9,500
		× 10%
Current cost depreciation	Cr.	950

As an expedient, computing current-cost depreciation and current-cost based operating income need not involve the use of a general price-level index if the measurements

EXHIBIT 12 HISTORICAL COST FINANCIAL STATEMENTS OF CRUZEIRO CORPORATION (000,000's)

Balance Sheet	19X6	19X7
Cash	Cr. 2,500	Cr. 5,100
Equipment, net*	4,000	3,500
Total assets	Cr. 6,500	Cr. 8,600
Current liabilities	Cr. 1,000	Cr. 1,200
Long-term debt	3,000	4,000
Owners' equity	2,500	3,400
	Cr. 6,500	Cr. 8,600

Income Statement		
Revenue		Cr. 10,000
Operating expenses	Cr. 7,700	
Depreciation	500	
Other	900	9,100
Net income		900
Owners' equity—19X6		2,500
Owners' equity—19X7		Cr. 3,400

* Equipment was acquired on 12/31/X5 and is being depreciated straight line over 10 years. There were no asset acquisitions or disposals during the year.

EXHIBIT 13 RELEVANT PRICE DATA

Exchange Rates:		
12/31/X6	Cr. 4,400 = $1	
Average 19X7	Cr. 4,800 = $1	
12/31/X7	Cr. 5,290 = $1	

General Price Level Indexes:	Brazil	U.S.
12/31/X6	30,000	281.5
Average 19X7	32,900	292.5
12/31/X7	36,000	303.5

Current Cost of Equipment at Year End:	19X6	19X7
Current cost (000,000's)	Cr. 8,000	Cr. 11,000
Acc. depreciation	(1,600)	(3,300)
Net current cost	Cr. 6,400	Cr. 7,700

are made in average-for-the-year currency units. Accordingly, current-cost depreciation in constant dollars is found by multiplying depreciation expense in cruzados by the average exchange rate or 198 (Cr. 950 × 1/4,800). Current-cost based operating income in constant cruzados is determined by adding back historical-cost depreciation (Cr. 500) to as reported earnings (Cr. 900) and subtracting the current-cost equivalent computed above (Cr. 950) to yield Cr. 450. Current-cost based income in constant dollars is $94 (Cr. 450 × 1/4,800).

The change in the current cost of equipment net of general inflation is calculated next. To measure the increase in the current cost of equipment in nominal cruzados, the effect of any exchange rate change during the period must be excluded. This may be accomplished by translating beginning-of-period and end-of-period current-cost balances to dollars at the average exchange rate and then restating these dollar equivalents to constant dollars. This is illustrated below.

	Current Cost (Cr.)	Translate (Avg. Rate)	Current Cost ($)	Restate for U.S. Inflation	Current Cost/ Constant $'s
Current cost, net					
12/31/X6	Cr. 6,400 ×	$\frac{1}{4,800}$ =	$1,333 ×	$\frac{292.5}{281.5}$ =	$1,385
Depreciation	(950) ×	$\frac{1}{4,800}$ =	(198)	=	(198)
Current cost, net					
12/31/X7	7,700 ×	$\frac{1}{4,800}$ =	1,604 ×	$\frac{292.5}{303.5}$ =	1,546
	Cr. 2,250		$ 469		$ 359

Since depreciation is measured in constant cruzados, it is assumed to be expressed in constant dollars upon translation at the average exchange rate. In this example, the difference between the nominal dollar ($469) and constant-dollar equivalent ($359) is the inflation component of the equipment's current-cost increase.

As Cruzado Corporation maintained a net monetary liability position during the year (see Exhibit 14) it experienced a gain in general purchasing power. Calculation of this monetary gain follows.

	Cruzados	Avg. Ex. Rate	Dollars	Restate	Constant $'s
Net monetary liabilities					
12/31/X6	Cr. 1,500 ×	$\frac{1}{4,800}$ =	$312 ×	$\frac{292.5}{281.5}$ =	$324
Decrease during year	(1,400) ×	$\frac{1}{4,800}$ =	(292)	=	(292)
Net monetary liabilities					
12/31/X7	Cr. 100 ×	$\frac{1}{4,800}$ =	$ 21 ×	$\frac{292.5}{303.5}$ =	20
Monetary gain					$ 12

Translation of cruzado balances to U.S. dollars during a period when exchange rates have changed yields a translation adjustment (i.e., translation gain or loss). This translation adjustment is the amount necessary to reconcile beginning owner's equity with ending owner's equity in constant dollars. It may be calculated as follows:

Owners' equity—12/31/X6
(in average 19X7 constant dollars)

$$\$1,113 \quad \times \quad \frac{292.5}{281.5} \quad = \quad \$1,156$$

+	Current cost operating income	$ 94
+	Purchasing power gain	12
+	Increase in current cost of equipment, net of inflation	359

465
1,621
− Translation adjustment   (236)

= Owners' equity—12/31/X7
  (in average 19X7 constant dollars)

$$1,437 \quad \times \quad \frac{292.5}{303.5} \quad = \quad \$1,385$$

The Restate-Translate Method. Under this inflation-currency translation option, procedures similar to the translate-restate construct are followed. The major difference is that adjustments for general inflation are made in cruzados using Brazilian inflation indexes prior to translation to dollars.

Current-cost depreciation in cruzados and operating income are determined as before. For Cruzado Corporation these figures would be Cr. 950 and Cr. 450, respectively. The increase in the current cost of equipment net of inflation is determined by restating both the beginning-of-year and end-of-year equipment current-cost balances using appropriate Brazilian inflation indexes. Thus:

	Current Cost (Cr.)	Restate for Brazil's Inflation		Current Cost/ Constant Cruzados
Current cost, net				
12/31/X6	Cr. 6,400	$\times \dfrac{32,900}{30,000}$	=	Cr. 7,019
Depreciation	(950)			(950)
Current cost, net				
12,31/X7	7,700	$\times \dfrac{32,900}{36,000}$	=	7,037
	Cr. 2,250			Cr. 968

Cruzado Corporation's monetary gain, expressed in constant cruzados, is calculated thusly,

	Nominal Cruzados	Restate for Brazil's Inflation		Constant Cruzados
Net monetary liabilities				
12/31/X6	Cr. 1,500	$\times \quad \dfrac{32,900}{30,000}$	=	Cr. 1,645
Decrease during year	(1,400)			(1,400)
Net monetary liabilities				
12/31/X7	Cr. 100	$\times \quad \dfrac{32,900}{36,000}$	=	Cr. 91
Purchasing power gain				Cr. 154

Translation of current cost/constant curzado balance to U.S. dollars under the restate/translate option gives rise to a translation adjustment. This figure is determined below.

	Constant Cruzados	Translate	Dollar Equivalents of Constant Cruzados
Owners' equity—12/31/X6*			
Cr. 4,900 $\times \dfrac{32,900}{30,000}$ =	Cr. 5,374	$\times \dfrac{1}{4,400}$ =	$1,221
+ Current cost operating income	450	$\times \dfrac{1}{4,800}$ =	94
+ Purchasing power gain	154	$\times \dfrac{1}{4,800}$ =	32
+ Increase in current cost of equipment, net of inflation	968	$\times \dfrac{1}{4,800}$ =	202
			$1,549
− Translation adjustment			(236)
Owners' equity—12/31/X7*			
Cr. 7,600 $\times \dfrac{32,900}{36,000}$ =	Cr. 6,946	$\times \dfrac{1}{5,290}$ =	$1,313

* in avg. 19X7 constant cruzados

Parity adjustment.   In addition to the translation adjustment, the restate-translate method, per F.A.S.B. 70, requires the calculation of a *parity adjustment.* What accounts for this adjustment? Whereas the restate-translate method produces current cost/constant cruzado performance measures expressed in U.S. dollar equivalents, the five-year supplementary current cost disclosures require that these performance statistics be expressed in constant dollars (i.e., this reporting requirement in effect calls for a restate-translate-restate procedure). The parity adjustment represents the effect of differential inflation rates between the parent and host country on restating beginning and ending owners' equity to average currency units and reconciles the restate-translate disclosures to the translate-restate disclosures.

Under the translate-restate method, the increase in owner's equity in average *constant dollars* was $229 ($1,385 – $1,156). Under the restate-translate method, the increase in the *dollar equivalents* of owners' equity expressed in average *constant cruzados* was $92 ($1,313 – $1,221). The difference between these two amounts constitutes the parity adjustment of $137 ($229 – $92).

The notion of the parity adjustment is confusing and logically inconsistent. The FASB is cognizant of this and is in the process of preparing another pronouncement that will address this issue along with all other current-cost/constant-purchasing power disclosures.

THE INTERNATIONAL RESPONSE.   The worldwide nature of the problem of disclosing the effects of changing prices has led to active development of inflation-accounting proposals internationally. Some major developments are briefly sketched. Addresses of organizations that will provide further information are appended to each subsection.

International Accounting Standards Committee.   Established with the objective of harmonizing accounting standards internationally, the IASC has maintained an accommodating posture in the area of inflation accounting.

In November 1981, the IASC issued I.A.S.C. No. 15, "Information Reflecting the Effects of Changing Prices." This pronouncement, which supersedes I.A.S.C. No. 6, recommends that large publicly traded enterprises disclose the following information using any method that adjusts for the effects of changing prices:

1. The amount of the adjustment to, or the adjusted amount of, depreciation of property, plant, and equipment.
2. The amount of the adjustment to, or the adjusted amount of, cost of sales.
3. A financing adjustment(s), if such adjustment(s) is generally part of the method adopted for reporting information on changing prices.
4. The enterprise results recomputed to reflect the effects of the items described in (1) and (2) and, where appropriate, (3), and any other items separately disclosed that the method adopted requires.

If a current-cost method is adopted, the current cost of inventories and of property, plant, and equipment should be disclosed. Disclosure of methods used to compute the inflation adjustment is also required.

The information should be disclosed on a supplementary basis unless inflation-adjusted accounts constitute the basic financial statements. It should be provided in financial statements covering periods beginning on or after January 1, 1983. (*International Accounting Standards Committee, 3 St. Helen's Place, London EC3 6DN, England*)

Other International Accounting Organizations.   In an effort to harmonize financial disclosures among member countries of the European Economic Community (EEC), the EEC Commission issued its Fourth Directive in 1978. In the area of asset valuation, the directive retains the historical-cost principle as its basic valuation method. However, it allows member states to authorize the use of replacement-value measurements or other methods based on current or market values. Any differences between historical-cost valuations and replacement-cost or current-market valuations must be aggregated and separately disclosed as an item of "revaluation reserve" in Owners'

Equity. The summarized revaluation reserves must be disaggregated according to the main asset categories to which they pertain. (U.S. Office, 245 East 47th Street, New York, NY 10017)

The U.N. Group of Experts on International Standards of Accounting and Reporting (GEISAR), whose major aim is harmonizing the disclosure practices of transnational corporations, has not yet concerned itself with accounting measurement rules. In its 1977 report *International Standards of Accounting and Reporting for Transnational Corporations,* the U.N. group simply calls for the disclosure of accounting policies including overall valuation methods such as historical cost, replacement value, general price-level adjustments, or any other valuation basis. (Center on Transnational Corporations, United Nations, Box 20, Grand Central P.O., New York, NY, 10017)

The Organization for Economic Co-operation and Development (OECD), which serves as a policy forum for its 24 member nations, has thus far adopted a posture similar to that of the U.N. group. (U.S. office, Suite 1207, 1750 Pennsylvania Avenue, N.W., Washington, DC 20006)

The United Kingdom. In a development pattern paralleling that in the United States, the U.K. Accounting Standards Committee (ASC) issued Statement of Standard Accounting Practice No. 16 (SSAP 16), *Current Cost Accounting,* in March 1980. Effective for financial reporting periods beginning on or after January 1, 1980, the U.K. standard differs from F.A.S.B. 33 in two major respects. First, whereas the U.S. standard requires both constant-dollar and current-cost accounting, SSAP 16 adopts only the current-cost method for reporting. Second, whereas U.S. inflation adjustments have an income-statement focus, the U.K. current-cost statements must include both a current-cost income statement and balance sheet, together with explanatory notes. The U.K. standard may be complied with by

1. presenting current-cost accounts as the basic statements with supplementary historical-cost accounts, or
2. presenting historical-cost accounts as the basic statements with supplementary current-cost accounts, or
3. presenting current-cost accounts as the only accounts accompanied by adequate historical-cost information.

SSAP 16 applied to all listed companies and unlisted companies that satisfy any two of the following criteria: sales of £5 million or more, total assets of £2.5 million or more, and 250 or more employees.

Owing to its unpopularity, S.S.A.P. 16 was suspended in May 1985 and is now subscribed to on a voluntary basis. In an attempt to secure agreement on a long lasting form of accounting for changing prices, the ASC has issued another exposure draft, ED 38.

ED 38 applies only to companies whose shares are listed on a recognized stock exchange or traded in the unlisted securities market. Companies will be required to disclose by way of a footnote in their financial statements, an adjusted income statement explaining the difference between earnings as shown in the income statement and earnings computed after maintaining the capital of the company. The latter may be either defined as "financial capital" (i.e., the general purchasing power of shareholders' equity) or "physical capital" (i.e., productive capacity).

Two adjustments will have to be shown: a depreciation adjustment and a cost-of-sales adjustment. Other adjustments, such as a *monetary working capital* (MWCA) and *gearing* adjustment, may be made at the option of the directors. The MWCA recognizes the effect of specific price changes on the total amount of working capital (basically trade receivables less trade payables) employed by the business in its day to day operations. The gearing adjustment reduces the *total* of the adjustments made to reduce historical-cost based income for the higher cost equivalents of depreciation expense and cost of sales, including MWCA. Based on the ratio of total debt to total capitalization, the gearing adjustment acknowledges that it is unnecessary to recognize in the income statement the additional replacement cost of assets to the extent they are financed by debt.

Similar to F.A.S.B. 33, no balance sheet information need be presented. A five-year trend summary must be published restated in units of general purchasing power showing sales, adjusted earnings, adjusted earnings per share, and dividends per share.

Given the long exposure period, it is unlikely that a revised inflation accounting standard will be produced before 1987. It appears that an additional period of experimentation is under way in the United Kingdom. (Chartered Accountant's Hall, P.O., Box 433, Moorgate Place, London EC2P 2BJ, England)

Argentina. A 1972 pronouncement of the Argentine Technical Institute of Public Accountants now mandates, in certain provinces, that publicly held corporations with paid-in capital exceeding 5 million pesos present complete restatements of all nonmonetary items using a general price index. The supplemental information may be disclosed in (1) a second column in the basic financial statements, (2) footnotes to the basic statements, or (3) a complementary set of financial statements.

More recently (September 1980), the Argentina Professional Council of Economic Sciences of the Federal District, which regulates the public-accounting profession in Buenos Aires, declared that basic financial statements should, in the future, disclose historical-cost/constant-dollar figures in one column and historical-cost in another. (Federacion Argentina de Colegios de Graduados en Ciencias Economicas, Avenida Cordoba 1261, 2 Piso 1055, Buenos Aires, Argentina)

Australia. In the last quarter of 1983, the Australian Accounting Research Foundation issued SAPI which supersedes a provisional standard issued in 1976 and revised in 1978. Based on this pronouncement, all listed companies with total assets exceeding A$20 million and government businesses with assets over A$100 million are to introduce supplementary income statements and balance sheets reflecting current-cost adjustments for depreciation, cost of sales, and gains or losses on monetary items. Reporting entities may elect to present current-cost accounts as their primary statements. In this event, supplementary financial statements based on a historical-cost basis are required.

As a noteworthy development, sections of the public sector are warmly embracing current-cost accounting principles. As a leading example, the State of Victoria has issued guidelines for semi-commercial undertakings such as power, gas, and port facilities to achieve a real rate of return. In addition, the Department of Management and Budget recently circulated guidelines for the form and content of a state reporting act. These guidelines mention current-cost accounting as a requirement. (Australian Accounting Research Foundation, 49 Exhibition Street, Melbourne, Victoria 3000)

Belgium.   An October 1976 *Royal Decree on Financial Statements of Enterprises* permits use of current-cost data with respect to inventories, fixed assets, cost of goods sold, and depreciation in the basic financial statements by means of footnote disclosure. Valuation differences are to be charged or credited to a revaluation account. (Institut des Reviseurs d'Enterprises, Rue Caroly 17, 1040 Brussels, Belgium)

Brazil.   Under the new Brazilian corporation law, companies are required to adjust both permanent assets (land, buildings, equipment, deferred assets, and investments, including investments in subsidiaries and affiliated companies) and equity accounts (capital, reserves, and retained earnings) for changes in the general price level using the ORTN, a Brazilian government treasury bond index, as a deflator. Depreciation is also restated and netted against the asset adjustment. Price-level-adjusted depreciation is deductible for tax purposes.

Inflation adjustments for permanent assets and owners' equity are netted with the excess reflected directly in current income. A permanent asset adjustment that exceeds the equity adjustment is treated as a gain owing to the benefits of leverage, and conversely. While a loss stemming from the balance sheet adjustment is tax deductible, a gain is recognized in taxable income only to the extent that it exceeds exchange losses on foreign currency accounts and charges for monetary correction of certain accounts in local currency (e.g., long-term debt in Brazil is indexed for inflation). In Brazil, inflation adjusted statements are basic as opposed to supplementary. (Instituto dos Auditores Independentes do Brazil, Rua Antonia de Godoi, 83-16 Andar, Conjunto 161, São Paulo, Brazil)

Canada.   The Accounting Research Committee (ARC) of the Canadian Institute of Chartered Accountants (CICA) approved the inclusion of Section 4510 into the CICA Handbook—the guide for chartered accountants—detailing the accounting procedures to be followed by large publicly-held enterprises in Canada. While referencing constant-dollar information, the CICA recommendations, entitled, "Reporting the Effects of Changing Prices," emphasize current-cost adjustments. Applicable to large public companies with inventories and fixed assets of at least C$50 million or total assets of at least C$350 million, the recommendations call for supplementary disclosure of (a) the current cost of goods sold and depreciation expense, (b) a financing adjustment similar in nature to the U.K. gearing adjustment, (c) income attributable to shareholders on a current-cost basis, and (d) current and deferred taxation. Additional disclosures include (e) changes in the current-cost equivalents of inventory and property plant and equipment during the period, (f) changes in the foregoing attributed to general inflation, (g) purchasing power gains or losses on monetary items, and (h) the current-cost equivalent of property, plant, and equipment as well as net assets at year end.

Section 4510 is regarded as a five-year experiment in the presentation of supplementary information on changing prices. A comprehensive review of the section will be undertaken before 1988. (The Canadian Institute of Chartered Accountants, 250 Bloor Street East, Toronto M4W 1G5, Canada)

France.   Listed companies in France were required to reflect in their basic financial statements the current replacement costs of fixed assets in 1978. Asset-revaluation adjustments were to be disclosed in Stockholders' Equity. Mandated by the French Finance Acts of 1977 and 1978, the disclosures were restricted to fixed assets and did not take into account the effects of inflation on debt and cost of goods sold. The disclosure requirements were also limited to one year.

More recently, French accountants have been successful in initiating a dual reporting experiment among some 20 firms in various industrial sectors. The firms agreed to supplement their official historical-cost accounts with another indexed for inflation. Specifically, the replacement costs of ending inventories are being recalculated using a retail price index while cost of sales is being determined on a last-in, first-out (LIFO) basis. Depreciation and fixed assets are also being adjusted to their current-cost equivalents using appropriate indexes. Experiences gained during this experiment, soon to be expanded, are expected to provide the basis for formal legislation. (La Documentation Française, 31 Quai Voltaire, Paris)

Japan.   With the exception of the early 1950s, when land and certain depreciable assets were revalued by legislative initiative, valuation principles in Japan have been based on historical cost. Owing to accelerating rates of inflation, especially in the area of property values, the Japanese Institute of CPAs and the Business Accounting Deliberation Council are actively studying the issue. No formal pronouncement has yet been issued. However, a memorandum issued by the Corporate Accounting Council, an advisory body, in May 1980, recommends voluntary disclosure of financial information concerning price changes. This means that Japanese companies may start making such disclosures should the rate of inflation rise again in Japan. (The Japanese Institute of Certified Public Accountants, the Kabuki Building, 4-12-15, Ginza, Chuo-Ku, Tokyo, Japan)

The Netherlands.   Despite the absence of any formal requirements to do so, a generally accepted accounting principle in the Netherlands is the inclusion of current replacement value measurements in annual accounts. Larger Dutch companies especially carry certain inventory and depreciable fixed assets at their current replacement values with corresponding replacement-value-based depreciation and cost-of-sales expenses in income statements, and replacement-valuation "reserves" in the Owners' Equity section of balance sheets. (Netherlands Instituut van Registeraccountants, Mensinge 2, Postbus 7984, Amsterdam 1011, Netherlands)

New Zealand.   In March 1982, the New Zealand Society of Accountants issued *Current Cost Accounting Standard No. 1* (CCAS No. 1), "Information Reflecting the Effects of Changing Prices." Applicable to companies listed on the New Zealand Stock Exchange, the standard permits flexibility in the restatement approach which can be adopted. Although CCAS No. 1 states a preference for supplementary current-cost disclosures based on the maintenance of productive capacity concept, it also allows alternative disclosures incorporating features of both productive capacity and financial capital concepts of wealth preservation. (New Zealand Society of Accountants, Willbank House, 57 Willis Street, P.O. Box 11342, Wellington, New Zealand)

West Germany.   As a result of a 1975 accounting standard, public companies in West Germany are encouraged to supplement their basic financial statements with information disclosing the effect on earnings of cost of goods sold and depreciation restated to their replacement-cost equivalents. However, that portion of inventories and fixed assets that is considered to be financed by debt, as opposed to equity, is excluded in determining the effect on net earnings. (Institut der Wirschaftsprüfer in Deutschland e.V., 4 Düsseldorf 30, Cecilienallee 36, West Germany)

OTHER REPORTING ISSUES

CONSOLIDATED FINANCIAL STATEMENTS. Consolidated financial statements (or group accounts) result from the line-by-line combination of the assets, liabilities, revenues, and expenses of a parent company and its principal subsidiaries. Reciprocal accounts stemming from intercompany transactions are typically eliminated.

Purpose. Statement 3 of the IASC (1976) describes the purpose of consolidated statements thus:

> Certain parties with interests in the parent company of a group, such as present and potential shareholders, employees, customers, and in some circumstances creditors, are concerned with the fortunes of the entire group. Consequently, they need to be informed about the results of operations and the financial position of the group as a whole. This need is served by consolidated financial statements, which present financial information concerning the group as that of a single enterprise without regard for the legal boundaries of the separate legal entities.

The preparation of consolidated accounts is being required in more and more countries. Practices, however, are not yet uniform. The United States and Canada, for example, present only consolidated results in their annual reports. In many other countries separate parent-company statements are presented together with group accounts. German annual reports often become rather voluminous because they contain not only consolidated financial statements and separate statements for the parent company, but also separate financial statements for two or three major subsidiary companies. In some German reports a dual set of consolidated statements is presented—one that includes only domestic subsidiaries, the other both domestic and foreign.

Requirements for Consolidation. In the United States, professional support for consolidated financial statements is contained in Accounting Research Bulletin (ARB) No. 51, Chapter 12 of ARB No. 43, and, more recently, F.A.S.B. statement No. 94 (1987). Although these pronouncements do not mandate consolidation in all instances, companies and their auditors are compelled to justify nonconsolidation. Governmental provisions are contained in the SEC's Regulation S-X. Rule 4-02 of that regulation states:

> The registrant shall follow in the consolidated financial statements principles of inclusion or exclusion which will clearly exhibit the financial position and results of operations of the registrant and its subsidiaries.

Private-capital market institutions, the New York Stock Exchange in particular, require as a condition for listing the provision of consolidated accounts. A consolidated balance sheet and income statement is permitted in lieu of financial statements of the corporation as a whole and each majority-owned corporate subsidiary.

International interest in consolidation is also very evident today. In 1976 the International Accounting Standards Committee, whose membership currently spans 61 professional accountancy bodies from 47 countries, issued a formal standard recommending that

> a parent company should issue consolidated financial statements, except that it need not do so when it is a wholly owned subsidiary. . . . Investments in associated

companies. . . . and in subsidiaries which are not consolidated. . . . should be included in the consolidated financial statements under the equity method of accounting.

Three developments at the governmental level are especially noteworthy. In 1983, the EEC issued its Seventh Directive calling for the preparation of consolidated accounts where either the parent or subsidiary company is a limited liability company, regardless of the location of its registered office. Legal power of control determines the consolidation requirement. Control exists if the parent company satisfies any one of the following criteria:

1. Majority voting rights.
2. The right to appoint a majority of the board of directors.
3. The right to exercise dominant influence pursuant to a control contract.
4. Control over majority of voting rights pursuant to agreement with other shareholders.

There are specific exemptions for sub-group consolidations within the EEC. Grounds for non-consolidation include:

1. Undertakings that are of negligible importance.
2. Severe long-term restrictions on subsidiary operations.
3. Disproportionate expense or undue delay in consolidating affiliate accounts.
4. Shares of investee companies are held for resale.

National implementation of the Seventh Directive is obligatory by January 1, 1988, with mandatory application to consolidated financial statements for financial years beginning January 1, 1990. Member states are afforded wide latitude for optimal implementation details.

In 1976, the Organization for Economic Cooperation and Development (OECD) issued a set of guidelines for the conduct of multinational corporations operating within the jurisdictions of its 24 member countries. The accounting dimensions of these guidelines, entitled *Declaration on Investment in Multinational Enterprises,* call for the annual publication of financial statements to each enterprise as a whole. Supplementary disclosures on a consolidated basis are also entailed.

A third noteworthy development was the issuance of a report in 1982 by an Ad Hoc Intergovernmental Working Group of the United Nations detailing minimum disclosure items for general-purpose reporting by multinational companies. The recommendations, refinements of a proposal issued in 1977, are intended to improve the availability and comparability of information made available by multinational corporations to host-government and other user groups. As presently constituted, they call for the disclosure of both financial and nonfinancial information by the consolidated enterprise, including separate reports by the parent company and individual member companies of the group.

Consolidation Issues. Multinational enterprises encounter a number of problems when consolidating the accounts of both domestic and foreign subsidiaries. Translation and the effects of inflation, were discussed earlier. Additional problems stem from differences between foreign and U.S. accounting methods, intercompany transactions, questions related to appropriate consolidation criteria, and information content of consolidated statements.

Consolidation mechanics would be straightforward were it not for differences in measurement bases underlying foreign and domestic accounts. Thus adding fixed-asset and accumulated-depreciation balances of a 100-percent-owned Philippine subsidiary to those of its U.S. parent for consolidation purposes would not be proper if the Philippine accounts were restated for local inflation. Even if asset valuation principles were the same in both countries, the resulting additions could still mislead, as most Philippine companies do not estimate the residual value of an asset when calculating depreciation. Additional differences in fixed-asset measurement internationally include the following:

1. Capitalization of interest expense on funds borrowed to finance construction of fixed assets is permitted in many countries; not so in others.

2. Depreciation of fixed assets is not a generally accepted practice in all countries (e.g., several countries on the African continent).

3. Whereas many countries employ straight-line depreciation for financial reporting purposes and accelerated depreciation for tax purposes, countries such as Japan and Korea use accelerated-depreciation methods for both.

4. Required in most countries, disclosure of the valuation basis of fixed assets remains the exception in countries such as Austria, Greece, Japan, Italy, and Switzerland.

These accounting differences are not limited to fixed assets but permeate almost all financial statement accounts. As a result, there is now a serious effort to reduce international accounting diversity. A leading force in the accounting-harmonization movement is the IASC. Established in 1973, the IASC has since issued over two dozen definitive accounting standards with many more in process. (Topics covered by IASC standards issued thus far include disclosure of accounting policies, inventory valuation, consolidated financial statements, depreciation, information disclosure, statement of changes in financial position, unusual and prior-period items and changes in accounting policies, research and development, contingencies and post-balance sheet events, construction contracts, income taxes, and presentation of current assets and liabilities, segment disclosures, effects of changing prices, property, plant and equipment, leases, revenue recognition, retirement benefits, government grants, and changes in foreign exchange rates.) Complementing the IASC's efforts are those of the International Federation of Accountants (an organization aimed at promoting the development of a coordinated worldwide accounting profession), the U.N. GEISAR group, the OECD, and several regional accounting organizations.

Despite this progress, accounting diversity continues to characterize the international accounting scene. Adjustments of foreign accounting principles to a basis consistent with those of the reporting parent is therefore necessary prior to consolidating foreign with domestic accounts.

When consolidated statements are prepared, intercompany receivables, payables, sales, profits, and the like are generally eliminated to avoid double counting. Elimination of intercompany profits can be troublesome, especially where a minority interest exists in the subsidiary. Thus whenever profits arise from a sale by the parent to a partially owned subsidiary ("downstream" sales), a common practice is to eliminate 100 percent of the intercompany profit. Sales from a partially owned subsidiary to a parent ("upstream" sales) may be accounted for either in terms of (1) a 100 percent elimination by a charge against consolidated income or (2) an elimination to the extent of the parent company's ownership interest in the subsidiary. The usual practice here is also 100 percent elimination. A view gaining support in the United States, however, is that 100 percent elimination should only apply when intercompany transactions are not at arm's length. Otherwise intercompany profits should be eliminated in proportion to the parent's ownership interest in the subsidiary where the equity method of accounting is used (Accountants International Study Group, 1972).

Watt, Hammer, and Burge (1977) provide helpful insights on the issue of complete versus partial elimination of intercompany profits. They favor 100 percent elimination of profits on downstream sales as a matter of practicality. The partial elimination method, for example, would require a case-by-case analysis of each transaction to determine timely realization of the profit recognized. In their words,

> This would involve an analysis of the financial position of the investee, an evaluation of the influence of the minority interest and assurance that the parent did not force "sales" to the investee near the period end to develop consolidated income. The application of this procedure, therefore, becomes burdensome to the point of impracticality in companies having a multiplicity of investments and intercompany sales.

Partial recognition, however, is preferred for upstream sales in the case of a subsidiary with a minority interest. Complete elimination in this case will involve a double charge against consolidated income; one for the minority interest's share in the profit of the selling subsidiary, and another in connection with the consolidating entry that eliminates the entire intercompany profit. Although the foregoing practice may not have a significant effect on reported earnings in any one year, the cumulative effect on consolidated results could. According to Watt et al.,

> The cost of the assets in consolidation should include the profit which accrues to the minority interest in a subsidiary on sales to the parent. This is a properly recognized cost element which the parent incurs as a result of the lack of complete ownership of the subsidiary, that is, using the capital of the minority interest. Moreover, an investor company brings into its income only its share of the profit reported by the investee on the intercompany transaction and that amount is all that should be eliminated. Income taxes, or the appropriate portion paid on intercompany sales, should be included in the cost of the asset that remains in the consolidation.

Consolidation criteria are called for when deciding whether or not to include the accounts of an associated company in consolidated results. An accepted consolidation prerequisite in many national jurisdictions is control over investee companies by the investor. Unfortunately, different interpretations exist as to what constitutes "control." In the United States, control is presumed to exist when 50 percent or more of the outstanding voting stock of an investee is owned by the parent (APB Opinion No. 18, par. 3). That this criterion is popular is evidenced by its embracement in International Accounting Standard 3, *Consolidated Financial Statements* (IASC, 1976). IAS 3, however, also acknowledges other interpretations of control, as follows:

> A company in which a group does not have control, but in which a group:
>   (a) owns more than half the equity capital, but less than half the voting power, or
>   (b) has the power to control, by statute or agreement, the financial and operating policies of the management of the company, with or without more than one half of

the equity interest, may be treated as a subsidiary and consolidated in the consolidated financial statements. In such circumstances, the reasons for consolidating the company should be disclosed.

The tenor of these provisions find expression in the EEC's Seventh Directive. In this document, control is associated with the power to exercise such dominant influence over group members that all related undertakings are managed on a central and unified basis. Hence the *power of control* is emphasized over the actual *exercise of control*. Based on these criteria, requiring horizontal consolidation of all entities operating within the EEC subject to a determined "dominant influence" is a member state option. For most MNC's this would mean at least one subconsolidation on a geographic basis. Such subconsolidation may include not only incorporated enterprises, but also partnerships, joint ventures or other forms of business organization.

Reasons justifying nonconsolidation of subsidiaries include the following:

1. Parent-company control is likely to be temporary.
2. Business activities of the subsidiary are so dissimilar to those of the parent that combined financial statements would not be meaningful (e.g., when finance companies are subsidiaries of industrial companies).
3. Host-government restrictions impair parent-company control (e.g., currency-exchange restrictions and the like).
4. Foreign accounts are insignificant in terms of amounts involved.

Surveys of corporate reporting practices suggest that exclusion of subsidiaries where parental control is temporary or that are not material is common. The problem here is that definitions as to what constitutes "temporary" or "material" for purposes of inclusion in group accounts often differ from country to country. In some instances, the concepts may not be defined at all.

While foreign restrictions on profit remittances are frequently cited as justification for exclusion, counter-arguments appear equally persuasive. Thus, restrictions on profit remittances alone may not constitute grounds for assuming that operational control is lacking. Indeed, the existence of funds available for dividends is itself an indication of successful operations. In highly industrialized countries, dividend restrictions often exist due to bond indentures, loan terms and government regulations. Yet, these factors seldom result in the exclusion of a domestic subsidiary from consolidation. Moreover, foreign profits may be remitted by indirect means such as transfer pricing, technical service fees and the like.

Opinions also differ on the matter of homogeneity of operations. Those arguing for exclusion from consolidation of dissimilar businesses point out that consolidations would impair the meaningfulness of the statements. On the other hand, the practice of not consolidating subsidiaries in lines of business that are different from the parent (e.g., finance and insurance subsidiaries) is increasingly criticized for obscuring the assets and liabilities of the group (Neuhausen, 1982).

Obtaining off-balance sheet financing by removing the subsidiary's debt from the consolidated balance sheet is a case in point. Many companies, for example, establish unconsolidated finance subsidiaries to purchase credit card receivables or installment receivables from the parent company. When this occurs, the receivables (economic resources) and associated debt (claims to those resources) disappear from the consolidated balance sheet. Yet, the parent company continues to control the receivables through its control of the subsidiary, and the parent often provides direct or indirect guarantees of the subsidiary's debt that obligate the parent to see that the debt is extinguished. The growing practice of disclosing segmental information by lines of business lessens any disadvantages of consolidating dissimilar businesses. Under F.A.S.B. No. 94, U.S. parent companies must now consolidate a majority-owned subsidiary even if it has "nonhomogeneous" operations.

Companies electing not to consolidate the accounts of foreign subsidiaries may account for these investments under one of two methods: cost or equity. Under the *cost* method, an investment in the securities of a foreign investor is recorded at cost. The parent company subsequently recognizes income from such an investment only to the extent that dividends are distributed by the investee (save for international tax considerations). Dividends received, however, may bear little relation to the actual performance of the investee, as dividends may be distributed to suit the income or cash needs of the parent.

To remedy this, more countries are requiring adoption of the *equity* method. Here the carrying value of the investee is adjusted to reflect the investor's proportionate share of the investee's profits or losses. Dividends received from an investee are treated, in turn, as reductions in the carrying value of the parent-company's investment.

While many countries are still struggling to adopt consolidation procedures, others are beginning to question the information utility of such procedures. To begin, consolidated statements depict a different set of relationships today than they did when they were first prepared. Around the turn of the century, most parent companies held 100 percent of the stock of their subsidiaries. There were no taxes on corporate incomes or distributions and holding companies and subsidiaries were considered separate legal entities. Under these circumstances, it was reasonable to regard consolidated statements as a representation of the affairs of the holding company. Today, consolidated statements often incorporate the results of subsidiaries that are less than wholly-owned. Accordingly, consolidated statements no longer depict the resources that are equitably owned by a homogenous group of shareholders. In addition, consolidated statements are prepared in a different accounting context than they were some 70 years ago. Over the years, significant changes have occurred in the conduct of business and in institutional arrangements. A variety of factors have also encouraged businesses to organize their affairs through a complex web of subsidiaries further reinforcing the need to re-evaluate consolidated reporting (Walker, 1976).

Perhaps the most compelling argument against consolidation relates to economic reality. To quote one writer:

> The entire process of consolidating the worldwide accounts of every multinational company can be criticized from the standpoint of rational behavior. So many assumptions go into the translation and consolidation process that the results are sometimes more a tribute to the ingenuity of the accountants than they are a measure of the achievements of the management. Stockholders looking for the amount of their dividend coverage will not find it in the consolidated statements of a company doing business in Indonesia or Argentina. Stockholders in a U.S.-denominated company expect a certain portion of the profits to be distributed to them, and who can say this expectations is irrational? But if the profits are locked in a foreign country with inflation measured in triple digits and with the inevitable exchange controls that accompany such inflation, real doubt exists that such profits should really be considered profits to U.S. shareholders (Hill, 1982).

As the previous quote suggests, consolidated financial statements of transnational corporations are such a conglomeration of restatements, translations, adjustments, eliminations and allocations that the economic reality of these statements has become a question of considerable substance. One reason for the existing turmoil surrounding MNC consolidations is the absence of a clear concept of what constitutes a transnational business entity. Do host country interests and controls extend far enough to invalidate the possibility of a single homogeneous worldwide business entity? To what limits can one reasonably push the notion of a single unique reporting currency to cover any and all events and transactions? If accounting standards and practices influence management decisions, how realistic is it to restate summary data prepared on the basis of one set of accounting rules to an arbitrarily selected different set, and retain the original information content of the data?

The problem of defining an appropriate reporting entity is so troublesome that the U.S. Financial Accounting Standards Board decided to re-examine the whole issue of consolidation reporting. The first stage of the FASB's consolidation accounting project develops the concept of a reporting entity and related conceptual matters, including the role of control in determining the boundaries of a reporting entity. The second stage addresses specific accounting policy issues by applying those concepts to problems identified in practice.

The Board has concluded that (a) the boundaries of a reporting entity should be determined on the basis of a parent company's control of a subsidiary's operating and financing policies and (b) all subsidiaries that qualify as components of the same reporting entity as their parent should be included in consolidated financial statements.

FOREIGN-OPERATIONS DISCLOSURE. The growth and geographic spread of business operations has stimulated public demand for information on a reporting enterprise's foreign operations. Proponents of such disclosures argue that consolidated statements, although desirable for their synergistic insights, do not allow investors and other financial analysts to assess the relative importance of foreign segments which experience patterns of profitability, growth, and risk that often differ from aggregate trends. Some express concern that foreign-operations disclosures may (1) harm a reporting company's competitive position, (2) be too detailed for general-purpose financial statements, or (3) confuse the reader. Others feel they are no more onerous than information currently provided in conventional accounting reports.

Arguments notwithstanding, there is today a push at both national and international levels to require more disclosure of a firm's foreign operations, which are viewed as useful supplements to consolidated information.

Reporting Requirements. Foreign-operations disclosure requirements are commonly treated in conjunction with reporting for business segments. In the United States, F.A.S.B. 14, *Financial Reporting for Segments of a Business Enterprise* (issued December 1976), is the authoritative pronouncement on such disclosures. In addition to information concerning industry segments, the statement requires separate information disclosure for an enterprise's foreign operations, which can be done in an aggregate fashion, or, if appropriate, by geographic area. This requires, however, that foreign operations contribute 10 percent or more of consolidated revenue, or the assets identifiable with the foreign operations must be 10 percent or more of consolidated assets. Excluding unconsolidated subsidiaries and investees, a foreign operation is defined as a revenue-producing operation located outside the United

States (for U.S. enterprises) that generates revenue either from sales to unaffiliated customers or from intercompany sales or transfers between geographic areas. Information sought by F.A.S.B. 14 for foreign operations includes the following:

1. Revenue, with separate disclosure of (a) sales to unaffiliated customers, (b) sales or transfers between geographic areas, and (c) transfer-pricing bases used.
2. Operating income, net income, or some other measure of profitability in between, as long as a consistent measure is used for all geographic areas.
3. Identifiable assets.

ARS No. 236 was issued by the U.S. Securities and Exchange Commission in 1978 to conform its earlier line of business reporting rules with F.A.S.B. 14. Now all SEC filings must contain revenue, income, and identifiable-assets information for foreign operations as required in F.A.S.B. 14.

Foreign-operations disclosure provisions, similar to those of F.A.S.B. 14, are also contained in *IAS 14*. IAS 14's intended purpose is "to enable users of financial statements to assess the effect that operations in different industries and in different geographical areas may have on the enterprise as a whole."

Governmental interest in foreign-operations disclosure stems from their concern over the economic and social effects of multinational corporation operations on the countries concerned, irrespective of the relative importance of such operations for the transnational corporation as a whole. Accordingly, the EEC, OECD, and United Nations have also joined the disclosure bandwagon. The EEC's Fourth Directive requires that sales be disaggregated by categories of activity and geographic markets to the extent that these categories and markets differ substantially from one another. The OECD's *Guidelines for Multinational Enterprises* include the following pertinent disclosure provisions:

1. The geographic areas where operations are carried out and the principal activities carried on therein by the parent company and the main affiliates.
2. The operating results and sales by geographic area and the sales in major lines of business for the enterprise as a whole.
3. Significant new capital investment by geographic area and, as far as practicable, by major lines of business for the enterprise as a whole.
4. The average number of employees in each geographic area.
5. The policies followed in respect of intragroup pricing.
6. The accounting policies, including those on consolidation, observed in compiling the published information.

Disclosures recommended by the U.N. Group of Experts on International Standards of Accounting and Reporting are set forth in Exhibit 15. Disclosure items listed there pertain to the enterprise as a whole. Similar provisions also apply to individual member companies of the multinational parent as well.

Policy Issues.   Policy decisions are required in at least three basic areas of foreign-operations reporting. The first concerns identification of the geographic segment(s) to be reported, on the premise that operations in different parts of the world may be

**EXHIBIT 14 CURRENT COST EQUITY IN NOMINAL
CRUZEIROS (000's) AND DOLLARS**

| | December 31 | | | | | |
| | 1983 | | | 1984 | | |
	Cr.	Ex. Rate	$	Cr.	Ex. Rate	$
Cash	Cr. 2,500	1/4,400	$ 568	Cr. 5,100	1/5,290	$ 964
Current liab.	(1,000)	1/4,400	(227)	(1,200)	1/5,290	(227)
LT-debt	(3,000)	1/4,400	(682)	(4,000)	1/5,290	(756)
Net monetary liab.	Cr. (1,500)		$ (341)	Cr. (100)		$ (19)
Equipment (net)	6,400	1/4,400	1,454	7,700	1/5,290	1,456
Equity at current cost	Cr. 4,900		$1,113	Cr. 7,600		$1,437

subject to different degrees of risk or profit opportunities. Although this operating characteristic provides a conceptual basis for identifying geographic areas, operationalizing the concept is difficult. Thus a U.S. subsidiary located in the Far East (e.g., Taiwan) may generate the bulk of its revenues from exports to the EEC. The appropriate geographic classification, assuming the Taiwanese operation is significant, is unclear. Whereas the foreign operation's revenue source may be in Europe, its political-risk complexion may be colored by its Far East location. Environmental risk, in turn, may change over time, often abruptly. Unfortunately, little help is provided by standard setters in suggesting appropriate geographic categories.

F.A.S.B. 14 offers the following guidance:

> For purposes of this statement, foreign geographic areas are individual countries or groups of countries as may be determined to be appropriate in an enterprise's particular circumstances. . . . Each enterprise shall group its foreign operations on the basis of the differences that are most important in its particular circumstances. Factors to be considered include proximity, economic affinity, similarities in business environments, and the nature, scale, and degree of interrelationship of the enterprise's operations in the various countries.

Guidance offered by international organizations such as the IASC and OECD are similarly phrased.

In a recent unpublished disclosure survey (Exhibit 16), geographical classifications employed by both U.S. and non-U.S. multinationals were subjectively ranked in decreasing order of informativeness. Despite within-group variances, most European companies employed geographical classifications that were considered informative. As a region, approximately 77 percent of European-based MNC's presented geographic categories either in terms of (a) individual countries, (b) individual countries and regions, separately disclosed, or (c) individual regions. In contrast, only 68 percent of American multinationals and 47 percent of Japanese MNC's employed similar categories. In the absence of more specific institutional guidance, geographic classifications must necessarily rely on subjective interpretations of existing guidelines.

Other segmental disclosure problems relate to (a) materiality criteria and (b) corporate allocations. Regarding the former, a particular geographic area per F.A.S.B. 14 is considered a separate reporting unit if area revenues from sales to unaffiliated customers or identifiable assets are 10 percent or more of worldwide totals. In addition

EXHIBIT 15   UN's FOREIGN OPERATIONS DISCLOSURE PROPOSALS

Segment and Disclosure Geographically:
Sales to unaffiliated customers
Transfers to other geographical area (eliminated in consolidation)
Operating results, such as profit before general corporate expenses, interest expense, taxes on
    income and unusual items
(Does not prohibit segmenting net income as well)

To the Extent Identifiable with a Geographic Area, Disclose:
Total assets or net assets or total assets and total liabilities, and at least:
    Property, plant and equipment, gross
    Accumulated depreciation
    Other long-term assets
New investment in property, plant and equipment
Describe principal activities in each geographical area or country
Disclose the basis of accounting for transfers between areas or countries
Disclose exposure to exceptional risks of operating in other countries
Comments: (1) Preference is expressed for segmenting assets according to the location of the
                assets and not necessarily the location of the records, and attributing revenue
                to the geographical area of the last significant value added by operations.
           (2) Amounts disclosed should aggregate to the total of the item shown in the
                consolidated financial statements, or reconciling amounts should be given.

Segment and Disclose by Line of Business
Sales to unaffiliated customers
Transfers to other lines of business (eliminated in consolidation)
Operating results, such as profit before general corporate expenses, taxes on income and
    unusual items
    (Does not prohibit segmenting net income as well)

To the Extent Identifiable with a Line of Business, Disclose:
Total assets or net assets or total assets and total liabilities, and at least:
    Property, plant and equipment, gross
    Accumulated depreciation
    Other long-term assets
Net investment in property, plant and equipment
Describe the principal products and services in each line of business
Disclose the basis of accounting for transfers between lines of business
Note: Amounts disclosed should aggregate to the total of the item shown in the consolidated
          financial statements or reconciling amounts should be given.

Source.   United Nations Center on Transnational Corporations, *Towards International Standardization of Corporate Accounting and Reporting* (New York: UNCTC, 1982), pp. 72–74.

to being completely arbitrary, the 10 percent criterion could suppress useful risk and
return disclosure by limiting the number of segments reported on. Under the 10 percent rule, a company whose multinational operations comprise less than 30 percent of
group totals is limited to two geographic segments; one, if multinational operations
are less than 20 percent. Exhibit 16 indicates that U.S. companies limit the number of
geographic reporting categories to 3.2 on the average. In contrast, the average for
Europe as a whole is 5.8 categories. Swedish companies are the best performers in this
respect, reporting 10.6 geographic categories on average. Companies wishing to emphasize the geographic breadth of their foreign operations would do well to increase

the number of their geographic partitions in the fashion of the Clark Equipment Company. Since 1977, Clark has reported at least five geographic areas, even though some segments do not meet the 10 percent materiality criterion.

In requiring disclosure of foreign operations' profitability by significant geographic areas, paragraph 10*d* of F.A.S.B. 14 requires that "operating expenses incurred by an enterprise that are not directly traceable to specific geographic areas should be allocated on a reasonable basis among those reporting segments." To the extent that such expense allocations are arbitrary, disclosed operating results will vary in their objectivity and relevance. Reporting entities must thus decide whether to (1) further improve upon the information being provided, or (2) in the absence of any theoretically correct or cost-efficient solution, alert statement readers to the data's limitations. Until further experience is gained on reporting foreign operations, the latter alternative, perhaps by means of a cautionary note, would appear to be a logical expedient.

TRANSNATIONAL FINANCIAL REPORTING.   The sale of corporate securities in foreign and international capital markets raises additional reporting problems for multinational companies, who must often report the results of operations and financial position to audiences of interest unfamiliar with the language, currency framework, accounting principles, auditing standards, and general business milieu of the reporting enterprise. Under these circumstances, the challenge is effective communication of intended messages to foreign readers. Failure might mean higher capital costs and other disadvantages.

Reporting Requirements.   At present, little formal attention has been accorded the transnational-reporting dimension. As a condition for listing their shares on the major U.S. securities exchanges, foreign companies must conform to the financial-reporting requirements of the SEC. In seeking comparability in financial statements issued to U.S. investors, the Commission permits, with certain exceptions, foreign issuers to prepare their financial statements in accordance with accounting principles generally accepted in their home countries. Any material differences between the foreign and U.S. generally accepted accounting principles must be reconciled by way of footnotes to U.S. GAAP. Although aware of it, the FASB chose to disregard the problem of transnational reporting in F.A.S.B. 52. With the exception of foreign disclosures, international accounting organizations have also been silent on the subject of reporting to foreign audiences of interest.

In the absence of enforceable transnational accounting and reporting norms, one must look to existing practice for guidance. Four distinguishable approaches are described next (Choi and Mueller, 1984).

Convenience Translations.   Many reporting entities continue to send copies of their *primary* financial statements to foreign readers, prepared in terms of the language, currency, accounting, and auditing framework of the reporting company's country of domicile. But many large multinationals in the United States and Europe with foreign shareholders regularly publish their annual reports in as many as six foreign languages. Japanese companies go a step further. In addition to language translations, companies such as Fujitsu Ltd. present monetary expressions in parallel columns, for example, Japanese yen and U.S. dollars when reporting to American readers.

EXHIBIT 15 FOREIGN OPERATIONS DISCLOSURES BY MULTINATIONAL CORPORATIONS—GEOGRAPHIC AREA DISCLOSURES, BY SELECTED COUNTRIES

Disclosure Item	European						North American		
	United Kingdom (N = 58)	West Germany (N = 28)	France (N = 13)	Netherlands (N = 9)	Sweden (N = 13)	Switzerland (N = 11)	United States (N = 94)	Canada (N = 11)	Japan (N = 34)
Foreign sales	93%	90%	87%	89%	100%	91%	100%	100%	65%
Sales by geographic areas	93	71	87	67	100	91	86	91	29
Foreign income	74	7	87	33	23	0	98	73	12
Income by geographic areas	67	0	40	22	23	0	84	64	0
Foreign assets	19	10	40	22	31	18	92	91	15
Assets by geographic areas	17	0	13	22	15	18	85	46	3
Exports from home country	78	61	13	11	62	10	25	27	53
Exports by geographic areas	14	10	0	0	8	0	5	18	21
Capital expenditures: foreign	19	36	20	33	39	46	15	9	15
Capital expenditures by geo. areas	19	23	20	33	15	46	11	9	3
Avg. no. of geo. areas reported	6.3	3.5	4.1	4.6	10.6	5.8	3.2	4.0	3.9

Source. F.D.S. Choi "A Cross-National Assessment of Management's Geographic Disclosures."

Although *convenience* translations lend an international appearance to primary statements and may offer some public-relations benefits, they may also mislead. For example, English language and/or U.S. dollar translations of Japanese financials often give the American reader the impression that the accounting principles underlying the convenience statements have been translated as well. If such is not the case, erroneous conclusions can be drawn. This problem may be minimized by disclosures that specifically identify the national accounting principles and auditing standards underlying convenience statements.

Special Information.   A small number of companies, notably those from Sweden, have made an effort to explain to foreign readers the major accounting principles behind their annual reports. Thus a company like Beijerinvest makes available to its U.S. readers an English language edition of its annual report, along with a little pamphlet explaining Swedish accounting principles employed. This practice, unfortunately, presumes that the foreign reader possesses accounting expertise and is able to quantitatively reconcile disclosed accounting differences. This is seldom the case.

Limited Restatements.   A partial remedy to the reconciliation problem just described is used by several Netherlands-based multinationals. For instance, in addition to language translations, the Philips Company estimates what earnings adjustments would be required if accounting principles generally accepted in the United States rather than in the Netherlands were followed. A direct result is that Dutch investors see earnings and per-share numbers that are consistent with local accounting practices, while their U.S. counterparts are at least provided with earnings numbers that are readily understood and can be used comparatively. The disadvantage of partial restatements are fairly obvious; that is, rate-of-return comparisons are hardly meaningful when earnings restated to U.S. GAAP are compared with total assets and other financial-statement categories that reflect Dutch accounting norms.

Primary-Secondary Statements.   In a 1975 study entitled *International Financial Reporting,* the Accountant's International Study Group (1975), which has since disbanded, recommends that two kinds of financial statements be recognized as part of a country's official set of generally accepted accounting principles. *Primary* financial statements, as previously defined, would be prepared for a reporting company's domestic readers. *Secondary* financial statements would be prepared specifically for foreign readers. These statements would reflect one or more of the following characteristics:

1.   The language of the reader's country of domicile.
2.   The currency of the foreign country.
3.   The accounting principles of the foreign country.
4.   The auditing standards of the foreign country.

An alleged advantage of the primary-secondary reporting system is that it accommodates more than a single set of accounting and reporting standards. In doing so, full recognition is afforded different national viewpoints. Tailoring published corporate reports to specific readership groups also eliminates the generalized traditional reporting formats, resulting in information more germane to user decisions.

But aside from considerations of production cost, the issuance of secondary statements can prove to be misleading. If one accepts the proposition that accounting principles are shaped by a particular social, economic, and legal environment, and that national accounting environments differ, translation of financial statements from one set of accounting principles to another could distort the original message. Even if accounting principles between two countries are similar, business and financial mores that affect the interpretation of accounting-based financial statement ratios may vary internationally. This could lead to further message distortion. As an example, high debt ratios, viewed with alarm in the United States, are an accepted part of the business scene in Japan.

Shortcomings of the AISG proposal can be remedied by footnote disclosure of the main differences between accounting principles of the reporting company's and reader's countries of domicile, together with their effect on net income and financial position. Environmental disclosures that assist foreign readers in properly interpreting secondary-statement information (i.e., financial ratios) should also be disclosed. Several Japanese companies have begun to provide such disclosures in their registration filings with the U.S. SEC as a result of past misunderstandings.

SOURCES AND SUGGESTED REFERENCES

Accountants International Study Group. *Consolidated Financial Statements*. New York: AISG, 1972.

———. *International Financial Reporting*. New York: AISG, 1975.

Accounting Standards Committee. *Current Cost Accounting*. Statement of Standard Accounting Practice No. 16. London: ASC, 1980.

American Institute of Certified Public Accountants, Committee on Accounting Procedure. "Restatement and Revision of Accounting Research Bulletins," in *Foreign Operations and Foreign Exchange*. Accounting Research Bulletin No. 43, Chapter 12, New York: AICPA, 1953.

American Institute of Certified Public Accountants. *Status of Accounting Research Bulletins*. Accounting Principles Board Opinion No. 6. New York: AICPA, 1965.

Arthur Young. *Financial Reporting and Changing Prices: A Survey of How 300 Companies Complied with FAS 33*. New York: Arthur Young, August 1980.

Business International Corporation. *Coping with Worldwide Accounting Changes*. New York: BI, 1984.

Choi, F.D.S., *et. al.* "Analyzing Foreign Financial Statements: The Use and Misuse of International Ratio Analysis," *Journal of International Business Studies,* (Spring-Summer 1983), pp. 113–31.

——— and G.G. Mueller. *International Accounting*. Englewood Cliffs, NJ: Prentice-Hall, 1984.

——— and G.G. Mueller. *Frontiers of International Accounting: An Anthology*. Ann Arbor, MI. University Microfilms International, 1985.

——— and A. Sondhi. "FAS No. 52 and the Funds Statement," *Corporate Accounting,* (Spring, 1984), pp. 46–56.

Dukes, R. *An Empirical Investigation of the Effects of Statement of Financial Accounting Standards No. 8 on Security Return Behavior.* Stamford, CT: Financial Accounting Standards Board, 1978.

"EEC Proposed Seventh Directive," *EEC Bulletin,* Supplement, September (1976).

Financial Accounting Standards Board. "Accounting for the Translation of Foreign Currency Transactions and Foreign Currency Financial Statements." *Statement of Financial Accounting Standards No. 8.* Stamford, CT: FASB, 1975.

Financial Accounting Standards Board. "Financial Reporting for Segments of a Business Enterprise." *Statement of Financial Accounting Standards No. 14.* Stamford, CT: FASB, 1976.

Financial Accounting Standards Board. "Financial Reporting and Changing Prices," *Statement of Financial Accounting Standards No. 33.* Stamford, CT: FASB, 1979.

Financial Accounting Standards Board. "Foreign Currency Translation." *Statement of Financial Accounting Standards No. 52.* Stamford, CT: FASB, 1981.

Financial Accounting Standards Board. "Financial Reporting and Changing Prices: Foreign Currency Translation." *Statement of Financial Accounting Standards No. 70.* Stamford, CT: FASB, 1982.

Financial Accounting Standards Board. "Financial Reporting and Changing Prices: Elimination of Certain Disclosures." *Statement of Financial Accounting Standards No. 82.* Stamford, CT: FASB, 1984.

Financial Accounting Standards Board. "Financial Reporting and Changing Prices," *Statement of Financial Accounting Standards No. 89.* Stamford, CT: FASB, 1986.

Financial Accounting Standards Board. "Consolidation of All Majority-owned Subsidiaries," *Statement of Financial Accounting Standards No. 94.* Stamford, CT: FASB, 1987.

Fitzgerald, R.D., A.D. Stickler, and T.R. Watts. *International Survey of Accounting Principles and Reporting Practices.* New York: Price Waterhouse International, 1979.

H.P. Hill. "Rational Expectations and Accounting Principles." *Journal of Accountancy.* (April 1982), p. 44.

Institute of Chartered Accountants in England and Wales. "The Accounting Treatment of Major Changes in the Sterling Parity of Overseas Currencies," in ICAEW. *Member's Handbook, Statement N25.* London: ICAEW, 1968.

International Accounting Standards Committee. "Accounting For the Effects of Changes in Foreign Exchange Rates." *International Accounting Standard 2.* London: IASC, 1983.

International Accounting Standards Committee. "Reporting Financial Information by Segment." *International Accounting Standard 14.* London: IASC, 1981.

International Accounting Standards Committee. "Information Reflecting the Effects of Changing Prices." *International Accounting Standard 15.* London: IASC, 1981.

International Accounting Standards Committee. "Consolidated Financial Statements." *International Accounting Standard 3,* London: IASC, 1976.

Lafferty, M., D. Cairns, and J. Carty. *1979 Financial Times Survey of 100 Major European Companies' Reports and Accounts.* London: Financial Times, 1979.

Lees, F.A. *Reporting Transnational business Operations,* Washington, DC: The Conference Board, 1980.

Neuhausen, Benjamin S. "Consolidation and the Equity Method—Time for Overhaul." *Journal of Accountancy.* (February 1984), pp. 54–56.

Organization for Economic Cooperation and Development. *International Investment and Multinational Enterprises: Accounting Practices in OECD Member Countries.* Paris: OECD, 1980.

Organization for Economic Cooperation and Development. *International Investment and Multinational Enterprises,* revised ed. Paris: OECD, 1979.

Reynolds, et. al. "Inflation Accounting—Ten Years On." *World Accounting Report.* (May 1984), pp. 7–14.

U.N. Commission on Transnational Corporations. *International Standards of Accounting and Reporting for Transnational Corporations.* New York: U.N. Economic and Social Council, 1977.

U.S. Securities and Exchange Commission. "Regulation S-X," in *Form and Content of Financial Statements.* Washington, DC: US SEC, 1972.

Vancil, R. "Inflation Accounting—The Great Controversy." *Harvard Business Review,* Vol. LIV, No. 2 (1976), pp. 58–67.

Watt, G.C., R.M. Hammer and M. Burge. *Accounting for the Multinational Corporation.* New York: Financial Executives Research Foundation, 1977.

COMPARATIVE ACCOUNTING SYSTEMS

CONTENTS

COMPARATIVE ACCOUNTING SYSTEMS

Konrad W. Kubin

Financial accounting principles and reporting practices of business enterprises around the world reveal a remarkable blend of diversity and homogeneity. Each nation's set of financial accounting and reporting standards is unique; yet many accounting concepts are universally accepted and have resulted in similar or even identical practices in different countries. This section discusses frameworks for the classification of national accounting systems, surveys the accounting practices in four foreign countries, analyzes the concerns of groups affected by international differences, and describes harmonization efforts.

TOWARD A TAXONOMY OF NATIONAL ACCOUNTING SYSTEMS

Classification frameworks for corporate accounting systems existing in various countries have been developed to accentuate similarities and differences, to help eliminate any unnecessary diversity, and to guide future accounting developments within countries as well as in the international realm. Early classification attempts relied largely on descriptive comparisons. Later, frameworks and morphologies for grouping national accounting systems were developed, and recently statistical investigations have identified clusters of countries exhibiting similar financial reporting practices.

DESCRIPTIVE COMPARISONS. Virtually all early articles in international accounting heralded certain foreign accounting practices unknown at home. Often the revelations were sensationalized and implied that the accounting practices abroad were inferior. The first more comprehensive and objective descriptive studies include Mueller's international business series on accounting practices in various countries (Mueller, various years starting in 1962), *Professional Accounting in 25 Countries* compiled by the American Institute of Certified Public Accountants (AICPA, 1964; see also the 1975 issue entitled *Professional Accounting in 30 Countries*), Zeff's historical analysis, *Forging Accounting Principles in Five Countries* (Zeff, 1972), and series of country studies published by various international CPA firms. For each of the countries included in the AICPA study, for example, information is provided about the accounting profession, auditing and reporting standards, and accounting principles.

EXHIBIT 1 CURRENT ACCEPTANCE OF ILLUSTRATIVE ACCOUNTING CONCEPTS IN SELECTED COUNTRIES

Accounting Concepts	Degrees of Current Acceptance[a]						
	Required	Insisted Upon	Predominant Practice	Minority Practice	Rarely or Not Found	Not Accepted	Not Permitted
Departures from the consistency concept are disclosed	a						
Departures from the historical cost convention are disclosed	a	UK					
Departures from the accrual concept are disclosed	a	S					
Revenues and costs are recorded in the financial statements of the period in which they are earned or incurred, and not as money is received or paid.	a	UK US					
Cost of sales is disclosed	B	US	N	UK	S		G
Leases are accounted for by the lessee as an installment purchase when the substance of the arrangement transfers the usual risks and rewards of ownership from the lessor to the lessee	US		N UK	S	G		B
Consolidated financial statements are prepared when an investor owning less than 50 percent of the voting-share capital has the power to control, by statute or agreement, the financial and operating policies of the management of an investee company	G S N		B	N	UK		US
Investments in less than 50 percent owned companies, over which the investor can exercise significant influence, are accounted for on the equity basis	UK US		B				G S

Source. Special tabulation based on data contained in Fitzgerald, Stickler, and Watts, 1979.

[a]B = Brazil, G = West Germany, N = Netherlands, S = Sweden, UK = United Kingdom, US = United States, a = all of the six countries listed above, except those identified as having a different "degree of current acceptance."

In 1973, Price Waterhouse published its first *Survey of Accounting Principles and Reporting Practices*. Now in its third edition (Fitzgerald, Stickler, and Watts, 1979), it is the most comprehensive comparative accounting study analyzing the degree of acceptance of 267 accounting practices in 64 countries. Illustrative concepts and practices for Brazil, Germany, the Netherlands, Sweden, the United Kingdom, and the United States are summarized in Exhibit 1. This exhibit shows unanimity of acceptance by these countries of the first four accounting concepts, but vast differences in the degree of acceptance of the last four. The disclosure of cost of goods sold, for example, ranges from "required" in Brazil to "not permitted" in Germany.

CLASSIFICATION FRAMEWORKS AND MORPHOLOGIES FOR NATIONAL ACCOUNTING SYSTEMS

Hatfield's Framework. Although Hatfield (1966) did not specifically have in mind to construct a classification framework, his keen observation and analysis of accounting practices as they existed in the United States and several European countries in 1911 can be viewed as an early form of a classification framework. Inductively derived, this framework classifies national accounting systems by the primary initiator of accounting progress. Using this criterion for differentiation, Hatfield identified a Continental European, a British, and an American model. On the Continent, jurists have been the primary initiators of accounting progress. They have codified even detailed bookkeeping requirements, valuation methods, and formats for financial statements. This legalistic approach to the promulgation of accounting principles contrasts sharply with the development of accounting in England, which came largely from chartered accountants, and the United States, where engineers pioneering cost and railroad accounting greatly influenced accounting progress, although public accountants had also made significant contributions. American accountants' inventiveness in designing bookkeeping systems, for example, was so admired on the Continent that any bookkeeping device having peculiar merit was, irrespective of actual origin, usually called "American bookkeeping."

Mueller's Framework. A more rigorous classification framework was developed by Mueller (1967). His inquiries into international accounting found that it was not as diverse as the more sensational descriptive literature suggested. Rather, he observed that differences in accounting standards and reporting practices among countries could be explained in terms of a limited number of patterns or cores of accounting thought. According to this classification scheme, accounting contains (1) a macroeconomic, (2) a microeconomic, (3) an independent, and (4) a uniform core of accounting thought. Although not a single accounting system has developed exclusively around only one of these cores, Swedish accounting practices typify the macro-economic pattern of accounting development; the Dutch accounting system can be considered a prototype of the microeconomic orientation; U.S. accounting reflects a strong independent core of accounting thought; and French and German accounting practices are illustrative of the uniform, or legal, pattern. The main concepts of these four models are contrasted in more detail in the "Survey of Major Accounting Systems" presented below.

The Seidler-Previts Framework. Seidler (1967) traces accounting practices of various countries to the "spheres of influence" of certain "mother countries." His tripartite classification scheme consists of a British, an American, and a Continental European model. The British model has influenced accounting in Australia and India as a result of strong colonial, traditional, and political linkages. Following the flow of investment capital, the American model has spread to Mexico and is now expanding into large parts of South America, Japan, and Israel. The Continental, primarily French, accounting model has had an impact on southern Europe, the Mediterranean and those South American countries with commercial codes patterned after the Napoleonic Code.

Elaborating on this classification framework, Previts (1975) associated Canada, New Zealand, South Africa, Nigeria, the British West Indies, Thailand, and Greece with the British model and assigned Germany to the American model.

As Seidler points out, the accounting system of the "mother country" is rarely adopted *in toto,* and in many instances, such as in Canada, spheres of influence overlap. Since accounting practices reflect the dynamic international business environment, classifications of countries according to their accounting practices are bound to change over time, and spheres of influence cannot be viewed as being mutually exclusive.

AAA's Framework and Morphology. A 1975–76 committee of the American Accounting Association (AAA) adopted a dual approach toward the international comparison of accounting practices ("Report of the American Accounting Association Committee," 1977). Based on historical-cultural-socioeconomic variables that have influenced financial accounting and reporting principles, the committee identified a classification framework consisting of the following five "zones of influence": (1) British, (2) Franco-Spanish-Portugese, (3) Germanic/Dutch, (4) United States, and (5) communistic.

EXHIBIT 2   A MORPHOLOGY FOR COMPARATIVE ACCOUNTING SYSTEMS

Parameters	States of Nature				
	1	2	3	4	5
P_1—political system	Traditional oligarchy	Totalitarian oligarchy	Modernizing oligarchy	Tutelary democracy	Political democracy
P_2—economic system	Traditional	Market	Planned market	Plan	
P_3—stages of economic development	Traditional society	Pre-takeoff	Takeoff	Drive to maturity	Mass consumption
P_4—objectives of financial reporting	◄————————Micro————————►			◄————————Macro————————►	
	Investment decisions	Management performance	Social measurement	Sector planning and control	National policy objectives
P_5—Source of, or authority for standards	Executive decree	Legislative action	Government administrative unit	Public-private consortium	Private
P_6—education, training, and licensing	◄————Public————►		◄————Private————►		
	Informal	Formal	Informal	Formal	
P_7—enforcement of ethics and standards	Executive	Government administrative unit	Judicial	Private	
P_8—client	Government	Public	◄————Enterprises————►		
			Public	Private	

Source. "Report of the American Accounting Association Committee," 1977.

At the same time, the committee developed a morphology that distinguishes financial reporting systems on the basis of eight environmental and endogenous accounting parameters, as shown in Exhibit 2. Within this morphology, the United States would be described in terms of P_1-5, P_2-2, P_3-5, P_4-1, P_5-4, P_6-4, P_7-3, and P_8-4.

In comparison with a strict taxonomy or classification framework, morphologies have the advantage of being more flexible and avoiding the need to force a particular accounting system into one of the basic models, categories, or zones of influence. Morphologies also mitigate the danger of unproductive, emotional discussions attempting to identify "the best" accounting system in the world or rank various national accounting systems without proper perspective for environmental differences.

STATISTICAL CLASSIFICATION SCHEMES.   Recent attempts to delineate classification schemes for national accounting systems rely on factor analysis to statistically uncover clusters of countries exhibiting homogeneity in financial accounting and reporting practices.

The Da Costa-Bourgeois-Lawson Clusters.   Da Costa, Bourgeois, and Lawson (1978) selected from the 1973 Price Waterhouse study (Price Waterhouse & Co., 1973) 100 accounting principles that were not uniform throughout the world and scaled the survey responses ordinarily from one to five as follows:

Survey Responses	Scale
Accounting practice is	
not permitted or found in practice	1
followed by a minority of reporting companies	2
followed by about half of reporting companies	3
followed by a majority of reporting companies	4
required of, or conventionally followed by, all reporting companies	5

In the second step of their analysis, highly correlated practices were grouped into common factors. This procedure resulted in the identification of seven underlying factors labeled as follows:

1. A measure of financial disclosure.
2. Company law as an influence on accounting practices.
3. Stress of reporting practices on income measurement.
4. "Conservatism" as a guiding principle.
5. Tax law as an influence on accounting practices.
6. Inflation as an environmental consideration.
7. Orientation of reported information toward capital market users.

The statistical analysis designed to identify those countries whose accounting practices are similar across all seven factors revealed two distinct groups. As can be seen in Exhibit 3, accounting practices in Group 2 apparently are patterned after those prevailing in the United Kingdom, since that country exhibits the highest correlation coefficient (.98) in that group. This is also the country most dissociated from Group 1 as indicated by the low (.004) coefficient in column 1. Although the United States does

EXHIBIT 3   COUNTRIES GROUPED ON THE BASIS OF THE ASSOCIATION AMONG THEIR FINANCIAL ACCOUNTING PRACTICES
(1973 survey data)

| Countries | Coefficient with | |
	Group 1	Group 2
Group 1 (nc = 26)		
Japan	.95	.28
Philippines	.94	.28
Mexico	.93	.32
Argentina	.93	.32
Germany	.90	.42
Chile	.90	.41
Bolivia	.89	.43
Panama	.89	.45
Italy	.88	.43
Peru	.88	.43
Venezuela	.88	.46
Colombia	.86	.50
Paraguay	.86	.48
United States	.86	.05
Pakistan	.85	.49
Spain	.85	.49
Switzerland	.84	.53
Brazil	.83	.51
France	.83	.53
Uruguay	.82	.52
Sweden	.81	.59
India	.81	.57
Ethiopia	.81	.57
Belgium	.79	.60
Trinidad	.76	.65
Bahamas	.75	.65
Group 2 (nc = 10)		
United Kingdom	.004	.98[a]
Eire	.19	.96
Rhodesia	.48	.87
Singapore	.50	.86
S. Africa	.51	.86
Australia	.51	.85
Jamaica	.54	.84
Kenya	.57	.81
New Zealand	.62	.78
Fiji	.65	.75
Factorially complex countries—unclassifiable		
Netherlands	.66	.74
Canada	.66	.47

Source.   Da Costa, Bourgeois, and Lawson, 1978.
[a]The British model: former British Empire members.

not enjoy a similar clear position, Exhibit 4 shows that the United states ranks first among Group 1 countries in terms of dissociation from the British model.

Frank's Clusters.   Contrary to the findings of Da Costa, Bourgeois, and Lawson, whose analysis did not support the existence of a Continental European group, Frank (1979), also using the 1973 Price Waterhouse survey responses, but different statistical methods, found the following four factor groupings:

Group I	Group III	Group II	Group IV
Australia	Argentina	Belgium	Canada
Bahamas	Bolivia	Colombia	Germany
Ethiopia	Brazil	France	Japan
Eire	Chile	Italy	Mexico
Fiji	India	Spain	Netherlands
Jamaica	Pakistan	Sweden	Panama
Kenya	Paraguay	Switzerland	Philippines
New Zealand	Peru	Venezuela	United States
Rhodesia	Uruguay		
Singapore			
South Africa			
Trinidad and Tobago			
United Kingdom			

The intuitive identification of these four groups with the British, the Latin American, the Continental European, and the United States models was supported by a supplementary multidimensional scaling analysis using various environmental variables, such as the country's language, several economic structure variables, and sets of variables reflecting trade patterns among the countries. According to this analysis, 83 percent of the countries were assigned to the same group under which they were classified on the basis of financial accounting practices.

Disclosure and Measurement Clusters.   Since in several countries financial disclosure standards are promulgated by one rule-making body, whereas valuation or measurement standards are set by a different regulatory body, Nair and Frank (1980) examined whether the classification of countries is the same using accounting measurement standards as it is using financial disclosure practices. Data from the 1973 and 1975 Price Waterhouse surveys relating to these two subsets of financial accounting served as the data base for the statistical inquiry. The groupings that emerged by analyzing measurement standards differed from those based on disclosure practices, as a comparison of Exhibits 5 and 6 reveals. Whereas the analysis of measurement practices is consistent with the classification frameworks proposed by Seidler and Frank with the addition of a fifth group, namely Chile, disclosure practices do not conform to these classification schemes. Contrary to popular belief, there seem to be more international differences in disclosure than in valuation or measurement practices.

However, a word of caution needs to be raised against placing too much reliance on statistical classification schemes. All attempts to delineate clusters of countries exhibiting homogeneity in financial accounting and reporting practices are only as

EXHIBIT 4   GROUP 1 COUNTRIES RANKED ON THE BASIS OF THEIR
DISSOCIATION FROM THE BRITISH MODEL OF GROUP 2 (1973 survey data)

Countries	Correlation Coefficient with Group 2
United States	.05[a]
Japan	.28
Philippines	.28
Argentina	.32
Mexico	.32
Chile	.41
Germany	.42
Bolivia	.43
Peru	.43
Italy	.43
Panama	.45
Venezuela	.46
Paraguay	.48
Spain	.49
Pakistan	.49
Colombia	.50
Brazil	.51
Uruguay	.52
France	.53
Switzerland	.53
India	.57
Ethiopia	.57
Sweden	.59
Belgium	.60
Trinidad	.65
Bahamas	.65

Source.   Da Costa, Bourgeois, and Lawson, 1978.
[a]The American model: international grouping of countries that dissociate from the British model.

good as the data on which they are based. Nobes (1981) has questioned both the reliability of the data used and their appropriateness for statistical analyses.

IMPLICATIONS OF INTERNATIONAL DIFFERENCES

In assessing the implications of international accounting differences, a distinction needs to be made between the concerns of at least six different interest groups. Briefly stated, the concerns about the comparability of various national accounting systems can be summarized as follows:

1.   *Multinational enterprises* are faced with having to maintain corporate accounting systems in many different national currencies, different languages, and different sets of accounting principles. Reports to satisfy the diverse

EXHIBIT 5   COUNTRIES GROUPED ON THE BASIS OF THE ASSOCIATION AMONG THEIR ACCOUNTING-MEASUREMENT PRACTICES (1975 survey data)

Group I	Group II	Group III	Group IV	Group V
Australia	Argentina	Belgium	Bermuda	Chile
Bahamas	Bolivia	Denmark	Canada	
Fiji	Brazil	France	Japan	
Iran	Colombia	Germany	Mexico	
Jamaica	Ethiopia	Norway	Philippines	
Malaysia	Greece	Sweden	United States	
Netherlands	India	Switzerland	Venezuela	
New Zealand	Italy	Zaire		
Nigeria	Pakistan			
Republic of Ireland	Panama			
Rhodesia	Paraguay			
Singapore	Peru			
South Africa	Spain			
Trinidad and Tobago	Uruguay			
United Kingdom				

Source.   Nair and Frank, 1980.

informational needs of numerous governments and international agencies must be prepared using various accounting measurement and reporting standards. To meet the informational needs of stockholders and management itself, countless reports from subsidiaries around the world have to be adjusted to reflect the same set of accounting principles, translated into one common language and monetary unit, and consolidated into a single set of financial statements.

A no-win situation exists in using a single standard for evaluating the performance of responsibility centers in various countries and the managers in charge of them. If a multinational enterprise employs the same standard throughout the world, environmental differences that have a bearing on the performance in various countries are disregarded. If, on the other hand, local standards are used to evaluate a subsidiary vis-à-vis its competitors in

EXHIBIT 6   COUNTRIES GROUPED ON THE BASIS OF THE ASSOCIATION AMONG THEIR FINANCIAL REPORTING PRACTICES (1975 survey data)

Group I	Group II	Group III	Group IV	Group V	Group VI	Group VII
Belgium	Australia	Bahamas	Bermuda	Argentina	Denmark	Italy
Bolivia	Ethiopia	Germany	Canada	India	Norway	Switzerland
Brazil	Fiji	Japan	Jamaica	Iran	Sweden	
Chile	Kenya	Mexico	Netherlands	Pakistan		
Colombia	Malaysia	Panama	Republic of Ireland	Peru		
France	New Zealand	Philippines	Rhodesia			
Greece	Nigeria	United States	United Kingdom			
Paraguay	Singapore	Venezuela				
Spain	South Africa					
Uruguay	Trinidad and Tobago					
Zaire						

Source.   Nair and Frank, 1980.

a given foreign country, a comparison of responsibility centers within the multinational enterprise is seriously hampered. An international harmonization of accounting principles would significantly simplify financial reporting, management planning and control, as well as decision making within multinational enterprises.

2.   *Investors and financial analysts* have to cope with similar problems of comparability. Since they are primarily familiar with financial reporting practices in their own country, they prefer annual reports in their country's language, currency, accounting principles, and auditing standards. Yet corporations issuing multiple financial reports to improve the effectiveness of transnational reporting would confuse those investors who happen to read financial statements intended for two different national audiences. Harmonization of accounting would improve the communication with the worldwide family of stockholders and thus contribute to a more efficient allocation of scarce investment capital on a global basis.

3.   *Host countries* are concerned about the multinational companies' ability to "manipulate" accounting data. Excess power ascribed to multinational corporations, which supposedly lifts them above the control of any one country, has resulted in charges of

   a. hiding information behind the veil of consolidation,

   b. evasion of local taxes,

   c. exploitation of local resources and capital,

   d. unfair competition with indigenous companies,

   e. perpetuation of technological dependence,

   f. lack of social responsibility and accountability, and

   g. disruption of the foreign-exchange market.

   Third World countries are concerned about North-South as well as East-West implications of accounting systems. Should an emerging nation pattern its accounting system after those prevailing in highly advanced Western countries, or should it adopt a system tailor-made for Eastern bloc countries? The system that is best for highly industrialized nations of the West may not necessarily be optimal for pursuing the goals of developing countries. On the other hand, the system utilized by centrally planned economies may contribute to a socioeconomic system that stifles private initiative and freedom of choice. Thus the developing countries are interested in international harmonization of accounting that considers their need for improved income measurement, financial disclosure, and social accountability.

4.   *Home countries* have almost similar concerns as host countries about the "supranational" power of multinational enterprises. They have started to question the validity of the saying "what is good for General Motors is good for the country." Some of the more frequently voiced concerns are the ability of large multinational corporations to export jobs, worsen the balance of payments, enjoy tax loopholes, and weaken the currency of any country, including that of the country of domicile. Although international harmonization of accounting cannot solve all of these problems, it can at least provide comparable data for establishing and maintaining sound international economic relations among sovereign nations.

5. *The International Labor Office* has voiced concern about the diversity of corporate disclosure standards among countries and the inadequacy of disclosure in general. Organized labor maintains that multinational companies have an unfair advantage by dealing with labor unions on a country-by-country basis. The corporations can readily avoid the bargaining power of a union by shifting production to their subsidiaries abroad without adequately disclosing their overseas involvement. Harmonized and improved disclosure would be a first step toward reestablishing bargaining parity between multinational companies and labor unions.

6. *The accounting profession* itself has been concerned over the years about the discrepancy of accounting practices among countries. If accounting is truly the language of businessmen, international accounting needs to become the language spoken in multinational companies. Only by harmonizing accounting around the world can international accounting improve communication among international business executives.

HARMONIZATION EFFORTS

The six interest groups—identified earlier—concerned about the diversity of accounting systems have become involved to various degrees in attempts to harmonize accounting practices around the world. The dominant forces behind setting international standards are the following organizations.

THE INTERNATIONAL ACCOUNTING STANDARDS COMMITTEE. Established in 1973 by the professional accountancy bodies of Australia, Canada, Germany, Japan, Mexico, the Netherlands, the United Kingdom and Ireland, and the United States, the IASC now has the support of national institutes in 43 countries representing more than 400,000 certified accountants. Each member organization of the IASC has agreed to use its best effort to ensure that (1) financial statements published in its country adhere to international accounting standards promulgated by IASC, (2) auditors satisfy themselves that the financial statements conform with these standards or that the fact of noncompliance is disclosed in the financial statements or the auditor's report, and (3) appropriate action is taken against auditors who disregard international standards.

The operating procedures of the IASC are similar to those followed by the FASB. The board of the IASC identifies the subject areas to be studied and appoints a steering committee for each area to write an exposure draft. After the exposure draft has been approved by a two-thirds vote of the board, the draft is sent to the professional accountancy bodies and others for comment. The steering committee reviews all comments and drafts the final standard, which must be approved by a three-fourth vote of the board to become effective. So far the IASC has issued the following international accounting standards:

IAS	1	Disclosure of Accounting Policies (1975)
IAS	2	Valuation and Presentation of Inventories in the Context of the Historical Cost System (1975)
IAS	3	Consolidated Financial Statements (1976)
IAS	4	Depreciation Accounting (1976)

IAS	5	Information to Be Disclosed in Financial Statements (1976)
IAS	6	Accounting Responses to Changing Prices (1977)
IAS	7	Statement of Changes in Financial Position (1977)
IAS	8	Unusual and Prior Period Items and Changes in Accounting Policies (1978)
IAS	9	Accounting for Research and Development Activities (1978)
IAS	10	Contingencies and Events Occurring after the Balance Sheet Date (1978)
IAS	11	Accounting for Construction Contracts (1979)
IAS	12	Accounting for Taxes on Income (1979)
IAS	13	Presentation of Current Assets and Current Liabilities (1979)
IAS	14	Reporting Financial Information by Segment (1981)

As of summer 1981, the following exposure drafts were outstanding:

Accounting for Foreign Transactions and Translation of Foreign Financial Statements

Accounting for Retirement Benefits in the Financial Statements of Employers

Information Reflecting the Effects of Changing Prices

Accounting for Property, Plant and Equipment in the Context of the Historical Cost System

Accounting for Leases

Revenue Recognition

Various steering committees are also currently working on the following:

Disclosures in financial statements of banks

Business combinations

Accounting for government grants

Accounting for the capitalization of finance costs

Related party transactions

The effectiveness of the IASC in harmonizing accounting practices has been questioned, since several member bodies, including the AICPA, do not have the power to set accounting standards and cannot enforce international standards under their respective codes of professional ethics. However, Nair and Frank (1981) found that considerable progress toward harmonization of accounting practices occurred between 1973 and 1979 with respect to topics on which the IASC had issued pronouncements. Nevertheless, it remains to be seen whether the United States would make substantial changes in its accounting standards in the interest of international harmony if the IASC should issue standards in conflict with U.S. principles.

THE INTERNATIONAL FEDERATION OF ACCOUNTANTS. Established in 1977, IFAC has a membership of 75 professional accountancy bodies from 57 countries. Its objectives are (1) to initiate, coordinate, and guide efforts aimed at (a) harmonizing technical, ethical, and educational aspects of the profession, and (b) granting recip-rocal recognition of qualifications for practice, (2) to encourage and promote the development of organizations working toward regional harmonization, and (3) to arrange the holding of international congresses of accountants. Seven standing com-mittees have been appointed to accomplish these objectives. As of spring 1981, IFAC has issued the following international auditing guidelines:

IAG	1	Objective and Scope of the Audit of Financial Statements (1980)
IAG	2	Audit Engagement Letters (1980)
IAG	3	Basic Principles Governing an Audit (1980)
IAG	4	Planning (1981)
IAG	5	Using the Work of an Other Auditor (1981)
IAG	6	Study and Evaluation of the Accounting System and Inter-nal Control in Connection with an Audit (1981)

Exposure drafts have been issued on the following topics:

Control of the Quality of Audit Work
Audit Evidence
Documentation
Using the Work of an Internal Auditor

THE UNITED NATIONS.   In 1974, a "group of eminent persons"—appointed by the U.N. secretary-general in response to a resolution of the U.N. Economic and Social Council—issued a report that noted the limited comparability of corporate reports and a serious lack of financial and nonfinancial information useful for assessing the activi-ties of multinational companies. At the recommendation made in this report, a "group of experts in international standards of accounting and reporting" was appointed to consider—under the auspices of the U.N. Commission on Transnational Corpora-tions—the promulgation of international accounting and reporting standards.

In 1977 this group issued a report, "International Standards of Accounting and Reporting for Transnational Corporations," which advocated extensive disclosures in financial and social accounting. In response to criticism, an "*ad hoc* intergovern-mental working group of experts on international standards of accounting and re-porting" was set up to review the report and issue a new one. The *ad hoc* group is consulting with the IASC, but will not necessarily adopt IASC standards in its own recommendations. So far it has issued an interim report entitled "Comprehensive Information System: International Standards of Accounting and Reporting," which deals with the feasibility of a proposed international code of conduct.

Other U.N. reports and background papers related to harmonization and im-proved disclosures are the following:

International Standards of Accounting and Reporting: Work of the United Nations (1979)

International Standards of Accounting and Reporting: A Comparative Study (1979)

International Standards of Accounting and Reporting: Regional and International Organizations Promoting Accounting and Reporting Standards (1979)

Ongoing Efforts of Harmonization (1980)

Information Disclosure: Numbers of Employees (1980)

Information on Gross Operating Profit and Depreciation (1980)

Besides striving for more disclosure and comparability, the United Nation's effort is also directed toward establishing a comprehensive financial data bank on multinational enterprises.

THE ORGANIZATION FOR ECONOMIC COOPERATION AND DEVELOPMENT   In 1976, OECD adopted the Declaration of International Investment and Multinational Enterprises. In essence, this declaration is a code of conduct for multinational companies and host governments. The "Guidelines for Multinational Enterprises," which are part of the declaration, call for, among other things, the disclosure of (1) geographic areas where operations are carried out and the principal activities carried on therein, (2) operating results and sales by geographic areas, (3) significant new capital investments by geographic areas, (4) the average number of employees by geographic areas, (5) transfer-pricing policies, and (6) accounting principles, including those on consolidation, observed in preparing financial statements.

The guidelines have been endorsed by the U.S. government and the International Chamber of Commerce. Australia uses them in deciding on applications by foreign companies for investments in Australia, and labor unions in Europe have cited them in disputes with management.

To assess compliance with the guidelines and review international accounting in general, the OECD Committee on International Investment and Multinational Enterprises (CIIME) organized a working group on accounting standards. Specific tasks of the working group are to (1) assist CIIME by clarifying the accounting terms contained in the OECD guidelines, (2) encourage exchanges of views between governments and professional accounting organizations, (3) provide technical advice relating to accounting and disclosure standards, and (4) consider ways to constructively further international accounting harmony. The working group's 1980 report "International Investments and Multinational Enterprises—Accounting Practices in OECD Member Countries" found a lack of standards for measuring items to be disclosed under the guidelines. It also identified areas of significant differences that need to be considered in future efforts toward harmonization.

THE EUROPEAN ECONOMIC COMMUNITY.   The harmonization efforts of the EEC are carried out under the provisions of Article 3 of the Treaty of Rome. This article states, among other things, that the objectives of the EEC are (1) the abolition of obstacles between member states to freedom of movement for persons, services, and capital, and (2) the institution of a system ensuring that competition in the Common Market is not distorted. To accomplish these objectives, the EEC has embarked on two major efforts contributing to the harmonization of accounting: the creation of a European company, and the issuance of "directives" dealing with accounting principles.

The creation of a European company, to be known by the Latin name Societa Europea (SE), would enable companies operating simultaneously in several

European countries to incorporate as supranational legal entities. A draft of a regulation, which would be binding in every respect and have direct force of law in every member country, was passed by the EEC Commission and submitted to the Council of Ministers in 1970. Although the economic and social committee of the EEC reported favorably on the draft, it is currently bogged down by extensive redrafting.

The harmonization in the form of directives has been more successful. Directives are binding on member countries with respect to the results to be achieved, but leave the ways and means of implementation to the discretion of the national authorities. So far the council has issued the following directive to achieve accounting harmony:

First Directive—Corporate Powers and Disclosures (1968)

Second Directive—Incorporation of Public Companies and Transactions in Capital Shares (1976)

Third Directive—Merger of Public Companies (1978)

Fourth Directive—Principles of Accounting and Disclosure (1978)

Directive—Coordinating the Conditions for the Admission of Securities to Official Stock Exchange Listing (1979)

Directive formerly titled the Sixth Draft Directive—Publication Requirements for Listing Securities (1980)

Directive—Protection of Employees in the Event of Insolvency of the Employer (1980)

By far the most important of these directives is the fourth, dealing with the preparation of annual financial statements by corporations operating in the EEC. It also prescribes accounting standards for intercompany investments, goodwill, research and development, and the valuation of fixed assets, inventory, and other current assets. Some of these standards as well as the formats to be used for the preparation of financial statements differ from practices adhered to in the United States and other non-EEC countries.

In addition to these directives, which have received final approval by the Council of Ministers, the European Commission has issued the following proposed directives for council action:

Proposal for a Fifth Directive—Corporate Management Structure and Employee Participation

Proposal for a Directive—Scissions of Public Limited Companies

Amended Proposal for a Seventh Directive—Consolidated Statements

Amended Proposal for an Eighth Directive—Auditor's Qualifications

Proposal for a Directive—Procedures for Informing and Consulting Employees of Companies with Complex Structures, Transnational Firms

Amended Proposal for a Directive—Interim Financial Data to Be Published by Listed Companies

The most important draft proposal is the one covering consolidated statements. If adopted in its present form, it would require enterprises operating within the EEC but domiciled elsewhere to prepare combined financial statements for all subsidiaries incorporated in the EEC and all companies controlled by them.

UNION EUROPÈENE DES EXPERTS COMPTABLES ECONOMIQUES ET FINANCIERS.   Similar to IFAC's worldwide harmonization efforts in auditing, the main objective of UEC is the mitigation of differences among auditing standards in Europe. Founded in 1951, UEC currently consists of 28 professional accounting organizations from 20 European countries. All member organizations have agreed to support UEC auditing statements by:

1. Informing their members about the content of UEC draft statements.
2. Either informing their members about the content of UEC definitive statements or incorporating these statements into their national auditing standards.
3. Using their best endeavors, in those countries where audit procedures are prescribed by law, to get the law adapted accordingly.
4. Using their best endeavors to ensure that bodies responsible for the maintenance of professional standards are aware of UEC auditing statements.

As of spring 1981, UEC has issued eight auditing statements, four additional exposure drafts on auditing, two statements on professional ethics with an additional three ethics statements in exposure form, and two studies by its technical and research committee that deal, among other things, with generally accepted accounting principles. These statements are not binding unless they have been incorporated into national auditing standards.

OTHER HARMONIZATION EFFORTS.   Over the years many other contributions toward harmonization have been made. The international congresses of accountants have highlighted the need for more accounting harmony since the first congress was held in St. Louis in 1904. The congresses in Sydney and Munich in 1972 and 1977, respectively, can take credit for the establishment of the IASC and IFAC. Regional conferences organized by UEC, the Confederation of Asian and Pacific Accountants, and the Inter-American Accounting Association have made indirect, albeit very valuable, contributions to the reduction of international accounting differences.

The international conferences on accounting education held in conjunction with the last four international congresses of accountants have focused attention on international accounting issues. World congresses sponsored by the Academy of Accounting Historians have traced the development toward international harmonization in accounting. University-based centers and institutes for international accounting studies have been established at the Universities of Illinois, Washington, Texas at Dallas, California State at Northridge, Lancaster in England, and other institutions. The international accounting section of the American Accounting Association has become a major vehicle for research and exchange of ideas related to international accounting issues. Its approximately 600 members not only have been active in teaching international accounting, but they also have researched international problems and have responded to exposure drafts issued by the IASC and other standard-setting organizations.

Although not all contributions to international harmonization can be properly acknowledged, one would go amiss by not mentioning the international public accounting firms. They continue to play an active role in the harmonization process by standardizing their accounting and auditing practices in offices around the world and establishing uniform training programs for their professional staff and clients.

Their international exchanges of staff and partners may not directly result in harmonization, but they create a greater awareness for the international dimension of the profession that is conducive to the eternal striving for harmony.

SOURCES AND SUGGESTED REFERENCES

Accountants International Study Group. *International Financial Reporting.* New York: AICPA, 1975.

American Institute of Certified Public Accountants. *Professional Accounting in 30 Countries.* New York: AICPA, 1975.

———. *Professional Accounting in 25 Countries.* New York: AICPA, 1964.

Arpan, J.S., and Radebaugh, L.H. *International Accounting and Multinational Enterprises.* Boston: Warren, Gorham & Lamont, 1981.

Arthur Young & Company. "Keeping Up-To-Date with International Accounting Developments." *Arthur Young Client Memorandum,* March 31, 1980.

Choi, F.D.S. and Mueller, G.G., *An Introduction to Multinational Accounting.* Englewood Cliffs, NJ: Prentice-Hall, 1978.

Coopers & Lybrand. *International Financial Reporting and Auditing.* New York: Coopers & Lybrand, 1979.

Da Costa, R.C., Bourgeois, J.C., and Lawson, W.M. "A Classification of International Financial Accounting Practices" *International Journal of Accounting,* Vol. XIII, No. 2 (1978), pp. 73–85.

Deloitte Haskins & Sells. *International Accounting Standards and Guidelines.* New York: Deloitte Haskins & Sells, 1981.

"Duties of Chief Accountants and CPAs, and Methods of Auditing of Financial Reports and Statements of State Enterprises." *Monitor Polski,* 1973, No. 37, Item 226.

Ernst & Whinney. *The Fourth Directive.* London: Kluwer, 1979.

Fitzgerald, R.D., Stickler, A.D., and Watts, T.R. *International Survey of Accounting Principles and Reporting Practices.* Scarborough, Ontario: Butterworths for Price Waterhouse International, 1979.

Frank, W.G. "An Empirical Analysis of International Accounting Principles." *Journal of Accounting Research,* Vol. XVII, No. 2 (1979), pp. 593–605.

"General Rules of Accounting of State-Owned Enterprises," *Monitor Polski,* 1972, No. 56, Item 300.

Hatfield, H.R. "Some Variations in Accounting Practice in England, France, Germany and the United States." *Journal of Accounting Research,* Vol. IV, No. 2 (1966), pp. 169–82.

Jaruga, A.A. "Problems of Uniform Accounting Principles in Poland." *International Journal of Accounting,* Vol. VIII, No. 1 (1972), pp. 25–41.

———. "Recent Developments in Polish Accounting: An International Transaction Emphasis." *International Journal of Accounting,* Vol. X, No. 1 (1974), pp. 1–18.

———. "Recent Developments of the Auditing Profession in Poland." *International Journal of Accounting,* Vol. XII, No. 1 (1976), pp. 101–09.

Kubin, K.W. and Mueller, G.G. *A Bibliography of International Accounting.* Seattle: University of Washington, 1973.

Lafferty, M. *Accounting in Europe.* Cambridge, England: Woodhead-Faulkner, 1975.

Mey, A. *On the Application of Business Economics and Replacement Value Accounting in the Netherlands.* Seattle: University of Washington, 1970.

Miller, E.L. *Accounting Problems of Multinational Enterprises.* Lexington, Mass.: Lexington Books, 1979.

Mueller, G. *Accounting Practices in (Various Countries).* Seattle: University of Washington, various years starting in 1962.

Mueller, G.G. *Accounting Practices in the Netherlands.* Seattle: University of Washington, 1962.

———. *International Accounting.* New York: Macmillan, 1967.

Nair, R.D. and Frank, W.G. "The Impact of Disclosure and Measurement Practices on International Accounting Classifications." *Accounting Review,* Vol. LV, No. 3 (1980), pp. 426–50.

———. "The Harmonization of International Accounting Standards, 1973–1979." *International Journal of Accounting,* Vol. XVII, No. 1 (1981), pp. 61–77.

Nobes, C.W. "An Empirical Analysis of International Accounting Principles: A Comment." *Journal of Accounting Research,* Vol. XIX, No. 1 (1981), pp. 268–270.

———. and Parker, R.H., *Comparative International Accounting.* Oxford, England: Irwin, 1981.

Oldham, K.M. *Accounting Systems and Practice in Europe.* Epping, England: Grower Press, 1975.

Previts, G.J. "On the Subject of Methodology and Models for International Accountancy." *International Journal of Accounting,* Vol. X, No. 2 (1975), pp. 1–12.

Price Waterhouse & Co. *Accounting Principles and Reporting Practices: A Survey in 38 Countries.* Toronto, Canada: Price Waterhouse International, 1973.

———. *Information Guide for Doing Business in Germany.* New York: Price Waterhouse, 1978.

———. *Information Guide for Doing Business in the Netherlands.* New York: Price Waterhouse, 1980.

———. *Information Guide for Doing Business in Sweden.* New York: Price Waterhouse, 1980.

"Report of the American Accounting Association Committee on International Accounting, 1974–75." *Accounting Review,* Vol. LI, supplement (1976), pp. 70–196.

"Report of the American Accounting Association Committee on International Accounting Operations and Education, 1975–76." *Accounting Review,* Vol. LII, supplement (1977), pp. 67–132.

Seidler, L.J. "International Accounting—The Ultimate Theory Course." *Accounting Review,* Vol. XLII, (1967), pp. 775–81.

Watt, G.C., Hammer, R.M., and Burge, M. *Accounting for the Multinational Corporation.* Homewood, IL: Dow Jones-Irwin, 1977.

Zeff, S.A. *Forging Accounting Principles in Five Countries.* Champaign, IL: Stipes, 1972.

INTERNATIONAL TAXATION

CONTENTS

INTERNATIONAL TAXATION

Lowell Dworin

COMPARATIVE TAX SYSTEMS

WHY INTERNATIONAL TAX PROBLEMS ARISE. Tax factors are likely to be of greater importance in the case of transnational activity than in a purely domestic context for several reasons:

1. The income generated in one country (the *host* country) may be subject to taxation by both the host country and the country in which the management of the business is located or the business organized (the *home* country). This overlap of taxing jurisdictions may result in the problem of *double taxation.*

2. Conversely, most countries do not tax the earnings of foreign corporations owned by resident individual or domestic corporations until such earnings are remitted to the resident stockholders (or until the disposal or liquidation of the foreign corporation). By operating through a foreign subsidiary, home-country *tax deferral* may generally be obtained. To the extent that financing, marketing, transportation, and other activities not requiring the existence of a *permanent establishment* in the host country are conducted by a foreign subsidiary located in a *tax haven* (a country that imposes little, if any, taxes on these activities), both home- and host-country taxation may be minimized.

3. Thus in contrast to domestic activity, where the income earned is roughly taxed at the same rate irrespective of the location or form of organization (ignoring differences between corporate and individual tax rates), the income earned by related entities engaged in foreign commerce may incur a tax burden ranging from full home- and host-country taxation to the absence of any current tax burden. Tax provisions such as the *foreign-tax credit* against home-country taxation for all or a portion of the profits taxes paid to the host country will likely mitigate the problem of double taxation. Other tax laws designed to preclude the improper shifting of income between related parties and limit tax-haven activities may reduce the benefits of tax deferral. Income earned abroad is thus likely to be taxed at an effective rate somewhere between the two extremes noted. However, by appropriate choice of business organization, dividend policy, or even method of tax accounting, this effective rate may be substantially reduced.

4. Not only may greater tax savings result from proper tax planning in the case of transnational activity, but because the reorganization of international operations is likely to incur tax costs (*toll charges*) that would not have arisen in a purely domestic reorganization, the penalty for rectifying an inappropriate plan is also greater.

KEY ELEMENTS OF ALL TAX SYSTEMS. Despite the multitude of taxing jurisdictions and variety of taxes that may be encountered in the conduct of international enterprise, all tax systems may be characterized in terms of certain basic features as follows:

1. The nature of the tax.
2. The scope of the tax.
3. The calculation of the tax base.
4. The treatment of losses.
5. The taxation of nonresidents.

Who is Subject to the Tax? Countries that tax the profits of commercial activities generally impose such tax on both resident individuals and resident corporations. The definition of a resident and the statutory rates of taxation differ. The residency of an individual is generally determined by reference to a number of factors, including the location of the individual's principal home and business activities. A number of countries (e.g., the United Kingdom, Japan, West Germany) define a resident corporation as one whose management or principal place of business is located within the country. Although several countries (e.g., Canada, the Netherlands, France, West Germany) presume a corporation organized within the country to be a resident corporation, other countries do not. The United States is nearly unique in subjecting the income of its citizens and corporations organized in the United States to the federal income tax even if they may be regarded by U.S. law as residents of other countries. This question is of importance in the determination of the maximum level of activities that may be carried out within the host country without subjecting such activity to host-country taxation, and is generally addressed in all *tax treaties* between home and host countries.

Taxation of Branch Income. The earnings of a domestic branch of a foreign corporation are generally taxed under the host country's corporate tax laws, although often at rates that differ somewhat from the corporate rates. Most countries require resident corporations to withhold a certain portion of the dividends remitted to nonresident stockholders. Generally no corresponding amounts need be withheld upon the remittance of branch earnings. To offset this comparative advantage given to branch operations, the tax rate on branch income is generally somewhat greater than the corporate rate. The rates are the same, however, in Canada and France, both of which impose a withholding tax on branch remittances (with some exceptions).

Statutory Tax Rates. Although profits taxes are generally imposed on the taxpayer's total operations within the country, a few countries (e.g., the United States, Norway, the United Kingdom) have enacted special taxes on oil-production income. It is not uncommon, however, for different sources of income (or income generated in different industries) to be subject to tax at different rates (generally manufacturing is taxed preferentially whereas oil production is taxed much less favorably). In many countries the various political subdivisions (provinces, states, prefectures, municipalities, etc.) levy an additional tax on the profits earned within the subdivision. Such jurisdictions generally apply the national corporate-tax laws (except as they relate to the taxation of foreign-source income) at substantially lower rates than the national corporate rates. These additional taxes are typically deductible from the national tax (in Canada a limited credit against the federal tax is given for the provincial tax incurred). When these additional taxes are included, the combined statutory rates of taxation on undistributed corporate profits for many of the major capital-exporting countries are seen to approximate the U.S. statutory combined federal and state tax rate of 46–51 percent, as follows:

Canada	
Normal rates	45–51 percent
Manufacturing and processing	39–45 percent
France	50 percent
The Netherlands	48 percent
United Kingdom	52 percent

The corresponding tax rates on undistributed profits are significantly higher in West Germany (61–64 percent) and Japan (53–54 percent).

Imputation Systems.   The above statutory rates may not be representative of the effective rates of taxation on corporate earnings for several reasons. More-liberal depreciation methods and other differences in the tax laws may result in a taxable income to which the above rates apply which differs significantly from that calculated under U.S. tax laws. Both West Germany and Japan utilize a *split-rate* tax system, whereby the statutory rate of taxation on distributed corporate earnings is lower than that on retained earnings, but both countries also impose a *withholding tax* at the corporate level on dividend remittances to resident stockholders (most countries, including all of those discussed above, impose such withholding tax on distributions to nonresident stockholders). Finally, several of these countries (e.g., West Germany, Canada, France, the United Kingdom) utilize an *imputation system,* whereby resident stockholders are allowed to credit a portion of the tax paid at the corporate level (as well as the tax withheld) against the tax imposed at the stockholder level. In such cases the stockholder must also gross up the dividends received by both the tax withheld and the credit allowed (i.e., add the imputation credit and withholding tax to the actual cash received to determine taxable income). Although the specifics vary, the overall effect is that the combined tax at both the corporate and stockholder level is substantially lower than it would have been if a *classical* system (as in the United States) were in use. Thus for a resident individual stockholder in the base-rate tax bracket (30 percent) in the United Kingdom, the imputation credit just eliminates the tax at the stockholder level, whereas for a resident stockholder in West Germany, the imputation credit just eliminates the impact of the corporate-profits tax. *These imputation credits are not generally allowed to nonresident stockholders,* although a 1970 amendment to the U.S.-France tax treaty allows such benefits to U.S. stockholders with less than 10 percent ownership interest. The recently adopted Third Protocol to the U.S.–U.K. tax treaty is unique in that it allows half of the imputation credit that would be available to a U.K. resident stockholder to be claimed by a U.S. parent corporation of a British subsidiary. The resulting benefit may be seen by comparing the statutory tax rates (including the appropriate withholding tax) if it is assumed that the wholly owned foreign subsidiary distributes all of its earnings (after tax payments to the foreign government) to its U.S. parent:

West Germany	51–55 percent
Japan	46–48 percent
Canada	
Normal rate	53–58 percent
Manufacturing and processing	45–53 percent
France	53 percent
The Netherlands	50 percent
United Kingdom	45 percent

Taxation of Foreign-Source Income.   Many countries (e.g., the United States, the United Kingdom, Japan) utilize a *global* tax system under which the worldwide income of its citizens or residents is subject to tax. Such countries generally allow a foreign-tax credit against home-country taxation for profits taxes paid to the host government. Although differences exist with respect to the ability to credit the underlying corporate taxes paid by the foreign subsidiary (rather than just the parent's foreign-branch tax and the tax withheld on subsidiary or branch remittances), the credit allowed is generally limited to the home-country tax that would have been imposed on the foreign-source income were such income earned in the home country. Thus—ignoring differences in the computation of taxable income, surtax exemptions, and certain other complexities—by comparing the statutory foreign tax rates on earnings remitted to a U.S. parent with the 46 percent U.S. corporate tax rate, it may be seen that dividends from a foreign subsidiary in each of the countries listed, with the exception of the United Kingdom and perhaps Canada, will generate *excess foreign-tax credits* (host-country tax payments that produce no corresponding home-country tax benefit). Some countries (e.g., West Germany, Canada, the Netherlands), although nominally using a global tax system, provide either through their internal tax laws or through bilateral tax treaties an effective exemption of foreign-source income earned in a particular set of host countries. A few countries (e.g., France with respect to the corporate tax, Argentina, Denmark) utilize a *territorial* tax system, under which all income earned outside the country is fully or partially exempt from tax. These countries thereby provide greater tax incentive to their domestic firms to invest abroad in low-tax-rate host countries than do countries such as the United States, which utilize a global tax system. Some of the advantage may be reduced in those countries that utilize an imputation system, since an additional tax (an *equalization* tax) may be imposed when such exempt foreign earnings are ultimately distributed to the parent corporation's stockholders. Moreover, a global system allows foreign losses to offset domestic income, whereas in a territorial system such losses will provide at best only temporary tax benefits.

Inventory Valuation.   Relatively few countries (e.g., the United States, Japan, the Netherlands) allow the use of last-in-first-out (LIFO) inventory valuation for tax purposes. Alternative methods designed to limit the taxation of inventory profits arising from the use of historical rather than current costs may be used (e.g., the stock-relief scheme in the United Kingdom, the inventory inflation adjustment in Canada, the reserve for inventory price increase in France). Both U.K. and Canadian allowances may provide permanent benefits, whereas LIFO and reserve methods in principle provide only tax deferral.

Depreciation Methods.   The rapidity with which the cost of fixed assets may be written off varies greatly. The cost of machinery and equipment (except cars) may be fully expensed in the year of acquisition in the United Kingdom, and if used for manufacturing and processing operations, in the first two years in Canada. If such rapid writeoff is not desirable (perhaps because of current losses), both countries allow the depreciation to be written off more slowly. In other countries (e.g., the United States, France, Japan, Norway) the cost of such assets must be depreciated over a period approximating the service life of the specific assets, although accelerated methods of depreciation may be used. Buildings and structures are not generally allowed to be written off as rapidly as machinery and equipment, but even for such assets as much as 50 percent of the cost may be written off in the year of acquisition in the United Kingdom. A number of countries (e.g., United States, France, West Germany) allow rapid writeoff of assets used for specific purposes (e.g., pollution-control equipment) or located in specific regions of the country. An *investment tax credit* (based on a percentage of the cost of qualifying assets acquired) is also allowed against the tax otherwise due by several countries (e.g., the United States, the Netherlands, West Germany, the United Kingdom). Such investment tax credits are generally not available for assets used outside the country. Expenditures for scientific research are often given preferential treatment, either through an allowance for additional depreciation (e.g., France) or the qualification of such investment for an investment tax credit (e.g., Japan, the Netherlands).

Intercompany Dividends.   Most countries substantially exempt dividends received by a corporation from another *domestic* corporation from taxation either expressly (e.g., the United Kingdom, Japan), through the allowance of a deduction (e.g., the United States, Canada, France), or by application of the imputation-credit system to the corporate stockholder (e.g., West Germany). Although the income out of which such dividends are paid has been subject to taxation at the corporate level, dividends paid out of such income to the recipient corporation's stockholders may either trigger the application of an additional equalization tax (e.g., France, if distributed more than 5 years after receipt) or not qualify for tax benefits otherwise available (e.g., the reduced tax rate in Japan).

Capital Gains.   Several countries (e.g., the United States, Canada, the United Kingdom) tax capital-gains income preferentially, generally by allowing a deduction equal to a fraction of the gains realized on the sale of capital assets held for more than a specific period of time. Other countries (e.g., West Germany, Japan, the Netherlands) generally tax such gains as ordinary income. Long-term corporate capital gains are taxed preferentially when realized in France, but the benefit is lost when the gains are distributed to the stockholders. Tax on the gains realized on the disposal of plant and equipment may often be deferred if replacement property is acquired within a specific period before or after the disposal (e.g., the United States, the Netherlands, West Germany). Gains realized from the sale of depreciable property, which might otherwise be subject to preferential capital gains treatment, may be taxed as ordinary income to the extent of all or a portion of the depreciation previously claimed with respect to the property (e.g., the United States, France, the United Kingdom).

Net Operating Losses.   Most countries that tax the profits from commercial activities allow losses incurred from one activity to offset the income from the taxpayer's other activity within the country. This general rule is most likely to be altered (if at all) in the case of mineral extraction, where there may be restrictions on the allowance of losses from other activities to offset mineral-extraction income (as in the *ring-fence* provisions of the British corporate tax) or even the allowance of losses from one mine or oilfield to offset income from other mines or oilfields (as in the United Kingdom's petroleum-revenue tax). Those countries that tax capital gains preferentially are also likely to allow *capital losses to offset only capital gains* (e.g., Canada, the United States, the United Kingdom). The tax treatment of a net operating loss from aggregate activities within the country varies. Many countries allow such losses to be carried back to the previous year (e.g., Canada, the United Kingdom if other than from accelerated depreciation, the Netherlands, Japan, and West Germany to a limited extent with respect to corporate tax) and allow the balance to be carried forward for varying periods. The United States provides more-liberal treatment by allowing such losses to be carried back 3 years and/or forward 7 years. In those countries where capital losses may only be offset against capital gains, a limited carryback and carryforward is also allowed (only an unlimited carryforward is provided in the United Kingdom, and a 10-year carryforward in France).

Consolidated Returns.   In some countries (e.g., the United States, the United Kingdom, France, the Netherlands, West Germany), a related group of corporations may be taxed as a single taxpayer. This may allow the deferral of the tax on intercompany profits and the utilization of one member's losses against another member's gains. Generally only domestic corporations controlled by a common parent corporation may be included, although even foreign subsidiaries may be included in France. In addition to minimum ownership requirements, certain other conditions (e.g., local ownership of the parent corporation in France, financial and organizational integration of the member corporations in West Germany) may be imposed on the group electing such treatment.

Foreign Losses.   Foreign losses may be used to offset domestic income in the case of countries that utilize a global tax system. However, such losses may also reduce the allowable foreign-tax credit for taxes paid with respect to other profitable foreign operations if an *overall* foreign-tax-credit limitation (the foreign-tax credit allowed is limited to the home-country tax on total foreign-source income) is used. For a company in an excess-foreign-tax-credit position, the tax benefits of the loss offset will just compensate for the reduced foreign-tax credits, resulting in no net benefit. In those countries (e.g., Canada, the United Kingdom) that utilize a *per-country* foreign-tax-credit limitation (the allowable foreign-tax credit from each country is limited to the home-country tax on the income from that country), the foreign-tax credits from profitable foreign-country operations are preserved. Although Japan uses an overall limitation, losses from foreign projects may be excluded from the calculation of aggregate foreign-source income producing the same effect. The United States requires the *recapture* of an overall foreign loss by reclassifying a portion of the subsequent foreign-source income as U.S.-source income, thereby reducing the allowable foreign-tax-credit limitation.

Taxation of Nonresidents.   If a nonresident alien or foreign corporation is considered to be engaged in a trade or business in the host country (and in some countries such as the United Kingdom and Japan if such trade or business is conducted directly or through an agent from some fixed place of business) the income from such activity is generally taxed at regular rates and in the regular manner. If not, the income earned in the host country (which would generally be of a passive nature such as dividend, interest, royalty, or rental income) is generally taxed at a *flat rate based on the gross payment;* this tax is required to be *withheld from the amount distributed.* Because of this diverse treatment, the characterization of a trade or business or the requisite establishment of a fixed place of business is an important issue that unfortunately is often inadequately defined in the internal tax laws of the host country. Even if the taxpayer conducts a business in the host country in a manner that calls for regular taxation, passive income of the type noted above may in some countries (e.g., the United States, West Germany, the Netherlands) be subject to the withholding tax rather than the regular tax unless such income is *effectively connected* to the trade or business (the economic nexus required being defined in the tax laws).

BILATERAL TAX TREATIES.   Although commonly thought of as conventions for the avoidance of double taxation, the major purpose of bilateral tax treaties is to limit the taxation *by one contracting state* of certain activities conducted by residents or citizens of *the other contracting state.* Thus, for example, most tax treaties preclude the host country from taxing business profits of a resident of the other contracting state unless such profits are attributable to a *permanent establishment* in the host country (the treaties moreover define the criteria by which such permanent establishment may be identified). Tax treaties also exempt from host-country taxation certain entire classes of income earned in that state by residents of the other state (e.g., shipping and air transportation income, income earned by a commercial traveler present in the host country for only a limited time, capital gains). Moreover, the applicable withholding rates on passive income that is not attributable to a permanent establishment are generally reduced below the nontreaty rates. Although bilateral tax treaties attempt to address many issues that arise from the disparity in the internal tax laws of the contracting states, not all such issues are expressly dealt with, nor is the interpretation of the treaty provisions always clear. For this reason many treaties establish a grievance procedure for residents of the contracting states who feel that the actions of one or both contracting states will result in a tax liability that is not in accordance with the objectives or provisions of the treaty. Such residents may request the *competent authority* of the state of residency to resolve the issue by consultation with the competent authority of the other state. Such authorities may agree on the same attribution of income for the residents' permanent establishments in the other state, the same allocation of income and expense between related entities (see "Inter Company-Transaction Problems"), the same source of income rules, and so forth. Without such uniformity of treatment, the problem of double taxation often cannot satisfactorily be resolved.

FOREIGN-TAX-CREDIT PROBLEMS

THE DIRECT FOREIGN-TAX CREDIT.   The foreign-tax credit (FTC) is the major unilateral mechanism for alleviating the problem of double taxation in countries such as the United States that tax the worldwide income of their citizens and residents. In practice it does not completely eliminate the problem of double taxation for a number of reasons:

1. The foreign jurisdiction may impose taxes other than income taxes, such as wealth taxes and turnover taxes, for which only a deduction, rather than a credit, may be claimed.
2. Many foreign countries levy income taxes at rates in excess of the U.S. tax rates (especially when the withholding tax incurred on the repatriation of the foreign earnings is included), but the United States limits the allowable credit to the U.S. tax on foreign-source income.
3. Many foreign countries have rules for calculating taxable income and for determining the source of such income that are quite different from the U.S. rules. These differences may result in foreign-tax payments for which no U.S. foreign-tax credit (computed according to U.S. laws) may be claimed, without competent-authority adjustments.

Creditable Foreign Taxes.   The United States allows a foreign-tax credit only for income taxes or taxes *in lieu of* income taxes paid or accrued by the taxpayer (the *direct*-tax credit) or deemed paid by the taxpayer (the *indirect*-tax credit). Whether or not a payment to a foreign government is a creditable income tax or a creditable payment in lieu of an income tax is based on U.S. standards. The most troublesome issue of classification has arisen in the context of foreign mineral extraction, where the distinction between an income tax and a payment that represents licensing fees, royalties, or other compensation for the privilege of conducting such operations in the foreign country is least clear. The general requirements for regarding a payment as an income tax are as follows:

1. The profits on which the foreign tax is levied must be realized according to U.S. standards of income recognition.
2. The tax must be on net gain. This does not preclude a tax on gross income, providing it is unlikely that taxpayers subject to the tax will be required to pay it when they have no net gain by U.S. standards.
3. The tax must be imposed on the receipt of income by the taxpayer rather than on specified activity of the taxpayer, such as the extraction and processing of minerals.

The general requirements for regarding a payment as being in lieu of an income tax are as follows:

1. The foreign government must have a general income-tax law in effect.
2. The taxpayer must be subject to the general income tax if the in-lieu-of payments are not made.

3. Both the in-lieu-of payments and the income-tax payments must not be imposed on the same activity in the same year.

In November 1980 the U.S. Treasury Department issued temporary and proposed final regulations that add the requirement that the tax not be compensation for the receipt of an economic benefit. A tax will be presumed to be compensation for an economic benefit if the charge on those receiving the economic benefit (such as the right to drill for oil) is significantly greater than the charge on those who do not receive such benefit.

The Foreign-Tax-Credit Election.   An individual who is a citizen of the United States and a domestic corporation are eligible to elect to utilize the foreign-tax-credit provisions rather than deduct the creditable foreign taxes. Such election is available on an annual basis. However, the option elected for a given year applies to *all* creditable foreign taxes paid or accrued during that year, even if some portion of such creditable taxes may not provide a current tax benefit because of the foreign-tax-credit limitations. Once made, the election may be changed at any time prior to the expiration of the statute of limitations for claiming refunds for that year (generally three years after the return is filed). Although the choice of the foreign-tax credit will generally be more advantageous, there may be cases, such as the occurrence of an overall net operating loss, when the deduction of creditable foreign taxes might be considered.

The Foreign-Tax-Credit Limitation.   The maximum amount of foreign taxes that may be credited in any year is limited to the U.S. tax that would be due on the taxpayer's *total* foreign-source taxable income (the *overall* limitation):

$$\text{maximum credit} = \frac{\text{U.S. tax on worldwide}}{\text{income before credits}} \times \frac{\text{foreign-source taxable income}}{\text{worldwide taxable income}}$$

Several points should be noted in connection with this formula:

1. Separate application of the formula must be made with respect to non-business-related interest income, dividend income from domestic international sales corporations (DISCs), foreign oil-related income (foreign-extraction income for individuals), and all other income. Thus creditable foreign taxes paid by an oil company with respect to oil production may not be used to reduce the U.S. tax that would otherwise be due on foreign petrochemical operations. However, foreign-source income from transportation, refining, and marketing of crude oil and gas (as well as extraction income) are regarded as oil-related corporate income, as are certain dividend and interest payments from subsidiaries engaged in such activities.
2. The U.S. tax on worldwide income does not include the accumulated earnings tax, the personal-holding-company tax, or the minimum tax. Foreign-tax credits may, however, be claimed against the alternative minimum tax.
3. The taxable income appearing in both the numerator and denominator in the limitation formula is calculated according to U.S. tax laws. An individual's personal exemptions, income excluded by various tax laws, and income for

which a Section 936 tax credit (see "The Section 936 Tax Credit") is claimed are excluded from the calculation.

4. Certain reductions in the amounts appearing in both the numerator and denominator must be made to reflect the reduced tax rates on capital gains. Moreover, gains from the sale of personal property sold outside the United States by a domestic corporation or sold outside the country of residency by an individual may *not* be included in the numerator if the country in which the property was sold taxes the gains at a rate less than 10 percent, subject to certain exceptions.

Creditable foreign taxes that may not be used in the current year because of the limitation formula may be carried back 2 years and forward 5 years. They may be used in these years only to the extent that the foreign taxes for the year to which the credit is carried, together with foreign-tax credits carried over to that same year from prior years, do not exceed the maximum credit allowed in that year. In addition, excess credits may not be carried to a year a deduction for foreign taxes rather than a credit was elected (although the credits remaining to be used in future years are reduced as if such excess credits could be carried to the deduction year).

Source-of-Income Rules. Since the FTC-limitation formula requires the determination of foreign-source taxable income, the rules by which the source of income is determined are of interest. These rules generally determine the source of *gross* income; *taxable income* is obtained by reducing the gross income by the allocable expenses. The general rules are listed in Exhibit 1. In the case where the income is shown as "part U.S., part foreign," the specific apportionment depends on whether an *independent factory price* may be established. If the taxpayer regularly sells the product to independent distributors, the income attributable to the country of production can be taken to be that obtained by assuming the product were sold by the manufacturer at the independent factory price. If no independent factory price may be established, the total taxable income generated by the taxpayer's sales of such goods must first be obtained taking into account all relevant expenses. *One half* of the total taxable income is then allocated to the United States *in proportion to U.S. gross sales* of such products, *and the other half* of total taxable income from the sale of such goods is allocated to the United States *in proportion to the value of the taxpayer's property that is U.S. property.* For this purpose, only property held or used to produce the goods is considered, and investment in foreign affiliates and accounts receivable from foreign purchasers are treated as non-U.S. property. In the simplest case, where goods are manufactured in the United States and sold abroad, at least one half of the total taxable income from such sales is treated as foreign-source income (the full gross-sales factor and some of the property factor). For the purpose of determining the source of income, a sale is considered to occur *where title to the property passes to the buyer.* When the seller retains mere legal title, the sale occurs where the risks of ownership pass to the buyer.

Allocation of Deductions. After several years of consideration, the U.S. Treasury Department in 1977 adopted Regulation 1.861-8 dealing with the allocation of expenses for the purpose of determining income from specific sources and activities. The regulation requires that all deductions for the year first be allocated to classes of gross (or *potential* gross) income in accordance with reasonable factual relationships

EXHIBIT 1   SOURCE-OF-INCOME RULES

Type of Income	Source of Income
Interest income paid by	
Domestic corporation	United States
Foreign corporation	Foreign country
Individual	Residency of debtor
Dividend income from	
Domestic corporation	United States
Foreign corporation	Foreign country
DISC	Foreign country
Compensation for personal services	Where performed
Rents and royalties	Where property located or used
Sale of real property	Where property located
Sale of purchased personal property	Where sold
Sale of personal property manufactured by taxpayer	
In United States and sold in United States	United States
Outside United States and sold outside United States	Foreign Country
In United States and sold outside United States	Part United States, part foreign country
Outside United States and sold in United States	Part United States, part foreign country
Losses on sale of capital assets	Where income would be sourced in absence of sale

between the deduction and the class of gross income. Deductions that are not directly related to any class of gross income (e.g., the zero-bracket amount) are to be allocated to all classes of gross income in proportion to the gross income in each class. Exempt or excluded income is also to be considered a class of income to which a portion of the deductions must be allocated. The deductions within each income class are then apportioned to the statutory groupings of interest (e.g., foreign-source taxable income) in a manner that reflects the factual relationship between the deductions and the statutory grouping. For many classes of income, apportionment will be automatic.

Allocation of Interest Expense.   The allocation of interest expense is predicated on the view that except in very limited circumstances a firm's interest expense is attributable to all activities and assets irrespective of the specific purpose for which debt was issued. The preferred method of allocation of interest is in proportion to the *value of the assets* utilized in generating each class of income. Either the average fair market value or tax basis for the year may be used for this purpose. As in the allocation of total taxable income from goods produced in the United States and sold abroad, foreign-related assets would include investments in foreign subsidiaries, loans to foreign corporations, foreign accounts receivables, and a portion of working capital and plant attributable to the supervision of the foreign subsidiary's activities. An optional *gross-income method* may also be chosen, in which the interest expense is allocated to the relevant classes of gross income in proportion to the gross income in each class. This method may be used unless the amount of interest expense so allocated to any class is less than 50 percent of the expense that would have been allocated to that class under the asset-value method. In such case an *alternative optional gross-income method* may be used, whereby 50 percent of the interest expense as determined under the asset-value method is allocated to that class that did not meet the test under the optional gross-income method (the balance allocated to the remaining classes). The same choice of allocation method must be made by all members of a consolidated-return group.

Allocation of Research and Development Expense.   Research expenses deductible under Internal Revenue Code (IRC) Section 174 are viewed as definitely related to specific classes of gross income based on the two-digit Standard Industrial Classification (SIC) Manual. Basic research not identifiable with any one SIC category is considered to apply to all classes of gross income. Research undertaken to meet legal requirements (such as federally mandated safety standards) imposed by one government that cannot be expected to benefit products marketed outside that government's jurisdiction may be apportioned solely to gross income from that country, but it may be difficult to convince the I.R.S. that no benefits from such research accrue elsewhere.

The preferred method of apportionment of R&D is the *sales method.* Under this method, if more than 50 percent of the costs of R&D are expended in a single geographic area (e.g., the United States) then 30 percent of the R&D expense after deduction of the legally imposed R&D costs may be *exclusively apportioned* to that geographic area (a greater exclusive apportionment may be claimed if there is very limited or long-delayed application outside the geographic area). The balance of the R&D expense is apportioned to the specific classes of gross income under consideration in accordance with the amount of sales in each product classification. Although it is only the taxpayer's R&D expense that is being allocated, the sales of both the taxpayer and the taxpayer's controlled subsidiaries enter into the apportionment calculation. The taxpayer may elect to apportion the R&D expense (after deduction of the legally mandated expense) on the basis of *gross income,* provided the resulting apportionment results in an allocation of 50 percent or more of the expense that would have been allocated to each relevant class of income under the sales method. If such is not the case for a particular class of gross income, an *alternative optional gross-income method* may be used, in which 50 percent of the expense is allocated to that class, with the balance of the expense allocated to the other classes. The same choice of allocation method must be made by all members of a consolidated-return group. It should be noted that if the foreign marketing and distributing function is conducted by a foreign sales subsidiary that does not engage in manufacturing, such sales subsidiary is viewed as a wholesale or retail subsidiary, with the result that none of the R&D definitely related to specific manufacturing categories need be allocated to income from that subsidiary. In addition, the establishment of a cost-sharing arrangement between foreign and domestic entities will preclude the need for allocation of the R&D (other than that called for in the cost-sharing agreement). In 1981 Economic Recovery Act suspends application of these rules for two years, during which time U.S. R&D is allocated entirely to U.S. source income.

THE INDIRECT FOREIGN-TAX CREDIT.   U.S. domestic corporations may claim an indirect (deemed paid) foreign-tax credit upon receipt of a *dividend* from a foreign subsidiary for a portion of the foreign taxes *paid by the subsidiary.* Such indirect credit may also be claimed with respect to a portion of the foreign taxes paid by second- and third-tier foreign subsidiaries when the earnings upon which the foreign taxes are levied are ultimately distributed through the chain of foreign corporations and remitted by the first-tier corporation to the domestic parent. In order to claim these credits, the domestic corporation must own at least 10 percent of the voting power of the first-tier foreign corporation, which in turn must own 10 percent or more of the second-tier corporation, which in turn must own at least 10 percent of the third-tier foreign corporation. In addition, the domestic corporation must have an indirect ownership interest in each of the second and third-tier foreign corporations of at least five percent.

The Deemed-Paid Credit.   The indirect-foreign-tax credit is obtained as a fraction of the foreign taxes paid (or deemed paid) by the first-tier foreign corporation as follows:

$$\text{deemed-paid-foreign-tax credit} = \frac{\text{foreign taxes paid}}{\text{or accrued}} \times \frac{\text{dividends paid}}{\text{accumulated profits after foreign taxes}}$$

A corresponding formula is used to determine the foreign taxes deemed paid by the second-tier foreign corporation for taxes paid by the third-tier corporation. *Such taxes are included together with the actual foreign taxes* paid by the second-tier corporation in the corresponding formula to obtain the foreign taxes deemed paid by the first-tier corporation (which are added to the actual taxes paid by the first-tier corporation in the above expression). If the dividends remitted from any tier reflect earnings from several years (rather than just the current year) the total deemed-paid credit is obtained by summing the product of the factors on the right-hand side of the expression for the individual years. Dividends paid within the first 60 days of the taxable year are assumed to be distributions of the previous year's earnings.

When dividends are received by the domestic corporation with an associated deemed-paid credit, the taxable (foreign source) dividend income is *grossed up* by the associated deemed-paid credit. If a withholding tax is imposed on the domestic corporation resulting in a reduced amount received, the dividend income is also grossed up by the taxes withheld (for which a direct-foreign-tax credit may be claimed).

Illustrative Example.   As an illustration of the indirect-foreign-tax credit and allocation of deduction rules, consider the situation described in Exhibit 2. Corporation X, a U.S. corporation, is the sole owner of Corporation Y, a foreign corporation. Corporations X and Y manufacture similar products, X sells its output in the United States and Y sells its output outside the United States, with the results shown in the exhibit. Note that the deemed-paid-tax credit that may be claimed by Corporation X is $9,200, resulting in a grossed-up dividend income of $20,000. Were it not necessary to allocate X's interest and R&D expense to its foreign-source income, the foreign-tax-credit limitation for X would be:

$$\$69,000 \; \frac{\$32,000}{\$150,000} = \$14,720$$

EXHIBIT 2   ILLUSTRATIVE EXAMPLE

	X	Y
Income		
Sales	$ 600,000	$200,000
Cost of goods sold	(232,000)	(80,000)
Gross income	368,000	120,000
Dividend income[a]	20,000	
Interest income[b]	12,000	
Interest expense	(150,000)	(12,000)
R & D expense[c]	(100,000)	
Taxable income	150,000	108,000
Gross U.S. tax[d]	(69,000)	
Foreign tax paid[d]		(49,680)
Net income	$ 81,000	$ 58,320
Assets		
Current and fixed assets	$3,200,000	
Investment in Y	600,000	
Loan to Y	200,000	
Total assets	$4,000,000	

[a]Cash dividend from Y to X: $10,800
   Deemed-paid credit: $49,680 (10,800/58,320) =   9,200
                                                                              $20,000

[b]Paid by Y on loan from X.
[c]All performed in United States; no federally mandated costs.
[d]Both U.S. and foreign tax rate taken as 46 percent of taxable income.

which exceeds the $9,200 deemed-paid credit; the entire deemed-paid credit may thus be utilized. However, the situation is quite different when the Regulation 1.861-8 rules are applied to X as follows:

	U.S. Source	Foreign Source
Gross sales income	$ 368,000	
Dividend income		$ 20,000
Interest income		12,000
Interest expense	(135,000)	(15,000)
R & D expense	(91,250)	(8,750)
Taxable income	$ 141,750	$ 8,250

Foreign-tax-credit limitation = $69,000 (8,250/150,000) = $3,795, where allocation of the interest and R&D expense was made using the alternative optional-gross-income method as follows:

$$\$15,000 = 0.5[\$150,000(800,000/4,000,000)]$$
$$\$ 8,750 = 0.5[(\$100,000 - \$30,000)(200,000/800,000)]$$

It may thus be seen that without a more-judicious organizational structure, less than half of the deemed-paid-foreign-tax credit may be used against X's current gross U.S. tax liability, resulting in a net U.S. tax liability of $65,205.

TAX-DEFERRAL PROBLEMS

CONTROLLED FOREIGN CORPORATIONS. An important modification of the general rule that a stockholder in a foreign corporation does not recognize income earned by the corporation until that corporation remits a dividend was introduced by Congress in 1962 and broadened in 1975. A set of new sections were introduced as *subpart F* (of Part III of subchapter N) of the Internal Revenue Code. Under subpart F, a U.S. stockholder owning directly or indirectly at least a 10 percent interest in a *controlled foreign corporation* (CFC) is liable for taxes on certain undistributed earnings of the CFC. The income so tainted is that which Congress felt may as easily have been earned by a domestic corporation, such as passive investment income or income from the sale by the CFC of goods produced by a related person for use or consumption in a country other than that in which the CFC is organized. Several other countries (e.g., Canada, West Germany, Japan) have also developed tax laws that result in the current taxation of a stockholder on the undistributed earnings of a foreign corporation, but these laws are generally less broad than the U.S. laws. It is important to note that all such laws *do not affect the home-country taxation of the CFC;* they only relate to the taxation of certain stockholders of the CFC.

When Is a Foreign Corporation a CFC? A controlled foreign corporation is defined as a foreign corporation of which more than 50 percent of the total voting power of the stock is owned by *U.S. shareholders*. A U.S. shareholder is any U.S. individual, corporation, or other entity *owning directly or indirectly 10 percent or more of the total voting power.* When several classes of voting stock are outstanding, these tests are made with respect to the stockholder's ability to elect the directors or cast the deciding vote. The substance rather than the formal measure of control is examined. In most cases (e.g., where a U.S. parent corporation is the sole owner of the foreign corporation), the identification of the U.S. shareholders and the characterization of the foreign corporation as a CFC is obvious. In cases where an attempt is made to avoid classification of the foreign corporation as a CFC (e.g., by spreading ownership over a set of related entities such that no one entity has 10 percent of the voting power) the relevant *attribution rules* under which one person's interest in the foreign corporation may be regarded (for the purpose of the ownership tests) as owned by another must be examined. The general thrust of these attribution rules is to preclude non-CFC status unless a significant degree of control over the foreign corporation has actually been given up by its majority U.S. stockholders.

Taxation of U.S. Shareholders. All U.S. shareholders of a foreign corporation that maintains CFC status for 30 days or more during the year are required to recognize their share of certain income of the CFC in proportion to their ownership of the CFC on the last day of the year. This income is viewed as a deemed distribution and increases the basis of the stock of the CFC. A later actual distribution of this previously taxed income will not again be taxed (but the basis of the stock of the CFC will be reduced). Since this deemed distribution is viewed as an actual dividend from the CFC, a deemed-paid-foreign-tax credit may be claimed by a corporate U.S. shareholder. When an actual distribution is made, the ordinary deemed-paid credit is available only to the extent that a credit had not previously been claimed at the time of the deemed distribution. In addition, the foreign-tax-credit limitation is increased in the year of the actual distribution to the extent the deemed distribution increased the limitation in the year it was taxed and such increase was not then absorbed by the corresponding deemed-paid credit. It should be noted that whereas actual distribution must flow from lower-tier foreign corporations to the parent corporation through the chain of intermediate foreign corporations and thus generate a lesser ordinary-deemed-paid-tax credit (because of the undistributed earnings of the intermediate corporations), the subpart F deemed distribution is viewed as flowing directly to the U.S. shareholder from the lower-tier CFC, generating in general a greater deemed-paid credit. It may thus sometimes prove more beneficial to have a lower-tier CFC loan funds to the domestic parent (which may give rise to a deemed distribution) than to remit such funds through a chain of foreign corporations. It is possible for an individual U.S. shareholder to elect to have the deemed distribution taxed as if the individual were a corporation (and thus enjoy the benefits of the deemed-paid credit), but these benefits are only temporary and are recaptured when actual distributions are made.

SUBPART F INCOME.   It is possible for a foreign corporation to be a CFC without having the U.S. shareholders taxed on the undistributed earnings (indeed, this is the more usual situation). The U.S. shareholders will be taxed currently only when the CFC either (1) earns *subpart F* income (or acts in a manner such that previously excluded subpart F income is currently recognized), or (2) increases its investment of earnings (whether subpart F or not) in U.S. property.

Foreign-Base-Company Income.   Subpart F income consists of three types of income—*income from the insurance of U.S. risks, bribe- and boycott-related income,* and *foreign-base-company income,* which is generally the major component. In computing the subpart F income, an allocation of expenses and deductions in accordance with Regulation 1.861-8 must be made. *Foreign-base-company income* is made up of four types of income as follows:

1.   Foreign-personal-holding-company income.
2.   Foreign-base-company sales income.
3.   Foreign-base-company services income.
4.   Foreign-base-company shipping income.

Regardless of the amount of subpart F income earned during the year, the deemed distribution is limited to the *earnings and profits* (an approximation of economic income) for the year.

Foreign-Personal-Holding-Company Income.   Passive investment income, such as dividends, interest, royalties, rents, and gains from the sale of securities may constitute foreign-personal-holding-company income of both a CFC or a foreign personal holding company (FPHC). If the corporation also qualifies as a FPHC, the foreign-personal-holding-company income will be taxed under the FPHC provisions; if not, the income will be foreign-base-company income of a CFC, unless the rents and royalties are received from unrelated parties in the active conduct of a trade or business, or the interest, dividends, and gains from the sale of securities are received from unrelated persons in the active conduct of a banking or insurance business. A *related person* is any person (individual, corporation, partnership, trust, or estate) that controls the CFC, a corporation controlled by the CFC, or a corporation that is controlled by the same person or persons who control the CFC. Control is ownership of more than 50 percent of the voting power. Dividend and interest income from a related corporation will not constitute FPHC income of a CFC if the related corporation is organized in the same country as the CFC and the related corporation's assets are substantially used in that country. This means that a holding company may be interposed between the U.S. shareholder and a foreign operating company provided the holding company is organized in the same country as the operating company. Likewise, rental or royalty income from a related person is not FPHC income if the property is located in the same country as the CFC.

Foreign-Base-Company Sales Income. As may be seen from the exceptions to FPHC income, the subpart F provisions are more likely to apply to income from transactions with a related person than to income from transactions with an unrelated person. Moreover, subpart F provisions are more apt to apply to income from transactions with a related person who has no business in the country in which the CFC is organized than to income when the related person is organized in or has property in that country. These same *antitax haven* concepts apply in the definition of foreign-base-company sales income. Thus income from the purchase of personal property from (or on behalf of) a *related person* and its sale to any person, or the purchase of personal property from any person on behalf of (or sold to) a *related person* is foreign-base-company sales income if the property is manufactured and sold for use outside the country of organization of the CFC. Thus the income from the sale of goods purchased by a Swiss sales corporation from its U.S. parent to French, West German, and Italian customers will be currently taxable to the U.S. parent as a subpart F deemed distribution. However, income from sale to Swiss customers or income from the sale of goods produced by a Swiss manufacturing subsidiary and sold to customers throughout the world is not foreign-base-company sales income. In order for the CFC to be regarded as producing or manufacturing the product (components of which may be purchased from a related person), the CFC must have substantially transformed the product or incurred conversion costs of 20 percent or more of the total cost of the product. Generally minor assembly and packaging operations will not suffice. To prevent the manufacturing operations of a CFC to shield from subpart F status the income from sales activities in other countries, the subpart F character of the income from such branch operations will be tested as if each branch were a separate corporation if the branch income is taxed by the host country at an effective tax rate that is less than 90 percent of (and at least five percentage points less than) the effective tax rate of the country *in which the CFC is organized.* A corresponding *branch rule* applies in the case of a manufacturing branch of a selling CFC.

Foreign-Base-Company Services Income. If a CFC performs services for (or on behalf of) a related person, and the services are performed outside the country in which the CFC is organized, the compensation of the CFC will constitute foreign-base-company services income. However, services performed in connection with the sale of personal property manufactured by the CFC are not included. If the related person performs substantial assistance to the CFC, the service performed by the CFC will be regarded as service on behalf of the related party; such would not be the case if the related party merely acted as guarantor for the CFC.

Foreign-Base-Company Shipping Income.   The income from the use or leasing of any aircraft or vessel in *foreign commerce* constitutes foreign-base-company shipping income. In addition, the performance of services related to such activity and the gains from the sale of shipping assets are included, as well as a portion of dividend and interest income from a foreign corporation engaging in such activities. However, to the extent the shipping income is reinvested in qualified shipping assets, the subpart F characterization is deferred until such investment is withdrawn.

Exclusions From Foreign-Base-Company Income.   If less than 10 percent of the CFC's gross income is foreign-base-company income, then none of the CFC's income is considered foreign-base-company income. This implies, for example, that each foreign manufacturing subsidiary may engage in a limited amount of foreign-base-company activity without triggering current taxation of the U.S. parent on such activity. Conversely, however, if more than 70 percent of the CFC's gross income is foreign-base-company income, then all of the CFC's gross income is considered to be foreign-base-company income. If the I.R.S. can be convinced that the creation or organization of the CFC and the effecting of the transaction through the CFC were not undertaken with tax avoidance as a significant factor, the income generated may be excluded from foreign-base-company income.

Insurance of U.S. Risks.   In addition to foreign-base-company income, subpart F income also includes income derived by a CFC from the insurance of U.S. property, life and health insurance of U.S. residents, and liability insurance in connection with U.S. activities. However, if the insurance premiums received by the CFC from the insurance of U.S. risks are less than 5 percent of the CFC's total insurance premium receipts, such income is excluded from subpart F characterization.

Bribe- and Boycott-Related Income.   Bribes, kickbacks, and other illegal payments paid by a CFC to any foreign official or government employee are not deductible, and the corresponding increase in taxable income is considered subpart F income. Income arising from operations in any foreign country requiring participation in an international boycott as a condition of doing business in that country is also considered subpart F income. If it is not possible to trace income to operations within the country, and *international-boycott factor* (essentially the ratio of boycott operations to total foreign operations, as measured by sales, purchases, and payroll) must be used. Such bribe- and boycott-related income also reduces the available foreign-tax credits.

Increase of Investments of Earnings in U.S. Property.   Even if none of the earnings of a CFC are subpart F income, the U.S. shareholder may be taxed currently on that portion of the earnings of the CFC that is invested in U.S. property. The actual calculation is rather complex, but the following points may be noted. First, U.S. property includes tangible property located in the United States as well as stocks and obligations of a U.S. person (including loans to the CFC's U.S. parent) and, with some exceptions, patents, know-how, and copyrights acquired or developed by the CFC for use in the United States. However, U.S. government obligations, the obligations of any U.S. person to the extent commensurate with the business transactions between the CFC and the U.S. person, the stock of a domestic corporation (other than a U.S. shareholder) provided the U.S. shareholders do not own directly or indirectly 25 percent or more of the voting power of such domestic corporation after the acquisition by the CFC, and certain other property may be excluded.

Second, the U.S. shareholder is not taxed currently on the increase of investment in U.S. property if such increase is out of undistributed earnings which were or are currently taxed to the shareholder as subpart F income (or effectively connected U.S. income).

Other Amounts Taxed Currently.   Foreign-base-company shipping income that was previously excluded because of investment in qualified shipping assets is included in the deemed distribution when such investment is withdrawn (either through depreciation or disposal). Since subpart F income could be excluded prior to 1975 to the extent qualified investments were made in certain less developed countries, the withdrawal of such investment is included in the deemed distribution (even though such deferral is no longer allowed).

CREATION, REORGANIZATION, AND DISPOSAL OF A FOREIGN CORPORATION.   The contribution of property to a domestic corporation in return for the corporation's stock does not generally result in the recognition of taxable income. Likewise, the acquisition, reorganization, and liquidation of a domestic corporation may often be effected without the recognition of taxable income. Because of the potential for avoidance of U.S. taxation of the gains on the sale of appreciated U.S. property or the undistributed earnings of a foreign corporation that might otherwise result, such *tax-free* transactions will generally require some income recognition if one or more of the corporations that are parties to the transaction are foreign corporations.

Transfers of Property from the United States.   The *outbound* transfer of property (other than stock or securities of a foreign corporation that is a party to the organization or reorganization) by a U.S. person in a transaction that would otherwise be tax-free if purely domestic entities were involved requires approval by the I.R.S. for corresponding tax-free treatment. Such approval must be sought within 183 days of the transfer of the property. Generally such approval will not be forthcoming in the case of the transfer of property to a foreign corporation unless such property is used in the active conduct of a trade or business and is needed in that business. Moreover, such permission will generally require that the gain that would have been recognized if the following properties had been sold be recognized by the transferor:

1. Inventory.
2. Copyrights.
3. Unrealized accounts receivable.
4. Stock or securities.
5. Property that the transferor leases or licenses (to parties other than the transferee).
6. Property that will be leased or licensed by the transferee.
7. U.S. patents, know-how, and so forth used in the conduct of a business in (or the manufacture of goods for sale in) the United States.
8. Foreign patents and other intangibles to be used in connection with the sale of goods manufactured in the United States.

Such income (*toll charge*) must also be incurred in connection with the liquidation of a U.S. corporation into a foreign parent corporation or acquisition of a U.S. corporation's assets by a foreign corporation in a qualified reorganization. Moreover, the toll charge required for the conversion of a foreign branch into a foreign subsidiary will include the recapture of any unrecovered foreign losses.

Transfers of Property to the United States.   A ruling request for tax-free treatment for transfers of property to the United States (or transfers that are purely foreign) is not necessary; such transactions are governed by recent temporary Treasury Department regulations. Under these regulations, when a foreign corporation is liquidated into a domestic parent, the parent is required to treat the transaction as if just prior to the liquidation the foreign corporation remitted all of its earnings and profits. The parent will thus pick up dividend income (effectively limited to the gain that would be realized if the foreign subsidiary were sold) and will be allowed to claim a deemed-paid-foreign-tax credit. Similar treatment is also generally required when a domestic corporation disposes of its foreign subsidiary in a tax-free reorganization. Although gain on the sale of a domestic corporation generally receives capital-gain treatment, all or part of the gain on the sale by a U.S. person who owned 10 percent or more of the stock of a foreign corporation that was a CFC at any time within the 5-year period preceding the sale may be treated as dividend income (and thus carry with it a deemed-paid credit). Such dividend income will be limited to the post-1962 earnings and profits of the corporation for the period during which the corporation was a CFC and the stock was owned by the U.S. person. Undistributed earnings that were already taxed to the U.S. shareholder as subpart F income are excluded from the determination of the dividend income. Additional limitations restrict the amount of such dividend income for both individual and corporate stockholders. Although the general thrust of these provisions is to reduce, at the stockholder level, the preferential taxation of the undistributed (and thus previously untaxed) earnings of the foreign corporation, for corporate stockholders the deemed-paid credit may in fact make dividend income more advantageous than capital gains.

INTERCOMPANY-TRANSACTION PROBLEMS

THE TRANSFER-PRICING PROBLEM.   A substantial portion of international trade occurs between related affiliates of multinational corporations (e.g., 50 percent of U.S. exports in 1970, 30 percent of British exports in 1973, 59 percent of Canadian exports in 1971). Since even a modest change in the prices at which goods are transferred between related entities may result in a significant shift of income from a high-tax-rate to a low-tax-rate country, the appropriateness of such prices has long been of concern to the fiscal authorities of many countries. Relying on the authority granted by Congress in *Section 482* of the Internal Revenue Code, which gives the Commissioner of Internal Revenue the right to allocate income among related taxpayers if such allocation is necessary to clearly reflect income or prevent the avoidance of tax, the I.R.S. has increasingly questioned the appropriateness of transfer price and charges for other intercompany transactions. In response to a specific request by the House-Senate conference committee considering the 1962 act (which introduced the subpart F provisions), the Treasury Department promulgated a set of *Section 482* regulations that attempt to provide guidance in an area where there may be no "correct" answer that would apply in every case. These regulations have also been generally approved in a 1979 OECD report, "Transfer Pricing and Multinational Enterprises."

THE SECTION 482 REGULATIONS.   The basic premise of the regulations (and the OECD report) is that the principal standard for the intercompany pricing of goods and services is the price that would be charged by unrelated parties (an *arm's-length* standard). When such price is readily apparent (e.g., when goods are sold to both unrelated distributors and related sales subsidiaries in comparable quantities and terms), the application of this standard presents no problems. In most cases, however, an arm's-length price cannot be unambiguously determined. For certain charges (interest rates, service fees, lease rentals) the regulations nevertheless provide *safe-haven* rules (generally favorable to the taxpayer), which establish a charge that will be acceptable to the I.R.S. even if such charge may be a poor approximation of the arm's-length standard (and for this reason the OECD report was generally critical of such rules). With respect to transfer prices, the regulations merely provide several methods (as well as a ranking of these methods) that must be used to determine an appropriate price. These methods are not meant to be used in a purely mechanical fashion. An appropriate adjustment reflecting the specific facts and conditions of each particular situation must be made.

Application of Section 482.   Section 482 applies to two or more entities that are owned or controlled directly or indirectly by the same interests (a *controlled group*). Control generally means ownership of at least 50 percent of the total voting power (or at least 50 percent of the total value of all classes of stock). When the I.R.S. makes an adverse change in the income of one member of the group, it is required to make a generally favorable *correlative adjustment* to the income of the other member engaged in the transaction in question (thus the total amount of income of the group is left unchanged). In the case of a foreign member, such correlative adjustment may be of no use if the adjustment is not recognized by the host government. In addition, the I.R.S. must allow adverse changes with respect to certain transactions to be *set off* against favorable correlative adjustments with respect to other transactions. In general, if a Section 482 adjustment results in an increase in income of a domestic parent corporation, the parent is allowed to receive a corresponding payment from its foreign subsidiary with no further U.S. tax imposed (either through the mechanism of a dividend-income exclusion or establishment of an account receivable).

Interest Charges.   When one member of a controlled group lends money to another member, if the interest rate charged is at least 11 percent but not more than 13 percent simple interest, the interest rate charged will not be questioned. If no interest is charged or the interest rate is outside the allowed range, 12 percent simple interest will be required, except in the following case:

1.   The funds were obtained by the lender from a creditor located in the same country in which the borrowing member is organized. In such a case the interest rate charged must reflect the interest charge to the lending member adjusted for the lender's transaction costs.

2. The market rate exceeds the rate charged and the rate charged is greater than 13 percent, or the market rate is lower than the rate charged, and the rate charged is less than 11 percent. In such case *the rate charged* is accepted.

3. The lender is in the business of making loans. In such a case the market rate will be required.

Service Fees.   When one member of a controlled group performs services for the benefit of another member and such activities are an integral part of the business activity of either member, an arm's-length charge is required. If such services do not constitute a significant portion of either member's operations, a safe-haven charge for such services is the cost (both direct and indirect) of such services to the performing member.

Lease Rentals.   When tangible property owned or leased by one member of a controlled group is leased to another member and either member is engaged in the business of renting such property, an arm's-length rental is required. When neither member is in the rental business, a safe-haven annual rental charge is the sum of the following:

1. The direct and indirect expenses of the owning member.

2. An allowance for depreciation for the period the property was used by the leasing member (using the straight-line depreciation method).

3. A return on capital equal to 3 percent of the *depreciable basis,* prorated for the period the property was used by the leasing member.

Sales of Tangible Property.   When one member of a controlled group sells tangible property to another member, the *comparable uncontrolled price* charged in similar transactions between unrelated parties must be used. Adjustment for differences in the quantity and quality of the product sold, the terms of the sale, the level of service provided to the buyer, and the condition and location of the market in which the product is sold must be made. However, if there are no comparable uncontrolled sales or the number of required adjustments would be excessive, the *resale-price method* must be used. The arm's-length price under this method is the price at which the product is resold by the buying member (within a reasonable time before or after purchase) in an uncontrolled sale, *less a markup* based on the uncontrolled activities of the buying member. If the buying member does not engage in corresponding transactions with unrelated parties, the markup may be determined by reference to industry experience, but adjustment for differences in markets, functions, or other relevant factors must be made. For example, if the selling member guarantees the buying member against loss, whereas independent distributors must bear the entire risk of loss, such a difference must be reflected in the markup used. If the buying member adds a substantial amount of value to the product before resale, the *cost-plus method* must be used. Under this method, the arm's-length price is the cost of producing the product, *plus a markup* based on the selling member's similar transactions with unrelated parties. As in the case of the resale-price method, if no comparable uncontrolled sales are made by the selling member, industry experience may be used to determine the appropriate markup, provided adjustment is made for all relevant differences. The taxpayer is entitled to use some other pricing method providing that it can be shown that such method is more appropriate than the suggested methods. Although frequently used in the past (particularly at the agent level), profit-allocation methods (such as a 50/50 split) that cannot be justified in terms of the business activities and risks of each member will not be sustained by the courts.

Sale or Licensing of Intangible Property.   When intangible property rights are transferred from one member of a controlled group to another, an arm's-length standard measured with respect to transfers of comparable rights to unrelated parties must be used. In the absence of comparative transfers, the regulations list a number of factors (but do not provide the weighting) to be used in establishing the appropriate charge. They do allow such a charge to be based on the profits earned by the transferee, which may prove more desirable than a charge based on sales in the initial years of a new foreign manufacturing operation. Cost-sharing arrangements will also be respected, providing they reflect each participant's share of the costs and risks of the development of intangible property.

SPECIAL TAX OPPORTUNITIES

EXPORTING THROUGH A DOMESTIC INTERNATIONAL SALES CORPORATION.   The Revenue Act of 1971 created a new type of domestic corporation for tax purposes—a domestic international sales corporation (DISC). The major advantage of exporting through a DISC (a DISC cannot itself manufacture or produce goods) as originally conceived was the ability to defer from U.S. taxation approximately 25 percent of the total income from the manufacture and sale of the goods exported. In the face of repeated Treasury Department studies that failed to detect an increase in U.S. exports resulting from the DISC provisions, these provisions were modified so as to provide reduced benefits for DISCs that failed to maintain an increased level of export sales.

Requirements for Qualification of a DISC.   Because Congress viewed the DISC provisions as an incentive for increased trade, the requirements for a domestic corporation to qualify as a DISC are quite modest. The major requirement is that 95 percent or more of the DISC's gross income must consist of qualified export receipts (receipts from the sale or lease of goods manufactured or produced in the United States for use or consumption outside the United States, provided not more than 50 percent of the value of such goods is attributable to imports). Crude oil, natural gas, coal, uranium, and certain intangible property such as patents, copyrights, and know-how are not qualified export property. A second requirement is that at least 95 percent of the DISC's assets must be export assets (assets used primarily in an exporting business, such as inventory and accounts receivable). In addition, the DISC must have at least $2,500 capital and only one class of stock, must maintain separate books and records, and must elect to be treated as a DISC. However, a DISC need not have any employees, nor (in the case of a commission DISC) have any tangible assets. A DISC may contract with its parent for a sales franchise whereby the parent will continue all export functions (except invoicing, which must be done by a buy-sell DISC) in return for the maximum commission allowable (for a commission DISC) or at transfer prices that provide the DISC the maximum profit allowable (for a buy-sell DISC).

Intercompany-Pricing Rules. The DISC provisions provide two safe-haven rules for determining the maximum allowable commission or profit. These rules are generally far more advantageous than the Section 482 rules (although the Section 482 rules may be used if desired). The first safe-haven rule allows the DISC an *income* equal to *4 percent of qualified export receipts,* plus 10 percent of the export promotion expenses incurred by the DISC (if any) on such sales. The second rule allows the DISC an income equal to 50 percent of the combined taxable income of the DISC and its related supplier, plus 10 percent of the export promotion expenses. In computing the total combined taxable income, the DISC may use marginal costing (including the export-promotion expenses to the extent that such expenses are used to increase the allowable profit), providing the ratio of the resulting income to the DISC sales does not exceed the *overall profit percentage limitation* according to the following formula:

$$\frac{\text{combined taxable income of DISC and related supplier + supplier's income from domestic sales of same product under full costing}}{\text{total gross receipts from above sales}} = \text{overall profit percentage limitation}$$

The DISC is given considerable flexibility in applying these rules by grouping transactions according to product lines and applying the method that generates the maximum income to each group (which need not exactly coincide with the grouping used in the overall profit percentage limitation computation). When the combined taxable income with respect to any grouping is positive, neither method may result in a loss to the related supplier. However, if the combined taxable income is negative, the DISC is nevertheless allowed the income calculated under the 4 percent gross receipts method to the extent that the ratio of the DISC income to the DISC sales does not exceed the overall profit percentage limitation for the particular grouping.

Taxation of DISC Income. A DISC is not subject to the corporate income tax. However, a portion of DISC income is taxed at the stockholder level as a *deemed distribution,* even if no earnings are actually distributed. Such deemed distribution does not qualify for the 85 or 100 percent dividend-received deduction. However, that portion of DISC income that is not deemed distributed is not taxed to the stockholder until such income is actually distributed, the corporation no longer qualifies as a DISC, or the DISC is sold, exchanged, or liquidated (unless the DISC or DISC assets are transferred to a corporation that is itself a DISC in what otherwise would qualify as a tax-free transaction). Actual dividend distributions are not taxable to the stockholders to the extent that they are out of earnings that had previously been taxed to the stockholders as deemed distributions. These rules are similar to the subpart F provisions regarding the taxation of a CFC. Unlike the subpart F provisions, however, a DISC *can* invest its earnings in U.S. property without subjecting to taxation the *accumulated DISC income* (the untaxed portion of the DISC's earnings). A DISC may loan its related supplier (or other U.S. export manufacturer) its accumulated DISC income, provided such *producers' loans* increase the export-related assets of the borrower. A producer's loan is a qualified export asset and the interest from such a loan a qualified export receipt.

Deemed Distributions.   The portion of DISC income taxed currently to the stockholders consists of:

1. Interest from producers' loans.
2. Gain on the sale or exchange of nonqualified export assets acquired in a nontaxable exchange.
3. Gain to the extent of depreciation recapture on the sale or exchange of qualified export assets acquired in a nontaxable exchange.
4. Fifty percent of the taxable income attributable to military property.
5. Taxable income attributable to *base-period export gross receipts.*
6. The amount of foreign investment attributable to producers' loans.
7. Fifty percent of DISC income in excess of items 1–5.

Item 5 is the mechanism by which DISC benefits have been tied to increases in export sales. Taxable income attributable to base-period export gross receipts is defined as:

$$\begin{array}{c} \text{taxable income attributed} \\ \text{to base-period export gross receipts} \end{array} = \begin{array}{c} \text{adjusted} \\ \text{taxable income} \end{array} \times \frac{\text{adjusted base-period} \; \underline{\text{export gross receipts}}}{\begin{array}{c}\text{export gross receipts} \\ \text{for current year}\end{array}}$$

Adjustable taxable income is the DISC income reduced by items 1–4, and adjusted base-period export gross receipts is 67 percent of the *average* of the export gross receipts for the base period (the fourth through seventh preceding taxable years). If the DISC has taxable income of $100,000 or less, this item may be ignored (and may be partly ignored to the extent the DISC income exceeds $100,000 but does not exceed $150,000). Item 6 arises when a DISC lends money to its related supplier to the extent there has been an increase in the foreign assets of the members of the controlled group to which the DISC belongs, and such increase results from foreign investment by the domestic members. In the simplest case, where items 1–6 are zero, the deemed distribution is 50 percent of the DISC income. If the 50 percent of combined taxable income method were used to determine DISC income, the tax on approximately 25 percent of the combined taxable income (50 percent of 50 percent) would be deferred. For a mature DISC, where items 1–6 may represent a fair portion of DISC taxable income, the deferral benefits may be significantly reduced. Moreover, since DISC income is generally foreign-source income that is free of foreign taxation, it may not be advantageous to use a DISC if the parent corporation is in an excess-foreign-tax-credit position.

THE SECTION 936 TAX CREDIT.   Prior to the Tax Reform Act of 1976, a domestic corporation engaged in an active business in Puerto Rico (and certain other U.S. possessions) was permitted, subject to certain requirements, to exclude from U.S. taxation all income earned in Puerto Rico or elsewhere outside the United States. Such a *possession corporation* was generally engaged in activities that qualified its Puerto Rican earnings for exemption from Puerto Rican taxes as well. As long as such a corporation did not remit dividends to its domestic parent (possession-corporation dividends did not generally qualify for the 85 or 100 percent dividend-received deduction), its earnings went untaxed, with the result that substantial accumulated earnings were invested *outside the United States and Puerto Rico.* Since such investments were not felt to provide the benefits to either the United States or Puerto Rico that were envisioned by Congress, the 1976 act made the income earned by the possession corporation taxable, but provided a new tax-sparing credit (the *Section 936 credit*) equal to the U.S. tax on the possessions-corporation income from the active conduct of a business in Puerto Rico and from *qualified possession-source* investment income. The foreign-tax-credit limitation does not apply to the Section 936 credit, and the income upon which the Section 936 credit is based is ignored in computing the limitation with respect to the ordinary foreign-tax credit.

Requirements for Claiming the Credit.   A domestic corporation must elect to claim the credit. Once elected, it remains in force for 10 years, provided the corporation satisfies the following two requirements:

1. Eighty percent or more of gross income from the 3-year period preceding the close of the taxable year must be derived from sources within a possession of the United States.

2. At least 50 percent of gross income for the same period must be derived from the active conduct of a trade or business within a possession. A corporation electing the Section 936 credit is not allowed to join in the filing of a consolidated tax return. However, the domestic parent of such corporation is eligible for the 85 or 100 percent dividend-received deduction on dividends received from such a corporation. Because qualified possession-source investment income is limited to income from investments that are made in Puerto Rico (and are not reinvested outside the possession), the general result of the 1976 act is to effectively continue to exclude from U.S. taxation income earned *in Puerto Rico* while encouraging repatriation of funds that had previously been invested outside the United States and Puerto Rico. The imposition of a Puerto Rican withholding tax (*tollgate* tax) on dividend remittances by a possession corporation to its U.S. parent may, however, reduce somewhat the desirability of repatriating the previously accumulated funds.

BORROWING THROUGH AN INTERNATIONAL FINANCE SUBSIDIARY.   If a domestic corporation borrows funds from a foreign creditor who is not otherwise engaged in a U.S. trade or business, the interest payments will be subject to a withholding tax. However, if the domestic corporation were to borrow from a creditor in a country such as the Netherlands Antilles, which has entered into a tax treaty with the United States that exempts from U.S. withholding tax interest payments from U.S. borrowers, payment may be made to the Netherlands Antilles creditor free of U.S. withholding tax. Moreover, if the treaty country itself does not impose any withholding tax on interest payments made to nonresidents, as is the case in the Netherlands Antilles, the Netherlands Antilles creditor could in turn borrow funds in the Eurobond market without subjecting the interest payments to foreign investors to any withholding tax. Thus by establishing a Netherlands Antilles finance subsidiary and structuring its payments to the finance subsidiary to match the Eurobond payments, a domestic corporation can tap the Eurobond market. Since the finance subsidiary's interest expense offsets its interest income, the finance subsidiary need not pay any taxes to the Netherlands Antilles. Despite the lack of any business activity with unrelated parties and the fact that the domestic parent generally guarantees the Eurobond loan (which often is convertible into stock of the domestic parent), the subsidiary has generally been recognized as a separate corporation for tax purposes, although the I.R.S. has indicated that such determination would have to be made on a case-by-case basis. This use of an intermediate entity located in a country with more-favorable tax-treaty provisions than those in effect directly between the United States and the foreign investor's country of residence is illustrative of the general practice of *treaty shopping*. The establishment of holding companies in the Netherlands, Netherlands Antilles, and British Virgin Islands in order to take advantage of favorable U.S. treaty provisions has also been frequently chosen by nonresidents seeking to invest in the United States. Such practice is expressly disallowed under the U.S. Model Treaty and some recently concluded treaties, but only if the treaty partner taxes holding-company income preferentially (as in the case in the Netherlands and Netherlands Antilles, but not the British Virgin Islands).

INTERNATIONAL TAX COMPLIANCE, TAX MORALITY, AND TAX HAVENS. The use of tax-haven corporations and trusts to maximize the benefits of tax deferral may serve the legitimate purpose of reducing a taxpayer's tax exposure. However, with the introduction of the subpart F provisions, the imposition of a *35 percent excise tax* on the transfer of appreciated property by a U.S. person to a foreign corporation or trust (other than in exchange for corporate stock), and other changes in the U.S. tax laws, the ability to use tax havens to shelter property and business income from U.S. taxation has been significantly reduced. However, because of their bank- and corporate-secrecy laws, many tax havens continue to be used by taxpayers who misrepresent or conceal facts in order to obtain by illegitimate means those benefits that no longer are legitimately available.

In addition to the filing of tax returns and supporting schedules, the Internal Revenue Code and the Bank Secrecy Act of 1970 establish a number of information-reporting requirements with respect to transactions with or relationships to foreign entities as follows:

1. Every U.S. person who owns more than 50 percent of the stock of a foreign corporation for 30 days or more during the year must file a Form 2952, which requires detailed information concerning the corporation, including summaries of certain transactions between the corporation and related persons as well as a listing of all U.S. stockholders owning more than 5 percent of the corporation's outstanding stock.

2. Every U.S. stockholder of a CFC must file Form 3646, which shows the shareholder's pro rata share of foreign-base-company income, increase in earnings invested in U.S. property, and previously excluded subpart F income withdrawn from investment in shipping operations and less developed countries.

3. Every U.S. officer or director of a foreign personal holding company must so indicate by filing an information return on Form 957 for the company's tax year, and must report operating results on Form 958.

4. Every U.S. officer or director of a foreign corporation must file Form 959 with respect to each U.S. person who acquires 5 percent or more of the corporation's stock or an additional 5 percent of such stock.

5. Every U.S. person who physically transports or causes to be transported into or out of the United States any currency or monetary instruments exceeding $5000 at any one time must file Form 4790 with the Customs Service.

6. Every U.S. individual (including trust beneficiaries) who has signature or other authority over a foreign-bank, securities, or other financial account, is required to file information return Form 90-22.1 with the Treasury Department, as well as indicate the existence of a foreign account or trust on Schedule B of tax return Form 1040.

7. Every financial institution covered by the Bank Secrecy Act must indicate each deposit, withdrawal, exchange of currency, or other transfer of currency in excess of $10,000 by or through a financial institution on Form 4789.

8. Every U.S. person who transfers property to a foreign trust that has a U.S. beneficiary must file an information return Form 3520-A and Form 3520 if the trust was created by a gift.

Because of the taxpayer's ability to structure certain transactions in such a way as to avoid the necessity of filing one or more of the information returns (or the outright disregard of the need to file such returns), the general level of tax enforcement with respect to tax-haven activity is rather poor, as evidenced by the results of the I.R.S. Project Haven investigation. In view of the difficulty of negotiating satisfactory agreements for the exchange of information with the tax-haven governments, the most likely method of attack on tax-haven abuse by the I.R.S. is through a more-comprehensive examination of those records of the U.S. banking, accounting, and legal professions that are currently available (e.g., Forms 4789 and 4790) or may be obtained by legislative or judicial action.

SOURCES AND SUGGESTED REFERENCES

Burns, O. "How I.R.S. Applies Intercompany Pricing Rules of Section 482." *Journal of Taxation,* Vol. LII (1980), pp. 308–14.

Commerce Clearing House. *Income Taxes Worldwide.* Chicago: Commerce Clearing House, 1976.

———. "OECD Model Double Taxation Convention on Income and Capital and Department of the Treasury Model Income Tax Treaty," in *Tax Treaties.* Chicago: Commerce Clearing House, 1965.

Committee on Fiscal Affairs of the OECD. *Transfer Pricing and Multinational Enterprises.* Paris: Organization for Economic Cooperation and Development, 1979.

Deloitte Haskins and Sells. *International Tax and Business Service.* New York: Deloitte Haskins & Sells, various years.

Diamond, W.H. *Foreign Tax and Trade Briefs.* New York: Matthew Bender, 1980.

Granwell, A., M. Amdur, G. Fritzhand, and A. Weiner. "Prop. Regs. on CFC's U.S. Property Contain New Concepts, Create New Problems." *Journal of Taxation, Vol. LII* (1980), pp. 368–73.

International Bureau of Fiscal Documentation. *European Taxation.* Amsterdam: International Bureau of Fiscal Documentation, 1961.

Kurtz, J., M.C. Ferguson, and D. Rosenbloom. "Statements on Foreign Tax Havens by I.R.S. Commissioner Jerome Kurtz; M. Carr Ferguson, Assistant Attorney General, Tax

Division; and International Tax Counsel David Rosenbloom Before the House Ways and Means Subcommittee on Oversight." *B.N.A. Daily Tax Report,* April 24, 1979. pp. J-1.

Moore, M.L. and R.N. Bagley. "U.S. Tax Aspects of Doing Business Abroad." *Studies in Federal Taxation No. 6.* New York: American Institute of Certified Public Accountants, 1978.

Prentice-Hall. *U.S. Taxation of International Operations.* Englewood Cliffs, N.J.: Prentice-Hall, 1973.

Price Waterhouse Information Guide. *Corporate Taxes in 80 Countries.* New York: Price Waterhouse, 1980.

Rhoades, R. von T. and M.J. Langer. *Income Taxation of Foreign Related Transactions.* New York: Matthew Bender, 1980.

Tax Management Foreign Income Portfolios. Washington, D.C.: Bureau of National Affairs, Inc.

Watt, G.C., R.M. Hammer, and M. Burge., *Accounting for the Multinational Corporation.* Homewood, IL: Dow Jones-Irwin, 1977.

INDEX